What others say . . .

Callaway has provided a thorough exposition and analysis of one of western Canada's most important religious educational institutions in the fifty-year period that spanned the 1920s through the 1970s. He shows that, through its iconic founder, L.E. Maxwell, the school was something of a northern outpost of American fundamentalism. In the process, the author complements and corrects the seminal work of John Stackhouse, Jr. and helps shed important light on the impact that this American-oriented fundamentalist school had on religion in Canada and beyond as its graduates moved into the world and into churches as workers, missionaries, and laity—in some instances as apostates. Callaway is able to offer a detailed, well-crafted overview of this unique school and its influence as someone who experienced it on the inside, yet stands back and draws on the tools of an historian and social scientist to interpret its nature and significance from the outside. This well-written tome is essential reading for anyone who wishes to understand the impact and legacy of Prairie Bible Institute.

Reginald W. Bibby, OC, PhD
Board of Governors Research Chair
Department of Sociology
University of Lethbridge
Lethbridge, Alberta, Canada

*   *   *

Callaway's work fills a significant hole in the research on religion in Alberta during the first half of the 20th century. Prairie Bible Institute has always been understood as a major force in the shaping of conservative Christianity, its influence extending far beyond the boundaries of Canada's Prairie Provinces as the school's alumni spread over the globe taking their understanding of faith with them. One of the unanswered questions has been the nature of the appeal of this small-town Alberta school for youth from across the continent. Callaway's research goes a long way to helping us understand how this was able to occur and be sustained.

Donald Goertz
Associate Professor of Church History
Tyndale University College and Seminary
Toronto, Ontario, Canada

A Militant Faith

"We need militancy in our faith before we shall get anywhere fighting the forces arrayed against us in these days. A soft life, a soft faith, a soft message, all these things sum up the average Christian life, even among the (so called) deeper life people. We speak not of modernists, for we have long maintained that the main trouble with the church is not its infidelic modernism and falsehood, as hellish as that is, but it is the deadness of those who have named the name of Christ—their utter indolence and indifference to the perishing souls all about them. They have lost their testimony. Laziness and secret sin have stopped their mouths. Their heads hang in the presence of the Devil and his crowd. Where there is no vision the people perish. Oh, that the blue flame of battle might once more be seen in the testimony of God's sagging servants!"

L.E. Maxwell in *The Prairie Pastor*—Vol. 4, No. 12; (December 1931), I.

TRAINING DISCIPLINED SOLDIERS FOR CHRIST

The influence of American fundamentalism
on Prairie Bible Institute (1922-1980)

---

for Brian, Barb + massive tribe!
with appreciation

TIM W. CALLAWAY

WESTBOW
P R E S S
A DIVISION OF THOMAS NELSON

WestBow Press books may be ordered through booksellers or by contacting:

WestBow Press
A Division of Thomas Nelson
1663 Liberty Drive
Bloomington, IN 47403
www.westbowpress.com
1-(866) 928-1240

ISBN: 978-1-4497-8989-3 (sc)
ISBN: 978-1-4497-8988-6 (hc)
ISBN: 978-1-449-78990-9 (e)

Library of Congress Control Number: 2013905835

Printed in the United States of America.

WestBow Press rev. date: 4/11/2013

TABLE OF CONTENTS

In grateful memory of my parents, Victor L. Callaway (1922-2005) and Bernice Marr Callaway (1923-2009), staff members at Prairie Bible Institute (1960-1987)

FOREWORD

If you grow up in a conservative evangelical Christian community in North America like I did, you will regularly be asked some version of a question that is supposed to indicate the measure of your true Christian experience: "What is your personal testimony?" And you will need to have an answer. The question is a way of placing the gospel story at the center of our identity. It is an invitation to say who you are and what your identity is in terms spelled out by the story of Jesus.

It is a question I was asked—and required to answer—many times over the course of my upbringing at Prairie Bible Institute during the 1970's and 1980's. What was being asked, of course, was the story of my conversion—how I "met Jesus" and "got saved" and how my life was transformed. There was a definite arc that my story was to reflect to our evangelical community including a decisive moment in which I turned from my sins to trust in Jesus as my Lord and Savior.

In many ways the question noted above is a very good one and asking it is an important community practice. Stories are important and we need to know who we are and whose we are and, as Stanley Hauerwas reminds us, we Christians are a community that lives through memory.

But being required to tell one's testimony certainly may create some confusion in an eight-year old boy. For one thing, it creates its own opportunities for temptation, particularly to break the Ninth Commandment (ie. lying). To tell a good testimony, I felt one had to have had a life of sin and debauchery which I did not exactly possess. If I have not confessed before, I do now: I lied on a few occasions about the depths of my depravity in order to make the story a little better. There were other times, however, where I just could not face up to what I had done and who I was, and I sometimes lied about that too.

Whatever the case, for most of us, I think our tendency is to make our stories seem a little better than they really are. There is an auto-correct feature in our memories that edits our stories to suit our fancies. However, telling the story properly means that we acknowledge and reveal our sin so that we can accept God's forgiveness of us in Jesus. So memory really is a moral exercise as we must pray to become the kind of people who are capable of remembering our failures and sins so that we may tell the story aright. We cannot just tell the bits we like and gloss over the rest.

The story of Canadian evangelicals is, like Canadians themselves, a tricky one to tell. One of the truisms about Canadians and our identity as such is that the only thing we know for sure is that we are not Americans! This could be said to be equally true of Canadian evangelicals. We inhabit a much smaller world than do American evangelicals and have experienced a very different set of social realities than our counterparts south of the 49th parallel—especially those concerning the relations between church and state.

Ours is also a different story with respect to how our national mythos connects to how we understand ourselves as evangelicals. We see clearly the ways in which evangelicals and conservatives in the United States have erred and strayed from faithfulness to the Gospel—principally in the ways in which they are different from us. This has produced in us a tendency to do all we can to distance ourselves from them to the point that, at times, we deny or forget or just simply cannot acknowledge the ways in which we are deeply implicated in the same practices and shortcomings. The trouble is, of course, that our ability to understand ourselves or be shaped differently is limited by the degree to which we can properly tell our collective story.

My point in saying all of this is that Tim Callaway tells the story of Prairie Bible Institute well—and in doing that he helps me tell my story and the story of Canadian evangelicalism, well. He remembers, he pauses over the details and allows the warts and the foibles to come to the surface, without ever casting aspersions on PBI and its leadership. He makes room for right remembering—and for healing and forgiveness, if that is required.

And for that I am in his debt.

The Reverend Myron Bradley Penner, PhD
Edmonton, Alberta, Canada
Third Week of Lent, 2013

INTRODUCTION

Readers will quickly discern an academic orientation informing what they encounter in this volume. This reflects the fact that an earlier edition of the manuscript was submitted in 2010 as a doctoral dissertation at the University of South Africa, Pretoria.

The comparative scarcity of academic attention given Prairie Bible Institute (PBI/Prairie) at Three Hills, Alberta, Canada, was indeed a motivating factor behind my initial inquiry. The original dissertation was written to augment and refine the limited research that exists regarding PBI during the L.E. Maxwell era (1922-1980). My work should therefore be regarded as an attempt to contribute to and refine how Prairie Bible Institute's first half-century should be understood and interpreted by students of North American church history.

As a significant part of this overarching objective, this book reflects both a belated response to and an eager interaction with the valuable foundational efforts of Canadian scholar, Dr. John G. Stackhouse, Jr. His work in this regard is represented in his 1993 book *Canadian Evangelicalism in the Twentieth Century: An Introduction to Its Character.*[1] Stackhouse's perspective on PBI has subsequently been affirmed by Dr. Bruce Guenther, another Canadian researcher who has made important contributions to the study of Canadian evangelical higher education.[2]

Although an evaluation of PBI represented only a part of Stackhouse's treatise, and that primarily as such related to his broader discussion of Canadian evangelicalism in the twentieth century, the former University of Manitoba professor kindly invited dialogue with his initiative by referring

---

[1] Dr. Stackhouse is presently the Sangwoo Youtong Chee Professor of Theology and Culture at Regent College, an international graduate school of Christian studies located near the University of British Columbia in Vancouver, British Columbia, Canada. His book (University of Toronto Press, 1993) is a revision of his PhD dissertation, "Proclaiming the Word: Canadian Evangelicalism since the First World War" (University of Chicago, 1987).

[2] Bruce L. Guenther, "Training for Service: The Bible School Movement in Western Canada, 1909-1960" (PhD dissertation, McGill University, 2001).

to it as "an outline that further research should fill in and modify."[3] In describing the intention of his study, he expressed the hope that it would:

> encourage scholars of Canadian history and religion to take more seriously this aspect of recent Canadian Protestantism—even inspiring, one might hope, studies that will go beyond and improve upon this one.[4]

Accordingly, and in the interest of reciprocating such goodwill, I attempt here to "improve upon" Stackhouse's conclusions regarding how Prairie Bible Institute's first half-century should be viewed by those interested in this particular component of religious history. Drawing on an insider's perspective of PBI, I challenge the adequacy of Stackhouse's comparatively narrow definition of fundamentalism. I also question the legitimacy of his inference that the kind of "sectish evangelicalism" he rightly claims typified PBI in the twentieth century was substantially different from the characteristics of the broader understanding of American fundamentalism that I advance from my analysis of the relevant data.

Toward this end, I endeavor to demonstrate that the following conclusion reached by Stackhouse, at least as it related to Prairie Bible Institute during the Maxwell era, is regrettably misleading, if not demonstrably false:

> The institutions portrayed here as central in the life of Canadian evangelicalism in the twentieth century were, without exception, indigenous Canadian products. However much they benefited in typical Canadian style from British or American initiative (for instance . . . the American model of Moody Bible Institute for PBI . . .) or from leaders from either place (for example, L.E. Maxwell at PBI . . .), the institutions were founded and funded and staffed predominantly by Canadians.[5]

---

[3] Stackhouse, *Canadian Evangelicalism in the Twentieth Century*, 12.

[4] Stackhouse, 17.

   Other Canadian church history scholars similarly appeal for more study to be undertaken regarding Canadian fundamentalism. See, for example, James W. Opp, "Culture of the Soul: Fundamentalism and Evangelism in Canada," (MA thesis, University of Calgary, 1994) 10-11: ". . . it is clear that fundamentalism as a movement deserves much closer study within the Canadian context."

[5] Stackhouse, 196.

My undertaking in these pages advances that PBI during the Maxwell era reflected the influence of American fundamentalism to a far greater extent than what Stackhouse allowed in his research.[6] I also present evidence to verify that, in the course of crafting a very helpful composite sketch of the infancy of Canadian evangelicalism, Stackhouse in fact did acknowledge the extent to which the American fundamentalist factor was active and evident at PBI during Maxwell's tenure. Nevertheless, he curiously chose to minimize it. Unfortunately, readers of Stackhouse's work are therefore likely to come away from his study with both an inadequate and an inaccurate

---

[6] Dr. Stackhouse is not the only Canadian scholar to minimize American fundamentalism's impact on PBI and possibly other Canadian Bible schools. Phyllis D. Airhart, "Ordering a New Nation and Reordering Protestantism 1867-1914) in George A. Rawlyk (ed.), *The Canadian Protestant Experience, 1760-1900* (Burlington, ON: Welch Publishing, 1990), 127, makes the very general claim that "[Toronto Bible Training School], later renamed Ontario Bible College, became the model for similar schools that sprang up across Canada in the 1920s, the 1930s, and the 1940s." Conversely, it should be noted, Canadian church historian, Bruce Hindmarsh's article, "The Winnipeg Fundamentalist Network, 1910-1940: The Roots of Transdenominational Evangelicalism in Manitoba and Saskatchewan" in George A. Rawlyk (ed.), *Aspects of the Canadian Evangelical Experience* (Montreal and Kingston: McGill-Queen's University Press, 1997), 303-319, very effectively documents the cross-pollination between Canadian and American fundamentalism as it related to the fundamentalist movement in the Canadian provinces of Manitoba and Saskatchewan, a dynamic this study will suggest was also prominent in the evolution of PBI. Similarly, Ian S. Rennie, "The Western Prairie Revival in Canada: During the Depression and World War II" notes that "A Mennonite Brethren Bible School was started in 1913 at Herbert near Swift Current in southwestern Saskatchewan, by men who had been influenced by the Bible Institute movement in the United States," 15.

Stackhouse's argument that PBI represented a unique form of Canadian evangelicalism is all the more curious in light of his claim that several colleagues, including Ian S. Rennie, carefully read some portions of his book. Rennie, in "The Western Prairie Revival in Canada . . ." (n.d.), 5, doesn't hesitate in drawing a parallel between the western Canadian frontier as "a very anemic cousin of its more lusty American counterpart" or in noting the American religious influence in western Canada (8-9) and on some of the Bible schools (15) in the Canadian West. Nor does Rennie shrink from using the terms "Fundamentalist" and "independent Fundamentalist ethos" with specific regard to Maxwell and PBI (15, 19). He also writes of Moody Bible Institute staffer Oscar Lowry who once came to Alberta at Maxwell's urging and, among other ventures, "For six weeks during November and December Lowry preached over CFCN, Calgary. In that short period he received almost a thousand letters a week telling him, in many cases of individuals coming to faith in Jesus Christ" (21).

picture of PBI's identity during the period of history that saw the school attain international acclaim.[7]

To reiterate an important consideration, the issue here is not so much a matter of Stackhouse's having overlooked evidence of the American fundamentalist factor at PBI as it is the manner in which he minimized—if not dismissed—this reality in his eagerness to identify PBI as part of a unique form of Canadian evangelicalism that emerged in the twentieth century. My contention is that whatever one wishes to conclude about the nature of the evangelicalism that prevailed at PBI during the better part of the twentieth century, it was decidedly not as uniquely Canadian in its nature as Stackhouse maintained in his research.[8]

---

[7]   It is perplexing that whereas Stackhouse's work over the years gives frequent indications he is well aware of Maxwell's strong fundamentalist leanings as reflected in PBI's magazines or of the strong American presence at PBI during the Maxwell era, he nonetheless consistently chooses to minimize such. See, for example:

   Stackhouse, *Canadian Evangelicalism*, 235-248, where he makes numerous references to articles in the *Prairie Pastor* and/or *Prairie Overcomer* that railed against such topics as women's dress, theological liberalism in The United Church of Canada, Roman Catholicism, Henry Emerson Fosdick, communism, the ecumenical movement, evolution, rock and roll, etc., all favorite "whipping boys" of American fundamentalism.

   John G. Stackhouse, "The Protestant Experience in Canada Since 1945), in George A. Rawlyk (ed.) *The Canadian Protestant Experience* (Burlington, ON: G.R. Welch Publishing Co., 1990), 204-205: "Prairie had grown dramatically since its founding in 1922. Under the powerful leadership of American L.E. Maxwell . . . the combined attendance reaching a peak of 900 in 1948-49 . . . Many of these students were Americans, and Prairie exemplified the cultural ties between Canadians and Americans on the plains." (See Appendix I, Table 1.6 of this book).

[8]   Michael Anderson, "Six Pilgrims Share Their Story," in Robert E. Webber, *Evangelicals on the Canterbury Trail: Why Evangelicals are Attracted to the Liturgical Church*, (Waco, TX: Word Books, 1985), 93. Anderson, who grew up in Yankton, South Dakota, and graduated from PBI in 1971 lends an "insider" perspective when he writes: "[PBI] was a good and healthy experience for me, and apart from some glaring eccentricities and a certain narrowness of vision, the school tutored me in a rather moderate form of fundamentalism . . . It would be hard to establish the theological pedigree of the Institute. It was preeminently a product of the rise of American Fundamentalism in the early years of this century. It has a strong Anabaptist strain, moderated by a mild Calvinism and the English Keswick movement."

Bruce Guenther views Stackhouse's work as an "institutional biography" of PBI that is "detailed and insightful."[9] As accurate as this claim may be in some respects, I will discuss PBI from an insider's point of view in an effort to modify Stackhouse's portrayal of the school. In so doing, I aim to demonstrate that Stackhouse constructed a perception of PBI as being more exclusively and uniquely Canadian in its origins and ethos than is justified by the data.

I maintain that Stackhouse's insistence on embracing a distinction between Canadian evangelicalism and American fundamentalism essentially focused on merely one element of American fundamentalism: *militant separatism.* I suggest that this approach unfortunately obfuscates matters. Observers in the twentieth century itself were not always clear or in agreement as to the basic criteria for determining what constituted *militancy* when it came to evaluating the rhetoric and behavior of American fundamentalists. The latter part of that century and the history of the twenty-first century to date, of course, have decisively demonstrated that concepts of militancy in the religious sector within North America have indeed been taken to previously unheard-of and even unanticipated levels as compared to the earlier twentieth century. The various attempted and successful murders of doctors who performed abortions are one example that immediately comes to mind to substantiate this claim. Such violence has sometimes had a distinctly religious motivation. The salient point is that it is now apparent that what constituted militant rhetoric and/or behavior throughout most of the 1900s pales in comparison to what constitutes militancy by twenty-first century standards.

Additionally, I argue in this book that at least some of those whom Stackhouse designates as Canadian evangelicals, like Maxwell himself, were of precisely the same theological and behavioral stripe as those who led self-designated American fundamentalist organizations such as Moody Bible Institute, Columbia Bible College, and The Christian and Missionary Alliance. Evidence is advanced to document that, particularly in his early years of ministry, Maxwell took a back seat to no one on either side of the forty-ninth parallel with respect to employing inflammatory imagery in his written and spoken rhetoric.

---

9   Guenther, 70-71: "While the institutional biographies of Prairie Bible Institute and Toronto Bible College are detailed and insightful, they do not on their own constitute an analysis of the Bible school/college movement."

Some of the flaws in Stackhouse's work along these lines have already been noted and briefly challenged by at least a couple of scholars.[10] My treatment of the topic at hand builds on these observations. I contend that throughout the Maxwell era, PBI consistently reflected an affinity for a broader understanding of the American fundamentalist movement that

---

[10] Michael S. Hamilton, "The Fundamentalist Harvard: Wheaton College and the Continuing Vitality of American Evangelicalism, 1919-1965" (PhD dissertation, University of Notre Dame, 1994) 16, 17: "In fact, scholars using Marsden's and Lawrence's definition have already begun retrospectively to define fundamentalists out of their own movement. John Stackhouse's recent *Canadian Evangelicalism in the Twentieth Century* correctly recognizes that the groups he studies—Toronto Bible College, Prairie Bible Institute, and Inter-Varsity Christian Fellowship—are not best characterized by the concept of militant anti-modernism. Stackhouse argues persuasively that their primary commitments were instead to the preservation of orthodoxy, evangelism, and spiritual growth of the converted. Less happily, however, he takes this to mean that the "mainstream" of Canadian conservative Protestantism was less militant and less separatistic than the mainstream of American conservative Protestantism. The problem with this argument is that it must carry an enormous freight of empirical difficulties such as the time the presumably less-militant L.E. Maxwell of the Prairie Bible Institute launched a vehement doctrinal attack on the presumably more-militant Wheaton College—something Edman would never have done to Maxwell. Ultimately, Stackhouse's argument tangles up the scholar's definition of fundamentalism with the American reality. Thinking of fundamentalism as militant anti-modernism hides the fact that centrist conservative Protestantism in America was every bit as non-controversialist in style, interdenominational in character, and dedicated to evangelism and the nurturance of spirituality as that in Canada. In short, if Stackhouse's Canadian "evangelicals" were not fundamentalists, then neither were most American "fundamentalists." Stackhouse's reluctance to apply the label of fundamentalism to the mainstream of Canadian conservative Protestantism stems primarily from the problematic definition of the term that prevails in scholarly writing (and perhaps secondarily from the characteristic Canadian eagerness to distinguish Canada's social institutions from those south of the border), for in fact his centrist conservatives more often called themselves "fundamental Christians" or "fundamentalists" than they called themselves "evangelicals.""

Stanley J. Grenz, review of *Canadian Evangelicalism in the Twentieth Century* by John G. Stackhouse, Jr., *Christian Century*, 111, no. 9; (March 16, 1994): ". . . Not all readers will be convinced that Canadian evangelicalism and American fundamentalism can be so neatly disentangled . . . Did Canadian institutions such as Prairie Bible Institute sufficiently differ from U.S. counterparts such as Bob Jones University to deserve the label "evangelical" rather than "fundamentalist?""

originally developed during the late-nineteenth and early-twentieth centuries than merely what was represented by the movement's militancy.[11]

It may be necessary to register an important caveat at this point. Although some key similarities did exist between the religious milieu and cultural ethos that prevailed at Prairie during the Maxwell years and a broader definition of American fundamentalism than that which Stackhouse posits, this book does not propose that PBI was a carbon copy of the American fundamentalist paradigm or any component or institution thereof. In fact, I will propose that when American fundamentalism eventually fragmented into two distinct camps during the 1940s, PBI attempted to steer a somewhat middle course between the two factions.[12]

Jeffrey Simpson, "Fighting hockey violence will give you a concussion," *The Globe and Mail*, A17, February 14, 2009, offers an informed perspective on the discussion often heard in North America that Canadians are generally a more irenic people than their American neighbors. Discussing the topic of fighting in ice hockey, he states: "Attend an NHL game in any arena. When a fight starts, fans throughout the building rise, shout and gesticulate as vigorously as when a goal is scored. A few Canadians like to insist that fighting really only appeals to Americans. Fighting exists in hockey to sell the game in U.S. markets where people carry guns, watch football players smash each other and where television is overrun with violence.

"Alas, such an argument merely reflects Canadian conceit about Americans in general, and American hockey fans in particular. Watch a fight in any Canadian city with a professional team, or attend a junior hockey game where fights break out even more frequently than in the NHL. Canadian fans eat up fighting.

"It's in Canada, don't forget, where the highest media priests who defend fighting reside . . ."

[11] I am indebted to personal discussions with James Enns, currently a member of PBI's faculty, for calling to my attention the notion of PBI as a "branch plant" of American fundamentalism, and to a July 5, 2007, e-mail exchange with Michael S. Hamilton of Seattle Pacific University in which he referred to Prairie as "an outpost of northern American fundamentalism."

As already suggested in footnote 6, Canadian church historian, Ian Rennie, demonstrated no hesitation whatsoever in associating PBI with American-style fundamentalism in "The Western Prairie Revival in Canada," 15. Similarly, Canadian sociologist, Harry H. Hiller, does not shy from linking PBI with American fundamentalism in "Alberta and the Bible Belt Stereotype," 372-383; Stewart Crysdale and Les Wheatcroft (eds), *Religion in Canadian Society*, Toronto: Macmillan of Canada, 1976.

[12] Part of the reason for this reality may have stemmed from the type of thinking reflected in one of L.E Maxwell's favorite sayings: "The hardest thing in the world is to keep balanced" as in L.E. Maxwell, *Quips & Quotes*; (Three Hills, AB: Action

This means that the school never officially embraced the ultra-strict "second-order separation" mandate advanced by the likes of mid-century American fundamentalist leaders such as Bob Jones Jr., John R. Rice and Carl McIntire (representative of the separatist camp). Yet neither did PBI whole-heartedly clamber aboard the "neo-evangelical" vessel that set out to sea under the guidance of Harold J. Ockenga, Carl F.H. Henry, and Billy Graham. Nor did the school ever officially endorse the entity that eventually became known as the National Association of Evangelicals (representative of the neo-evangelical camp).

In the course of establishing my basic argument, therefore, this book affirms that the best lens through which to view the type of Christian fundamentalism that prevailed at PBI during the Maxwell era is that which regards the school during that period as a hybrid. That is, it was a combination of a broadly defined American fundamentalism and one of its particular components, the British Keswick movement with its attendant emphasis on the victorious Christian life.

It is apparent to me that, particularly in Prairie's first twenty or so years of operation (1922-1942), Maxwell was very dependent on certain of the belligerent elements of American fundamentalism to lead the way in defining the basic stances PBI would adopt on various religious and cultural controversies. When American fundamentalism divided into the separatist and neo-evangelical camps, however, the evidence indicates that PBI's preference was to focus on the pietistic and holiness emphases of Keswick while maintaining its international reputation as a missionary training center.[13]

By the time the 1950s arrived, Maxwell's evolving theological orientation demonstrated he was more at home with the kind of emphases that characterized the Keswick culture than with those issues that preoccupied the interests of either the feuding fundamentalists or the fledgling neo-evangelicals.

International Ministries, 1992), 3. Students at PBI often referred to this dictum as Maxwell I:I.

[13] Rennie, "The Western Prairie Revival," 16, hints at this type of interpretation for PBI when he states in reference to L.E. Maxwell: "He stressed holiness of the mystical Keswick type with his hero being—mirabile dictum—the extreme French Roman Catholic Quietist, Madame Guyon."

In summation then, the primary purpose of this book is to spotlight the strong connection that existed during the Maxwell era between Prairie Bible Institute and a broader understanding of American fundamentalism than what Stackhouse allowed. As a part of that overall objective, Prairie's affinity for the revivalism and holiness theology characteristic of Keswick is briefly explored.[14] In so doing, it is demonstrated that the revivalist and holiness emphases were also important components of a broader understanding of twentieth-century American fundamentalism than what was accounted for in Stackhouse's work.

A brief explanation of the Insider/Outsider perspectives

This inquiry into the theological and cultural ethos that prevailed at Prairie Bible Institute under L.E. Maxwell attempts an interpretive analysis of the topic incorporating qualitative research with my own personal experience growing up on the campus of the school from 1960 to 1977. Appendix I presents a superficial quantitative assessment of PBI in support of my overall argument although such a focus was but a minor component of my research and is offered here merely as a "snapshot" of where further research in that direction might lead.

As a qualitative effort, my work here reflects an inductive orientation as well as an attempt to contextualize various emphases, teachings and events that held sway and/or transpired at PBI during the years under review. A holistic view of phenomena is intended throughout in a manner that allows for subjectivity along with an emphasis on description and an exploration for meaning. It should be apparent throughout this work that I have attempted to participate in and collaborate with the data presented.

By way of an interpretive analysis, it is imperative for readers to be aware that my interest in and exposure to the topic explored within these pages has a distinctly personal dimension. In March of 1960 following my third birthday, my parents, Victor and Bernice Callaway, joined the staff

---

[14] Maxwell's first and best received book, *Born Crucified*, (Chicago, Moody Press, 1945) was based on a series of editorials he'd written for the staunch American fundamentalist journal *The Sunday School Times*. It contains significant evidence that Maxwell's thinking had been influenced by teachings referred to as "the Deeper Life" and "the Victorious Life" that were associated with Keswick. Note especially Philip E. Howard, Jr.'s *Forward* in the book.

of the Prairie Bible Institute.[15] Although my father initially worked in the mail-order department of the institute's bookstore, he eventually went on to assume roles as Director of Public Relations, a member of Prairie's Board of Directors and of its Operating Executive Committee (OEC). Prior to his retirement in 1987, "Vic" (as my father was known to colleagues) also served for several years as the Executive Secretary of the institute. The tasks of board member, member of the OEC and Institute Secretary required his participation at the highest levels of Prairie's decision-making processes.

While growing up as a "staff kid" at PBI, I thus completed programs in Prairie's elementary school (K-8; 1961-1970), high school (9-12; 1970-1974) and Bible school (four-year Pastoral Diploma program; 1974-1977 including spring sessions).[16] Over a span of seventeen years therefore, I not only experienced life at PBI for myself but was often able to interact with my parents regarding the rationale behind certain thinking, decisions and policies that prevailed on the school's campus where we lived.[17]

---

[15] Norman F. Cantor and Richard I. Schneider, *How to Study History* (Arlington Heights, IL: Harlan Davidson Inc., 1967), 19: "It is true that forty or fifty years ago it was widely believed that history was merely a record of the past, a journal about what happened, and that the historian's responsibility was merely to collect the data ("The facts, and only the facts!") of the past for present readers . . . This older view of history, we have come to see, is also false because it is based on a naïve belief that the historian can dispassionately separate himself from the events he is describing and can be "unbiased." Modern psychology and philosophy have taught us that every historian comes to his material with a previous set of assumptions about what is important and what is not. The historian cannot tell us every fact of what happened in the past; he invariably selects from a great number of events and facts the ones that he thinks are important."

[16] L.L. Langness, *The Life History in Anthropological Science,* (New York: Holt, Rinehart and Winston, 1965), 3: "It is probably safe to say that the more the data are based upon direct observation the more accurate they are, the more they are based upon what one has been told the less accurate they are. The problems involved stem mostly from the personal biases of both observer and observed. It is this fact which has led in the past to the rejection of introspective accounts and to the development of extreme forms of behaviorism. The science of man demands, however, that all human behavior, introspective as well as any other, be taken into account . . . to simply record controlled observations of behavior in the absence of verbal accounts and introspection, although it might prove very amusing, would be absurd."

[17] Leonard I. Sweet, "Wise as Serpents, Innocent as Doves: The New Evangelical Historiography," *Journal of the American Academy of Religion,* LVI:3, 397-416, discusses the negatives and the positives of the contributions of "insider" or "observer-participant"

During their years of active service at the school, both of my parents were good friends of and colleagues with Prairie's first five presidents: J. Fergus Kirk (1922-61), A. Henry Muddle (1961-65), L.E. Maxwell (1965-77), Paul T. Maxwell (1977-86), and Ted S. Rendall (1986-92), as well as with many other members of Prairie's core leadership teams. Following retirement, my parents continued to live within the PBI community offering varying levels of volunteer involvement until my father's death in July 2005 and my mother's passing in June 2009.

---

evangelical scholars Joel A. Carpenter, Nathan Hatch, George Marsden, Mark Noll, Harry Stout and Grant Wacker to evangelical historiography. When it comes to portraying the history of Prairie Bible Institute, then, there are similar pluses and minuses to my status as an "observer-participant." One of the keys Sweet identifies to "understanding the phenomenon of observer-participant history" (401) is recognizing the personal backgrounds of the historians named above who are "second generation evangelicals." They grew up, he writes, in environments where "they were not subjected to fundamentalism's harsh schooling." He credits their upbringing at some distance from fundamentalism for their ability to be somewhat dispassionate when writing about it. Comparatively speaking, I grew up in an environment where it was both expected and demanded of PBI "staff kids" that they adhere to the expectations arising from how PBI taught and practiced the Christian faith. Open rebellion usually met with drastic results such as the child being expelled and the parents being asked to leave staff. Although my parents were open enough to allow their children to question/ challenge (within the privacy of "home") certain of PBI's regulations and expectations, they fully expected behavior of a manner which reflected my father's standing as a part of PBI's leadership team. Youthful incidents that cast aspersions on their reputation were cause for great concern at home. Part of what I am attempting in this book thus has an element of what Sweet says the Germans call *Vergangenheitsbewaltigung*, (402): "coming to terms with and overcoming the past by recognizing oneself as a product of the past and by mastering the history of one's own past." It is my responsibility, Sweet would suggest, (404), to try and recover what he calls the "Protestant-Principle,"— "the ability and willingness to be self-critical without defensiveness or spite." Sweet accordingly applauds the historians he discusses for learning "the art of critique in polite, discreet, kind, and even loving ways" (404). While such nobility is commendable, there is a sense in which I must leave my success in these respects to the judgment of readers. To be sure, this is not a problem-free undertaking as is apparent when Sweet states: "What Marsden identifies as "innocent" and "alleged" (1987:105) can appear rather brutal and blatant to the outsider" (405). Hopefully, the research represented in this book will contribute in some way to the existence of "absorbing critiques of fundamentalist sectarianism, anti-intellectualism, personalities, and populism" (406). That hope is offered bearing in mind Sweet's reminder that Marsden "denies the possibility of writing completely "objective history" (411) and Noll argues that "no one writes about the past with objectivity" (412).

Accordingly, my personal connection to Prairie Bible Institute warrants a forthright acknowledgement of the potential complications associated with what is commonly referred to as the Insider/Outsider problem in studies of this nature.[18] A truncated identification of such is therefore important to mention here.

In brief, as presented by Russell T. McCutcheon, the Insider/Outsider problem as it relates to studies in religion identifies members of the group under investigation as "insiders." It asks whether a researcher or an "outsider" who does not share the assumptions and beliefs of the "insiders" is actually capable of offering an accurate and effective critique of the actions and beliefs of that group. Furthermore, can an outside researcher adequately leave behind their own background, biases and experiences in order to effectively "climb into the skin" of the "insider" and see reality from the "insider" perspective even if they happen to share some of the assumptions and beliefs of the "insiders?"

As it concerns the perspective I bring to the topic at hand, the fact is that for the better part of twenty years, I was some kind of an "insider" by virtue of spending most of my childhood as well as all of my adolescent and early young adult years as a member of the Prairie Bible Institute community. As such, I therefore shared or was perceived to share the assumptions and beliefs that prevailed at the school. For better or worse, therefore, I cannot help but bring some of the baggage of an "insider" to this study.[19]

Some participants in the Insider/Outsider debate would hasten to suggest that since my life following those years has been lived as a participant in the broader North American evangelical community, I more than qualify as an "insider" with regard to the topic of Prairie Bible Institute. Conversely, it should be acknowledged that other voices in the discussion might consider

---

[18] Russell T. McCutcheon, (ed.) *The Insider/Outsider Problem in the Study of Religion: a Reader* (London and New York: Cassell, 1999), 1-22. As McCutcheon and others indicate, the issues related to the Insider/Outsider debate are significant.

  Michael H. Agar, *The Professional Stranger: An Informal Introduction to Ethnography* (New York: Academic Press - Harcourt Brace Jovanovich, Publishers, 1980); see especially Chapters 1-3, 6.

[19] As many of my former fellow "staff kids" could affirm, the question might well be asked as to whether we ourselves qualify or qualified as true "insiders" or were merely the children of "insiders." The matter as to when, if ever, a "staff kid" truly became an "insider" would doubtless be suitable fodder for some animated conversations among those of us who grew up at PBI.

me to now be an "outsider" since over thirty-five years have elapsed since I left PBI.

Given the nature of the general topic in view in this work, Christian fundamentalism, it is perhaps significant to also point out that approximately fifteen years of my life after leaving PBI were spent as the pastor of two congregations associated with the Baptist Union of Western Canada (BUWC), now known as Canadian Baptists in Western Canada (CBWC). In addition to being a member of the Baptist World Alliance, CBWC is one of three bodies that comprise the Canadian Baptist Federation (CBF). The CBF is perhaps best known in Canadian church history as the organization that the fiery Canadian fundamentalist pastor, T. T. Shields, charged with heresy and eventually abandoned in the mid-1920s to start another group that now exists as the Fellowship of Evangelical Baptists in Canada (FEBC), or, as they are more commonly identified, the "Fellowship Baptists."

While a pastor in Toronto in the 1920s, Shields repeatedly maintained that one of the CBF's schools, the well-known McMaster University in Hamilton, Ontario, harbored theological modernists on its divinity faculty. The point here is to simply note that, in the eyes of some people affiliated with PBI, the Baptist Union with which I once served was accordingly considered a theologically "suspect" organization owing to its affiliation with McMaster Divinity School.[20]

The relevant point of this information for the discussion at hand is simply to note that a significant period of my adult life has been spent outside strict fundamentalist circles which may prompt some to label me an "outsider" as it concerns the focus of this book. Having thus divulged my background, and in recognition of the fact that both the "insider" and "outsider" roles have their own strengths and weaknesses, perhaps it is best left to readers to draw their own conclusions with regard to where I best fit

---

[20] My own parents had roots in the Fellowship of Evangelical Baptist Churches in Canada, a descendant denomination of the group T.T. Shields founded after breaking with the Baptist Convention of Ontario and Quebec (or "Convention" Baptists as they were commonly known) over his views of theological modernism at McMaster. When I advised my parents following seminary that I was taking employment with a church affiliated with the Baptist Union of Western Canada, a sister organization to the Baptist Convention of Ontario and Quebec, they expressed moderate concern owing to their awareness of the historic events involving Shields and McMaster. Right up until shortly before her passing, my mother derived amusement by reminding me that "the jury is still out regarding your orthodoxy, Timothy!"

on the Insider/Outsider scale with respect to the matter of my relationship to PBI.[21]

As intimated, my upbringing at Prairie presents certain advantages as well as some disadvantages for the purposes of this study. It is therefore appropriate to acknowledge at least some of the more important of each category in a work that consists of an interpretive analysis.

As to the former, because I was a PBI "staff kid" for almost one-third of the time period in view in this study, there is a definite sense in which I bring an "insider's" perspective to the realities of the culture that prevailed at Prairie at the time. I know the topic of this study very well as a result of having lived in Prairie's fundamentalist sub-culture for a substantial and formative period of my life. Some of the perspectives advanced in this project, therefore, arise from personal memories of numerous experiences and people encountered during the years I spent growing up on the campus of Prairie Bible Institute.[22]

---

[21] L.L. Langness, 47, writes: "It has often been suggested that anthropological fieldworkers should undergo psychoanalysis before going into the field. The purpose of such an analysis is, of course, to give the investigator insight into his own personality and thus enable him to understand better how much of his work reflects himself and how much reflects objective reality. Although it is not necessary to go to this extreme, it is an idea of considerable merit; the personality of the investigator can obviously play an important role both in the kinds of material that will be gathered and in what subsequently happens to it." While my wife and children—the two youngest of which are pursuing graduate studies in clinical psychology—would doubtless affirm that I am a worthy candidate for ongoing psychoanalysis, let the record show that, for better or worse, such was not received prior to undertaking the research for this book.

[22] Paul Thompson, *The Voice of the Past: Oral History* (Oxford: Oxford University Press, 1978), 2: "The challenge of oral history lies partly in relation to this essential social purpose of history. This is a major reason why it has so excited some historians, and so frightened others. In fact, fear of oral history as such is groundless. We shall see later that the use of interviews as a source by professional historians is long-standing and perfectly compatible with scholarly standards." Later, 20, Thompson offers an apt reminder that in pre-literate societies, "all history was oral history" and that even in literate societies, most history begins as the spoken word.

Largely because so many of the main players on the PBI stage during the years under review in this book are now either deceased or aged and infirm, the only pure interview conducted for this study was taped with Dr. Ted Rendall over four hours on August 14, 2006, at the Ted S. Rendall Library on the PBI campus. (Thompson, 98: ". . . the recording is a far more reliable and accurate account of a meeting than a purely written record.") Due to his wife's poor health, Paul T. Maxwell declined my

One of the reasons this factor is important is due to the various "myths" that have circulated far and wide regarding life at PBI under Maxwell's administration. I still occasionally encounter people today who are eager to advance their misinformed perceptions of the PBI of Maxwell's day as solid facts. Unfortunately for them, I know with certainty that many of these "facts" are simply false.[23] I readily confess to a certain amount of sinister delight derived from allowing people to feverishly paint themselves into a corner with their ignorance concerning the PBI of the Maxwell era prior to revealing to them the fact that I spent virtually all of my youth at the institution they evidence an eagerness to dissect.

My parents first moved to Three Hills in 1946 when my father enrolled as a Bible school student at PBI following domestic service in the Canadian Army during World War II. My mother took a number of classes at Prairie while simultaneously managing duties as a wife, mother and homemaker. My father graduated from Prairie in 1952 before returning to work in the Prairie Book Room as a staff member in March 1960. After moving into the position of PBI's Extension Director, a role that included scheduling various music teams of PBI students to promote the school in numerous churches across North America, he encountered most of the "myths" and perspectives that were in circulation during those years regarding Prairie and its curious ethos. He frequently relayed the same to Mom often unaware that youthful ears were listening.

The perspective I reveal in this book will hopefully contribute to exposing, clarifying and correcting certain historical fallacies concerning

---

request for an interview. I conducted numerous informal interviews with my parents in the months and years preceding their deaths. Additional informal interviews were periodically conducted with several former PBI "staff kids" in an effort to clarify my own memory of events and dynamics referred to here.

That being said, there is a sense in which this book reflects what amounted to an ongoing interview with myself as I've recalled incidents and people from years gone by. In that respect, Thompson's documentation of several studies on memory and mental retention is encouraging, 100-102: "It is clear that on all counts the loss of memory during the first nine months is as great as that during the next forty-seven years. Only beyond this do the tests suggest any sharp decline in average memory . . ." See also his observation, 112, that: ". . . significant memory persists in most people over an interval of fifty years."

[23] One story that circulated in the mid-1960s claimed that L.E. Maxwell owned two Cadillacs. In fact, he had recently undergone eye surgery for cataracts!

Prairie Bible Institute. Perhaps some of the information and interpretation shared here will also enlighten readers concerning lesser or little-known realities about Prairie.

It is my judgment that the few written works in circulation regarding the history of PBI might generally be classified in two categories. On one hand are several books written at the popular level that present a very positive and, on occasion, a somewhat idealistic view of the Kirk family, L.E. Maxwell and Prairie Bible Institute.[24] This is not surprising since most of these volumes were written, commissioned or funded by Prairie Bible Institute itself or by people with close ties to Prairie, the Kirks and/ or L.E. Maxwell.

On the other hand, there are a small number of academic studies that, although insightful and somewhat more objective than the first group in their analysis of Prairie and its founders, cannot help but occasionally reflect superficial if not inaccurate analysis. Such inevitably arises when a researcher merely visits or interviews the subject of their study for or during comparatively brief periods of time.[25] It is my conclusion that such limited exposure to Prairie's people, culture and history has contributed to the propagation of certain misperceptions about an institution that was my home for seventeen years.

Having been away from PBI for now more than three decades, I thus draw on my first-hand, long-term experience of growing up at Prairie in combination with my subsequently acquired academic and professional experiences to advance a perspective I suggest is more critically informed on the topic than some of those available to date.[26] Certain of the views tendered

---

[24] For example, see Chapter Four's review in this book of works by Keller (1966), Callaway (1987), Epp (1973) and Fuller (2002).

[25] For example, see Donald A. Goertz, "The Development of a Bible Belt," (MCS thesis, Regent College, 1980) and Stackhouse, *Canadian Evangelicalism*. The latter is a revision and expansion of Stackhouse's PhD dissertation earlier submitted to the University of Chicago. See also David R. Elliott, David R., "Studies of Eight Canadian Fundamentalists," (PhD dissertation, University of British Columbia, 1989).

[26] Perhaps the best way to describe what is being attempted in this book is to direct readers' attention to a work that is somewhat difficult to classify. One of L.E. Maxwell's grandsons, Stephen M. Spaulding, prepared a very helpful thesis entitled "Lion on the Prairies: An Interpretive Analysis of the Life and Leadership of Leslie Earl Maxwell 1895-1984" as part of his studies while a student at Fuller Theological Seminary's School of World Missions. It is obvious in reading Stephen's work that he had the

here will therefore evidence a quality that students, observers and researchers like Stackhouse who came to Prairie from elsewhere for comparatively brief periods of time cannot legitimately be expected to have fully absorbed.[27]

Conversely, I hasten to state that I am aware of some of the shortcomings that my being a former "staff kid" brings to this study. For one thing, I recognize that while there are some positive connotations of being an "insider," such a designation also presents certain limitations. I have undoubtedly been influenced in my view by having been completely immersed in the Prairie culture for most of my formative years. Even a rudimentary acquaintance with basic principles of psychology suggests that my perspectives at times may be skewed in ways that I do not yet grasp.[28]

---

benefit of "insider" perspectives on L.E. Maxwell (his mother, Eleanor, was Maxwell's oldest daughter) which in turn enhanced the credibility of his critical analysis of Maxwell's life as a leader. However, in an e-mail exchange with Steve Spaulding on August 16-17, 2009, he advised me that he ultimately did not submit this work for credit at Fuller. Nonetheless, the document offers a very useful, if personal, overview of L.E. Maxwell's life and ministry.

That being said, it should be recognized that the challenges of oral history are quite significant. For example, Spaulding's parents recall L.E. Maxwell's tendency to occasionally preach almost an entire sermon after a featured speaker had finished in this way (p. 75): ". . . L.E. also had the rare gift of bringing others' messages to a greater level of intensity and application, or actually rescuing poor messages from utter uselessness and pouring new light from Scripture or some insight upon the matter." Others, meanwhile, considered Maxwell's penchant in this regard to be rude and inconsiderate.

[27] L.L. Langness, 42: "The longer the anthropologist has in the field, whether in one period or by returning several times to the same place, the greater is the likelihood that his data will be reliable."

[28] Arthur Marwick, *The Nature of History*, (London: Macmillan and Company Ltd., 1970), 109: "Later commentators have rightly remarked that so long as the historian continued to back his psychological insights without reference to the discoveries of modern psychology he was producing, if not literature, certainly fiction . . . Today no historian could write a biographical study without betraying something of the influence of Freudian and post-Freudian psychology."

As previously noted, two of my children are presently pursuing graduate studies in clinical psychology and take great delight in reminding me of the considerable power of the formative years in constructing one's overall psychological orientation. I absorb their not-so-subtle insinuations by reminding them that whereas they may be using their mother's brains for their education, they're using my credit cards which I alone retain the right and, indeed, the privilege, of canceling at will.

For all practical purposes, my initial worldview was completely formulated in and by the PBI milieu and I had a minimum of other experiences or contexts to compare it with as a child, adolescent or young adult. Whereas most young people came to Prairie for eight to ten months of the school year and then went home during summer, Christmas and spring vacations, my home was at Prairie for twelve months of the year. Even many of my childhood summer vacations were taken at property that PBI owned at Pine Lake, a rustic lakeside campground located about an hour's drive northwest of the campus. Fellow campers there were usually families from Prairie or other similar Christian ministries that were in some way associated with or supportive of PBI.

Since to some extent we are all products of our respective upbringings, I am well aware that some of my perspectives on Prairie Bible Institute may reflect a subjectivity that could serve to actually hinder the kind of clear analysis that more objective observers might bring to this topic. If I fault previous researchers for not being close enough to the institution under analysis, it may be that they could legitimately fault me for indeed being too close to it. That being said, as a guiding light for this study I have attempted to bear in mind the observation that "the historian cannot help but make moral judgments, if only by implication or by virtue of his selection of the facts . . ."[29]

To be candid, when one of my academic supervisors first suggested I engage in research on PBI, my immediate inclination was to dismiss the suggestion owing to personal reservations that I could not be objective enough concerning the topic.[30] It was only after concluding that an important vacancy existed in what limited research has been done on Prairie that I opted to proceed.

It should also be noted that by virtue of being a "staff kid," my experience of life at PBI differed in certain ways and at specific times from those who experienced Prairie as residential students. For one thing, I never lived in

---

[29] Marwick, 102.

[30] The problem of objectivity in historical research is, of course, well documented in the discipline. See, for example, James E. Bradley and Richard A. Muller in *Church History: An Introduction to Research, Reference Works, and Methods* (Grand Rapids: Wm. B. Eerdmans Publishing Co., 1995), 48ff, and Michael A. Agar, *Speaking of Ethnography: Qualitative Research Methods* (vol. 2) (Beverly Hills, CA: Sage Publications, 1986), 11-25, whose insights were particularly helpful in researching this project.

the dormitories or student residences at Prairie thereby inevitably missing out on certain important dynamics of that particular component of the PBI experience. The military-style discipline that governed the lives of Prairie students was certainly not a part of my experience to the same extent that it was for those who lived in the "dorms."

For instance, at least some of us as "staff kids" had access to radios, phonographs and cassette recorders long before such were ever permitted in PBI's dormitories. As well, it was generally far easier for the children of staff members to leave campus with their parents and travel to nearby cities like Red Deer, Calgary or Edmonton than for those who lived in the dormitories to do so. Further, when I was in high school, my parents chose to regularly attend a church that was some distance away from the PBI campus thereby enabling me to have a more normal exposure to members of the opposite sex than was the case for resident students at Prairie High School.

Privileges such as these were enough to make some of my friends who lived in the PBI dormitories frequently remark to the effect that "you staff kids have it far easier than we do." Accordingly, as my wife who was a dormitory student at Prairie frequently reminds me, it would be somewhat misleading for me to imply that my experience of Prairie should be considered the "norm." To reinforce the important point then, readers should bear in mind that those of us who lived in staff homes had more freedoms than did the dormitory students, a factor that may skew my perspective on PBI at some important points.[31]

Nonetheless, having weighed at least some of the "pros" and "cons" of my personal relationship to the topic at hand, and having sought the perspective of several respected academics on the matter, it is important to mention again that more than thirty-five years have now elapsed since I graduated from Prairie Bible Institute and left my boyhood home at PBI.

---

[31] For example, the children in Victor and Bernice Callaway's family were never early-risers. Consequently, arising at 6 a.m. on weekdays as required in the PBI dorms was not a part of our regular routine. And, since it is widely rumored that confession is good for the soul, let the record show that I had regular access to the splendors of rock-and-roll music while such was *verboten* in the school's dormitories where radios were not permitted. Indeed, my biggest worry in this regard consisted in successfully switching off tunes like Alice Cooper's beloved "School's Out" before my parents came within earshot of such "jungle-jive" as my father consistently derided it.

Hopefully, any tendencies to be too subjective in my analysis of the topic are somewhat mitigated by these realities.

It may be beneficial for me to comment on one more reality that will be apparent at various points in this book. Such relates to the role that personal memory played in the construction of some of the contents of these pages. As most readers can appreciate, since more than thirty-five years have passed since I resided at and attended Prairie Bible Institute, I have inevitably forgotten and possibly even misinterpreted or misrepresented certain details and experiences from those years. These possibilities represent what some might consider as merely another weakness of the "insider" perspective that I bring to the study.

Having acknowledged such, however, it is useful to consider the work of Eduardo Hoornaert who points out that, notwithstanding the challenges associated with the reality, memory has always played a key role particularly in Judaism and Christianity.[32] On the one hand, he reminds us, the essence of Christianity and the associated hope it offers is inextricably linked with the memories of the early saints who eventually "sought to replace their purely oral memorials with written documentation."[33] Following in the tradition of Eusebius and Aquinas, Hoornaert argues, "Church history will always have its role to perform in the mission of reanimating the memories of the Christian community."[34] Nonetheless, he cautions, even the most revered historians "cannot but be the prisoners of their own categories when it comes to an analysis of the data of the past." What this means in practical terms, Hoornaert asserts, is that "our memory is conditioned by social influences of which we are unaware."[35]

Important factors regarding the parameters of this study

This study of Prairie Bible Institute focuses primarily on the approximately sixty years that L.E. Maxwell was active in the founding, teaching, preaching

---

[32] Eduardo Hoornaert, *The Memory of the Christian People* (Maryknoll, NY: Orbis Books, 1988), 3: "Judaism and Christianity are "memory religions." Unlike other religions, they are based primarily on a fund of historical data engraved on the memory of the faithful throughout the course of their history."

[33] Ibid., 4-5.

[34] 9.

[35] 20.

and leadership duties associated with the school (1922-1980). It was during this period that Prairie established an international reputation for its training of missionaries, pastors and other Christian workers. Practically speaking, then, this inquiry is really a study of the PBI of yesteryear and does not take into consideration the significant changes the school has undergone to date in the post-Maxwell era.[36]

It may be helpful to note with regard to some of the changes in ideological orientation that have occurred at PBI since Maxwell's tenure that four presidents have now served the school following Maxwell-protege T.S. Rendall's retirement in 1992 to serve as Chancellor. Dr. Paul Ferris, an American, held the position from 1992-1998 followed by Canadians Richard Down (1998-2002), Dr. Charlotte Kinvig (interim) and Dr. Jon Ohlhauser, who took over in early 2003. Ohlhauser was succeeded in 2010 by Mark Maxwell, the grandson of L.E. Maxwell and nephew of Paul T. Maxwell, who had served as PBI board chairman during much of Ohlhauser's tenure.[37]

In the Winter 2008 issue of PBI's alumni publication, *Prairie Harvester*, Ohlhauser stated that since 1922 more than 15,000 men and women have "completed a personal journey of study and growth in the understanding of Scripture" at PBI. He also announced the formation of two new divisions at PBI to augment the ministry of the Bible College: Prairie School of Mission Aviation and Prairie College of Applied Arts and Technology.[38]

The major reasons for limiting this study to the Maxwell era will be readily appreciated by most readers. For one thing, the historical and economic realities that impacted both Alberta and Canada during Maxwell's tenure left the broader society that PBI was part of a very different place by the early 1980s than it was when classes began there in an abandoned farmhouse in 1922.

---

[36] It should perhaps be noted that although, as previously mentioned, I left PBI over thirty-five years ago, my awareness of changes at the school remains current in that two brothers and a sister still live in Three Hills and have all served on PBI staff at some point. As of this writing, my two brothers are on PBI staff while my sister still resides in Three Hills.

[37] An October 24, 2009, e-mail to PBI Alumni advising of recent developments at PBI stated: ". . . the Board and the President discussed how to best move forward. They mutually concluded that this was an appropriate time for a change of Presidency. Dr. Ohlhauser will be concluding as President at the end of December."

[38] *Prairie Harvester*, (Winter 2008), 2.

The province of Alberta joined Canada in 1905 at a time when the western frontier consisted of mile after mile of rugged terrain beckoning for development by hardy homesteaders. The burgeoning population of Europe needed food and the soil of Western Canada was viewed as a primary potential answer to this demand. As a result, "settlers flocked to the empty prairies" so that by 1930 there were approximately ten times as many people in Alberta as there had been in that area at the start of the twentieth century.[39]

Despite the promising economic prosperity that began to be quickly realized in Western Canada, there were those who made haste to sound the alarm right across North America that affluence and abundance were creating a spiritual famine in the nation's western provinces.[40] The onset of a severe economic depression in the 1930s prompted some to suggest such should be viewed as the judgment of God on man's spiritual waywardness.[41]

---

[39] J.M.S. Careless, *Canada: A Story of Challenge* (Toronto: Macmillan, 1970), 301-2: "Only in the 'last, best West' of Canada was there a great reserve of fertile soil whose crops could feed the factory population of Europe. Now at last there was good reason to settle the Canadian West. Settlers flocked to the empty prairies, from Britain, from the United States, from continental Europe. Year by year the rustling wheat fields reached further into the western grasslands, year by year the crops poured eastward through the narrow funnel of the Canadian Pacific [railroad], and yet the demand for grain continued to grow."

[40] M.B. Ryan, "Provinces of Western Canada Call for the Restoration Message," *Christian Standard*, vol. LXIII, No. 8, (February 25, 1928), 1: "Western Canada is just now one of the most interesting communities in the world. In its newness it is full of inspiring possibilities . . . We share here with all parts of the western world, in the rampant materialism, born of the machine age, stimulated by profuse inventiveness and deified by popular acclaim as the supreme good . . . We are beset in a thousand forms with the evil spirit of our age, the lawlessness, the mad chase after pleasure, the scorn of the ancient sanctities of life, the absorption in the making of money . . . There is only one influence that can save this new community from blight and abortion. That is the gospel of Christ. We can no more survive a devotion to materialism than could Babylon or Rome."

[41] As will be seen in Chapter Nine of this book, this was a perspective shared by J. Fergus Kirk. See also, L.E. Maxwell, "Healing for a Sick World," *Prairie Pastor*, Vol. 6, No. 9, (September 1933), 2: "The present depression is a result of an apostate church having either forgotten or willfully repudiated her calling and settled down to make this world serve her; rather than to recognize in this world enemy-territory out of which God's people are to be saved."

In 1935 the residents of Alberta elected a Social Credit government, an evolving administration that survived until 1971 under the leadership of three premiers: William Aberhart, Ernest C. Manning and Harry Strom, each of whom was an outspoken fundamentalist Christian.[42] Indeed, for years both Aberhart and Manning broadcast weekly radio programs by which they preached a fundamentalist version of the Christian gospel, a reality that also enabled them to maintain a timely profile before thousands of prospective voters.[43]

The importance of these facts for this book is that for a significant portion of the Maxwell era, a unique religious environment prevailed in Alberta as compared to other political jurisdictions in Canada: the top politician in the province was well-known as a fundamentalist Christian.[44] The overlap of the political and religious spheres in Alberta under the Social Credit administrations created an environment in which the general population of the province was at least tolerant and knowledgeable, if not entirely supportive, of the emphases of fundamentalist Christianity.

---

[42] Social Credit was a monetary theory based on the writings of Major Clifford Hugh Douglas, a Scottish engineer and cost accountant. For a helpful discussion of this philosophy, see John J. Barr, *The Dynasty: The Rise and Fall of Social Credit in Alberta* (Toronto: McClelland & Stewart, 1974), especially Chapter Three.

Harry Strom's brother, Clarence, was one of the pastors of the congregation at Prairie Tabernacle where I attended for a good part of my youth. Clarence Strom was also a part-time instructor at Prairie Bible Institute during the brief time (1968-71) that Harry Strom was premier of Alberta. Clarence Strom and my father along with other men from PBI periodically attended meetings of The Canadian Protestant League, an anti-Catholic organization of which Canadian fundamentalist pastor, T.T. Shields, was founding president.

[43] By 1925, long before he entered politics, Aberhart, a full-time school teacher and part-time pastor, had "a weekly two-hour radio program reaching over 350,000 listeners every Sunday" (see Barr, 39). In 1929 he launched the Prophetic Bible Institute in Calgary (a school even more fundamentalist in its orientation than Prairie by virtue of its insistence on using only the King James Version of the Bible along with other distinctive and unique perspectives). Aberhart incurred criticism from some, including L.E. Maxwell, when he left religious life to enter politics. I vividly recall Sunday nights as a youth hearing Premier Ernest Manning preach on "Canada's National Back to the Bible Hour" over radio station CJDV—Drumheller.

[44] As will be noted later, in his early years Maxwell was generally content to keep his distance from politicians, including those who were professing Christian fundamentalists. He did however develop a friendship with Aberhart's successor as the premier of Alberta, E.C. Manning.

By the last decade (1970s) of the Maxwell era, however, both Alberta and Canada had witnessed significant changes emerge on the economic and political scenes. At the national level, a man widely considered by fundamentalist Christians to be a socialist and a Communist-sympathizer, Pierre Elliott Trudeau, was elected Prime Minister of Canada in 1968.[45] Social issues like gay rights and the morality of capital punishment were soon being openly debated in Canadian popular culture.

When Canada celebrated its 100th birthday in 1967 by hosting an international extravaganza at Montreal under the banner "Man and His World," it was a designation perceived by many conservative Canadians as a shockingly secular theme. Moreover, the country began cutting the apron strings to its British origins by designing and adopting its own national flag in 1965, then repatriating its Constitution and creating its own Bill of Rights and Freedoms in 1982.[46]

The discovery of underground crude oil in 1947 at Leduc in central Alberta garnered international attention for Alberta's economy as it became obvious the province had more to offer the world than grain, lumber, beef and coal.[47] Although the province of Alberta already had a significant number of American residents, this discovery of ample hydrocarbons brought even more Americans north.[48]

---

[45] I recall as an eleven year-old being beset by fear listening to various authorities at PBI including L.E. Maxwell warn that Trudeau was a Communist and had once attempted to row to Cuba to visit Fidel Castro in a small boat. About the only thing I knew about communists at the time was that they put Christians in concentration camps. The "Red Scare" or the communist factor was, of course, something that certain mid-century American fundamentalists such as Carl McIntire feverishly warned was at work in the United States.

[46] The power to amend the Constitution now rests in Canadian hands, no longer with the British Privy Council.

[47] Catherine Ford, *Against the Grain: An Irreverent View of Alberta* (Toronto: McClelland & Stewart Ltd, 2005), 4-5: "Under our feet is 77 per cent of Canada's conventional oil and 91 per cent of its natural gas and bitumen and synthetic oil resources . . . It is the energy business and its wealth that makes the bullies back down. The business is huge. its companies inject $30 billion into the economy, generate a trade surplus of $14 billion or more, depending upon prices, employ directly and indirectly more than 240,000 Canadians, and hand over some $6 billion every year in taxes."

[48] John J. Barr, "The Impact of Oil on Alberta: Retrospect and Prospect" in A.W. Rasporich (ed.), *The Making of the Modern West: Western Canada Since 1945* (Calgary:

The major American oil companies in time began setting up branch offices in Alberta's largest cities of Calgary, Red Deer and Edmonton. When the Social Credit government was defeated in 1971 by the more cosmopolitan Progressive Conservative party, it was evident that urban Alberta would now command a larger say in provincial affairs than had previously been the case.

As the immediate world in which PBI was situated encountered significant changes, it was no surprise that some at Prairie periodically expressed opinions that, so too, it was time for the school to change certain emphases and patterns of thinking that had been entrenched at the school for years. For most of those on the inside, however, it was generally accepted

---

University of Calgary Press, 1984), 98-99, indicates the very significant changes the discovery of oil at Leduc introduced in Alberta when he writes:

"I realize Turner Valley was an interesting and significant oil development, but Alberta didn't really enter the ranks of significant oil and gas producers until Leduc No. 1 blew in on 13 February 1947.

"It came in at a remarkably propitious time. E.J. Hanson points out in his book *Dynamic Decade* that Alberta had been losing people steadily since 1931 and unless something dramatic happened, we were due for a further outflow after the war. It's estimated about 80,000 people left the province between 1936 and 1946, leaving us with a population of 803,000; Hanson says it would have dropped as low as 750,000 by the early 1950s if oil had not injected new life into Alberta . . .

"The discovery of oil touched off a boom that added up to 600,000 people to the western provinces along with huge amounts of capital and economic opportunity. The impact on population was dramatic. Instead of declining, Alberta's population grew 40 percent between 1946 and 1956, faster than any other province. The labor force was changed radically. Oil created a demand for people with university or technical training in everything from engineering, geology, geophysics and the hard sciences through to a wide variety of skilled trades. Suddenly we had a need for whole new occupations, a new source of demand for university graduates, and the sudden emergence of a much more sophisticated labor force.

"The oil industry generated a tremendous number of direct and indirect jobs. Twenty-two thousand direct new jobs were created between 1946 and 1956 in oil exploration and production, plus a vastly larger number in associated trades, construction, manufacturing, services, government and so forth. In this decade we saw the emergence of the modern Alberta economy. The best evidence is that employment in agriculture dropped from 40 percent of the labor force to 26 percent in the decade after 1946. In 1947, oil and gas generated five percent of Albertans' personal income, ten years later, it was 45 percent. And during the same period, income from farming dropped from 78 percent of Albertans' total personal income to 41 percent . . .

as unlikely and even unnecessary that there should be any major changes while Maxwell was in a state of good health and leading the school.

A second reason for limiting the scope of this book to the Maxwell era is that the nature of L.E. Maxwell's personality and character was such that he had a very distinct influence on the school's identity during its first sixty years in existence. In the view of many people conversant with PBI's ethos during these years, there was indeed a sense in which "L.E. Maxwell" and "Prairie Bible Institute" were virtually synonymous terms. Stackhouse succinctly and correctly captures this reality by stating with regard to Maxwell:

> His presence looms large over everything at Prairie—he was the founding principal, he set up the distinctive Bible study method here, he edits the school's magazine, he runs the show.[49]

Given this scenario, it was inevitable that whoever succeeded Maxwell at PBI would operate under the long shadow cast by Maxwell's "commander-in-chief" persona.[50] Those acquainted with the spirit of Prairie fully understand that there truly was a distinctive "L.E. Maxwell era." In fact,

---

"Oil cracked this tight little world and let in dazzling rays of change. Suddenly, on the streets of Edmonton, there were all those swaggering, super confident Marlborough Men with Oklahoma or Texas accents who winked at the girls, drove big cars, and came from a different world. The Edmonton Eskimos hired a coach who later returned to the States and came to symbolize big-time college football. His name was Darrel Royal, and he lived down the street from me. He was handsome, he had a beautiful blonde wife who used to be a cheerleader and he called his little girl "Sugar." He symbolized the beginning of a different kind of Alberta.

"It was "Americanization," and we loved every minute of it. America was big-time. The big-league. Suddenly we were somebody, we were somewhere, and we were getting a piece of the action. Deep down, no Albertan who grew up in the 1950s could ever be truly anti-American. The Americans introduced us to the big-time. They made it possible to be first-class Canadians for the first time, instead of just the dumb hicks from the West."

[49] Stackhouse, 74.

[50] The title of W. Harold Fuller's book cited in this work, *Maxwell's Passion and Power,* rightly captures this idea as does the title of Stephen Spaulding's (Maxwell's grandson) research, "Lion on the Prairies."

there remain those in the school's supporting constituency today who struggle with accepting that this era is indeed over.[51]

A third consideration here is that beginning in the last few years of Maxwell's life (d. 1984), the administration of Prairie Bible Institute did begin to initiate some significant changes in the school's identity.[52] Within months of his passing, in fact, some of those changes had become somewhat controversial and divisive.[53] Mark Maxwell is the sixth man to have succeeded L.E. Maxwell as president following the latter's decision to step down in 1977. One of the results of this reality is that the Institute today is a noticeably different place physically and, at least to some extent, ideologically than it was in the time period under review here. I am of the opinion that the numerous changes that have occurred at Prairie since L.E. Maxwell's passing properly merit their own study, perhaps as they relate to topics such as organizational and leadership transition. Consequently, I have chosen to leave that initiative to other researchers.

Considering the additional factor of the inevitable passage of time, the number of people active at Prairie today who were present during the Maxwell era is comparatively few. Many of those who are still alive are in the late stages of life and in poor health. This reality essentially restricted much of the research conducted for this project to what is available in written and auditory records. On those occasions when a conversation could be secured with a former influential instructor, administrator or personality from the Maxwell era, arrangements were made to conduct such although I was less successful in this regard than I had hoped.

---

[51] My youngest brother, Phil Callaway, is a popular Christian author and currently the editor of PBI's *Servant* magazine which began publication in the latter 1980s as successor to *The Prairie Overcomer*. He has shared numerous anecdotes and periodically forwards me letters from readers who, struggling to accept some of the changes that have occurred at PBI over the past twenty-five years, demonstrate by their attitudes and comments that they continue to regard the Maxwell era as the guiding template for what Prairie should continue to stand for and exemplify as a Christian institution.

[52] For example, regulations governing male-female relationships, music, academic credentials for faculty, the school's accreditation status, etc. have changed significantly since I left Prairie in 1977. As well, the school today has new divisions that include Prairie College of Applied Technology and Prairie Aviation School.

[53] For example, the PBI Board of Directors' minutes reveal that the 1986 decision to permit television on campus and in staff homes was that type of change.

This study thus draws on extensive research in the written and auditory records found in the PBI Archives in tandem with my own personal experience and memories. Additional information was acquired via personal conversations and informal interviews with PBI alumni who represent a variety of positions on the spectrum of religious perspective.

This study will show that many of the contentious theological and social issues that occupied American fundamentalism in the time period under review were also reflected to a greater or lesser extent in community life at PBI. As well, evidence will be presented to argue that L.E. Maxwell sought and received counsel on issues that concerned fundamentalists as well as general leadership considerations, not from his counterparts in Canada, but primarily from the leadership of American schools. Leaders at Moody Bible Institute in Chicago and Columbia Bible School (now Columbia International University) in Columbia, South Carolina, were particularly favorite advisors.

In addition to information gleaned from the literature detailed in Appendix II and that identified in the book's Bibliography, the primary sources for the information that serves as the foundation of this study were the Ted S. Rendall Library Archives and the PBI Records Office, both located on the campus of Prairie Bible Institute in Three Hills, Alberta, Canada. Among the items in the Rendall Library Archives that I found of particular benefit were the personal files and correspondence of L.E. Maxwell; back issues of *Prairie Pastor, Prairie Overcomer* and *Young Pilot*; decades' worth of minutes and notes from Prairie's Board of Directors, Operating Executive Committee, Administrative Team and Academic Committee; samples from the hundreds of reel-to-reel and cassette tapes going back to the 1950s that contain: scores of messages delivered by various speakers at Prairie's annual Spring Missions and Fall Bible conferences, PBI's various radio programs over the years, sermons and class lectures by L.E. Maxwell, Ted Rendall and Paul Maxwell, plus a broad menu of special meetings from the every-day life of a busy Bible school; an almost complete set of "The Prairian," the school's annual yearbook; several files containing a variety of Prairie Staff directories, telephone books and monthly prayer calendars.

Equally helpful was data found in the PBI Records Office which contained PBI's various Manuals and Catalogues covering every year back to the first handwritten "Prospectus" for the 1923-24 school year that is penned in L.E. Maxwell's distinctive scrawl. This office also holds the Bible

School Handbooks dated back to 1946 that spelled out various guidelines and regulations for students.[54]

Personal memories as verified, clarified and augmented in personal conversations with various family members, fellow "staff kids" and PBI alumni who shared the author's PBI experience contributed an important element to this study. Although most of these exchanges were extemporaneous, unofficial and perhaps somewhat unorthodox for academic purposes, they nevertheless were a vital element in helping retain and reclaim key pieces of the PBI puzzle.[55] A lengthy taped interview with Dr. Ted Rendall in August 2006 was of particular value for the purposes of my research.

Finally, I retain ample class notes from my days as a student in the Bible school division at PBI (1974-77). These were consulted in an effort to particularly bring to memory the "pluses" and the "minuses" of PBI's famous "search question" method of Bible study as well as to re-create a feel for those days of long ago.[56]

---

[54] Harold W. Fuller, "The Legacy of Leslie E. Maxwell," 130, footnote 8: "As a result of incomplete record keeping in the early years of the school, statistics about graduates are necessarily approximate. As Maxwell explained to researcher Aaron Goertz, "In the early years we were so sure that Christ would return right then, we didn't think it worth keeping records" (of graduates and their places of ministry). "We possessed only three file cabinets. When the third got full, we threw out the contents of the first and started over again." See Donald Aaron Goertz: "The Development of a Bible Belt: The Socio-Religious Interaction in Alberta Between 1925 and 1938." (M.A. Thesis, Univ. of Alberta, 1976), p. 97; further details in interview with the author." (NOTE: Fuller's identification of this thesis is in error; Goertz's thesis is that referred to in footnote 25 of this Introduction)

[55] For example, I attended a reunion of approximately fifty former PBI "staff kids" held in Three Hills on July 12, 2008. Their assistance was especially helpful in assembling some of the data contained in Appendix I of this book.

[56] PBI Archives in Ted S. Rendall Library: L.E. Maxwell personal file—"Education and Christianity." The file contains a document entitled "Missionary World Supplement," an undated publication by W.C. Stevens. It quotes Maxwell as follows on the value of the "search question" method of studying the Scripture which Maxwell learned from Stevens while the former was a student at Midland Bible School in Kansas City: "First, we studied the Bible, rather than books about the Bible. Within the past week the secretary of one of the very evangelical Home Mission Boards said to me in commenting upon this course of study: "I wish I had that course; I studied so many books about the Bible, rather than the Bible itself . . . Secondly . . . Under the guidance of select questions, the student searches the Bible for his own findings. As arrows by

Among other benefits, the class notes assisted me in recalling the emphasis at PBI on "directing the student to the Bible which in turn reveals itself powerfully to the student's understanding."[57] For instance, despite the frequent rhetoric encountered at PBI regarding the value of the "search question" method of Bible study, the fact was that any interpretation of Scripture which varied significantly from that which a given instructor preferred was usually accorded a low score. In other words, there were definite limits to the extent to which a PBI student could go in "securing his own rich original findings from the Book of Truth."[58]

---

the roadside direct the traveler to his destination, so these questions direct the student in the Book of truth . . ."

[57] *Manual of Prairie Bible Institute, 1946-47,* 17.

[58] *Prospectus of the Three Hills Bible Institute, 1924-25,* 1.

CHAPTER ONE

A concise history of Prairie Bible Institute (1922-1980)

The simple road sign on the outskirts of town that identifies Three Hills, Alberta, as the home of Prairie Bible Institute is easily overlooked by motorists. Similarly, there is little to distinguish Three Hills from scores of other small farming communities located on the rolling prairies of Western Canada. Accordingly, few would ever suspect that this non-descript village served as the stage for one of the most remarkable dramas to occur in both Canadian and international religious history throughout most of the twentieth century.[1]

This surprising reality is underscored, however, in an article entitled "Miracle at Three Hills" that appeared in the December 15, 1945 issue of *Maclean's*, Canada's national news magazine. Reporter James S. Gray stated:

> "The most famous place in Canada? Ottawa? Perhaps. Or Montreal or Toronto, Niagara Falls, Winnipeg, Banff, Vancouver? Maybe. But if you were set down in the wilds of Africa, India, the West Indies or China, and found shelter in the nearest mission, there's a good chance your host would say to you: 'You from Canada? How are things back in Three Hills?' Chances are you've never heard of Three Hills, but your missionary friend could quickly enlighten you. He'd tell you about the remote Alberta village of Three Hills and its most famous institution, The Prairie Bible Institute, the biggest missionary college in Canada and the second largest on the continent."

Prairie Bible Institute indeed earned an international reputation during the twentieth century as a leading center for the training of evangelical

---

[1]   J. Robert Clinton, *Inspirational Life Changing Lessons From Eight Effective Christian Leaders Who Finished Well* (Altadena, CA: Barnabas Publishers, 1995), 391, accurately reflects the thinking of many when he writes: ". . . a most unlikely location to become a Christian center of influence on the world, the prairies of Alberta, Canada . . ."

missionaries, pastors and Christian workers. Operations formally began on October 9, 1922, when six young people and two adults enrolled for Bible classes offered in a borrowed farmhouse near the small village situated approximately an hour northeast of the "Stampede" city of Calgary.

J. Fergus Kirk, a local farmer who was the product of a devout Scottish Presbyterian home near Kingston, Ontario, was serving as a lay Bible teacher in the Three Hills area. As the years immediately following World War I unfolded, Kirk believed God was giving him a passion for the spiritual welfare of youth in south-central Alberta and began to contemplate the possibility of starting a small Bible school.[2] In all likelihood it never crossed his mind that his initiative would develop over time into one of the largest Bible institutes in the world.[3]

Kirk's eventual search for someone with more expertise in teaching the Bible than he felt he possessed resulted in an invitation being extended to

---

[2] Juanita C. Snyder, *Raise Up the Foundations!* (Three Hills, AB: Prairie Bible Institute, 1966).

Bernice A. Callaway, *Legacy: The Moving Saga of Our "Prairie Pioneers"* (Three Hills, AB: MacCall Clan, 1987).

Both authors relate the story of Andrew and Maria Kirk's missions-minded home in southeastern Ontario, Canada, where Fergus was raised. Later in life, his parents moved into western Canada as lay Presbyterian missionaries, eventually settling in the Three Hills, Alberta, area, as did several of their children.

Mark A. Noll, *A History of Christianity in the United States and Canada* (Grand Rapids, MI: William B. Eerdmans Publishing Co., 1992), 275. Noll briefly discusses early Canadian Presbyterianism noting its missionary outreach particularly into the Canadian west.

[3] PBI Records Office files; PBI's *Prospectus for 1924* states: "The aim of the School is to produce a Bible Teaching and Missionary Ministry under the unction of the Holy Spirit. By "Bible Teaching" is meant the opening up of the whole horizon of the Book of God, as a self-evident body of revelation to the student, who will in turn be prepared to open the same to the heart and mind of others." This was a direct reflection of the philosophy of learning that prevailed at Midland Bible School where L.E. Maxwell studied prior to coming to Three Hills.

PBI Archives in Ted S. Rendall Library, Three Hills, Alberta: L.E. Maxwell personal file - "Education and Christianity." A document entitled "Missionary World Supplement" in the file states: "The distinguishing feature of this School is that of taking the whole Bible consecutively without "Helps" or "Light on the Scriptures," in the confidence that it will reveal itself to the patient searcher so that he will in turn become a zealous and competent guide to others throughout the world into the same pathway of Scriptural Light."

Leslie Earl Maxwell to come to Three Hills. Maxwell, born July 2, 1895, and raised near Salina, Kansas, arrived on the rolling prairies of western Canada in the fall of 1922 in time for classes to begin following completion of that year's harvest season.

After overseas service in France during World War I with the United States Army, the former soldier enrolled at Midland Bible Institute in Kansas City, a small school established by W. C. "Daddy" Stevens.[4] A former principal of the Missionary Training Institute of the Christian and Missionary Alliance in Nyack, New York, Stevens would become highly respected by Maxwell and would register a considerable influence on the younger man's theological development and orientation to Christian ministry.[5]

Several of Kirk's siblings had studied at the school in Nyack and Hattie, one of his sisters, had shared with her brother the "search-question" method of Bible study that Stevens had introduced there.[6] Fergus Kirk thus

---

[4]   Philip W. Keller, *Expendable! With God on the Prairies: the ministry of Prairie Bible Institute, Three Hills, Alberta, Canada* (Three Hills, AB: Prairie Press, 1966), 44: "On September 22, 1922, Maxwell finished his studies at the Midland Bible Institute. The school existed for only one more year. During [Midland's] five years of operation in Kansas City Leslie Maxwell was the only man from that city to attend its classes, complete its course and graduate from its halls."

[5]   PBI Records Office files; Stevens, (b. August 24, 1853, in Parma, Ohio; d. October 5, 1929, in Seattle, Washington), is listed as the Honorary President of PBI's Board of Directors in publications from the school's earliest years, Kirk as Chairman and Maxwell variously as Principal, Secretary and Treasurer.

L.E. Maxwell personal file—"Obituaries." "A Friend of Arabia," Simpson's obituary, reads: "After his grammar school and collegiate training, Brother Stevens entered The Western Reserve, a college then in Hudson, Ohio, which is now located in Cleveland. He attended the Reserve only one year and then entered Beloit, Wisconsin, of which he was a graduate. From Beloit he went to Union Seminary, N.Y., finishing with two years in Germany and a trip through other parts of Europe. He was a student of Hebrew, Greek, Latin, German and French. He won for himself many titles but for many years after he came into the fullness of Jesus, wished only to be addressed as brother, or pastor."

[6]   Following missionary service in Central America and Cuba, Hattie Kirk and her husband, Ephraim Monge (pronounced and sometimes spelled Mon-hay) were instrumental in establishing a Bible school in northern Alberta. Similar to her brother's request to W.C. Stevens in Kansas City, they appealed to PBI for someone to come and teach the Bible whereupon PBI graduate Walter W. McNaughton founded the Peace River Bible Institute (PRBI) in 1933. The first mail-out concerning PRBI dated November 3, 1933, clearly reveals its affinity with PBI with regard to a "no-debt" policy, doctrine, an unsectarian position and the "guide-question method of study."

employed this approach in preparing for Sunday afternoon Bible studies he began conducting near Three Hills.[7] The "search-question" or "inductive" method of study would become a staple in PBI's educational philosophy concerning how its students were to study and interpret the Bible. In an environment that discouraged the use of aids such as commentaries, students were directed to rely on the Scriptures and the teaching ministry of the Holy Spirit alone to formulate their answers.[8]

Capitalizing on the enthusiasm of several families near Three Hills to have their young people study the Bible in a context beyond the traditional Sunday worship and Christian education classes, Kirk wrote Stevens in 1921 to inquire if he might recommend someone to come and teach the Christian Scriptures in a more formal educational context. Kirk's letter to Stevens articulated his growing concern that liberal or modernist teaching was entering many churches.[9] In time, Maxwell responded favorably to

---

(I obtained a copy of this document while attending PRBI's 75th anniversary weekend, August 8-10, 2008.)

[7] Kirk served as PBI's first president until 1961 and then, until his death in 1981, as President Emeritus.

[8] Prairie earned a reputation for its use of the "search-question" or "inductive" method of Bible study, an important link with nascent American fundamentalism. PBI Records Office files; PBI's *Prospectus for 1923-24* states: "The whole Bible is studied consecutively and constructively under the guidance of select questions to each student. This method enables each student to produce his own original findings from the Scriptures and thereby secure the Book as his own possession, his very own. This is the culminating object of the School." (emphasis in original)

George M. Marsden, *Fundamentalism and American Culture* (New York: Oxford University Press, 1980), 60. Marsden attributes the origins of the inductive method of Bible study to Reuben A. Torrey who taught at both Moody Bible Institute and the Bible Institute of Los Angeles (BIOLA) around the turn of the twentieth century.

L.E. Maxwell personal file—"Bible Orientation." One is uncertain what to make of Maxwell's claim in a document in this file that: "It is generally conceded, and is a fact, that here at Prairie Bible Institute we have a rarely used and different method of Bible study. It is what we call the Search Question or Study-Guide method." In any event, the same file contains a booklet entitled *The Inductive Method of Bible Study*, written by Daniel P. Fuller while Instructor of English Bible at Fuller Theological Seminary, Pasadena, California, in 1956. Fuller went on to become president of the school named after his famous father, revivalist Charles E. Fuller. A note on the title page of the booklet reads: "To my good friend L.E. Maxwell from Dan Fuller, Acts 17:11."

[9] Harold W. Fuller, *Maxwell's Passion & Power* (Memphis, TN: The Master Design, 2002), 9. This is an important detail to bear in mind as it relates to PBI's connection

Stevens' suggestion that he would be a good candidate for the position and, immediately following graduation from Midland a year later, the young man traveled north to Alberta.[10]

Maxwell arrived in Alberta some twenty-five years before the province achieved international fame by virtue of the discovery of massive reservoirs of underground crude oil and natural gas. Calgary, situated on the eastern doorstep of the Canadian Rocky Mountains, would in time become home to the Canadian headquarters of numerous multi-national energy firms and become a sister-city to Houston, Texas. At the time of Maxwell's initial arrival in Canada, however, Alberta's economy was primarily based on agriculture-related industries such as grain and beef.

The early years at PBI

In addition to his teaching responsibilities that first year at what was initially called The Three Hills Bible School, Maxwell used the experience he had gained on the family farm in Kansas to assist the families he had come to serve in their milking, haying and other agricultural duties. Local religious leaders were bemused by the young teacher's willingness to roll up his sleeves and get involved in the day-to-day life of the farming community.

Nevertheless, it was a quality that would characterize Maxwell for the duration of his life. Even in his senior years, he could often be seen shoveling snow from a PBI sidewalk or pulling persistent weeds from a campus flower-bed. These attributes demonstrated his firm commitment to equality and to servant-leadership and greatly endeared Maxwell to the Bible school constituency.

The second year of operations saw the small student body more than double in size thereby immediately establishing a pattern of rapid growth

---

to early American fundamentalism which initially distinguished itself as a strong resistance movement to theological modernism.

[10] Virginia Lieson Brereton, *Training God's Army: The American Bible School, 1880-1940* (Bloomington, IN: Indiana University Press, 1990), vii. Brereton's definition of a "Bible school" is helpful at this point: "As it had evolved by 1920, a Bible school was an institution—sometimes denominational, sometimes non-denominational—operating at roughly a high school level and training men and women as evangelists, missionaries, religious teachers, musicians, pastors, and other workers for the conservative Protestant evangelical churches."

at PBI.[11] In the summer of 1924, the small group of believers pooled their meager resources to facilitate the construction of an all-purpose classroom building that measured 30 x 60 feet. Scornful local residents were overheard to remark that they looked forward to using the facility as a dance hall once the religious madness had dissipated.[12]

The scoffers were to be disappointed, however. Despite the crash of the North American stock market in 1929 that unleashed an unprecedented economic depression resulting in the devastation of the agriculture industry in Western Canada, progress at PBI proceeded virtually undeterred.[13] A chapel building containing additional classrooms was erected that year. As the wind whipped the black topsoil across the barren prairie farmland throughout "The Dirty Thirties," an increasing number of students enrolled at PBI. Drawing on the assistance of local believers, staff members continued building the required facilities despite the desperate economic times.[14]

---

[11] PBI Records Office files; according to information in various files the school was called the "Three Hills Bible School" for the 1922-23 and 1923-24 school years. In 1925-26 it was known as the "Three Hills Bible Institute" and thereafter as "Prairie Bible Institute."

PBI Records Office files; a chart labeled "Bible School Enrollment" lists the school's enrollment as follows:

1922-23 10	1923-24. 25	1924-25 37	1925-26 . . . .*35
1926-27. . . . .*40	1927-28. . . .*45	1928-29 69	1929-30. 65
1930-31. 90	1931-32 152	1932-33 230	1934-35. . . .280
1935-36 . . .280	1936-37. . . .294	1937-38 295	1938-39. . . .325
1939-40. . . 408	1940-41 . . .500	1941-42. . . .500	1942-43 475
1943-44. . . 544	1944-45 415	1945-46 472	1945-47 . . . *670
1947-48. . . 757	1948-49 900	1949-50 865	
			(* = approximate)

[12] Keller, 102.

[13] Ibid., 104: "They came in such overflowing numbers that adding to the original structure became a virtual scramble from year to year, to keep ahead of the enrollment."

[14] Eric Hanson, *Local Government in Alberta* (Toronto: McClelland & Stewart Ltd., 1956), 44: "Alberta recovered slowly after 1933. It was not until the 1940s that agricultural conditions became prosperous and that unemployment in the urban centers disappeared. The average price for wheat was $1.20 per bushel for the period 1926-29; it was only $.0.43 for the five-year period 1930-34 and $0.72 for the five-year period 1935-39."

Davidson, 32, states that as early as the summer of 1926 Maxwell and other faculty members undertook speaking engagements at camps and churches in both Canada

A spirit of sacrifice

Crucial to PBI's survival and progress during the early days was a sacrificial mindset eagerly embraced and exemplified by the Kirks, McElherans, Maxwell and other members of the fledgling Bible school community. Fergus Kirk had been raised in a home where material sacrifice to further God's work was diligently taught and practiced.[15] Prior to Maxwell's arrival in Three Hills, Kirk had sold farm land at a financial loss and cancelled plans to build a new home in order to support his vision of establishing some kind of a Bible training center for the region's young people.[16]

Material sacrifice thus became a defining concept woven into the embryonic fabric of the emerging PBI culture and an enduring component of PBI's reputation throughout the Maxwell era.[17] Following the first year of classes at Three Hills, Maxwell served as a summer pastor at an established church in Alberta that then offered him an attractive salary to continue as their full-time minister.[18] Praying for direction in this regard, he later

---

and the United States. This appears to have been a primary method of advertising for the school at the time. It should also be noted that Maxwell spent many weeks of his summers travelling in the U.S. Bill Gothard, whose Institute in Basic Youth Conflicts (now called Institute in Basic Life Principles) achieved prominent attention in some North American evangelical circles beginning in the 1970s, reports that his father was greatly influenced through Maxwell's ministry at Gull Lake Bible Camp in Michigan in the 1940s. See http://www.billgothard.com/bill/about/lifechapters/3/ (accessed September 14, 2009.)

[15] L.E. Maxwell, *Crowded to Christ* (Grand Rapids: Wm. B. Eerdmans Publishing Co., 1950), 88: "My mind recalls the history of Grandma and Grandpa Kirk (as we knew them), who lived on a poor Ontario farm with a modest family of ten children. Yet they managed to give hundred of dollars to missions . . . During one year alone, after they were seventy years of age, they gave one thousand dollars to foreign missions and spent only eight dollars on themselves . . ."

[16] McElheran, Chapter 4.

[17] Callaway, *Legacy*, 38-39, relates how Andrew and Maria Kirk's children would go without Christmas gifts and butter on their bread in order to make sure missionaries received funds the Kirks had promised them.

[18] David R. Elliott, "Three Faces of Baptist Fundamentalism in Canada: Aberhart, Maxwell, and Shields." In David T. Priestley, (ed.), *Memory and Hope: Strands of Canadian Baptist History* (Waterloo, ON: Wilfred Laurier University Press, 1996), 175: "After the first year, Maxwell was approached by Bonnie Doon Baptist Church in Edmonton. The congregation wanted him to become their minister, but the BUWC [Baptist Union of Western Canada] requested that he take more education at the University

related, the only leading which came to him from Scripture was contained in the words "hoping for nothing" found in Luke 6:35. He interpreted this as God's directive he was to live a life of bold faith with regard to his monetary compensation, confident that whatever amount God supplied would be sufficient for his necessities in life. Maxwell consequently turned down the church's offer and returned to Three Hills.

To what extent the believers at Three Hills influenced Maxwell's views on the matter of material sacrifice is probably debatable.[19] Fergus Kirk's first words to the young teacher when the latter stepped off the train at Three Hills in late September 1922 were: "I'm very sorry that we can't offer you more!"[20] Yet, prior to his graduation at Midland, Maxwell had experienced a specific spiritual brokenness he later claimed was essential in prompting him to "die to self" and to follow God anywhere under any circumstances.[21]

It appears that a firm commitment to material sacrifice was an issue that both Kirk and Maxwell dealt with individually to some extent even before the new graduate came to Three Hills. Thereafter, the men likely cross-pollinated one another in this regard since, as previously noted, significant material sacrifice quickly became a cornerstone in PBI's theological and economic orientation.

Leaders and followers alike became strongly committed to this distinctive.[22] For example, in preparing to construct the first classroom building in 1924, the core families who supported the Bible school pulled

---

of Alberta. Maxwell turned down the offer/requirement and remained at Three Hills . . ."

[19] Goertz, 99: "Fergus Kirk was the president of the school from its beginning and brought to it a strong emphasis on missions and above all, sacrifice . . . Sacrificial giving of one's self, time and money was to characterize Three Hills like no other factor and this came as a result of the Kirk influence."

[20] Keller, 74.

[21] Ibid., 43, and Goertz, 98: "During that last year [at Midland, Maxwell] became increasingly sensitive to missions and this change continued until he found himself ready to go even to rural Alberta, a place of very little glamour."

[22] Davidson, 24: "Under the title "History of the Work" in the early school catalogues, Mr. Maxwell writes: "One of the first essentials for a Bible school is a spiritual background of like-minded persons. In His pre-vision and provision, God 'determined the times before appointed and the bounds of their habitation' when He led to this district certain families who were later to form the initial spiritual constituency of this school.""

together $1,400, a substantial amount of money at the time.[23] In addition to cash, some donors offered entire railroad cars full of grain. Typically, Fergus Kirk led by example, selling a new car at a loss in order to contribute to the new edifice.[24]

There thus emerged a pattern of thinking in the Institute's early days that would later be translated into a firm policy at Prairie for the duration of Maxwell's tenure: the school would not borrow money or go into debt to fund any capital project. Instead, staff would publicize plans and needs only in a manner that communicated a sole reliance on the sacrificial giving of God's people to accomplish God's work. The strategy met with remarkable success throughout the continent-wide economic destitution of the 1930s and indeed for the duration of Maxwell's tenure at PBI.[25]

Remarkable growth and international fame

By the time the mid-1940s arrived, PBI's campus was well on its way to covering 120 acres. The school also operated a 1,000 acre farm that

---

[23] Hanson, 34-35: "There was a sharp recession in 1920-22. Prices of agricultural products in Alberta fell by forty-two per cent while the prices of commodities and services purchased by farmers in Western Canada fell by only fifteen per cent. Both 1921 and 1922 were poor crop years. This reduced the net incomes of Alberta farmers seriously . . . The decade of the 1920s was not a particularly prosperous one for Alberta. The economy was highly dependent upon agriculture which proved to be unstable from year to year because of weather and price fluctuations."

Davidson, 16: "In the fall of 1919, the price of wheat, the main crop in this area, started increasing in price and at the end of harvest buyers were paying $2.75 to $2.80 per bushel for No. 1 wheat. In the spring of 1920, the same quality of wheat was down to $1.50 per bushel . . . the price of wheat declined during the 1920's and hit an all time low in 1932 when buyers were paying only $0.19 to $0.20 per bushel. The cost of machinery did not decrease for a much longer time. Crop yields in 1920, 1921, and 1922 were below average while cost of production was at its peak." See also p. 47: "Following the 1923 bountiful harvest, crop yields and prices declined throughout the remainder of the twenties, reaching an all-time low in 1930 . . . All farm produce was below the cost of production!"

[24] Keller, 83; 98-102.

[25] PBI Records Office files. The *1925-26 Manual of the Prairie Bible Institute* states: "The Institute stands upon faith principles throughout. The maintenance, expansion and further enlargement of the School are dependent upon the unsolicited, free-will offerings of friends who believe in such a ministry. We believe that God will supply all of our needs, and therefore, proceed upon the principle of incurring no indebtedness."

supplied the burgeoning student body with fresh milk, eggs and other dairy products. As well, the farm generated revenue by virtue of its ample fields of grain. With a student body population that by the late 1940s rivaled that of the Moody Bible Institute in Chicago, Prairie was regularly enrolling close to 800 men and women in the Bible school division and around another 250 in Prairie High School (grades 9-12), an initiative launched in 1938.[26] The formation of an elementary school (kindergarten through eighth grade) for the children of staff members, Bible school student families and local believers followed in 1941.

In time, of course, news publications around the globe were taking note of what was occurring at PBI and regularly featured stories regarding what was considered a modern miracle unfolding on the Canadian prairie.[27] As has already been indicated, over the years journalists and academics would comment to the effect that PBI was largely responsible for enabling people around the world to locate the town of Three Hills, the province of Alberta and even the country of Canada on a map of the world.[28]

---

[26] Gene A. Getz, *MBI: The Story of Moody Bible Institute* (Chicago: Moody Press, 1986), 206, Figure 4, indicates the enrollment in Moody's Day School program around 1960 was just below 700. Moody, however, also ran an Evening School program as well as a number of extension school programs in various cities around the United States. Consequently, it is accurate to state that Moody's student body was always larger than Prairie's, although Harry Hiller "Alberta and the Bible Belt Stereotype," in *Religion in Canadian Society*, (eds.) Stewart Crysdale and Les Wheatcroft (Toronto: MacMillan of Canada, 1976), 381, and Ian S. Rennie, "The Doctrine of Man in the Bible Belt," (unpublished paper c. 1977), 3, both assert that Prairie was the largest theological school on the North American continent.

[27] PBI Archives in Ted S. Rendall Library; L.E. Maxwell personal file—"Articles on PBI," contains several articles written in the 1930s-1940s from news sources in Australia, England and Denmark in addition to ample coverage from North American media. J.H. Hunter, "With God on the Prairie: The Story of Prairie Bible Institute," *The Evangelical Christian*, August 1943, 337; Theo Hoel, "Prairie Bible Institute in Canada: Amazing Development in 23 Years . . . ;" *New Life* (Melbourne, Australia) Thursday, November 29, 1945, vol. 8, no. 22, p. 7; (no author) *Kirkenlokken* (Denmark), 27 January 1957; Paul Wright, "Prairie Bible School: Alberta College is Missionaries' Training Field," *The Standard*, February 1950, 14.

[28] PBI Archives in Ted S. Rendall Library; James S. Gray, "Miracle at Three Hills;" *Maclean's*, December 15, 1947, 16, (see first page of this chapter)

Howard Palmer (with Tamara Palmer), *Alberta: A New History* (Edmonton, AB: Hurtig Publishers Ltd., 1990), 242: "Many people in the Third World first heard of Alberta, and often of Canada, either through contact with evangelical missionaries

Even before PBI celebrated its twenty-fifth anniversary in 1947, the school was regularly included in conversations and discussions concerning the noteworthy American Bible schools of the day such as Moody (Chicago), Biola (Los Angeles), Columbia (South Carolina) and Gordon (Boston).[29] In addition to Prairie's soaring enrollment, another part of the explanation for its comparison with large American Bible schools was that following World War II an unusually large component of Prairie's student body were citizens of the United States who came to study at Three Hills.[30]

On the one hand, Prairie quickly earned widespread fame for the hundreds of students it graduated who proceeded to join various faith-mission agencies such as the China Inland Mission and the Sudan Interior Mission to go abroad as missionaries.[31] A book written to celebrate the school's fiftieth anniversary in 1972 reported on the author's visits with PBI alumni serving as missionaries in northern Canada, Colombia, Ecuador, Peru, Bolivia, Venezuela, Brazil, Aruba, Puerto Rico, Haiti, Zaire, Nigeria, Kenya, Ethiopia, Japan, Korea, Taiwan, Hong Kong, Singapore, Indonesia, Philippines, India, Austria, Germany, Belgium and France.[32]

---

trained in the province's Bible schools or from the hundreds of Mormon missionaries from southern Alberta."

[29] Joel A. Carpenter, *Revive Us Again: The Reawakening of American Fundamentalism* (New York: Oxford University Press, 1997), 17.

[30] Appendix I, Table I.6
   Davidson, 56: "The Bible school student body increased from about 300 in the middle 1930's to about 1200 including high school, in the fall of 1945. This was due in part to some who had started school prior to World War II and who had either enlisted or were conscripted in the American or Canadian armies. Following the war, both governments gave financial assistance to those who served in their forces to receive further training to prepare for their futures."

[31] Gray, "Miracle at Three Hills," reported: "More than 3,000 of its graduates are in foreign missions and several thousand more spread the gospel in the United States and Canada."
   Davidson, 34-35, indicates the pattern PBI set from the very outset in placing a priority on foreign missionary service when he relates concerning the school's first graduating class: "Of these seven, six spent a lifetime of fruitful ministry on different mission fields."

[32] Margaret A. Epp, *Into All the World: the missionary outreach of Prairie Bible Institute* (Three Hills: Prairie Press, 1973).

PBI's famous and infamous alumni

Among the scores of Prairie students from the L.E. Maxwell era that went on to distinguished careers in Christian service were:

1. Elmer V. Thompson, who married Fergus Kirk's niece and went to Latin America in the late 1920s where he founded the Cuba Bible Institute and The West Indies Mission. The latter continues to operate as WorldTeam.[33]
2. Norman and Evelyn Charter, a Canadian couple who served with the China Inland Mission in mainland China in the late 1930s and throughout the 1940s alongside Isobel Kuhn, the author of numerous popular books regarding ministry in China prior to the Communist takeover in 1949.[34]
3. Albert E. and Evelyn Brant, a couple appointed to service with the Sudan Interior Mission in the mid-1940s. The Brants established numerous churches that grew to represent some 50,000 believers among the Gedeo tribe in south-central Ethiopia.[35]
4. Elisabeth (Betty) Howard, a Wheaton College graduate whose father, Philip E. Howard, served as editor of *The Sunday School Times*, the prominent American fundamentalist journal to which L.E. Maxwell frequently contributed. Phil Howard thought so highly of Maxwell that he recommended his daughter attend Prairie before going to the mission field. She later married fellow Wheaton graduate, Jim Elliot, one of five American missionaries murdered

---

[33] Joseph F. Conley, *Drumbeats That Changed the World: a history of the Regions Beyond Missionary Union and The West Indies Mission 1873-1999* (Pasadena: William Carey Library, 2000) relates the stories of numerous PBI alumni who served with these two missions that eventually merged in 1995 to become WorldTeam.

[34] The Charter family graciously made available to me a collection of fascinating biographical notes related to Norman and Evelyn's ministry in China. See also the story of Marvin and Miriam Dunn, (Marvin was another PBI graduate from this era who served in China) as recorded in Miriam Dunn, *My Children or the Cross: one woman's sacrifice in pre-communist China* (Dalton, OH: P. Graham Dunn Publishing, 2011).

[35] Albert E. Brant, *In the Wake of the Martyrs: A Modern Saga in Ancient Ethiopia* (Langley, BC: Omega, n.d.) records the occasionally harrowing story of the Brants' ministry in Ethiopia.

by Auca Indians in Ecuador in early 1956, an event that garnered worldwide media attention.[36]

5. W. Harold and Lorna Fuller, who served with Sudan Interior Mission in Africa during the 1950s and '60s where Harold functioned as editor of *African Challenge* and authored several books based on their missionary experiences;[37]

6. The Janz Brothers Quartet, consisting of Hildor, Adolph, Leo Janz (brothers from a farming community in Saskatchewan) and Cornelius Enns who traveled with L.E. Maxwell on publicity tours for PBI in the late 1940s. Following their schooling and service at Prairie, the quartet founded the Janz Brothers Gospel Association in (West) Germany where they conducted numerous evangelistic campaigns and established the Black Forest Academy. The ministry continues to operate as Janz Team/Teach Beyond.

7. Ralph D. Winter, prominent American missiologist and founder of the U.S. Center for World Missions and William Carey International University located in Pasadena, California, interrupted post-graduate studies in anthropology and linguistics at Cornell University to attend PBI for a couple of semesters.[38]

---

[36] Elisabeth Elliott is the author of numerous books including: *Through Gates of Splendor* (New York: Harper & Row, 1958); *Shadow of the Almighty: the Life and Testament of Jim Elliott* (Grand Rapids, MI: Zondervan Publishing House, 1958); *A Chance to Die: the life and legacy of Amy Carmichael* (Old Tappen, NJ: Fleming H. Revell, 2005 repr.); *A Path Through Suffering* (Ann Arbor, MI: Vine Books, 1992); *Let Me Be a Woman* (Wheaton, IL: Tyndale House Publishers, 1976).

[37] Fuller, 161: "In God's mercy, *African Challenge* became better known than Coca-Cola . . . In circulation, it became the highest monthly in West Africa and second highest on the continent." See also Fuller's books: *Run While the Sun is Hot* (Cedar Grove, NJ: Sudan Interior Mission, 1967); *Fire God—And other African Adventures* (Chicago: Moody Press, 1972); *Mission-Church Dynamics: how to change bi-cultural tensions into dynamic outreach* (Pasadena: William Carey Library, 1980); *The Ends of the Earth* (Cedar Grove, NJ: Sudan Interior Mission, 1983); *Tie Down the Sun* (Toronto: SIM, 1990); *Celebrate the God Who Loves* (Toronto: SIM International Media. 1992); *People of the Mandate: the story of the World Evangelical Fellowship* (Grand Rapids, MI: Baker Book House, 1996);

[38] Ibid., 78
When I was a first-year seminary student at TEDS (Chicago) in 1981-82, Dr. Winter was a visiting chapel speaker and made comments to the effect that he had interrupted his university studies and gone north to Canada to study where he had discovered "some pretty good fundamentalists up there," or words to that effect. Dr. Winter passed away in May 2009.

8. Don and Carol Richardson, served with Regions Beyond Missionary Union (now WorldTeam) in Kalimantan (Borneo), Indonesia, in the 1960s and '70s. Don authored several books including *Peace Child* which was condensed as a *Reader's Digest* story. *Peace Child* was also made into a motion picture that attained significant attention among students of cross-cultural ministry.[39]

By the middle of the twentieth century Prairie Bible Institute had earned a reputation around the world for the percentage of its graduates who were serving as foreign missionaries or as pastors and Christian workers in North America.[40] L.E. Maxwell's grandson, Steven Spaulding, estimates that when

---

L.E. Maxwell personal file—"Revised Standard Version." The file contains April 1953 correspondence from Winter to Maxwell while the former was a student at Cornell in which he expressed great concern to Maxwell about the latter's contribution to the negativity surrounding the Revised Standard Version (RSV). Winter, an anthropologist and linguist, considered it "simply the most accurate and reliable translation of the Word of God now existing in the English language!" He urged Maxwell to reconsider a strong statement against the RSV that had appeared in *The Prairie Overcomer*.

[39] Don Richardson, *Peace Child* (Glendale, CA: Gospel Light Publications/Regal Books, 1974); *Lords of the Earth* (Glendale, CA: Gospel Light Publications/Regal Books, 1977); *Eternity in their Hearts* (Glendale, CA: Gospel Light Publications/Regal Books, 1981).

[40] PBI Records Office; PBI's *1970-71 Student Catalogue* reported that 1,581 graduates were serving as missionaries around the world while another 1,000 were involved as pastors and Christian workers in North America.

In the interests of constructing as accurate a historical overview of PBI as possible, it would be misleading to suggest that all of Prairie's alumni went on to establish stellar reputations of Christian service that the school was/is proud to acknowledge. For example:

Fred Phelps, current pastor of Westboro Baptist Church in Topeka, Kansas, attended Prairie from 1949-51. He presently leads a militantly anti-homosexual church/crusade whose agenda can be viewed at www.godhatesfags.com. In e-mail correspondence dated May 20, 2007, his daughter Shirley L. Phelps-Roper wrote me: "Yes, Pastor Phelps attended PBI. The years were 1949 and 1950 . . . In October 2001 I was with a group of people when we made our last trip into Canada to deliver words of warning to those people. We were treated so badly by your government that we knew God had cursed that nation. We would never set foot upon your soil again. God hates Canada." A news story entitled "Protesters banned from entering U.K." in *The Buffalo (New York) News*, (Saturday, February 21, 2009, A5) reported that the British government had banned Fred Phelps and his daughter Shirley Phelps-Roper from entering the United Kingdom where they had hoped to protest a play about the

PBI reached its zenith in the 1950s, "the school was putting out about five percent of the entire Protestant missionary force from North America."[41]

A distinctive reputation around the world

On the other hand, by the middle of the twentieth century Prairie had also obtained a renowned if controversial reputation for a peculiar distinctive pertaining to its "pink" and "blue" sidewalks, an apocryphal legend stemming from the school's stringent "social regulations" that governed relationships between male and female students.[42] Indeed, many people

---

murder of an American gay man that occurred in Wyoming in 1998. The play was to be held at Queen Mary's College in Basingstoke. The same news story indicated that members of the Westboro Baptist Church planned to picket memorial services being held in the Buffalo area for victims of Continental Connection Flight 3407 which crashed on approach to the Buffalo Niagara International Airport on February 12, 2009, killing all 49 people aboard and one man in his home on the ground.

Wendell Krossa graduated from PBI in 1975 and his parents served on the Institute's staff for a number of years. He spent eleven years as a missionary with Overseas Missionary Fellowship serving in small villages in the Philippines before abandoning evangelical Christianity. In e-mail correspondence with the author dated March 6, 2007 he stated: "I have no idea how to refer to myself. I see myself as continually moving forward in discovery and understanding of the great Mystery that sustains all in existence . . . I have left religion entirely depending on how one defines religion . . ." Krossa outlines his fundamentalist experience, including his PBI years, on his website at www.wendellkrossa.com (see especially *Autobiography: Leaving My Religion*).

Linda M. Fossen, *Out of the Miry Clay* (self-published, n.d.) writes that she was repeatedly sexually abused as a young girl by her father, Chuck Phelps (no relation to Fred Phelps above), while he was a student at PBI for several years in the mid-late 1960s. She states that Phelps, who has served as an evangelist with Open Air Campaigners and a prison chaplain since leaving PBI, maintains his innocence and continues his career despite being confronted by Linda and her husband. See www.lindafossen.com.

[41] Stephen Maxwell Spaulding, "Lion on the Prairies: An interpretive analysis of the life and leadership of Leslie Earl Maxwell 1895-1984," 85, a document prepared for the Missiology program at Fuller Theological Seminary, Pasadena, California, May 1991.

[42] Although there is minimal mention of Prairie's "social regs" in the school's Manual until the 1958-59 edition, there is little doubt that such rules had long been in use at PBI. Davidson, 31-32, 37, for example, (a member of the first class at PBI), indicates rigid social regulations were in force at PBI from the outset. One assumes that these were communicated to students via an application packet, school year orientation

who never set foot on Prairie's campus vigorously insisted, not always in jest, that PBI so tightly controlled the relationship between the genders that campus sidewalks were actually painted according to the traditional colors associated in North American folklore with girls (pink) and boys (blue). The point of the fabricated legend was that females could walk only on pink sidewalks and males on blue, thereby enabling PBI to minimize and control interaction between the genders.[43]

Such fanciful claims regarding the colors of the sidewalks were in fact the product of someone's creative imagination. Nonetheless, the truth of the matter is that students were indeed carefully monitored by virtue of the "social regulations" that prevailed at Prairie during the Maxwell era. Such rules became a defining feature of the very rigid nature of the variety of Christianity embraced and advanced by the school under the J.F. Kirk—L.E. Maxwell administration.[44] Rigorous self-discipline and

---

sessions or in some other way. Unfortunately, the copies of the school's *Student Handbook* available in PBI's Records Office don't begin until the late 1940s. It is unknown if that is because such wasn't published until then or that no copies were retained until then. The *1958-59 Manual* states: "Social relations between men and women students are strictly regulated during their years in school in order that all students may be unhindered in the serious business of study and preparation for the Lord's work."

Specific regulations governing male-female student relationships were not uncommon in the Bible school movement in general. See Virginia Lieson Brereton, "The Bible Schools and Conservative Evangelical Higher Education, 1880-1940." In Joel A. Carpenter and Kenneth W. Shipps, (eds.), *Making Higher Education Christian* (St. Paul, MN: Christian University Press, 1987), 126: "Rules regarding recreational activities and relations between male and female students were becoming especially stringent. Sexual segregation or close supervision became the norm."

[43] Richard W. Flory, "Development and Transformation Within Protestant Fundamentalism: Bible Institutes and Colleges in the U.S.,1925-1991" (PhD dissertation, University of Chicago, 2003), 332f, states that the very same "apocryphal" story regarding pink and blue sidewalks circulated concerning student life at Bob Jones University in South Carolina, U.S.A.

He also relates that men and women students at BJU were allegedly not permitted to come closer than six inches to a member of the opposite sex. The version of this myth that circulated regarding Prairie was that there had to be at least a Bible's-width between male and female students. One assumes that the originators of this fabrication no doubt had a family or ample-sized pulpit Bible in mind.

[44] Mark Taylor Dalhouse, *An Island in the Lake of Fire: Bob Jones University, Fundamentalism & The Separatist Movement.* (Athens, GA: The Univ. of Georgia Press, 1996), 143f, offers a look at the social regulations that prevailed at BJU. In this regard, PBI's social regulations during the Maxwell era were very similar in nature to those at one of the strongest

repeated decisions to subject one's own will and preferences to those of God were essential to the duo's interpretation of the Christian gospel as it was dispensed at PBI under the motto "Training Disciplined Soldiers for Christ."[45] This theme served as the school's self-description for most of the era under consideration in this volume.[46]

The scrupulous self-discipline that characterized the culture at PBI under Maxwell's leadership was directly linked to his understanding of the meaning of the cross in the life of the believer. In constructing his theology at this point, he drew on what he had learned while a student at Midland Bible School studying favorite authors such as Horatius Bonar, Army Carmichael, F.J. Huegel, Oswald Chambers, William Law, Robert Murray McCheyne, Madame Guyon, A.J. Gordon and others, as well as his own study. Maxwell considered the Apostle Paul's words in Galatians 2:20 to identify what the normal objective and experience of the Christ-follower is to be: "I am crucified with Christ: nevertheless I live; yet not I, but Christ liveth in me: and the life which I now live in the flesh I live by the faith of the Son of God, who loved me, and gave himself for me."

As summarized in the Preface to his first book, *Born Crucified*, published in 1945, this meant:

---

fundamentalist institutions in the United States. In fact, PBI for the majority of the Maxwell era was even more stringent than BJU in that, as a general rule, no dating whatsoever was officially permitted at PBI.

[45] L.E. Maxwell personal file—"Social regulations." An April 9, 1955, letter from Maxwell to "Dear Board and Staff Members" reads: "I am confident that God spoke to me regarding the boy and girl relationships that first month in 1922, when we had only ten students. At the present time some external agitation is on foot to have us let down in these matters. Should anyone within our staff favour our "having dating here within a year" no one need wonder that we are apprehensive lest pressure from without find foothold and encouragement within our ranks. While I think it may be desirable that we henceforth have a little more supervised group activity among the young folks during the school year, we must not entertain the idea, or practice, of dating among our attendants at Prairie."

[46] Dalhouse, 145, speaks of a "separated lifestyle" that prevailed at BJU. In what could easily be a page out of the PBI culture of the Maxwell era, he presents a "sampling of the characteristics that a separated life should encompass: 1) Do you have a daily devotional time reading God's Word? 2) Do you have good music standards, and have you eliminated rock music? 3) Are you getting victory over sinful habits? 4) Are you submissive to authority and responsive to correction? . . ."

The Cross is the key to all situations as well as to all Scripture. If I lose that key, I miss the road not only in the Bible, but also in the whole of my life. If, through the years, the Cross in the life of the believer had been adhered to as strenuously as the Cross for salvation, the Church would not today be so plagued with modernistic infidelity . . . This book is written to show the believer that, from the moment he is saved, he is so related to the Cross, that, if he henceforth fails to live by the Cross, he is an utter ethical contradiction to himself and to his position in Christ.[47]

This is what Maxwell consistently referred to as "the crucified life," a theological perspective that garnered him considerable acclaim within certain Christian circles in North America and beyond. This somewhat mystical concept advances that at the moment of salvation, the believer dies to sin and self

through identification with our Substitute in His death and resurrection . . . When God declares the ungodly sinner just, He makes no mere legal and lifeless imputation of righteousness apart from a real and deep life-union of the believer with Christ . . . Indeed we are to be partakers of the divine nature; and the doorway into such an experimental participation of the life of Christ is through identification—identification with Christ in His death and resurrection.[48]

In the course of daily life, then, believers reveal that they have been crucified with Christ by demonstrating that such pursuits as are of primary importance to natural man, or the unbeliever, (e.g. romantic interests, the acquisition of material assets, peer recognition, social standing, professional merit and accomplishment, etc.) are now of secondary importance in comparison to the noblest endeavor of all, to know and serve Jesus Christ. As the Christ-follower conscientiously and daily draws on this life-union with the empowering Christ, his priorities are so transformed that sacrifice of all but the quest to know and emulate Christ is comparatively inconsequential. Ostensibly, the discipline and sacrifice of "the crucified life" is therefore not a burden but a delight.

---

[47] L.E. Maxwell, *Born Crucified* (Chicago: Moody Press, 1945), 7.
[48] Ibid., 15-18.

Such an emphasis has prompted some observers to posit the existence of a distinct ascetic or "monastic" element in the PBI culture during the Maxwell era.[49] This was due in part to the rigid guidelines that applied governing how male and female students were expected to relate to one another.[50] Some observers considered the rural setting of Three Hills to be conducive to removing students from the attractions and distractions of "the world" so abundant in urban settings. The meager financial compensation that PBI staff members received for their service and the overall emphasis on material sacrifice in order to further God's work around the world were additional factors in creating the ascetic or monastic perception of PBI held by some.

The arrival of Ted S. Rendall

A significant and new chapter in PBI's history began in 1953 when Ted S. Rendall, a young preacher from Edinburgh, Scotland, enrolled for studies at the school.[51] His assignment as a student worker was to assist L.E. Maxwell in the production of PBI's monthly magazine, the *Prairie Overcomer*.[52]

---

[49] Ian S. Rennie, "The Western Prairie Revival in Canada: During the Depression and World War II," (unpublished paper c. 1974),16: ". . . the quasi-monastic discipline, expounded in Born Crucified, was defended as a necessary element in the lives of that cadre of heroic souls who were to be gospel pioneers."

Spaulding, 149, uses the word "monastic" several times in reference to PBI.

[50] Flory's research compares a number of factors at Wheaton College, Moody Bible Institute, Biola and Bob Jones University. One of the facts that emerges from his helpful study is that each of these schools (Wheaton, less so) had fairly rigid standards when it came to regulating relationships between the genders. Nevertheless, each of these colleges always permitted some variety of "dating" for at least some of their students, something that was virtually non-existent at PBI until near the end of L.E. Maxwell's tenure in the 1970s.

Spaulding, 85-86, discusses the rationale behind PBI's strict discipline.

[51] Prior to his arrival in Three Hills, Rendall had become familiar and sympathetic with Prairie's emphasis on material sacrifice, self-denial and "the crucified life," an important factor given the roles he would assume at Prairie in the following years. See Fuller, 173, quoting Rendall, "I'd heard of Prairie through some of its graduates . . . There were several fine Bible and theological schools in Scotland, but I was attracted by Prairie's emphasis on the crucified life. I know God led me here—otherwise why should I leave the beautiful city of Edinburgh, with its ancient castles, its university life, and its museums, and come to Three Hills!"

[52] *The Prairie Pastor* served as Prairie's primary publication beginning in 1926 (Davidson, 33), although it didn't begin off-campus distribution until 1928. In January 1930 the

Following graduation in 1956, Rendall was appointed as Maxwell's resource assistant, a position that entailed reading books, magazines and newspapers for the president's teaching, preaching and writing ministries. During this time Rendall began developing his own writing skills and enhancing his preaching and teaching ministry under Maxwell's tutelage.[53]

When Rendall indicated to Maxwell in 1957 that he intended to return to Scotland, the senior man convinced the younger to remain at Prairie whereupon Rendall began teaching the Bible school's primary second-year course known as Bible II. PBI's board subsequently appointed Rendall as Vice-Principal of the Bible Institute in 1960, Vice-President in 1966 and then Principal/Vice-President in 1968. He eventually took over as editor of the *Prairie Overcomer* and it was assumed by most that, for all practical purposes, he was being groomed as Maxwell's heir-apparent.[54]

Prairie Overcomer began as a publication for young people. It merged with the *Prairie Pastor* in mid-1943 and starting in January 1946, when the *"Pastor"* component of the title was dropped, the *Prairie Overcomer* functioned as Prairie's primary communiqué with its constituency for the duration of Maxwell's tenure. The *Young Pilot*, a magazine for children to which my mother frequently contributed, was published by the school from 1954-1988.

[53] This marked the beginning of what would become a prolific ministry for Rendall. During his tenure at PBI (retired 1998) he wrote numerous books including: *Living the Abundant Life.* (Three Hills, AB: Prairie Press, 1969); *In God's School* (Three Hills, AB: Prairie Press, 1971); *Fire in the Church.* (Chicago: Moody Press, 1974) (reprinted by G.R.Welch/Prairie Press, 1982); *Jeremiah: Prophet of Crisis.* (Three Hills, AB: Prairie Press, 1979); *Nehemiah: Laws of Leadership.* (Three Hills, AB: Prairie Press, 1980); *Discipleship in Depth.* (Three Hills, AB: Prairie Press, 1981); *Give Me That Book.* (Burlington, ON/Three Hills, AB: G.R.Welch/Prairie Press, 1982).

While still a student at Prairie, Rendall began preaching at Bethel Fellowship Church, a local, independent congregation that met several miles east of Three Hills. He continued there in addition to his duties at Prairie until 1975 when he was asked to succeed Maxwell as Pastor of Preaching at the Prairie Tabernacle, the congregation that met regularly on PBI's campus. My family attended Bethel Fellowship Church from 1971-1977.

Fuller, xiii, speaking of Maxwell, Rendall states: "Although I never called him "mentor," that is truly what he was to me. Eventually when my office was moved next to his, I had full access to him any time he was alone. He answered my questions, lent me books . . ." Fuller, 174, refers to the Maxwell-Rendall relationship in terms of the Paul-Timothy model from the New Testament.

[54] Ted S. Rendall Library: Tape AC 207.71). Maxwell acknowledges as much in this 1970 interview on "Forum," CHQR radio, Calgary.

The return of Paul T. Maxwell

By 1973 however, Maxwell's younger son, Paul, had returned to teach at Prairie after serving as a missionary in Colombia, South America. He was appointed Vice-Principal of the Bible School in 1974 and then, in a move that surprised most in PBI's ample constituency, was named successor to his father as President of PBI in 1978. Ted Rendall eventually became President when, owing to poor health, Paul Maxwell resigned in 1986, two years after the death of the latter's father.[55] Rendall held that position until 1992 when he was named the school's Chancellor.

Another important development in Prairie's history took place in time for the 1980-81 school term that immediately followed the completion of L.E. Maxwell's active involvement at the school. Prairie's catalogue for that term announced that, on the basis of authorization by the Alberta Legislative Assembly, the school would begin offering several degrees as the core of the curriculum: Bachelor of Theology, Bachelor of Religious Education and Bachelor of Biblical Studies. One-year and three-year diplomas in Bible were also offered as was a Certificate of Biblical Studies.[56]

This was a significant change at Prairie since, as will be visited later in this study, Maxwell firmly opposed academic accreditation throughout most of his tenure. It is sufficient at this point to simply point out that, although Prairie began granting degrees in the early 1980s, a development

---

[55] This development was controversial at the time and remains somewhat so even years later. I had several conversations with my late father who was a member of both Prairie's Board of Directors and the Operating Executive Committee at the time the decision was being made to appoint Paul Maxwell as President rather than Ted Rendall. He reported that two of the important considerations related to the matters of name recognition among Prairie's constituency and the personalities of the younger Maxwell and Rendall. Firstly, some board members apparently felt that the uniqueness of Prairie's ethos made it advisable to retain the Maxwell name at the top of the leadership structure (Flory, "Development and Transformation Within Protestant Fundamentalism," 284-288, discusses a similar dynamic with regard to Bob Jones University where Bob Jones Sr., Bob Jones Jr., and Bob Jones III were the first presidents of that school). Secondly, although Rendall excelled in the areas of preaching, teaching and writing, certain decision-makers apparently were of the opinion he did not have the necessary social skills they felt were an essential quality for the person who held the position of President of Prairie Bible Institute.

[56] PBI Records Office files: *Catalogue of the Prairie Bible Institute, 1980-81.*

L.E. Maxwell apparently approved of, the school did not achieve full accreditation with the American Association of Bible Colleges until 1997.

Hiebert adequately summarizes PBI's history during the second half of L.E. Maxwell's leadership of the school. He states:

> When Prairie Bible Institute (one of my *alma maters*) passed nine hundred in student enrollment in 1947-48 under the dynamic teaching, preaching and itinerant ministries of founding Principal, L.E. Maxwell, likely no one foresaw this school's decline in enrollment to the low six hundreds in the decade following, only to rebound to near nine hundred another decade following.[57]

In 1980, nearly sixty years after that original handful of students gathered for Bible instruction in an abandoned farmhouse near Three Hills, L.E. Maxwell retired from active teaching at Prairie Bible Institute. He may have begun his ministry at Three Hills "hoping for nothing," but by the time he left the classroom for the last time at the conclusion of the 1979-80 school year, it was apparent the young man from Kansas had truly accomplished something! W. Harold Fuller aptly records the nature of that "something" by noting that "in 2002, the [Prairie] Alumni Association stated that alumni-numbering 17,000 with the majority serving in missions or churches—were working in 114 nations."[58]

---

[57] Al Hiebert, *Character with Competence Education: The Bible College Movement in Canada* (Steinbach, MB: Association of Canadian Bible Colleges, 2005) records the history of accreditation of Canadian Bible institutes/colleges and how such related to the work of the American Association of Bible Colleges. See chapter 4: "Competition or Collaboration? How Have Bible Colleges in Canada Related to Each Other?"

[58] Harold W. Fuller, "The Legacy of Leslie E. Maxwell," *International Bulletin of Missionary Research*, Vol. 28, No. 3, (July 2004), 127. Fuller's footnote to this statistic is insightful regarding Prairie's milieu and Maxwell's persona: "As a result of incomplete record keeping in the early years of the school, statistics about graduates are necessarily approximate. As Maxwell explained to researcher Aaron Goertz, "In the early years we were so sure that Christ would return right then, we didn't think it worth keeping records. We possessed only three file cabinets. When the third got full, we threw out the contents of the first and started over again." See Donald Aaron Goertz: "The Development of a Bible Belt.""

CHAPTER TWO

Definition of Terms (Part I)

Several terms used frequently throughout this book require a properly contextualized definition if readers are to meaningfully engage the nuanced topic under discussion. Because certain labels have now acquired somewhat dated definitions as employed by various church history scholars, it is important that readers understand how I use them here and why. Further, because of their relevance to the history of Prairie Bible Institute, a clear definition of these terms is necessary particularly as it concerns how the school perceived and identified itself during the Maxwell era.

Two main factors influence my attempt to usefully define these terms. First, a consultation with a selection of the most prominent and relevant literature was carried out in an effort to obtain as comprehensive a definition as possible to illuminate the study at hand. The second consideration concerned, as applicable, how L.E. Maxwell and/or Prairie Bible Institute confirmed or differed from such a definition in their use and understanding of the same terms.

Bible school, Bible institute

In a work widely regarded as the original history of the North American Bible school movement, S.A. Witmer advances that the primary function of the first Bible schools and institutes was to prepare students for church vocations or other Christian ministries by offering a program of Biblical and practical training.[1]

Virginia L. Brereton augments this introduction by documenting that by 1920 dozens of denominational and non-denominational Bible schools were offering men and women an education at "roughly a high school level."[2] Such

---

[1] S.A. Witmer, *The Bible College Story: Education With Dimension* (Manhasset, NY: Channel Press, 1962), 23-26.

[2] Brereton, vii; see also 55: "The first known American school of this type was the Baptist Missionary Training school for women (1881) in Chicago. The earliest Bible

an education was intended to prepare them for practical ministry vocations as evangelists, missionaries, religious teachers, musicians and pastors within Protestant churches of a conservative evangelical orientation.

Guenther affirms a similar academic orientation and purpose for the early Canadian Bible schools.[3] An important observation regarding the comparatively low entrance requirements that existed for admission to these schools is offered by Hiebert.[4] McKinney does not hesitate to directly associate the early North American Bible schools with the fundamentalist movement.[5] He also notes that the majority of Bible school instructors were not highly educated themselves.[6]

Witmer states that two key attributes characterized Bible school life. First, the study of the Bible itself was at the core of the curriculum supplemented by courses that enabled students to practically apply the Bible's teaching to daily life. Secondly, in keeping with the primary purpose of the

---

training schools—Simpson's Missionary Training Institute, Moody's Bible Institute, and Gordon's Boston Missionary Training School followed shortly afterward, between 1882 and 1889."

[3] Bruce Guenther, "Slithering Down the Plank of Intellectualism? The Canadian Conference of Christian Educators and the Impulse Towards Accreditation among Canadian Bible Schools During the 1960s" in *Historical Studies in Education* Vol. 16, No. 2 (2004), 198: "Bible schools typically offered a Bible-centered, intensely practical, lay-oriented post-secondary theological training. As educational institutions, they operated in a zone between the upper years of secondary education and the undergraduate years of post-secondary education."

[4] Hiebert, 39: ". . . prior to the 1950s a relatively small proportion of North American adolescents (particularly those in western Canada) completed high school, and many fewer still went on to post-secondary education of any sort. Hence, it is understandable that the Bible institutes of those times often did not require high school graduation as entrance requirements. These trends changed dramatically in the 1950s and 1960s so that requiring high school graduation as entrance requirements became feasible for Bible institutes and it became feasible for these institutions to upgrade the academic rigor of their programs to a Bible college (university equivalent) level."

[5] Larry J. McKinney, "Protestant Fundamentalism and Its Relationship to the Bible College Movement in North America," in *North American Religion* 5 (1996/7), 112-113: "In the period immediately following World War I, when fundamentalism was a major recognized influence on North American church life, the Bible schools served as a base of operations for the movement . . . It was from these schools that fundamentalism gained the strength to deal with the theological controversies of the 1920s and to become a legitimate religious force in the decades that followed."

[6] Larry J. McKinney, "The Growth of the Bible College Movement in Canada," in *Didaskalia* (Fall 1998), 45.

Bible schools to train students for Christian service, a major emphasis was placed on the cultivation of the student's personal spiritual life—growing faith, fervent prayer, devotional Bible study and sensitivity to the work of the Holy Spirit.[7]

William C. Ringenberg's reminder that Bible schools represented a reaction to the growth of modernistic thinking in American Protestantism in general and its colleges in particular is a key element to the definition of the "Bible school" or "Bible institute" as the terms are used in this book.[8] Mark Noll helpfully points out that the Bible schools went along with the larger stream of evangelical academia in rejecting a revolution in educational philosophy that emerged near the end of the nineteenth century.[9]

The first American Bible schools such as Nyack, Moody and Gordon had their philosophical origins in the European training centers for missionaries and religious workers that were motivated by a strong interest in missions. Their intent was to establish religious training that differed from that offered by the formal ministerial preparation available in church colleges or seminaries.[10] Accordingly, the founders of these schools placed a strong emphasis on either foreign missions (A.B. Simpson, a Canadian, in

---

[7]   Witmer, 24.

[8]   William C. Ringenberg, *The Christian College: A History of Protestant Higher Education in America* (Grand Rapids, MI: Christian University Press & Eerdmans Publishing Company, 1984), 157.

   Hiebert, 5, offers a modifying perspective on the notion of Bible schools/institutes as being formed only or primarily in reaction to modernism by referring to a citation (from Richard Niebuhr) in Richard Niebuhr, Daniel Day Williams and James M. Gustafson, *The Advancement of Theological Education*, (New York: Harper & Row, 1957): ". . . the growth of the Bible school movement in the 20th century is not always to be regarded as a phenomenon of the opposition of 'conservatives' to 'liberals;' it is an increased participation of certain groups in the United States and Canada in the general movement toward education. The conservative schools seem to have their origin less in antagonism to the 'liberal' schools than in the desire of conservative groups to provide education of a Christian type for their young people and particularly of their ministers."

[9]   Mark A. Noll, "The Revolution, the Enlightenment, and Christian Higher Education in the Early Republic," 56-76; "The University Arrives in America, 1870-1930," 98-109, in Carpenter and Shipps (eds.), *Making Higher Education Christian* (Grand Rapids: Eerdmans Publishing Co., 1987).

[10] Brereton, 57.

the founding of Nyack) or Christian ministries at home (D.L. Moody in the founding of Moody), and usually a hybrid of both themes.[11]

The first such school to take lasting root in Canada was the Toronto Bible Training School established in 1894 (later renamed Toronto Bible College, then Ontario Bible College, and now known as Tyndale University College).[12] Whereas the established universities, church colleges and seminaries of the day were committed to producing professional clergy, the focus of these newer training centers was on preparing practitioners for active service as opposed to bestowing respectable academic or professional credentials on graduates.[13]

Prairie Bible Institute during the Maxwell era was a proudly inter-denominational community that attached minimal significance to the emphases of academia while training willing men and women for vocations

---

[11] Virginia Lieson Brereton, "Bible Schools and Evangelical Higher Education" in Carpenter and Shipps, (eds.), *Making Higher Education Christian*, 112: "The first Bible schools, then, belonged to this wider heterogeneous group of missionary training schools," and 125: "The Bible schools' inner culture was devoted to the missionary enterprise."

[12] The historiography of the Canadian Bible School movement, although somewhat sparse compared to that of the American Bible School movement, is thankfully growing. In addition to the work by Stackhouse that has already been identified, readers should also consult Bruce L. Guenther, "Training for Service: the Bible School Movement in Western Canada, 1909-1960," (PhD dissertation, McGill University, 2001); Burkinshaw, Robert K., *Pilgrims in Lotus Land: Conservative Protestantism in British Columbia 1917-1981* (McGill-Queen's University Press: Montreal & Kingston, 1995); James Enns, "Every Christian a Missionary: Fundamentalist Education at Prairie Bible Institute 1922-1947," (M.A. thesis, University of Calgary, 2001); Hiebert, *Character With Confidence Education*, etc.

[13] Ronald J. Sawatzky, "Looking for that Blessed Hope: the Roots of Fundamentalism in Canada 1878-1914," (PhD dissertation, University of Toronto, 1986) offers an informative treatment of how the Niagara Bible and Prophecy conferences held during the late nineteenth century contributed to the founding of the Toronto Bible Training School. Sawatzky makes two important points regarding the eventual founding of T.B.T.S. First, the eschatology of those he calls "proto-fundamentalists" promoted a sense of urgency that Christ's return was near, prompting them to provide practical Bible training for as many young people as possible who would in turn declare the truth of Christ's soon return. Secondly, the "proto-fundamentalists" perceived the established church colleges to be increasingly irrelevant to the needs of the day: ". . . the proto-fundamentalists were concerned that the theological training being received by their youth in the church colleges was too scholarly and not practical enough," 270. See especially 256-294.

in keeping with the school's passion for foreign missions and church-related ministries in North America.[14] The Bible was the anchor of the school's curriculum and served as the primary basis for the strong emphasis on the cultivation of a disciplined personal faith, prayer life and commitment to Christian vocational service.[15] The focus on the Bible was regularly augmented by exposure to presentations by visiting missionaries from around the world who would share their acquired experience and wisdom in classes, chapel services and other public meetings.

It is important to reiterate here that PBI came into being partly due to J. Fergus Kirk's concern about the inroads that liberal thinking was making into local churches.[16] The mistrust of modernism as well as of secular colleges and universities was prominent throughout Maxwell's tenure at Prairie. Well into classes and sermons in the 1970s, Maxwell would occasionally still vigorously berate some aspect of Harry Emerson Fosdick's theology or behavior.

---

[14] PBI Records Office files. The school's published *Prospectus* for the 1924-25 school year included the term "interdenominational" immediately beneath the document's title. The school's 1954-55 *Catalogue* states: "As an independent school it offers a place where persons of all evangelical denominations can feel happy together . . ."

The "Conditions of Matriculation" in the 1924-25 *Prospectus* stated simply: "Persons applying for admission should have a fixed Christian principle and purpose, should be unexceptionally considerate of others, and obedient to those who are over them in the Lord. Rather than advance ideas and methods contrary to the spiritual harmony of the Institute as an interdenominational school, students are expected to withdraw."

The first Application for Admission appeared in the *1928-1929 Bulletin of The Prairie Bible Institute* and simply asked, "How much schooling have you had?" An expanded application form introduced in 1941-42 directed applicants to forward their high school transcripts as a part of the application process.

[15] James Enns, "Every Christian a Missionary: Fundamentalist Education at Prairie Bible Institute 1922-1947," 7-8, contends it is essential to understand that PBI's primary function was the training of overseas missionaries. Indeed, those of us who grew up at PBI understood this to be the case and had a standing "joke" that if you weren't committed enough to go overseas, perhaps God might accept your choice of Christian service in the homeland as an acceptable alternative.

[16] See Chapter One of this book, footnote 9.

Guenther, 57, makes passing reference to Ronald G. Sawatzky's claim in "The Bible College/School Movement in Canada: Fundamental Christian Training" in *Canadian Society of Church History Papers 1986* (n.d.) and "Bible schools/Bible colleges" in *Canadian Encyclopedia*, vol. 1 (Edmonton, AB: Hurtig, 1985)) that most Canadian Bible schools were reacting against the "liberalism" of established theological colleges.

Prairie consistently identified itself as a "Bible school" and usually referred to itself as "the Institute." Thus, for the purposes of this study, the terms "Bible school" and "Bible institute" are considered and used as synonyms.

Bible college

Witmer minimizes the differences between the terms "Bible college" and "Bible school" or "Bible institute." The one distinction he does allow for the "Bible college," an additional year of general education, is an important one for this study, however.[17] As will be noted later on, in the 1960s PBI specifically chose not to join the American Association of Bible Colleges lest so doing would require the school to offer courses it considered to detract from its strong and unique Biblical focus.

As the twentieth century progressed, many Bible institutes chose to change their names from "Bible institute" to "Bible college" in keeping with decisions by administrators to pursue a broader and more rigorous academic orientation.[18] While retaining a focus on the Bible and Bible-related courses at the core of the curriculums, stricter entrance requirements were introduced for Bible colleges and course offerings expanded to include

---

[17] Witmer, 26: "There is no fundamental difference between the Bible college and the day Bible institute. Both offer Bible-centered programs for which the chief purpose is to prepare students for Christian ministries. . . The one principal difference is that the Bible college includes one additional year of general education. Bible institutes limit general education to only 16 to 32 semester hours, while Bible colleges require from 32 to 64 hours in their four-year program."

  Reference was made in the opening paragraph of this chapter to the different nuances of meaning adhered to by different scholars in how they use certain terms. Evidence of this is found within Witmer's own thinking. In the citation just referred to from his work (footnote 17), he speaks of a Bible college as being somewhat different from a Bible institute. A few pages later (37), however, he speaks of two types of Bible schools. "It is significant that the first two schools, Nyack and Moody, represent quite typically the two chief types of Bible schools. Moody has throughout its history represented the more specialized "Bible institute" with its three-year diploma courses. Nyack is an example of the degree-conferring Bible college whose curriculum includes more liberal arts or general education courses."

[18] Thomas A. Askew, "The Shaping of Evangelical Higher Education Since World War II," 137-152, in Carpenter and Shipps, (eds.), *Making Higher Education Christian*.

classes in the liberal arts, humanities and general education.[19] The program was usually accredited by a recognized accrediting association such as the American Association of Bible Colleges and, in time, various degrees were regularly conferred on graduates.[20]

In his comprehensive study of Canadian Bible schools, Bruce Guenther reports that in contrast to developments in the United States where numerous Bible schools transitioned into Bible colleges, very few such Bible colleges appeared in Canada prior to 1960. Nonetheless, the few Canadian Bible colleges that did exist were accredited, conferred degrees and included significantly more liberal arts courses in their curriculum. They also had "more rigorous entrance requirements and higher academic standards."[21] Such factors thus account for what distinguishes the term "Bible college" from "Bible school" and/or "Bible institute" as they appear in this book.[22]

Within the time period under review in this study, Prairie Bible Institute made a conscious choice to remain a Bible institute rather than become a

---

[19] For the purposes of this study, it is important to again stress that the distinction between Bible schools/institutes and Bible colleges is not an exact science. For example, the school A.B. Simpson founded in New York was initially called the Missionary Training College for Home and Foreign Missionaries and Evangelists (1883), then The Training College (1890), the New York Training Institute (1894) and The Missionary Training Institute upon moving to Nyack, NY, in 1897. Various scholars refer to it as essentially the first Bible school in the U.S. Nonetheless, Witmer in *The Bible College* Story, 35, indicates that from its humble beginnings in 1882, the school offered courses in logic, philosophy, natural sciences, ancient and modern history, and geography which, in keeping with the definitions being developed in this study, would have made it more of a Bible college than a Bible institute.

[20] Ringenberg, 167: "The most significant recent development in the academic organization of the Bible-college movement has been the tendency for institutions to evolve from Bible institutes to Bible colleges and even, in a few cases, from Bible colleges to Christian liberal arts colleges . . . As an educational institution, a Bible college occupies an intermediary position between a Bible institute and a Christian liberal arts colleges . . . A Bible college curriculum is generally four years long and results in an A.B. degree, whereas a Bible institute program is shorter—frequently three years—and results in a diploma."

[21] Guenther, 11.

[22] Robert K. Burkinshaw, "Evangelical Bible Colleges in Twentieth-Century Canada," 369-384, in George A. Rawlyk (ed.), *Aspects of the Canadian Evangelical Experience*, (Montreal-Kingston: McGill-Queens Univ. Press, 1997) also touches on some of these differences as they related to the Canadian scene.

Bible college. The reasons for that important decision by the school's leaders will be visited at a later point in the book.

Christian liberal arts college

Whereas Bible institutes and Bible colleges gave a prominent place in their curriculums to the study of the Bible, theology and courses related to Christian service, Ringenberg reports that the distinctive of the Christian liberal arts school is that the Bible and Christian theology formed the platform for a curriculum that primarily focused on the study of the liberal arts and sciences.[23] Except for students majoring in religion, students at Christian liberal arts schools did not explicitly study the Bible except as such was required or encouraged through chapel services, special emphases and personal study. In other words, although the direct study of the Bible is not as prominent in a Christian liberal arts school, the Biblical or Christian worldview informs the study of the very same disciplines and courses that are taught at mainstream universities or colleges.[24]

The history of conservative Christian liberal arts schools in Canada is comparatively brief when compared with the movement in the United States. Wheaton College, for example, one of the most prominent conservative Christian liberal arts schools in the U.S., was established in the mid-nineteenth century.[25] On the other hand, as Burkinshaw relates, conservative Christian liberal arts schools were virtually unknown in Canada prior to the 1960s.[26]

---

[23] Ringenberg, 167: "The Christian liberal arts college student can choose from a wider variety of general education courses and major disciplines; however, the academic experience of a Bible college student compares closely to that of a student who majors in religion in a Christian liberal arts college."

[24] Witmer, 25: "The liberal arts college goes on from a foundation of general education in the humanities and sciences to prepare students for the many professions and vocations. Emphasis is on a liberal arts education."

Askew, 145: "Indeed, the evangelical institutions had convinced parents that their children could receive intellectual grooming and credentialing for professions without eschewing moral and spiritual nurture."

[25] Flory, 6: "Wheaton College was founded in 1843 as the Illinois College, a secondary school, and in 1860 became Wheaton College and graduated its first class."

[26] Burkinshaw, "Evangelical Bible Colleges. . ." 369, in George A. Rawlyk (ed.), *Aspects of the Canadian Evangelical Experience*: "In the virtual absence of seminaries and liberal arts college under conservative evangelical control until the 1960s, evangelicals in twentieth

As already seen, Prairie Bible Institute during the Maxwell era intentionally retained its identity as a Bible institute. This study will verify that it specifically rejected overtures to become a Bible college or to seek accreditation with any kind of outside regulating body. Since becoming a Christian liberal arts school was never a serious possibility at PBI in the time frame under review in this study, the use of the term here is minimal.

"Non," "un," "inter" and "trans"-denominational Bible schools

It is helpful to note at some point in a study like this that the Bible institute movement in North America must be viewed against the historical background of higher education in general in both the U.S. and Canada. Christian churches, in general, and various church denominations, in particular, were the dominant factors in the initial establishment of centers of higher education on both sides of the international border as the United States of America and Canada each developed their national identities.[27]

However, as many of the mainline denominations and their related colleges gradually embraced theological modernism if not outright

---

century Canada were typically trained in Bible institutes and colleges. And despite the dramatic development of evangelical seminaries and liberal arts colleges in Canada over the past three decades, Bible schools consistently remained the choice of the great majority of students enrolling in evangelical post-secondary institutions."

[27] Witmer, 27: "For more than two centuries, Protestant, evangelical Christianity gave leadership to American higher education and stamped it with its faith and spirit. Each of the nine colleges founded during the colonial period was prompted by Christian motivations." See also 28: "While the first Canadian institutions were not established until the latter part of the 18th century and the first part of the 19th, religious motivations were dominant. King's College was founded by the Anglicans in 1790, Acadia University by the Baptists in 1839, and Bishop's College by the Anglicans in 1845."

Michael Gauvreau, *The Evangelical Century: College and Creed in English Canada from the Great Revival to the Great Depression* (Montreal-Kingston: McGill-Queen's Univ. Press, 1991), 8, in reference to the Methodist and Presbyterian denominations in Canada states: "Of greater significance for this study is the early and highly visible role of these two churches in the promotion of institutions of higher learning. These colleges formed the central components of the modern Canadian university system."

Ringenberg, "The Old-Time College, 1800-1865," 77, in Carpenter and Shipps (eds.), *Making Higher Education Christian*: "Almost without exception, to be a college in America before the Civil War was to be a Christian college."

secularism, certain conservative Protestants responded by establishing Bible schools as alternative learning centers. Their intent was to educate their young people in keeping with their understanding of truth and to provide personnel for their churches and missionary endeavors.[28] Although some of these latter schools were started by specific denominational groups, many of them were of a multi-denominational or interdenominational orientation.[29]

Thus, terms such as "nondenominational," "undenominational," "interdenominational" and "transdenominational" frequently appear in the literature with reference to these institutions. In the case of an approach such as that employed in Guenther's dissertation where he examines the different types of Bible schools established in Western Canada, it is necessary to distinguish between these terms.[30]

Since this study interacts with Stackhouse's representation of Prairie, it should be pointed out that his definition and use of the term "trans-denominational evangelicalism" to refer to organizations like P.B.I. is appropriate given that such a term aligns with Prairie's own description of itself.[31] Where this analysis parts ways with Stackhouse in this regard

---

[28] Ringenberg, *The Christian College*, 115: "Some scholars have observed that the secularization process in higher education is an outgrowth of the secularization of America in general during the last century. To a certain extent this is true; however, one must note that the colleges secularized more than did society as a whole. Before the Civil War, the colleges, as agents of a church dominated by orthodoxy, were much more Christian in their convictions than was society. By contrast, higher education today is considerably more secular than is the populace in general." See also 147: "Between 1890 and 1925 ... Also in this period the small religious groups, in part as a response to the general secularization pattern, began to organize autonomous Bible institutes and Bible colleges, thus creating a largely new form of higher education."

[29] Brereton, 71-77, offers a lengthy list of North American Bible institutes founded by 1945 and their sponsoring denominations. She consistently uses the term "interdenominational" to refer to those that were not the initiative of one particular denomination.

See also Ringenberg, *The Christian College*, 173-187.

[30] Guenther, 11.

[31] Stackhouse, *Canadian Evangelicalism in the Twentieth Century*, 9: "... these Christians were committed to 'transdenominational evangelicalism,' the belief that the evangelical 'basics' are most important in Christianity and that transdenominational cooperative action should be undertaken on this basis."

PBI Records Office files; *Catalogue of the Prairie Bible Institute, 1980-81*, 9: "... There are great fundamental doctrines of the Bible which bind us together as true believers—for

relates to his insistence on a significant difference between Canadian "trans-denominational evangelicalism" and American fundamentalism specifically as such relates to an accurate depiction of PBI's identity.

It is expedient to note that most of the recognized Canadian church history sources that make reference to PBI identify it as either "nondenominational" or "undenominational."[32] Nonetheless, it is sufficient to reemphasize that PBI immediately identified itself as "inter-denominational" and intentionally emphasized that identity in the earliest of its publications.[33] This was possibly influenced by the fact that J. Fergus Kirk came from a Presbyterian background, W.C. Stevens held allegiances to the Christian and Missionary Alliance while L.E. Maxwell in his early

example, the inspiration and inerrancy of the Bible, the vicarious death of Christ and His resurrection, etc. There are certain interpretations of Bible teaching which if propagated with zeal in an unbalanced way can become divisive. For example, there are among Christians various interpretations of holiness, of the second coming of the Lord, of the sovereignty of God and the free will of man, and of the order of events in the experience of salvation. In these areas we must strive to keep the unity of the Spirit."

[32] Douglas J. Wilson, *The Church Grows in Canada*, (Toronto: Canadian Council of Churches, 1966), 148, and Robert A. Wright, "The Canadian Protestant Tradition: 1914-1945," 166, in Rawlyk, George A. (ed). *The Canadian Protestant Experience 1760-1990* (Burlington, ON: Welch Publishing Co., 1990) and William E. Mann, *Sect, Cult and Church in Alberta* (Toronto: Univ. of Toronto Press, 1955), 4, all refer to Prairie as "non-denominational." H.H. Walsh, *The Christian Church in Canada* (Toronto: The Ryerson Press, 1956), 321, and John Webster Grant, *The Church in the Canadian Era (updated and expanded)* (Burlington, ON: Welch Publishing Co., 1988), 128, identify P.B.I. as "undenominational."

[33] Prairie Records Office files; *Manual of the Prairie Bible Institute, 1926-27*, 4-5: "As an Institute we seek and enjoin upon our students the most cordial fraternal relations with all Evangelical denominations. Seven denominations are represented on our Board of Directors, three on our faculty, and twelve denominations were represented last year in our student body. The Institute exists, therefore, under God, to be of service to all bodies of Christians." *Bulletin of the Prairie Bible Institute 1928-29*, 10, quoted W.C. Stevens, the honorary president: "This School, while independent of denominational auspices, yet is not anti-denominational. While it does point out the reproof and correction which the Word of God makes of the spirit of sectism—the spirit of schism and division (I Cor. 1:10; 12:25)—yet the School holds itself in cordial fraternal relationship with all evangelical divisions of the Church." *Catalogue of the Prairie Bible Institute, 1980-81*, 9: "Although the school holds itself in cordial, fraternal relationship with evangelical divisions of the Church, it holds a denominationally unrelated viewpoint . . ."

years had developed associations with several conservative denominations and had been ordained a Baptist.[34] As well, the local believers at Three Hills who supported the school in its infancy likely represented a variety of conservative Christian traditions. There emerges, nevertheless, some basis for informed speculation that PBI's early decision to retain a non-denominational orientation was not unanimous among the school's initial leadership core.[35]

---

[34] Keller identifies Presbyterian (29-33), Christian Endeavor Society (37) and Baptist (38) influences in Maxwell's conversion and early Christian experience. And, of course, Maxwell would have encountered the Christian and Missionary Alliance influence when he studied under Stevens at Midland Bible Institute in Kansas City.

[35] Davidson, 23, stresses PBI's early, conscious decision to establish an undenominational school by mentioning a Christian and Missionary Alliance pastor from Edmonton, Rev. Woodward, whom Maxwell had invited to speak at PBI at the end of the 1924 spring term. Woodward's input on the future of PBI was that "there were no other Bible schools in the west so why not build a Christian and Missionary Alliance school in a city?" by which he was suggesting that PBI relocate to a city as a C&MA school. This anecdote is enlightened by the following.

Lindsay Reynolds, *Rebirth: the redevelopment of the Christian and Missionary Alliance in Canada* (Willowdale, ON: C&MA in Canada, 1992), 337-338, writes concerning Rev. Woodward and District Superintendent Roffe (C&MA District of Canada): ". . . neither Roffe nor Woodward had lost their convictions for the need of some form of Alliance-controlled instruction in the west. In October 1923, Roffe and Woodward visited Maxwell in Three Hills. To the visitors, Maxwell appeared to welcome the possibility of some connection with the Alliance. Indeed, on his return, the superintendent reported that "it was the unanimous desire of the school (at Three Hills) to affiliate with the Canadian District. It would seem that fancy had taken over from fact. In March 1924, an article appeared in the *Alliance Weekly* about Maxwell's school, which stated:

"The school, feeling its development to be of God, asked Mr. Roffe, Canadian Superintendent, to take over the school. While arrangements have not yet been completed for the transfer, students from the Canadian West are being sent there in preparation for Nyack.

"Maxwell had no such intentions. He was prepared to have Woodward assist with the teaching, to have Roffe address the student body, to take up annual collection for Alliance missions, and, in the event that the Alliance opened a school in Edmonton, to recommend it to his students living in Edmonton. However, he was not prepared to turn over his school to them. For the sake of his school, it was just as well that Maxwell remained obdurate."

Spaulding, 106, 177: "Maxwell's first inclination had been to establish, if they were to be an incorporated school, a Christian and Missionary Alliance institute like Nyack in New York. This was firmly resisted by the local people who were now his

In this study the term "inter-denominational" informs descriptions of Prairie Bible Institute. This is the manner in which the school consistently identified itself throughout the Maxwell era.

Sect

From its earliest days, Prairie Bible Institute made a point of stressing its unsectarian identity.[36] This remained an important emphasis for the school throughout the Maxwell era.[37] It is necessary to clarify, however, that the definition Prairie attached to the notion of "sect" or "sectarian" varied

---

trusted friends and advisors. This would be their school and would be open to as many students of the various local traditions as possible."

[36] PBI Records Office files. The first time the term appears in the school's promotional literature is in *the Manual of the Prairie Bible Institute 1925-26* which stated (5): ". . . The School cannot, however, as a servant of all, begin to trim to the sectarian preferences of God's children, for it will then lose its consistent unsectarian character and forfeit its service to those who prefer the undivided body to a particular division. As an independent School it offers a place where persons of all sects can feel happily together, and that for two reasons; first, because the School itself is wholly unsectarian; secondly, because those who come to it as students are expected to prefer it on that account; that is, they prefer the whole undivided body to any one division thereof, while yet remaining consistent and warm-hearted members of their particular sects."

[37] PBI Records Office files. The school's 1980-81 catalogue stated, 9: "When we speak about an unsectarian position we mean something like this: There are great fundamental doctrines of the Bible which bind us together as true believers . . . inspiration and inerrancy of the Bible, the vicarious death of Christ and his resurrection, etc. There are certain interpretations of Bible teaching which if propagated with zeal in an unbalanced way can become divisive . . . various interpretations of holiness, of the second coming of the Lord. Of the sovereignty of God and the free will of man . . . **There are particular current interpretations of Bible teaching which the Institute does not endorse** . . . the claim that speaking in tongues is the necessary evidence of the fullness of the Holy Spirit, the claim that healing is unqualifiedly available to every believer, and other aspects of teachings which are variously labeled, such as neo-pentecostalism, charismatic renewal, charismatic ecumenism, etc. The Institute wishes it to be known that it does not permit the propagation on campus of these views . . ." (**emphasis** in original)

Hector A. Kirk, *Balanced Security*, (Maple, ON: The Beacon Press, n.d.) is an example of the middle-ground PBI endeavored to walk on such polarizing theological issues as the eternal security of the believer. J. Fergus Kirk's brother was an early PBI graduate and faculty member who also served as a missionary in Nigeria.

significantly with how the term was and is used in the relevant literature. This is not surprising for a couple of reasons.

For one thing, as in most of its undertakings, PBI took its cue for how it defined anything, including the concept of "sect," from the Bible itself with minimal regard for any other influence. In this instance, such passages as I Corinthians 1:10, 11:18 and 12:25 were directive.[38] Accordingly, the term "unsectarian" as used by PBI had a distinctly theological and Biblical meaning which was intended to convey that the school did not emphasize or promote those points of theology that, in its view, promoted schism or division among believers.

Secondly, Prairie was using the term in this manner prior to the time the sociological definition given it by such European thinkers as Max Weber (1864-1920) and Ernest Troeltsch (1865-1923) became popular in North America.[39] In the European context, the term "church" came to refer exclusively to the established state churches or denominations such as the Lutheran church in Germany. On the other hand, "sect" was the term of choice for referring to dissenting religious bodies such as the Mennonites, Hutterites or Doukhobors that broke away from the state-authorized church. The key sociological distinction was that whereas the "church" was perceived to accept or embrace the sinful world in order to sanctify it, a "sect" was seen to reject the world and any notion of accommodation or adjustment to it.[40]

---

[38] *The New American Standard Bible* translates the verses cited: "Now I exhort you, brethren, by the name of our Lord Jesus Christ, that you all agree and that there be no divisions among you, but that you be made complete in the same mind and in the same judgment" (1:10); "For, in the first place, when you come together as a church, I hear that divisions exist among you (11:18); "so that there may be no division in the body, but that the members may have the same care for one another" (12:25).

[39] Ernest Troeltsch, *The Social Teaching of the Christian Churches* 2 vols; (translation by Olive Wyon); (New York: Harper and Brothers, 1960); Max Weber, *Essays in Sociology* (London: Routledge & Keegan Paul Ltd., 1974); see also Joachim Wach, *Sociology of Religion* (Chicago: Univ. of Chicago Press, 1962).

[40] S.D. Clark, *Church and Sect in Canada*, (Toronto: University of Toronto Press. 1948), xii: "The church seeks the accommodation of religious organization to the community; the welfare of society is something for which it feels responsible. The sect emphasizes the exclusiveness of religious organization; the worldly society is something evil of no concern to the spiritually minded. While no sharp line can be drawn between the two forms of religious organization (the church always contains some of the attributes of the sect while the sect is never "pure," completely other-worldly in character), within

Although the development of Canadian religious life did not exactly parallel the European experience, the "church-sect" typology, as Stackhouse maintains, proves somewhat helpful for understanding the Canadian evangelical experience prior to the 1960s as portrayed by the standard reference works on Canadian church history.[41] Stackhouse affirms that the "church-sect" model is correct to some extent in helping us understand Canadian evangelicalism in the first half of the twentieth century: it was "sectarian" and "played the role of 'outsider,' estranged from the larger culture."[42]

Useful to this study is Stackhouse's identification of Prairie Bible Institute as "sectarian" in its conscious separation from the larger Canadian society including the mainline denominations.[43] As this book will clarify,

---

the church the spirit of accommodation tends to dominate, with the sect the spirit of separation. It is the difference in outlook, in attitude of mind, which is so important in setting the one off from the other."

[41] Stackhouse, *Canadian Evangelicalism in the Twentieth* Century, 12-13: "In Canada, scholarly treatment of evangelicalism in the twentieth century has been limited almost entirely to a 'church-sect' typology, in which the mainline denominations (the Roman Catholic, United, Anglican, and Presbyterian—and, for some, the groups making up the Canadian Baptist Federation) are 'churches' and groups like the Salvation Army and Pentecostals are 'sects.' The original meanings of these terms, as formulated by Max Weber and Ernst Troeltsch in a Europe of state churches, do not apply exactly to the Canadian situation in which there are no established churches and dissenting sects. By derivation, however, the terms have come to denote something like the following. A 'church' is a denomination that enjoys status in the culture, participates in the culture and indeed manifests something of a proprietorial interest in the culture. It includes many whose allegiance is only nominal and typically comprises a variety of views and practices (remnant of the 'territorial church' idea) as part of its stature as a broadly 'accepted' and 'accepting' denomination. The 'sect,' by contrast, enjoys no status in the culture but rather consciously separates itself from it. It is made up only of 'believers,' only of those who consciously join it and who maintain its intellectual and behavioral discipline."

For an example of the Canadian scholarly treatment that Stackhouse refers to, see John S. Moir's "Sectarian Tradition in Canada" in John Webster Grant (ed.), *The Churches and the Canadian Experience: A Faith and Order Study of the Christian Tradition* (Toronto: The Ryerson Press, 1963), 119-132.

[42] Ibid., *Canadian Evangelicalism in the Twentieth Century*, 13.

[43] Stackhouse, 14: "Part 2 traces out this attitude of alienation from society and its institutions in the history of two key institutions: Prairie Bible Institute, which trained youth for evangelism and church leadership with no interest in broader cultural influence . . ."

there was a definite sense in which L.E. Maxwell himself was a "dissenter" to the influences of Canadian religious culture at large, particularly those of the Roman Catholic Church and the United Church of Canada. Accordingly, he intentionally led PBI in establishing a strong identity as the "sectish" type of organization that Stackhouse identifies as one of two "dispositions" or "mentalities" that emerged in twentieth-century Canadian evangelicalism.[44]

While fully appreciative of the theological significance that Prairie Bible Institute attached to identifying itself as "unsectarian," this study accepts that there is value in identifying the school during the Maxwell era as a "sect" in keeping with the sociological connotation of the term. As has already been observed, like many of its sister institutions, Prairie was founded in part as a reaction to the theological modernism of the North American mainline denominations. L.E. Maxwell intentionally established an environment of discipline at Prairie that he perceived essential in setting it apart from both worldly society and the mainline churches. Practically speaking, in matters related to dress, social standards and separation from worldliness, there was a sense in which Prairie followed in the train of earlier groups of dissenting believers who were proud to be visibly different than the "status quo" of the day.

Finally, in this regard, Prairie Bible Institute during the Maxwell era reflected several characteristics of the "sect" as identified by William E. Mann in his important work *Sect, Cult and Church in Alberta*.[45] For instance,

---

[44] Stackhouse, 16-17: "Canadian evangelicalism, therefore, cannot be described adequately by the traditional denominational or 'church-sect' typologies of Canadian church history . . . It appears, in fact, that two different dispositions, two *mentalities*, were evident within this fellowship. One involved itself more with the culture at large and tended to embrace a wider diversity of Christians: this I will refer to as the 'churchish' type of evangelical . . . The other type separated itself from the culture and tended to include a smaller and more clearly delineated spectrum of constituents; this I will refer to as the 'sectish' type of evangelical. . ."

[45] Mann, 5: "The sect is defined as a social institution distinguished from the church type of structure by certain basic social characteristics. These include an ascetic morality which renounces many so-called "worldly" values and mores . . . a high degree of equality and fraternity among the members along with an unusual degree of lay participation in worship and organizational activities. Sects are usually exclusive and selective in membership and hence tend to be small and homogeneous . . . sectarian groups tend to show great respect for leaders with charismatic powers and a casual indifference to, or an energetic protest against, the professionalization and hierarchization of the

the "social regulations" that governed the relationship between male and female students might be considered a form of "ascetic morality" which reflected both the school's disdain for worldly values and its subjugation of the natural desires for a higher purpose.

The structure of compensation at PBI during this period challenged some of the presuppositions of free-market capitalism. The equal value of each member of the community's contribution and their sacrificial contribution to the work of the school was emphasized and every staff member was compensated and valued equally. As a charismatic leader held in high regard by the PBI community, public criticism of Maxwell by members of the school's community was discouraged and seldom tolerated. In his writings and speaking, Maxwell himself frequently criticized both individuals and perspectives that he believed represented not only theological modernism but, to quote Mann, "the professionalization and hierarchization of the clergy."[46]

The importance placed on individual religious experience at Prairie was another attribute of the "sect" that prompts this study to see certain validity in Stackhouse's judgment of the PBI of the Maxwell era as "sectish."[47] Although PBI did not consider itself as such by virtue of its theological

clergy. They are often suspicious of sacramental forms of theology and worship, such as infant baptism. This standpoint is usually accompanied by an emphasis upon individual religious experience, a requirement that generally limits full membership to adults. Furthermore, most sects rigidly eschew membership in the district councils of churches and the national associations of the Protestant denominations . . . while the spirit of the church is largely this-worldly and accommodative, that of the sect is distrustful of the secular world and its supporters, and is basically separatist."

[46] For example, the United Church of Canada and its ministers were one of Maxwell's favorite targets as was Harry Emerson Fosdick even years after Fosdick had passed from the public stage and was deceased. In the interview I conducted with Ted S. Rendall on August 14, 2006, inquiry was made as to whether or not Maxwell had ever been granted an honorary doctorate. Rendall responded that he was not aware that such had ever been offered and/or conferred, stating: "I think he would have turned it down if he had been offered an honorary doctorate—I think he would have felt that in accepting it and being called "Dr." he was compromising his position that was critical of degrees. That would be my hunch. He probably associated the term "Dr." with the German rationalists and liberal scholars that had caused so many problems."

[47] Stackhouse, *Canadian Evangelicalism in the Twentieth Century*, 75: "Prairie Bible Institute . . . represented the 'sectish' form of Canadian evangelicalism and therefore the 'Bible Institute' type of school with its homegrown teachers, its independence from accrediting institutions, and its greater concentration upon Bible instruction."

understanding of such language, it is both necessary and useful to grasp and apply the broader sociological use of "sect" since this is how it is generally understood and used in the study of religious history. Such a reality thus dictates how the term is understood and employed in this project.

Evangelicalism

Church history scholars are in general agreement that "evangelicalism" represents a complex theological designation that is somewhat difficult to define.[48] In the estimation of some observers, the twentieth century did little to clarify things in this regard.[49]

To complicate matters further, even attempts to precisely identify when that component of the Christian community now labeled "evangelical" first emerged pose a challenge.[50] And, as if these considerations are not sufficient

---

[48] Guenther, 12: ". . . the search for a precise definition is complicated by the fact that neither evangelicalism nor fundamentalism is a clearly defined religious organization with a membership list." See also: Timothy P. Weber, "Premillenialism and the Branches of Evangelicalism," 12, in Donald W. Dayton and Robert K. Johnston (eds.), *The Variety of American Evangelicalism* (Downers Grove, IL: Inter-Varsity Press, 1991); Bernard Ramm, *The Evangelical Heritage: A Study in Historical Theology* (Grand Rapids, MI: Baker Book House, 1973), 13; John R. Stone, *On the Boundaries of American Evangelicalism* (New York: St. Martin's Press, 1997) 3; George M. Marsden, *Understanding Fundamentalism and Evangelicalism* (Grand Rapids, MI: Eerdmans Publishing Co., 1991), 1; Sam Reimer, *Evangelicals and the Continental Divide: The Conservative Protestant Subculture in Canada and the United States* (Montreal and Kingston: McGill-Queen's Univ. Press, 2003), 6; Leonard I. Sweet, "The Evangelical Tradition in America" in Leonard I. Sweet (ed.), 85, in *The Evangelical Tradition in America* (Macon, GA: Mercer Univ. Press, 1984): "[i]t looks as if everyone at times has either been drawn into the loosely twined evangelical camp or claimed the label, thereby stripping the concept of Evangelicalism of much analytic purchase."

[49] "CT Predicts: More of the Same," *Christianity Today* 43, No. 14, (December 6, 1999); 36. Cited in Stanley J. Grenz, *Renewing the Center: Evangelical Theology in a Post-Theological Era* (2nd ed) (Grand Rapids, MI: Baker Academic, 2006), 19: ". . . evangelicals are still confused about their role in society, divided as a body, and even bewildered about what *evangelical* means.""

[50] Jeffrey Sheler, *Believers: A Journey Into Evangelical America* (New York: Viking/Penguin Group, 2006), 39: "I decided to. . . [confer] . . . with Mark Noll . . . one of the most knowledgeable people on the planet regarding evangelical origins. An evangelical himself, Noll has written more than twenty-five books and dozens of articles on the history of evangelicalism and of early American Protestantism in general . . . So when I telephoned and told him I was looking for the place where it all began, I knew I

to disorient the average inquirer, a handful of scholars have recently argued that evangelicalism itself is in dire need of deconstruction or, at minimum, a major overhaul.[51] In identifying a useful definition of the movement, therefore, it may be of help to review specific events and developments that occurred at different points in church history.

As a backdrop to this undertaking, a few comments are in order regarding the etymology of the word. Since the English term "evangelical" derives from the Greek word 'euangelion' as used in the New Testament with reference to the "good news" or the "gospel" proclaimed by Jesus, some are inclined to view evangelicalism as having been initially established during the earthly ministry of Christ.[52] "Evangelicalism" as an identifiable entity, then, it is claimed, consists of those believers and churches that have faithfully adhered to Christ's core message ever since he first articulated it.[53] This contention helps underscore evangelicalism's historical affinity with the practical application of the teachings of Jesus in the lives of those who claim to be his followers.

That being said, many scholars prefer to affix the advent of evangelicalism to the Protestant Reformation (c. 1517-1648), viewing it as a school of thought firmly grounded in the distinctive theological convictions

---

could count on him to steer me to just the right spot. Noll responded to my query as any distinguished scholar would when asked to summarize a lifetime of academic work in a three-second sound bite. He chuckled. "There really is no such place." . . . I asked him to explain. "The evangelical movement—some people think 'tradition' may be a better word—cannot be traced to a single place or time," he began. "There is no single founder or instigator as such—no one like Martin Luther for the Protestant Reformation or Joseph Smith for the Mormons." . . . The evangelical movement was more "a confluence of a multiplicity of sectarian and denominational streams," each with its own unique history and setting."

[51] David F. Wells, *No Place for Truth: Or Whatever Happened to Evangelical Theology?* (Grand Rapids, MI: Eerdmans Publishing Co., 1993), 106-115.

D.G. Hart, *Deconstructing Evangelicalism: Conservative Protestantism in the Age of Billy Graham* (Grand Rapids, MI: Baker Academic, 2004. See particularly 13-32 and 175-191.

[52] John D. Woodbridge, Mark A. Noll and Nathan O. Hatch, *The Gospel in America: Themes in the Story of America's Evangelicals* (Grand Rapids, MI: Zondervan Publishing House, 1979), 13-14.

[53] Mark Elllingsen, *The Evangelical Movement: Growth, Impact, Controversy, Dialog* (Minneapolis, MN: Augsburg Publishing House, 1988), 46; Richard Quebedeaux, *The Worldly Evangelicals* (San Francisco, CA: Harper & Row, 1978), 6-7; Ronald H. Nash, *Evangelicals in Action* v (Nashville, TN: Abingdon, 1987), 40-53.

of emergent Protestantism.[54] The initial theological infrastructure of evangelicalism thus reflected a commitment to the key beliefs of the magisterial Reformers: *sola Scriptura, solus Christus, sola fide* and *sola gratia.* Given Martin Luther's important role in the Reformation, evangelicalism and Protestantism were once considered virtually synonymous in places such as Germany where Lutheranism prevailed.[55] The label was eventually applied to both Lutheran and Reformed fellowships in Germany although the domination of the church by civil rulers drained the movement of much of its spiritual vitality.

Richard Pierard maintains that evangelicalism was restored to vibrancy as a result of three European influences—German pietism, Methodism, the Great Awakenings—that were transported to the United States in the seventeenth and eighteenth centuries. He links each of these influences to Puritanism with its strong emphasis on biblical authority, divine sovereignty, human responsibility, personal piety, and discipline.[56]

---

[54] Woodbridge, Noll and Hatch, 14; Donald G. Bloesch, *The Future of Evangelical Christianity: A Call for Unity Amid Diversity* (Garden City, NY: Doubleday and Co., 1983) 14-15; John H. Gerstner, "The Reformed Perspective," 23; Vinson Synan, "The Arminian Tradition," 38-39; Kenneth S. Kantzer, "Unity and Diversity in Evangelical Faith," 58-59, all in David F. Wells and John D. Woodbridge (eds.). *"The Evangelicals: What They Believe, Who They Are, Where They Are Changing* (Grand Rapids, MI: Baker Book House, 1977); Richard Lovelace, "A Call to Historic Roots and Continuity," 46-47, in Robert Webber and Donald Bloesch (eds.). *The Orthodox Evangelicals: Who They Are and What They Are Saying* (Nashville: Thomas Nelson Inc., 1978); James Davison Hunter, *American Evangelicalism: Conservative Religion and the Quandary of Modernity* (New Brunswick, New Jersey: Rutgers Univ. Press, 1983), 7; Kenneth S. Kantzer, "The Future of the Church and Evangelicalism," 127-129, in Donald E. Hoke (ed.), *Evangelicals Face the Future,* (South Pasadena, CA: William Carey Library, 1978) points out that the word "Evangelical" was used by the Reformers even before the term "Protestant" was in use.

[55] The website for The Institute for the Study of American Evangelicals http://www.wheaton.edu/isae/defining_evangelicalism.html (accessed 04 April 2009) states: "During the Reformation, Martin Luther adapted the Greek term, dubbing his breakaway movement the *evangelische kirke,* or "evangelical church" - a name still generally applied to the Lutheran Church in Germany." See also Sydney E. Ahlstrom, "From Puritanism to Evangelicalism: A Critical Perspective," 289, in David Wells and John D. Woodbridge (eds.), *The Evangelicals: What They Believe . . . ":* "For Lutherans, who have probably used the word longer and more tenaciously than any other communion, it became in effect a synonym for Christian, that is, for one who lived by faith alone . . ."

[56] R.V. Pierard, "Evangelicalism" in Walter A. Elwell (ed.), *Evangelical Dictionary of Theology* (Grand Rapids, MI: Baker Book House, 1984), 380.

Evangelicalism found a home in North America when famous British preachers such as George Whitefield and John Wesley traversed the Atlantic declaring the necessity of a specific transforming encounter with God through Jesus Christ in experiences they variously identified as "the new birth," "regeneration" or "conversion."[57] Successful revivals conducted in the U.S. by Jonathan Edwards and Charles G. Finney that were characterized by "the proclamation of Christ's saving work, the necessity of personally trusting him for eternal salvation," brought to evangelicalism a heightened awareness of man's urgent need for purity and holiness.[58]

The late eminent Canadian church historian, George A. Rawlyk, wrote of a "radical evangelicalism" that emerged in British North America that was, he claimed, more demonstrative and populist than its sister movements

---

[57] Douglas A. Sweeney, *The American Evangelical Story: A History of the Movement* (Grand Rapids, MI: Baker Academic Books, 2005), 23-24: "Evangelicals comprise a movement that is rooted in classical orthodoxy, shaped by a largely Protestant understanding of the gospel and distinguished from other such movements by an eighteenth-century twist." See also Douglas Jacobsen, *Church History* 75:2, 464-65, who applauds Sweeney's contention that evangelicalism's uniqueness is found in its simultaneous adherence to the beliefs of the Protestant Reformation and to the practices of the Great Awakening. See also: George A. Rawlyk and Mark A. Noll (eds.), *Amazing Grace: Evangelicalism in Australia, Britain, Canada and the United States* (Grand Rapids, MI: Baker Books, 1993), 16ff; Randall Balmer, *Encyclopedia of Evangelicalism* (Waco, TX: Baylor Univ. Press, 2004), 244-248; Martin Marty, "Tensions Within Contemporary Evangelicalism: A Critical Appraisal," 191, in David Wells and John D. Woodbridge (eds.), *The Evangelicals . . .* ; G.A. Rawlyk, *Is Jesus Your Personal Saviour? In Search of Canadian Evangelicalism in the 1990s* (Montreal & Kingston: McGill-Queen's Univ. Press, 1996), 9; D.W. Bebbington," *"Evangelicalism in Modern Britain: A history from the 1730s to the 1980s* (New York and London: Routledge, (repr. 2002)), 20f.

[58] Marsden, *Understanding Fundamentalism and Evangelicalism*, 2.
Mark A. Noll, *The Rise of Evangelicalism: the Age of Edwards, Whitefield and the Wesleys* (Downer's Grove, IL: Inter-Varsity Press, 2004), 64-102.
Mark A. Noll, David W. Bebbington, George A. Rawlyk (eds.). *Evangelicalism: Comparative Studies of Popular Protestantism in North America, The British Isles and Beyond* (New York: Oxford Univ. Press, 1994), 6: "The contributors here do not claim exclusive use of the term. Rather, they assume that, whatever its other legitimate uses may be, "evangelical" is also the best word available to describe a fairly discrete network of Protestant Christian movements arising during the eighteenth century in Great Britain and its colonies. This historical sense of "evangelical" is complemented by a parallel use of the term designating a consistent pattern of convictions and attitudes." The last sentence here is a reference to Bebbington's four terms as discussed later in this chapter—see footnote 69.

in the United States. At its center was the aggressive witness of preachers like Henry Alline around the time of the American Revolution and William Black who advanced such themes as conversionism, revivalism, Biblicism, activism, crucicentrism, pietism and mysticism.[59] Another Canadian church history scholar, Michael Gauvreau, focuses an entire volume on the authority of Scripture as the essence of evangelicalism in his review of the important role played by the Methodist and Presbyterian churches and colleges in Canadian life from 1820-1920.[60]

Christian Smith writes that throughout the nineteenth century in the U.S., conservative Protestantism or evangelicalism was "the establishment."[61] By mid-century, the rising popularity of millenarianism in Britain and North America served to cloak much of evangelicalism in an eschatological robe. Men like John Nelson Darby and William Miller introduced to the movement a preoccupation with prophecy and the belief in the imminent second coming of Christ. The populist appeal of millenarianism in the United States as advanced through Bible conferences and prophecy conferences led by leaders like Dwight L. Moody eventually contributed to a polarization among American Protestants into two camps that might be provisionally called "mainline" and "revivalistic," a development that paved the way for the rise of fundamentalism.[62]

The revivalistic or holiness branch of evangelical Protestantism became increasingly attentive to spreading the gospel message of salvation by faith alone in preparation for what it perceived to be the imminent return of

---

[59] G.A. Rawlyk, *The Canada Fire: Radical Evangelicalism in British North America 1775-1812* (Montreal and Kingston: McGill-Queen's Univ. Press, 1994), xiv-xv; G.A. Rawlyk, *Ravished by the Spirit: Religious Revivals, Baptists, and Henry Alline* (Montreal and Kingston: McGill-Queen's Univ. Press, 1984), 1.

[60] Gauvreau, 10.

[61] Christian Smith, *American Evangelicalism: Embattled and Thriving* (Chicago: The Univ. of Chicago Press, 1998), 2-4.

[62] Martin E. Marty, *Modern American Religion (vol. 1): The Irony of It All 1893-1919* (Chicago: The Univ. of Chicago Press, 1986), 210: "Under Moody and his colleagues evangelism began to take turns toward what was called premillennialism and, with it, new kinds of culture-negation."

  Ernest R. Sandeen, *The Roots of Fundamentalism: British and American Millenarianism, 1800-1930 (repr.)* (Grand Rapids, MI: Baker Book House, 1978); chapters 1-3.

  Ronald G. Sawatzy, "Looking for That Blessed Hope: The Roots of Fundamentalism in Canada, 1878-1914."

Christ.[63] As the twentieth century approached, such an emphasis helped prompt evangelicalism to distance itself from mainline denominations where German rationalism and other elements of liberal theology had found a home.

The first third of the twentieth century saw two developments unfold in the United States that added new dimensions to the definition of evangelicalism. Pentecostalism was born out of the nineteenth century holiness emphasis and the dramatic early twentieth century revivals such as the 1906-1909 Azuza Street events in Los Angeles to secure a place on the evangelical spectrum.[64] Although this new focus attached a theological significance to the miraculous events associated with the Day of Pentecost in the New Testament book of Acts thereby disquieting many in the evangelical camp, Pentecostals nonetheless affirmed such major theological tenets of evangelicalism as Biblical authority and the necessity of a specific and individual conversion experience.[65]

In response to theological liberalism that by the turn of the twentieth century had infiltrated many of the mainline denominations, a school of thought now known as the "Princeton Theology" took on renewed significance as a cornerstone of evangelicalism. Following in the tradition of staunch proponents of orthodoxy at Princeton Theological Seminary such as Archibald Alexander, Charles Hodge, A.A. Hodge and Benjamin B. Warfield, encroaching liberalism at Princeton was challenged in the 1920s by J. Gresham Machen. Although his defense of orthodoxy did not prevail and he eventually left the Presbyterian school in New Jersey to help establish Philadelphia's Westminster Theological Seminary, Machen's

---

[63] Woodbridge, Noll and Hatch, 37-38.

[64] Randall Balmer, *Mine Eyes Have Seen the Glory: A Journey into the Evangelical Subculture in America (third ed.)* (New York: Oxford Univ. Press, 2000), xvii; Martin Marty, *Modern American Religion (vol. 1)*; 237-247.

[65] Differing perspectives on including Pentecostalism within evangelicalism can be found in Vinson Synan, "Theological Boundaries: The Arminian Tradition," 38-39, in Wells and Woodbridge, (eds.) *The Evangelicals*, (1977), vs. Donald W. Dayton, "The Limits of Evangelicalism: The Pentecostal Tradition," chapter 4 in Dayton and Johnston (eds.), *The Variety of American Evangelicalism*, (1991).

For the riveting story of a Canadian woman who made a significant contribution to the spread of Pentecostalism in the United States, see Edith L. Blumhofer, *Aimee Semple McPherson: Everybody's Sister.* Grand Rapids: William B. Eerdmans Publishing Co., 1993.

rigorous defense of such ideals as the inerrancy of Scripture assured the orthodox Princeton scholars the esteem they enjoy yet today among many evangelicals.[66]

Against this general background regarding evangelicalism, the work of British historian David Bebbington proves very useful for our purposes. His influential book, *Evangelicalism in Modern Britain: A History From the 1730s to the 1980s*, offers a sufficient definition of "evangelicalism" as the term is used in this book.[67] Drawing on the background of reformation theology, Bebbington writes that evangelicalism has existed in Britain since the 1730s and has demonstrated a remarkable ability to unite people across denominational lines.[68] Although evangelicalism reflects a wide

---

[66] Mark A. Noll, "Princeton Theology, Old," 877-878, in Walter A. Elwell (ed.), *Evangelical Dictionary of Theology*.

[67] David Bebbington, *Evangelicalism in Modern Britain: A History from the 1730s to the 1980s* (London and New York: Routledge, 2002).

[68] Kenneth J. Stewart challenges Bebbington's widely embraced assignment of evangelicalism to an eighteenth century British origin and raises a number of thought-provoking caveats in this regard. See "Did evangelicalism predate the eighteenth century? An examination of David Bebbington's thesis," *Evangelical Quarterly*, (77:2), April 2005, 135-153.

Stewart's work eventually led to collaboration with other similarly minded scholars that resulted in the publication of Michael A.G. Haykin and Kenneth J. Stewart, (ed.) *The Advent of Evangelicalism: Exploring Historical Continuities*, (Nashville, TN: B&H Academics, 2008), a collection of essays "concerned with rethinking Bebbington's claim that evangelicalism began in the 1730s" to quote from Timothy Larsen's opening chapter, "The reception given *Evangelicalism in Modern Britain* since its publication in 1989," 23.

Concerning the cross-denominational nature of evangelicalism, see George M. Marsden, "The Evangelical Denomination," in George M. Marsden (ed.), *Evangelicalism and Modern America* (Grand Rapids, MI: Wm. B. Eerdmans Publishing Co., 1984), viii: "Evangelicalism is certainly not a denomination in the usual sense of an organized religious structure. It is, however, a denomination in the sense of a name by which a religious grouping is denominated. This ambiguity leads to endless confusions in talking about evangelicalism. Because evangelicalism is a name for a religious grouping, - and sometimes a name people use to describe themselves—everyone has a tendency to talk about it at times as though it were a single, more or less unified phenomenon."

See also: Timothy L. Smith, "The Evangelical Kaleidoscope and the Call to Unity," *Christian Scholar's Review* 15, No. 2, (1986), 125-40, who outlines the concept of evangelicalism as a "kaleidoscope" rather than a "mosaic" as he had earlier described it.

It bears repeating that both Guenther in "Training for Service" (16) and Stackhouse in *Canadian Evangelicalism in the Twentieth Century* (9-10) follow George M. Marsden in

diversity of personalities and viewpoints, Bebbington's work effectively
crystallizes the discussion. He identifies four main themes that adherents
of evangelicalism consistently emphasize in order to distinguish themselves
from other branches of Christianity: conversionism, activism, Biblicism and
crucicentrism.[69]

Conversionism points to the imperative nature of a personal experience of
that which the reformers described as "justification through grace by faith
alone." Such is characterized by a specific, identifiable encounter with God
that leads men and women to turn away in repentance from their sins and
toward Christ in faith. Although evangelicals differ over such matters as the
roles of the sovereignty of God and the free-will of mankind in conversion,
it is agreed that the personal nature of the conversion experience is an
indispensable component of what it means to belong to evangelicalism and
to be an evangelical.

Activism represents the activity of believers subsequent to conversion
wherein they consider their lives a mission devoted to the purpose of
convincing unbelievers to embrace the gospel of Christ. This conviction
eventually led to the development of the modern missionary movement
which stressed the importance of evangelizing people in the far-off regions
of the world.[70] Activism also manifests itself through the efforts of social

---

using the term "transdenominationalism" in defining their understanding of the kind
of "evangelicalism" that prevailed in organizations like Prairie Bible Institute. See
George M. Marsden, *Reforming Fundamentalism: Fuller Seminary and the New Evangelicalism*
(Grand Rapids, MI: Eerdmans Publishing Co., 1995), 2: "Second, evangelicalism has
also always been a transdenominational movement."

[69] Bebbington, 2-3.

[70] The modern foreign missions movement is based on certain well-documented events
such as: 1) March 8, 1698; British missionary Thomas Bray and four laymen found
the Society for Promoting Christian Knowledge (S.P.C.K.) *"to advance the honor of God and
the good of mankind by promoting Christian knowledge both at home and in the other parts of the world by
the best methods that should offer;"* 2) March 20, 1747—David Brainerd, colonial American
missionary, concluded his labors among the Indians of New Jersey and Delaware due
to deteriorating health. He had started 2.5 years earlier but was continually plagued
with illness. Brainerd died of tuberculosis seven months later. His diary, published
by Jonathan Edwards, became a major force in promoting missions work, inspiring
missionaries like William Carey, Henry Martyn and Thomas Coke; 3) 1792; William
Carey of Britain establishes the Baptist Missionary Society and by 1793 was pioneering
its operations in India.

action in which believers attempt to impact society by practically addressing and opposing such ills as child labor, alcoholism, slavery and prostitution.

Biblicism refers to the particular regard evangelicalism holds for the supreme authority of the Bible as the final arbiter of Christian doctrine and practice. Although the introduction of ideas concerning the Bible's "inerrancy" or "infallibility" did not surface until the early nineteenth century, evangelicals have always maintained a strong commitment to the Bible as the inspired and authoritative Word of God which merits fervent study and consistent application to daily life.

Crucicentrism speaks of evangelicalism's focus on the cross of Christ as the symbol that represents Christ's blood shed as the vicarious atonement for mankind's sin. The theological significance of what Christ accomplished by his death on the cross is considered by evangelicalism as that which reconciles sinful humanity to a holy God's standards of justice and perfection. In more recent times the meaning of the cross for evangelicals has reflected itself in a quest for sanctification and a thirst for holiness of life. For some evangelicals, including L.E. Maxwell of PBI, the importance of the cross has spawned enthusiasm for a mystical brand of spirituality that manifests itself in rhetoric concerning "the deeper life" and "the crucifixion of self."[71]

Many other historians have identified a theological infrastructure of evangelicalism that features only minor variations from Bebbington's construct.[72] While such definitions should be viewed as primarily descriptive,

---

[71] As will be noted later in this book, these latter themes are directly and indirectly addressed in L.E. Maxwell's early books: *Born Crucified* (Chicago: Moody Press, 1945), *Crowded to Christ* (Grand Rapids, MI: Eerdmans Publishing Co., 1950) and *Abandoned to Christ* (Grand Rapids, MI: Eerdmans Publishing Co., 1955).

[72] Marsden, *Fundamentalism and American Culture*, ix-x, identifies five emphases of evangelicalism: 1) the Reformation doctrine of the final authority of Scripture; 2) the real, historical character of God's saving work recorded in Scripture; 3) eternal salvation only through personal trust in Christ; 4) the importance of evangelism and missions; 5) the importance of a spiritually transformed life.

Balmer, xvi: 1) Luther's theology save for his ideas about polity and worship which evangelicals consider too formal and "papist;" 2) a "born-again" experience during which one acknowledges personal sinfulness and Christ's atonement; 3) a literalistic hermeneutic for understanding the authority of the Bible which, in turn, led to an emphasis on "inerrancy;" 4) proselytizing zeal.

John G. Stackhouse, Jr., "Who Whom? Evangelicalism and Canadian Society," 56, in George A. Rawlyk (ed.), *Aspects of the Canadian Evangelical Experience* lists: 1) evangelicals affirm the good news (the evangel) of God's salvation in Jesus Christ, both

Guenther accurately notes that many evangelicals attach creedal significance to these planks in their movement's theological platform.[73] Indeed, as Guenther observes, it is thus not uncommon to meet individual Christians who consider their identity as a part of evangelicalism's worldwide family to be of greater significance than their particular denominational allegiance.

A consideration of the theology of evangelicalism alone, however, does not supply enough information for a sufficient definition of the term. As intimated by certain features of the theological beliefs identified by Bebbington and others, particularly *activism*, some attention should be paid to the practical realities of how these ideological convictions have been lived out in everyday life by those who consider themselves to be stakeholders in evangelicalism.

In this regard, Randall Balmer offers a succinct comment acknowledging the immense significance of the character-development dimension of evangelical identity:

"Part of what defines an evangelical, however, transcends mere doctrine or belief; in greater or lesser degrees, evangelicals place a good deal of emphasis on spiritual piety."[74]

---

accomplished and symbolized primarily in his Cross and resurrection; 2) evangelicals believe this good news is expressed most authoritatively in the Bible; 3) evangelicals understand this good news to require personal transformation; 4) evangelicals are evangelists, people active in proclaiming this good news.

Hunter, *American Evangelicalism*, 7, identifies: 1) the belief that the Bible is the inerrant Word of God; 2) the belief in the divinity of Christ; 3) the belief in the efficacy of Christ's life, death, and physical resurrection for the salvation of the human soul; 4) an individuated and experiential orientation toward spiritual salvation and religiosity in general; 5) the conviction of the necessity of actively attempting to proselytize all nonbelievers to the tenets of the Evangelical belief system.

It should be noted that not all scholars agree with such summations of the key features of evangelicalism's theological convictions. See, for example, the essays assembled by Donald W. Dayton and Robert K. Johnston (eds.) under the title *The Variety of American Evangelicalism* identified previously. See also Donald W. Dayton, *Discovering an Evangelical Heritage*, (New York: Harper and Row, Publishers, 1976), 137-141.

[73] Guenther, 14.

[74] Balmer, xvi: To illustrate what he means by "spiritual piety," Balmer writes: "On May 24, 1738, John Wesley attended a religious gathering on Aldersgate Street in London. There, as someone read Luther's preface to his commentary on the book of Romans, Wesley felt his heart "strangely warmed" and felt an assurance that "Christ

As part of an eagerness to fan the flames of personal piety, nineteenth century leaders of North American evangelicalism promoted the movement's history via a strong emphasis on personal Bible study, preaching and revivalism. They launched initiatives such as importing the Young Men's Christian Association and Young Women's Christian Association organizations from England to serve as centers of evangelism for young people flocking to the rapidly expanding metropolitan centers of North America.

Sunday school movements such as the American Sunday School Union and the Canadian Sunday School Mission followed the example of British agencies in efforts to evangelize children, young people and adults alike. The British zeal for both home and foreign missions likewise found a home among evangelicals in North America especially toward the end of the nineteenth century.[75]

As noted previously, the Bible school movement of which PBI was a part arose out of evangelicalism's passion to train and provide effective leadership for its churches during a time when many believed abundant evidence existed that Christ's return was imminent. Such organizations as the Christian Endeavor Society, where L.E. Maxwell once publicly testified as a youth, were developed to provide training for Christian service and to support the fight against numerous signs of social disease that characterized a period of rapid urbanization and industrialization.[76]

"had taken away *my* sins, even *mine*, and saved *me* from the law of sin a model for many . . . evangelicals. They like him . . . aspire to the kind of warmhearted piety so characteristic of Wesley's spiritual life."

[75] Marsden, *Understanding Fundamentalism and Evangelism*, 22f.

[76] Keller, 37; Marsden, *Understanding Fundamentalism and Evangelism*, 24: ". . . Francis E. Clark, a Congregationalist minister, founded [the Christian Endeavor Society] in Maine in 1881 "to promote earnest Christian life" and to provide raining for Christian service. Typically, Christian Endeavor groups held weekly devotional meetings and monthly meetings for special consecration. "Trusting in the Lord Jesus Christ for strength," read the simple pledge, "I promise Him I will strive to do whatever He would have me do." Clark's organization grew so rapidly among young people that by 1885 he could found an international organization claiming 3.5 million members by 1910, with perhaps two-thirds of these in the United States and Canada. Such enterprises had the important side effect of uniting Protestants from almost every denomination. In this context the more famous crusades of the era should be viewed. Of these the most successful was the temperance movement, which attempted to ban the use of alcoholic beverages."

A wide variety of such organizations and ministries were founded to support and promote the practical implications of embracing and advancing the theology of evangelicalism. At its core today there throbs a powerful motivation to meld theology with zealous passion in the course of demonstrating the eternal importance of a personal experience of saving faith in Jesus Christ.

Although evangelicalism preceded that entity which in the early twentieth century became known as fundamentalism, it is important for the purposes of this study to underscore that the latter arose out of the former and came to exist as a subset of evangelicalism.[77] Such a reality therefore prompts many critical commentators to minimize differences between the two movements and to use the terms as virtual synonyms.[78]

The nature of the evangelical ethos that prevailed at Prairie Bible Institute during the Maxwell era aligns well with the each of the four theological themes identified by Bebbington in tandem with the kind of spiritual piety acknowledged by Balmer. Within the context of an environment that stressed a disciplined and intense sensitivity to the work of the Holy Spirit of God in individual lives, the school consistently promoted the following themes: the necessity of a personally meaningful experience of having been justified through grace by faith alone (conversionism); the individual believer's responsibility to be active in soliciting unbelievers near and far to make a similar profession of faith (activism); the uncontestable authority and reliability of the Bible as the Word of God (Biblicism); and the vicarious suffering and death of Christ on the cross as the sole basis for the sinner's acceptance by the holy God (crucicentrism). All of these pursuits were practiced at PBI within the context of a relentless cultivation of deep personal piety.

The resources consulted in the course of researching this study in combination with my own experience as a member of the Prairie Bible

---

[77] See, for example, George M. Marsden, *Understanding Fundamentalism and Evangelicalism*, 1: "In either the long or the short definitions, fundamentalists are a subtype of evangelicals . . ."

[78] Bruce Bawer, *Stealing Jesus: How Fundamentalism Betrays Christianity* (New York: Crown Publishers, Inc. 1997); Steve Brouwer, Paul Gifford & Susan D. Rose, *Exporting the American Gospel: Global Christian Fundamentalism* (New York and London: Routledge, 1996); Bruce Lawrence, *Defenders of God: The Fundamentalist Revolt Against the Modern Age* (San Francisco: Harper & Row, 1989); Esther Kaplan, *With God on Their Side* (New York and London, The New Press, 2004).

Institute community from 1960 to 1977 prompts me to unequivocally support Bebbington's definition of historical evangelicalism. When one bears in mind the close relationship between evangelicalism and fundamentalism as briefly noted above and elaborated on later in this work, there is ample legitimacy in Stackhouse's judgment with regard to organizations like Prairie:

> this group looks back to the Protestant Reformation for its emphasis upon the unique authority of Scripture and salvation through faith alone in Christ. It adds to these convictions concern for warm piety in the context of a disciplined life and for the evangelism of all people. And this group holds these convictions as so important that members of it join with Christians—often of other denominations—in order to further these concerns, even if these others hold different view of important but less crucial matters.[79]

---

[79] Stackhouse, *Canadian Evangelicalism in the Twentieth Century*, 7.

CHAPTER THREE

Definition of Terms (Part 2)

Proto-fundamentalism

In his doctoral dissertation examining the roots of fundamentalism in Canada, Ronald G. Sawatzky employs the term "proto-fundamentalism" in a manner that proves helpful for the purposes of this book particularly as it relates to the attempt to establish some kind of meaningful distinction between the terms "evangelicalism" and "fundamentalism." He wrote:

> It has been pointed out above that the fundamentalist movement existed both before and after the controversy of the 1920's and that the name was only self-consciously applied in 1920. From the point of view of the period under discussion here (1875 to 1914), it is not quite accurate, then, to refer to the movement prior to 1920 as fundamentalist. Therefore, throughout this study the term "proto-fundamentalist" will be used to refer to the late nineteenth and early twentieth century of the Canadian movement which is being analyzed here.[1]

Sawatzky uses "proto-fundamentalism" strictly within the context of his examination of the 1885 international Bible and prophecy conference held at Niagara-on-the-Lake, Ontario, Canada. There is at least some value, however, in applying the term even more broadly to developments that occurred in the last quarter of the nineteenth century when figures such as A.B. Simpson and Dwight L. Moody rose to prominence in the United States with their respective Bible schools at New York and Chicago.[2] It

---

[1] Sawatzky, "Looking for That Blessed Hope," 19-20.
[2] Smith, 5: "During the last quarter of the nineteenth century, a series of profound, social, demographic, and intellectual transformations began to challenge evangelical Protestantism's security, influence, and relevance. Within the church, liberal theology, biblical higher criticism, and an increased skepticism about supernaturalism began to question the old orthodox verities . . . Outside of the churches, the shift from the

was during this period of time that some of the influential forefathers and prominent themes of emerging American fundamentalism came to the fore to establish a unique theological energy that was eventually articulated in the book entitled *The Fundamentals* and also demonstrated on the sawdust trails of evangelistic crusades led by preachers such as Billy Sunday.[3]

It bears repeating that elements of overlap are inevitable when discussing evangelicalism and fundamentalism. Accordingly, this study sees merit in using the term "proto-fundamentalism" to identify a particular period of time (the late nineteenth century) when a group of spiritual leaders including A.B. Simpson, D.L. Moody and A.J. Gordon were establishing Bible schools as well as organizing and conducting Bible conferences. These initiatives promoted a pietistic interpretation of Christianity while advancing strategic themes such as world missions, revival, an ongoing experience of the filling of the Holy Spirit, and the imminent, pre-millennial second coming of Christ. Although some of these same emphases became a part of the fundamentalist platform in the 1920s, the terms "proto-fundamentalism" or "proto-fundamentalists" will surface occasionally in this book. They refer to the beliefs, practices and personalities of late nineteenth century leaders such as Simpson, Moody and Gordon who played a very influential role in the theological and ideological orientation of both L.E. Maxwell and the Prairie Bible Institute.

Fundamentalism

The comments of Professor Roger W. Stump serve as a succinct and useful introduction to an effort to define fundamentalism. He wrote:

> As the twentieth century began, the effects of modernism and secularism on American culture produced a growing sense of alarm among conservative Protestants, who believed that these innovations threatened to undermine the traditional values and moral authority of evangelical Christianity. They responded by asserting their unyielding commitment

---

Newtonian paradigm of science and the collapse of Scottish Common Sense Realism seriously undermined in scientific circles any role for the Bible in scientific inquiry."

[3] Richard J. Mouw, *The Smell of Sawdust*, (Grand Rapids, MI: Zondervan Publishing House, 2000), provides an excellent overview of the integration and overlap that exists between and within the evangelical and fundamentalist communities.

to certain fundamental beliefs, such as the divine authorship and literal truth of the Bible, and by working to ensure the survival of those beliefs in American institutions and public life. By the 1920s, this movement came to be known as fundamentalism, and, since that time, its views have permeated swathes of the social and cultural fabric of America.[4]

Stump's observations underline the veracity of Marsden's and Carpenter's important reminders that the term "fundamentalism" was originally used to define a religious movement.[5]

The difficulty involved in distilling a definition of the term "fundamentalism" that is sufficiently comprehensive yet utilitarian enough to distinguish it from "evangelicalism" or "neo-evangelicalism" is underscored by a comment offered by Frank Schaeffer when he concisely refers to modern evangelicalism as "fundamentalism-lite."[6] Although it might be argued that Schaeffer's judgment reflects the reality of the late 1900s in North America more than it does the situation in that century's earlier years, his point is well taken since there is no universally agreed-upon line of demarcation between "evangelicalism" and "fundamentalism."[7] Add to this consideration the frequent observation in the literature that whereas all fundamentalists are

---

[4] Roger W. Stump, "Fundamentalism," in Sara Pendergast and Tom Pendergast (ed.), *St. James Encyclopedia of Pop Culture* (Detroit: St. James Press, 2000), 181.

[5] Marsden, *Fundamentalism and American Culture*, 3: "From its origins, fundamentalism was primarily a religious movement."

Carpenter, "Fundamentalist Institutions and the Rise of Evangelical Protestantism, 1929-1942," 64, in *Church History* Vol. 49, No. 1, March 1980: ". . . fundamentalism is a distinct religious movement which arose in the early twentieth century to defend traditional evangelical orthodoxy and to extend its evangelistic thrust."

[6] Frank Schaeffer, *Crazy for God: How I Grew Up as One of the Elect, Helped Found the Religious Right, and Lived to Take All (Or Almost All) of It Back* (New York: Carroll and Graf Publishers, 2007), 117: "Other figures like Carl Henry, founder of *Christianity Today* magazine . . . criticized fundamentalism's failure to address the world's intellectual and social trends. A movement was born—modern evangelicalism, a fundamentalism-lite where everyone could more or less do their own theological thing, long as they "named the name of Christ" and paid lip service to the "inerrancy" of the Bible."

What Schaeffer identifies here as "modern evangelicalism" is what this chapter of this book identifies as "neo-evangelicalism."

[7] Malise Ruthven, *Fundamentalism: The Search for Meaning* (London: Oxford University Press, 2004), 8, succinctly suggests concerning fundamentalism: ". . . no single definition will ever be uncontested."

evangelicals, not all evangelicals are fundamentalists, and the complexity of establishing a problem-free definition for "fundamentalism" quickly comes into focus.[8]

This conundrum is compounded by writers who speak, for example, of "conservative evangelicals and fundamentalists" without clarifying what they perceive to be the apparent difference(s) between the two designations.[9] The fact that the meaning of the term "fundamentalist" encountered several revisions or refinements over the course of the twentieth century further complicates the endeavor to establish a sufficient definition.[10]

Regardless of these challenges, George Marsden offered a helpful starting point in our quest when he wrote:

---

[8] See, for example, a helpful summation by Sean David House, "Pentecostal Contributions to Contemporary Christological Thought: A Synthesis With Ecumenical Views," (ThM thesis, University of South Africa, 2006), 9. http://etd.unisa.ac.za/ETD-db/theses/available/etd-08152007-101024/unrestricted/dissertation.pdf (accessed 15 April 2009).

Joel A. Carpenter, "The Fundamentalist Leaven and the Rise of an Evangelical United Front," 260, in Leonard I. Sweet (ed), *The Evangelical Tradition in America* (Macon, GA: Mercer Univ. Press, 1997).

George M. Marsden, "Fundamentalism and American Evangelicalism," 23, in Dayton and Johnston (eds), *The Variety of American Evangelicalism.*

[9] Robert A. Wright, "The Canadian Protestant Tradition 1914-1945" in G.A. Rawlyk (ed.) *The Canadian Protestant Experience,* 143. Wright uses this phrase twice on the same page without having clarified the distinction between what he obviously considers two different groups. His terminology becomes even more confusing when on p. 158 he then identifies fundamentalism as coming out of "the right wing of conservative evangelicalism in both Canada and the United States." It is only later on p. 158 that he states fundamentalists distinguished themselves from conservative evangelicals by "stressing the wrath of God in place of a paternalistic interpretation of His relation to man."

[10] George M. Marsden, *Fundamentalism and American Culture (New Edition)* (New York: Oxford University Press, 2006). See the new "Part Five: Fundamentalism Yesterday and Today (2005)," 235f, where Marsden reviews the rise of fundamentalism as a political power in the late 1900s and acknowledges the ongoing murky distinction between the terms "evangelicalism" and "fundamentalism" by introducing the term "fundamentalistic evangelical." He then proposes a view of history according to the following grid: 19th century—Evangelicalism; 1920s—Fundamentalism; 1950s-mid 1970s—New Evangelicalism and Fundamentalism; late 1970s to early 21st century—Fundamentalistic Evangelicalism.

Fundamentalism was a mosaic of divergent and sometimes contradictory traditions and tendencies that could never be totally integrated. Sometimes its advocates were backward looking and reactionary, at other times they were imaginative innovators. On some occasions they appeared militant and divisive; on others they were warm and irenic. At times they seemed ready to forsake the whole world over a point of doctrine; at other times they appeared heedless of tradition in their zeal to win converts.[11]

Of particular significance in Marsden's words here is his judgment that fundamentalism was not a monolithic movement or entity.[12] In other words, there were significant differences within its ranks owing to both the variety and complexity of the personalities and themes that coalesced to make it an identifiable movement. Further, Marsden acknowledges the very important reality that there was a definite psychological dynamic at play in the personalities of fundamentalist leaders. Accordingly, and as will be noted again later in this section on fundamentalism, it is fair to suggest that any definition which fails to take into account both the theological and psychological elements of the collective entity should ultimately be considered incomplete and insufficient.

The movement that officially became known as fundamentalism in the 1920s had roots among the activities of proto-fundamentalist Protestants in the United States and Canada in the last quarter of the nineteenth century. Among the best known figures of these years were men such as Dwight L. Moody, A.J. Gordon, A.T. Pierson and Reuben A. Torrey.[13] Other leaders who had lesser yet important profiles were W.H. Howland, S.R. Briggs and Alfred Sandham.[14]

---

[11] Marsden, *Fundamentalism and American Culture*, 43. This reference is to the original 1980 version of the book.

[12] Leonard I. Sweet, "Wise as Serpents, Innocent as Doves: The New Evangelical Historiography," 399, in referring to James Davison Hunter's assessment of fundamentalism as "a richly diverse cultural tradition," Sweet remarks: "with a veritable fairground of forms, styles, subgroups, and temperaments—as varied response to the Revised Standard Version (from being burned in Georgia to being brandished at Fuller) attests."

[13] Carpenter, *Revive Us Again*, 6.

[14] Sawatzky, 79-85. These men formed the Executive Committee for the Niagara Prophecy and Bible Conference held at Niagara-on-the-Lake, Ontario, Canada, in the summer of 1885.

Numerous Christian leaders of that day found themselves increasingly alarmed by what they viewed as the pernicious impact of such troubling innovations as German scholarship's higher-criticism of the Bible and Charles Darwin's evolutionary theory regarding the origins of the universe.[15] Of particular concern were the advances theological modernism was making into the mainline denominations and their leading educational institutions. Many wary evangelicals, including observant laymen such as J. Fergus Kirk in Three Hills, Alberta, Canada, believed the historic Christian faith was under siege.[16]

"Modernism," declared James M. Gray, the president of Moody Bible Institute as the twentieth century approached, "is a revolt against the God of Christianity" and a "foe of good government."[17] In the judgment of William Jennings Bryan, three-time Democratic nominee for President of the United States: "The evolutionary hypothesis is the only thing that has seriously menaced religion since the time of Christ."[18]

The emphasis among proto-fundamentalists in the late nineteenth century of such themes as dispensational pre-millennialism, prophecy, revivalism, and holiness theology led to the establishment of annual conferences to study these matters. Such gatherings were held at various

---

[15] Nancy T. Ammerman, "North American Protestant Fundamentalism," 10-11, in Martin E. Marty and R. Scott Appleby (eds.), *Fundamentalisms Observed* (Chicago: Univ. of Chicago Press, 1991): "Darwin's theory of the relationships between simple and more complex organisms led him to propose that even *Homo sapiens* be seen as part of this natural, evolving order and thus as the product of natural selection (rather than a special creation). It was a theory that would make Darwin the fundamentalists' symbol of all that was wrong with modern science . . . But no aspect of nineteenth-century intellectual life proved more challenging than the turning of a scientific eye on the Scripture itself . . . The message of the new biblical scholars was that the Bible is neither the unique "word of God" nor the historical document it seems on the surface to be. Critical study disclosed that it is both much more and much less than it seems to the commonsense, faithful reader."

[16] Fuller, 9: "'Liberal teaching is beginning to enter the church,' Kirk wrote to Stevens in Kansas (sic), Missouri. "We'd like a teacher from a Bible school. Can you send us one for a couple of years?"

[17] Irving Hexham, *A Concise Dictionary of Religion* (Downer's Grove, IL: InterVarsity Press, 1993) 149, refers to modernists as those ". . . who rejected the theology and metaphysics of traditional Christianity in favor of a Kantian epistemology, evolution, biblical criticism and comparative religion."

[18] Marsden, *Fundamentalism and American Culture* (1980), 3-4.

locations in the U.S. and in the Niagara region in Canada.[19] These assemblies helped fuel growing opposition to liberal teachings and assisted in the development of the kind of organizational infrastructure necessary to mount an effective resistance movement to liberalism.

The perceived need to rigorously defend the historic beliefs of the church eventually led to the publication of a series of booklets called *The Fundamentals* in 1910-1915. This ambitious project was financed by California oil millionaires Lyman and Milton Stewart and featured the publication of short scholarly essays on what were considered fundamental Christian doctrines. The essays were edited by A.C. Dixon, pastor of Moody Church in Chicago, who had distinctly impressed Lyman Stewart in a sermon the former had preached attacking the teachings of a modernist university professor.[20]

Millions of copies of *The Fundamentals* were distributed free of charge to every pastor, missionary, theology student or instructor, Sunday school superintendent and religious broadcaster who would receive them.[21] The multi-volume series denounced higher criticism, evolution and Roman Catholicism and vigorously defended traditional views on such matters as the authority of Scripture, the deity of Christ, the atonement, justification by faith and the personal return of Christ. The essays also underscored the urgency of evangelism.[22]

---

[19] Sawatzky, "Looking for that Blessed Hope."

[20] Marsden, *Fundamentalism and American Culture* (1980), 101: "As A.C. Dixon put it at (of all places) an ecumenical missions conference in 1900, "Above all things I love peace, but next to peace I love a fight, and I believe the next best thing to peace is a theological fight."" Clearly, the militant element in emerging fundamentalism surfaced early.

[21] Charles L. Feinberg (ed.), *The Fundamentals for Today* (2 vols.) (Grand Rapids, MI: Kregel Publications, 1958), Forward.

Stewart G. Cole, *The History of Fundamentalism* (New York: Richard R. Smith Inc., 1931), 61: "The far-reaching influence of *The Fundamentals* can scarcely be measured."

It should be noted that there is ample evidence in the literature that whereas some scholars attribute the naming of the fundamentalist movement to the publication of *The Fundamentals*, others prefer to reserve that honor for Baptist magazine editor Curtis Lee Laws who applied the term "fundamentalism" to the growing movement in a 1920 article. Further, it should also be observed that there are also differing perspectives regarding the overall importance of the publication of *The Fundamentals* to the rise of the popular movement that came to be known as Fundamentalism.

[22] Martin E Marty, *Modern American Religion*, (vol. 1): *The Irony of It All 1893-1919* (Chicago: The Univ. of Chicago Press, 1986), 237: "No other theme appeared more than four

In addition to a sense of unfolding theological crisis, an atmosphere of alarm gripped post-World War I North America when widespread demobilization and a number of discordant labor strikes took place. The increasing industrialization and urbanization of the American population served as an impetus to the development of social ills such as alcoholism and prostitution. This unrest was augmented by a growing fear of foreign powers brought about by the Bolshevik Revolution that occurred in Russia in 1917.[23]

In response to the significant social changes taking place in American culture, the popularity of new interpretations of science and the international challenges underscored by World War I, theological modernists insisted that man's understanding of Christianity should adjust accordingly.[24] For traditionalists, however, the numerous signs of modernity served to validate passages of Scripture such as II Thessalonians 2 and II Timothy 3 that warn of the increase of sin and a measureable cooling of spiritual fervor in the last days. For many evangelicals, ample evidence of such realities merely served as proof to them that Christ's return was imminent.[25]

---

times in these tracts, yet twenty-seven of ninety-four topics opposed the higher criticism of the Bible as proposed by modernists."

[23] This dimension of the social and economic environment in which fundamentalism was birthed is clearly portrayed in:

John Braeman, Robert H. Bremner, and David Brody (eds.). *Change and Continuity in Twentieth Century America: the 1920s.* Columbus, OH: Ohio State University Press, 1968.

See also, James H Gray, *The Roar of the Twenties.* Toronto: Macmillan of Canada, 1975.

[24] Martin E. Marty, *Modern American Religion,* (vol. 2): *The Noise of Conflict 1919-1941* (Chicago: The Univ. of Chicago Press, 1991. Symbolic of the strong feelings and critical rhetoric that characterized the debate was a sermon preached by modernist pastor, Henry Emerson Fosdick, in 1922 entitled "Shall the Fundamentalists Win?" 168: "The golden-voiced pulpiteer spoke up for magnanimity, liberality, and tolerance of spirit. "What immeasurable folly," he cried, was the effort by some to drive from the Christian churches all who did not agree with their own view of the inspiration of scripture. Tragically, Fosdick went on, all this activity was occurring at a time when believers ought to be working for other sets of answers in the presence of colossal problems . . . In Calvary Baptist Church in New York a Fundamentalist warrior, John Roach Straton, replied to Fosdick with an anti-evolutionary sermon title which bore a question mark and which showed how quickly the fights could descend to lower depths: "Shall the Funny-Monkeyist Win?"

[25] Thaddeus Coreno, "Fundamentalism as a class culture," in *Sociology of Religion* (Fall 2002), 1-24: "Most sociologists and historians agree that fundamentalism is a reaction to the effects of modernization . . . The social changes accompanying

As World War I came to an end, a number of the leaders of the Bible school and prophecy conference movements proposed the establishment of the World's Christian Fundamentalists Association in 1918.[26] Baptist magazine editor Curtis Lee Laws applied the term "fundamentalism" in 1920 in an article concerning the growing movement.[27] The word was initially associated therefore with its religious or theological roots to categorize those who were unswervingly loyal to the historic, orthodox teachings of the evangelical Christian church and were convinced, at least to some extent, of the urgency to aggressively and militantly combat and resist modernist teachings.[28]

---

modernization, especially accelerated urbanization, catalyzed the decomposition of Protestantism's institutional and cultural hegemony and triggered fundamentalism as a social movement in the early decades of the twentieth century . . ."

[26] Carpenter, *Revive Us Again*, 26, points out that the editor of the *Sunday School Times* during the 1930s, Charles G. Trumbull, was both "a leading "Victorious Life" holiness advocate" and "one of the organizers of the World's Christian Fundamentals Association." This is an important detail to bear in mind given L.E. Maxwell's affinity for holiness teaching and the fact that the *Sunday School Times* under the guidance of Philip E. Howard, Jr., later published a series of essays that eventually constituted Maxwell's first book, *Born Crucified*, published in 1945.

[27] Marsden, *Fundamentalism and American Culture* (1980), 159.

Nancy T. Ammerman, "North American Protestant Fundamentalism," 2, points out that whereas fundamentalism initially arose out of the perceived need among many evangelicals to "*defend traditional beliefs*," by 1920 a defensive cause had adapted an offensive thrust as was evident when Lees wrote that a "fundamentalist" is a person willing to "do battle royal" for the fundamentals of the faith. (emphasis added)

[28] The terms "militant" and "militancy" are important to the overall argument of my thesis in this book. Accordingly, reference to such will occur several times in the study. At this point, it is sufficient to simply flag the primacy given the concepts of "militancy," "struggle" and "resistance" by several writers as such terms relate to the essence of fundamentalism. See:

George M. Marsden, *Fundamentalism and American Culture* (1980), 4: "Briefly, [fundamentalism] was militantly anti-modernist Protestant evangelicalism . . . Fundamentalism was a loose, diverse, and changing federation of co-belligerents united by their fierce opposition to modernist attempts to bring Christianity into line with modern thought."

George M. Marsden, "Defining American Fundamentalism," 22-23, in Norman J. Cohen (ed.), *The Fundamentalist Phenomenon: A view from within, a response from without* (Grand Rapids, MI: Eerdmans Publishing Co., 1990): ". . . a fundamentalist is an evangelical Protestant who is militantly opposed to modern liberal theologies and some aspects of secularism in modern culture. This definition refers to fundamentalism in its classic

It is important to briefly interject here that when Prairie Bible Institute was founded in 1922, it unashamedly identified with the emerging fundamentalist movement and those who originally shaped it such as Dwight L. Moody, A. J. Gordon, A.T. Pierson, Reuben A. Torrey and the contributors to *The Fundamentals*. The handwritten PBI Prospectus for 1923-24 clearly states: "The school stands for every whit of the "Fundamentals,"" presumably a reference to the essays financed by the Stewart brothers and edited by A.C. Dixon.[29] The writings of Moody, Gordon, Pierson and Torrey were staples in both the PBI Book Room and the PBI Library throughout the Maxwell era.

As the 1920s unfolded, outspoken pastors and Bible teachers like John Roach Straton, William B. Riley, J.C. Massee, J. Frank Norris and T.T. Shields, who held pulpits in prominent cities across North America, helped stoke the rapid spread of fundamentalism.[30] T.T. Shields was a fiery orator of British extraction who was pastor of a large Baptist church in Toronto. He earned a reputation for his repeated allegations that modernism was creeping into Canadian Baptist circles and, among other ventures, was involved in a controversial and somewhat bizarre attempt by fundamentalists to take control of Des Moines University in the United States.[31]

---

historical American sense, the Protestant evangelical movement that was so named in 1920. It also applies to those Protestants who call themselves fundamentalists today."

Clark H. Pinnock, "Defining American Fundamentalism: A Response," 42, in Cohen (ed.), *The Fundamentalist Phenomenon*: "In my opinion, fundamentalism is orthodoxy in a desperate struggle with secular modernity."

James Davison Hunter, "Fundamentalism in its Global Contours," 58, in Cohen (ed.), *The Fundamentalist Phenomenon*: "I would maintain that fundamentalism derives its identity principally from a posture of resistance to the modern world order."

29 PBI Records Office files.
30 William Vance Trollinger, Jr., "One Response to Modernity: Northwestern Bible School and the Fundamentalism Empire of William Bell Riley," (PhD diss., University of Wisconsin-Madison, 1984) is an example of some of the excellent research that has been done to date on individual fundamentalists of this era that successfully highlights the passion and power of these men. Trollinger's work has subsequently been published in book form as *God's Empire: William Bell Riley and Midwestern Fundamentalism* (Madison, WI: Univ. of Wisconsin Press, 1991).
31 Leslie K. Tarr, *Shields of Canada* (Grand Rapids, MI: Baker Book House, 1967) gives a comprehensive if uncritical treatment to Shield's controversial career as a cantankerous but multi-talented pastor. See 105-106 regarding bizarre incidents involving Shields at Des Moines University in Iowa. Because Shields was so obstinate and given his

People from a variety of denominations coalesced in the increasingly belligerent fundamentalist cause believing society's problems could and should be attributed not to political, economic or social considerations, but to America's rapid drift toward theological liberalism.[32] Rifts that developed in the Northern Baptist and Presbyterian denominations were particularly bitter and public.[33]

As denominational conferences and institutions became centers of rancorous and heated debate, the fundamentalist identity inevitably acquired a psychological or temperamental connotation.[34] The term "fundamentalism" therefore earned an even more militant connotation than merely that of a school of thought which vigorously advocated and defended the historic, orthodox teachings of the Christian church.

Surges of bitter acrimony ultimately led to such hostile conflicts as the infamous 1925 "Scopes monkey trial" in Tennessee, widely regarded by many even today as the ultimate showdown between fundamentalists and modernists.[35] Ironically, although the fundamentalist cause actually prevailed

---

association with prominent American fundamentalist leaders like John Roach Straton and J. Frank Norris, Stackhouse, *Canadian Evangelicalism in the Twentieth Century*, 23-34, assigns him a place outside the mainstream of Canadian evangelicalism. Part of the objective of my book is to demonstrate that, particularly in his early years at PBI, the record indicates that L.E. Maxwell was equally persistent in denouncing modernists and in decrying Roman Catholic interests in Canada. Although Maxwell did not publicly associate with the leading American fundamentalists in the manner that Shields did, his rhetoric was often equally strident.

[32] George Dollar, *A History of Fundamentalism in America* (Greenville, SC: Bob Jones Univ. Press, 1973), 105-143, "The Prima Donnas of Fundamentalism," contains biographical sketches of some of these men.

[33] Peter J. Boyer, "The Big Tent: Billy Graham, Franklin Graham, and the transformation of American evangelicalism" in *The New Yorker* (August 22, 2005), 4: "As Kevin Bauder, a fundamentalist theologian and the president of Central Baptist Theological Seminary in Minneapolis, puts it, "The result was, for a period of about twenty years, there was all-out war in most of the major Protestant denominations.""

[34] Marsden, "Defining American Fundamentalism," 22, in Cohen (ed.) *The Fundamentalist Phenomenon*: "My own offhand definition of a fundamentalist is "an evangelical who is angry about something.""

[35] The event popularly known as "the Scopes monkey trial" pitted the state of Tennessee versus John Scopes, a Dayton, TN, biology teacher charged with teaching Darwinism in contravention of state law. The American Civil Liberties Union provided three prominent lawyers to defend Scopes, led by Clarence Darrow of Chicago. The prosecutor was William, Jennings Bryan, erstwhile American politician, who under

in the court battle in that John Scopes was found guilty of teaching evolution in violation of state law, fundamentalism was thereafter widely discredited. Clarence Darrow, counsel for the defense, and curmudgeonly journalists like H.L. Mencken effectively combined to portray fundamentalist Christianity as synonymous with the ignorance and backwardness associated with prevailing stereotypes of the rural population in America.

For better or worse, it is this acrimonious dimension of fundamentalism and the resulting caricature of its adherents as uneducated and unsophisticated dogmatists that have consistently been associated by many with the terms "fundamentalism" or "fundamentalist." It is not without due cause that in the minds of many observers the psychological dimension of fundamentalist identity eventually came to overshadow the theological features of the movement.[36]

One of the first attempts to adequately define fundamentalism contained elements of an obituary.[37] Explaining that the movement had existed from 1918 to 1928, in 1931 Richard Niebuhr wrote of it strictly in the past tense. In his view, fundamentalism had been a brief hiccup on the American religious scene that featured the short-sighted thinking of predominantly

---

cross-examination by Darrow emerged unable to answer the latter's skeptical questions and openly admitted to his ignorance of other religions and the science of Biblical criticism. Scopes was found guilty of teaching evolution although the verdict was later reversed on a technicality. Nonetheless, fundamentalism's moment in the national spotlight was generally considered a failure as the press painted Bryan and company as backwoods, half-educated obscurantists.

[36] Mortimer Ostow, "The Fundamentalist Phenomenon: A Psychological Perspective," 100, in Cohen (ed.) *The Fundamentalist Phenomenon*: "One of its most visible and unfortunate qualities is its tendency to split into quarrelling subunits which contend with each other over their differing positions on religious and social issues, and frequently on the degree of accommodation that they are willing to extend to the outside community and to the realities of modern life."

[37] Carpenter, *Revive Us Again*, 13-14: "In the wake of the Scopes trial, the *Christian Century* described the fundamentalist movement as "an event now passed," a brief, dysfunctional mutation away from the main line of religious evolution. Theologian H. Richard Niebuhr's article on fundamentalism in the 1931 edition of the *Encyclopedia of the Social Sciences* assumed that the movement was finished, for Niebuhr referred to it exclusively in the past tense. While these diagnoses probably owed much to wishful thinking, secular figures with less at stake in the church fights, such as H.L. Mencken and Walter Lippmann, observed that the movement, if not dead, certainly was no longer a significant force in American thought and culture."

rural people who were resistant to those inevitable cultural changes being welcomed by city-dwellers who were ostensibly better educated.[38]

Niebuhr's perspective was premature, however, as demonstrated by subsequent history and by the fact that the term remains popular yet today in referring to militant pockets of strident defenders of orthodoxy as found in numerous religions.[39] The rise of the so-called "Religious Right" in the

---

[38] Attempts to better define and understand fundamentalism are ongoing. See, for example, Edward Farley, "Fundamentalism: A Theory," in *Crosscurrents*, (Fall 2005), 378-402: "The term, fundamentalism, initially described a trans-denominational movement among conservative Protestant Christian groups in the United States which, in the first part of the twentieth century, vigorously and publicly defended biblical inerrancy against historical criticism and biblical geology and cosmology against the theory of evolution . . . Given the similarities between modern fundamentalism and the perennial self-maintaining behaviors of religion, is it possible that fundamentalism, rather than a distinctive phenomenon, is simply the present-day name for a perennial feature of tradition-maintaining religion? Is fundamentalism traditional religious behavior in a new (modern) setting? Or is it something new and distinctive, a way of being religious never before seen in human history. This is the problem that calls for a theory of fundamentalism, and the task of that theory is to uncover fundamentalism as a new historical phenomenon distinguishable from perennial self-maintaining ordinary religion." (378, 380)

[39] Martin Riesebrodt, *Pious Passion: The Emergence of Modern Fundamentalism in the United States and Iran*, (Los Angeles: Univ. of California Press, 1993), 2: "Fundamentalist movements have emerged in other countries as well. Gush Emunium in Israel represents a militant variety of Jewish fundamentalism. Radical-traditionalist Catholic movements of the twentieth century have had close connections with fascist movements, especially in Eastern and Southern Europe. More recently, traditionalist and integralist subcurrents within the Catholic church have strengthened. Fundamentalism among the Sikhs in India and the Sinhalese Buddhists in Sri Lanka suggests that such movements are possible in all religions of salvation and redemption. Fundamentalism is therefore neither an exclusively Shi'ite, Islamic, or Iranian phenomenon, nor a specifically Protestant, Christian, or North American one. It is found worldwide."

Karen Armstrong, *The Battle for God* (New York: Ballantine Books, 2000), xiii: "There have always been people, in every age and in each tradition, who have fought the modernity of their day. But the fundamentalism that we shall be considering is an essentially twentieth-century movement. It is a reaction against the scientific and secular culture that first appeared in the West, but which has since taken root in other parts of the world."

An example of the enduring and spreading reality of American Christian fundamentalism and the intense dislike many continue to have for it is evident in Brouwer, Steve, Paul Gifford & Susan D. Rose, *Exporting the American Gospel*, 9: "The new Christian fundamentalism is a reconfiguration of patriarchal power; it may

United States during the last quarter of the twentieth century introduced the concept of "fundamentalism" to a new generation of Americans.[40] As well, it is widely perceived that radical Muslim fundamentalists were responsible for the terrorist attacks on New York, Washington and Pennsylvania that took place on September 11, 2001.[41]

---

welcome female participation and celebrate womanly qualities, but only when it can subordinate women to male control." See also Bruce Bawer, *Stealing Jesus*: 5: ". . . it is extremely misleading to suggest that the kind of theology to which conservative Christians subscribe is truly more traditional, in the deepest sense, than that of liberal Christians. Likewise, labels like *biblical Christian* and *Bible-believing Christian*, which many conservative Christians attach to themselves, wrongly suggest that there is something unbiblical about the truth of liberal Christians."

An example of the realities that exist within the world of Islamic fundamentalism is recorded by Ayaan Hirsi Ali, *Infidel* (New York: Free Press, 2007). Bruce Bawer articulates alarm for the proliferation of Muslim fundamentalism in Europe and the United States in *While Europe Slept: How Radical Islam is Destroying the West from Within* (New York: Doubleday, 2006) and *Surrender: Appeasing Islam; Sacrificing Freedom* (New York: Doubleday, 2009).

[40] Perry Deane Young, *God's Bullies: Power, Politics and Religious Tyranny* (New York: Holt, Rinehart and Winston, 1982), 57-58: "We assumed the flames of backwoods fundamentalism were put out during that famous exchange between William Jennings Bryan and Clarence Darrow in Dayton, Tennessee in July 1925 . . . And every way you look, the ghost of William Jennings Bryan now stalks the land in a hundred different new embodiments."

Bruce B. Lawrence, *Defenders of God*, 83, defines fundamentalism in relation to its polar opposite—nationalism.

See also: Esther Kaplan, *With God on Their Side*, 2004; Chris Hedges, *American Fascists: The Christian Right and the War on America* (New York: Free Press, 2006); *Jesus Camp*, A&E IndieFilms and Magnolia Pictures, 2006.

[41] Mark LeVine, "What is Fundamentalism, and How Do We Get Rid of It?" in *Journal of Ecumenical Studies* Vol. 42, No. 1 (Winter 2007), 17-18. While acknowledging the widespread application of the term "fundamentalists" to resistance efforts in other religions, LeVine cautions against equivocating its meaning. "There are, then, many good reasons to be cautious in using the term "fundamentalism" when speaking of Muslim religious and/or political movements. Among the most important are that while most self-described Christian fundamentalists are united by their agreement on the nine principles that first defined the movement, Sunni and Shi'a "fundamentalists" have shared few theological or political principles. They are united primarily in their disdain for each other, the U.S. Israel, and Western culture more broadly. Outside of common enemies and a desire to achieve some sort of Islamic government, which in turn can return their societies toward a more Islamic path, the wide variety of goals of these movements makes them hard to categorize under one rubric."

The standard early works on fundamentalism by Stewart Cole and Norman Furniss reflect Niebuhr's judgment that fundamentalism's adherents were predominantly staunch opponents of social change cut from a traditionalist cloth who stubbornly, and somewhat ignorantly, insisted upon preserving standard values largely because such had been universally accepted for centuries.[42] Richard Hofstadter identified more of a psychological element in the anti-intellectualism of fundamentalists and argued that such people saw an opportunity for "a militant type of mind" to come to the fore in a cause that provided "an outlet for animosities."[43] Historian Winthrop Hudson dismissed fundamentalism as "much more cultural than religious in its orientation" and criticized its alignment with conservative economic, political and social perspectives.[44] William McLoughlin argued that fundamentalism should be understood as an inevitable side-effect of the passing of an old cultural order.[45]

A couple of objections were registered in the mid-twentieth century, however, regarding the prevailing tendency to view fundamentalism as merely a passing aberration on the religious or social scene. William Hordern complained that no system of thought should be assessed solely on the basis of what certain fanatics do in its name.[46] And, as Michael

---

[42] Stewart G. Cole, *The History of Fundamentalism* (New York: Richard Smith, 1931), 53: "Fundamentalism was the organized determination of conservative churchmen to continue the imperialistic culture of historic Protestantism within an inhospitable civilization dominated by secular interests and a progressive Christian idealism. The fundamentalist was opposed to social change, particularly such change as threatened the standards of his faith and his status in ecclesiastical circles. As a Christian, he insisted upon the preservation of such evangelical values as at one time had been accepted universally . . ." See also 34 where Cole defines fundamentalism in terms of its strict adherence to belief in 1) inerrancy, 2) the virgin birth, 3) the atonement of Christ, 4) the resurrection of Christ, and 5) the miracle-working power of Christ.

Norman F. Furniss, *The Fundamentalist Controversy 1918-1931*, (Hamden, CT: Archon Books, 1963), 35f, Furniss advanced that fundamentalists held to their views out of fear, ignorance and illiteracy, a longing for certainty, a personal love of militancy and abusive personal attacks and compared them to the Ku Klux Klan.

[43] Richard Hofstadter, *Anti-Intellectualism in American Life* (New York, Vintage Books, 1962), 118.

[44] Winthrop S. Hudson, *American Protestantism* (Chicago: Univ. of Chicago Press, 1961), 148.

[45] William McLoughlin, "Is There A Third Force in Christendom?" *Daedalus* XCVI (Winter, 1967), 43-45.

[46] William E. Hordern, *A Layman's Guide to Protestant Theology* (rev. ed) (New York: Macmillan Publishing Co., 1968), 68.

Hamilton records in his dissertation referred to earlier in this book, Paul A. Carter published an important article in 1968 arguing that, contrary to standard liberal perspectives, fundamentalism was anything but dead and its passing had been celebrated prematurely. In fact, Carter contended, fundamentalism was not even in decline; it was alive and well.[47] Such a state of affairs, Carter suggested, therefore required a new understanding of fundamentalism.

Two important works on fundamentalism were published just after the mid-point of the twentieth century, one of which pointed out the British contribution to the kind of thinking that eventually blossomed in the American fundamentalist movement. Ernest Sandeen argued that fundamentalism should not be merely equated with evangelical Protestantism but that it contained a couple of distinctive beliefs qualifying it as a new religious movement. He rooted fundamentalism in a millenarian theology that had surfaced in England in the early part of the nineteenth century prior to being transported to America by John Nelson Darby in the form of dispensationalism. He also argued that faith in an inerrant Bible was as much a hallmark of fundamentalism as its eschatology.[48]

Representing another perspective on fundamentalism, Louis Gaspar argued that the zenith of the movement was not the Scopes monkey-trial as many believed. He advanced that fundamentalism actually reached its peak following 1930 due to the primary influences of two divergent groups of fundamentalists: the conservative, separatistic American Council of Christian Churches and the more widely-embracing National Association of Evangelicals which this study will later identify as neo-evangelicalism.[49]

British scholars James Barr and Harriet A. Harris are representative of a school of thought that perceives minimal differences between

---

[47] Paul A. Carter, "The Fundamentalist Defense of the Faith" in John Braeman, Robert H. Bremner, and David Brody (eds.), *Change and Continuity in Twentieth Century America: the 1920s* (Columbus, OH: Ohio State University Press, 1968), 186-187.

[48] Ernest R. Sandeen, *The Roots of Fundamentalism: British and American Millenarianism, 1800-1930* (Chicago: Univ. of Chicago Press, 1970). See especially chapters 1-6, noting xix: "For it is millenarianism which gave life and shape to the Fundamentalist movement," and p. 132f where Sandeen identifies fundamentalist theology with the 14 point theological creed of the Niagara Bible Conference.

[49] Louis Gasper, *The Fundamentalist Movement, 1930-1956* (Grand Rapids, MI: Baker Book House, 1963).

fundamentalism and evangelicalism.[50] Interestingly enough, this perspective is also advanced by Sandeen in the Preface to the New Edition of his work reissued in 1978.[51] This possibly indicates that views of fundamentalism which take into account certain behaviors and developments in Christendom outside of North America tend not to share the kind of fine distinctions between the two theological camps that many North American scholars appear eager to maintain.

Barr maintains that the core of fundamentalist thinking represents a particular kind of religious tradition and sees a close parallel between the terms "fundamentalist" and "conservative evangelical."[52] Harris's work posits a strong connection between the Scottish school of philosophy known as Common Sense Realism and fundamentalism. Although she is sympathetic to Barr's views, she is particularly anxious to point out that the doctrine of an inerrant Bible as shared by both fundamentalists and evangelicals in North America has never been widely accepted among evangelicals in Britain.

Nancy Ammerman's work in *The Fundamentalism Project* is helpful in clarifying why some scholars see minimal differences between evangelicalism and fundamentalism. Bearing in mind what was reviewed in the last chapter regarding Bebbington's four defining characteristics of evangelicalism (conversionism, activism, Biblicism, crucicentrism), it is instructive to note what Ammerman advances as four defining features of North American fundamentalism: evangelism, inerrancy, premillennialism and separatism. When careful attention is paid to specific ideas behind several of these defining

---

[50] Comparatively speaking, some of the works referred to in footnote 39 of this chapter that view fundamentalism and evangelicalism as virtual synonyms are arguably written in a more popular vein than the works of Barr and Harris.

[51] Ernest R. Sandeen, *The Roots of Fundamentalism: British and American Millenarianism, 1800-1930 (repr.)* (Grand Rapids, MI: Baker Book House, 1978), ix: "...I would like to make it clear that I have been as surprised as everyone else at the remarkable recent popularity of Fundamentalism, or Evangelicalism, the name preferred by contemporary members of the movement."

[52] James Barr, *Fundamentalism* (London: SCM Press Ltd., 1977), 5 and 11: "As a practical course of procedure within this book, I shall therefore continue to use the term "fundamentalism" for a certain basic personal religious and existential attitude, which will be described. This attitude I consider to be a pathological condition of Christianity, and one which, when it appears, commonly appears within, and overlaps with, the ecclesiastical grouping known as "conservative evangelical." I do not say therefore that all conservative evangelicals are also fundamentalists; but the overlap is very great."

characteristics as interpreted by Bebbington and Ammerman, it is apparent that the two designations do, in fact, share several clear similarities.[53]

The co-editors of the multi-volume *The Fundamentalism Project*, Martin E. Marty and Scott Appleby, offer a comprehensive if somewhat cumbersome definition of fundamentalism when they state:

> In these pages, then, fundamentalism has appeared as a tendency, a habit of mind, found within religious communities and paradigmatically embodied in certain representative individuals and movements, which manifests itself as a strategy, or set of strategies, by which beleaguered believers attempt to preserve their distinctive identity as a people or group. Finding this identity to be at risk in the contemporary era, they fortify it by a selective retrieval of doctrines, beliefs, and practices from a sacred past. [54]

The technical accuracy and broad scope of this definition of "fundamentalism" is important to note, as is its applicability to the international scene and to religions other than Christianity. This broader application reflects the reality that fundamentalism has earned renewed significance in the last thirty-five to forty years with the rise of an aggressive political wing of the movement that has come to include various forms of international terrorism carried out in the name of a variety of religious faiths.[55] Marty and Appleby's approach also reminds us that it is unwise to think of fundamentalism as a monolithic entity and that, as compared to

---

[53] Bebbington, *Evangelicalism in Modern Britain*, 2-17, and Ammerman, "North American Protestant Fundamentalism," in Marty & Appleby (eds.), *Fundamentalisms Observed* (Chicago: Univ. of Chicago Press, 1991), 4-8. Bebbington's *conversionism* and *activism* are roughly equivalent to Ammerman's *evangelism* in light of her words: "When fundamentalists describe how they are different from other people, they begin with the fact that they are saved. They clearly affirm their kinship with other evangelicals on this point. Much of their organized effort is aimed at seeking out converts . . . Evangelism and the salvation of individual souls remains at the heart of the message fundamentalists proclaim to American society in the late twentieth century." Similarly, Bebbington's *Biblicism* and Ammerman's *inerrancy* are closely related in that both emphasize a strong devotion to the authority of the Bible.

[54] Marty & Appleby, (1991), 835

[55] See "Fundamentalism and the Modern World: a dialogue with Karen Armstrong, Susannah Heschel, Jim Wallis, and Feisal Abdul Rauf," in *Sojourners*, March/April 2002, 20-26. Armstrong states: "Fundamentalism has erupted in every single major

the situation that existed one hundred years ago, there is at least some value to be found today in thinking of multiple fundamentalisms.[56]

George M. Marsden's unparalleled research on fundamentalism primarily inform the terms "fundamentalism" and "fundamentalist" as they are used in this study.[57] His numerous books and articles on the topic collectively underscore two defining characteristics of fundamentalism that are assumed here.

Firstly, in explaining fundamentalism's relationship to evangelicalism, Marsden succinctly identifies fundamentalism as "a subspecies of evangelicalism."[58] By this he means that fundamentalism originated as a movement within American evangelical Christianity and, for the most part, shared that constituency's attendant theology.[59] What this observation establishes in practical terms is that the core theological beliefs of evangelicals and those of fundamentalists are not significantly different.[60]

---

faith worldwide . . . the term has come into popular parlance and tends to stand for a group of militant pieties . . ." (emphasis added)

[56] Harry H. Hiller, "Continentalism and the Third Force in Religion," in *Canadian Journal of Sociology*; Vol. 3, No. 2 (Spring, 1978), 183-207: ". . . important differences do exist between the many varieties of fundamentalism. . ." (p. 185)

[57] Leonard I. Sweet, "Wise as Serpents, Innocent as Doves: The New Evangelical Historiography," 398, 400: "Marsden is the closest thing one can imagine to a pontiff of evangelical history . . . Marsden has become to fundamentalism what Kochel is to Mozart—the name everyone knows and no one can do without."

[58] George M. Marsden, "Evangelical and Fundamental Christianity" in Mircea Eliade (ed.) *The Encyclopedia of Religion* (New York: Macmillan Publishing Company, 1987), 190.

[59] Marsden, *Fundamentalism and American Culture*, (1980), 3: "From its origins fundamentalism was primarily a religious movement. It was a movement among American "evangelical" Christians, people professing complete confidence in the Bible and preoccupied with the message of God's salvation of sinners through the death of Jesus Christ. Evangelicals were convinced that sincere acceptance of this "Gospel" message was the key to virtue in this life and to eternal life in heaven; its rejection meant following the broad path that ended with the tortures of hell. Unless we appreciate the immense implications of a deep religious commitment to such beliefs—implications for one's own life and for attitudes toward others—we cannot appreciate the dynamics of fundamentalist thought and action."

[60] Marsden, *Fundamentalism and American Culture*, 4. This is evident, for example, when Marsden states: "Militant opposition to modernism was what most clearly set off fundamentalism from a number of closely related traditions, such as evangelicalism, revivalism pietism, the holiness movements, millenarianism, Reformed confessionalism, Baptist traditionalism, and other denominational orthodoxies."

Accordingly, as Marsden points out, there is a certain amount of overlap between fundamentalism and several other movements all of which held evangelical theology in common.[61]

Joel Carpenter's important work, *Revive Us Again: the Reawakening of American Fundamentalism*, addresses the fracturing of American fundamentalism during the 1930s and 1940s. Carpenter augments Marsden's work by identifying four theological emphases that crystallized during this period and gained recognition as distinctive hallmarks of fundamentalism: 1) an intense focus on evangelism as the church's overwhelming priority; 2) the need for a fresh infilling of the Holy Spirit after conversion in order to live a holy and effective Christian life; 3) the imminent, pre-millennial second coming of Christ; 4) the divine inspiration and absolute authority of the Bible, the very words of which are free from error.[62]

While fundamentalists were certainly evangelicals in their affirmation of each of the four motifs identified earlier in Bebbington, evidence suggests their commitment to the four evangelical distinctives had an even more specific application. *Conversionism* was understood as more than merely a point-in-time event; it was an ongoing dynamic requiring the continuous infilling of the Holy Spirit in order to experience what was often spoken of as "the higher life" or "the victorious Christian life." *Activism* was interpreted primarily with regard to foreign and home missionary efforts. A commitment to *Biblicism* for fundamentalists usually involved a pointed rejection of Darwin's evolutionary theory and an equally strong insistence on a literal understanding of the Genesis account of the origins of the universe and mankind. *Crucicentrism* for many fundamentalists took on the importance of their being visibly rejected by the world in a manner similar to that experienced by Christ at Calvary. It also had implications of a daily decision by the believer to die to the interests of self in favor of a disciplined pursuit of holiness.

Each of the distinctive theological hallmarks of fundamentalism as identified by Carpenter received significant emphasis at Prairie Bible

---

[61] Marsden, 4: "Fundamentalism was a "movement" in the sense of a tendency or development in Christian thought that gradually took on its own identity as a patchwork coalition of representatives of other movements. Although it developed a distinct life, identity, and eventually a subculture of its own, it never existed wholly independently of the older movements from which it grew."

[62] Carpenter, *Revive Us Again*, 6.

Institute during the Maxwell era. This fact is an important consideration that contributes to the contention of this book that the influence of American fundamentalism at PBI was much stronger than Stackhouse acknowledges.

American fundamentalism had a unique focus in the way it understood and practiced evangelical theology. This contributed to a fundamentalist ethos that was virtually the same regardless of whether one was a student at Moody Bible Institute or Columbia Bible College in the United States or at Prairie Bible Institute in Canada.

For Carpenter, fundamentalism's emphasis on a fresh infilling of the Holy Spirit after conversion in order to live a holy and effective Christian life was a reflection of the influence of both Wesleyan holiness and Pentecostal theologies.[63] He helpfully emphasizes fundamentalism's link with the Keswick-holiness tradition which, as has already been acknowledged, was a very strong influence in the fundamentalism practiced at PBI, just as it was in the fundamentalism practiced at American schools like Moody and Columbia.[64]

This is partly why, in assessing the influence of American fundamentalism at PBI during the Maxwell era, this study insists there is far more to be taken into consideration when discussing fundamentalism than merely the militancy motif that Stackhouse focuses on. That being said, militancy is indeed the second key characteristic of Marsden's definition of fundamentalism that cannot be overlooked in understanding the term "fundamentalism" as used in this book.

Marsden's work consistently posits a perspective that is perhaps best encapsulated by his statement that "a fundamentalist is an evangelical who is angry about something."[65] This is the American scholar's somewhat idiosyncric way of identifying the militant mindset of those evangelicals who:

---

[63] Carpenter, 8f.

[64] Carpenter, 81-85.

[65] Marsden, *Understanding Fundamentalism and Evangelicalism*, (Grand Rapids, MI: Eerdmans Publishing Co., 1991), 1. See also Marsden, *Fundamentalism and American Culture* (2006), 235: "My own unscientific shorthand for this broader usage is that a fundamentalist (or a fundamentalistic evangelical) is "an evangelical who is angry about something."

Michael Hamilton, 20, conversely, maintains that a good percentage of fundamentalists "were not particularly angry about anything."

consider it a chief Christian duty to combat uncompromisingly "modernist" theology and certain secularizing cultural trends. Organized militancy is the feature that most clearly distinguishes fundamentalists from other evangelicals.[66]

Given the popular sentiment Marsden acknowledges that whereas all fundamentalists are evangelicals, not all evangelicals are fundamentalists, it may be helpful to suggest that a fundamentalist is an evangelical who is angry about what they perceive to be an overt attack on or the steady erosion of historical evangelical theology or practice. Such a definition has the advantage of viewing fundamentalism to be as alive and well in Christian circles in the early part of the twenty-first century as it ever was in the early twentieth century.[67]

As mentioned several times so far, it is this militant component of the fundamentalist identity that Stackhouse sees as particularly definitive of American fundamentalism and largely absent at Canadian schools like PBI.[68] While this study disagrees with Stackhouse's judgment on the absence of this aspect of American fundamentalism at PBI, it concurs with both Stackhouse and Marsden that militancy was indeed a key element in a

---

[66] Marsden, "Evangelical and Fundamental Christianity,"190-191.

A good example of what Marsden has in mind when he speaks of "militancy" is demonstrated in Dollar, *A History of Fundamentalism in America*, xv, where in bold type the following definition (declaration?) is found: "**Historic fundamentalism is the literal exposition of all the affirmations and attitudes of the Bible and the militant exposure of all non-Biblical affirmations and attitudes.**"

Marsden, "Defining American Fundamentalism," 23, in Cohen (ed.) *The Fundamentalist Phenomenon*: "In Dollar's definition, as in my own, militancy is one of the leading features that distinguishes fundamentalism from other forms of revivalist evangelicalism. A fundamentalist is ready to stand up and fight for the faith."

[67] Witness the firestorm of protest that arose among some American fundamentalists in 2011 in response to Rob Bell's book, *Love Wins: A Book About Heaven, Hell and the Fate of Every Person* (New York: HarperOne, 2011). Bell was rebuked by prominent American evangelical preachers like John Piper for denying traditional evangelical theology regarding the existence of a literal hell. See http://therevealer.org/archives/6111 (accessed March 11, 2012).

[68] Stackhouse, *Canadian Evangelicalism in the Twentieth Century*, 11: "The controversies of the 1920s, however, brought out its chief characteristic of militancy, of a crusading spirit against what it saw to be modern threats to the faith."

multi-faceted movement. Prominent as this militant element may have been, however, it was but one part of a more complex entity.

The part does not and cannot adequately represent the whole in this instance. Without doubt, American fundamentalism gained notoriety as a visceral reaction to modernity. That obvious externality, however, should not obscure the reality that fundamentalism was and is a complex hybrid of select theological emphases advanced in a distinctive manner and defended by a collective psyche of a decidedly combative nature.

To be sure, Marsden's view regarding fundamentalism's distinctive association with militancy is not flawless. For one thing, such a claim does not definitively triumph over other interpretations of fundamentalism.[69] Nor does it adequately answer the simple objection that whereas some observers may be greatly offended by said militancy, others may consider such an entirely appropriate demonstration of strength of conviction or of strength of character, both worthy of emulation. Further, in light of the September 11, 2001, terrorist attacks on the United States, it could be objected that modern notions of "combat" or "militancy" now carry a freight of implications that in no way accurately characterized Christian fundamentalism as it existed at any time during the twentieth century.[70]

---

[69] Hamilton, 1-28. In the Introduction of his PhD dissertation, Hamilton helpfully engages the discussion regarding how fundamentalism should be viewed. Was it primarily a religious or theological movement or, as argued by various liberal scholars, more of a social protest? Hamilton identifies three schools of interpreting fundamentalism: 1) the (old/new) liberal school which saw fundamentalism as a defense of rural culture, a defense of medieval Christianity, a political movement, an appeal to Americans' worst moral instincts; H. Richard Niebuhr, Stewart Cole, Norman Furniss, Richard Hofstadter, James Barr and Paul A. Carter are among those associated with this view; 2) another school of thought views fundamentalism as part of a global phenomenon, a global social protest movement that manifests itself in many of the world's religions by resisting cultural change; Martin Riesbrodt, Bruce B. Lawrence, Martin E. Marty and Scott Appleby's *The Fundamentalism Project* are representative of this perspective; 3) the conservative school of thought sees fundamentalism as primarily a religious protest movement as opposed to a social protest movement; George Marsden, Louis Gasper, Ernest Sandeen, Randall Balmer, Douglas Frank are spokesmen for this view, as also, presumably, would be Joel Carpenter and John Stackhouse, Jr.

[70] John D. Woodbridge interview, "The Fundamentalist Label," in *Trinity Magazine* (Spring 2009), 9: "Well, several years ago, I got a call from Swiss Radio, the equivalent of National Public Radio, to talk about American fundamentalism as compared to Muslim fundamentalism . . . A poll in France had revealed that something like two-thirds of French people believed that there was going to be a third World War,

In light of more recent history, it may now be more accurate to represent Marsden's point of view regarding militancy by employing terms such as "vociferous," "rigorous" and "harsh," or to speak of "aggressive rhetorical resistance" to clarify what he has in mind when he speaks of the militant nature of twentieth century Christian fundamentalism.[71] Generally speaking, it appears accurate to suggest he is referring to severe, upbraiding and

---

which would be precipitated by American fundamentalists fighting against Muslim fundamentalists . . . For the next two hours we talked. An hour of the interview was played on Swiss Rad . . . The misconceptions that many Europeans apparently had about this matter were huge. Many did not understand that American fundamentalists, regardless of how they may on occasion lapse into harsh rhetoric, do have a motif that they are to love their neighbors as themselves, they are not to kill, they are to follow the teachings of Scripture. Due to the clumping of American fundamentalists with violent non-Christian religious groups, many Europeans entertained negative misperceptions of American fundamentalism . . ."

On the other hand, it could be argued that the use of firearms in the service of Christian fundamentalism is not without precedent as represented by the 1926 incident in which Baptist fundamentalist pastor J. Frank Norris of Fort Worth, Texas, shot and killed D.E. Chipps when the latter threatened Norris by phone and later came to his study where he was apparently shot to death by Norris (see Marsden, *Fundamentalism and American Culture* (1980), 190. Further, the late twentieth century and early twenty-first century has featured certain self-identified Christian fundamentalists in North America shooting and, in some instances, killing medical doctors that they believed offered abortion services.

[71] See footnote 59 in this chapter. Armstrong (footnote 55 of this chapter) nonetheless states in "Fundamentalism and the Modern World: a dialogue with Karen Armstrong, Susannah Heschel, Jim Wallis, and Feisal Abdul Rauf," 20, 22, 24: "Fundamentalism is not simply extremism. Fundamentalism is not simply conservatism . . . Fundamentalism represents a kind of revolt or rebellion against the secular hegemony of the modern world. Fundamentalists typically want to see God, or religion, reflected more centrally in public life . . . When people feel that their backs are to the wall and they're fighting for survival, they can, very often, turn to violence. So fundamentalism often develops in a kind of symbiotic relationship with a modernity that is felt to be aggressive and intrusive."

Martin E. Marty and R. Scott Appleby, *The Glory and the Power: the Fundamentalist Challenge to the Modern World* (Boston: Beacon Press, 1992), 24, 34. The authors refer to fundamentalisms as "protest movements of a particular kind" and offer a somewhat less aggressive definition of fundamentalism than they do in *The Fundamentalism Project* by defining it as "a religious way of being that manifests itself as a strategy by which beleaguered believers attempt to preserve their distinctive identity as a people or group."

demanding rhetoric when he uses the term "militant."[72] The kind of militancy now associated with the fundamentalist religious views of suicide bombers who have become virtually a ubiquitous part of political and religious rancor in parts of the twenty-first century world is not what Marsden has in view.

Having raised a caution regarding the appropriateness of applying the term "militancy" to historic Christian fundamentalism in light of twenty-first century realities, it nevertheless stands that this second aspect of Marsden's view of fundamentalism is in fact shared broadly by observers and is a particularly relevant point of reference for the purposes of this study.[73] Not only did Prairie Bible Institute come into existence (1922)

---

[72] Bruce Lawrence, *Defenders of God*, 169-170: ". . . [Fundamentalism is}. . . above all, a religious protest against modernism . . ." It appears obvious that the majority of the "militancy" or "protest" of twentieth-century American fundamentalism was rhetorical in nature.

[73] Martin E. Marty and R. Scott Appleby, (eds.), *Fundamentalisms Observed*, ix-x: "It is no insult to fundamentalisms to see them as militant, whether in the use of words and ideas or ballots or, in extreme cases, bullets. Fundamentalists see themselves as militants." The authors proceed to describe fundamentalists as fighting back, fighting for, fighting with, fighting against and fighting under God.

Paul David Numrich, "Fundamentalisms and American Pluralism," *Journal of Ecumenical Studies*, (Winter 2007, Vol. 42, No. I), 9, draws his definition of fundamentalism from both *The Fundamentalism Project* and Gabriel A. Almond, R. Scott Appleby and Emmanuel Sivan, *Strong Religion: The Rise of Fundamentalisms Around the World* (Chicago and London: Univ. of Chicago Press, 2003) when he writes: "I offer here a definition of "fundamentalism" taken from the book *Strong Religion*, the title an apt shorthand phrase for the phenomenon. I recognize that scholars disagree over usage of the term, but I find this definition immensely helpful in clarifying the heart of the fundamentalist worldview and agenda: Fundamentalism is "a discernible pattern of religious militance by which self-styled 'true believers' attempt to arrest the erosion of religious identity, fortify the borders of the religious community, and create viable alternative to secular institutions and behaviors." This definition confines the notion of fundamentalism to religious contexts. Political or other kinds of nonreligious groups may be militant, but fundamentalist militance stems from religious motivations, seeks religious goals, and battles a secular (that is, nonreligious, even anti-religious) enemy. Definitionally, the term "religious fundamentalism" is thus redundant—"fundamentalism" per se is a religious worldview and pattern of behavior."

Fisher Humphreys and Philip Wise, *Fundamentalism* (Macon, GA: Smyth & Helwys Publishing Inc., 2004), 9-10: "The association of the word *fundamentalist* with violence and terrorism is becoming so close that Bob Jones III, the president of Bob Jones University, has announced that he will no longer refer to himself and his colleagues

at approximately the time American fundamentalism was unleashing its aggressively defensive nature, but the arduous rhetoric, flamboyant personality and method of Biblical interpretation employed by L.E. Maxwell when confronting modernists was fanned by his love for the militant imagery of the Christian life employed in the New Testament.[74] As will be seen, it is evident in the early issues of the *Prairie Pastor* that Maxwell frequently identified with that beleaguered element of North American Christians who considered themselves to be under siege by theological modernists.[75]

---

as *Fundamentalists*, even though they have proudly called themselves by that name for more than half a century. If this trend continues, there could come a time when few people are willing to describe themselves as fundamentalists . . . Fundamentalism is a religious impulse that drives a religious movement, and any interpretation of fundamentalism that does not include an account of its religious character is to that extent incomplete and misleading."

[74] Marsden, "Defining American Fundamentalism," 24, in Cohen (ed.) *the Fundamentalist Phenomenon*: "Central to being a fundamentalist is perceiving oneself to be in the midst of a religious war. Fundamentalists are particularly fond of the metaphors of warfare."

At this point it is sufficient merely to call attention to several facts: 1) As represented by the title of this book, PBI's motto for much of Maxwell's tenure was "Training Disciplined Soldiers for Christ;" 2) One of the last books Maxwell wrote (presently being revised under another title) was *World Missions: Total War* (Three Hills, AB: Prairie Press, 1977); 3) Maxwell's lectures, sermons and writing were filled with metaphors, illustrations and challenges likening the Christian life to various elements of military battle. For example, see the *Prairie Pastor* (Vol. 4, No. 12, (Dec. 1931), 1, as quoted in the *frontispiece* of this book: "We need militancy in our faith before we shall get anywhere fighting the forces arrayed against us in these days. A soft life, a soft faith, a soft message, all these things sum up the average Christian life, even among the (so called) deeper life people . . ."

Similarly and particularly in the prime of his ministry, Maxwell chastised the likes of Harry Emerson Fosdick as in *The* Prairie *Pastor* Vol. 4, No. 9, (Sept. 1931), 1: "Dr. Fosdick has been the leading critic of God's Word for several years and has lived long enough to see the fruit of his own handiwork, yet he is so blinded by his own wisdom and the god of this world that he cannot recognize the children of his own doings. Both are blind and both going toward the ditch." See also the *Prairie Overcomer* Vol. 20, Nos. 4-5, (April-May 1947), 102-103: "In the March issue of *Reader's Digest* is an article by Harry Emerson Fosdick which is typical of the man. He has always been able to use terms with two meanings. He is mystifying and illusive, double-minded and contradictory . . . This modernist is without doubt the triumphant expression of last-day religion, "Having a form of godliness, but denying the power thereof.""

[75] *The Prairie Pastor* Vol. 4, No. 8, (August 1931), 2-3; Dorothy Ruth Miller reported favorably on The Fundamentals Convention that had been held at Philadelphia on May 17-24 of that year.

Maxwell's vehemence in his spoken and written communications, particularly in Prairie's early years, often had much in common with that of vociferous fundamentalists like John Roach Straton and more moderate fundamentalists like J.C. Massee or Clarence E. Macartney.[76] Reference has already been made to similarities between PBI and Bob Jones University, but it may be helpful to again call attention to a convergence of thought between Maxwell and the Bob Joneses on the matter of seeing their institutions as training bases of spiritual militancy.[77]

As this book will show, particularly in his younger years, Maxwell was second-to-few in his strident rhetoric against theological modernism and modernists. And, as will also be demonstrated here, whereas he was decidedly less militant when it came to the kind of "second-order" separation insisted upon by the Bob Jones, John R. Rice and Carl McIntire breed of American fundamentalists, that factor alone is not sufficient to completely disconnect Maxwell from the broader stream of American fundamentalism.

In the interests of balance, it should be said that important as the militancy motif in Marsden's research on fundamentalism has proven to be, as was noted with regard to the work of Carpenter in elaborating on Marsden's view of fundamentalism as a "sub-species" of evangelicalism, there is in fact more to the fundamentalist identify for Marsden than the militancy motif alone. He clearly acknowledges that various strains of evangelical theology coalesced in American fundamentalism. Specifically, he identifies dispensational premillennialism, the holiness movement and its implications for social reform, efforts to defend the faith, and views of Christianity's relationship to culture as "distinctive emphases that came to characterize fundamentalism."

---

[76] C. Allyn Russell, *Voices of American Fundamentalism* (Philadelphia: Westminster Press, 1976) presents an overview of the careers of J. Frank Norris, John Roach Straton, William B. Riley, J.C. Massee, J. Gresham Machen, William Jennings Bryan and Clarence E. Macartney. Generally speaking, although L.E. Maxwell was not usually as cantankerous a personality as a J. Frank Norris, nor as scholarly as a J. Gresham Machen, it is fair to say that his personality and ministry reflected characteristics similar to many of these individuals.

[77] Dalhouse, 140: "Another principle undergirding student rules at BJU is the conviction that Christians are in an armed conflict with the devil and need to be trained for battle. Bob Jones III called the university a "training camp for Christian soldiers . . . We tell our students the war with the devil, with the flesh, with sin is out there."

Again, given this broader understanding of American fundamentalism which even Marsden makes allowance for, this study contends that it is not prudent to minimize PBI's close association with American fundamentalism solely on the "militancy" criterion as Stackhouse does. Although neither Maxwell nor the PBI of his day were particularly strong on the dispensational or social reform elements of fundamentalism that Marsden identifies, this book will show they certainly did qualify for fundamentalist status with regard to their stances on pre-millennialism, holiness, defense of the faith, and particular views of Christianity's relationship to culture.[78]

Various attempts have been made over the years to articulate a theological definition of fundamentalism by pointing out its association with a five-point creed, a fourteen-point statement or other similar formulations.[79] Helpful as each of these efforts is, the particular purposes of this study are best served by conflating the research of George Marsden, Nancy Ammerman and Joel Carpenter to construct a three-part portrait of fundamentalism as it existed at Prairie Bible Institute in the period under review.

---

[78] Marsden, *Fundamentalism and American Culture* (1980), 6: "The second section of this book turns from accounts of prominent individuals to discussion of the emergence of the distinctive emphases that came to characterize fundamentalism. Among these, four are especially important—dispensational millennialism, the holiness movement and its implications for social reform, efforts to defend the faith, and views of Christianity's relationship to culture."

J.F. Kirk, *Jesus Christ, the same yesterday, and today, and forever.* Although replete with numerous uses of the term "dispensation" and several affirmations of the dispensational view of eschatology, Kirk's strong emphasis on seeing the grace of God at work in/through/behind the Old Testament is in harmony with L.E. Maxwell's rejection of the type of strong dispensationalism that insists on making a radical distinction between the age of law and the age of grace.

[79] Marsden, *Fundamentalism and American Culture* (1980), 117, refers to the "five points of fundamentalism" that some fundamentalists in the 1920s adopted from a five-point identification of essential doctrines established in 1910 by the Presbyterian General Assembly: 1) the inerrancy of Scripture, 2) the virgin birth of Christ, 3) his substitutionary atonement, 4) his bodily resurrection, 5) the authenticity of the miracles. Marsden (p. 262, note 30) points out that fundamentalists often substituted "the deity of Christ" as #2 and would combine the resurrection with the second coming of Christ as #5 in place of miracles.

Sandeen, 273-274, outlines the fourteen point Niagara Creed from the 1878 Niagara prophecy conference. It was presented to the conference by Rev. James H. Brookes in 1878 and officially adopted in 1890.

First, each of these scholars in their own way identifies the issue of Christianity's relationship to culture as a major theme addressed by American fundamentalism. Generally speaking, this consideration requires that two sides of the same coin be affirmed. On the one hand, fundamentalists were passionate about evangelism; that is, they sought to be instrumental in enabling unbelievers to come to a personal experience of salvation by trusting in the efficacious atonement of Jesus Christ for acceptance before God. On the flip side of the coin, unbelieving culture was simultaneously considered a pernicious threat to living the kind of circumspect and holy life that was of such importance to fundamentalists. Modern culture was therefore something to be wary of, at minimum, and aggressively resisted, opposed and separated from, at best.

Three of the emphases of fundamentalism that Marsden identifies can properly be associated with fundamentalism's view of the proper attitude of Christianity toward culture: the holiness movement and its implications for social reform, efforts to defend the faith, and views of Christianity's relationship to culture. Ammerman's identification of evangelism and separatism as hallmarks of fundamentalism similarly fit here as do Carpenter's references to evangelism and the fresh, infilling of the Holy Spirit in order to lead a holy and effective Christian life and keep oneself unstained by the world.

Secondly, Marsden, Ammerman and Carpenter concur that American fundamentalists maintain a rigid adherence to the authority of Scripture as the inerrant record of the Christian faith.[80] In general, fundamentalists prefer a literal reading and interpretation of the text whenever doing so makes, what they consider to be, common sense. Thus, for example, Darwin's theory of evolution was seen as a clear attack on the plain teaching of the early chapters of Genesis.

Thirdly, the trio of historians identifies the importance of pre-millennial eschatology in fundamentalism's theological platform. A firm conviction regarding the imminent return of Jesus Christ fueled the fundamentalists'

---

[80] Harold Bloom, *The American Religion: The Emergence of the Post-Christian Nation* (New York: Simon & Schuster, 1992), 224, states somewhat uncharitably and with the later 1990s in mind: "The literal inerrancy of the Protestant Bible, and premillennialism, are the authentic stigmata of American Fundamentalism, the first bedrock of their dogmatic anti-intellectualism."

zeal to travel the world in efforts to convert the unbelieving as quickly as possible.

A more recent but very useful work on fundamentalism worthy of brief mention is *Fundamentalism* co-authored by Fisher Humphreys and Philip Wise. Drawing on the work of Marty and Appleby in *The Fundamentalism Project*, the authors concisely identify nine "family resemblances" of fundamentalism they claim will consistently surface regardless of which religion one is investigating: 1) fundamentalism is almost always associated with a religion; 2) fundamentalists are traditionalists albeit selective about the aspects of tradition they retain; 3) fundamentalism reacts against aspects of the modern world; 4) fundamentalists believe their faith and community are under siege from aspects of modernity; 5) fundamentalists react to modernity by fighting against it, often demonizing their enemies; 6) authoritarian males lead fundamentalist movements; 7) fundamentalism's view of history is to remember the past as better than the present; 8) fundamentalists distinguish clearly between true believers and others, drawing clear, definite lines between insiders and outsiders, and they keep the outsiders outside; 9) fundamentalists do not work toward coexistence with those they perceive as their enemies, but toward control of their society or what Marty and Appleby refer to as *totalitarian impulse*.[81]

Most, if not all of the theological and behavioral characteristics of American fundamentalism as identified by Marsden, Ammerman, Carpenter, Humphreys and Wise were visible in the kind of Christianity articulated and practiced at Prairie Bible Institute during the Maxwell era. The same was true with regard to the variety of Christianity expected to be part of the experience of everyone associated with the school. This study will document examples of most of these affirmations and attitudes.

The tendentious spirit generated by leading early fundamentalists in their efforts to defend their beliefs and attack the proponents of modernism eventually resulted in internal discord. Accordingly, a movement that had begun with a sense of urgency to reaffirm the fundamental tenets of evangelical theology began, over time, to be perceived by many as an environment wherein the acerbic psyche of its most outspoken constituents eventually dominated. For numerous observers, the term "fundamentalism"

---

[81] Humphreys and Wise, 10-14.

or "fundamentalist" thus deteriorated into an appellation of derision and "gathered considerable symbolic power to evoke negative images."[82]

"Fundamentalism" or "fundamentalist" are therefore terms often used today to sarcastically caricature or marginalize those who display an inhospitable rigidity in their interpretation of Scripture or to the aggressive manner in which they seek to impose their perspectives on others.[83] Understandable as this may be, as Guenther suggests, it needs to be acknowledged that this development is somewhat unfortunate:

> Although the generic use of the term as a typological label for militant religious conservatism may indeed have value, it also obscures the fact that the word referred first to a specific religious phenomenon that emerged out of evangelical Protestantism during the early twentieth century in North America.[84]

---

[82] Guenther, 18.

See footnote 55 of this chapter: "Fundamentalism and the Modern World . . . " 22, where Heschel says: "For some people fundamentalism is about bigotry and rigidity. For others, it's about nostalgia and more . . ."

[83] Barr, 2: "Now fundamentalism is a bad word: the people to whom it is applied do not like to be so called. It is often felt to be a hostile and opprobrious term suggesting narrowness, bigotry, obscurantism and sectarianism. The people whom others call fundamentalists would generally wish to be known by another term altogether."

John D. Woodbridge, "The Fundamentalist Label," 8: "I think it's important to say something first about the power of words before attempting to give a definition of the word "fundamentalism." Words can heal, words can hurt, words can inflame, words can inspire, words can scar, words can soothe, words can provoke, words can praise. The power of words is really quite enormous. People's perceptions of a religious movement are often shaped by their understanding of the words commonly used to describe the movement . . . The use of negative descriptors can lead non-Christians to think they need not bother to consider the truth claims of a particular Christian movement. As we saw in the special report, CNN used the word "fundamentalist" variously to refer to conservative Christians who self-identify as fundamentalists, other Christians who would not so self-identify, and more broadly to religious groups deemed "militant," whether Hindu, Buddhist, Islamic or Jewish. Some scholars have loaded up the word "fundamentalist" with connotations these religious groups allegedly share in common . . ."

[84] Guenther, 18.

Indeed, as certain researchers have pointed out, the Bible institutes and colleges—PBI among them—played a key role in establishing and promoting such a militant religious sub-culture.[85]

There have been a number of deserving attempts at a popular level to define fundamentalism in pragmatic rather than merely theological or psychological terms. At least two of these efforts merit brief mention here in order to familiarize readers with what growing up in fundamentalist circles actually "looked like" and "felt like" on a daily basis.

Stefan Ulstein describes this aspect of his knowledge of fundamentalism in a manner that virtually parallels my own experience while growing up at PBI:

> But fundamentalism is more than a theological movement. It is a subculture with a complete value system that encompasses aesthetics, education and politics. The fundamentalism that white baby boomers grew up with during the fifties and sixties was concerned with biblical inerrancy, personal piety and the imminent, physical return of Christ, but it was also on the right end of the political continuum . . . As small children, the boomers watched breathlessly as Sunday-school teachers presented Bible stories on the flannelgraph. They earned points for memorizing Scripture verses and bringing their Bibles with them every Sunday, and more points for bringing unsaved friends. At summer camp the boomers recommitted their lives to Christ before returning to the worldly snares of the public schools. At Sunday-evening services, with every head bowed and every eye closed, they were exhorted to accept Christ, or recommit to him if they had backslidden.[86]

Similarly, in a page that might have been taken directly from the lives of those of us who experienced childhood and adolescence on the campus of PBI, David B. Currie, a fellow alumnus of Trinity Evangelical Divinity School, writes:

> On a practical level, being fundamentalist meant keeping myself separate from the evils of the world and from the errors of liberal Christianity.

---

[85] Carpenter, *Revive Us Again*, 16-22.
[86] Stefan Ulstein, *Growing Up Fundamentalist: Journeys in Legalism & Grace* (Downers Grove, IL: Inter-Varsity Press, 1995), 11-12.

And so I did not dance, attend movie theaters or the ballet, use tobacco, drink any sort of alcohol, swear, play cards, gamble, or date non-fundamentalists. (Our Southern counterparts accepted the use of tobacco but forbade mixed swimming.) It may sound rather strict, but it did keep me out of trouble. I was almost thirty when I first stepped into a tavern. I was impressed by the free peanuts available with my Pepsi. When I took my own children to see old Walt Disney reruns like *Bambi*, I too was seeing the movies for the first time.[87]

Long before those of us born and raised in fundamentalist circles even knew what a "fundamentalist" was or, for some of us, became aware that not every child in North America was not being raised the way we were or did not believe what we believed, we were participants in the fundamentalist sub-culture that was a practical expression of fundamentalist theology and ideology. In many respects, it was an all-encompassing world.[88]

In summary then, for the purposes of this book, the terms "fundamentalist" and/or "fundamentalism" will identify individuals or organized groups of people of evangelical theological orientation that

[87] David B. Currie, *Born Fundamentalist, Born Again Catholic* (San Francisco: Ignatius Press, 1996), 15. The expectations at PBI were essentially the same as Currie describes, albeit my younger brother and a friend once confessed to smoking an entire package of cigarettes they found and, as mentioned previously, dating was not permitted whatsoever for PBI high-school students. I was twenty years of age before I entered a movie theatre for the first-time to see *Jaws* (Part I). Currie writes further, 20-21: "I had friends who attended Bob Jones University, Wheaton College, Columbia Bible College, Biola, Prairie Bible Institute, Moody Bible Institute, or Grand Rapids School of Bible and Music. I attended Bible school after high school graduation, transferred in order to complete my degree in philosophy at Trinity College (now Trinity International University) in Deerfield, Illinois, and entered full-time ministry in Chicago. I had been scheduled to start at Dallas Theological Seminary, but because of my commitments in Chicago I entered Trinity Evangelical Divinity School (TEDS) in the Masters of Divinity program instead." I also attended TEDS (1981-84) but, as far as can be remembered, I never met David Currie. (emphasis added)

[88] Two other works that provide very useful insights into the fundamentalist sub-culture by those who were raised in it are:
Randall Balmer, *Growing Pains* (Grand Rapids, MI: Brazos Press, 2001). Balmer is another fellow-TEDS alumnus and now Professor of American History at Barnard College/Columbia University, New York City.
Christine Rosen, *My Fundamentalist Education: A Memoir of a Divine Girlhood* (New York: Public Affairs, 2005).

demonstrate(d) both a separatistic belligerence against modernity and a distinct affinity for certain theological emphases and expression. Such individuals or groups simultaneously promote(d) the cultivation of a deeply pietistic relationship with God in the revivalist/holiness tradition within the context of a highly-regulated community life that was/is cross-denominational in nature. The end result was/is the promotion of a distinctive Christian sub-culture wherein, as was the case at Prairie Bible Institute, earnest devotion and blatant legalism often co-existed.[89]

Neo-evangelicalism

It is perhaps not surprising that the strident rhetoric and militant disposition of some of the leading American fundamentalists eventually led to strife within the fundamentalist camp itself as the twentieth century unfolded.[90] A New Jersey Presbyterian pastor, Dr. Carl McIntire, had sided with J. Gresham Machen in leaving the Presbyterian Church USA to establish the Orthodox Presbyterian Church. The former subsequently abandoned that group to form the Bible Presbyterian Church. In September of 1941

[89] Thaddeus Coreno, "Fundamentalism as a class culture"; "There are important differences that distinguish evangelicals and fundamentalists . . . Overall, evangelicals are not quite as repulsed by modernity as the fundamentalists. Evangelicals are not as committed to biblical literalism as the fundamentalists and are less enamored with premillenial dispensationalism. Additionally, they relate more inclusively with other faiths and frequently engage in ecumenical activities. Fundamentalists, especially small, Southern denominations, tend to endorse a stronger commitment to separatism."

Opp, 108: "The worship, work, and study within these unique self-contained communities formed the clearest isolated expression of the fundamentalist sub-culture."

[90] Dalhouse, 52: "Since the days of the fundamentalist-modernist controversy, many fundamentalists, such as William B. Riley, had elected to stay within their denominations and fight modernism there. Others, such as J. Gresham Machen, regarded continued fellowship in a modernist denomination as intolerable and promptly withdrew. Though adopting divergent approaches, both groups of fundamentalists were united by the common enemy of modernism. But as theological modernism began to decline in the 1930s, many fundamentalists wished to adopt a less strident and more inclusive attitude. Others still held to the war-like attitude of the 1920s and insisted on maintaining complete separation. By the early 1940s this division could be neatly charted with the formation of the extreme separatist American Council of Christian Churches in 1941 and the more moderate National Association of Evangelicals in 1943."

McIntire created the American Council of Churches in firm opposition to the modernism he perceived within the Federal Council of Churches and called on all true fundamentalists to join this initiative.[91]

But not all fundamentalists by now remained interested in aggressively opposing modernists or spending their best energies attacking unbelief. Interestingly enough, Drs. Bob Jones, Sr. and Bob Jones, Jr. were among those who disappointed the McIntire faction by helping form the National Association of Evangelicals (NAE) in 1942.[92] Among other causes, this group was committed to scholarly dialogue and interaction with those in the mainline denominations and beyond. Within a few years, however, the Joneses left the NAE and two new terms, "first degree separation" and "second degree separation" were thereafter introduced into the fundamentalist debate.[93]

---

[91] Dalhouse, 54: "Having separated from the Presbyterian Church, USA, to help Machen form the Orthodox Presbyterian Church, and having then separated from Machen to form his own Bible Presbyterian Church, McIntire was a man constantly in search of a foe."

[92] Joel Carpenter, "The Fundamentalist Leaven and the Rise of an Evangelical United Front" in Leonard Sweet, *The Evangelical Tradition in America*, 257-288, provides a useful contextualization for understanding the establishment of the National Association of Evangelicals.

[93] Dalhouse, 99: "The division between Jones Jr. and Rice introduced two new terms into the separatist debate, "primary" and "secondary" separation. Primary, also called "first degree" separation, was separation from a modernist. Secondary, or "second degree" separation was disassociating oneself from a fellow fundamentalist who was not sufficiently separatist." Dalhouse's work is an excellent overview of the evolution of the "separatist" debate among fundamentalists.

Dollar, *A History of Fundamentalism in America*, is a sympathetic treatment of the "fighting fundamentalists'" contention for second degree separation (see particularly the last part of "Revulsion and Revolt" and the first part of "Reconstruction, Revival and Retreat.")

Smith, 7-8: "Particularly by the 1940s, separatism became a new fundamentalist strategy for dealing with suspect Christians and the modern world. Among some, the doctrine of "double separation" became the litmus test of purity: a good fundamentalist had to separate not only from modernists and liberals but also from any otherwise-orthodox believer who refused to break all ties with liberals. This meant that any moderate conservative who chose to remain with a mainline denomination, or even to cooperate with those who did so, was shunned for consorting with the enemies of the Gospel."

See also Camille Kaminski Lewis, "Whatsoever Things Are Lovely: Bob Jones University and the Romantic Rhetoric of Separation," (PhD diss., Indiana University,

Simply put, "first degree" separation was used to refer to those who separated from and broke fellowship with modernists; "second degree" separation identified those who not only separated from and broke fellowship with modernists but also from those fellow fundamentalists who would not satisfactorily separate and break fellowship with modernists.[94] A significant schism thus developed within the fundamentalist camp between those who wanted no association whatsoever with modernists or modernism and those fundamentalists who believed they needed to engage modernism and contemporary scholarship in order to offer a credible defense of orthodox doctrine and practice.[95]

The latter group included rising conservative luminaries such as Harold J. Ockenga, Charles E. Fuller and Carl F.H. Henry, who urged more congenial fundamentalists to move beyond the polarizing spirit of

---

2001) and Howard Edgar Moore, "The Emergence of Moderate Fundamentalism: John R. Rice and "The Sword of the Lord" (PhD diss., George Washington University, 1990) for further examination of the fundamentalist notion of "separation."

[94] Jack Van Impe, *Heart Disease in Christ's Body: Fundamentalism . . . is it sidetracked?* (Royal Oak, MI: Jack Van Impe Ministries, 1984) aptly describes the rancor and divisive spirit that came to characterize the "second-order" separatists. Fed up with such behavior, Van Impe's work is a plea for love and respect to prevail among fundamentalists. He uses the term "historic fundamentalism" to refer to the movement's origins and borrows the term "neo-fundamentalists" from Carl McIntire to identify the strife-oriented fundamentalists who were always eager to pick a fight. In turn, he demonstrates that the "neo-fundamentalists" referred to historic fundamentalists such as Van Impe as "pseudo-fundamentalists." Van Impe unequivocally faults Dr. Bob Jones, Jr. and a host of "informers" (= Bob Jones University graduates) for focusing on issues such as length of hair/sideburns on men, women wearing pantsuits, popular music, to divide fundamentalists.

[95] Sweet, *"Wise as Serpents, Innocent as Doves,"* 407: ". . . the new evangelicalism separated from fundamentalism not over questions of deep theological meaning but over the very principle of separatism against which the new evangelicals were struggling."

Currie, 21: ""First-degree" separationists would not fellowship with Christians who had compromised with error, including liberals and Catholics. Being "second degree" meant we did not fellowship even with Christians with whom we *did* agree if *they* fellowshipped with those with whom we did not agree."

Peter J. Boyer, "The Big Tent," 3: "Once fundamentalists parted from the mainstream, there was nowhere to search for error but among themselves, where much error was found. (One Baptist group separated on the doctrine that only the King James translation of the Bible contained God's pure word.) Within months of its founding, even [Gresham] Machen's new church suffered its own schism, as, eventually, did the new splinter sect."

perpetual contention and "adopt a more irenic posture toward the world in general and other Protestants in particular."[96] They desired to counter the perception earned by fundamentalists as being anti-intellectual and consequently appealed to fundamentalist academics with reputable qualifications to join them in establishing a more respectable face for a new kind of evangelicalism.[97]

From this component of fundamentalism were born initiatives such as the National Association of Evangelicals, the Fuller Theological Seminary and *Christianity Today* magazine.[98] Billy Graham emerged as a successful crusade evangelist in 1949 to become the public face of what became known as "neo-evangelicalism," a term coined by Ockenga.[99]

Although neo-evangelicals by and large remained loyal to fundamentalist theology on such issues as the inerrancy of Scripture and the deity of Christ, they antagonized their separatist brethren by questioning the assumptions of dispensational theology and seeing certain merit in some aspects of the literary criticism of the Biblical text. Billy Graham's association with Roman Catholic and liberal Protestant clergy during his 1957 New York City evangelistic crusade garnered significant criticism from the separatists and became a watershed in the fundamentalist world.[100] Accordingly,

---

[96] Randall Balmer, *Encyclopedia of Evangelicalism*, 486.

[97] Daniel P. Fuller, *Give the Winds a Mighty Voice: The Story of Charles E. Fuller*, 189-220, recounts the founding of Fuller Theological Seminary in Pasadena, California, which represented this new face for evangelical academia.

[98] David F. Wells, *God in the Wasteland: The Reality of Truth in a World of Fading Dreams* (Grand Rapids, MI: Eerdmans Publishing Co., 1994), 24: "When *Christianity Today* was launched in 1956, its first editorial spoke of evangelicals as having been "neglected, slighted, misrepresented," and it promised that now a clear voice would be heard advocating historic Christian faith in place of the tired liberalism that had failed both the individual and society."

[99] George M. Marsden, *Reforming Fundamentalism: Fuller Seminary and the New Evangelicalism* (Grand Rapids, MI: Eerdman's Publishing Co, 1987) perhaps contains the most detailed treatment available of the development of "neo-evangelicalism."

Boyer, "The Big Tent," 3: "Ockenga had been a student of Machen's at Princeton, and he had followed when Machen established his own school. But Ockenga became one of fundamentalism's severest critics, castigating its self-created importance. "Their plan is division in every denomination and every church where Modernism or error appears. The absurdity of division ad infinitum has become apparent."

[100] Dalhouse, 83-84: "One observer noted that shortly after New York, "at the grass roots level the question soon became simply, 'are you for or against Billy Graham?'" a

where organizations such as Prairie Bible Institute stood on the matter of endorsing or not endorsing Billy Graham's ministry became a defining issue for whether or not a fundamentalist church or pastor would recommend a particular Bible school or college to its young people.

The cause of neo-evangelicalism was carefully and capably articulated in 1947 with the publication of *The Uneasy Conscience of Modern Fundamentalism* by Carl F.H. Henry.[101] Henry was also instrumental in organizing the Berlin Congress on Evangelism in 1966. Rather than spending their energies bickering among themselves, this portion of American fundamentalists was committed to perseverance in declaring the Christian evangel to the entire world. Accordingly, Billy Graham was a leading architect of the International Congress on World Evangelization held in Lausanne, Switzerland in 1974.

As will be seen later in the book, Prairie Bible Institute during the Maxwell era attempted to walk a middle ground between the disparate camps that developed within American fundamentalism. This study will present evidence that although L.E. Maxwell himself may have been initially eager to align the school with Billy Graham's popularity, he eventually reconsidered this position as controversy escalated in North America regarding Graham's bold association with modernists.

Evidence will also be advanced in this study to suggest that during and following the emergence of neo-evangelicalism in the U.S., Maxwell opted to keep a very low profile in terms of openly endorsing the neo-evangelical agenda. This stance prevailed despite the fact that definite overtures to join their cause were received by Maxwell from prominent neo-evangelical spokesmen.

"Neo-evangelicalism," then, as used in this study, is a reference to the more inclusive branch of fundamentalism that developed following the fundamentalist-NAE split in the early 1940s.[102] Most North Americans today who call themselves "evangelicals" identify with this entity.

---

reference to Ernest Pyles, "Bruised, Bloody, and Broken: Fundamentalism's Internecine Controversy in the 1960s," *Fides et Historia* 18 (October 1986), 50.

[101] Carl F.H. Henry, *The Uneasy Conscience of Modern Fundamentalism* (Grand Rapids, MI: Eerdman's Publishing Co, 1947).

[102] George M. Marsden, *Reforming Fundamentalism*, Chapter 11. Neo-evangelicals were not always in agreement as Marsden indicates in recording that eventually the faculty

Pietism

Prairie Bible Institute during the Maxwell era placed a very strong emphasis on the daily demonstration of disciplined Christian devotion in the lives of all who were a regular part of the community. In short, priority was placed on the condition of one's heart or spirit over the capabilities or accomplishments of one's mind or intellect. Thus, this section on "definitions" would be incomplete without at least a paragraph or two on "pietism."

As Randall Balmer explains it, the Pietist movement arose through the efforts of Philip Jacob Spener (1635-1705) of Frankfurt, Germany who was concerned for revival and the advancement of piety in the Lutheran church. It was an emphasis characterized by devotion to religious feeling or to strictness of religious practice. Balmer states:

> Pietism covers the spectrum from conservative, orthodox, liturgical members of state-church traditions to separatist groups who reviled the "four dumb idols" of the state churches—baptismal font, altar, pulpit, and (in Lutheran lands) confessional—to radical prophetic groups alienated from both social and institutional church life. All pietists, however, emphasized the importance of experiential (or, in the argot of the day, "experimental") religion, a warmhearted piety that was more important than mere intellectual assent to prescribed dogmas. Indeed, Pietism in Europe very often arose as a protest against a cold orthodoxy, which bordered on scholasticism, a highly intellectualized or ratiocinated theology.[103]

Richard J. Mouw defines pietism as "a pattern of Christianity that has emphasized the experiential dimensions of the Christian faith." He amplifies this by adding:

> Early pietist groups protested what they saw as the intellectualistic excesses of rationalistic orthodoxy, whose fascination with "head knowledge"—to

---

of Fuller Theological Seminary broke into "progressive neo-evangelicals" and "conservative neo-evangelicals" camps.
[103] Balmer, *Encyclopedia of Evangelicalism*, 543.

use a favorite pietist way of putting things—seemed to be crowding out "heart knowledge."[104]

Although Prairie Bible Institute during the Maxwell era existed as an educational institution, it is important to stress that primary emphasis was always placed on the personal and collective experience of God. The classroom was not a place for dry discussion of ancient history, abstract metaphysics or the intriguing paranormal. It was considered a vibrant spiritual greenhouse where lives were nurtured on the sustenance provided by serious contemplation of the personal meaning of the text of the Bible. There was therefore no such thing as a "Dean's List" or an "Academic Honor Roll" recognizing superior academic achievement. Rather, students were encouraged to attain recognition from God by regular participation in a prayer group for a particular part of the world, by developing their musical talents or by cultivating a meaningful devotional life.

Weekly "testimony meetings" were a part of the routine where, following the evening meal in the campus Dining Hall, all students (including those of us who did not live in the dormitories) were required to assemble for an hour to spontaneously articulate how God was working in our lives. Such sessions typically featured reports from students of having recently been awakened by God's Spirit to a component of their lives that yet needed to be yielded to Christ, to an area of unconfessed sin, or to the recognition of which faith mission or foreign country they were being called by God to consider for full-time service.[105]

In such an environment, it was the order of the day to hear people speak in terms that would not have been understood by anyone foreign to the fundamentalist sub-culture. Piety was encouraged and expressed through claims such as "the Lord has been teaching me," "I believe God is calling me to Bolivia" or "the Holy Spirit has been speaking to me through the Word

---

[104] Mouw, 21.

[105] It is likely not difficult for readers to imagine that such an environment created excesses of its own and occasionally led to someone saying something in public that leadership considered inappropriate such as male students confessing sexual lust. Nor was it uncommon for students to use such a platform to create the impression that they were playing a game of "spiritual one-upmanship." Such realities prompted these "testimony meetings" at PBI to earn such sarcastic designations from some as "test-o-fest" and "brag-a-mony."

about my hardness of heart" or "my critical spirit." The annual Spring and Fall conferences frequently featured speakers who would advance missionary or Keswick themes related to "the deeper life" or "living the victorious Christian life." It was not uncommon for the conference sessions or special meetings to include a call for some kind of public indication that God had revealed something of spiritual significance to those in attendance. More intense sessions considered to be "mini-revivals" or "a real moving of God" would periodically unfold at PBI wherein classes were suspended in lieu of additional school-wide gatherings to accommodate the "unusual sense of God's presence and blessing."

Another feature of the pietistic environment that prevailed at Prairie was evident in the directives given students regarding how assignments were to be completed. The use of commentaries and other resources for Bible, Theology and Doctrine classes was openly discouraged. Students were directed instead to interact with the text of the Bible in prayerful consultation with the Holy Spirit and additional passages of Scripture rather than seek the interpretation of the commentaries that lined the shelves of the Institute's ample library. Courses that did require the use of a text-book were always augmented by significant instruction from the teachers. At all times it was clear that the preferred study method for PBI students was that of prayerfully seeking God's wisdom as opposed to consultation with reference works.

Modernism/worldliness

Humphreys and Wise succinctly capture the essence of the modernism or liberalism to which American fundamentalists were united in opposition. They speak of the latter's "four enemies."[106]

Firstly, they write of the characteristics of the Enlightenment which came to pose nefarious implications for fundamentalism: individualism, reason, freedom and progress. Secondly, Biblical Criticism introduced a new method for approaching the understanding and interpretation of the Bible that posed significant challenges to the traditional understanding regarding the authority of Scripture. In the third instance, the speculations of Charles Darwin as contained in the book *The Origin of the Species* (published

---

[106] Humphreys & Wise, 18-21.

1859) introduced a novel view of the origins of the universe popularly called "evolution" which had major ominous implications for Biblical authority as well as an impact on anthropological and sociological considerations. Lastly, Humphreys and Wise identify Liberal Theology or "the work of academic theologians who attempted to incorporate into their thinking about God insights from the Enlightenment, biblical criticism, and biological evolution" as one of the components of modernism or liberalism.

Useful as these accurate observations are, it is essential to point out that fundamentalists perceived these more academic influences to be the motivating factors behind a more sinister reality which they identified. This they frequently referred to as "worldliness," a reference to what they considered to be a secular assault on the church as the holy people of God. They perceived this attack to primarily present itself via the avenue of popular culture which through such venues as Hollywood and Madison Avenue and via enticements such as smoking, drinking and dancing served to divert the attention of the masses from considerations of the eternal and divine to a preoccupation with the mundane and temporal.

Accordingly, the term "modernism" is employed in this project to refer to the more academic or theological aspect of the new breed of thinking that fundamentalists reacted against. On the more practical or existential side of the issue, terms like "the world," "worldly" or "worldliness" will identify those components of popular culture that glorified wealth, hedonism, sex, entertainment and fashion from which fundamentalists desired to be strictly separated.

CHAPTER FOUR

Important literary influences
on this study (Part I)

This chapter and the one following identify the existing literature that substantially engages some aspect of the history of Prairie Bible Institute and has been influential in what appears here with regard to my interpretation of the school. A few comments regarding the significance of each source to the basic premise being advanced in this book are then offered. Readers are encouraged to consult Appendix II for other works on PBI considered of lesser value for the purposes of this study.

The focus of this chapter is on books or booklets devoted in their entirety to either L.E. Maxwell or PBI. This is followed by a review of the few academic projects entirely pertaining to Maxwell or PBI that have been carried out to date.

A. Books/booklets entirely devoted to L.E. Maxwell and/or PBI

I. *Expendable!*—by W. Phillip Keller (Three Hills, AB: Prairie Press, 1966) 224 pp.

Written by a veteran missionary and seasoned author/photographer who lived in Three Hills for a time, *Expendable!* was commissioned by PBI's Board of Directors to serve a dual role as the definitive history of the school as Canada's centennial year (1967) approached. It was also considered the standard biography of L.E. Maxwell. By its author's own admission, however, the book was ultimately intended to serve a more pietistic purpose:

> the format of this book is not that of a straightforward documentary history. It is, rather, an attempt to recount in simple layman's language the unremitting faithfulness of God to His children—those who are

prepared to obey His instructions by putting into practice what they are told in "the Book." (18)

In the writing of the following pages, therefore, I am much more concerned with the concepts of discipleship, sacrifice, simplicity, and singleness of purpose, which have made "Prairie" a household word around the Christian world, than I am with its concrete heating tunnels, steam turbines, or sprawling campus, that stretches itself broadly upon these windswept Canadian wheat plains. (19)

Beginning with a sketch of Maxwell's boyhood and adolescent years in Kansas which included a dramatic salvation experience, Keller emphasizes the rigid discipline that prevailed in young Maxwell's life following his conversion. He also reveals that a similar discipline was at work in the family life of Andrew and Maria Kirk, devout Scottish Presbyterians in central Canada and the parents of J. Fergus Kirk, who would eventually co-found Prairie Bible Institute with L.E. Maxwell.

Keller details the role of traumatic spiritual battles in the life of both parties that eventually saw Maxwell as a Bible institute student in Kansas City reach a place "of utter capitulation to the commands of Christ" and be "brought to a point of utter mortification." Meanwhile, despite a devotion to the support of foreign missions that prompted the Kirk family to go "without butter on their bread for two whole years" and Andrew Kirk to "cancel all his insurance," Kirk encountered a period during which he wrestled with the conviction that he was becoming too attached to material wealth. This prompted the Kirks to enter missions work in western Canada which eventually brought them to the Three Hills area.

Having moved to western Canada as a young adult, Fergus Kirk pursued a farming career on the frontier. Keller reveals that during a period of broken health, the young man encountered a time where he was "broken, humbled, and malleable under the impact of God's Word." Kirk responded to this experience with these words:

What I do must cost. It must cost me something to do something for God. I must be prepared to sacrifice and sacrifice and sacrifice for my Savior. (66)

Accordingly, Fergus began to sell off his farmland "at a time when most people were looking for acreage and thought any man a fool for selling off part of his farm." At the same time, he began to use some "search questions" for Bible Study that had been given him by his sister, Hattie, who had studied with "Daddy" Stevens at the Christian and Missionary Alliance denomination's Bible school in Nyack, New York. Kirk then became a lay preacher under the Presbyterian Church. It was during this time he contacted Stevens in Kansas City to inquire about the availability of a Bible teacher who might come to Three Hills.

The balance of *Expendable!* recounts the remarkable growth PBI experienced shortly after its formal launch in October 1922. Among the themes Keller presents are the school's immediate passion for world missions, the "hoping for nothing" and self-sacrifice motifs that characterized PBI's collective attitude toward material wealth and professional advancement, the emotional intensity that frequently accompanied the belief that "God was at work," and the environment of military discipline that prevailed at PBI.

Although Keller claims "outsider" status (17) in penning *Expendable*, nothing whatsoever of a critical element surfaces in the work save for brief interactions with some of the standard criticisms that had come Prairie's way after forty plus years in existence. Nonetheless, one of *Expendable's* most helpful contributions for the purposes of this study is the clarity with which Keller presents the militant fundamentalism that characterized PBI and Maxwell in the opening decade of the school's existence. Writing concerning the debut of the school's publication, the *Prairie Pastor*, in January 1928, Keller leaves no doubt concerning Prairie's early commitment to a militant and separatist form of fundamentalism:

> the very first words appearing at the top of the first page were both prophetic and poignant. "For wherein shall it be known that I and Thy people have found grace in Thy sight? Is it not in that Thou goest with us? So shall we be separated, I and Thy people, from all the people that are upon the face of the earth" (Exodus 33:16).
>
> This was a strong statement—a positive declaration of independence—the nailing of the flag to the masthead. Now all who read would know where the school stood.
>
> Just a few paragraphs farther down in the first column this same affirmation of a "Prairie principle" was reiterated.
>
> "The Church had never such influence over the world as in those days when she had nothing to do with the world."

These were fighting words, flung into the face of a world, just then maddened with money. It was in the late twenties when people wallowed in prosperity—when money was made and squandered in reckless abandon—when money was the "god" most people pursued.

Continuing in that same first column of the first page, Maxwell opened his attack with these cannonading bursts of fire: "Money never stays with me: it would burn me if it did. I throw it out of my hands as soon as possible, lest it should find a way into my heart" (John Wesley) . . .

"When William Carey first went to India, he was receiving $250 as yearly salary. This was all that he required for his living; but when he was receiving $7,500 per year, he was still living on $250 per annum and giving the rest to the mission."

With such opening salvos of shattering statements the little paper blazed its way into print. It was a pattern of bold, forthright attack on the ramparts of the world that were to characterize the paper's entire history . . .

. . . Maxwell, the teacher, had taken up the pen, which was to become a flashing weapon, mightier than any human sword in his hand. (148-9)

Similarly, Keller did not shrink in his presentation of Maxwell's militant rhetoric that characterized him in both spoken word and print:

There is about Mr. Maxwell's writing the same intangible quality that pervades his teaching and preaching. Somehow it gives one the impression that the stony heart and will must be broken under the sledge-hammer blows of repeated attacks. Instead of striking swiftly and surely with one fatal and paralyzing stroke, going in a direct line to a fixed point, he hammers from every angle.

If a parallel can be drawn from physical warfare, it is the difference between pinpoint and saturation bombing. During the last war there were aircraft equipped with exceptionally accurate bomb sights that enabled them to pinpoint their target with a single bomb. Others relied upon gigantic loads of bombs that demolished everything in view through sheer mass of explosive fire power.

This is an important point to understand about Maxwell's ministry. It explains in part why some students and many strangers have recoiled from him. They become bewildered by this bombardment that is aimed at demolishing their self-confidence.

Those who are broken by it through the application of the Word live again to bless the day it happened. Unhappily, others get only bruised in the battering. They retreat from it into disillusionment with a tinge of bitterness beneath their tongues.

The great saving grace in all of this is that it is all done without malice. He is a man hot with enthusiasm for God. He himself is utterly committed to the cause of Christ. He drives and disciplines himself with great gusto, far exceeding the demands he puts upon others. Not everyone is this keen for the Kingdom. Some drag their feet and wonder why he's so on fire.

In vivid contrast to all this is the testimony of those who have had to work closely with him across the years. They find him a great-hearted man, warm, utterly approachable, and beautifully balanced with his hilarious sense of humor.

This side of his character, unfortunately, seldom finds expression on paper or in the pulpits of churches. The upshot is that he has been misunderstood by many and sadly maligned by those who never really knew him. It is part of the price to pay for being impassioned about the ongoing of God's work. (156-7)

In addition to noting Keller's tendency to spiritualize if not completely justify Maxwell's militancy, it is important for the purposes of this book to call attention to the fact that both L.E. Maxwell and Ted S. Rendall "scrutinized" the contents of *Expendable!* (see the book's Acknowledgements) and were seemingly comfortable with Keller's portrayal of Maxwell as a militant fundamentalist. Since the matter will be revisited later in this book, suffice it to state at this point that the early L.E. Maxwell could certainly hold his own in terms of the vehemence of his rhetoric when compared with that of the great American fundamentalists of his day.

2. *The Prairie Bible Institute . . . whither bound?*—by Marvin L. Fieldhouse (Nagano Ken, Japan: Bibla-Books/Oriental Bible Study Fellowship, n.d), 45 pp. (First and Second editions)

No date is recorded for the publication of this aggressive critique of Prairie Bible Institute by a 1950 graduate of the school who had served nineteen years as a missionary in Japan at the time it was written. Nonetheless, several time references in its pages indicate that both its first and second editions would have appeared toward the end of the 1960s, likely in 1969 or 1970.

Small in size and length, the publication of the booklet nevertheless arrested the attention of the leadership of Prairie Bible Institute. I vividly recall as a young teenager overhearing parts of several hushed conversations between my parents regarding the scandalous *"Whither bound?"* Furthermore, whenever my oldest brother wanted to annoy our parents, a mere suggestion of the legitimacy of some of the viewpoints articulated in *"Whither bound?"* was usually sufficient to uproariously accomplish that objective.

The booklet holds particular significance for the purposes of this study because of Fieldhouses's conviction that, as compared to when he attended PBI in the late 1940s, the school at the end of the 1960s had abandoned its fundamentalist moorings and was on the path to association with the World Council of Churches:

> I am now going to make a clear and a bold prophecy about the Prairie Bible Institute, and it will surely come to pass if they turn a cold shoulder to the cure (in at least its essence) for their ills, which I have outlined in the closing section of this booklet. Unless there is a great change of heart in the School's leadership towards the authority of the Scriptures, an utter crucifying of the fear of man, and a loathing for human politics, policy and cunning, within eight years (by 1977) the Prairie Bible Institute will have been so infiltrated by the ecumenical movement as to be turning out pastors and missionaries under the direct control of the World Council of Churches . . . (44, 2nd edition)

Although apparently many, if not most, of PBI's leadership personnel at the time dismissed Fieldhouse's criticisms and prophecy as the musings of a crank, there is evidence to support the conclusion that at least a couple of his complaints were not without some validity.[1] True, the missionary's

---

[1] Ted S. Rendall, personal interview, Three Hills, Alberta; August 14, 2006. Dr. Rendall indicated he had known Fieldhouse fairly well and found him to be "quite a unique character . . . Marvin wrote quite a bit including commentaries on Genesis, Job, a whole book of poetry, brief articles on all kinds of topics; but running through them all is his strong negative attitude toward the evangelical establishment as if he got soured on it." After suggesting he considered Fieldhouse's writing style to be the closest to Mr. Maxwell's of any alumnus of PBI, Rendall reported that Fieldhouse

prediction regarding Prairie coming under the control of the World Council of Churches has never been realized. Nevertheless, two of his concerns require brief mention.

Fieldhouse states that when he was home on furlough from Japan at the time of PBI's fortieth anniversary (i.e. 1962), the Social Credit premier of the province of Alberta, Ernest C. Manning, was the guest speaker at a large banquet and public meeting held on Prairie's campus. What troubled Fieldhouse about this event was what he perceived to be a 180 degree about-face by PBI on the matter of the school's relationship to politicians and political matters.[2] Reflecting on his student days at Prairie during 1946-50, Fieldhouse recalled:

> Mr. Maxwell had reminded us of how God so deeply dealt with them as a School board about not having anything to do with this political party when first it came in under Mr. Aberhardt (sic) in the early 1930's. How he thundered on keeping politics out of principles in the Church! But now? (17)

---

had once said concerning him: "what Ted Rendall needs is a period in the Bastille!" When asked if there was any kind of credibility given by PBI to Fieldhouse's critiques, Rendall responded: "I think if there were any staff members that picked up on that they would have had some root of bitterness themselves to ally with somebody like Marvin."

[2] See Enns, "Every Christian a Missionary," 67-68, where he quotes from PBI Board Meeting minutes to show PBI's decision as early as 1929 not to allow political functions to use its facilities in order to adhere to its "one true call" to "make Christ known among the nations."

PBI Archives in Ted S. Rendall Library: L.E. Maxwell personal file—"PBI-Miscellaneous." A loose, undated document simply records these four paragraphs:

"Whereas, we as an Institute have been called to the one task of preaching and the teaching the simple Gospel, and of course, exemplifying the same by proper personal conduct toward all men everywhere, and

Whereas, the tendency of political and economic problems is to divide God's children over the land, and

Whereas, we as an Institute have been given the task, as was timothy (sic), of committing these things (of the Gospel) to faithful men and that we therefore, come under the injunction not to become "entangled with the affairs of this life,"

Be it resolved that as the Board of the Prairie Bible Institute we reaffirm our full confidence in the "one thing" of our original call, to make Christ known among all nations."

As is noted in the next chapter of this book regarding Donald Goertz's research on PBI, Maxwell had been openly critical of Aberhart's departure from the Christian ministry and the latter's entrance into Alberta politics, leaving no uncertainty regarding Maxwell's view that Aberhart had abandoned the work of the real kingdom for lesser pursuits.[3] Similarly, as this work will later document, J. Fergus Kirk once wrote a tract that was particularly critical of Aberhart's theology.

Partisan politics aside, Fieldhouse's consternation over his perception of a regrettable change on the part of Maxwell and the Institute in this regard is worth drawing to the attention of readers. This book posits an evolving ethos at Prairie that is evident when comparing Maxwell's early years with his later years. In this case, the change in perspective with respect to openly supporting a particular politician was both obvious and troubling to Fieldhouse.[4] This is but one example of Maxwell's mellowing on certain matters concerning which he had once held very rigid positions.

Of even more relevance to this work is the criticism Fieldhouse leveled at Maxwell and Prairie for ducking the controversy surrounding the rise to prominence of the American evangelist, Billy Graham. Again, evidence will be presented later to show that, in fact, when Graham first came to fame following the Los Angeles crusade of 1949, Maxwell was eager to have the evangelist visit Prairie. By the time Fieldhouse wrote, of course, Billy Graham's association with modernists had generated no small controversy in fundamentalist circles. Graham had become a key factor in cementing the division that had seen neo-evangelicalism separate from the American fundamentalist movement.

It is apparent from Fieldhouse's extensive criticism of PBI for "deliberately avoiding the Billy Graham issue" and additional comments he offers

---

[3]   Davidson, 10, points out that, interestingly enough, in 1919 just at the time J. Fergus Kirk's vision for a Bible school was beginning to form, "the Kirks invited Mr. Aberhart, a high school teacher and Bible student from Calgary, to come for a series of meetings on prophecy. Mr. Aberhart was very able in his teaching and in his study of the Bible. His ability to impart the Biblical teachings made quite an impression on many in this community."

[4]   L.E. Maxwell, "Mess," *The Prairie Overcomer*, 25, No. 2; (February 1953), 36: "As an Institute we have no part with politics or parties. But we wonder: Will the people of Canada awaken to the need of putting such a man as our Christian Premier, E.C. Manning, at the head of this dominion? We believe it is something to pray for." And, one presumes, to vote for.

regarding neo-evangelicalism that not only did he consider himself a loyal fundamentalist. He also saw PBI's reluctance to take a strong stance against Billy Graham as evidence the school had abandoned its fundamentalist moorings, was leaning to neo-evangelicalism and the inevitable "slippery-slope" into outright modernism.

Therefore, as brief as Fieldhouse's critique of PBI is, he serves the purposes of this inquiry well by putting his finger on a couple of significant changes he identified at the school between his student days and what he witnessed at Prairie a couple of decades later. Regardless of what one may think of Fieldhouse's perspectives, what is important for the purposes of this book is to note that his observations support the view that the Maxwell and PBI of later years did in fact begin to move away from as rigid a fundamentalist identity as that which had characterized the school's earlier decades.

3. *Into All The World: The missionary outreach of Prairie Bible Institute*—by Margaret Epp (Three Hills, AB: Prairie Press, 1973) 406 pp.

Into All The World was written by a Prairie alumnus and professional free-lance writer in recognition of PBI's 50th anniversary in 1972. At the urging of Maxwell and my father, who was PBI's Director of Public Relations at the time, Margaret Epp spent five months travelling to more than twenty-five countries around the world to visit and compile a record of the ministry of Prairie graduates living there as overseas missionaries. In a volume that reads somewhat like a diary, Epp registered the activities of PBI alumni who were occupied in diverse pursuits such as church planters, medical personnel, Bible teachers, radio broadcasters, aircraft pilots, dorm parents and evangelists.

The anecdotes and testimonies recorded in *Into All the World* represent Prairie Bible Institute in its finest hour since overseas missions was the primary passion of Maxwell and the cause for which PBI was, and at least to some extent today, is still best known.[5] The book is a fitting tribute to

---

[5] Rennie, "The Western Prairie Revival in Canada," 23, suggests L.E. Maxwell and Henry Hildebrand, his counterpart at Briercrest Bible Institute in Caronport, Saskatchewan, Canada, "emerge as two of the greatest recruiters of missionaries in the history of the Christian Church, and the western prairies of Canada as one of the most fruitful areas in the western world for the production of missionary personnel."

the primary and zealous burden Maxwell maintained throughout his life for those in far-off places who had never heard the gospel of Christ. As he stated in the Forward to Epp's volume: "the home fields at their blackest are almost white when compared with the dense darkness of heathenism."

Ken Grant, who made a commitment to go to Ecuador following the slaying of five American missionaries there by the Auca Indians in 1955; Albert Brant, who took the message of Christ to the murderous Arrusi at Shashamane, Ethiopia where on his initial visit he was initially surrounded by a menacing circle of spear-wielding warriors;[6] Phyllis Masters, who returned to missionary service in West Irian Jaya (Indonesia) along with her five children after her husband, Phil, and another missionary had been murdered and cannibalized there in 1968 by Kimjal tribesmen they were attempting to convert; Beryl Finch, who overcame a chronic fear of missionary service and in particular, India, to spend several terms with the Bible and Medical Missionary Fellowship in that very land.

These are but a few of the "disciplined soldiers" Epp visited who had taken their Bible school training at PBI prior to departing for the little-known, and occasionally dangerous, regions beyond. To again quote Maxwell from the book's Forward: "This volume sets forth the good soldiery of some disciplined ones."

4. *Legacy*—by Bernice Callaway (Three Hills, AB: MacCall Clan Publishing, 1987) 154 pp.

Beginning with the early years of J. Fergus Kirk's parents, Andrew and Maria Kirk, this volume was penned by my mother. It draws on interviews with Kirk himself to convey a very favorable view of the devout Presbyterian home he was raised in and his own experiences leading up to the arrival of

---

[6] Albert E Brant, *In the Wake of the Martyrs*, records Brant's remarkable experiences in the course of building a church of some 50,000 Gedeo believers in Ethiopia. A significant part of Brant's story is that his son, Howard, followed his parents as a second-generation student at PBI and then a second-generation missionary in Ethiopia. One of my memories of childhood at PBI is of watching in awe as a shirtless and sweaty "Howie" Brant ran the short distance from PBI's Men's gymnasium to J-K Dorm, the men's campus residence, on a sub-zero winter's morning. A later memory of Howie is as a classmate at Trinity Evangelical Divinity School in 1984 where he earned his Doctor of Missiology degree. Today, Howard and Joanne Brant have a worldwide ministry based from their home base in Nairobi, Kenya.

L.E. Maxwell to teach Bible classes at Three Hills in 1922. Written at a popular level, the book reflects the high regard, if not virtual reverence, that most PBI staff members over the years held for the Kirks and Maxwells and, as was observed regarding Keller's work, does not contain any kind of critical assessment.

Callaway emphasizes the simplicity, sacrifice and discipline that typified the Kirks' lives along with their remarkable support of foreign missions and delicate sensitivity to what they believed to be the prompting of God's Spirit. They took humble pride in being considered "fanatical" by neighbors and the unsettling events of everyday life were usually met with a spiritual interpretation.

In her presentation of Maxwell's early years, Callaway notes, as does Keller, that the accidental, farm-accident death of a younger brother prompted Maxwell in his early adolescence to ponder eternity and acquire a very strong fear of hell. Openly caustic toward Christians at one point in his youth, he faithfully went along to church with his aunt strictly as an expression of gratitude to her for landing him a good job. Prior to joining the U.S. Army and being shipped off to France in World War I, Maxwell committed his life to Christ.

Callaway's story is rife with emphases on the miraculous elements of the establishment of PBI: the town of Three Hills offering the nucleus at the Bible school two lots in town for a mere ten dollars; the arrival at the last-minute of desperately needed funds which was interpreted as God's blessing upon the group's debt-free policy; the sacrificial giving of local sympathetic families such as the McElherans, Davidsons, Grants and Crawfords.

Of particular relevance to the focus of this book are two incidents to which Callaway makes brief reference that give minor insight into the kind of fundamentalism that held sway in the thinking of Kirk and Maxwell during the early years at PBI. In an event that has overtones of the infamous Scopes' "monkey trial" in 1925 and of the civil disobedience that has characterized some American fundamentalists in a more recent era, Callaway relates how Fergus Kirk was briefly jailed in the late1930s for keeping his sons from attending the local public high school. His actions were owing to his concerns about elements of the curriculum:

> The subtle influences of humanistic teaching in the English curriculum
> of the public school system had not escaped his discerning and largely

self-educated mind, and if something had to give, it wasn't going to be Fergus Kirk!

Into the local "jail" the president of Prairie Bible Institute went! He could sit in prison if necessary, he pointed out boldly, but his children would never, as long as he had anything to say about it, be forced to learn from school textbooks of which he could not approve. (121)[7]

With regard to Maxwell's reputation as a combative preacher, Callaway points out that in the mid-1960s when he was hospitalized with a detached retina, Maxwell painfully reflected on his record up until that point:

Suddenly the acid test came. "A detached retina," was the doctor's verdict in 1966. Physical darkness zeroed in and threatened to freeze his very soul as this intense, energetic dynamo was laid flat for more than ten weeks. Was his ministry to end in blindness? And what of that ministry? Had, he through the years, been guilty of the accusations hurled at him? How well he knew that his sermons had often been cutting, lacing, negative! He had been criticized, misunderstood, labeled legalistic, strict, unsympathetic. The school he had founded was frowned upon, heckled by many in his own fundamentalist camp.

How aware he was of his faults and failures and blunders! Though naturally an outgoing optimist, he had not sailed through life unscathed. Well he knew that he deserved some of the criticism. A born actor, he had been known to leap over the pulpit, stand on the front pew and point an accusing finger at his listeners—all most odious to some decorous souls. This prophet's sermons, too, had often hit the nerve. (133)

As was seen in Keller's work, Callaway is quick to defend Maxwell's shortcomings and hastens to credit his distaste for sin as the motivating factor in his frequent vehement rhetoric. Nonetheless, certain of her observations support the argument of this book that, at times, Maxwell's aggressive rhetoric made him right at home with the militant American fundamentalists of the 1920s-1940s.

---

7   Enns, *"Every Christian a Missionary,"* 66-67, cites PBI Board minutes to detail the school's decision to start its own high school. See also Davidson, 61.

5. *God's Plan on the Prairies*—Roy L. Davidson (Three Hills, AB: Roy L. Davidson, 1986) 71 pp.

This brief but insightful overview of the first twenty-five years of PBI's history was penned by a member of the school's original class of students and one of PBI's earliest graduates. The work reflects Davidson's occupation as a competent farmer and thereby reflects the unique perspectives of a tradesman in its portrayal of PBI's early years.

The book's value to this study is evident by the several references made to it already and will be seen again particularly in the chapter on L.E. Maxwell. It is sufficient here to indicate that Davidson helpfully points out that beginning in the 1930s and on into the '40s, many people from the United States came north to serve in strategic staff positions at PBI, a reality that persisted at the school for the duration of the period under review in this project.[8]

6. *Maxwell's Passion & Power*—by W. Harold Fuller (Memphis, TN: The Master Design, 2002) 302 pp.

Initiated by the Maxwell Foundation, an entity established by L.E. Maxwell's grandson and the current president of Prairie Bible Institute, Mark Maxwell, *Maxwell's Passion & Power* has essentially replaced *Expendable!* as the primary biography of the co-founder of Prairie Bible Institute. It also serves as an

---

[8] At least with regard to PBI, Davidson's work effectively challenges Stackhouse's assertion that the Canadian institutions he cites in *Canadian Evangelicalism in the Twentieth Century* were "founded and funded and staffed predominantly by Canadians" (196). In addition to Davidson's own parents who moved from the state of Vermont to Alberta in 1911 (9), he writes of: Ernest "Pop" Gowdy (49f), an experienced dairyman and heavy-equipment operator who was from Chicago; the David Hartt family (61f), electrical department manager from Washington State; the Clarence Mumford family (61f) from Washington State, both Mr. and Mrs. Mumford taught in the elementary and high schools (Mrs. Mumford was my kindergarten teacher); sisters Flo and Marjorie Dixon (62) from Washington State, the latter who was a librarian at Prairie High School for the duration of her life including while I was a student there; sisters Kathleen and Ruth Dearing (62) also from Washington State—Kathleen was a staple in the PBI Music Department until her retirement, and Ruth was the initial principal of Prairie High School before she joined the Bible school division where she was Registrar and also taught Doctrine and Greek until her retirement. The latter was also a member of the PBI Board of Directors for many years.

anecdotal history of PBI and documents some of the changes that have taken place there following L.E. Maxwell's death in 1984.

The work, written by a Prairie graduate and veteran missionary journalist, is a very sympathetic treatment of the passionate charisma that characterized L.E. Maxwell in the public eye. Replete with descriptive terminology such as "fireball," "prophet," "histrionic" and "bursting with vigor," Harold Fuller combines experiences from his years as a student at Prairie and as a missionary colleague in Africa with Maxwell's son, Ernest, to paint a glowing portrait of Maxwell's passion in carrying out the vision to see lost souls come to Christ.

As noted regarding the books by Keller and Callaway, Fuller's objective is not so much to offer a definitive biography of Maxwell as it is to tap into the spiritual insight and power he believes Maxwell radiated in his pursuit of a somewhat mystical interpretation of "the crucified life." Fuller states:

> How did a careless youth end up as a prophet for his day? That's what this book is about. It doesn't pretend to be a definitive (as in "exhaustive") history—rather a first-hand opportunity to know L.E. Maxwell's secret of passion and power . . . I've also sought to reveal secrets of his powerful message and passionate life. (2)

The theme of Maxwell's commitment to "self-denial" appears early in Fuller's work and resurfaces periodically throughout as a primary theme of Maxwell's life and message. Fuller emphasizes that Maxwell's original willingness to come to the Canadian prairies as a young Bible school graduate was remarkable in that "he never wanted to live in a cold climate or a rural setting."

In the summer following his first year at Three Hills, Maxwell undertook pastoral duties at three rural churches north of Three Hills. These responsibilities led to an invitation from a congregation in the city of Edmonton for Maxwell to be its pastor, an undertaking that would have enabled him to pursue studies at the University of Alberta. However, because the church's official "call" did not arrive until the day after a deadline Maxwell had established, he concluded God was not guiding him in that direction and returned to the impoverished Bible school at Three Hills where he agreed to stay on with no compensation other than his meals.

Fuller incorporates numerous insights from Prairie staff members and alumni in fashioning a portrait of Maxwell's translating the theme of self-denial or "death to self" into a theology of "crucifixion with Christ" based on his understanding of the teaching of Galatians 2:20. Given the somewhat ominous implications of a theology that is best articulated in Maxwell's first book, *Born Crucified*, Fuller is eager to point out that beneath Maxwell's frequent abrasive rhetoric and demeanor was a very sensitive spirit that did not hesitate to publicly apologize for having spoken too severely in a lecture or sermon. In this respect, Maxwell set the tone for regular periods of personal spiritual revival at Prairie.

Depicting a scene from life at Prairie in the late 1940s which was virtually identical to what this writer experienced regarding PBI's sensitivity to "revival" while a student at Prairie High School in 1972, Fuller describes how "the Holy Spirit began to convict us of sin and righteousness."

> At lunchtime, students didn't hurry off as usual to be first in line at the dining room. Many stayed in their seats, praying or talking quietly with each other. Some fell to their knees by their benches. There was a quiet hush in the Tab, broken only by murmurs of prayers or an occasional sob. Back in the dormitories students asked forgiveness of each other, and roommates met together for prayer.
>
> By the second morning, the session leader announced that a few students had asked for time to confess something the Lord had spoken to them about. "I've had a proud, critical spirit!" began one. "I ask the forgiveness of my dorm mates!" said another. Some simply wept, unable to speak. L.E. would sometimes place an encouraging hand on the student's shoulder or quietly lead us in prayer. More quickly left their seats and lined up for a turn at the microphone. (32)

Fuller attributes the strict rules and social regulations that PBI became so famous for to the fact that "the founding families were from strict Scottish Protestant lineage, and early faculty and staff reflected Victorian values." As for Maxwell's contribution to PBI's distinctive rules, he notes: "L.E.'s own military background gave him an appreciation for self-discipline" as did his fondness for the prose of missionary Amy Carmichael. Fuller's background in the Canadian Navy prompts him to observe that in the post-World War II years when he attended Prairie, students who were accustomed to the discipline and regimentation of the war years didn't find Prairie's rules as onerous as was the case with later generations.

In Fuller's view, holiness of life and victory over sin formed the essence of Maxwell's Keswick-influenced theology which was always of a practical orientation. Contrary to the teaching of the strong dispensationalists, Maxwell believed the Old Testament law carried out a practical function in the lives of God's people by shepherding them to the grace of God ultimately unveiled in the Christ of the New Testament. This component of Maxwell's theology, Fuller suggests, found expression in the numerous rules and demanding regimen that prevailed at PBI. Added to this was Maxwell's affinity for the writings of mystics such as Madame Guyon and Jessie Penn-Lewis which together with his own stringent self-discipline promoted a disdain for what society at large considered rational or normal behavior.

Several sections of Fuller's work serve the purpose of this work in a limited way yet offer fleeting glimpses into facets of Maxwell's life thereby confirming he was as an ardent fundamentalist particularly in the first two or three decades of his career at Prairie. On one occasion, Maxwell experienced severe anxiety over a threat he had received from a local elder and minister regarding comments Maxwell had made in a PBI publication to the effect that the elder's son had returned from seminary with his faith in ruins. In Maxwell's judgment, the young man's preaching made it apparent that he now embraced the tenets of modernism. Enraged by Maxwell's perspective, the father suggested the Bible school principle had libeled his son and threatened to put Maxwell in jail for three years.

Similarly, in an instance after Maxwell had preached against modernism on one of PBI's radio broadcasts, a trusted colleague at PBI observed, "Well, you said all you dare say, didn't you?" Although Maxwell was distressed by his associate's estimation that he could be too outspoken or rash, Fuller claims he learned to deal with such criticisms by "embracing the Cross in his own life."

These incidents help underline the argument of this book that at times Maxwell's fundamentalist rhetoric was indeed acidic. He was capable of generating heated reactions from friend and foe alike.

Fuller lists a number of writers and thinkers that Maxwell regularly "devoured" in preparation for his teaching and preaching. Included are such names as Horatius Bonar, Amy Carmichael, Oswald Chambers, Robert Murray MacCheyne, Charles G. Finney, A.J. Gordon, H.C.G. Moule,

Reuben A. Torrey, James M. Gray, Andrew Murray, Jessie Penn-Lewis, Hannah Whitehall Smith and Charles Spurgeon.

In addition to writers who indulged Maxwell's interest in the cause of world missions and the Keswick-holiness theme, it is clear that Maxwell was conversant with the perspectives of those who helped mold and shape the thinking of the American fundamentalists of the early twentieth century. Fuller also makes brief mention of Maxwell's close friendship with Robert C. McQuilken, founding president of Columbia Bible College, an institution that was another product of the fundamentalist cause that flourished in the 1920s.

By way of assessing the value of Fuller's work, it should be noted that it is a popular and highly affirming treatment of its subject. Similar to the works by Keller and Callaway, it avoids any kind of critical treatment of either Maxwell or PBI, choosing instead to be defensive where the two did encounter criticism from outside the PBI community. As well, Fuller refrains from placing Maxwell in any particular theological camp although he notes that people have used many different labels in an attempt to locate Prairie's co-founder on some kind of a theological grid. He prefers to simply advance that Maxwell's "message was very much his own, for it resulted from his walk with God and his saturation in the Scriptures."

B. Academic work entirely devoted to L.E. Maxwell and/ or PBI

I. *"Lion on the Prairies: An interpretive analysis of the life and leadership of Leslie Earl Maxwell"*—by Stephen Maxwell Spaulding; 1991, 275 pp.

Stephen Spaulding's work is a refreshingly candid portrait of his maternal grandfather viewed from the perspective of one attempting an interpretive analytical biography.[9] Because of his "insider" or "observer-participant" relationship to his subject, much of Spaulding's project represents oral history that contains numerous insightful anecdotes and perspectives likely unavailable to the average researcher. These lend a highly personal touch to Spaulding's investigation yet do not appear to have unnecessarily or

---

[9] See the explanatory note regarding the nature of Spaulding's research in this book's Introduction, footnote 26.

significantly skewed his attempts to be suitably objective. While a significant portion of the thesis is devoted to the technicalities associated with an interpretive analysis, the work helpfully contains significant biographical data as well as a critical element not found in the sources identified in the previous category.[10]

The usefulness of *"Lion on the Prairies"* to the central thesis of this book is evident at the outset of the work where, after introducing Maxwell's birth into an America "torn by religious debate and cultic proliferation," Spaulding identifies the cleavage that had emerged between "the mainline Protestant churches and the younger, sectarian and rising fundamentalist groups." Following reference to the roles of D.L. Moody and A.B. Simpson in launching the Bible school movement and helping lay the groundwork out of which early twentieth century American fundamentalism arose, Spaulding offers this instructive summary of his grandfather's life: "his whole life would become an extension of the debates and ideological storms of this preliminary and formative period." (18) Of significance for our purposes here is the clarity Spaulding employs not only in placing Maxwell squarely in the fundamentalist camp for the duration of his ministry, but also in the clear references to his standard mode of operation as a militant fundamentalist:

> L.E. Maxwell, like us all, was a child of his age. The critical elements listed above: the evolution debate, the social gospel, the rise of communism, higher critical methods of biblical study, the rise of the student volunteer missionary movement, along with the number of other primary events and trends at the time of his birth, are themes which L.E. would debate, laud or lambast throughout his life as a leader. His reception of or reaction to the above movements would impact his educational, theological, ideological and personal worlds. (18)

---

[10] This is both a commendable and bold element of a "participant-observer" perspective for a number of complicated reasons. Sweet, "Wise as Serpents, Innocent as Doves," 408, brings to light the difficulties involved in the use of candor when commenting on George Marsden's book *Reforming Fundamentalism*: "Marsden finds it necessary to deodorize his presentations on Fundamentalist leaders, especially those still living or recently dead. His portraits of people are so even-handed that the ugly, sordid features are flattened out or explained away."

Spaulding writes of Maxwell's exposure in his youth to "old-time Methodist "hell-fire and brimstone" preachers," "an early response to altar calls," an encounter with a book containing a chapter entitled "Forty-eight Hours in Hell," and a godly aunt who took young Leslie to her Presbyterian church where regular invitations to salvation were extended. His conversion at age twenty in his rooming house bedroom came about as the result of these elements of fundamentalism's understanding of the gospel and how it should be effectively presented.

Maxwell's decision to study at Midland Bible Institute introduced him to the emerging fundamentalist community in that two of his instructors there, W.C. Stevens and Dorothy Ruth Miller, "had spent eleven years on the faculty of Nyack Bible Institute in New York city (sic), A.B. Simpson's training base for Alliance missionaries." Meanwhile, in Alberta, a shy farmer named J. Fergus Kirk was studying a W.C. Stevens' correspondence course on the recommendation of his sister who had studied with Stevens at Nyack.

Another section of *"Lion on the Prairies"* directly supports identifying L.E. Maxwell as a staunch fundamentalist particularly in his early days. Spaulding writes:

> The era of which we speak was characterized by the ongoing battle between "modernists" and "fundamentalists." L.E. Maxwell was no idle observer of this debate. When the first publications rolled out of the tiny Prairie press in the late 1920s, called the Prairie Pastor, one of the clear objectives of the paper was to draw a fundamentalist line in the sand for all to see. Prairie would not compromise the integrity and finality of the Word of God and the fundamentals of the faith to diluting effects of German higher criticism or various theological aberrations such as a growing universalism. (34)

Similarly, in a paragraph describing PBI's distinctive beliefs in the early years, Spaulding identifies "a commitment to the fundamentalist position regarding Scripture, salvation and the lost, world missions . . ." (36)

A couple of passing comments by Spaulding lend support to the contention of this book that Maxwell and PBI's fundamentalist ardor waned somewhat following the splitting of the American fundamentalist camp into fundamentalist and neo-evangelical components. He mentions that Charles E. Fuller visited PBI to speak at the Spring conference in 1947. Fuller, after whom Fuller Theological Seminary in Pasadena, California, is named, was close friends with Harold J. Ockenga, a prime motivator behind the formal organization of the neo-evangelicals in the early 1940s. Fuller Seminary was launched in September 1947 as:

> a school that should provide scholastically sound training in scriptural exegesis, theology, and church history and at the same time imbue students with a vision for missions and evangelism. Harold Ockenga felt that the needs of the evangelical cause would be served best by a school providing postgraduate theological training on a seminary level, as Charles Fuller had originally planned.[11]

As well, Spaulding notes that Maxwell was a speaker at the first annual missions conference convened in Toronto by Inter-Varsity Christian Fellowship that took place just after Christmas 1946.[12] Clearly, there was

---

[11] Daniel P. Fuller, *Give the Winds a Mighty Voice: The Story of Charles E. Fuller* (Waco, TX: Word Books, 1972), 198. Interestingly enough, as indication of yet another American influence at PBI, Fuller records that Ernest Buegler, "an ex-army chef who had used his culinary skills to feed students at Prairie Bible Institute in Canada and later at Moody" (203), was involved in setting up the kitchen and dining room facilities when Fuller Seminary opened. PBI's kitchen was under the firm control of yet another former member of the U.S. Army, Ed Giger, during much of the author's youth at the school.

    See also George M. Marsden, *Reforming Fundamentalism: the History of Fuller Theological Seminary.*

[12] The conference was transferred to the University of Illinois in Urbana, Illinois, and is now popularly called simply "Urbana." It continues to meet every third year during the week between Christmas and New Year's Day. Urbana always had a high profile at PBI during my years in Bible school there, 1974-1977.

    John G. Stackhouse, Jr., "The Protestant Experience in Canada Since 1945," 205, in George A. Rawlyk, ed., *The Canadian Protestant Experience*, may actually put his finger on the challenges Prairie faced in positioning itself on the fundamentalist/neo-evangelical spectrum when he writes: "Indeed, one observer of the Christmas missions conference sponsored by IVCF at the University of Toronto in 1946-47 noted that while L.E. Maxwell was on the program as one of several prominent speakers, the IVCF leaders from Toronto and the Prairie folk who accompanied Maxwell found each other distressingly alien in outlook on world affairs, attitudes toward Canadian mainline denominations, and habits of personal piety." As a PBI student in the mid-late 1970s toward the end of Maxwell's tenure at Prairie, this writer affirms that

an effort made by Maxwell to cooperate at least to some extent with the neo-evangelical agenda.

In a commendably frank overall assessment of Maxwell's life which he titles "Negative Patterns," Spaulding acknowledges the existence of those who "flatly rejected Maxwell's overbearing preaching style and fundamentalism." He then proceeds to detail a number of his grandfather's shortcomings, some of which might best be categorized under the rubric of "insensitivity."

Although these insensitivities may well have arisen out of a passion for God and Christian ministry, Spaulding states clearly that Maxwell's wife and family (particularly the two youngest children) experienced neglect by their husband and father.[13] He also suggests the youthful Maxwell's "misappropriated theology of healing in the atonement" that he learned from W.C. Stevens' Christian and Missionary Alliance background very nearly cost his wife, Pearl, her life early in the Maxwells' marriage. At one point, Maxwell's relationship with his youngest son, Paul, became so strained that, in Spaulding's words, "L.E. initially took to preaching at Paul from the Sunday pulpit" until cautioned by board members that such an approach was not prudent. (60)[14]

Such insensitivities contributed to the perception that some PBI students and staff, along with many outsiders, gained of Maxwell as an overbearing fundamentalist who regularly left some of his listeners "feeling beat up" or "verbally assaulted."[15] Although Maxwell's staunch defenders at PBI tended

---

neither Maxwell nor PBI ever did fully embrace a neo-evangelical identity during that time frame.

[13] PBI Archives in Ted S. Rendall Library (Box 78). James Enns, "Hothouse Fundamentalism on the Prairies: The early years of Prairie Bible Institute through the private eyes of Dorothy Ruth Miller," 21-22, quotes from Dorothy Ruth Miller's February 24, 1930 diary entry: "I must say that on the subject of matrimony Mr. Maxwell tries me. He thinks that he knows a lot about it but he knows nothing of women, even if he has a wife." Miller was Maxwell's right-hand woman at PBI at the time.

[14] In faithfulness to the discipline of historical investigation, it should be noted that some authorities caution students of history to be wary of imposing the social practices/ standards of one era/generation on another. Davidson, 48, notes that in the early 1930s (a time when L.E. and Pearl Maxwell had five young children), Maxwell came to the Davidson home two or three times a week to sleep overnight for the "quietness," thereby leaving the care of the children entirely to his wife, a scenario that many in the post-feminist 21st century would doubtless find alarming.

[15] I extend appreciation to lifelong friends from Prairie High School days, John Pace, (Vermont) and his younger brother and my former classmate, Robert Pace, (Tennessee)

to dismiss such perceptions as mere harmless indications of his "zeal for the Lord" or "his prophetic anointing," his wit, sarcasm and authoritarian rhetoric were definitely offensive to some.[16]

If, as Stackhouse argues, T.T. Shields rightfully deserves the designation of an American-type "fundamentalist" for his cantankerous and militant rhetoric or hard-nosed personality, Maxwell's own grandson sets the record straight that Maxwell's similar zeal in the fundamentalist cause occasionally harmed not only his own family but also others who came under his influence. Thankfully, following reconciliation with his son, Paul, after the latter's high school rebellion, Maxwell was able to say, "I quit the mudslinging with Paul." As Spaulding notes:

> In other words, he found it much more difficult to point out the errors and sons of incompetent or undisciplined parents and Christians in general after facing his own defeat with Paul. (61)

---

for their willingness to be quoted in this regard (e-mail exchange with John on August 17, 2007, and Robert on September 6, 2007).

[16] Spaulding, 49, indicates that following Maxwell's eye surgery in 1966 he went through a "dark night of the soul." Afterward he told others: "From here on to the end of my life I want to be kind, to be gentle to every person I meet." In this regard it is instructive to note that John and Robert Pace, referred to in footnote 15 above, were at PBI during 1971-1973, several years after Maxwell expressed such sentiments. Wendell Krossa, likewise, who attended PBI in the early 1970s states at http://www.wendellkrossa.com/?attachment_id=36 (accessed October 27, 2012): "LE did not so much lead us as drive us with fear. He, better than anyone else I have ever met, knew how to communicate the wrath of God in his preaching. He could shout and glare and freeze people in their seats with stern warnings of Hell ("where the worm dieth not and the fire is not quenched") or at least serious loss of reward for careless, sinful moments in the Christian life. When LE frowned from the pulpit, you could feel that God was angry with you."

Such perspectives suggest that Maxwell's affinity for harsh rhetoric was something he struggled with for most of his life. In at least some respects, then, and based on the perspectives of those who, unlike Stackhouse, actually sat under Maxwell's teaching and preaching for some time, he could be more like T.T. Shields than Stackhouse is qualified to pass judgment on . . .

Clinton, 403, identifies a softer side of Maxwell when he writes: "Several times during his ministry at PBI he will make statements or write things which were wrong or at least unwise. But, under conviction from God about them, he would make a public confession before the faculty, staff and students."

Nevertheless, it should be noted that my friends identified in footnote 15 of this chapter attended PBI some fifteen years or more after Maxwell and his son reconciled. The salient point is that Maxwell's tendency to be overbearing and insensitive, rhetorically and otherwise, was a characteristic he wrestled with for the balance of his life. It made a substantial contribution to the perception of a component of those who encountered him during his lifetime who deemed him a cantankerous fundamentalist.[17] In any event, his fitness to be considered a fundamentalist should probably not stand or fall on this qualification alone lest it be claimed that so doing is merely to engage in reasoning similar to what this book faults in Stackhouse's work.

One additional component of Spaulding's work requires comment because of its usefulness to the purposes of this project. In a section entitled MILITANT FUNDAMENTALISM that critiques Maxwell's theological and intellectual leanings, Spaulding asserts:

Maxwell was born again into the heart and soul of fundamentalism. He wrote tyrades (sic) against the modernists (the "beknighted (sic) Church of Canada" for United Church of Canada) and put a high premium on the scriptural precept of separation from false Christianity . . . With a bent against intellectualism, one of L.E.'s prominent commitments especially in the early decades of the school was this battle between liberals and fundamentalists. He gave vent to the battle in his writings in the PRAIRIE PASTOR, later the PRAIRIE OVERCOMER . . . As will be seen with other faults, L.E. at times misused his power of language to lambast churches which he felt were killing people spiritually through their departure from the historic, biblical faith. (65)

---

[17] For obvious reasons, it would be difficult, if not impossible, to quantify the number of people who had or have a negative perception of L.E. Maxwell. Suffice it to say thatI am frequently asked to "explain L.E. Maxwell" when people learn I grew up at PBI. In the course of such conversations, it becomes apparent that he was and is a figure that inspires strong emotions. Most would agree that given the nature of his flamboyant personality and the daunting speaking schedule he maintained when he was in his prime, it is not difficult to conceive that his militant orientation likely would have offended at least a percentage of his audience at any particular time. Disparate personalities will invariably draw different conclusions on outspoken figures like L.E. Maxwell and their role as spokesmen for God.

Note that Spaulding dates Maxwell's outspoken fundamentalist perspectives as "especially in the early decades of the school" which is a foundational claim of this book. That being said, it is appropriate to note that Maxwell never did lose his love for denigrating the modernists. When I attended Bible school at PBI in the mid-1970s, it was not uncommon for Maxwell to periodically verbally harangue the modernist Harry Emerson Fosdick as if it was the 1920s all over again and Fosdick was still preaching his inflammatory messages at Riverside Church in New York City.

B. *"Every Christian a Missionary: Fundamentalist education at Prairie Bible Institute 1925-1947"*—James Enns, 2000, 146 pp.

James Enns, the youngest son of PBI alumni and former staff members, is currently Professor of History at PBI and prepared this thesis in the course of acquiring the Master of Arts degree at the University of Calgary. The relevance of this "insider's" work for the purposes of this study is apparent from the outset when, after presenting statistics that PBI's student body (Bible school and high school) in 1947 consisted of 658 Canadians, 420 Americans and 20 non-American foreign students, he states:

> From the above data, one is tempted to draw the same conclusion as Canadian sociologist, William E. Mann, that PBI and schools like it were simply branch plants of American fundamentalism. This thesis, however, has been challenged by a recent wave of Canadian religious historians, who have argued that Protestant fundamentalism operated only on the margins of Canadian evangelical Christianity, and is therefore an inaccurate term for describing evangelical educational institutions, such as Bible schools. Both sides tended to treat Bible schools as an (sic) homogeneous group, selecting data from various schools to create a kind of composite stereotype, with larger schools, such as PBI, frequently providing the basic template for these studies. While the fruits of their labor have been helpful in opening up the Bible school movement for scholarly inquiry, both camps have produced simplified, and therefore inadequate, pictures of these Canadian schools. Mann and his followers have simply seen these schools in terms of what they have in common with their theological cousins to the south, while recent scholars such

as John Stackhouse and Robert Burkinshaw, have chosen an arbitrarily narrow definition of fundamentalism, and thus neatly eliminated it from playing a role in Canadian evangelicalism. As a result, PBI and other western Canadian Bible schools, are reduced to a "sectish" voice in a broader, more irenic, evangelical tapestry . . . The purpose of this thesis is to address the inadequacies of both perspectives . . . (6-7)[18]

As this book will also attempt to portray, it is the judgment of Enns that the influence of American fundamentalism in at least some of the western Canadian Bible schools, PBI in particular, cannot be as easily dismissed as the Stackhouse-Burkinshaw-Guenther school of thought suggests.[19]

Enns proceeds to effectively argue that PBI "needs to be understood as an individual institution, not simply as a representative type" and insists that any effort to interpret Prairie that does not take into account its central purpose of training overseas missionaries will be inevitably deficient. He adds that a more nuanced understanding of fundamentalism than Stackhouse or Burkinshaw allow for is "both possible and necessary if one is to understand more accurately what was happening in North American evangelicalism from the 1920s to the 1940s." Accordingly, he asserts, it is sensible to place PBI in a fundamentalist context:

Preparing students for foreign missionary service became the central organizing principle behind PBI's growth and development. The impetus for such a mandate came out of a stream of fundamentalist Christianity, which stressed personal revival and a form of devotional quietism, known as holiness theology, over the bombastic rhetoric of militancy, and the end-times fatalism of dispensational premillennialism . . . Under Maxwell's leadership, PBI stood squarely in the fundamentalist

[18] Bruce Guenther in his dissertation, "Training for Service," adheres to the Stackhouse and Burkinshaw perception as summarized here by Enns.

[19] Readers may already have picked up on the fact that three researchers who represent "insider" perspectives on PBI concur regarding L.E. Maxwell/PBI's fundamentalist orientations, particularly in the earlier years. I grew up at PBI and, as a "missionary kid" and grandson of L.E. Maxwell, Stephen Spaulding spent furloughs from Japan and Brazil at PBI prior to graduating from the school in 1979. Although James Enns did not attend PBI as a student, his parents and his older siblings—David, Lauren, and Carol—did attend PBI prior to his joining the faculty there. Lauren and Carol graduated from PBI with me in April 1977.

camp in its Bible teaching . . . Although PBI did have some strong separatist tendencies, these were more than counter-balanced by holiness theology's strong emphasis on missions and evangelism. Militancy, while a prominent metaphor in describing campus life was always channeled toward spreading the gospel, not cultural apologetics. (8-9)

One of the primary contributions of Enns' work in terms of supporting the overall contention of this book is his reminder that the holiness-revivalist emphasis must be recognized as an important emphasis within historic North American fundamentalism. He particularly cites the research of Joel Carpenter to point out that although the separatist and militant emphases of the post-1920 fundamentalists have always received significant attention, an equally important element of the fundamentalist paradigm was its affinity for the pursuit of personal holiness.[20] Fundamentalists believed that the best argument to support their belief in the supernatural (inerrant) character of Scripture was a transformed life, Enns states. Thus, they emphasized evangelism and the use of available technology (i.e., radio and television) to promote that end. Enns' attention to this component of the fundamentalist heritage supports the suggestion of this work that, following the parting of ways between fundamentalists and neo-evangelicals, PBI opted to identify more readily with the holiness-revival emphasis in historic fundamentalism than it did with many of the characteristics of neo-evangelicalism.

Another helpful contribution from Enns in his portrayal of PBI as thoroughly fundamentalist in its orientation is the brief treatment he gives to the evolution of the school's doctrinal statement in the early years. He notes that PBI's first doctrinal statement in 1925 "expressed the central tenants (sic) of fundamentalist belief" and a 1934 revision "helped define PBI as a thoroughly fundamentalist institution to both its supporting constituents and to missionary agencies."

Employing a broader definition of fundamentalism than Stackhouse allows for enables Enns to convincingly claim that "through its charismatic leader, PBI's reputation as a leading missionary training school was firmly

---

[20] Enns cites Carpenter's *Revive Us Again*, 28-31, and Carpenter's essay "From Fundamentalism to the New Evangelical Coalition," 3-16, in George Marsden, (ed.) *Evangelicalism in Modern America* (Grand Rapids, MI: Wm. B. Eerdmans Publishing Co., 1984) in this regard.

established in the fundamentalist community on both sides of the forty-ninth parallel." Such a judgment also prompts him to comment:

> By the early forties, PBI's reputation as a dynamic missionary training school was well established in North America and, because of this some of the best known, and most influential, fundamentalist leaders appeared as speakers at its mission conferences. In 1943 the conference featured, in addition to the usual slate of missions' representatives, the senior editors of three prominent evangelical periodicals. J.H. Hunter, editor of the Toronto based *Evangelical Christian*, shared the conference podium with Earl Frid, editor of *World Conquest*, and, most well-known of all, Philip Howard, editor of the *Sunday School Times*, the fundamentalist periodical with the largest readership in North America. Both Hunter and Howard subsequently featured favorable pieces about PBI in their respective magazines, which served to place the school firmly in the fundamentalist camp and give it invaluable exposure to prospective students. (99)[21]

In sum, the work of James Enns is the only thesis or dissertation up until the research undertaken for this book that reflects extensive interaction with PBI's own archives. His concise but thorough thesis very capably and clearly places PBI within the twentieth-century North American fundamentalist community. That being said and in light of the fact that Enns' work covers roughly only the first half of L.E. Maxwell's tenure at Prairie, the burden

---

[21] My father, who initially worked in PBI's bookstore and accordingly travelled to Christian Booksellers' annual conventions in places like Milwaukee, Chicago, and Miami, closely followed L.E. Maxwell's personal advice in the compilation of his personal library and the selection of his reading material. *The Sunday School Times*, and as it became later, *The Sunday School Times and Gospel Herald*, as well as prominent American fundamentalist John R. Rice's *Sword of the Lord* were staples of my father's subscriptions along with *Moody Monthly*, the *Good News Broadcaster*, Billy Graham's *Decision* magazine, and other neo-evangelical publications. Having inherited a good portion of my father's library, I retain numerous sets/works by writers such as A.J. Gordon, F.B. Meyer, G. Campbell Morgan, A.T. Pierson, Charles Spurgeon, W. Griffith Thomas, Bishop Moule and the South African holiness writer, Andrew Murray.

Among what was always the very tightly controlled material available in the PBI library, the Bob Jones University periodical, *Faith for the Family*, was available during my years in attendance at PBI (1974-77).

of proof falls to this inquiry to present evidence from Maxwell's leadership after 1947 that justifies retaining such an identity for the school he led.

C. *"Hothouse Fundamentalism on the Prairies: The early years of Prairie Bible Institute Through the Private eyes of Dorothy Ruth Miller"*—by James Enns (paper located in PBI Archives, Box 78, n.d.) 24 pp.

This short paper appears to have been published shortly after Enns submitted his thesis identified above and was apparently circulated strictly for use at PBI. It briefly examines the extensive collection of Dorothy Ruth Miller's diaries available in the PBI archives in an effort to gain an understanding of the spiritual ethos that prevailed at Prairie in what Enns calls "the spiritual hothouse sub-culture of missionary-minded fundamentalism" (3).

Miller, who taught with W.C. Stevens at Nyack prior to instructing L.E. Maxwell at Midland Bible Institute in Kansas City, left Simpson Bible Institute in Seattle in 1928 to teach at PBI where she served until her death in 1944.[22] A graduate of both New York (history major) and Columbia (English major) universities in New York City, she taught Bible and doctrine courses at Prairie and also served as women's dorm Superintendent and co-editor with Maxwell of the *Prairie Pastor*. Enns claims that next to L.E. Maxwell himself, "Miller exercised the greatest influence in shaping the identity of the school" (2). The purpose of his short treatise is "to give a more particular and nuanced understanding of one expression of fundamentalist Christianity on the Canadian prairies" (4).

Enns contributes to our understanding of the kind of piety that characterized PBI in its early days by identifying three general themes in Miller's diaries: 1) the monastic-like commitment to prayer and devotional discipline; 2) the culture of scarcity evident in her references to her spartan living conditions and meager personal finances; 3) an overriding concern for students to heed the call to missionary service. As he traces these emphases, Enns serves the purposes of this book by pointing out PBI's early and strong affinity for Keswick-holiness teaching concerning "the deeper life."

---

[22] Miller taught at three Christian & Missionary Alliance schools (Nyack, Kansas City and Seattle) prior to her arrival at PBI.

CHAPTER FIVE

Important literary influences on this study (Part 2)

This chapter briefly examines several sources that only partly examine PBI yet have been influential in how the school has been perceived over the years. Reference is made to several books and academic works that are partly devoted to addressing some component of PBI's history. A brief discussion is also offered regarding a couple of more obscure sources that nonetheless contain insights on Maxwell or PBI that are relevant for the purposes of this study.

C. Books/booklets partly devoted to Maxwell and/or PBI

I. *"Canadian Evangelicalism in the Twentieth Century: An Introduction to Its Character"*—by John G. Stackhouse, Jr. (Toronto: Univ. of Toronto Press, 1993) 319 pp.

This volume's key relationship to the topic at hand has already been introduced. Given what was previously stated about my book's interest in modifying Stackhouse's characterization of Prairie Bible Institute, it may be worthwhile to point out that in this volume's *Preface* wherein Dr. Stackhouse identifies colleagues who read some portions of his manuscript prior to publication, there is no mention that anyone associated with PBI reviewed the sections on Prairie.

The reason for this reality is unknown and perhaps was beyond Stackhouse's control. However, since representatives of each of the other institutions he profiles did review relevant parts of the manuscript prior to publication, this is a most unfortunate omission. Stackhouse's perspective on Prairie may have benefitted by some editorial attention from Ted S. Rendall or Paul Maxwell. Failing their availability or interest, perhaps someone on Prairie's faculty or staff at the time of the book's publication could have taken on that role.

The significant value of Stackhouse's work in sparking interest in the study of Canadian evangelical centers of higher education is apparent by the handful of theses or dissertations that have followed publication of this volume.[1] The Canadian evangelical community as well as Canadian scholarship in general is indeed indebted to his vision and initiative in stimulating study of an area of national life that, apart from the work of George Rawlyk, had been virtually ignored prior to Stackhouse's efforts. The caveats registered in my study are offered in an effort to refine and not detract from Dr. Stackhouse's original noble foray into unchartered territory.

In the course of drawing a distinction between the terms "evangelicalism" and "fundamentalism" in the *Introduction* of the book, Stackhouse asserts that the neo-evangelical community in the United States:

> retained the doctrinal orthodoxy of their fundamentalist forebears, but denounced the insularity of this community, its fear of modern learning, and its abandonment of social responsibility. 'Fundamentalism,' then, especially after 1960, became the more marked by separatism and, in particular, by the distinctive practice of 'second-degree separatism': separation not only from those who compromise the faith ('first-degree separation'), but also from those, admittedly fully orthodox, who none the less do not themselves separate from the unorthodox. (The most conspicuous *bête noire* here was Billy Graham who, while indubitably conservative in theology, yet included liberals and Roman Catholics in his crusades). (11)

He then proceeds to construct a Canadian understanding of evangelicalism by distinguishing "'fundamentalist Protestantism' from the larger category of 'evangelicalism' that includes it as a constituent" (12). According to Stackhouse, the characteristics of fundamentalist Protestantism are decidedly American in orientation, namely: 1) militant opposition to modernity—especially modern ideas (liberal theology, biblical criticism,

---

[1] See, for example, the works by Burkinshaw, Opp, Enns and Guenther that are identified in this book.

and evolution), and 2): separation from all who are not wholly pure in their convictions and associations.

He claims his study will demonstrate the existence of "a Canadian fundamentalism *of this sort* in the twentieth century . . . but that it was not in fact central to Canadian evangelicalism" (12) (*emphasis* in original). The Canadian religious figures he assigns to this Canadian fundamentalist category are the fiery Toronto preacher, T.T. Shields, and Alberta high-school principle turned Bible institute founder/pastor/radio evangelist turned politician, William Aberhart.[2]

Stackhouse excludes Prairie Bible Institute from the Shields-Aberhart type of Canadian fundamentalism arguing that PBI should rather be classified as a prominent example of what he labels "transdenominational evangelicalism."[3] On the basis of "Prairie documents or the observation of the author during a research visit in 1986" (236, footnote 7), Stackhouse deems the religious culture that prevailed at Prairie Bible Institute from 1922 up until the time of his visit as a uniquely Canadian form of "sectish" evangelicalism.[4] He describes such as follows:

> these Christians were committed to 'transdenominational evangelicalism,' the belief that the evangelical 'basics' are most important to Christianity and that transdenominational cooperative action should be undertaken on this basis . . . So as the twentieth century dawned, evangelicalism in Canada had established a variegated heritage. Within it was a prophetic, spiritual, 'outsider' tradition reaching back to Henry Alline in eighteenth-century Nova Scotia but continuing among the Millerites, Plymouth Brethren, and Salvation Army in the nineteenth. Within it also, however, was a pastoral, socially conscious, 'insider' tradition reaching back to

---

2   James W. Opp, 12: "By focusing on individuals and controversies, and relegating fundamentalism to the far edge of evangelicalism, Canadian historians have seriously misrepresented the depth and meaning of this unique phenomenon." The phenomenon to which Opp refers is that of fundamentalism as a popular movement with its own leaders, institutions, publications, etc.

3   David R. Elliott, "Three Faces of Baptist Fundamentalism in Canada: Aberhart, Maxwell, and Shields," 171-182, is much less hesitant to associate Maxwell with Aberhart and Shields than is Stackhouse.

4   Spaulding, 65, "Militant Fundamentalism; "With a bent against intellectualism, one of L.E.'s prominent commitments especially in the early decades of the school was this battle between liberals and fundamentalists."

Edgerton Ryerson and coming to dominate Anglophone culture—albeit with regional differences—in both the Maritimes and Ontario. Both types of this complex heritage would become manifest among evangelicals in the twentieth century as well, as this narrative will demonstrate."[5]

Referring to standard Canadian scholarly treatment of evangelicalism in the twentieth century, Stackhouse borrows from the popular "church-sect" notion to posit the existence of "two different dispositions" or "mentalities" among Canadian evangelicals: the "churchish" type of evangelical and the "sectish" type of evangelical. He places PBI in the latter category among that group of Canadian evangelicals which "separated itself from the culture and tended to include a smaller and more clearly delineated spectrum of constituents" (16-17).

Without doubt, such an approach to Canadian evangelicalism has its merits. As noted earlier in this work, however, it is my purpose to demonstrate that Stackhouse's failure to grasp the prominent American influence at PBI clouds the very real possibility of a clear and abundant overlap between Canadian "sectish" evangelicalism and American fundamentalism. It is my contention that part of the reason for such overlap is directly related to the strong American effect and presence at what was, for a significant period of time in the twentieth century, Canada's largest Bible school.

To be sure, L.E. Maxwell and Prairie Bible Institute were duly proud of their inter-denominational or trans-denominational identity. Statistics frequently appeared in the school's various publications calling attention to this reality.[6] And, in discussing the definition of "sect" earlier in this book, the legitimacy of considering PBI to be "sectish" in its orientation was acknowledged.

---

[5]   Stackhouse, *Canadian Evangelicalism in the Twentieth Century*, 9.

[6]   L.E. Maxwell, "Surveys," in *The Prairie Pastor* 4, No. 3, (March 1931), 3: "Denominations represented at the school this year are as follows: Undenominational—103, Baptist—55, Christian & Missionary Alliance—9, Presbyterian—9, United Church—6, Brethren—6, Lutheran—6, Church of England—4 . . ." Altogether in the list, Maxwell lists twenty different denominations.

   PBI Archives in Ted S. Rendall Library; L.E. Maxwell personal files—"United Church." In a December 23, 1950, letter to Rev. Wm. Aitken Harvey, pastor of Westminster United Church in The Pas, Manitoba, Maxwell wrote: ". . . and believing you will rejoice to know that we have in our midst persons out of 100 different denominations. . ."

Nevertheless, there is something sharply paradoxical about Stackhouse using PBI as one of his examples of the uniquely Canadian "transdenominational evangelicalism" that he identifies. For one thing, as will come into focus several times in this book, *Canadian Evangelicalism in the Twentieth Century* contains several references that clearly depict Stackhouse's awareness of PBI's militant fundamentalist orientation and its unique nature in that regard when compared to the other Canadian evangelical organizations he profiles. As the following citations from his book reveal, what Stackhouse opts to call "sectish evangelicalism" or a different disposition or "mentalitie" (16-17) is, at best, minimally different from essentially the same characteristics that flourished within American fundamentalism. See, for example, the following citations:

Prairie Bible Institute maintained its separatist stance . . . (14)

A small battle was fought in letters and over the radio between Aberhart and leaders of the Prairie Bible Institute in rural Three Hills, Alberta . . . (43)

'The school stands for every whit of the "Fundamentals' (77)

the appropriate metaphor, at least in Prairie's case, is military. (82)

So Prairie's regulations are understood better as a part of a missionary 'boot camp' experience (82)

The three most frequently mentioned foes were modernism (and its supposed offspring, the ecumenical movement), communism, and Roman Catholicism. As did other fundamentalists, Prairie's leaders often linked the three. (85-86)

Communism and Roman Catholicism especially were dangerous because of their commitments to world domination, and the Prairie editors were quick to spot attempts by either to extend its influence in Canada or the United States. (86)

Prairie's avowed identity as a militant opponent of modernism. (86)

The usual fundamentalist targets of alcohol, dancing, television, and rock-and-roll do come in for frequent attack (87)

More than a few remnants of the old code remained, to be sure. In the late 1980s students were still forbidden to attend movies or dances, to drink or to play cards. Hairstyles and dress were still regulated, with women to be in skirts or dresses and men in ties for all classes (134)

But PBI remained largely unchanged in ethos and program, and stood somewhat apart from its evangelical relatives, like Ontario Bible College and Inter-Varsity Christian Fellowship, in concentrating almost exclusively on missionary and ecclesiastical vocations, even as it stood with them in the broad fellowship of Canadian evangelicalism. (137)

not to mention Prairie Bible Institute's distinctiveness right from its very start. (145)

[Prairie Bible Institute] . . . manifested much more caution, and even suspicion of or outright hostility toward modern ideas (190)

Secondly, in Stackhouse's brief description of the defining characteristics of neo-evangelicalism on page 11 of his book, it is instructive to bear in mind that PBI was openly aligned on several counts with the very kind of fundamentalism Stackhouse claims the neo-evangelicals "denounced."

Stackhouse states, for example, that neo-evangelicals denounced the insularity of the fundamentalist community. While, as will be documented in a later chapter here, PBI's early publications contain frequent denunciations by Maxwell of the open-mindedness of modernists and their theology, one would be hard pressed to produce any kind of similar record wherein he denounces the narrow-mindedness of militant American fundamentalists. Presumably, the reason for such is found within the abundant evidence which exists that Maxwell considered PBI to have much in common with the American fundamentalist community.

Indeed, as will be reviewed later in this book, the early years of the *Prairie Pastor* periodically contained articles or citations from prominent figures in American fundamentalism such as William B. Riley, John Roach Straton or Bob Jones, Sr. As well, former PBI president, Dr. Ted Rendall, advised me that the prominent American fundamentalist, John R. Rice, once spoke at a PBI conference.[7]

Stackhouse also notes that the neo-evangelicals denounced fundamentalism's fear of modern learning. This book will point out that for the majority of his tenure at PBI, L.E. Maxwell was openly skeptical, suspicious and, at times, downright denigrating toward the kind of scholarly pursuits the neo-evangelicals advocated. Regardless of stories that might be

---

[7] Ted S. Rendall, personal interview, August 14, 2006. "I don't think Carl McIntire was ever here. John R. Rice was here because I heard him speak in chapel in the '50s. Neither of the Bob Jones's were here."

cited to indicate Maxwell's personal support of those who pursued advanced education, the fact of the matter is that Maxwell opposed accreditation at a critical juncture in PBI's history and consistently spoke disparagingly of a Christianity that in his estimation was "dying by degrees."[8] He delighted in caricaturing the pursuit of studies in the liberal arts such as philosophy as "fool-osophy."[9]

Despite his respect for some with impeccable academic credentials such as his former teacher and later colleague, Dorothy Ruth Miller, Maxwell was far more interested in promoting the "deeper life" of the spirit than he ever was in encouraging the cultivation of the human intellect. With respect to this component of the neo-evangelical agenda, even militant American fundamentalists like the Bob Jones, Sr. and Jr. tandem, Carl McIntire and John R. Rice demonstrated a more sympathetic spirit to academic pursuits than Maxwell ever did.[10] For those of us who spent years under the preaching and teaching of Maxwell, the record is such that he requires

[8] Fuller, 214, cites PBI "staff kid" Miriam Charter: ""I was making decisions about going on to university after Bible school rather than 'straight to the field' as some thought every Prairie grad should do!" Miriam remembers. "To my surprise, Mr. Maxwell applauded my thoughts.""

[9] PBI students from my era will readily recognize "dying by degrees" and "fool-osophy" as two of the sarcastic phrases Maxwell often used to communicate his disregard for higher education.

[10] Ted S. Rendall, personal interview, August 14, 2006. When asked about "Dr. Maxwell" as he was sometimes called, Rendall replied: "That was just what some people did when addressing a person in his position. I don't know if he was ever offered an honorary doctorate and he turned it down, I don't know unless there's some correspondence to that effect. I never saw anything from anybody offering him an honorary doctorate. I think it was more a polite way of referring to him as president of the school, especially in the States. I think he would have turned it down if he had been offered an honorary doctorate. I think he would have felt that in accepting it and being called "Dr." he was compromising his position on degrees—that would be my hunch. He probably associated the term "Dr." with the German rationalists and liberal scholars that had caused so many problems."

Fuller, 213-214: "Rightly or wrongly, L.E. himself felt that accepting an honorary doctorate might make him and his message appear "man-made" . . . It is true that his depiction of universities and seminaries as the graveyard of faith could come across an anti-intellectual. Actually, his concern was anti-academic—not without reason. Evangelical centers of higher learning (among them Harvard, Princeton and Yale) had been founded to train church leadership but were hijacked by liberal theology and secularism in the name of academic freedom.""

categorization among those fundamentalists who, to use Stackhouse's own words, had a deep suspicion or "fear of modern learning."[11]

Stackhouse points out that the neo-evangelicals were also critical of fundamentalists for abandoning a strong sense of Christian social responsibility. On this count as well, PBI had much in common with American fundamentalism.

The Prairie Bible Institute of my youth had a modest sense of Christian social duty. The various outreaches the school conducted into mainstream society were primarily of an evangelistic nature and intent. Weekly trips to rescue missions and jails in nearby cities like Calgary, Drumheller and Red Deer were carried out by staff and student volunteers. Another regular activity was street evangelism in larger centers that involved tract distribution, personal conversations and, on occasion, open-air preaching. As well, the school targeted local aboriginal reservations at villages such as Gleichen and Morley (Alberta) for evangelistic outreach. A significant number of "Indians," as they were popularly identified in the mid-twentieth century, frequently attended PBI conferences as guests of students or graduates from the school who were carrying out Christian service on the reservations.[12]

Similarly, PBI's concern for the "regions beyond" or what today are often referred to as "third-world countries" was primarily evangelistic in nature. L.E. Maxwell often wrote and spoke of the communist menace, yet his emphasis usually concerned the suppression of the gospel message and the Christian church in communist lands as opposed to the nationalistic concerns pertaining to the United States as articulated by American fundamentalists like Carl McIntire.

Hiebert, 45: "Prairie's L.E. Maxwell critiqued scholarly educational research as breeding pride, which contradicted the "crucified to self" emphasis of the Cross in the life of the believer."

[11] Spaulding, 44-45, "Anti-intellectualism;" "Maxwell was born again into the heart and soul of fundamentalism. He wrote tyrades (sic) against the modernists (the "beknighted (sic) Church of Canada" for United Church of Canada) . . . Part of his armory was a staunch anti-intellectualism . . ."

[12] Bernice and Victor Callaway, *The Spirit of Prairie*, 20. It should be noted that some of PBI's alumni did pursue careers or ministries involving the social aspects of the gospel. For example, Harvey Jesperson, a 1942 PBI graduate, founded Bethany Homes for children near Wetaskiwin, Alberta, where for over forty years he and his wife "provided love, care and Christian training for 700 children from broken homes."

Seldom, if ever, did PBI focus on issues such as racism, systemic poverty or injustice, third-world debt or exploitive North American and European capitalism as realities to be exposed and opposed in the course of carrying out Christ's great commission.[13] By and large, the impression generated more by what was not said on these issues at PBI rather than by what was actually said was that social issues of such a nature were the domain of the liberal mainstream denominations and organizations such as the World Council of Churches.

Thus, PBI during the Maxwell era gave a decidedly minor emphasis to Christian social responsibility. Indeed, Christian activism of any variety that did not primarily and aggressively seek or attain the conversion of lost souls was considered a dereliction of duty to Christ's command to "make disciples" and a concession to the agenda of the modernists. Even Stackhouse affirms this detail of PBI's theological and philosophical emphases.[14]

In light of PBI's similarity to American fundamentalism with respect to insularity, the fear of or disregard for modern learning and the low profile given social responsibility, the school's contribution to the "transdenominational evangelicalism" category that Stackhouse uses to categorize PBI contained distinct similarities to certain components of militant American fundamentalism. Consequently, one has to posit that, at least as it concerned PBI, the difference between Canadian "transdenominational evangelicalism" and American fundamentalism was simply not as apparent as Stackhouse infers.

True, Maxwell definitely did not openly affiliate with the kind of cantankerous American fundamentalists that were the regular company

---

[13] Palmer, *Alberta: A New History*, 263: "L.E. Maxwell, principal of the Prairie Bible Institute, counseled other fundamentalists that while Christians should vote, they had no business trying to bring about social reform."

[14] Stackhouse, *Canadian Evangelicalism in the Twentieth Century*, 43: "A small battle was fought in letters and over the radio between Aberhart and leaders of the Prairie Bible Institute in rural Three Hills, Alberta, over Aberhart's espousal of political solutions to the Depression. Like most evangelicals, the Prairie people believed the Depression to be a divine judgment on a civilization that had rejected God. They thought that Christians should vote intelligently and prayerfully, to be sure, but also that Christians had no business trying directly to bring about social reform. The real problem was personal sinfulness, and the real solution was evangelism."

Stackhouse, 87, (quoting Maxwell): "Is it not our one business as believers to send starving peoples the Bread of Life?"

of T.T. Shields. Nevertheless, as will be seen, there are good reasons to challenge the conclusion that he was any less "contentious" than Shields or Aberhart, those figures that Stackhouse designates as authentic Canadian fundamentalists.[15]

In an effort to supply a suitable Canadian angle to the definition of fundamentalism, Stackhouse advances (12) that ". . . we can provisionally appropriate the leading characteristics of American fundamentalism" which he then identifies as: militant opposition to modernity—especially modern ideas (liberal theology, biblical criticism, and evolution chief among them), and separation from all who are not wholly pure in their convictions and associations. It is not entirely clear to me why Stackhouse considers the "militancy" and "separatistic" elements of American fundamentalism to be its "leading characteristics" and uses only those two criteria to determine what constitutes a fundamentalist in the Canadian context. It appears that he somewhat arbitrarily chooses to focus on only one wheel of a two-wheeled cart, namely the movement's psychological characteristics. He simultaneously assigns the theological strains of revivalism, holiness theology, resistance to popular culture, and the imminent second-coming of Christ that existed at PBI and which Carpenter, Marsden and others identify as leading theological themes in the fundamentalist movement to a Canadian "sectish" evangelicalism. His choice in this regard thus begs the question: theologically speaking, what distinguishes Canadian "sectish" evangelicals from American fundamentalists? Presumably, Stackhouse would respond that the absence of militancy sets Canadian "sectish" evangelicalism apart from American fundamentalism. Does this distinction truly survive close scrutiny, however?

While acknowledging there was a militant Canadian fundamentalism that surfaced in the twentieth century, Stackhouse chooses to disassociate L.E. Maxwell and PBI from the rancorous type of fundamentalism that typified early American fundamentalists such as J. Frank Norris and William B. Riley. Instead, he reserves that designation for prominent Canadian preachers T.T. Shields and, to a lesser extent, William Aberhart, suggesting that Maxwell and PBI embodied a more irenic type of fundamentalism or,

---

[15] Ted S. Rendall, personal interview, August 14, 2006. "T.T. Shields' *Gospel Witness* came to Mr. Maxwell's desk weekly and he found it useful particularly for its exposure of Roman Catholicism in Quebec."

in his words, qualified as "the best representative" of a distinctive type of Canadian evangelicalism.[16]

The argument of my book advances and attempts to document that drawing such a distinction between L.E. Maxwell (especially the early Maxwell) and figures like Shields and Aberhart ventures into the territory of a subjective judgment that is not as clearly supported by the facts as Stackhouse claims. Further, as will be demonstrated, when applying Stackhouse's comparatively objective "Canadian" angle on fundamentalism (=militant opposition to modernity, separation from all who are not wholly pure in their convictions and associations) to Maxwell and PBI, this study will substantiate that both elements of Stackhouse's "Canadian" fundamentalism were unquestionably present in some form at PBI during the period of time under review. If the "militant" or "separatist" element of Maxwell's fundamentalist orientation was not as well-known as that of Shields and Aberhart, perhaps the explanation for that should be sought in other considerations such as PBI's comparatively rural location and its corresponding comparative isolation from the kind of public scrutiny often associated with urban leaders and settings.

From an insider's perspective, it was well known at PBI that most aspects of modernity as represented by popular culture and theological liberalism were considered a threat to the pietistic version of Christianity the school prized. Certainly, it was also a standard expectation during the 1960s and '70s that those of us at Prairie would have minimal contact with local unbelievers including people who were participants in the churches of the mainline denominations represented in town. As well, it was not uncommon to hear overtones of the "first-order separation" theme emanating from the leadership of Prairie Bible Institute.[17]

---

[16] Stackhouse, *Canadian Evangelicalism in the Twentieth Century*, 11-13. Curiously, at no point in his volume does Stackhouse make any reference whatsoever to the fiery Canadian fundamentalist, Perry F. Rockwood, who, following a public falling-out in 1943 with the Presbyterians, advocated a "King James Version only" variety of fundamentalism. Rockwood's radio program, "The People's Gospel Hour," based in Halifax, Nova Scotia, is still heard on the airwaves across North America continuing beyond Rockwood's death which occurred in March 2008 just prior to his 91st birthday. Stella Jarema, a PBI classmate of my father's in the early 1950s, was the featured soloist on "The People's Gospel Hour" for many, many years.

[17] T.S. Rendall, *Nehemiah: Laws of Leadership* (Three Hills, AB: Prairie Press, 1980), 250-251: "The Word of God is crystal clear on the matter of separation from the enemies

Any meaningful evaluation of PBI during the Maxwell era will quickly establish that opposition to modernity and separation from unbelievers were staples of the PBI milieu. When placed alongside the theological emphases of American fundamentalism then, there are good reasons to question whether, as far as it relates to PBI, Stackhouse's Canadian evangelicalism is truly as substantially different from American fundamentalism as he claims.

2. *Character with Competence Education: The Bible College Movement in Canada*—by Al Hiebert (with Char Bates and Paul Magnus) (Steinbach, MB: Association of Canadian Bible Colleges, 2005) 110 pp.

This brief but comprehensive treatment of the history of the Canadian Bible college movement reflects the work of Al Hiebert, a PBI graduate from the early 1960s, who went on to earn a PhD at New York University and devote his career to teaching at Providence (formerly Winnipeg Bible) College and also Briercrest Bible College in Canada. Additionally, he served on staff at the Association for Biblical Higher Education (formerly American Association of Bible Colleges) in the United States, and thus brings a wide range of expertise to the project. Contributors Char Bates, Ph.D., has a lengthy association as an instructor and administrator at PBI from which she graduated, and Paul Magnus, Ed.D. served as professor (later President) at Briercrest College and Seminary for the better part of his career.

In addition to mapping out the distinguishing elements of the Canadian Bible institute/college movement, the work contains a number of valuable charts, graphs and appendixes. It includes a list of relevant research projects compiled in a manner that enables readers to grasp a clear sense of the progress that has been made on studying the Canadian Bible college

---

of God's people . . . This is one of the serious consequences of modern-day co-operative evangelism. During the duration of the evangelistic crusade, men who are known to be liberal in their theology are invited to associate with men holding to the fundamental doctrines of God's Word. The people on "the outside" are led to believe that all those co-operating in the campaign share the same views, and that the liberal pastors endorse the preaching of the evangelist; whereas in actual truth there has been no change in the view of the majority of the liberal participants. Tobiah does not have a change of heart because he has a room in the Temple; nor does a liberal preacher have a change of heart because he participates in a fundamental evangelistic campaign."

movement. Not only does the volume look back at what has transpired to date in the Canadian Bible college movement, Magnus's chapter looks ahead to the movement's future potential and posits some practical suggestions concerning areas where progress remains to be made.

Of particular value to this book is an observation that brings into focus what might best be identified as "PBI's fundamentalist heritage." Referring to a work by J. Burchaell on the demise of evangelical schools, Hiebert reports that when PBI began issuing degrees in 1980 and became Prairie Bible College in 1986, thereby expanding its course offerings to include liberal arts and social sciences, "word began to circulate among some of its radical right-wing alumni that Prairie was on the road to liberalism and eventual secularism" (61).[18]

This statement accurately reflects a development that can be traced in part to L.E. Maxwell's longstanding personal bias against the academic world which has already been referred to in this study. The rumor likely also stemmed from Maxwell's resistance to allowing any kind of outside influence or control to dictate the contents of Prairie's curriculum, a matter that will be documented in a later chapter of this book.[19]

3. *Focused Lives: Inspirational Life-Changing Lessons From Eight Effective Christian Leaders Who Finished Well*—by J. Robert Clinton; Altadena, CA: Barnabas Publishers, 1995. (E-book edition)

J. Robert Clinton is Professor of Leadership in the School of Intercultural Studies at Fuller Theological Seminary in Pasadena, California. The portion of his book devoted to the life of L.E. Maxwell is exclusively dependent on Stephen M. Spaulding's work identified in the last chapter which Clinton identifies as a "pre-doctoral dissertation." He considers Spaulding's effort

---

[18] J. Burtchaell, *The Dying of the Light: The Disengagement of Colleges and Universities from their Christian Churches* (Grand Rapids, MI: William B. Eerdmans Publishing Co., 1998).

[19] Although the scope of this book does not cover the 1980s at PBI nor was I living at Three Hills then, phone conversations with family members and periodic visits to Three Hills during those years frequently contained discussions related to how changes at PBI were being received by those associated with the school during the Maxwell era. As well, as one who has devoted significant time and resources to acquiring additional education since leaving Prairie, questions and comments from people at Prairie that I have known my entire life have often reflected certain presuppositions and occasional suspicions regarding the status of my orthodoxy as a result of acquiring such.

"... a relatively objective study which paints the picture "warts and all" and labels it "a Type 4 Chronological Interpretive Biographical presentation." (391: footnote 3)

Clinton reviews Maxwell's life according to a proprietary leadership grid that he has developed in his extensive writings on leadership and a series of what Clinton calls "macro-lessons."[20] He defines "macro-lessons" as:

> major lessons which seem to apply in many of the six leadership eras in the Bible. One such is the timing lesson. EFFECTIVE LEADERS ARE INCREASINGLY AWARE OF THE TIMING OF GOD'S INTERVENTIONS IN THEIR LIVES AND MINISTRY. THEY MOVE WHEN HE MOVES. THEY WAIT. THEY CONFIDENTLY EXPECT. (391: footnote 4)

Accordingly, numerous terms developed by Clinton such as "Divine Contact," "positive testing pattern," "double confirmation," "integrity check," "literary processing," and others are applied to the biographical details of Maxwell's life and leadership as supplied by Spaulding.

Since Clinton's work is largely dependent on Spaulding and focuses primarily on Maxwell's leadership style, it has limited usefulness for the purposes of my book. That being said, it should also be noted that Clinton's work suffers from the presence of editorial sloppiness and factual inaccuracies that reflect his personal unfamiliarity with Canada, Prairie Bible Institute and the backgrounds of certain of the school's leaders.[21]

---

[20] J. Robert Clinton, *The Making of a Leader: Recognizing the Lessons and Stages of Leadership Development* (Boulder, CO: NavPress, 1988); J. Robert Clinton, *Leadership Emergence Theory: A Self-Study Manual for Analyzing the Development of a Christian Leader* (Altadena, CA: Barnabas Publishers, 1989); J. Robert Clinton, *Leadership Perspective—How to Study the Bible for Leadership Insights* (Altadena, CA: Barnabas Publishers, 2006); J. Robert Clinton, *Conclusions on Leadership Style* (Altadena, CA: Barnabas Publishers, 1986); J. Robert Clinton, *A Short History of Leadership Theory* (Altadena, CA: Barnabas Publishers, 1986); etc.

[21] See, for example, p. 419 where he refers to "the McClean article" and then a few sentences later rightly identifies it as "Maclean's." On p. 422 he states that Maxwell "... selected young Ted Rendall as Vice-Principal and an ongoing leader. Rendall was a brilliant and loyal follower who had shown Maxwell the importance of a theological education. He had had sound Biblical training in the British seminary environment." In fact, not only is the British seminary virtually non-existent, but Rendall trained at the Bible Training Institute in Glasgow and the London Bible College before coming to PBI (see Chapter Nine, footnote 55). To be sure, Rendall established a sterling

D. Academic work partly devoted to Maxwell and/or PBI

I. *The Development of a Bible Belt*—by Donald A. Goertz; Master of Christian Studies thesis, Regent College, Vancouver, B.C., Canada; 1980

Written by a current Professor of Theology and History at Tyndale College and Seminary in Toronto, this thesis represents the first significant academic work to examine the phenomenon of L.E. Maxwell and Prairie Bible Institute. Placing L.E. Maxwell alongside the life of Alberta radio preacher turned politician, William Aberhart, Goertz concludes that, despite Aberhart's political prominence, Maxwell was the arbiter of the Alberta fundamentalist mainstream and the figure who developed "the theology and lifestyle which was to characterize Alberta for a generation" (iii).

As several references in these pages to Goertz's work have already indicated, it makes a number of important contributions to the fundamental premise of this book. From the outset of his thesis, Goertz clearly refers to Maxwell as a fundamentalist and to PBI as a center of fundamentalism.[22] He is nevertheless careful to portray the fundamentalism that prevailed at Three Hills in terms of its distinctive "blend of holiness and missions" that arose out of a firm commitment to orthodox theology (2). Similar to the work of Marsden, Carpenter and Enns, therefore, Goertz posits a broader definition of fundamentalism than does Stackhouse.

Although separatism of the first and second-order variety was as yet not clearly defined in the early 1930s, Goertz contends that the young Maxwell was "strongly separatist" in that "he rejected Aberhart's involvement in politics as an evil compromise" (2). Goertz offers the clearest reference of any source to the public exchanges of criticism that took place between Aberhart and Maxwell, two Alberta fundamentalists. This reality is somewhat prescient of

---

reputation in Canada as an avid reader and a disciplined self-learner with a keen mind, a fact recognized by Providence Theological Seminary in Manitoba, Canada, that awarded him the honorary Doctor of Divinity in the late 1980s.

[22] One of the significant differences between the timing of Goertz's research and that carried out by Stackhouse is that both J.F. Kirk and L.E. Maxwell were still alive and interviewed by Goertz at the time the latter researched and wrote his thesis whereas both Kirk and Maxwell had passed away by the time Stackhouse visited PBI in 1986.

the discord that would lead to the parting of the ways between fundamentalists and neo-evangelicals approximately a couple of decades later.

Goertz's work notes the prominent influx of American immigrants into the Canadian west, an estimated fifty thousand by 1901. He states that whereas these newcomers were proud of their new country, their "worldview remained that of their country of origin" (10), an important observation, it is suggested, in helping to understand L.E. Maxwell. In identifying the political populism that developed early in Alberta's history, Goertz comments that not only did it have a very powerful religious element, but he attributes populism's taking root to the large influx of American immigrants to the Canadian west. This population exodus from the American Midwest, he notes, was sufficient to alarm both American politicians as well as British nationalists, albeit for different reasons (25).

The warm reception given American politician William Jennings Bryan on his visit to Alberta in 1909 is given several pages by Goertz. He suggests the reasons for Bryan's popularity in the province were directly tied to the number of Americans in Alberta and the similarity of the political grievances fostered by Americans and the residents of Canada's West (26-29). He also calls attention to the social theory of American-born Henry Wise Wood and its significant effect on the United Farmers of Alberta that formed Alberta's government between 1921 and 1935.

The research in Goertz's thesis included a personal interview with L.E. Maxwell as well as ongoing written correspondence between the two. This led the former to record what is perhaps the most detailed account in print of the intense fear of death and hell that Maxwell acquired as a youth by virtue of his exposure to various "hell-fire" preachers of the fundamentalist persuasion. This aspect of Goertz's work offers an important insight into an essential component of Maxwell's theology that found ultimate expression in his passion for the missionary endeavor to "reach the lost" whom he believed were headed for everlasting torment without Christ. Goertz establishes this point in the revealing statement: "For Maxwell evangelism was carried out primarily by creating fear through preaching on hell" (196).

Maxwell's adherence to the concept of separation from all appearances of worldliness, Goertz points out, was something he picked up in his youth from the influence of Plymouth Brethren preacher and author, Dr. Walter Wilson. This indeed was the type of fundamentalist separation "from the world" so familiar to me while growing up at PBI. The prevailing assumption at Prairie was that the only prolonged contact one should have with unbelievers was for the specific purpose of attempting to convert them. People who belonged to "the world" were invariably viewed as ominous threats to devout Christian commitment and were therefore best avoided.[23]

In observations gleaned from a personal interview with J. Fergus Kirk, Goertz establishes that in Kirk's judgment, the one church that existed in Three Hills at the time of his arrival there around the time of World War I, "didn't preach the gospel." This congregation was associated with what would eventually become the United Church of Canada, a modernist denomination that Maxwell frequently inveighed against in *The Prairie Pastor*. Goertz's comments in this regard clearly confirm that both young men, Kirk and Maxwell alike, were clearly sympathetic to the American fundamentalist orientation and perspective at the time PBI was established.

Goertz's conviction that the early decades of PBI's history placed the school solidly in the camp of American fundamentalism is clearly evident in this excerpt from his fifth chapter:

Prairie Bible Institute was the first of the Alberta Bible schools and was responsible for setting much of the tone of the developing fundamentalist milieu. Here the theology was formed, the lifestyles cemented, and the workers trained. The resultant Prairie ethos was largely the result of L.E. Maxwell and Fergus Kirk. *In its teaching Three Hills made no attempt to adjust its message to the specific needs of society. There was one message, centered around an emphasis on man's sinfulness and God's salvation, and this they preached without compromise. Society and Christianity were at war and there would be no middle road. Because of this they became very strict moral and social isolationists, practicing a rigid separation from the world.* This type of theology seems to be more of an extension of the great American revivals of the late 1900s and the resultant premillennialism with its convictions about religious and social apostasy on the one hand,

---

[23] I recall several times in high school days pleading with my parents to be allowed to play on the various ice hockey teams in the town of Three Hills since, I argued, Three Hills was my hometown. As a member of PBI's board, of course, my father was well aware that such was against the school's policy. When I would persist, my father would reply that it had to do with the belief of the school's leaders that we were to be separate from "the world." This particular policy eventually changed after my years at Prairie High School (1970-74).

and extreme holiness on the other, than something developed in Canada. Maxwell, coming up from Kansas, brought this separatist theology with him and it stood in stark contrast to the traditional themes of a Christian Canada which dominated the Canadian church up to this point, including, to some extent, even William Aberhart. (119—*emphasis* added)

I have intentionally emphasized a portion of the above quotation to point out that Goertz accurately summarizes the essential spiritual environment that prevailed at Prairie during my years as a "staff kid" there. Again, to pick up on a point made by James Enns in the title of his paper identified earlier, PBI was only moderately less a hothouse of fundamentalism in the 1960s and 1970s than it was in its earlier years. True, as Stackhouse avers, the school may not have distinguished itself by regularly crossing swords with other believers or via a T.T. Shields-like preoccupation with modernism. Yet the fact that PBI in the Maxwell era became virtually a self-sustaining community is, at least in part, testimony to the militancy with which the notion of separation from the world was enforced.

Lest there be any doubt as to Goertz's assessment of L.E. Maxwell and Prairie Bible Institute as a thoroughly fundamentalist institution, his work includes a depiction of both J. Fergus Kirk and L.E. Maxwell as involved and promoting the very kind of militant opposition to modernity that Stackhouse wants to reserve strictly for T.T. Shields and the American fundamentalists. In describing the public acrimony that arose between PBI and William Aberhart in the early 1930s when the latter translated his theology into a form of populist politics, Goertz refers to Kirk's circulating a letter "in which he attacked Aberhart for turning to materialism, lawlessness and communism" (166). Kirk accused Aberhart of ". . . joining hands with the world against the evil day which we see straight ahead, instead of looking to the Lord alone . . ." (167)

Kirk and Maxwell were also outspoken in their criticisms of what they perceived to be Aberhart's attempts to preach a social gospel. Quoting extensively from Kirk's missives against Aberhart and Social Credit, Goertz portrays the founding president of PBI articulating invective against Social Credit's social gospel, socialist and outright communist ideas in a manner similar to that popularized by American fundamentalist Carl McIntire during the Cold War of the later 20th century.

Goertz concludes his very useful survey of PBI in its first twenty years by documenting the remarkable success of American radio evangelist, Oscar Lowry, whom Maxwell credited with putting "us back on the map" after PBI's public conflict with Aberhart had taken a toll on the school's finances and its popularity in Alberta. [24] It is instructive to note that it was an American affiliated with Moody Bible Institute and preaching "the old time gospel . . . on such subjects as "Hell and Who's Going There"" that Maxwell entrusted with PBI's radio ministry for a period of weeks in late 1938. The results, to quote Goertz, "were phenomenal."[25]

Referring to Lowry and other American radio evangelists who followed him on the airwaves, Goertz aptly summarizes his work by noting: "these men preached a similar type of fundamentalism as that of Maxwell" (228). The last paragraph of the thesis summarizes Alberta's fundamentalist movement by making reference to the theological orientation of the province's last Social Credit premier, Harry Strom, a devout fundamentalist.

2. *Studies of Eight Canadian Fundamentalists*—by David R. Elliott, PhD dissertation at University of British Columbia, Vancouver, B.C., Canada; 1989; 460 pp.

David Elliott, who works as a historian in the Canadian province of Ontario, carves a somewhat novel portrait of fundamentalism. Portraying it as a movement with roots firmly embedded in eighteenth and nineteenth century schismatic movements, he suggests it had "structural, intellectual, and behavioral similarities to earlier medieval heresies" (ii). He links the eight Canadians profiled in his work with earlier figures in Christianity who rejected ecclesiastical authority and promoted popular theologies that diverged from the creeds of the established Protestant churches. A.B. Simpson, P.W. Philpott, Aimie Semple McPherson, T.T. Shields, William

---

[24] David R. Elliott, "Studies of Eight Canadian Fundamentalists," 269: "That "holy war" adversely affected both sides of the dispute, but Prairie Bible Institute suffered the most; it lost two-thirds of its financial support because of its attack on Aberhart."

[25] Goertz, 218-219: "In six weeks Lowry received 5, 700 letters, 3,700 from Alberta, with the rest coming from the provinces of Saskatchewan, Manitoba and British Columbia. Donations surpassed 10,000 and there were over a thousand reported conversions. Maxwell devoted complete issues of the school's magazines solely to reprinting letters."

Aberhart, Clem Davies, L.E. Maxwell and Oswald J. Smith are identified as "radicals" who operated in an "intellectual underworld."

Elliott advances that a part of the "intellectual underworld" that impacted fundamentalism was the Keswick-holiness movement which he links to the ancient heresy of Manichaeism (a form of dualism).[26] As has already been affirmed in my book, the Keswick-holiness emphasis certainly had a dominant role at PBI in the period under review.[27] Accordingly, should one accept Elliott's convincing portrayal of the Keswick influence in fundamentalism, it is obvious that PBI in the Maxwell era definitely qualified as a fundamentalist institution. Elliott's argument at this point has significance since, as I experienced growing up at Prairie during the 1960s and 1970s, both the militancy motif that Marsden and Stackhouse emphasize in fundamentalism and the Keswick-holiness influence that Carpenter and Elliott identify in the movement were prominently visible in PBI's daily life.

Elliott's work is helpful for pointing out that L.E. Maxwell was ordained as a Southern Baptist minister. The work also clearly portrays the influence of the Catholic mystic, Madame Guyon, in Keswick-holiness thought. Guyon's occasionally bizarre musings often figured in the thinking and writings of L.E. Maxwell in the *Prairie Pastor* and *Born Crucified* (pub. 1945) era. A biography on Guyon's life was once a standard textbook used at Prairie High School.

Elliott's dissertation also contains a very candid assessment of the mental illness that dogged the life of Robert Pearsall Smith, Keswick evangelist and husband of Hannah Whitehall Smith, author of *The Christian's Secret of a Happy Life*. As noted previously in this study, Smith's well-known volume which advocates a pursuit of the "higher Christian life" and the "crucifixion of self" was very influential in the home in which J. Fergus Kirk was raised.

Elliott notes that Keswick-inspired hymns and gospel songs by such writers as Frances Ridley Havergal, Fanny Crosby, Philip Bliss and Ira Sankey were popularized in North America by Dwight L. Moody and Sankey, song leader for Moody's evangelistic services. Not only did the

---

[26] Elliott, 59, includes an informative diagram that traces fundamentalism's links with such ancient influences as Donatism, Gnosticism, Persian Dualism and Manichaeism.

[27] The archives in the PBI library contain hundreds of reel-to-reel tapes of PBI conference speakers during the mid-twentieth century. Among them are dozens of sermons by speakers who had Keswick connections such as Alan Redpath, Stanley Collins, etc.

songs of these writers become "standards" in many evangelical hymnbooks in North America throughout the twentieth century, they were staples in the spiritual environment that prevailed at PBI during the Maxwell era. Such songs were often used in services at PBI to enhance the very introspective task of crucifying another aspect of one's carnality in the pursuit of the victorious Christian life.

A significant value of Elliott's work for the purposes of this book is to note that his details regarding the primary emphases at PBI as "mystical spirituality" and "promotion of foreign missions" within the context of strict fundamentalism are decidedly accurate with respect to my experience at Prairie. In fact, it is perhaps necessary to acknowledge that a part of Elliott's perception of daily life at PBI was acquired by virtue of an interview he conducted with me while researching his "Eight Canadian Fundamentalists" dissertation back in 1986.[28]

In elaborating on the "mystical spirituality" and "promotion of foreign missions" that dominated life at PBI during the Maxwell era, Elliott accurately alludes to Maxwell's dependency on opinions published in American fundamentalist publications for his views on international affairs. As verified by my own research, Maxwell's personal files were amply filled with such and also dominated by news clippings and stories from standard American news publications such as *TIME* and *Newsweek*. It is apparent that Maxwell, as was the case with many Americans at PBI, was concerned to remain conversant with the perspectives of the U.S. media despite living most of his life in Canada.[29]

Elliott makes reference to Maxwell's frequent written bromides against Communism, Roman Catholicism and evolution, popular targets of American fundamentalists in the early and mid-twentieth century. He also rightly depicts Maxwell's pulpit presence particularly in his younger

---

[28] Elliott, 402, footnote 91.

[29] While growing up at PBI, I frequently scanned *U.S. News & World Report*, still a prominent American weekly news magazine. My father borrowed issues of the magazine from his good friend, Donald Crites, an American from Illinois, who served as PBI's Personnel Director from the mid-twentieth century until his retirement toward the end of that century. It was a well known fact that many of the Americans who served as PBI staff members followed U.S. politics/history very closely and often voted via absentee ballots on American election days. L.E. Maxwell remained an American citizen for the duration of his life as verified in a conversation I had with Paul T. Maxwell on August 18, 2008.

years as similar to the dramatic antics of the American fundamentalist evangelist, Billy Sunday.

In summary, Elliott's work faithfully captures the prominent themes of self-sacrifice, rigid discipline, mystical spirituality and foreign missions that prevailed at PBI during the L.E. Maxwell era. The connection he posits between ancient church heresies and the fundamentalist movement, although no doubt an annoyance to some, is nonetheless plausible. His portrayal of PBI as a solid fundamentalist institution during the Maxwell era, therefore, supports the broader understanding of the term "fundamentalist" that this book affirms.

3. *Training for Service: the Bible School Movement in Western Canada, 1909-1960*—by Bruce Guenther, PhD dissertation at McGill University, Montreal, Quebec, Canada, 2001; 423 pp.

Bruce Guenther, a Canadian Mennonite Brethren scholar, offers a valuable treatment of the vital role played by Bible schools in the unfolding of Protestant evangelicalism throughout western Canada during the first two-thirds of the twentieth century. Intended as a more multi-faceted explanation of Bible schools than previous efforts which depicted them as part of an American fundamentalist reaction to Protestant liberalism, Guenther effectively emphasizes the ethnic, theological and denominational concerns that motivated the establishment of the approximately one hundred Bible schools that existed in western Canada prior to 1960.

Guenther's work reflects the influence of John Stackhouse who stepped in to serve as the former's advisor following the unexpected death of the original supervisor who had been working with him (vii). Guenther briefly discusses PBI as one of four institutions he assigns to the transdenominational category. Taken as a whole, he asserts, the four organizations he surveys reflect the significant influence of fundamentalism within the transdenominational cluster of Bible schools "and its southward links to American fundamentalism" (299).

As with Stackhouse's work, Guenther acknowledges the significant number of American students that were a component of the student body at PBI beginning in the 1930s and reaching almost 40% in the 1940s.[30] He

---

[30] Stackhouse, *Canadian Evangelicalism in the Twentieth Century*, 84, 243.

points out that Prairie was the only Bible school in western Canada to have had such a significant proportion of non-Canadian students. In response to this reality, it should be noted that anyone conversant with the American nationalist psyche can readily appreciate that this fact alone would have helped distinguish PBI from other western Canadian Bible schools in terms of its American orientation.[31]

Guenther is unequivocal in stating that PBI "intentionally aligned itself with fundamentalism" (317, n. 70) but, in a manner similar to Stackhouse, tempers that judgment by noting that Maxwell openly affirmed his intention to maintain cordial relations with all evangelicals. Although he portrays Maxwell's affinity for the Keswick-holiness teaching and its emphasis on "the victorious Christian life" or "the deeper life" as emphases that kept Prairie from being militantly anti-modernist, he nonetheless does not shrink from describing the school as "a major part of a larger international fundamentalist network" and "a major influence in popularizing a particular fundamentalist ethos throughout Alberta and western Canada" (320-321).

It is difficult to read Guenther's treatment of PBI and the other transdenominational evangelical Bible schools in western Canada without noting again the significant overlap that exists between that specific designation and the original understanding of historic American fundamentalism.[32] If, as Stackhouse posits and Guenther appears to accept, militant anti-modernism is the primary factor that distinguishes American fundamentalism from Canadian transdenominational evangelicalism, I must maintain that at least with regard to Prairie Bible Institute, that line

---

[31] For example, American presidential elections always had a significant profile at PBI during my time at the school. Part of the reason for that was that the weekly "testimony meetings" that were a regular part of the PBI regimen were always held on Tuesday nights which coincided with American elections which are always held on the first Tuesday of every other November (every fourth November for presidential elections). Accordingly, U.S. students who testified on these dates often spoke openly of "the elections going on at home" and the importance of praying that "God's sovereign will would prevail in the results."

[32] See, for example, Guenther's treatment of Winnipeg Bible Institute (331) where in consecutive sentences he identifies that institution as both "a unique influence . . . that occasionally extended into the larger world of transdenominational evangelicalism in Canada" and "an important centre of fundamentalist influence."

of demarcation alone is not sufficient to exempt PBI from the camp of American fundamentalism.

As has already been noted and will be documented in this work, Maxwell's rhetoric at times was militantly anti-modernist. When that reality is combined with other attributes of American fundamentalism such as the missionary focus, holiness theology and revivalism, there are good reasons for challenging the assertion embraced by both Stackhouse and Guenther that Canadian transdenominational evangelicalism as typified by PBI was substantially different from or independent of American fundamentalism.

E. Other works that offer brief but helpful insights of Maxwell or PBI

Two other works deserve brief mention here. In both instances, although these publications are comparatively obscure and somewhat difficult to obtain, their perspectives shed important light on matters of relevance to this book.

Thine Hand Upon Me: He tells it like it was is a self-published memoir by the late David E. Enarson, a founding father of Trinity Western College (now University) in Langley, British Columbia, Canada. A graduate of Prairie Bible Institute, Enarson served as a pastor and Christian educator in a number of locations in western Canada including a term as a faculty member at PBI from 1952 to 1957. He then moved west to help launch Trinity Western (originally Trinity Junior College) where he labored for approximately the last twenty years of his career.

Enarson's story is of interest to this study because of its revelations about the thinking which prevailed at PBI throughout the 1950s and on into the 1960s. As has already been referred to in this book, PBI was resistant to accreditation and the offering of academic degrees until the last few years of the Maxwell era. Enarson's memoirs document that resistance and, in conjunction with several other works, helpfully illuminate several important factors in that regard which contribute to this study's fundamental thesis.

Several references have already been made in this book to a number of independent papers by Ian S. Rennie that make important contributions to understanding L.E. Maxwell and Prairie Bible Institute. Although three of these papers are in circulation among historians of Canadian evangelicalism, at least two of them—"The Doctrine of Man in the Bible Belt" and "Theological Education in Canada: Past and Present"—are simply identified as notes or transcripts from lectures given by Rennie during the mid-1970s. The third paper, "The Western Prairie Revival in Canada: During the Depression and World War II," appears to have been prepared for a more academic exercise since it contains endnotes.

Rennie's unpublished "papers" contain significant observations of L.E. Maxwell and PBI that represent one of the first assessments of the school to come from a Canadian evangelical perspective. As has already been seen, some of Rennie's observations with respect to Maxwell's fundamentalist identity are very helpful for the purposes of this study. The balance of this book will draw further on these insights. [33]

---

[33] I am indebted to Dr. John Stackhouse and Dr. Bruce Guenther for their assistance in locating these now somewhat obscure papers.

CHAPTER SIX

American influence
in Canadian history (Part I)

It is my judgment that Stackhouse's inaccurate portrayal of PBI in *Canadian Evangelicalism in the Twentieth Century* is due in part to an inadequate consideration of the ubiquitous American influence in Canadian history in general. While the important research of Canadian church history scholars such as William Westfall and Michael Gauvreau effectively profiles the domestic and British aspects of the development of Christianity in Canada, the influence of various Americans in the religious life of "the true north, strong and free" is very capably explored by Canadian scholars like George A. Rawlyk and Eric R. Crouse.[1] To neglect or minimize the latter reality that goes back to the earliest days of Canada's emerging identity, as Stackhouse appears to do, introduces the risk of promoting certain faulty conclusions regarding Canadian church history.

This part of the book thus paints an essential background against which to interpret the perspective advanced herein concerning the significant American influence on Prairie Bible Institute during the L.E. Maxwell era. This chapter and the one following demonstrate that this work's fundamental thesis requires at least some familiarity with the conspicuous

---

[1] William Westfall. *Two Worlds: The Protestant Culture of Nineteenth Century Ontario* (Kingston and Montreal: Queen's-McGill University Press, 1989). Chapters 2-3 detailing the rivalry between Anglican John Strachan and Methodist Egerton Ryerson and Methodism's displacement of Anglicanism as the new national church of Protestant Canada are particularly engaging and informative.

Michael Gauvreau, "History and Faith: A Study of Methodist and Presbyterian Thought in Canada 1820-1940," (PhD dissertation, University of Toronto, 1985); see for example, 152-158, where Gauvreau discusses the impact the 1860 publication in Britain of Essays and Reviews had on evangelical Presbyterians and Methodists in Canada.

Books by Rawlyk and Crouse are considered in Chapter Seven of this book.

Canada's national anthem, *O Canada*, refers to Canada as "the true north, strong and free."

American influence that has always been a reality in Canadian history in general and, specifically, with respect to Canada's religious scene. Of particular import, it calls attention to the strong American effect that has been present in western Canada from the earliest days of the region's settlement.[2]

In using the word "influence" to describe the relationship of the United States with its northern neighbor, the attention of readers is directed to the impact of specific individuals and movements from south of the international border whose thinking or behavior strategically affected or altered the way Canadians thought about and pursued life in general and their practice of the Christian faith in particular. Further, as the United States became an increasingly prominent player on the cultural, military, economic and political stages of the world, this book assumes its geographical proximity to Canada has had, in turn, a significant effect on the behavior and thinking of Canadians in all areas of life. Whether or not Canadians have always been consciously aware of this dynamic is beside the point.

This book affirms a stronger connection between a Canadian religious institution, Prairie Bible Institute, and American fundamentalism than has been documented to date. It would be a major error however, for readers to conclude that such an argument in any way implies that Canadian culture, religious or otherwise, is a mere microcosm of the cultural realities that prevail in the United States of America.[3] In many instances, this

---

[2] G.A. Rawlyk, *Revolution Rejected 1775-1776* (Scarborough, ON: Prentice-Hall of Canada Ltd, 1968). Rawlyk insightfully discusses why Nova Scotia and Quebec refused to join the American Revolution in 1775-76. He points out the significant number of New Englanders living in these regions at the time of the revolution and their influence in all three options that surfaced at the time for embryonic Canada: 1) resist revolution; 2) remain neutral, 3) join the revolution. In so doing, Rawlyk affirms the reality of American influence in Canada from at least the point of the American Revolution on. His work solidly reflects the consensus of other historians who affirm the substantial American influence in Canada from the latter's earliest days.

[3] *Maclean's* (special double issue) 121, nos. 26 & 27, (July 7 & 14, 2008), devoted a Special Canada Day Report to the topic of Canadians vs. Americans: The Startling Facts. The lead article by Duncan Hood, "How Canada Stole the American Dream" underscores Canadians' perennial interest (some might call it a persistent paranoia) in comparing ourselves to our American neighbors (51-52):

"To be an American is to be the best. Every American believes this. Their sports champions are not U.S. champions, they're world champions. Their corporations aren't the largest in the States, they're the largest on the planet. Their armies don't defend just America, they defend freedom.

is assuredly not the case as it relates to Canadian society in general or with specific regard to Canadian religious life.[4] Let there thus be no equivocation on the matter: there always have been and indeed, continue to be, many significant differences between Canadian and American societies including

"Like the perpetual little brother, Canadians have always lived in the shadow of our American neighbors. We mock them for their uncultured ways, their brash talk and their insularity, but it's always been the thin laughter of the insecure. After all, says University of Lethbridge sociologist Reginald Bibby, a leading tracker of social trends, "Americans grow up with the sincere belief that their nation is a nation that is unique and special, literally called by something greater to be blessed and to be a blessing to people around the globe." Canadians can't compete with that . . ."

[4] Among the more relevant differences outlined in the *Maclean's* feature are:

"Americans have almost twice as many marriages per 1,000 unmarried women each year as Canada does, and far fewer couples living in sin. In Canada, an amazing 18.4 per cent of all couples are now "cohabiters," whereas in the U.S., the figure is 7.6 per cent. Even when we do marry, we put it off for as long as we can. Here, the average age of first marriage is 28.5 for women and 30.6 for men. In the U.S., the ages are much younger, 25.1 and 26.7 respectively. So why are we so reluctant to get that little piece of paper? There are three reasons: we're less traditional, less religious, and we have Quebec. Quebec, it turns out, leads not just Canada but the world in common-law couplings. There, a whopping 35 per cent of couples cohabit rather than marry. Family experts say that after the Quiet Revolution in the 1960s when the Church lost much of its influence in the province, religion—and marriage—simply ceased to matter . . . Montrealer Benoit Laplante, the director of demography programs at the Institut national de la recherché scientifique, says Quebecers don't marry because ". . . When people decided to leave religion out, they began to disregard it in anything they did."" (Barbara Righton; 55)

Per cent who say that religion is very important to them: Canada 28, U.S. 60 (55, citing "Worlds Apart: Religion in Canada, Britain and U.S.;" Gallup)

There are 30 guns per every 100 people in Canada . . . The U.S—the world's most heavily armed society—has 90 guns per every 100 people. As a result, in Canada firearms only account for one-third of homicides, while more than two-thirds of American murders involve guns . . . The Canadian Centre for Justice Statistics, using data from 2000, neatly sums up the difference: "the U.S. has much higher rates of violent crime, while Canada generally has much higher rates of property crime." (Ken MacQueen; 58)

Lifetime number of sex partners reported by men: Canada 23, U.S. 13; by women: Canada 10, U.S. 9; number of teen pregnancies per 100,000 teen females: Canada 3,050, U.S. 7,200; number of teen girls with Chlamydia per 100,00 population: Canada 1,367, U.S. 2,863 (p. 60 citing 2007.08 Durex Sexual Wellbeing Global Survey, conducted by Harris Interactive; Statistics Canada and the U.S. National Center for Health Statistics; Public Health Agency of Canada, U.S. Centers for Disease Control)

notable distinctions between the geographical neighbors' religious cultures.[5] In no way is this book an effort to minimize this complex reality. Indeed, it readily affirms the existence of many such distinguishing characteristics.[6]

On a related point, it should also be noted that the point under discussion is not intended to insinuate in any way whatsoever that the relationship between the United States and Canada is or ever was primarily one-directional. Just as surely as noting the significant manner in which the U.S. has influenced Canada, there is ample evidence that such influence has flowed north to south as well. For example, as it relates to the general topic of this book, David R. Elliott has capably documented the impact of various Canadian fundamentalists such as A.B. Simpson, W.H. Griffith Thomas,

---

[5]   Nigel Hannaford, "If U.S. can ask leaders what they believe, why not Canada?" *Calgary Herald*, A16, August 19, 2008. Following a prominent American pastor's interview with both U.S. 2008 presidential candidates at an evangelical mega-church in suburban Los Angeles, Hannaford, a Canadian newspaper columnist wrote: "Pity we're not likely to get that kind of a discussion this side of the border. For, while separation of church and state is a fine thing, politicians will continue to bring their faith, or its lack, to politics . . . surely Canadians have no less an interest in understanding how their leaders think, than do the Americans . . . Yet, Canadians let their politicians off this incredibly important hook. Instead, faith is treated as something intensely private, about which it is indelicate to ask."

   Helpful general treatments of Canadian religious life include:

   Pierre Berton, *The Comfortable Pew*, (Philadelphia: J.B. Lippincott, 1965); Reginald W. Bibby, *Fragmented Gods: the Poverty and Potential of Religion in Canada* (Toronto: Irwin Publishing, 1987); Reginald W. Bibby, *Unknown Gods: The Ongoing Story of Religion in Canada* (Toronto: Stoddart Publishing, 1993); Reginald W. Bibby, *Restless Gods: The Renaissance of Religion in Canada* (Toronto: Stoddart Publishing, 2002); Mark A. Noll, *What Happened to Christian Canada?* (Vancouver: Regent College Publishing, 2007), see particularly pp.7-19.

[6]   The *Maclean's* feature underscores that many Americans tend to minimize differences between the new nations. They view Canada primarily in terms of how the comparison relates to their frame of reference which is comparatively Ameri-centric. The feature quotes Eric Nay who moved to Toronto from California, 54: ""Left-wing urban Americans," he says. "Canada is just a country of left-wing urban Americans," and "an airport limo driver in Los Angeles, 59, to the effect: ""We're really not much different," he said. "You folks are just disarmed Americans."" Nonetheless, the *Maclean's* feature capably identifies some of the key differences between the two cultures.

P.W. Philpott, Aimee Semple McPherson, T.T. Shields, and Oswald J. Smith on American religious life.[7]

Most Canadians, nonetheless, are familiar with the legendary notion that since the American elephant and the Canadian mouse sleep in a common geographical bed, when the elephant rolls over, the mouse is invariably affected.[8] The simple reality that the population of the United States has consistently been approximately ten times larger than that of Canada is but one helpful fact in grasping the inevitable spillover effect that life

---

Seymour Martin Lipset, *Continental Divide: The Values and Institutions of United States and Canada* (New York: Routledge, 1990), 8: "My central argument is that the two countries differ in their basic organizing principles. Canada has been and is a more class-aware, elitist, law-abiding, statist, collectivity-oriented, and particularistic (group-oriented) society than the United States ... the United States remained throughout the 19th and early 20th centuries the extreme example of a classically liberal or Lockean society, one that rejected the assumptions of the alliance of throne and altar, of ascriptive elitism, of mercantilism, of noblesse oblige, of communitarianism."

Michael Adams, *Fire & Ice: The United States, Canada and the Myth of Converging Values* (Toronto: Penguin Canada, 2009), xxii: "The central claim of *Fire and Ice* is not that Canadians and Americans are the most irreconcilably dissimilar groups of people on earth; it is simply that we are different and in many ways becoming more so, and that our respective values are part of that picture. In essence, what I see as these countries mature is an America that is becoming more American and a Canada that is becoming more Canadian."

[7] David R. Elliott, "Knowing No Borders: Canadian Contributions to American Fundamentalism," 349-374, in George A. Rawlyk and Mark A. Noll (eds.) *Amazing Grace: Evangelicalism in Australia, Britain, Canada and the United States* (Grand Rapids, MI: Baker Books, 1993).

[8] Editorial, *Winnipeg Free Press*, July 19, 2007, attributes the origin of this metaphor to former Canadian Prime Minister, Pierre E. Trudeau, who held that office for all but a few months during June 1968-June 1984.

Editorial, *Calgary Herald*, February 11, 1909, celebrating the 100th anniversary of the birth of American president Abraham Lincoln is a good example of how Canadians have perceived American history to profoundly impact their own. The editorial, reprinted in the *Herald's* February 9, 2009, edition to remember the 200th anniversary of Lincoln's birth stated, A8: "The United States owe much to Lincoln—more than to any other one man. So does Canada. When Lincoln struggled for the right of all men to liberty the principle was hardly established in this country. Canada was in a very plastic state and its future was immediately influenced by Lincoln's victory. Democracy was on trial and who can say to what extent the course of this new country was affected by the fortunate result of the contest to the south of it?"

James Travers, "Obama makes Americans of us all," *Toronto Star*, February 19, 2009, A6.

in the United States has always had on Canadian society.[9] The immediate access most Canadians have to American culture as propagated in movies, television, radio and other media is another major source of American influence in Canadian daily life.[10]

Observations drawn from general histories of Canada

A basic premise that is quickly encountered when consulting works that offer a general history of Canada concerns the inescapable differences in thought and deed that led to the formation of Canada as compared to that which prevailed in the founding of the United States of America. In order to fully appreciate the argument being developed here, it is imperative to grasp a fundamental difference between the orientations of the two peoples that surfaced early in their respective histories.

The citizens of the United States take great pride in the Declaration of Independence from British rule that formally established that nation on July 4, 1776. Theirs is a republic born of an intense desire for a freedom they believed could only be achieved by seeking independence from what Americans had come to view as the oppressive regime of Great Britain's King George III.

Comparatively speaking, Canadians have always demonstrated a more loyal if somewhat dependent frame of mind towards Britain, a truth reflected

---

[9] At a conference I attended in June 2008 at Princeton University in Princeton, New Jersey, I enjoyed several conversations with various Americans regarding the amount of international trade that exists between Canada and the U.S. (each is the other's primary trading partner). Those discussions confirmed impressions gained while attending seminary in the U.S. from 1981-1984 that many, if not most, Americans essentially view Canada as a 51st state and do not consider us to be as "foreign" as countries like China, Germany or South Africa.

[10] Joe Volpe, M.P., "New Year, New Leaf, New Agenda: Why the American Presidential Race Should Take Second Place," January 10, 2008, 1: "So the New Year begins with our "National Newspapers" and "National Media" replete with stories about the American presidential primaries. I know there is merit to staying current with "what is going on in our neighbor's backyard" but surely it makes sense for our national institutions (of which the press and media are a part) to focus on matters in and over which their readers and viewers could possibly have some influence? . . . Not surprisingly, but unhappily, the American elephant occupies a large space in our daily (government) lives." (Public mail-out received January 15, 2008, from a Liberal member of the Canadian Parliament.)

in the historical realities surrounding the establishment of the Dominion of Canada on July 1, 1867. Whereas Americans chose to go to war in order to reject their British heritage, early Canadians and particularly the United Empire Loyalists who made up a significant percentage of those early Canadians, chose to retain and embrace their British ties.[11] Works such as Brown's *The Illustrated History of Canada* consistently advance the comparative deference and loyalty to the British Empire typical of the major figures in pre-confederation Canadian society, the specific Fathers of Confederation and the majority of Canadians since confederation.[12]

Stated in whatever terminology one chooses, the important consideration to note here is that in comparison to the strong spirit of independence so clearly demonstrated by our American neighbors, Canada opted for a more dependent association with the British. It was a conscious decision that Canadians initially made at the time of the American Revolution in 1776. Arguably, it is a decision Canadians have made several times since, perhaps most notably at the time of the War of 1812.

Craig Brown (ed.)

A collection of essays under the title *The Illustrated History of Canada* illustrates the deferential element of the emerging Canadian psyche by highlighting the dominant roles and influences the Anglican (Church of England) church enjoyed in Canadian life as compared to the numerous expressions of Protestantism that prospered in the U.S.[13] This reality contributed to

---

[11] United Empire Loyalist was the term given those who moved north to Canada from the emerging United States of America as a result of looming and eventual American independence from Britain.

[12] Craig Brown, (ed.). *The Illustrated History of Canada* (Toronto: Lester Publishing, 1991), x: "There was little thought of independence, of emulating the American colonies of 1776. The goal of the Confederationists was, rather, to achieve self-sufficiency within the British Empire. That meant expanding self-government to a widening range of responsibilities, transforming the imperial relationship into what Macdonald called a "healthy and cordial alliance.""

[13] Ibid., 216, referring to the aftermath of the American-British North America War of 1812, Graeme Wynn observes: "Rising numbers of Methodists and Baptists in the pioneer communities of Upper Canada were considered an American threat to the Church of England."

various differences between the assumptions that prevailed in Canadian society versus the philosophy of life that held sway in the United States.[14]

The emerging northern nation's preference for its own way of life over that unfolding in the U.S. is particularly evident in Peter Waite's discussion. He notes the haste with which confederation talks in Canada accelerated when word spread that influential Yankees were of the opinion that a U.S. takeover of Canada would constitute appropriate compensation for their belief that a British conspiracy with the Confederate Army had prolonged the American Civil War by a year or two at great expense to the Americans.[15]

In the early twentieth century, Canadian nationalism and loyalty to Britain spawned firm resistance to the possibility of American annexation of Canada's western provinces. In fact, the preference of westerners to remain within Canadian confederation was a contributing factor to the results of the 1911 federal election that saw Prime Minister Wilfred Laurier's Liberal government lose decisively to Robert Borden's Conservatives.[16]

---

[14] Brown, 275: "Yet the belief in an individualistic, egalitarian way of life was never as pervasive in British North America as it was to the south. In an increasingly introverted French-Canadian society, family ties, the parish, and the close-knit settlements of the lowlands heightened a sense of community. Obligations and respect were due the priest and *seigneur*. Retrospection and an attachment to traditional institutions were strong . . . Loyalty was the cornerstone of English-speaking conservatism in British North America, and provincial conceptions of that term encompassed not only allegiance to the British Crown but also general approval of the established church, British liberties, and English imperialism—all of which, contemporary British North Americans hoped, would make their manners, politics, and social arrangements "different from, and superior to" those of the United States."

[15] Ibid., 321f. A Confederate ship named *Alabama* was built in Liverpool ostensibly as a merchant ship although the Yankees were suspicious that it looked quite warlike. After being finally outfitted in France, the *Alabama* in fact began a murderous two-year rampage against the North before it was finally sunk. "The American State Department, and American newspapers argued that the *Alabama* had prolonged the Civil War by two years; because the war had cost the American government $2 billion a year, indirect claims against Great Britain added up to 2 x $2 billion, or $4 billion. Yours sincerely! A nice way of settling this bill, the Americans intimated not too delicately, could be British North America."

[16] 405-406: "As events proved, the new trade agreement, while welcomed in some parts of the West, was not the winning issue that Laurier had expected. The Conservatives played upon the fears aroused in the country's industrialized areas that the agreement was only a beginning. Once implemented, it would so alter the east-west pattern of

Why is it important to identify a significant difference between American (independent) and Canadian (dependent) thinking in an effort to introduce American influence in Canada? The important dynamic to be noted here by calling attention to the early Canadian preference for the British way of life is to highlight storied Canadian deference to established authority within the context of a rapidly and simultaneously developing strong American identity. Although the people of early Canada consistently opted for political loyalty to Britain by virtue of their deferential mindset, they were nevertheless geographically situated beside a more populous nation that was rapidly crafting an established authority of its own.[17]

---

trade that free trade in manufactured goods would be the next necessary step, and that would mean flooding the Canadian market with cheap American goods, the destruction of local industries, rising unemployment, and perhaps even annexation to the United States . . . aided by the indiscretions of a few American politicians who spoke openly about the prospects of annexation, so that the Liberals found it increasingly difficult to focus on trade rather than loyalty."

[17] Most Canadians are conversant with the debate regarding the existence of a Canadian deference as it has been advanced by some and questioned by others with regard to our national psyche. See, for example:

Patrick Boyer, *The People's Mandate, Referendums and a More Democratic Canada* (Toronto: Dundurn Press, 1992), 112: "Canada has remained a timid democracy. The establishment that has run our country has proceeded comfortably—not always in the interests of the people, nor indeed of the country itself—supported by Canadians' deference to authority and a strange willingness to be passive spectators in our own land. We have become what anthropologists call 'participant observers.'"

Michael Adams, *Sex in the Snow: Canadian Social Values at the End of the Millennium* (Toronto: Viking, 1997), 9: "Over the past three decades, the Canadian personality has evolved from one that could be described as shy and mostly deferential to one that is characterized by a more autonomous and ironic individualism." Also, pp. 162-3:" As countless commentators—most prominently the eminent sociologist Seymour Martin Lipset—have pointed out, historically, Canadians have been much more deferential to institutional authority than was the case among Americans. However, in the space of a single generation, Canadians have, for better or worse, by necessity and by choice, become much less deferential. On many registers we are now even more critical of institutional authority and of our elites than Americans are of theirs. Canadians can be likened to children on the last day of school, running and squealing in the schoolyard, free at last from the rules and discipline imposed by tradition. A nation of "repressed hedonists" . . . has decided that "peace, order and good government" is not enough, and, like citizens around the world, we want some of the "life, liberty and happiness promised in America's founding declaration.

This combination of the deferential mindset of a significantly smaller population co-existing alongside the much larger, independent American economic and political clout as it rapidly materialized created an important dynamic: the inevitability of ongoing American influence which indeed has long been present in the Canadian ethos. It is not unreasonable to therefore suggest that over time, whether consciously or unconsciously, at least some Canadians began to transfer their deferential mindset from far-off England to the expanding American cultural behemoth next door. Although this transfer of deference from Great Britain to the United States has never been sufficient to prompt Canadians to join the United States or adapt its political model, it has contributed to opening wide the channels of American influence into virtually every sphere of Canadian life.

J.M.S. Careless

J.M.S. Careless, the late distinguished professor of history at the University of Toronto, in a work entitled *Canada: A Story of Challenge*, summarizes the surprising emergence of Canada as a viable national entity. This occurred despite the fact that 80 per cent of the population of the world's second largest country lives in close proximity to the American border.

An aspect of the Careless study that proves particularly useful in helping explain the rapid growth of Prairie Bible Institute derives from his observations concerning the topographical realities of North America.[18] Since such natural dividers as the Rocky Mountains, the Great Central Plains and the Pre-Cambrian Shield cover North America in a north-south direction, it stands to reason that the prairie provinces of Canada where PBI is located were exposed to both the benefits and the challenges of what Careless calls "sectionalism."

---

[18] J.M.S. Careless, *CANADA: A story of challenge* (Toronto: Macmillan of Canada, 1970), 8: "Furthermore, because the lines of geographic division that mark off the regions of Canada tend to run north and south across the continent, and because so much of the Canadian population lies near the American boundary line, Canadians in one section have often had easier contacts with the neighboring American region to the south than with the other parts of Canada that lie east or west. Hence the 'north-south pull,' heightening sectionalism, has played a significant role throughout Canadian history."

That is, due to being located on the prairie of south-central Alberta, the residents of Alberta, including PBI, had more in common with their American neighbors on the prairies to the south and east than they did with their fellow Canadians to the west since the Rocky Mountain range forms a natural barrier to British Columbia. As even a cursory survey of a topographical map of North America immediately indicates, the population in the grain-growing Canadian provinces of Alberta, Saskatchewan and Manitoba have more in common with respect to vocation and weather with grain-growers in the states of North and South Dakota, Nebraska, Kansas and Iowa than it does with Canadians in the heavily forested provinces of British Columbia or (northwest) Ontario.[19] Similarly, parts of Alberta and Saskatchewan are naturally linked to the states of Montana, Wyoming and Colorado by virtue of sub-surface similarities that yield a vibrant hydrocarbons industry.[20]

By calling attention to these topographical realities, Careless enables us to better understand why it would have literally been natural for certain American influences to come into play at PBI. For example, as noted previously, the number of American students and faculty at Prairie during the Maxwell era was always considerable.[21] This would have been for reasons similar to why L.E. Maxwell fit in so well with the agricultural folk at Three Hills. He had been born and raised in Kansas where grain-growing dominated rural life in much the same way it did in rural Alberta.[22] It is thus not difficult to see why prospective students from America's

---

[19] See the discussion in Chapter Seven of this book regarding what Canadian sociologist, Harry H. Hiller, refers to as "continentalism."

[20] Archie McLean, "Border no barrier to many issues," *Calgary Herald*, A4, July 1, 2008: "They may not know anything about equalization payments or funding public medicine, but when it comes to energy, water and wildlife, the western U.S. governors share many issues with Alberta and other western provinces. "Geography defines the relationship," Wyoming Gov. Dave Freudenthal said Monday. "And history defines the relationship in that the economies are much more interrelated. The economy of Wyoming is more related and more typical of the western provinces of Canada than we are the state of New York . . ." . . . Alberta Sustainable Resource Development Minister Ted Morton—who grew up in Wyoming and is attending the meeting with Premier Ed Stelmach—said . . . "I send my mother copies of [the Edmonton Journal] and [the Calgary Herald] occasionally, or she comes up and looks at them and says, 'this looks like Wyoming.'"

[21] See Appendix I of this book.

[22] See Chapter One of this book.

"breadbasket" would have concluded they could better relate to the rural if international setting of PBI than to the inner-city, urban world of Moody Bible Institute in Chicago or the Bible Institute of Los Angeles in that city, even though Chicago and Los Angeles were located in their home country, the United States of America.[23]

Careless also emphasizes the deference to established authority that typified early Canadian society. In particular, he identifies the significant control the Roman Catholic Church exercised from the earliest days in French Canada.[24] In religious matters, the French component of early

---

23 Sam Reimer, *Evangelicals and the Continental Divide* (Montreal-Kingston: McGill-Queen's Univ. Press, 2003) is an excellent resource that presents Reimer's findings while doing PhD research regarding the similarities and differences among evangelicals in Manitoba and New Brunswick, two Canadian provinces, and evangelicals in Minnesota and Mississippi, two American states. His research identifies surprising uniformity among evangelicals both north and south of the international border. Although Reimer's use of the term "continental divide" in the title of his research is understandable and politically accurate, it also generates some misleading expectations since the term "continental divide" traditionally designates several North American geographical divisions that run north and south, whereas his "continental divide," namely the international border, traverses the continent in an east-west direction. Thus, one could mistakenly assume that Reimer's work traces the kind of north-south "sectionalism" that Careless identifies in his work which he attributes to the topographical constitution of the North American continent. Having been born and raised in Western Canada, where one of these geographical "continental divides" forms part of the provincial boundary between Alberta and British Columbia, my earliest recollections from elementary school of the term "continental divide" is a reference to The Great Divide, the name given to that portion of the North American mountainous ridge running more or less north and south that demarcates the watersheds that drain into the Pacific Ocean (to the west) from those that drain into the Arctic Ocean (to the north) and those that drain into the Atlantic Ocean (to the east). Due to the geographic definition of the term "continental divide" as it relates to North America, I therefore initially concluded Reimer's work was tracing evangelical beliefs in Careless's north-south "sectional" sense as opposed to north or south of the 49th parallel which, as mentioned above, runs in an east-west direction.

24 Careless, 64-66: "Furthermore, while New France was being built in the seventeenth century . . . Its Catholicism was more devout and the power of the Church greater than in Old France. Thanks both to the energy and determination of the religious leaders, and to their early hold in New France, the Church came to occupy a place of great authority in the colony. Much of that authority was unquestioned . . . The Church, moreover, carefully censored thought and reading for layman, and no newspapers or other organs of public opinion developed. Once more this air of quiet and obedience

Canadians (generally speaking, Lower Canada/Quebec) were loyal to the established Catholic authority.[25] In that part of early Canada where the British settled (generally speaking, Upper Canada/Ontario), the Anglican Church, although sometimes outnumbered in size by other forms of Protestantism, assumed similar privilege to the point where one-seventh of crown lands were held in reserve for the support of the clergy, usually the ministers of the Church of England.[26]

---

to authority was very different from the free and lively mental climate of the English colonies to the south."

[25] Careless, 59-68: "Yet in matters of religion, government, and relations between classes of people, French Canada readily accepted direction from above. There was little of the demand for religious independence and self-government, or the leveling of social distinctions which generally marked the English colonies to the south . . . while New France was being built in the seventeenth century, a high tide of religious enthusiasm was running in the Catholic Church. Devoted priests, nuns and missionaries came to Canada and entered into the task of shaping New France. They left their mark on the colony. Its Catholicism was more devout and the power of the Church greater than in Old France. Thanks both to the energy and determination of the religious leaders, and to their early hold in New France, the Church came to occupy a place of great authority in the colony. Much of that authority was unquestioned . . . There was no secular education, no attempt to inquire into and certainly no attempt to criticize the authority of Church teachings. The Church, moreover, carefully censored thought and reading for laymen, and no newspapers or other organs of public opinion developed. Once more this air of quiet and obedience to authority was very different from the free and lively mental climate of the English colonies to the south. The ordinary Canadian habitant was cheerfully uninformed, though simply, straightforward, and contented."

[26] Ibid., 170: "The Anglican church, as the established church in England, had claimed that it was also the official church in Canada, and its ministers the Protestant clergy named in the Act."

120: "In further attempts to strengthen authority and to waken the 'popular' element, the Constitutional Act [1791] also envisaged setting up a colonial aristocracy and an established church. The former scheme was never carried out—the thought of backwoods dukes pitching hay was too much—but the latter was effected in the provision for clergy reserves. In either province, so the Act ran, an amount equal to one-seventh of the public, or crown, lands granted, should be reserved in order to create a fund for the support of 'a Protestant clergy.' This for some years was taken to mean the clergy of the state Church of England. Through this clause, and later additions, the Anglican church became a powerful state-endowed body in Canada, where it worked on the side of the governors and the conservative ruling groups against any radical tendencies among the mass of the colonists."

Again, of particular relevance here is to stress that one way of interpreting the religious deference present in the thinking of the early settlers in embryonic Canada is to assert that, historically speaking, Canadians are a people more easily led or influenced by others as compared to their American neighbors. Since the American democratic experiment was formally already a quarter century old when the nineteenth century opened, that nation was in full expansionist mode. In fact, Careless indicates this is precisely what happened as the nineteenth century unfolded on the western frontier of what in 1867 became the nation of Canada: many Canadian settlers were attracted to the message and the style of American circuit-riding preachers.[27] It is not at all unreasonable therefore to suggest that the deference originally granted by Canadians to religious authorities from the Old World over time began to be transferred by at least some Canadians to emerging religious influences and personalities that originated in the United States.

As they relate to the fundamental thesis of this book, Careless's comments with regard to the rapid population influx that occurred on the Canadian prairies in the early decades of the twentieth century are also important. He points out that a significant portion of the approximately one million immigrants who came to western Canada around 1905, the year Alberta became a new Canadian province, came from the U.S. as either new immigrants or returning Canadians. Accordingly, both groups would have brought at least some important elements of American identity and/or influence with them.[28]

---

[27] Careless, 161: "The preacher was a most important figure on the frontier. His regular visits supplied almost the only release from the monotonous toiling round of daily life, and so it is small wonder that religious services among the pioneers were emotional in the extreme. The services held in the little log churches build for traveling ministers, or in great 'camp meetings' under the trees were religious revivals, popular holidays, and exciting public festivals all rolled in one. As a result, the more formal and restrained Church of England, which claimed religious control in the principal English-speaking colonies, was not widely popular on the frontier. Indeed, its clergy tended to stay among the officials and well-to-do merchants in the towns and left the back-country to Presbyterian, Methodist and Baptist ministers. The Methodist 'circuit-riders,' in particular, who were often from the United States, built up the power of Methodism among the pioneers of British North America."

[28] Ibid., 305: "Altogether, about a million new inhabitants went to the prairies and British Columbia in the peak period, 1901 to 1911. Probably the majority were [returning] Canadians and Americans, and the rest British and continental Europeans in about equal numbers."

Careless indicates it was not uncommon for such disagreements as the dispute over the Alaska-Canada border in 1903 to periodically surface as the younger nation sought to establish its own sovereign identity. Nonetheless, "the plain fact was that Canadians and Americans got on well together and the Canadian way of life was closely tied to the American."[29] Because the latter was more formally developed than the former, at least some of the easily-led Canadians would have been susceptible to the influence of American newcomers.

Desmond Morton

Desmond Morton in *A Short History of Canada* makes several contributions to the argument being advanced in my book. Morton is particularly helpful in those sections of his work that describe the nature of a struggling Canadian cultural identity that began to emerge in the 1920s and 1930s.[30] To be succinct: it was profoundly impacted by its American neighbors.

Morton shows that the 1920s, the decade in which Prairie Bible Institute was established, is of particular significance to properly understanding the development of Canada since it was the first decade in which North Americans were exposed to mass-produced culture. Not surprisingly, the vast majority of that mass-produced culture emanated from the United States.[31] Canadians were therefore introduced to both the nefarious

---

[29] Careless, 321.

[30] Desmond Morton, *A Short History of Canada* (Edmonton, AB: Hurtig Publishers Ltd., 1983). The section of the book in view here begins with the following quote on 168 and runs through to 187: "The twenties brought American investment and American markets, and these would make Canada a north-south nation once again . . . Almost every development of the twenties contradicted national unity. Ottawa had always managed railways; roads had been left under provincial control as unimportant. Now they mattered. The expansion of secondary education and new allowances for widows, the blind and the disabled were paid for from provincial coffers. Sir John A. Macdonald had planned an east-west country; now the branch-plant factories, the mineral exploration, the floods of American films, magazines, and radio programs were switching Canada to a north-south axis."

By "north-south" Morton is referring to what Careless calls "sectionalism," the notion of the natural affinities of North Americans owing to the topographical north-south character of the continent.

[31] G.A. Rawlyk, *Champions of the Truth: Fundamentalism, Modernism, and the Maritime Baptists* (Montreal/Kingston: McGill-Queen's Univ. Press, 1990), 73, 74: "Most Maritime

elements of American culture such as the Ku Klux Klan and the more promising components of Americana such as the introduction of powerful radio broadcasts. In Morton's view:

> [Canada's] own frail culture was shrinking before the excitement and prosperity of the United States. No cultural force broke down the international barriers more swiftly than radio. By the mid-twenties, powerful American stations carried signals into most populated parts of Canada, and the technology of a crystal set receiver was not beyond a dexterous youngster. Canada, with its frugal comforts, its low wages, its backwater vision of itself, had never been more immediately or more dangerously challenged.[32]

Morton outlines the profound impact that radio and, in particular, American programming had on Canadian listeners by referring to Canadian Prime Minister R.B. Bennett's 1932 decision to establish the Canadian Radio Broadcasting Commission. This followed Bennett's being alerted by "young enthusiasts in the Canadian Radio League who insisted that it would be either the State or the States."[33]

Today, in direct succession to Bennett's action, the Canadian Broadcasting Corporation broadcasts in both English and French on AM and FM radio and on television. It is an entity committed to bringing a uniquely Canadian perspective to world affairs and to specifically profiling Canadian artists, entertainers and newsmakers.[34] Some Canadians cynically view the CBC as

---

Baptists in the 1920s and 1930s could not really empathize with the main North American fundamentalist or modernist propagandists, because they perceived religion in a radically different manner. Unlike many of their Baptist cousins in Central Canada and the West, they had not, as yet, experienced the profound Americanization of their popular culture and were quite successful in the interwar years in resisting the fundamentalist-modernist bombardment from the south. Is it surprising that the two Baptist conventions in Canada most greatly influenced by the osmosis of Americanization were the two conventions most significantly affected by the fundamentalist-modernist controversy?"

[32] Morton, 172.
[33] Ibid., 176.
[34] D.C. Masters, *The Coming of Age* (Montreal: The Canadian Broadcasting Corporation, 1967) is the fourth book in *The CBC International Service History of Canada*. Each book reprints 13 half-hour radio programs with Masters' work focusing on "The Modern Era: 1914 to 1967." Chapter 5 in the book, "The Canadian Spirit" is a good example

a government funded beacon that exists to keep Canadian tax-payers from being swamped by American culture.[35]

A Short History of Canada makes an even more useful contribution to our understanding of the powerful American influence on Alberta's society in the 1920s and 1930s by depicting how William Aberhart, high-school principal and fundamentalist preacher in Calgary during this era, creatively harnessed the potential of radio to introduce the financial doctrine of Social Credit to tens of thousands of his listeners. Claiming that "rarely had medium and message been better combined," Morton relates how Aberhart strategically employed his Sunday afternoon radio broadcasts as founder of Calgary's Prophetic Bible Institute in the cause of eventually seeing a Social Credit provincial government elected in Alberta in 1935.[36]

Aberhart served as the Premier of Alberta, the highest elected office in provincial politics, and the province's education minister for the next eight years. Following a sudden illness and his death in 1943, he was succeeded

---

of the CBC's mandate to profile Canadian culture and accomplishments with reference being made to a Canadian vessel called the *Bluenose* that won the International Fisherman's Trophy in October 1921 and is now featured on the Canadian ten cent piece. Other references are to the achievements of Drs. Banting, Best and Macleod of the University of Toronto who in January 1922 isolated insulin and demonstrated its beneficial effect on diabetes as well as to the Group of Seven, seven Canadian artists in 1920 who painted Laurentian Shield landscapes north of Lakes Huron and Superior, 48-50.

[35] Barry Cooper, *Sins of Omission: Shaping the News at CBC TV* (Toronto: Univ. of Toronto Press, 1994) is a critical analysis of how CBC shapes the news to what Cooper believes is a predetermined agenda.

My older brother, Dan, who in the late 1970s studied broadcasting at Mount Royal University in Calgary, Alberta, relates that the term "Can-con," an abbreviation for "Canadian content" was often used derisively among students to refer to Canadian broadcasting regulations that require a percentage of broadcasting content on Canadian radio stations to be written or performed by Canadian artists. The point of the derision was the belief of some that Canadian musical artists were generally considered to be inferior to their American or European counterparts. Proud Canadians, however, point to the accomplishments of Canadian musicians like Neil Young, The Guess Who, Bruce Cockburn, Anne Murray, Gordon Lightfoot, Leonard Cohen, Celine Dion and Justin Bieber, authors like Michael Ondaatje, Margaret Atwood, Carol Shields, Timothy Findlay and Alice Munro, as well as actors Jim Carrey, Mike Meyers, Dan Ackroyd, Christopher Plummer, Donald and Kiefer Sutherland as evidence that Canadians need not take a back seat to anyone when it comes to competency in the performing and literary arts.

[36] Morton, 181.

by Ernest C. Manning, a close associate who shared Aberhart's religious and political views. Manning, who ruled as Alberta's Premier until 1968, was, simultaneous to the time he served as Premier, host and preacher on the radio program *Canada's National Back to the Bible Hour.*[37]

During this era, Prairie Bible Institute became convinced of the value of a presence on the airwaves and launched a Sunday broadcast near the end of the 1920s on a Red Deer station before moving to a Calgary station in the early 1930s.[38] For a period of several weeks in 1938, PBI's airtime over CFCN in Calgary was devoted to the preaching of Oscar Lowry, an American Bible teacher and evangelist, who had come to PBI as part of his role on the extension staff at Moody Bible Institute in Chicago.[39]

Morton's identification of the impact American radio programming had on the emerging Canadian culture serves as a solid example of American influence on Canadian thought and behavior as both countries developed. Religious leaders in Alberta such as Aberhart (a Canadian) and Maxwell (an American) both saw the value of broadcasting and quickly determined to use radio for their own purposes.

The importance Morton places on American influence in Canadian life in *A Short History of Canada* is further evident in the attention he draws to two other spheres of Canadian society. Not only does he write concerning the impact the U.S. had on Canada's popular culture, he also identifies American influence in the northern nation's political and economic realms.

In terms of political influence, Morton makes passing reference to the fact that during the 1920s both major Canadian political parties, the Liberals and the Conservatives, experimented with an "American-style leadership convention."[40] Of perhaps even greater significance, however, is

---

[37] Opp, 117-146, offers a succinct overview of the importance radio broadcasting played in Canadian fundamentalism noting: "Considering the entertainment value of radio, it is somewhat surprising that fundamentalists considered it useful when other forms of entertainment such as theatre and film were condemned as frivolous . . ." (118)

[38] Goertz, see particularly chapters 3 and 8 for a discussion of Aberhart and Maxwell's radio preaching experiences. Goertz points out that on occasion there were verbal jabs exchanged on air owing to Maxwell's view that Aberhart was abandoning the preaching of the gospel for the preaching of politics.

Davidson, 65, indicates Prairie began broadcasting over CKRD in Red Deer in 1929.

[39] Davidson, 65-66.

[40] Morton, 175.

what he reveals concerning the attraction many Canadians felt for American president Franklin D. Roosevelt when he swept into the White House in 1932 and launched the famous New Deal program. Stealing a page from Roosevelt's policy manual, Canadian Prime Minister R.B. Bennett surprisingly announced that the federal government would intervene in the economic depression that was devastating particularly western Canada by introducing unemployment insurance, minimum wages, a maximum number of work hours, marketing legislation for farmers and measures against price-fixing.[41]

As far as American influence in the economic realm was concerned, Morton indicates that the immediate cause of the Great Depression in Canada was not the crash of the Wall Street stock market in 1929. Rather, he faults "the enormous 1928 wheat crop" and the fact that farmers in western Canada listened to the advice of "a persuasive American lawyer named Aaron Sapiro" to pool the huge wheat harvest and sell it with the added power of the united bargaining strength associated with any good cartel. The idea worked well, Morton says, as long as there was no glut and no serious competition. However:

> By 1928, there were both: 567 million bushels at a Pool-guaranteed price of $1.28 a bushel, to be sold in a world that could now buy much more cheaply from the United States, Argentina, Australia, and even the Soviet Union.[42]

Morton's work thus offers convincing evidence that at the time of Prairie Bible Institute's founding in 1922 and continuing into the 1930s, American influence in the cultural, political and economic spheres of Canadian life was particularly apparent. It is against this broader background, therefore, that this book calls for seeing a larger degree of American influence in the ethos of Prairie Bible Institute during the L.E. Maxwell era than that evident in either Stackhouse's work in particular or in related historiography in general.

---

[41] Morton, 183, 184.
[42] Ibid., 173-174.

Observations drawn from general histories of Alberta (or "The West")

Bruce Guenther's exhaustive overview of the historiography of western Canada capably points out the comparative dearth of useful references to the role of religion in works primarily concerned with a general history of Alberta or the prairie provinces of Canada as a whole.[43] While this study affirms the legitimacy of Guenther's assertion, some attention should nevertheless be called to the frequency with which reference is made in many of these works to the general American influence in the emerging Canadian West.

One source notes that in 1905, the year Alberta officially became a Canadian province, 55,000 Americans arrived in the jurisdiction, prompting supporters of the British Empire to begin "fretting over Americanization." The same work states that about 80,000 Americans entered Alberta during the first decade of the 1900s, "the largest immigrant group entering Canada." By 1911 they accounted for 22 per cent of Alberta's population, "although many were returning Canadians and a third were European born."[44]

---

[43] Guenther, 90: "One cannot examine the history of the Canadian prairies without consulting the work of Gerald Friesen. And yet, despite its magisterial stature in the field, there is hardly a mention of religion in the entire study."

  Among the sources Guenther cites that affirm Canadian historians' curious disregard for religious history in general is Carl Berger, *The Writing of Canadian History: Aspects of English-Canadian Historical Writing Since 1900 (second ed.)* (Toronto: Univ. of Toronto Press, 1993), 292: "Historians who wrote on aspects of cultural history explored many subjects . . . Of all the subfields that accorded priority to ideas, convictions, and values, the history of religion experienced the most curious fate. While historians had acknowledged its pervasive presence in the past, they tended to treat it as subsidiary to other topics . . . The history of religion, however, existed on the margins of historical scholarship; as for a history that treated religion as a way of defining self, of feeling and faith, this was hardly developed at all . . . Historians after the sixties continued to subordinate religion to other presumably more important subjects even when they tried to demonstrate its impact on society at large."

[44] Ted Byfield, (ed.), *Alberta in the 20th Century, (vol. 2): The Birth of the Province* (Edmonton: United Western Communications Ltd., 1992), 141-144, 154.

  There is a direct connection between these immigrant Americans and Prairie Bible Institute. Roy L. Davidson (b. 1906), author of *Miracle on the Prairies* and member of the original class at PBI moved from Vermont, USA, to Calgary with his parents and three brothers in February, 1912 and then on to Three Hills in 1915. An early graduate of PBI, he later served on the school's board and then on the institute's staff for a number

Other informative comments one comes across in the literature on Alberta's early history are statements like: "So Calgary elbowed its way into the twentieth century with an American pedigree" and "Canadian newspapers in the 1920s adopted an "American" style . . . a heavy reliance on American wire services for international coverage."[45] Additional contributions include: "American settlers came . . . [with] . . . the Jeffersonian physiocratic notion that the soil was the sole source of wealth guided their thinking," and "Canadian government propaganda which employed . . . prominent features of American liberal mythology."[46]

Gerald Friesen

As Guenther avers, Gerald Friesen's *The Canadian Prairies* contains few references to the role of religion on the Canadian prairies. Nevertheless, it does underscore a couple of important dynamics that serve to confirm the direction of the argument in this book.

As was seen in Careless's work, Friesen indicates that a significant portion of the new immigrants that flooded western Canada in the late nineteenth and early twentieth centuries came from the United States.[47] He points out that an aggressive campaign to recruit immigrants in both Britain and the U.S. was introduced with the appointment of Clifford Sifton as Canada's federal Minister of the Interior in 1897.[48] Although

---

of years. His mother, Mrs. W. B. Davidson, and brother, Andrew, a member of PBI's first graduating class, both served on PBI's first Board of Directors.

[45] Aritha Van Herk, *Mavericks: An Incorrigible History of Alberta* (Toronto: Penguin Canada, 2002), 316.

R. Douglas Francis, Richard Jones and Donald B. Smith, *Destinies: Canadian History Since Confederation* (4th ed) (Scarborough, ON: Nelson Thomson Learning, 2000), 281.

[46] R. Douglas Francis, Donald B. Smith, *Reading Canadian History* (Scarborough, ON: Nelson Thomson Learning, 2002), 286.

[47] Gerald Friesen, *The Canadian Prairies* (Toronto: Univ. of Toronto Press, 1987), 245: "The third infusion of immigrants, and by far the largest, occurred between 1897 and 1913, and was comprised in equal parts of British, Canadian, American and continental European arrivals, with a sprinkling of others from around the globe. The fourth, an extension of the third in terms of national origin, took place in the 1920s."

[48] Ibid., 245-246; 249-250: "[Sifton] enlarged the immigration service in the United States from 6 agents to 300 and asked them to pursue recruits rather than wait for

Friesen acknowledges that insufficient research has been done to permit the conclusion that life on the Canadian western frontier was a carbon copy of that which existed in the American West, he states that the immigrants contributed to creating an atmosphere that sometimes resembled British

---

enquiries. He ensured that a similarly aggressive campaign was undertaken in the rural areas of England and Scotland."

See also D.J. Hall, "Clifford Sifton: Immigration and Settlement Policy 1896-1905" in R. Douglas Francis and Howard Palmer (ed.) *The Prairie West: Historical Readings* (Edmonton, AB: Pica Pica Press/Univ. of Alberta Press, 1985), 290: "[Sifton's] program was a great success, as the number of United States immigrants increased from 2,400 in 1897 to nearly 12,000 in 1899, and between 40,000 and 50,000 annually in the years 1902-05." By means of comparison, Hall affirms that Great Britain always received the best of Sifton's promotional efforts: "Britain continued to receive the greatest promotional expenditure: in 1902-03, for example, this amounted to 205,000 dollars, compared to 161,000 in the United States, and 60,000 in Europe."

In the interests of not over-stating the case regarding American influence in western Canada, it should be noted that Hall indicates not all Canadians were pleased by Sifton's promotional ventures into the U.S., 292, 297: "Many Canadians were angered that the government was spending too much time and money on encouraging "foreigners" to come, while the Dominion was losing thousands of her own people annually to the United States . . . To those who suggested that the flow of American immigrants into the Canadian West spelled the beginning of the end for an independent and British Canada, the *Free Press* retorted: [They] are coming into a country where they will very soon realize that the will of the people rules. There is a greater freedom, a better administration of justice and greater respect for the law, guaranteeing the equal rights of all, in Canada than there is in the United States. The security of life and property is greater. The accessions to our population which we are now receiving from the United States are very largely of British origin. They are of our own stock. Their interests, once they make their homes on Canadian soil, become Canadian. So it has always been; and that it will continue so is not to be doubted."

Lewis H. Thomas in "A History of Agriculture on the Prairies to 1914" in Francis and Palmer (ed.), *The Prairie West*, 227, points out that the efforts to attract American immigrants didn't shrink from the occasional exaggeration of the facts: "[John Macoun's] *magnum opus*, the 687-page volume entitled *Manitoba and the Great-North West*, was widely distributed and generated much enthusiasm among would-be settlers. A St. Paul newspaper later urged Minnesota readers to: Buy farmlands in Saskatchewan. You can leave home after Easter, sow your grain and take in the harvest and come home with your pockets full of money in time for Thanksgiving dinner." Of this boosterism Grant MacEwan quotes an unknown author: "Where everyman's a liar, that's where the West begins." Certainly the record of homestead cancellations bears this out."

society but at other times was "much closer to the American Midwestern Model."[49]

It is significant that Friesen makes it a point on several occasions in his narrative to specifically identify aspects of the American influence on life in western Canada. He repeatedly states that the Alberta natural gas and oil industries which came to dominate Alberta's economy in the middle of the twentieth century were developed according to "American precedent," the "American example" or "as in the United States."[50] If anything, the American factor in Alberta has increased in the years since the discovery of oil to the point where it is presently estimated that an estimated 80,000 Americans reside in Calgary, Canada's most "American" city.[51]

Friesen identifies the influential role played by two American gentlemen in the development of western Canadian society. Henry George was a Christian with training in economics who strategically promoted the social gospel that led him to "condemn the effects of private landholding—a revolutionary stance in that day—and to argue that land should be taxed in order to give the entire community the rents that now accrued to wealthy individuals."[52]

Henry Wise Wood, a religious American from Missouri, was a dominant figure on the labor and political fronts in Alberta. He served as president of the United Farmers of Alberta (UFA) from 1916-1930. Although Wise Wood's experience with American farm organizations prompted him to initially discourage the UFA from becoming involved politically, the entity eventually formed the government of Alberta from 1921-1935.[53] Among

---

Howard Palmer in "Strangers and Stereotypes: The Rise of Nativism—1880-1920" in Francis and Palmer (ed.), *The Prairie West*, 312, points out that while "the Alberta elite, as elsewhere on the Prairies, regarded British and American immigrants as the most desirable settlers," not all Albertans were pleased with the arrival in southern Alberta between 1887 and 1908 of Mormons from Utah, 311-313.

[49] Friesen, 308-312.

[50] Ibid., 440-442.

[51] Jason Fekete, "City abuzz with U.S. conventions fever," *Calgary Herald*, A6, 26 August 2008.

[52] Friesen, 350.

[53] Masters, *The Coming of Age*, 28: ". . . Wood did not believe in political parties in the old sense. He favored "group government," a system in which Parliament should be composed of groups, each consisting of the representatives of a particular class. This was the Alberta point of view."

its significant accomplishments, the UFA secured the transfer of natural resources from federal to provincial control, an accomplishment that with the later discovery of oil in Alberta has resulted in Alberta's modern status as one of the wealthiest political jurisdictions in the world.

At least some similarity should be seen between the roles of Henry Wise Wood on the social and political fronts in the province of Alberta and that of L.E. Maxwell on the province's religious scene.[54] Wise Wood was influential in the merging of religious and agrarian energies, influencing the unique role that religion would play in Alberta politics for decades to come. At the other end of the idealistic spectrum, Maxwell opposed anything that detracted from the Christian's primary duty to proclaim a gospel of personal salvation through Christ and was responsible for thousands coming to Alberta for training to then carry that message around the world. The prominent roles of these two Americans in the history of Alberta are

Friesen, 410: "And Wood, a native of Missouri, brought a distinctive combination of Christianity and social reform to his work."

Richard Allen, "The Social Gospel as the Religion of Agrarian Revolt," in Francis and Palmer (ed.), *The Prairie West*, 440, 443: "The identification of western agrarianism with religion motives was even closer than the foregoing implies, for both the leadership and the membership generally espoused religion with a will. Henry Wise Wood, the great Alberta agrarian leader of the time, though not an active churchman in his Alberta days, was a very religious man who viewed the United Farmers in Alberta as a religious movement . . . Henry Wise Wood was not a member of any church in Canada, but brought a liberal leaning religious outlook from an upbringing and training under the Campbellite church in Missouri."

[54] Walter D. Young in "The C.C.F.: The Radical Background" in Francis and Palmer (ed.), *The Prairie West*, 539-540: "Agrarian politics in Alberta were more radical and more class-conscious, a result of the activities of the United Farmers of Alberta and the Non-Partisan League . . . Two of the early antecedents of the CCF deserve some comment. The Non-Partisan League and the United Farmers of Alberta represented the purely North American strain in the CCF's pedigree. Both had something in common with British socialism, which helped attract support from those immigrants familiar with that body of doctrine, but American ideas were more dominant. Henry Wise Wood, leader of the UFA, for example, was born in Missouri, and came to Canada in his forties. Like many of his compatriots who had emigrated to Alberta, he had been a member of the Populist party and put an emphasis on active non-partisan citizenship that was clearly more an American than a British concept."

representative of a visible American influence that came to bear on life in western Canada during the early decades of the twentieth century.[55]

C.B. Macpherson

Democracy in Alberta: Social Credit and the Party System by C.B. Macpherson is another useful resource that helps underscore the American influence on Alberta politics in the early years of the province. Its primary contribution to the focus of this book is the light it sheds on the role of the Non-Partisan League in Alberta and on American Henry Wise Wood's importance in the formation of the United Farmers of Alberta.

Students of Alberta history are familiar with the fact that the province has acquired a peculiar political distinctiveness since entering Canadian confederation in 1905. Whereas it had been standard procedure in the early years of Canada's nationhood for the two main political parties, the Liberals and the Conservatives, to establish provincial counterparts to manage provincial affairs, the Liberals were elected to serve as the first provincial government in Alberta.

By 1910 however, as Macpherson points out, "Alberta voters began to doubt whether parties were consistent with honest, efficient administration."[56] Indeed, farmers right across western Canada were becoming united in their distrust of the traditional political parties and discussions began to surface proposing that farmers' associations should initiate farmers' parties or, at

[55] Grant MacEwan, *Fifty Mighty Men* (Vancouver, BC: Greystone Books, 1995) recounts the history of fifty men who significantly impacted the development of the Canadian West. At least eight of these individuals were American-born or had spent part of their lives in the U.S. including Guy Weadick (123-129), widely regarded as the father of The Calgary Stampede. The first Stampede was held in 1912, is held annually during the first half of July and as The Calgary Exhibition and Stampede is known around the world as "The Greatest Outdoor Show on Earth." Thousands of Americans come to Calgary every year as visitors and/or participants in the event. For additional information on Guy Weadick, see Fred Kennedy, *Alberta Was My Beat: Memoirs of a Western Newspaperman,* (Calgary, AB: The Albertan, 1975), 92f. Kennedy claims Weadick was born in Portage la Prairie, Manitoba, Canada, whereas MacEwan says he was born in Rochester, New York, in 1885 (124). In any event, he came to Alberta from Wyoming, U.S.A.

[56] C.B. Macpherson, *Democracy in Alberta: Social Credit and the Party System (2nd ed.),* (Toronto: Univ. of Toronto Press, 1962), 25.

the very least, enter candidates in every constituency who were sympathetic to the concerns of farmers.

By 1916, the Non-Partisan League had moved into Canada from North Dakota, U.S.A., to experience rapid growth.[57] The organization had been established south of the border in 1915 in response to the concerns of farmers there regarding exploitation by out-of-state milling companies, the railroads and eastern capital markets. Under the leadership of a Canadian clergyman, William Irvine, who successfully exploited similar sentiments among farmers in western Canada, the Non-Partisan League played a significant role in the eventual emergence of the United Farmers of Alberta as a political force.[58]

Beginning in 1921 with the election of the U.F.A. as the provincial government, Alberta introduced a virtual one-party system to Canadian politics. The U.F.A., an Alberta novelty, ruled from 1921-1935 with only a handful of opposition members regularly elected to the provincial legislature. Social Credit, another Alberta innovation as it applied to the

---

[57] Macpherson, 25-26: "The party system itself, as well as the old parties, came under heavy fire after 1916 from the rapidly growing Non-Partisan League. The League spread into Canada from North Dakota in the summer of 1916 and was particularly effective in Alberta. In the provincial election of 1917 it ran four candidates and elected two, and its propaganda was increasingly successful in the next two years."

Young, "The C.C.F.: The Radical Background," 541: "The Non-Partisan League was a direct import from the United States, fresh from its triumphant capture of the government of North Dakota."

[58] Macpherson, 21: "But the needs of the prairie provinces were different. In them, two characteristics, not found together in any of the other provinces, combined to discourage the introduction and development of a party system. One was their relatively homogeneous class composition, the other was their quasi-colonial status . . . The quasi-colonial position of the western provinces made it a primary requirement of their provincial political systems that they should be able to stand up to the national government, that is, able to make effective demands on it and to resist national legislation which they regarded as exploitive. That they should be able to do so was all the more important as their quasi-colonial status was not only economic but political. Unlike the provinces which had entered Confederation at the beginning, the prairie provinces were creations of the federal government; and the federal government retained control over their natural resources until 1930. They were not equal members of a federation; the federal government was to them not only a federal but an imperial government. It was therefore essential to the purposes of the provincial community that its government should be an effective offensive and defensive weapon against this imperial power."

Canadian scene, was then elected in 1935 and governed until 1971 with, again, only a very few members from other political perspectives elected in provincial elections as the official Opposition. The Progressive Conservative Party in Alberta has been elected repeatedly since 1971 with huge majorities including the most recent election of March 3, 2008 in which over seventy Conservatives were elected whereas less than ten members of other parties won seats in Alberta's legislature.

In effect, since the advent of the Non-Partisan League in 1916 and its eventual merger with the U.F.A., Alberta has essentially been a one-party province, with the U.F.A. and Social Credit administrations having the added significance of essentially being home-grown movements. Of particular, albeit minor, significance for this book's argument is the recognition that a political ideology originating in the United States had a profound impact on the thinking of Alberta farmers at roughly the same period of time that J. Fergus Kirk, a farmer in the small agricultural community of Three Hills was envisioning Prairie Bible Institute in its embryonic form.

One particular aspect from Macpherson's summary of Henry Wise Wood's well-developed social theory merits brief mention. In detailing Wood's role as the philosopher behind the popularity of the U.F.A., Macpherson makes passing reference to the fact that in addition to the articulation of Wood's views in various publications and in his annual presidential addresses, Wood also gave "Chautauqua addresses" in Alberta.[59]

Chautauqua was a traveling festival that originated at Chautauqua Lake, New York, in the early years of the twentieth century and was brought to Alberta from the U.S. in 1917 by John M. Erickson.[60] Influenced by the

---

[59] Macpherson, 30.

[60] See www.thecanadianencyclopedia.com (accessed April 25, 2009). "Chautauqua programs consisted of 4 to 6 days of musical numbers, lectures, dramatic productions and magic or puppet shows. A different performance was presented daily, and performers then moved on to the next town on the circuit. Keeping workers, artists, tents and equipment moving smoothly along the circuits required careful organization and many employees. A total of some 50 young men handled the tents and approximately 80 young women helped organize local committees and directed the operation. These people, mainly university students, developed initiative, self-confidence and skills that gave them an excellent foundation for success in life. Chautauqua was good family entertainment and the people loved it. To many it provided their only opportunity for a cultural experience. It broadened horizons and brought colour and beauty into many lives. "

Methodist emphasis on temperance, Chautauqua ran for several days as a mobile family show that the United Farm Women of Alberta utilized to promote the betterment of rural life.[61] Erickson established "Dominion Chautauquas" or, as such were called after 1926, "Canadian Chautauquas," that were headquartered in Calgary and operated until 1935.

Of significance to my purposes here is to simply draw attention to the scenario of an American like Henry Wise Wood articulating social theory via an American instrument such as Chautauqua to the farmers of Alberta, many of whom were Americans themselves or were farmers that had been influenced by the Non-Partisan League, another organization from south of the Canadian-American border. This is but another glimpse of American influence in the type of society that was emerging in Alberta at precisely the time the ideas leading to the establishment of Prairie Bible Institute were being conceived.[62]

John J. Barr

The portrait of significant American influence in early Alberta is confirmed by John J. Barr in *The Dynasty: The Rise and Fall of Social Credit in Alberta*. This reality is particularly evident in a brief section from the book's opening chapter which merits full citation here:

> By 1910 most of the West's aching emptiness had been filled. By 1920 one Canadian in every four lived in the West.
>
> In the cold, clear air of this lonely last frontier, this society of immigrants began to define its own identity.

---

[61] See www.thecanadianencyclopedia.com (accessed April 25, 2009). "[UFWA] initiated changes in legislation affecting credit for young farmers, income tax reform, mothers' allowances and widows' pensions. It was a major contributor to the UFA's successful elections to govern Alberta through the years 1921 to 1935, after being a major player in the suffrage campaign, which granted women the vote in 1916. The organization's first president, Irene Parlby, was appointed as the first female cabinet minister in Canada after winning a seat in the 1921 election."

[62] Kenneth A. Epp, "The Impact of the Theological Views of William Jennings Bryan Upon His Educational Ideas," (PhD dissertation, Loyola University of Chicago, 1995). See Chapter III, "Chautauqua—Bryan's Link with the Common Man" which contains several useful insights into both Chautauqua itself and Bryan's association with the movement.

A major part of that identity was the experience the American settlers brought with them from the fast-disappearing U.S. frontier. By 1920 Alberta was thirty per cent foreign-born, and over half the settlers were Americans. With them they brought ideas about temperance, women's rights, radical social democracy.* (*The three movements frequently coincided: Alberta was a hotbed of women's liberation and produced a score of early feminist leaders, including the Empire's first female magistrate. Some of the most important Social Credit figures in the early years were female reformers and temperance supporters). Many of them had worked in The Grange, fought the U.S. railways and grain companies, supported the Non-Partisan League. A number had worked in William Jennings Bryan's great populist Presidential campaign in 1896, which came heartbreakingly close to victory.

South of the border the frontier was closing, and an ugly industrialism was starting to appear. On the Canadian frontier, they hoped, they would find or create the old life with its solid agrarian values.[63]

Several points from this part of Barr's work deserve brief comment as they relate to the overall theme of my book. Firstly, I vividly recall my early elementary school days (c. 1961-66) at Prairie Grade School on the campus of PBI where the annual Women's Christian Temperance Union poster contest was a major event. Prizes were awarded for the best posters depicting the evils of alcohol and tobacco use. Although I never won any of the coveted awards for "best poster," I distinctly remember the creativity expected and employed in attempting to communicate the message that drinking alcohol and smoking tobacco were harmful to individuals, families and society at large.[64]

---

[63] John J. Barr, *The Dynasty: The Rise and Fall of Social Credit in Alberta* (Toronto: McClelland & Stewart Ltd., 1974), 14.

[64] Careful scholarship requires it be pointed out that the Women's Christian Temperance Union was established in the United States at Cleveland, Ohio, and in Canada at Owen Sound, Ontario, in the same year, 1874, so it is questionable to imply as Barr does that the temperance matter was solely a matter of American influence. Wendy Mitchinson, "Women's Christian Temperance Union," 614, in A.I. Silver (ed.) *An Introduction to Canadian History* (Toronto: Canadian Scholars' Press Inc., 1991) suggests that Canadian temperance advocates followed the lead of a law passed in the state of Maine prior to 1874 that favored prohibition.

Secondly, as will be noted later in the book, one of the unique aspects of L.E. Maxwell's theology and philosophy of ministry from the outset of his tenure at PBI was the importance he assigned to permitting women a public profile in teaching and preaching. In this respect, Maxwell was far ahead of his time as compared to other schools such as Moody Bible Institute, Wheaton College and BIOLA where women were largely restricted to teaching courses in language arts or Christian Education.[65] Interestingly enough, Maxwell's promotion of women in this regard from virtually the very beginning at PBI parallels the new places women were discovering on the political and social fronts in Alberta during the 1920s.[66]

Thirdly, Barr's reference to William Jennings Bryan, a thrice defeated U.S. Democratic presidential candidate, is particularly useful for my purposes in that Bryan himself visited Alberta in October 1909 where he was warmly received by government officials, businessmen and large crowds alike. Suffice it to simply call attention to the influence of a very prominent American in Alberta's emerging political culture by referencing Goertz who points out that the grievances among residents in the American and

Sharon Anne Cook, "Evangelical Moral Reform: Women and the War Against Tobacco, 1874-1900," in Marguerite Van Die (ed.), *Religion and Public Life in Canada: Historical and Comparative Perspectives* (Toronto: Univ. of Toronto Press, 2001), 177-195, discusses the seldom-profiled battle against tobacco fought on both sides of the Canada-U.S. international border by the Salvation Army and the Women's Christian Temperance Union.

[65] Chapter Nine of this book refers to Flory's research on faculty gender at Wheaton, Moody and Biola.

[66] Further, anyone conversant with Alberta history is well aware of Nellie McClung, who secured the right for women to vote in Canada in 1916 and later was one of "The Famous Five," a group of Alberta women (also Emily Murphy, Henrietta Muir Edwards, Louise McKinney, Irene Parlby) held in high regard for their role in obtaining recognition for women as persons under the British North American Act in 1929. See www.abheritage.ca/famous5 (accessed April 25, 2009) for further information on these important figures in Alberta history. Again, it is debatable to imply as Barr does that the elevation of women's rights in western Canada was strictly or primarily a matter of American influence.

Nellie McClung, *Clearing in the West: An Autobiography* (Toronto: Thomas Allen & Son Ltd., 1976. See especially Chapters 34, "The Young Evangelists," and 36, "My First Political Meeting."

Canadian West were so similar that Bryan's articulation of U.S. problems resonated with audiences right across the plains."[67]

As has been demonstrated, it is the consistent indication of a selection of reference works that outline the history of Alberta or western Canada that the American factor was a significant influence in various sectors of the society emerging in Alberta at precisely the time Prairie Bible Institute was being conceived and established. True, L.E. Maxwell's legacy was not as Alberta-centric as that left by such figures as Henry Wise Wood or Guy Weadick in that Maxwell's "products" were disseminated around the world.[68] Nonetheless, the international profile attained by Prairie Bible Institute during the balance of the twentieth century suggests that his being included as an American who significantly impacted the history of the province is indeed warranted. The comparatively low-profile accorded both he and PBI in mainstream Alberta historiography is partially explainable in terms of the evidence Guenther refers to concerning the virtual silence of historians in general regarding religion in western Canada.[69]

---

[67] Goertz, 28-29: "Politically Bryan was very unpopular with Canadian leadership, but among the ordinary people Bryan was popular for both his religious and political beliefs. Grievances of the American and Canadian West were so similar that his articulation of U.S. problems hit a responsive cord (sic) right across the plains . . . Bryan was the popularizer of this fight. Speeches against tariffs, trusts and the plutocracy could be given on either side of the border with few changes and draw excited cheering. Both Bryan and the Canadian agrarians had the same agenda, something compounded by the arrival of American veterans of the Populist crusade, who did not abandon their heritage. This combination of religious and political idealism did not die out but was expressed in varying forms in both the United Farmers of Alberta and the Social Credit, climaxing of course in William Aberhart who combined the idea of the man of God with a radical political stance. In many ways Bryan prepared and made possible the way for Aberhart."

Kenneth A. Epp, 38, points out that "Throughout his life, William Jennings Bryan would be found strongly advocating the rights and worth of the common person. Hence, he was known as *The Great Commoner*." Bryan, who also served as Secretary of State under U.S. President Woodrow Wilson, also published a popular periodical called *The Commoner*.

[68] Rennie, "The Western Prairie Revival in Canada," 23, aptly summarizes Maxwell's and his colleague Henry Hildebrand's - president of Briercrest Bible Institute in Saskatchewan - legacies this way: "L.E. Maxwell and Henry Hildebrand emerge as two of the greatest recruiters of missionaries in the history of the Christian Church . . . "

[69] See footnote 43 in this chapter.

CHAPTER SEVEN

American influence
in Canadian history (Part 2)

Observations drawn from religious histories of Canada

S.D. Clark

The opening chapter of S.D. Clark's sociological treatise *Church and Sect in Canada* conveys how following the collapse of the French Empire in North America around 1760, aggressive New England Congregationalism contributed to the rapid disappearance of the authority of the Roman Catholic church in the Acadian or Maritime region of Canada's east coast.[1] For Clark, this marked the arrival of the more "sectish" expressions of Christianity to a region that would eventually be a part of the new nation of Canada.[2] As Congregationalist churches began to be formed in Nova Scotia and Prince Edward Island due to the influence of immigrants from New England, independent groups of

---

[1]   S.D. Clark, *Church and Sect in Canada*, 3-4: "Growth of settlement along the Atlantic seaboard and in Nova Scotia after 1760 was indicative of the strength of expansive forces within the New England farming and fishing villages and commercial towns. The bitter opposition of New England Protestantism to efforts of the Roman Catholic Church to maintain the attachments of the Acadian and native populations in Nova Scotia was reflected in the insistence upon the evacuation of the Acadians and in the lack of any sympathetic understanding between the new settlers in Nova Scotia and the natives. The destruction of Roman Catholic influence in Nova Scotia was made complete with the establishment of New England dominance in the Maritime fisheries and with the settlement of New England farmers on the vacated lands of the Acadians. The controls of empire gave way to the controls of the local village, and the religious sect established itself in place of the church."

[2]   See Chapter Two of this book, footnotes 38 and 39, where it is noted that Clark follows Troeltsch's European perspective wherein a "sect" is essentially considered a religious group that separates itself from the established state church and becomes a dissenting entity. For this reason, Clark frequently summarizes religious development in Nova Scotia in the late 18th century with statements such as above: "the religious sect established itself in place of the church" (4).

worshipers were established under the influence of American-born preacher Henry Alline and his "New Light" gospel.[3]

The most important theme from Clark for my purposes is his depiction of the longstanding tradition of influence from "south of the border" upon an emerging Canadian religious life. It was a dynamic that continued even after American independence as scores of United Empire Loyalists who favored political affinity with Britain nevertheless furthered the spirit of religious independence with which they had become comfortable while residing in New England.[4] Clark documents that as the eighteenth century unfolded, one of the major concerns of British officials north of the U.S. border became how to bring the numerous religious dissenters who had been influenced by American "sectism" such as aggressive Methodism into the fold of the Anglican church.[5] He also points out that American

---

[3]   Clark, 47ff, indicates that "New Light" or "Newlight" services were led by the American-born Alline who had not been formally ordained by any established church. The services were often accompanied by visible demonstrations of emotion such as loud weeping, calling out, exuberant rejoicing, people falling down purportedly under the Holy Spirit's power, as well as spontaneous adult baptisms.

[4]   Clark., 46: "The American frontier was an area of religious experimentation. In Kentucky, West Virginia, upper New York State, and Maine new religious forms emerged with the advance of the frontiersman. Inevitably, the religious influence of the American frontier extended across the border in the Maritime Provinces. The sect spirit, which had gained its early strength in Nova Scotia through the connection with New England, found new strength through the connection with the American West."

[5]   Ibid., 90-96; 150: "In religious appeal as in form of organization, the Methodist movement served as an effective socially reorganizing influence in the Canadian backwoods settlements. The strength of that appeal lay largely in the fact that it was directed towards the emotions and feelings and relied little upon reason. The close American connection of the movement in Canada inevitably determined the highly emotional character of its appeal."

160: "Before 1832, the Canadian population was predominantly of American origin, and the close American connection of the Methodist movement gave it a great advantage in winning the support of the people it sought to serve. Most of the early Methodist preachers were drawn from the United States; those who were not tended to have something of an American outlook. Methodism grew up in Canada as a distinctively American movement."

Presbyterians and Baptists had a marked influence as the Canadian frontier pushed westward.[6]

Clark is persistent in his view that part of the reason American religious influences were so strong in Canada was not only because of the number of American immigrants who came to Canada as civilization moved westward, but also because the upper-class orientation of the ministers of the Church of England hindered their ability to relate to the "commoner" identity of many North Americans.[7] The anecdote mentioned in Chapter One of this book regarding how the local clergy at Three Hills were bemused by L.E. Maxwell's eagerness to help area farmers with their duties suggests how deeply entrenched this notion of "superiority complex" was for ministers of the established Protestant traditions in Canada.

Clark suggests that American influence in Canadian religious life was not always welcomed north of the border and, in fact, he devotes an entire chapter of his book to "The Break with American Sectarianism."[8] Therein he unveils that British Methodism and American Methodism were

---

[6] Clark, 102: "American Presbyterian and Baptist preaching supported the general movement of religious reorganization of the Canadian frontier settlements secured through Methodist influence. Religious revivalism cut across traditional lines of social class and denominational attachment to produce a new sense of spiritual fellowship. The religious sect emerged to take the place of the church . . . Growth of revivalist influence led particularly to a serious weakening in the position of the Church of England."

165: "The considerable dependence upon American direction and reliance upon American preachers emphasized the frontier relationship of Canada to the United States."

[7] 128: "The Church [of England] remained English as well as upper class in outlook, and, while such a disposition strengthened its hold upon the population of overseas origin, it weakened its influence among those of American origin and among those coming increasingly to think of themselves as Canadian in attachment . . . such clergymen of an old world background could not win the sympathy of people with a new world, American background."

[8] Nor should it be assumed that the Loyalists' influence was always or only positive. See George Rawlyk, *Champions of the Truth: Fundamentalism, Modernism and the Maritime Baptists* (Montreal/Kingston: McGill-Queen's Univ. Press, 1990), 16: "The arrival of the Loyalists to peninsular Nova Scotia at the end of the Revolution seemed to accelerate a process of social disintegration already underway in some regions of the colony. The Loyalists, according to Edward Manning, the influential Baptist patriarch, had a "bad and . . . dreadful" effect on the colony since they "corrupted" societal values and made many Nova Scotians "adepts in wickedness.""

TIM W. CALLAWAY

often at odds in Canada as were Scottish Presbyterianism and American Presbyterianism.[9] In a somewhat humorous section of the work, Clark indicates that many residents of Canada simply could not countenance the uneducated and unrefined approaches they encountered in American Methodism.[10]

---

[9] Clark, 194: "The character of Methodist preachers and of Methodism preaching weakened the influence of the movement among certain elements of the population. As dependence increasingly came to be placed after 1790 upon preachers from the United States, antagonism to these preachers because of their American background became more pronounced. "I made bold to open matters to Mr. Wesley," Garrettson wrote to Asbury in 1786, "and begged of him to send one preacher from England, as a number of people would prefer an Englishman to an American.""

Ibid., 198: "After 1815, however, the Canadian society ceased to be simply a projection of the American frontier; population increasingly was drawn from older-settled areas of the United States, and from Great Britain, and new channels of communication developed. Conservative influences evident in the development of Methodism in the eastern United States and in England made themselves felt in the development of Methodism in Canada."

202: "The agreement of 1818 shut out the Wesleyan missionaries from Upper Canada but opposition to the Methodist Episcopal preachers, many of them Americans, remained strong. Organization in 1824 of an annual conference in Canada to control Methodist work in the country was part of a general move to free Canadian Methodism from American control. In 1828 the Canada Conference was formed and the Methodist Church in Canada became completely independent of the Methodist Episcopal Church in the United States."

205: "[After 1837] American Presbyterianism as a distinctive evangelical movement disappeared in Canada."

[10] 214-215: "The itinerant preacher was something of a rustic serving a rustic population . . . With the growth, however, of towns, the increase of wealth, and the immigration from overseas of people of education and social standing, the limitations of a movement depending upon uneducated preachers became increasingly more evide . . . The homely style of preaching of the Methodist itinerants, and their lack of any great philosophical or theological understanding of the problems with which they dealt, while no handicap in the country districts, placed them at a disadvantage in the towns where they came in competition with ministers who set a high standard of pulpit oratory."

Roger Finke and Rodney Starke, *The Churching of America 1776-1990: Winners and Losers in Our Religious Economy* (New Brunswick, NJ: Rutgers Univ. Press, 1992), 57. Finke and Starke point out that the American Congregationalist preacher of this era, Lyman Beecher, was equally condemning of certain tactics of American Baptists and Methodist preachers. He referred to them as "ignorant and unlettered men,"

184

Clark demonstrates that there was a definite slowing of American influence in Canadian religious life following the War of 1812. As Canadians moved closer to eventual confederation as a nation in 1867, it is fair to say that what had at one time been a virtual flood of American religious influence was reduced to a swift river.[11] Nonetheless, when Dwight L. Moody visited Toronto to preach December 3-5, 1884, his meetings were front page news in the *Toronto Globe* which reported: "the Christian convention last week attracted more widespread interest than any similar event in the religious history of this city." Two years later, the "Georgia evangelists," Sam Jones and Sam Small, came to Toronto and held revival services for close to three weeks.[12]

H.H. Walsh

In a work entitled *The Christian Church in Canada*, H. H. Walsh strongly affirms the prominent role that Clark assigns American influence in the evolution of Canadian Protestantism. He similarly begins his book with reference to the strong influence of "sects" in the development of a religious

---

suggesting "illiterate men have never been the chosen instruments of God to build up his cause."

[11] Clark, 219-221: "The strengthening of imperial sentiment in the country after the War of 1812, and the emergence of feelings of strong antagonism to the United States ... The bitterness of feeling aroused by the war favoured the shift to the support of Wesleyanism on the part of many of the Loyalists in the country as well as on the part of the British immigrants ... By 1831 Methodism had progressed very far in the direction of becoming a Canadian movement."

Ibid., 351-352: "William Davies wrote of the influences at work within the [Baptist] denomination which led to the construction of the Jarvis street church, June 15, 1876: "There has been built in this city [Toronto] recently a large Baptist Chapel (Jarvis Street Baptist Church), gothic, brown stone, spire pointing upward if not heavenward, marble bapistry (sic) & cost $100,000 & odd, & the organ $7,000 besides, & I believe it is all paid for ... One of the members, a M.L.C., say a Senator, very wealthy, married an American, natural result they soon had an American minister, then this new building also American, then the Lady & the minister lay their heads together & get a professional singer a sort of *prima donna* & she is paid $300.00 per year and many are very much hurt about it ..."

[12] 401-402. See discussion later in this chapter regarding the visits of Moody, Jones, Small, et al, to Canada.

identity in North America, but is careful to qualify that "sects" in Canada have never enjoyed the success they encountered in the United States.[13]

Walsh emphasizes that a component of the Anglican tradition in Canada arrived via New England and notes that the Church of England was carrying out missionary work in the U.S. sometime before the Puritans landed at Plymouth Rock. In fact, Anglicans who had departed England because of the Puritan influence there were already settled in Virginia, Maryland and the Carolinas when the Puritan pilgrims arrived in America. Descendants of these settlers later made up a large component of the Loyalist immigration to Canada. The Anglican Church's development in the Thirteen Colonies consequently contributed ingredients to Canadian church history.[14]

Another helpful angle that Walsh presents is his focus on the influence of former New England residents in the political and religious life of the city of Halifax in particular and the Acadian region in general. Not only did New England Congregationalists contribute to the virtual disappearance of Roman Catholicism in Acadia, as Clark also notes, Walsh points out how they also introduced township government to Nova Scotia. This development was a direct challenge to the traditional British patriarchal system which consistently granted preference to the Anglican Church as part of a centralized government based in Halifax.

The Congregationalists insisted on more authority at the township level which, among other innovations, challenged the Church of England's sole

---

[13] H.H. Walsh, *The Christian Church in Canada* (Toronto: The Ryerson Press,1956), 4: "There can be no question as to the significance of sectarianism in creating new cultural and religious values on the North American frontier, as all American church historians are now aware; but sectarianism never attained the same chaotic proportions in Canada as in the United States, evidenced by the fact that there are now only some thirty separate denominations listed in the Canadian census, whereas there are well over three hundred still listed as active denominations in the *Handbook of Denominations in the United States.*"

Interestingly enough, Walsh's footnote to his reference to the Canadian census states, 9: "The Canadian Census has ignored some very small sects. The registration forms at the Prairie Bible Institute, Three Hills, Alberta, indicate a student body representative of 47 religious denominations or sects. W.E. Mann in his study of *Sect, Cult, and Church in Alberta* (Toronto, 1955) has identified 35 fundamentalist sects in Alberta, p. 30."

[14] Walsh, 15: "The Virginia episode, however, is relevant to our story, as it established an Anglican tradition in North America, which greatly influenced Anglican church development in Canada."

right to perform marriages and to keep the records for marriages, births and deaths.[15] These relocated New Englanders thus introduced into British North America the concept of liberty in ecclesiastical matters in a similar fashion to what their counterparts south of the border accomplished in the political realm with the Declaration of Independence in 1776.

Walsh helps balance our grasp of the impact of the quest for American independence on Canadian life including its religious sphere by contrasting the "Americanization" of Canadian religious life with the recognition that "Loyalism" was enhanced between 1776 and 1784 when thirty or forty thousand English-speaking "refugees" from the United States moved into the predominantly French colonies in Canada.[16] In effect, Walsh suggests it would be erroneous to conclude that American influence in Canadian religious life has always and only been to "Americanize" Canadians.[17] On the contrary, Walsh contends, the Loyalist influence helped reverse or balance some of the liberating elements introduced into Canadian religious life by New Englanders who came to Canada yet nevertheless adhered to the spirit of American independence.

---

[15] Ibid., 94-95: "In England parish registers were the responsibility of the parochial clergy, and this gave them a civil status not enjoyed by dissenting clergymen. The paucity of the Anglican clergy in Nova Scotia soon made the English system unworkable, and in 1761 civil registers were permitted where there was no parish; this was confirmed by a law in 1782, whereby town clerks were made responsible for keeping registers, and clergymen who solemnized marriages were required to send in returns to the nearest town clerk, a decided victory for the New England township system."

[16] George A. Rawlyk, *Wrapped Up in God: A Study of Several Canadian Revivals and Revivalists* (Burlington, ON: Welch Publishing Co. Inc., 1988). Rawlyk speaks of the general disorienting effect of the American Revolution for many in that part of British North America close to the New England colonies. The political turmoil had implications for religious life as well. See, for example, 14, regarding Henry Alline's ministry (c. 1775-1784): "His audacity—some would call it "spiritual hubris"—appealed to those many Nova Scotians who were particularly confused and disoriented by the divisive forces unleashed by the American Revolution." Also, 35: "The Anglo-American crisis furthered helped to shape Alline's resolve "to preach the gospel . . ." and 53: "The implication of this conjunction of events, of civil war in neighboring New England and an unprecedented outpouring of the Holy Spirit in Nova Scotia, must have been obvious to Alline and to the thousands who flocked to hear him."

[17] Walsh, 103: "The Loyalists . . . also held firmly to the idea of a hierarchical society in which rights and privileges adhered to certain classes by virtue of their wealth or birth; and the dutiful recognition of such rights and privileges by all classes, they considered the best assurance of a well-ordered and well-mannered society."

There is thus a sense in which the Loyalist influence which came via the U.S. helped strengthen Canada's ties with Britain. It is in this light then that Walsh makes this important statement:

This sudden increase of English-speaking inhabitants reduced drastically the disproportion between the French and English and made certain that Canada would now become an integral part of the British Empire. In other words, modern Canada, with its pre-dominantly Anglo-Saxon culture and institutions, is as much a creation of the American Revolution as the United States itself.[18]

An additional aspect of Walsh's work deserving mention here is the connection he makes between both of the Great Awakenings that occurred in the United States and their impact on religious life in Canada. In both instances, Walsh suggests that what transpired in terms of religious awakening south of the Canada-U.S. border had a distinct influence on later developments in Canadian religious life.

With regard to the First Great Awakening (c. 1735-70), after noting the controversial nature of what many considered to be "the emotional extravagance it engendered," Walsh points out that "it was towards the end of this religious awakening that the immigration of New Englanders into Nova Scotia began." According to Walsh, this contributed to "an outburst of mystical enthusiasm in Nova Scotia that almost duplicated the events that followed upon the revival in Northampton, Massachusetts, some fifty years earlier."[19]

Similarly, Walsh attributes the "great religious revival" that occurred in Canada during the opening years of the nineteenth century to the Second Great Awakening (c. 1790-1830) that occurred in the U.S. Significantly, he pointedly argues that this revival had very little connection with a similar one in Maritime Canada. Nonetheless, by the time the revival had run its course, "the social and cultural institutions of Upper Canada resembled more closely those of the Maritime Provinces than any of the neighboring American states."[20]

---

[18] Walsh, 102.
[19] Walsh, 118-119.
[20] Ibid., 134.

Again, Walsh calls to our attention the fact that American influence on Canadian religious life did not necessarily always result in the Americanization of Canada. Ironically, it sometimes had the very opposite effect, leading Canadians to strengthen their loyalties to the British models of political and religious life.

Considerable additional space might be spent in demonstrating that Walsh identifies an American influence in numerous aspects of an emerging Canadian religious life. Like Clark he writes of the influence of American circuit-riding preachers who entered Canada, of the disdain for the same that characterized particularly the Anglican clergy, and of an American influence in virtually every denominational stripe that was established in Canada.

One last statement from Walsh will therefore suffice to summarize his perspective on this aspect of American influence on Canadian religious life:

> When the British finally conceded the independence of the Thirteen Colonies, almost every religion and racial group were represented in the great trek northwards.[21]

Douglas J. Wilson

Another source that informs the perspective of American influence in Canada as it is being advanced in this book is *The Church Grows in Canada*. Author Douglas J. Wilson refers to how the Anglican Church's progress in New England directly affected Canada. The establishment of the Protestant Episcopal Church of the United States of America under the Bishop of Connecticut in 1784 introduced to Canadian Anglicans a representative governing body with lay delegates, a marked difference to how the Church of England functioned.

Rev. Charles Inglis, a prominent Anglican rector in New York and a governor of what is now Columbia University in New York City was consecrated Bishop of Nova Scotia in 1787 with jurisdiction over Quebec, Nova Scotia, Ontario, Prince Edward Island, Cape Breton, New Brunswick and Newfoundland. Among his significant accomplishments were the securing of a Jesuit chapel in Montreal for use by the Anglicans (Christ Church) and the initiation of plans for King's College which is now affiliated

---

[21] Walsh, 104.

with Dalhousie University in Halifax. Just as the Christian church was instrumental in founding many of the great universities in New England, the influence of Inglis ensured the same was to be true in Canada.[22]

The section of Wilson's book dealing with the arrival of the United Empire Loyalists in Canada from the U.S. contains this instructive comment: "It is an axiom of Canadian history that the Loyalists exerted a religious and political influence out of all proportion to their actual number."[23] He proceeds to demonstrate that whereas "the incoming Loyalists and the subsequent waves of Americans" may have preferred allegiance to the British monarchy, they nevertheless brought with them such republican practices as self-government and adequate schools, views with significant theological implications.[24]

One of Canada's most famous native sons from this era, Egerton Ryerson, a religious and educational figure for whom Ryerson University in Toronto is named, was born of Loyalist parents in 1803. Wilson indicates that five Ryerson brothers were ordained as Methodist ministers at a time when many Methodist preachers were "trained in theological colleges of the Methodist Episcopal Church in the United States."[25]

Again, Wilson is careful to acknowledge the anti-Americanism that prevailed in some places in Canada, especially following the War of 1812. Yet along with those writers already identified in this chapter he underscores the American influence among Canadian Anglicans, Presbyterians, Congregationalists, Lutherans, Methodists, Mennonites, Quakers and Baptists.[26]

---

[22] Douglas J. Wilson, *The Church Grows in Canada* (Toronto: Canadian Council of Churches, 1966), 21-22.

[23] Wilson, 48.

[24] 48-49.

[25] 54-55.

[26] G.A. Rawlyk, *Is Jesus Your Personal Saviour? In Search of Canadian Evangelicalism in the 1990s* (Montreal-Kingston: McGill-Queen's Univ. Press, 1996), 11. Commenting on the anti-Americanism unleashed by the War of 1812 and its influence on the ultimate nature of evangelicalism in Canada, Rawlyk makes this important observation: "Anti-Americanism triggered by the War of 1812, especially in Central Canada, and the demographic transformation of British North America in the post-War of 1812 period meant, among other things, that radical evangelicalism would no longer be the evangelical norm and the dominant strain in Canadian Protestantism. Rather, it would be quickly pushed to the periphery of Protestantism by a burgeoning formal evangelical movement that owed a great deal to the growing middle class preoccupied

With regard to the latter, he writes of how Canadian Baptists welcomed Negro slaves fleeing slavery in the United States via the "Underground Railroad" throughout the nineteenth century. The escaped slaves brought the unique culture of the African-American to Canada and established black churches that carry on that tradition today in many of Canada's large cities.[27]

John Webster Grant

John Webster Grant offers several helpful insights regarding American influence in Canadian religious life in *The Church in the Canadian Era*.[28] The samples cited here refer only to dynamics not already identified in the three works previously mentioned in this section.

For example, in describing the state of affairs in Canadian religious life at the time of Canadian confederation in 1867, Grant points out that contrary to most rural areas of Canada East (Quebec) which were solidly French Catholic, Protestants formed a majority of the population in six counties in the region's Eastern Townships. This area had originally been settled by New England Yankees and had a reputation as one of the most religiously volatile in Canada, due in part to the presence of three thousand Second Adventists and two thousand Universalists.[29]

Meanwhile, several of the Baptist groups in a number of counties north of Lake Erie in Canada West (Ontario) were known as "people who took their religion seriously" and "traced their origins to American-style revival."[30] In fact, Grant reports, many of the people who came to Canada West from the U.S. brought with them a religious heritage that had already "undergone a mutation or two on the American frontier."[31]

---

with British order, British respectability, and a growing suspicion of democratic evangelical and American-style enthusiasm."
[27] Wilson, 68-69.Harry A. Renfree. *Heritage and Horizon: The Baptist Story in Canada* (Mississauga, ON: Canadian Baptist Federation, 1988), 74.
[28] John Webster Grant, *The Church in the Canadian Era* (Burlington, ON: Welch Publishing Company Inc., 1988). This volume was originally published in 1972 by McGraw-Hill Ryerson Ltd. under the title *The Church in the Canadian Era: Volume Three* of *A History of the Christian Church in Canada*.
[29] Ibid., 5.
[30] 7.
[31] Grant, 11.

Grant identifies several innovations of American origin that soon came to be staples in the life of Canadian Protestant churches including the office of deaconess for women, Christian education programs that included among other things the International Lessons for continent-wide use in Sunday school, and the Christian Endeavor Society.[32] He also acknowledges the influence of American educator John Dewey with regard to the pedagogical philosophy that prevailed in Canadian Christian education programs.[33] As well, Grant points out that the intensified search for holiness following the moral slackness of the U.S. Civil War "affected Canadians of several denominations."[34] On a more nefarious note, he states that the "Ku Klux Klan flourished in Saskatchewan in the 1920s."[35]

Grant briefly covers the modernist-fundamentalist controversy of the early twentieth century and its impact in Canada with reference to fundamentalism's inroads into all evangelical denominations in the U.S. He notes that Toronto pastor, T.T. Shields, attempted to make his church, Jarvis Street Baptist, the center of Canadian fundamentalism by "importing many American preachers." He further links the development of "sectarian movements" like Prairie Bible Institute in western Canada with the fact that many westerners had come from the U.S. where they had absorbed the populist religious and political fundamentalism of figures like William Jennings Bryan.[36]

Instructively, as it relates to the primary argument being established here, Grant speaks of the post-World War I popularity of church gymnasiums and summer camps in Canada as modeled after the direction taken by churches in the United States at this point in time. Popular mid-week youth programs such as the United Church of Canada's Canadian Girls in Training are also viewed by Grant as being "adapted from American models."[37]

Grant's work is filled with frequent brief comments such as the above that elucidate the significant impact of American thinking and programming on Canadian religious life following Canadian confederation in 1867. He

---

[32] Grant, 58-60.
[33] 60.
[34] 75.
[35] 118.
[36] 123-129.
[37] 131.

attributes the strong strain of social radicalism that emerged in some churches on the Canadian prairies in the 1930s to the fact that many prospective ministers from this region took their training at U.S. schools like Rochester Seminary where Walter Rauschenbusch fanned the flames of the social gospel.[38] He notes that Harry F. Ward, "perhaps the most prominent clerical advocate in the United States of close collaboration with Communists" was a popular speaker at places like the Alberta School of Religion during the late 1930s.[39] The demand for greater recognition of the role of the laity was spurred by the American Quaker, Elton Trueblood, whose books were widely read after he visited Canada to address United Church laymen in 1953.[40]

So prevalent has the American influence in Canadian religious life been in Grant's judgment that, appropriately, his review of Canadian church history up to the Canadian centennial celebrations in 1967 concludes with the suggestion that perhaps Canadians' affinity for traditionalism would spare the nation from "a temptation to take refuge in "fortress America.""[41] Conversely, as mentioned in the previous chapter of this book, perhaps at least some of the traditional deference of Canadians for established authority has over time merely been transferred, at least to some extent, from Great Britain to the United States.

David B. Marshall

David B. Marshall, professor of history at the University of Calgary, claims that many of Alberta's immigrants in the early twentieth century were Americans with evangelical leanings. He suggests that because they could not identify with mainline religious groups such as the Methodists or Lutherans, they clustered into sectarian forms of Protestantism.[42]

Marshall's observations resonate with what was mentioned in this book's previous chapter regarding the significant influx of Americans into Alberta in the early years of the 1900s. They also serve to introduce the

---

[38] Grant, 142.
[39] Ibid., 154.
[40] 170-171.
[41] 219.
[42] Graham Chandler, "Loosening our Bible Belt: The Changing Faith of Alberta," *Alberta Views*, November/December 2001, 31.

important role played by American citizens in the development of evangelical Christianity in Alberta following 1905 when the region officially became a province of Canada. Marshall's perspective reflects a prominent theme that emerges in the following standard work on church life in Alberta.

William E. Mann

The early chapters of William E. Mann's detailed, if somewhat dated, study entitled *Sect, Cult and Church in Alberta* overflow with references to the American influence behind the establishment of the numerous sects that took root in the province.[43] Indeed, on the basis of Mann's presentation, it would take less time to identify which of these groups did not have American ties than those that did. In a footnote at the outset of his study, for example, Mann states: "The history and theological roots of nearly all the groups dealt with in this study are described in the latest edition of E.T. Clark, *The Small Sect in America* (Nashville, Tenn., 1937)."[44]

Mann begins his overview with reference to the establishment of congregations in Alberta by such groups as the German Baptist Church of North America and the Evangelical Swedish Mission Covenant of America which came to Alberta via the respective German and Swedish immigrants to the United States who eventually came north.[45] He attributes the planting of the Church of the Brethren or "Dunkards," as they were popularly known, to planned emigration from the United States, noting that this group's subsequent decline can be attributed to theologically liberal congregations in the U.S. from where most of its pastors originated.[46]

Mann repeatedly uses phraseology such as "from the United States," "from the Dakotas," "from South Dakota," "originating in the northwest United States," "with headquarters in California" and "another American-born group" when he speaks of various Christian groups that came to Alberta. These included The Church of Christ, The Church of Christ

---

[43] As noted previously, Mann follows S.D. Clark (Mann was one of Clark's doctoral students) in using the term "sect" to refer to religious groups outside the mainline denominations that tended to reject popular culture and maintain a comparative exclusivity from the established denominations.

[44] Mann, *Sect, Cult and Church in Alberta*, 9.

[45] Ibid., 9-10.

[46] 10-11.

Scientist, The Seventh Day Adventists, The Hutterites, The Church of the Nazarene and The Rosicrucian Fellowship.[47]

At the time of my birth at Rose Valley, Saskatchewan, Canada, in December 1956, my father, Rev. Victor L. Callaway, was the pastor of a congregation associated with the Evangelical Free Church of America, a group Mann rightly identifies as originating in "the mid-western States" that first planted a church in Enchant, Alberta, in 1917.[48] The Evangelical Free Church of Canada did not become a separate entity from its American parent until the early 1980s.[49]

Mann's lengthy list continues. The Foursquare Church founded in Los Angeles in the 1920s by Canadian-born Aimee Semple McPherson started a congregation in Calgary in 1934 following several visits to the city by McPherson.[50] American based cults such as The Church of Truth and The Great I Am were also influential in Alberta in the 1930s.[51]

---

[47] 12-18.

[48] Mann, 19.

[49] On another personal note, prior to moving to suburban Chicago in 1981 to attend Trinity Evangelical Divinity School (TEDS), a seminary owned and operated by the Evangelical Free Church of America, I was personally encouraged by several leaders of the embryonic Evangelical Free Church of Canada to stay in Canada for seminary training. Ironically, Evangelical Free Church of America leaders were simultaneously encouraging me to attend TEDS since that school was offering a significant tuition grant to attract Canadian "Free Church" students. I did attend TEDS where 50% of my MDiv tuition was provided as a grant with the understanding that I would repay it upon completing the program via three years of service to either the EFCA or the EFCC.

Bill Taylor, *From Infancy to Adolescence: The Evangelical Free Church of Canada, 1984-2005* (Belleville, ON: Guardian Books, 2007) recounts the story of the EFCC's separation from the EFCA and its subsequent development. The book also indicates the significant number of PBI graduates who went on to pastor Evangelical Free Churches in Canada.

[50] Mann, 23. McPherson's remarkable and occasionally bizarre story can be found in Edith L. Blumhofer, *Aimee Semple McPherson: Everybody's Sister* (Grand Rapids, MI: Wm. Eerdmans Publishing Co., 1993). McPherson was a Canadian-born woman who found fame and success as a traveling evangelist in the United States. Informed speculation suggests that, given the number of American pastors/Christian leaders who came to Canada in the early 20th century, similar to McPherson's influence south of the border, (and arguably on a far less flamboyant scale), these American Christian leaders had an influence in Canada. L.E. Maxwell would be one example of this dynamic.

[51] Mann, 24-25.

In one of his work's boldest assertions, Mann claims the fundamentalist movement in Alberta was, in many respects, an extension of the great upsurge of fundamentalism he says began around 1877 in the United States. In documenting this aspect of American religious influence in Canada, he interestingly cites personal interaction with the United Church Superintendent of Missions for Alberta who indicated to him that perhaps 80 per cent of the United Church membership in Alberta was inclined to fundamentalism.[52]

In Mann's judgment, the popularity of the revival meeting or conference in Alberta during the 1940s had a definite American flavor. In commenting on the well-orchestrated planning that went into these sessions, he states that "most of the professional evangelists came from the American middle and far West."[53]

Mann is careful to point out that American religious influence was not always successful or even welcome in Alberta. For example, he identifies correspondence he had with the Alberta secretary of the "Dunkards" who indicated the trouble that particular group experienced in retaining American pastors for longer than two or three years. He states:

> Our experience with the American Pastors has not been too successful . . . They are somewhat inclined to consider Canada an adjunct to the U.S., which idea just will not go hand in hand with success for their pastoral work . . . [The mission board leaders] see only the likeness between the U.S. and Canada and not the few but vital differences and their underlying significance. [August 23, 1947][54]

What is readily apparent in Mann's volume on Alberta is a reality similar to that encountered in most of the other works already referenced in this chapter: American religious influence in Canada has always been present. Even in those situations where that influence was pointedly rejected by those helping forge the new country or one of its regions, the American influence served to help Canadians identify certain characteristics they did not want as a part of their religious experience.

---

[52] Grant, 29.
[53] 68-69.
[54] II.

Mark A. Noll

Mark Noll's *A History of Christianity in the United States and Canada* is a more recent religious history that deals with the broader theme of North American Christianity. It too makes an important contribution to establishing an adequate background against which to consider the main argument of this book. While Noll carefully outlines both the British and American influences in Canada's emerging religious culture, at one point going so far as to posit a Canadian "third way" as a combination of sorts of the two influences, he is unequivocal in his presentation of how certain aspects of American religious behavior and thought impacted Canada both before and after Canadian confederation.

Early in his narrative, Noll indicates that as early as the mid-eighteenth century, "a large contingent of New Englanders" were influential in introducing "instant religious pluralism" into what was primarily Catholic Nova Scotia.[55] He is nevertheless careful to balance the implications of this development by noting that the "Roman Catholic-Protestant admixture" and "a tighter relationship between governmental authority and religious life" would always distinguish Canadian religious life from that unfolding in the U.S.

Noll states that by the 1760s the majority of immigrants in the Canadian Maritime region consisted of New Englanders "and most of them shared the Puritan or evangelical convictions that were merging so easily with republican patriotism."[56] Although the Canadian deference for British political and religious authority always prevailed in British North America, the influence of New England Congregationalists helped set the stage for the ministry of Henry Alline, the American-born, Canadian-raised itinerant revivalist who introduced the contagious "New Light" emphasis to Nova Scotians.[57] Interestingly enough, Noll sees the popularity of Alline's

---

[55] Noll, *A History of Christianity in the United States and Canada*, 73.

[56] Mann, 127.

[57] G.A. Rawlyk, *Champions of the Truth*, 23: "Garrettson and Alline, so alike and yet so different, were an extraordinary team. The religious landscape of the Maritimes was permanently altered because of the charismatic preaching of these two American-born evangelists.

"New Light" gospel as a significant factor in keeping the residents of Nova Scotia from joining the American Revolution.[58]

When 35,000 loyalists left New England at the outbreak of the American War of Independence to settle in Halifax, the population of that region tripled. Noll suggests this loyalist influx not only brought such influences as Methodist preacher Freeborn Garrettson to Canada but also helped strengthen the Anglican Church.[59] Again, we see a sense of the irony in which one might say that American influence helped keep Canadians from becoming Americans or, at a minimum, helped strengthen certain early Canadian characteristics that helped distinguish them from Americans. Although Maritime Protestantism, to use Noll's words, "had been born within an American context," he is careful to present the region's religious life as a hybrid of U.S. oriented Protestant plurality and a Canadianized version of British traditionalism.[60]

In the tenth chapter entitled "Christian Canada," Noll steers a delicate balance in terms of explaining the emerging religious life in mid and late nineteenth century Canada. He states that although "there was much in Canada to remind observers of what was also transpiring in the United States," nonetheless "there was also much that was different."[61] If, as Noll asserts, the War of 1812 was a second firm rejection by Canadians of the bold American independent approach to politics and religion, he balances this claim by adding that the most effective religious leaders in Ontario "were much more likely to be Methodist evangelists in the populist mold

---

[58] Noll, 128.

    Rawlyk, *Champions of the Truth*, 25-26, offers another angle to this reality when he writes: ". . . the [Alline] revivals were viewed by the Maritime elite as being almost revolutionary threats to the *status quo*. These people tended to equate revivalism with American and, later, French republicanism and they did everything in their power to eradicate from the land what they disparagingly referred to as "New Light Fanaticism.""

[59] Noll, 17-18: "Soon after landing in Halifax, Garrettson had elbowed William Black [an English clergyman] aside and become the most influential Methodist leader in Nova Scotia . . . Though he spent only twenty-six months in Nova Scotia, Garrettson "left an abiding impression on the whole life of the province.""

    Rawlyk, *Wrapped Up in God*, 57: "[Garrettson's] influence in Nova Scotia, according to J.M. Buckley, author of *A History of Methodism in the United States*, "was almost equal to that of Wesley in Europe and Asbury in the United States.""

[60] Noll, 129.

[61] Ibid., 246.

of Francis Asbury than socially conservative Anglicans of the sort desired by Canada's British governors."[62]

As for choosing between British and American influence in important matters including religion, it is Noll's judgment that Canadians wanted the best of both and the worst of neither. This preference for a middle ground is what, as was noted earlier, Noll designates the Canadian "third way."

The context Noll establishes for Canadian religious life in the years leading up to the establishment of Prairie Bible Institute is decidedly a combination of British and American influences. Was religious life in Canada a 50%-50% mixture of the two? Noll never really says, preferring to describe it as a "uniquely Canadian" balance. What he does make clear in a manner that is helpful for my purposes here, however, is that American influence in Canadian religious life has always been both prominent and profound. He even employs terminology that could be interpreted to tie the inductive Bible study method that PBI prided itself on throughout the Maxwell era to American affection for the Baconian scientific method.[63]

Harry H. Hiller

The work of University of Calgary sociologist, Harry H. Hiller, merits brief mention here because of its value to the central argument of the book. In a 1978 *Canadian Journal of Sociology* article, Hiller advanced the importance of "continentalism" in the growth and development of sectarian Christianity in Canada. Picking up on John Webster Grant's application of the term "third force" to identify the fundamentalist/Pentecostal/evangelical

---

[62] 267.

[63] Noll, 276: "Canada's dominant Protestant theology at the end of the nineteenth century was well nourished by the evangelical stream that had begun in eighteenth-century Britain and broadened out in nineteenth-century North America. It was uniquely Canadian in balancing an American openness to innovation, optimism, and personal liberty with a British commitment to order, stability and tradition. Late nineteenth-century Canadian Protestant theology also owed a great deal to America in its full embrace of Baconian scientific procedure, since the United States was the place where a commitment to empirical induction had the longest and most vigorous life in the Western world. Finally, this Canadian theology also reflected British influence, especially in its endorsement of Christianized versions of evolution and modest views of biblical criticism alongside traditional commitments to evangelical doctrine and piety."

challenge to the prevailing influence of the mainline denominations in Canadian religious life, Hiller attributes the impressive growth of the "third force" in Canada to "continentalism." He presents a variety of statistics to validate that, because of proportionately greater activity among the "third force" in the United States, the remarkable growth of the "third force" in Canada is due to "continentalism" or the forging of "strong continentalist relationships, dependencies, and alliances" between Canadian "third force" groups and their more numerous "third force" American brethren.

In other words, in the time frame represented by the statistics that Hiller offers (1940-1974), he suggests there is ample evidence of a strong Canadian orientation to American "third force" organizations. Tellingly then, Hiller states: "Zwerman (1974) has applied Rex Lucas' term "branch plant mentality" to this Canadian relationship to American religious organizations."[64] In summing up his findings, Hiller writes:

> Canadian sectarians then have always had to look south of the border for direction, sustenance and social support as head office, publishing facilities, dynamic orators, educational institutions, and large local congregations provided models to inspire. Proximity to the United States, internal east-west communication difficulties in Canada, and a relatively small Canadian population have been some of the additional factors conducive to third force continentalism.[65]

It is necessary to emphasize that the situation in this regard has changed somewhat in Canada since Hiller made his initial observations. For example, both the Southern Baptists and the Evangelical Free Church that, at the time Hiller wrote his article, did not list separate statistics for their Canadian churches, now have vibrant, independent Canadian bodies.[66] Obviously, this

---

[64] Harry H. Hiller, "Continentalism, and the Third Force in Religion," *Canadian Journal of Sociology 3* (Spring 1978), 189.

[65] Ibid., 191-192. See also his comments (192) regarding the famous "frontier thesis" and Clark's suggestion that the evangelical movement in Canada only furthered closer ties with the movement across the international border.

[66] Taylor, *From Infancy to Adolescence.*

Richard Blackaby states regarding the Canadian Convention of Southern Baptists: "By February 1984 the committee had decided to recommend the formation of an autonomous Canadian convention with an organizational structure similar though not identical to that of a state convention in the United States. The Southern Baptist

means that at least some of the Canadian "third force" groups Hiller studied have sufficiently matured to the point where they have left their American parent's "nest" and become something more than a "branch plant."

Nevertheless, it is significant to point out that the findings which Hiller published in 1978 cover the period of time when Prairie Bible Institute was in its prime. Accordingly, it is not unreasonable to posit that PBI could very easily be viewed as a part of the Canadian "third force" that reflected a strong association with its American counterparts. In fact, as will be documented later, L.E. Maxwell consistently sought the counsel of colleagues at American Bible schools like Moody and Columbia for direction in his leadership of PBI. Indeed, as Hiebert points out, although there really was not much of an organized fraternity among the leadership of Canadian Bible institutes and colleges until the later years of Maxwell's tenure at PBI, when such did come into operation in the early 1960s it initially had a decidedly American influence.[67]

T.W. Acheson

An essay by T.W. Acheson calls attention to the very significant influence that the New England colonies' agitation for independence from Britain had on religious life in that part of Canada now known as the province of New Brunswick.[68] Acheson asserts that although New Brunswick became the designated "refuge for those who rejected the revolution and its values" and "a place where early leaders attempted to create a British social order, including an established Church of England," such an experiment was hardly a success. In fact, Acheson points out, "the religious institutions and assumptions of New Brunswickers after 1830 increasingly resembled American rather than British society."[69]

Convention adopted this proposal at its 1984 Convention thus presumably settling the "Canada question.'" See www.ccsb.ca/national-ministries/the-history-of-the-ccsb (accessed 25 April 2009).
[67] Hiebert, 37-38.
[68] T.W. Acheson, "Evangelicals and Public Life in Southern New Brunswick, 1830-1880" in Marguerite Van Die (ed.), *Religion and Public Life in Canada* (Toronto: Univ. of Toronto Press, 2001), 50-68.
[69] Ibid., 50.

Interestingly enough, Acheson claims, "the dominant thread in this transition was the growing influence of evangelicalism, a transdenominational Protestantism characterized by biblicism, conversionism, crucicentrism, and social activism." By 1860, he writes further, about a generation later than it occurred in the U.S., "evangelicals, organized denominationally, had become the culturally dominant civil religion in New Brunswick . . . remnants of the traditional religious establishment, increasingly found themselves on the political periphery." This was a pattern of development very similar to that which held sway in neighboring New England.[70]

George A. Rawlyk

Several footnotes in this section of the book have already called attention to the invaluable work of the late, esteemed Canadian church historian, George Rawlyk, as it relates to the matter of U.S. influence on Canadian religious life. Rawlyk's expertise on emerging Canadian religious life around the time of the American Revolution is indispensable in tracing the active and passive aspects of American influence on the political and religious sensitivities of its northern neighbor.

Throughout the numerous lectures and essays that form a large component of Rawlyk's written legacy is a consistent emphasis on the "acute disorientation and confusion" that the American War of Independence created in Nova Scotia.[71] For Rawlyk, there is little doubt that the disorientation generated by the conflict between Great Britain and the New England colonies left Nova Scotians ripe for the preaching of influential figures such as Henry Alline and Freeborn Garrettson.[72]

---

[70] Acheson, 50-51.

[71] George A. Rawlyk, *Wrapped Up in God*, 5. Rawlyk frequently uses the ideas of confusion and disorientation in discussing the impact of the American Revolution in Nova Scotia. See also p. 56.

[72] Ibid., 56-57: "And, as might have been expected, sometime "bizarre but emotionally satisfying ways of relating to God and others" became increasingly widespread phenomena as many Nova Scotians sought a renewed sense of "community belonging" in order to neutralize the powerful forces of alienation then sweeping the colony. It was a period when, it had been perceptively observed, "everything was believable" and "everything could be doubted." "Radical enthusiasts and visionaries," regarding themselves as the disciples of Henry Alline and as propagators of his tradition, became

Although these two American-born gentlemen differed significantly in their theological perspectives, such was the nature of their influence that Rawlyk suggests had Garrettson stayed longer than just two years in Nova Scotia, "the religious landscape of the Maritimes would have been radically different in the nineteenth and twentieth centuries."[73] Citing Buckley, Rawlyk indicates that Garrettson's twenty-six months in Nova Scotia enabled him to leave "an abiding impression on the life of the whole province."[74]

As for Alline, Rawlyk speculates that both Alline's conversion experience as well as his embracing and proclaiming a highly mystical understanding of Christianity might be explained at least in part in terms of the social upheaval associated with the New England colonies' quest for political independence. For instance, Rawlyk writes that Alline's conversion at twenty-seven years of age in February 1775 was "significantly shaped" by three factors: a finely developed morbid introspection, a fear of imminent death, and "by the considerable pressure he felt to commit himself one way or another during the early months of the American Revolutionary struggle."[75] Although Rawlyk at times appears to shy away from suggesting that Alline's conversion was related to the unrest unfolding in the New England colonies, he nevertheless advances Alline's view that the Nova Scotia "Yankees" had a "special predestined role to play in God's plan for the world" and such was directly related to "the tragic backsliding of New England."[76]

Of particular significance here for the purposes of this brook is that, regardless of what conclusions one ultimately draws regarding the motivation behind Alline's dramatic conversion experience, the reality is

---

the "advanced guard" of the renewed "popular evangelical movement with which they shared a common hostility to orthodox authority.'"

[73] Rawlyk, 75.

[74] Rawlyk, 58.

[75] G.A. Rawlyk, *Ravished by the Spirit: Religious Revivals, Baptists and Henry Alline* (Montreal/Kingston: McGill-Queen's Univ. Press, 1984), 3.

[76] Ibid., 17-21; Rawlyk vacillates somewhat on the nature of the influence of Anglo-American matters on Alline's life. For instance, after acknowledging legitimacy in the view of some that Alline's religious commitment was influenced by "Revolutionary ideology," he writes: "Outside temporal events did not, in any way, impinge on his "New Birth" experience" (17). A few pages later (21), however, he notes: ". . . the Anglo-American crisis helped to shape Alline's resolve "to preach the gospel . . .'"

that this man who so significantly influenced the religious life of what is now a part of Canada did so within the context of a constituency that was greatly impacted by political and religious developments in New England. Alline's ministry was carried out among a people who lived within range of the shadow cast by a revolutionary political experiment with all of its implications for notions of liberty, authority and the self.

That developments in New England directly impacted Alline himself and therefore indirectly impacted Nova Scotians is evident by seemingly incidental developments such as his decision to desert his plans to go to Boston for theological education in light of the political upheaval going on there.[77] Would Henry Alline ever have returned to Nova Scotia had he gone to Boston to train for the ministry?

Although it is somewhat foolish to speculate on such matters, one thing appears certain: Canadian church history was substantially impacted by developments in New England that served to keep Henry Alline in Nova Scotia. This simple incident is a telling vignette from the life of one man as it relates to this book's call to give due and proper attention to the enormity of American influence on Canadian religious life.

Robert K. Burkinshaw

In a collection of essays entitled *Amazing Grace* and edited by George Rawlyk and Mark A. Noll, the Canadian historian, Robert K. Burkinshaw, makes several observations that are useful to the core argument of this book.[78] In the course of tracing the history of evangelicalism in British Columbia (B.C), Canada's most westerly province, Burkinshaw points out the following realities.[79]

Despite the fact that B.C. is often referred to as the "California of Canada" given its reputation as a bastion of materialism and hedonism, and the reality that its evangelical population eventually exceeded that of Alberta's in the latter stages of the twentieth century, Burkinshaw writes:

[77] Rawlyk, 20-21.
[78] Robert K. Burkinshaw, "Conservative Evangelicalism in the Twentieth Century "West:" British Columbia and the United States," 317-348, in George A. Rawlyk and Mark A. Noll (eds.), *Amazing Grace: Evangelicalism in Australia, Britain, Canada and the United States.*
[79] Ibid., 317-319.

"it is clear that American influences and characteristics were not prevalent within British Columbian evangelicalism to the same extent that they were in the neighboring province of Alberta." To substantiate this claim, Burkinshaw identifies some of the same dynamics that either already have been or will yet be identified in this book: the significant influx of Americans into Alberta in the early twentieth century that saw Americans account for up to 50 percent of the farmers in southern Alberta by the 1920s; radio preaching in the prairie provinces by American evangelists; L.E. Maxwell of Prairie Bible Institute who retained his American citizenship all his life, and PBI's "powerful influence" in providing pastors and Christian workers for denominations like the Christian and Missionary Alliance, Evangelical Free Church, Associated Gospel Churches, as well as "independent churches and home-mission organizations."

By way of contrast, in an effort to enhance his argument regarding the more British orientation of B.C. as compared to Alberta, Burkinshaw reports that B.C. received "by far the highest number of British immigrants" of any Canadian province; that the proportion of American immigrants in B.C. in 1911 was "considerably less than half that in Alberta" while approximately one-third of B.C.'s residents at the time were "recent British immigrants;" and that "organized conservative resistance to liberalism" arrived later in British Columbia than it did in the western United States.

As noted previously, this book provides documentation indicating Maxwell sought counsel for strategic leadership decisions at PBI from leadership personnel at American institutions like Moody Bible Institute, Columbia Bible College, and Fuller Seminary. Conversely, Burkinshaw indicates that fundamentalists in British Columbia looked to the influences of the eminent British pastor Charles Spurgeon and the British ex-patriate, Toronto pastor T.T. Shields, as their role models.

This is not to suggest that American religious influence in B.C. was entirely inconsequential. Indeed, as Burkinshaw reveals, the first Bible institute in western Canada, established as Vancouver Bible Training School (VBTS) in 1918, had close ties with the rationale associated with the first American Bible schools. He writes that the purposes of VBTS's founder, Walter Elllis, were very similar to the emphases of the founders of the earliest American Bible schools. Such emphases were identified in Brereton's work referred to earlier in this overview.[80]

In documenting that fundamentalists in B.C. were far more British-oriented than their brethren in the provinces of Alberta and Saskatchewan, Burkinshaw calls attention to a "rather interesting reversal of the usual view of the American influence on Canadian fundamentalism." He notes that "Baptists in the more American-oriented provinces of Alberta and Saskatchewan were much less inclined ⸤to separatist fundamentalism" than were their more British-influenced counterparts in B.C. Although a substantially higher proportion of Baptists in the two prairie provinces were American-born and a much larger number of Baptist ministers on the prairies were trained in the U.S. than was the case in B.C., Burkinshaw notes that separatist fundamentalism had nowhere near the kind of impact in Baptist churches on the Canadian prairies that it did in the same circles in B.C. He attributes this reality to the fact that whereas the Baptist pastors and professors of the prairies had attended American seminaries associated with the Northern Baptists such as Crozer, Rochester, and Chicago, "many British Columbian Baptists, in contrast, viewed the Northern Baptist Convention with great suspicion."[81]

As to how this latter element of Burkinshaw's research relates to my overall argument, writing via the lens of the religious history of British Columbia, Burkinshaw corroborates the reality documented here concerning the significant American presence in western Canada and its corresponding influence, particularly as such related to the province of Alberta. Nevertheless, his work also calls to our attention that American religious influence in western Canada did not always or only advance the interests of American fundamentalism. With particular regard to the prairie provinces of Alberta and Saskatchewan, it also served to enhance the interests of modernist theological perspectives.

---

[80] Burkinshaw, 332-333: "In many ways Ellis's emphases were much like those of the founders of the earliest American Bible schools in the years well before the heat of the controversies in the period of World War I and the 1920s heightened the mood of defensiveness and militancy. He did not see his school as competing with the denominational theological colleges. Instead, his purpose of the new school was to train a generation of evangelists. It "aims to furnish a thorough and practical use of the English Bible, and to send forth the workers with an extreme love of souls, and a full realization of the presence and power of the Holy Spirit in their life and service.""

[81] Burkinshaw, 342-343.

Eric R. Crouse

Perhaps the clearest portrait of the powerful influences of American populist revivalism at a particular point in Canadian history is that portrayed by Eric R. Crouse. Drawing on his doctoral research at Queen's University, Crouse traces the very warm reception that Canadian audiences and the secular media extended to the forerunners of the American fundamentalist movement, or proto-fundamentalists. This included figures such as Dwight L. Moody, Reuben A. Torrey and J. Wilbur Chapman who visited Canada immediately preceding the arrival of the twentieth century until just before the First World War.[82]

Almost forty years before the establishment of Prairie Bible Institute, these Americans, whose names, reputations and writings would come to be held in high regard at PBI throughout the L.E. Maxwell era, captivated large audiences from Fredericton on the east cost of Canada right across to Vancouver and Victoria in the far west. Indeed, the meetings of Moody, Torrey and Chapman were so well attended that they garnered front page headlines in major newspapers in Canadian cities such as Brantford, Ottawa, Fredericton, Winnipeg, Orillia and Toronto. Crouse also documents that even lesser-known American evangelists such as southerners Sam Jones and Sam Small conducted well-attended meetings "in at least seven urban centres throughout central Canada in 1886 and 1887."[83]

Of particular usefulness to the intent of this book is to note that Crouse openly acknowledges that many of the recognized historians of religion in Canada have been somewhat reluctant to acknowledge the extent of

---

[82] Eric R. Crouse, *Revival in the City: The Impact of American Evangelists in Canada 1884-1914* (Montreal-Kingston: McGill-Queens' Univ. Press, 2005), 4. Crouse follows Ronald Sawatzky in designating these men "proto-fundamentalists" in viewing them as "forerunners of the fundamentalist movement." Sawatzky's PhD dissertation, "Looking for that Blessed Hope," already referred to several times in this book, is similar to Crouse's work in showing the similarity of interests that existed among Canadian and American "proto-fundamentalists" in the last couple of decades of the nineteenth century. As Sawatzky shows, Canadian and American believers worked side by side in the preparation and execution of the various Prophecy and Bible conferences that were held during this time including the Niagara Bible Conference which is the focus of Sawatzky's research.

[83] Ibid., 6.

American influence in the northern country's Protestant life.[84] Nevertheless, Crouse suggests that insufficient attention has been paid to these visiting American evangelists who proclaimed conservative evangelicalism at the grass-roots level. He convincingly maintains that:

> a careful examination of the press coverage of revivalism will underscore the important role that conservative as opposed to "progressive" evangelicals played in attracting American evangelists to Canada. Moreover, a more detailed examination not only of the means but also of the revival message may indeed conclude that the popularity and impact of American revivalists in Canada, particularly among the working class, depended precisely on their preaching a conservative evangelical message that maintained rather than sacrificed biblical truths."[85]

It is important to emphasize that while the viewpoints of the seasoned authorities Crouse refers to above certainly merit due respect, their failure to pick up on the influence of the American proto-fundamentalist evangelists in English Canada during the thirty-year period immediately before and after 1900 may contribute to why Stackhouse minimizes the impact of American fundamentalism in Canada in general and at PBI in particular. Yet newer studies such as Crouse's make it increasingly difficult to overlook the significant implications of American influence in Canadian Christianity. His work and that of other Canadian scholars such as Dr. Sam Reimer serve as a clarion call for a more nuanced understanding of American influence in Canadian religious life than has held sway to date.

Despite the allowance Crouse makes for Canadian religious scholars' preoccupation with establishment Protestantism, the Introduction of his book is an urgent call for academics to recognize the profound effect the visiting American evangelists had on Canadian popular culture as the twentieth century dawned. There may even be an element of implicit rebuke in his pointed rhetoric in this regard. That is, regardless of one's personal opinion of a religious appeal that catered to the working classes, there is no denying its strong influence among the Canadian populace at the time. Crouse writes:

[84] Crouse, 163, note 7: "Historians who distance Canadian Protestants from the American experience include George Rawlyk, Michael Gauvreau, and Nancy Christie, to name only a few."
[85] Crouse, 10-11.

In a cultural sense, the American-Canadian border became remarkably fluid, and, consequently, contrary to arguments that claim Canadian Protestant exceptionalism, the American Protestant experience played a significant role in shaping Canadian evangelicalism . . . throughout all of English Canada, the impact of the American evangelists was exponential since local Protestant clergy and evangelists often modeled their message and methodology after the well-known evangelists. Moreover, the proliferation of revival reports in local newspapers brought an American brand of popular conservative evangelicalism to many thousands of households in most regions of English Canada.[86]

He is emphatic in his concern to establish his point:

Before the sounds and images of American radio, talking movies, and television, there was an onslaught of American popular religion into the lives of a surprising number of English Canadians. As a result of the emergence of famous Protestant evangelists in the United States from the mid-1870s to the First World War, populist forms of American conservative evangelicalism flourished in Canada. Many English-Canadian workers embraced the revivalism and conservative evangelicalism of visiting Americans who held meetings from coast to coast in churches, roller rinks, halls, theatres, and other public urban spaces. The attendance exceeded one and a half million for the approximately eight hundred revival meetings held by the best-known American evangelists of the late nineteenth and early twentieth centuries.[87]

Crouse even goes so far as to suggest:

"The Americanization of Canada," which scholars debate in regard to social, political, and economic issues of the twentieth century, began to occur in the late nineteenth century as a result of visits by well-known American evangelists who upheld conservative theological, social, and economic ideals . . . In many ways a significant number of Canadians looked to mother Britain for cultural and national guidance (although

---

[86] Crouse, 5.
[87] Ibid., 3.

this became less so in twentieth-century Canada), but, on the matter of religion, large masses of Canadian Protestants found American popular evangelists especially attractive.[88]

As my book documents, the form of Protestant Christianity that characterized Prairie Bible Institute in the L.E. Maxwell era reflected a number of attributes that defined the religious experience made popular by these visiting American evangelists. For example, PBI opposed an intellectual approach to divine matters, choosing rather to emphasize a subjective approach to faith. Individuals were primarily preoccupied with what God was doing for them or saying to them personally that very hour or day through their studies and their participation in Prairie's community life. The viewpoint of the revered clergy in the key churches of established denominations or the perspectives of learned academics in the mainline seminaries was by and large both disdained and ignored. Of far greater importance were the gripping tales of visiting revivalists or missionaries who related "what God was doing" on the other side of the world. Prairie's conferences even featured a special hymnbook called "Hymns That Live" containing many of the songs written by D.L. Moody's musical counterpart, Ira D. Sankey, or Charles Alexander, who held a similar role in meetings where R.A. Torrey was the preacher.

In this respect, the following observation by Crouse concerning the spirit of popular religion that these visiting Americans brought with them aptly captures similar emphases and attitudes that prevailed at PBI years later.

the old-fashioned gospel message, the popular hymns, and the methods of the major American evangelists, all of which received such lavish press attention, also represented an expression of popular religion. Popular religion seeks to reject both the clerical mediation between humankind and God and an over-intellectualized form of religious practice. It usually exists in tension with established religious groups, represents beliefs channeled by word of mouth or by popular literature rather than be seminaries of established religion, and rejects the "modernization" that is accepted by official religion.[89]

---

[88] Crouse, 4-5.
[89] Crouse, 6.

Although Crouse is careful to point out that the primary impact of American revivalism in Canada was over before the First World War began, it should be noted that Reuben A. Torrey was preaching in Canada at precisely the same time a couple of California businessmen were preparing *The Fundamentals* for publication. Torrey, of course, contributed several essays to that initial theological treatise which outlined what fundamentalists believed. In this respect, it is significant to call attention to the fact that one of the fathers of American fundamentalism was part of a series of popular American evangelists whose visits to Canada, as verified by Canadian media, had an impressive influence on religious life in Canada.[90]

Crouse summarizes well the unmistakable importance of this period of Canadian history as the young nation entered the rocky twentieth century. Given the fluidity of the international border between Canada and the U.S. at the time, it is hardly surprising that a young American from Kansas, L.E. Maxwell, headed north in the early 1920s to help nurture seeds sown by Moody, Torrey, Chapman and others.

To cite Crouse again in this regard:

For the time period investigated here, there was no doubting the popularity of American revivalism among Canadian workers . . . When the accelerated pace of change tore at Canadian society, the American evangelists represented the paradoxical spirit of the era, maintaining past certitudes and adapting modern ways as they preached . . . During the late nineteenth and early twentieth-centuries, American revivalism was a dominant element in a Canadian Protestantism buffeted by modern stresses.[91]

*   *   *

The last two chapters have established the existence of a prominent American influence in British North American and Canadian life since the time of American independence. It might effectively be argued that such influence is diminishing as Canada grows and matures as a national entity.

[90] Marsden, *Fundamentalism and American Culture* (1980), 47: "Torrey was one of the principal architects of fundamentalist thought."
[91] Crouse, 12-13.

Nevertheless, the historical record as it relates to the purposes of this book is clear: American influence in Western Canada at the time Prairie Bible Institute was founded and establishing its core identity was significant. This reality was reflected prominently at the school in the nature of the Christian fundamentalism that prevailed at PBI throughout the Leslie Earl Maxwell era.

CHAPTER EIGHT

Leslie Earl Maxwell

The brief sketches of the personalities visited in the next two chapters are presented in affirmation of Marsden's words noted earlier that describe fundamentalism as "a mosaic of divergent and sometimes contradictory traditions and tendencies that could never be totally integrated."[1] If this characteristic is true of fundamentalism as a collective movement, such an assessment is also helpful in describing the temperaments and personalities of many of the constituency's individual leaders. A combination of winsome graciousness and combative dogmatism was often evident in their unique personal constitutions.

From the early fall of 1922 when he completed his studies at Midland Bible Institute in Kansas City until his death at Three Hills in February of 1984, the life of L.E. Maxwell was inextricably linked with the history of Prairie Bible Institute. In many ways, Maxwell both defined and embodied the school. His personality, his theology and his philosophy of Christian community played a dominant role in the school's identity particularly during its first fifty years of existence when Maxwell was in the prime of his career. Any attempt to accurately define PBI during the Maxwell era, therefore, requires that we establish a basic portrait of this intriguing individual. [2]

L.E. Maxwell frequently used the term "fundamental folk" in reference to himself, PBI and that expression of Christianity he was most comfortable with and considered to most accurately reflect the lifestyle and theology he believed were endorsed by Scripture. His public discourses and writings were replete with references to "we fundamental folk" and quotations from the standard-bearers of American proto-fundamentalism such as

---

[1] See Chapter Three of this book, footnote 11.

[2] The following composite is primarily taken from material found in Keller (1966), Goertz (1980) who had several extensive interviews with Maxwell, Maxwell's grandson Spaulding (1991) and my personal recollection.

R.A. Torrey, A. J. Gordon, A.W. Tozer and D.L. Moody.[3] And, as noted previously, Maxwell was definitely not averse to employing a militant rhetoric or temperament when he considered such to be necessary.

A dynamic briefly spoken of earlier in this book again deserves brief mention. As noted, while fundamentalism has been interpreted by many primarily in terms of its theological or religious characteristics, some scholars prefer to view it mainly as a social protest movement based on an affinity for tradition and anti-intellectualism.[4] It is impossible, however, to read the various histories of fundamentalism without realizing there is also a psychological factor at work in the personalities of those who are so adamant and rigid in their beliefs.[5] Similarly, fundamentalist communities frequently develop a collective psyche with distinct characteristics. This is a reality that is perhaps too often overlooked in some efforts to understand fundamentalism as a movement and the fundamentalist as an individual.[6]

[3] L.E. Maxwell, "Jonah and His Gourd: God's Dealings With a Selfish Servant," *Prairie Overcomer*, 20, No. 9, (Sept. 1947), 237: "As Bible-loving fundamentalists, we claim that "there is none other name under heaven given among men, where by we (yea, and all others) must be saved."" L.E. Maxwell, *World Missions: Total War*, Preface: "It might be expected that missionary interest would be minimal among the liberals as a natural consequence of their false theology. But when fundamental folk fail to fulfill the Great Commission, we must needs ferret out the cause thereof." T.S. Rendall Library at P.B.I. audio tape entitled "The Laodicean Church" (AC 228 MAXW; n.d.): "We fundamental folks, orthodox and evangelical, are not frozen stiff like the modernists and Pharisees. Neither are we hot. We're not boiling for God as we should be, we're just half-baked, half-hearted . . ."

[4] The assessments of Niebuhr, Cole, Furniss and Hofstadter all contain elements of this perspective.

[5] Arthur Marwick, *The Nature of History*, 110: "Just how far the historical biographer should penetrate into the depth psychology of his subject is by no means a settled matter, even among those historians who are most receptive to the influences of the social sciences . . . Although there is in practice no rigid line between the *individual* psychology . . . and the *group* or *social* psychology which must be of utmost value to the historian, the distinction is one which should always be borne in mind."

[6] Ralph W. Hood, Jr., Peter C. Hill, and W. Paul Williamson., *The Psychology of Religious Fundamentalism* (New York/London: The Guilford Press, 2005) is a recent excellent work that brings this reality into clearer focus. See also Riesbrodt, *Pious Passion*.

See Chapter Three of this book, footnote 55: *"Fundamentalism and the Modern World . . ."* where Rauf states, 25: "Much of what we call fundamentalism today in the Muslim world is less accurately described by that term. It's more a psychology, a reaction to a perceived attack . . ." In the same article, Armstrong observes, 22: ". . . every fundamentalist movement that I've studied—in Judaism, Christianity, and Islam—is

Part of what leads me to contend that the Prairie Bible Institute of the Maxwell era had much in common with early American fundamentalism is the ample evidence that exists of Maxwell's combative temperament, particularly during the first half of his tenure.[7] As seen previously, during the prime of his career he did not shrink from calling Wheaton College to account when rumors circulated regarding its purported drift into modernism.[8] Similarly, in what was often referred to by supporters as Maxwell's "prophetic" nature, he was not hesitant in castigating the teachings and behavior of such individual modernists as Harry Fosdick. Contrary to what Stackhouse asserts and as Chapter Fourteen of this book will clarify, organizations that were considered theologically corrupt such as The United Church of Canada and the Roman Catholic Church were also a frequent target of Maxwell's ire.[9]

rooted in a profound fear. They are convinced, even here in the United States, that modern liberal secular society wants to wipe out religion in some way or is destructive to faith."

[7] *The Prairie Pastor*, P.B.I.'s official publication from 1928 until it merged with the *Prairie Overcomer* in the early 1940s contains numerous brief notations or articles which bang the fundamentalist drum against the perceived ills of German rationalism: "The Looting of a Legacy" in 4, No. 10; (October 1931), 6; modernism: "A Word for Modernists" in 2, No. 3; (March 1929), 4-5; worldliness in the church as evidenced by movies being shown in churches: ("What Are We Coming To?" in 2, No. 6; (June 1929), 1; communism: in "Awake Thou That Sleepest," 3, No. 11; (November 1930), 1; declining standards in women's dress: "Women's Dress," 1, No. 9; (September 1928), 1; intellect/reason: "Poor Puny Reason," 1, No. 10; (October 1928), 1; and evolution: "Is It True? Is Man Coming Up or Going Down?" in 2, No. 6; (June 1929), 4. *Prairie Pastor* also contained articles supportive of many fundamentalist causes such as the imminence of Christ's return: "Nearing the End?" in 3, No. 5; (May 1930), 1; Bible schools as defenders of the faith: Defenders of the Faith" in 3, No. 12; (December 1930), 3; missions: "Every Christian a Missionary" in 1, No. 6; (June 1928), 7; the need for fundamentalists to have backbone: "Wishbones or Backbones?" in 1, No. 6; (June 1928), 1; the joy of revival: "Rejoice With Us" in 4, No. 12; (December 1931), 9; the ideal of martyrdom: "The Martyr in the Making" in 5, No. 1; (January 1932), 3; the reality of hell: "A Vision of Hell" in 5, No. 4; (April 1932), 1.

As well, early issues of the *Prairie Pastor* carried articles by leading American fundamentalists such as Bob Jones, Sr.: "A College Tragedy" in 4, No. 12; (December 1931), 3, and W. B. Riley "The Grief of Parents" in 2, No. 3; (March 1929), 3.

[8] See Introduction of this book, footnote 10.

[9] L.E. Maxwell, "Rotten!" in the *Prairie Pastor*, 4, No. 10, (Oct. 1931), 1: "Dr. Ernest Thomas, leader of the United Church and regular contributor to the *New Outlook* says:

Maxwell's upbringing

A review of Maxwell's early years reveals that the Kansas grain-farming couple who brought him into the world demonstrated greater concern for the material aspects of life than for spiritual matters. Young Leslie consequently knew little about God in his early years and later summarized them as a period when he "played ball, played pool and played the fool."[10] The tragic death of a younger brother in a farm accident when Maxwell was eleven years of age was a rare occasion when he saw a soft side to his father who tearfully speculated that "maybe Ernest went to heaven." Maxwell would later recall being overwhelmed at the time with the realization that, should his turn come to die, he had no certainty he would ever see his brother again.

His first encounter with preaching and church life occurred when a fire-and-brimstone Methodist evangelist held meetings at a local church. Maxwell attended with a number of other young teenagers. The evangelist's wife apparently dramatized the horrors of hell so effectively that a sense of fear and judgment drove young Leslie to the altar that night along with some of his friends. A few days later when he responded to being kicked by a horse with a stream of profanity, he ruefully concluded his salvation wasn't genuine and returned to his worldly ways.

The Christian witness of a faithful aunt who had been praying for Leslie since before his birth was to yield results however. Despite the fact that he went to work with his father in the pool hall business while still an impressionable youth, Maxwell could not shake the conviction that he was a sinner and that, as such, an eternal and fearful punishment awaited him.

"Every element of 'possessive morality' in the relations of men to women is being rejected. Every vestige of the idea of a man's property or monopoly in his wife must be set aside." We say, 'rotten.' Sunken doctrine leads to sunken living." The same issue of the *Prairie Pastor* contains a lengthy commendation of a booklet by a United Church preacher "who has rendered a valuable service to all the members of that constituency who wish to know the truth about the official teachings of their denomination. Quoting from the *New Outlook* and from many leading church officials, J.N. Sturk, Winnipeg, Lay-preacher of the United Church in his book *"The Looting of a Legacy,"* shows how the current teachings of his church are contradictory to all the historic creeds of Christendom . . ."

10 Maxwell frequently employed this catchy phrase in sermons and lectures when describing his early years.

Following his high school graduation, the praying aunt secured a job for him in Kansas City and encouraged Maxwell to attend chapel services with her on Sundays. Despite having acquired a disdain for Christians by then, his respect for his aunt prompted him to accompany her to worship where the persistent, if perfunctory, message of the pastor to "come to Christ and the church" in time penetrated Leslie's calloused conscience.

He soon found himself regularly wrestling with the knowledge of his sin and a distinct fear that he was headed for hell. This battle eventually led to another intense spiritual experience wherein Maxwell knelt by his bed one night while his roommate slept and cried out to God to forgive his sins. The very strong emotional element involved in Maxwell's conversion is conveyed by Keller when he writes:

> Immediately a sense of being right with God swept like a billow over him. From that moment he knew he had been converted. Although he had met God, he had no knowledge whatever of the grounds or the merit upon which he had been justified before God. He knew only that his heart was right with God. In that knowledge he rejoiced.[11]

Shortly after his conversion, Maxwell was taken by his aunt to hear Dr. Walter Wilson, a prominent Bible teacher who also happened to be a medical doctor. Wilson's beliefs followed in the theological footprints of the famed proto-fundamentalist, Dwight L. Moody, and were published in several books by Moody Press.[12]

Following service in France with the U.S. Army during World War I throughout which he courageously maintained his Christian testimony, Maxwell prepared to follow up on his desire to go into God's service. Although encouraged by his pastor, a Moody Bible Institute graduate, to attend that school, Maxwell explained that he had a widowed mother to help support financially and simply could not go to Chicago.

Recalling the new Bible school that W.C. Stevens was starting in Kansas City, the pastor then advised Maxwell to seek the counsel of the veteran Bible teacher. One visit with the former Nyack instructor was sufficient to convince the former soldier of what he needed to do. He immediately

---

[11] Keller, 32.
[12] Walter L. Wilson, *The Romance of a Doctor's Visits* (Chicago: Moody Press, 1935) is an example of such.

enrolled in Midland Bible Institute, a commitment that enabled him to work half-days at a Kansas City financial enterprise in order to support his mother back in Salina.

It is somewhat significant for the purposes of this historical account to note that the early years of Maxwell's life were characterized by periods of intense spiritual turmoil. Keller indicates, for instance, that even prior to meeting Stevens, Maxwell:

> wrestled with problems arising from his desire for a closer walk with God. Hour after hour, night upon night, he agonized in tears and turmoil, attempting to "pray the old man out and the new man in." He lived and relived the experience that is drawn so vividly by Paul in Romans 7: "O wretched man that I am! Who shall deliver me from the body of this death?" How he longed for deliverance from the power of sin—for victory in Christ! So brutal had been the battle that raged within his heart that by summer's end he had shed fifteen pounds of body weight in his struggle.[13]

Keller also relates a key incident during Maxwell's final year of Bible school in Kansas City that helps us comprehend the latter's life-long understanding of the Christian experience as an intense battle wherein he believed it was his responsibility "to reach a place of utter capitulation to the commands of Christ."[14] Choosing to become involved in a matter at the school which apparently was really none of Maxwell's concern, Keller speaks of the incident as "an open-handed demonstration of ""self" asserting itself" which eventually resulted in Maxwell being "brought to a point of utter mortification" wherein "God's gracious Holy Spirit revealed to him the utter loathsomeness of himself." The matter was finally resolved, Keller conveys, when, weeping bitterly before the Lord and the entire student body, Maxwell "died" to "self."

It was shortly after this excruciating inner experience that Maxwell travelled north to Alberta, Canada, to be the primary instructor of what was to become Prairie Bible Institute. With such crisis experiences deeply etched on his consciousness, it is not surprising that Maxwell's view of the

---

[13]   Keller, 39.
[14]   Ibid., 43f.

Christian life as an intense spiritual battle was woven into the fabric of PBI's emerging culture from the very beginning.

Mention was made earlier in this book that fundamentalism is characterized by a number of defining characteristics including militant aversion to modernity and a corresponding belief that fundamentalists are under siege by modernity. Although more specific examples of these realities at play at PBI during the Maxwell era will be presented later in this study, it is important at this point to identify the evidence of this fundamentalist dynamic in a generalized way in the formative years of L.E. Maxwell.

As has been observed, struggle and battle were a part of Maxwell's spiritual experience from the outset. His initial Christian awakenings involved intense spiritual battle as he wrestled with the turmoil of believing he was a sinner and headed for hell. An important moment of victory for him in this crisis was the night in his rooming house when he cried out to God to forgive his sins.

As was also evident in the life of J. Fergus Kirk, both men endured crisis spiritual experiences of no small import while they were young adults. This reality not only portrayed their personal experience of the Christian life as a battle but also made a substantial contribution to an environment at PBI wherein personal spiritual battle and crises were viewed as the norm in the lives of those involved in the Bible school community. Accordingly, the "battle" motif that came to define the normal Christian experience for "disciplined soldiers" at PBI was essentially present from the very beginning. Both in this generalized manner as well as in specific ways yet to be identified, this emphasis at PBI was in harmony with the emerging fundamentalist notion of the Christian life being one wherein various forms of spiritual battle were the norm.

In such an environment, significant attention was paid at PBI to such emphases as "surrendering to God," "doing battle with the enemy," or "doing business with God," to cite one of Maxwell's favorite expressions. Specific areas of one's life that had, as yet, to be "crucified," were to be identified and abandoned. Modernist theology and worldly influences were considered prospective instruments of corruption and thus part and parcel of the spiritual battle we were engaged in and in need of being banished from one's life.

Further, it should be noted that L.E. Maxwell's theological orientation at Midland Bible Institute included experiences and counsel wherein the believer was perceived to be under siege by "self." Thus, notions such as "dying to self" and "crucifying the flesh" that became distinguishing emphases in Maxwell's theology and frequent themes in his writings, sermons and lectures, surfaced quite early in his theological experience and education. It is not surprising then that community life at PBI during the Maxwell era reflected the conviction that believers were under siege by the world, the flesh and the devil. It was a belief derived from his own fundamentalist education that, in turn, was quickly incorporated into the theological orientation of PBI and tied the school to the broader fundamentalist movement.

Maxwell's writings

A. The Prairie Pastor/The Prairie Overcomer

Maxwell's first published articles began to appear in 1925 with the launch of a newsletter called *The Prairie Pastor* of which he was the editor.[15] In 1928 the *Pastor* became a monthly offering in a small magazine format of several pages in length. Identified on the front page as the "Organ of the Prairie Bible Institute," it was circulated primarily to the school's alumni and supporting constituency.[16]

In addition to advertising various events at PBI that were open to the public, the journal regularly contained commentary on contemporary news and world developments. As well, a variety of pieces were included by Maxwell and his first co-editor, Dorothy R. Miller, on spiritual themes they considered important. Articles or citations from such that had originally appeared in similar publications regularly consulted by the editors were also frequently reprinted in the *Pastor*.[17]

---

[15] Davidson, 33.

[16] Copies of *The Prairie Pastor* that are available in the PBI Library Archives begin in 1928. The Masthead declared: "Published monthly in the interest of good Bible Teaching and Missionary appeal, and setting forth the position of the Prairie Bible Institute as an unsectarian institution for the Wide-West."

[17] Given the format that was used in laying out the structure of *The Prairie Pastor* it is not always clear whether an article is by Maxwell, Miller or another PBI instructor or even if the article is an original by Maxwell or Miller or a reprint borrowed from another publication.

From its inception the *Pastor* sounded a strong voice in support of the fundamentalist cause.[18] In addition to prominent exposure given to articles that advanced PBI's passion for holiness and overseas missions, many of the journal's initial pieces advocated leading fundamentalist perspectives including: 1) established universities and colleges as being under the control of modernists intent on undermining the Christian faith; 2) the historic Christian faith as being under assault by German rationalism and evolutionary theory; 3) the faithful who belonged to the true church as being under siege; 4) the importance of believers being on guard against the evils of Hollywood and the entertainment and fashion industries; 5) the necessity of believers maintaining separation from the world, and so forth.

Maxwell, for example, would opine as follows in the *Pastor*:

It is a sad fact that during the past generation, our high schools, colleges, and publishing houses (religious as well as secular) have largely come under the control of destroyers of the faith. The majority of our higher educational institutions are impregnated with an evolutionary modernistic philosophy, which is utterly destructive of faith in God's Word. The heart of the natural man cannot but welcome such "philosophy and vain deceit." . . . A missionary who gives much of her time to working amongst young men attending one of the higher schools in this country, tells me with what avidity they devour and digest anything of German philosophy, which seems to prove that God is non-existent . . . [19]

Behold, the gathering clouds of Modernism and atheism unitedly doing their best to crush the very life out of God's chosen ones. Shall Modernism triumph and be able to say, "Aha, aha, so would we have it!"[20]

---

[18] It bears repeating that whereas Stackhouse demonstrates he is indeed conversant with many of these themes as they appeared in the *Prairie Pastor*, he nonetheless chooses to minimize these clear indications of the influence of American fundamentalist thought in L.E. Maxwell's and Dorothy R. Miller's (who were both Americans) perspectives. See Introduction of this book, footnote 7. Opp, 139, clearly views Maxwell as a fundamentalist: "Maxwell . . . like many other fundamentalists . . ."

[19] *The Prairie Pastor*, "The Progress of Modernism," I, No. 10; (October 1928), 1-2.

[20] *The Prairie Pastor*, "Forward"—"Amen!" 5, No. 3; (March 1932), 3. See also: *The Prairie Pastor*, "The Anesthesia of Modernism and Modernism, or The Devil's Dirty Water," 9, Nos. 11, 12; (November-December 1936), 3-4.

During the early years Maxwell proudly acknowledged in the *Pastor* that he considered the opprobrium of modernists to be a badge of merit: "As a School our best commendation from the Lord is that the Atheists and Modernists UNITEDLY hate us."[21]

On occasion Maxwell did not hesitate to boldly upbraid his fellow fundamentalists or display a hint of the kind of pride that developed among fundamentalist spokesmen. Some fundamentalists assumed their particular initiatives or views were perhaps just a little more faithful to the fundamentalist cause than those of other fundamentalists:

> While Fundamentalists are attempting to check the Modernistic enemies of God's Word, it behooves them to take stock of their own spiritual assets and resources. We hear much about deeper-life Conferences, Keswicks, and Holiness Conventions, (and for all such endeavors in these days, we thank God) but who does not know that there is a terrible scarcity of powerful heart-searching messages in fundamental circles?[22]
>
> Only a Bible School with a Christ-centered curriculum can possibly stem this present wave of apostasy and emerge with an evangelistic message. "Telling a student what he knew not, means little; but *making him what he was not* and what he will *remain forever*, is everything. This kind of training involves more than intellectual broadening. It centers in spiritual deepening, brought about not by mere sentiment or example, but by direct contact with God and His Word, the only source of true spiritual life.[23]

An article in an early issue of the *Pastor* demonstrates a reality that was consistent throughout Maxwell's years at the helm of PBI: a keen awareness of developments in religious life in the United States. Indeed, as verified by the research conducted for this book, Maxwell regularly and closely followed developments in his home country via reading such news magazines as *TIME*, *Newsweek* and other American publications.[24]

---

21 *The Prairie Pastor*, "Modernism Aids Atheism," 4, No. 12; (December 1931), 2.

22 *The Prairie Pastor*, "Putting Teeth in the Fundamentalist Message," 8.

23 *The Prairie Pastor*, "Principles and Methods of Prairie Bible Institute," 5, No. 6; (June 1932), 2.

24 *The Prairie Pastor*, "America's Need," 10, No. 7-8; (July-August 1937), 1: "The *Wall Street Journal* recently published this amazing report: "What America needs more than . . .

This particular article contains reference to a questionnaire that had recently been sent to 436 ministers representing twenty denominations in the Chicago area. Responses indicated growing disbelief among clergy regarding the legitimacy of the creation account of Genesis, the virgin birth of Christ, the accuracy of the Bible, the authenticity of miracles, and so forth. Although these statistics represented the thinking of a U.S. audience, it is instructive to note the assumption of the editors of the *Pastor* as evidenced in the following caution that such waning of faith was indicative of a spiritual demise they considered to be virtually identical in Canada as well:

> In view of these prevailing conditions we believe that parents should more carefully guard the placing of their sons and daughters in higher schools of learning. Pathetic indeed have been the results of destructive teaching which we have witnessed right in the province of Alberta. Furthermore, members of churches should know positively whether their pastors truly believe the great cardinal truths of Scripture, such as the verbal inspiration, the Virgin Birth of Christ, His essential Deity, His substitutionary Atonement, His bodily Resurrection and His Return to this earth.[25]

This citation also clearly indicates what Maxwell, Kirk and the early leadership at PBI had in mind when, as previously observed, an early catalogue of the fledgling institution stated: "The school stands for every whit of the "Fundamentals.""[26] It confirms that in Maxwell's view many of the nefarious spiritual realities that fueled American fundamentalism existed on both sides of the international border between Canada and the United States. In the early years at PBI, it is apparent that in Maxwell's judgment, the 49th parallel was of minimal significance as far as the necessity for establishing one's position within the fundamentalist-modernist controversy.[27]

---

is a revival of religion."

[25] *The Prairie Pastor*, "The Progress of Modernism," 2.

[26] See Chapter Three of this book, footnote 29.

[27] *The Prairie Pastor*, "Sowing Soviet Seed," II, No. 9-10; (September-October 1938), I. The editorial note inserted before the article reads: "The following article, printed in "*The National Republic*," concerning our sister nation, just across the border, may serve as a warning to Canadians as well. The danger which threatens that land menaces us also. It is time for us to awake to a realization of impending disaster, before civilization itself is overthrown."

Maxwell's life-long delight in issuing fiery rhetorical darts is frequently evident in the early years of the *Pastor* when he recorded such comments as: "We presume our readers know that Modernists and Liberals are merely unhatched Unitarians;"[28] "Is it any wonder that a Bolshevistic atheistic citizen of Three Hills expressed great glee over another addition to their infidel ranks?"[29] or "But, oh! oh! oh! how about the hundreds of young lives blasted by the booze of Modernism! This modern adultery in religion is slaying its thousands!"[30] and "Just another instance of the Catholic stranglehold on Canada's life."[31]

His rhetorical confrontations were particularly noticeable in the numerous theological indictments he flung at the United Church of Canada following the 1925 organization of that institution which arose from the amalgamation of Methodist, Congregationalist and about two-thirds of Canadian Presbyterian congregations.[32] Maxwell frequently articulated in the pages of the *Pastor* ongoing criticism of evidences of modernism at various United Churches in Calgary under the care of ministers such as Rev. Norwick Kelloway and Dr. R. Paton.[33]

That Maxwell in his early days of leading PBI was conversant with, sympathetic to and influenced by some of the leading publications and

---

28 *The Prairie Pastor*, from "The Bible Under Fire," 5, No. 1; (January 1932) 3.

29 *The Prairie Pastor*, "A Local Tragedy," 4, No. 12; (December 1931), 2.

30 *The Prairie Pastor*, "False Guides of Youth," 5, No. 10; (October 1932), 3.

31 *The Prairie Pastor*, "Chaplaincy," 15, No. 11; (November 1942), 2.

32 *The Prairie Pastor*, "Further Exposure of United Church Teachings," 5, No. 4; (April 1932), 6.

  The Prairie Pastor, "Rotten!" 4, No. 10; (October 1931), 1: "Dr. Ernest Thomas, leader of the United Church and regular contributor to the *New Outlook* says: "Every element of 'possessive morality' in the relations of men to women is being rejected. Every vestige of the idea of a man's property or monopoly in his wife must be set aside." We say, 'rotten.' Sunken doctrine leads to sunken living!"

33 *The Prairie Pastor*, "Deeds and Doctrine," 7, No. 12; (December 1934), 4f.

  The Prairie Pastor, "A Religion to Die By," 8, No. 1; (January-February 1935), 4.

  The Prairie Pastor, "Modernism, or The Devil's Dirty Water," 9, Nos. 11, 12; (November-December 1936), 3.

  Stackhouse (1993), 86, curiously discounts PBI as fundamentalist in this regard in that "there is little evidence of actual engagement with these foes, whether in debate, public protest, or political action." In addition to suggesting that Stackhouse underestimates the reality of Prairie's rural location on this matter, I will present evidence later in this book to show that Maxwell did not hesitate whatsoever to confront the liberal beliefs of a United Church in the Three Hills area.

figures associated with the American fundamentalist-modernist debate is consistently apparent in the pages of *The Prairie Pastor.* He would occasionally publish cartoon diagrams ridiculing some aspect of modernism or its spokesmen.[34]

He reprinted articles or segments of articles by Bob Jones, the founder of the fundamentalist Bob Jones University, as well as by other prominent American fundamentalists such as J.C. Massee and W.B. Riley, the latter writing in the *Christian Fundamentalist.*[35] William Jennings Bryan was extolled as "a virtual victim of Darrow."[36] And, as noted earlier, one of Maxwell's favorite targets throughout his life was the famous New York modernist, Rev. Dr. Harry Emerson Fosdick, who was at the center of a much publicized scandal in 1922 when he preached a sermon entitled "Shall the Fundamentalists Win?"[37]

By the 1940s Maxwell's rhetoric in *The Prairie Pastor* and its successor, *The Prairie Overcomer,* became somewhat less strident than in the early days of the *Pastor.* More attention began to be paid to articles advocating "the deeper life" and holiness themes. Nonetheless, Maxwell consistently and frequently identified with and advanced many of the standard fundamentalist themes of the day such as: lamenting the spiritual demise apparent within established universities and colleges; the dangers of Communism; the degeneration within the mainline denominations, public schools and society in general; the urgent need for revival.[38]

---

[34] *The Prairie Pastor,* "The Highway of Modernism," 2, No. 3; (March 1929), 5, is a cartoon by a PBI student that looks exactly like those that frequently appeared in such American fundamentalist publications as *The King's Business,* the official publication of the Bible Institute of Los Angeles (Biola).

[35] *The Prairie Pastor,* "A College Tragedy," 5, No. 2; (February 1932), 3; *The Prairie Pastor,* "The Grief of Parents," 2, No. 3; (March 1929), 3; *The Prairie Overcomer,* "The Only Key," 35, No. 4; (April 1962), 142.

[36] *The Prairie Overcomer,* "Crime of the Century," 31, No. 4; (April 1958), 122-123.

[37] *The Prairie Pastor,* "Dr. Fosdick," 4, No. 9; (September 1931), 1; 4, No. 3; (March 1931), 3; *The Prairie Overcomer,* "Fosdick," 20, Nos. 4, 5; (April-May 1947), 102. Marsden, *Fundamentalism and American Culture* (1980), 172-173.

[38] *The Prairie Pastor,* "Briefs on Bolshevism," 4, No. 3: (March 1931), 5; "Socialism, Communism, Facism: Three Unclean Spirits like Frogs," 8, No. 6-7; (June-July 1935), 2-5; "Communism and the Church,"15, No. 6; (June 1942), 9; *The Prairie Overcomer,* "Sacramental," 20, No. 1; (January 1947), 2; "The Pendulum," 3-4; "Spurious or Genuine Revivals—Which?" 13f; "Spank or Not," 20, No 2; (February 1947), 34; "Declension," 35; "What For?," 36; "Vicars," 37; "Blindness," 20, No. 3; (March

An even more moderate tone is evident in Maxwell's writings in the *Overcomer* once the 1950s arrived although every now and then he would erupt as in his earlier years. Possible factors for this reality might be: the possibility that Maxwell was mellowing somewhat with age and experience, the cleavage that had appeared between the militant fundamentalists and the neo-evangelicals in the early 1940s, and Maxwell's realization that he really did not wish to side with the more openly cantankerous American fundamentalists such as the Bob Joneses and Carl McIntire; the arrival and broadening influence of Ted S. Rendall at PBI, an avid reader whose duties included functioning as the associate editor of the *Overcomer*.

That being said, a section of the *Overcomer* entitled "The World of Today in Light of the Word" steadfastly reiterated typical American fundamentalist perspectives on such topics as alcohol consumption; tobacco and drug abuse; the threat of Communism; evolutionary theory; dancing, etc.[39] As well, Maxwell continued his periodic challenges to Canada's secular media when an appropriate opportunity arose.[40]

1947), 68; "Hope," 70; "Savagery," 20, No. 6; (June 1947), 132; "Teachings," 132; "Deterioration," 20, No. 7; (July 1947), 163; "Standards," 164; "Two Worlds," 167; "Communism," 20, No. 8; (August 1947), 193; "Preparation," 194; "Liberties," 195; "Protest," 20, No. 9; (September 1947), 225; "Reprimand," 226; "Education," 20, No. 10; (October 1947), 259; "Dreadful," 259; "Curtain," 20, No. 11; (November 1947), 290; "UNESCO," 295; "Juveniles," 20, No. 12; (December 1947), 321; "Slaughter," 322.

39 *The Prairie Overcomer*, "The Devil's Holiday," 31, No. 1; (January 1958), 4; "Alberta's "Problem Drinkers," 4; "Deception," 4; "Russian Boast," 5; "Exciting Prospect," 6; "Ban on Dancing," 7; "Under New Management?" 31, No. 2; (February 1958), 42; "No Longer Earthbound," 43; "Catholics in America, 47; "Cigarette War," 31, No. 4; (April 1958), 127f; "Deception," 128; "Alcohol at the Wheel," 128f; "Communistic Fifth Column," 31, No. 5; (May 1958), 168; "The Challenge of Communism," 31, No. 6; (June 1958), 210; "Papist President," 31, No. 9; (September 1958), 329; "Papist Plot," 329; "Men and Monkeys," 31, No. 10; (October 1958), 362; "Horror Films," 31, No. 11; (November 1958), 403; "Liquor Ads," 404; "Cigarette Sales," 404; "Popery," 31, No. 12; (December 1958), 449.

40 Ibid., "PROTEST," (January 1958), 9-10 reprints ". . . a letter which we have sent to "Canada's National Magazine," *Maclean's* of Toronto." The opening paragraph reads: "Dear Sirs: As Editor of *The Prairie Overcomer* I wish to register the strongest protest against your writers who delight in their subtle and cynical aspersion upon God's Word and the teachings of Christ."

When PBI celebrated its 50th anniversary in 1972, a portion of the public celebration was recorded for broadcast by the Canadian Broadcasting Corporation (CBC). A grade

The *Overcomer* in the 1960s continued to employ its major articles to focus on issues related to Bible study, "the deeper life," holiness, world missions and revival.[41] And again, the "The World of Today in Light of the Word" section persisted in highlighting concerns that reflected the school's orientation to a fundamentalist readership. These included: the ills associated with liquor and smoking; Roman Catholicism; dancing; Communism; and a new perceived evil, the Ecumenical movement.[42] On occasion, the *Overcomer's* perspective during this time sounded like the political rhetoric of the American "Religious Right" although some fifteen or twenty-years were yet to elapse before that movement formally arrived on the American scene.[43] As well, Maxwell still periodically delighted in launching a few rhetorical salvos at modernists:

> Is it not a fact that Protestant leaders of today who are promoting this "ecumania," actually believe much less Bible truth than did those

---

II student at the time, I recall a public meeting wherein Maxwell guffawed in the glare of the TV lights and on camera something to the effect that "never has the CBC shed so much light on the gospel as it is doing tonight." His quip was included in what the CBC later broadcast.

[41] Chapter Eleven of this book will expand on these themes as they relate to PBI's embrace of a broader understanding of American fundamentalism than what Stackhouse allows.

[42] *The Prairie Overcomer*, "Alcoholic America," 35, No. I; (January 1962), 6; "Alcohol and Civilization," 7; "Home in Rome," 7; "The Twist," 9; "Catholic Killing," 35, No. 2; (February 1962), 45; "Better Dead Than Red," 47f; "Ecumania," 48ff; "No Other Authority," 35, No. 3; (March 1962), 90; "Liquor Profits," 35, No. 4; (April 1962), 121; "Moscow's Own Mouth," 35, No. 7 (July 1962), 243; "Lenin and Lawlessness," 245; "Censorship Needed," 249; "Vatican Clean-Up," 35, No. 9; (September 1962), 324; "Another "Missing Link,"" 330f; "American Morality," 331; "Callous Communism," 35, No. 10 (October 1962), 367.

[43] *The Prairie Overcomer*, "On Right-Wingers," 35, No. 2; (February 1962), 46: ". . . Now another attitude has taken the public mind. There has been so much pleading for "peaceful coexistence" with Communism that the convictions of Americans have largely collapsed There is the collapse of conviction, the collapse of "capacity for righteous indignation." Ex-president Eisenhower is to be pitied, for saying, "I don't think the U.S. needs superpatriots." That is just what America needs. But the new slogan is "Right-Wing Extremists." Any man who is avowedly against the Communist enemy is dubbed an extremist. He is bigoted, intolerant-not open-minded. This new slogan is working successfully for the Soviets preparing America for a quiet takeover."

against whom Reformation fathers protested to the death? This kind of "reformation" may not be institutional, in the sense of forming a new lot of sects, so much as in a discernment that severs true believers from any complicity or compromise with the present Protestant apostasy.[44]

By way of summary, the *Prairie Pastor* clearly reflects Maxwell's purpose to position Prairie Bible Institute alongside established American Bible institutes such as BIOLA and Moody as a defender of the faith against the onslaughts of modernism. Although there is some evidence that Maxwell's tone became somewhat less strident with regard to modernism by the early 1940s when the *Pastor* was absorbed into the *Prairie Overcomer*, it is nonetheless apparent that Maxwell maintained certain sympathies for the distinctives of American fundamentalism that had come to the forefront of the American religious scene in the 1920s.[45]

---

[44] *The Prairie Overcomer*, 35, No. 2; (February 1962), 49-50.

[45] Stackhouse's insistence on maintaining a significant difference between Canadian evangelicalism and American fundamentalism merits further notation here. On the one hand, as it relates to PBI's official publications, he writes (Stackhouse, *Canadian Evangelicalism*, 85-86): "The three most frequently mentioned foes were modernism (and its supposed offspring, the ecumenical movement), communism and Roman Catholicism. As did other fundamentalists, Prairie's leaders often linked the three." He then proceeds (86) to suggest, somewhat selectively as I contend elsewhere in this book, that Prairie did not significantly engage the modernism of the United Church of Canada or have much to say about the evolution debate, thereby qualifying it as more evangelical than fundamentalist in its orientation. Accordingly, he argues (87) that *The Prairie Overcomer* should not be viewed as "a typical fundamentalist magazine" before confusingly recording, just a few lines later, "The usual fundamentalist targets of alcohol, dancing, television and rock-and-roll do come in for frequent attack in these pages." I again suggest that Stackhouse's reasoning at this point is, at best, perplexing. In fact, as will be documented later in this book, the United Church of Canada did come under frequent fire from Maxwell in his sermons and in PBI's publications. Moody Bible Institute's film series, *Sermons From Science*, which challenged the presuppositions of evolutionary science were regularly shown on campus including in Prairie's elementary and high school while I was a student there. At least as it relates to Prairie Bible Institute, the distinction Stackhouse insists on making between Canadian evangelicalism and American fundamentalism is simply not as clear-cut as he maintains.

B. Maxwell's primary books

I. *Born Crucified*

With the publication in 1945 of Maxwell's first book, *Born Crucified*, it became apparent that the nature of the American fundamentalist schema to which he was committed encompassed more than the militancy motif that Stackhouse elects to focus on in his assessment of American fundamentalism and PBI.[46] Writing in the Forward to *Born Crucified*, the then editor of the resilient American fundamentalist journal, *The Sunday School Times*, affirms that Maxwell's theology as revealed in the volume reflects the influences of such Christian sages as Brother Lawrence, William Law, Hudson Taylor, Hannah Whitall Smith and Charles G. Trumbull.[47] The latter three names, of course, are virtually synonymous with the faith-missions movement, the "victorious" or "deeper" Christian life emphasis as popularized by Keswick, and American fundamentalism.[48]

In *Born Crucified* Maxwell outlined his views of "the crucified life," a theme for which he became best known at and beyond PBI and the theological emphasis for which he is most remembered today. In so doing, he nevertheless indicated that he maintained concrete sympathies for certain emphases of separatistic fundamentalism. This contention had played a prominent role in the split between fundamentalists and neo-evangelicals as it had played out in the early 1940s around the time he was writing the contents of *Born Crucified*.

---

[46] As will be seen in Chapters Ten and Eleven of this book, both Marsden in *Fundamentalism and American Culture* and Carpenter in *Revive Us Again* maintain there were more planks in the American fundamentalist platform than merely the militancy motif.

[47] I visited the archives of the main library at Biola University in La Mirada, California, on August 1, 2007, to review old copies of *The Sunday School Times*. The visit verified that PBI had a prominent profile in the journal particularly during the 1940s when the school regularly ran advertisements for its "Unique Method of Bible Study" and for its publications. PBI was also regularly featured on *The Times'* list of "Bible Schools True to the Faith." A winning submission to The Illustration Round Table in the February 5, 1944, issue of *The Sunday School Times* came from Mrs. Robert Vining of Piedmont, West Virginia, U.S.A. Her source for the illustration was *The Prairie Pastor!*

[48] J. Hudson Taylor (1832-1905) was founder of the China Inland Mission; Hannah Whitall Smith (1832-1911) was the author of *The Christian's Secret of the Happy Life*; Charles G. Trumbull (1830-1903) was an earlier editor of *The Sunday School Times*.

For example, Maxwell identified his disdain for modernism and its "handmaid," intellectualism, which he considered to be an attribute of worldly-mindedness, a characteristic of the sinful flesh and something to be crucified:

> However, the infinite cunning and craft of the world-spirit are beyond the natural mind to detect. It is an enchantment, a witchery, a pageantry vastly seductive. Worldly-mindedness in multiple form has thrust its cancerous roots into the very fibre of our religious life. It is a deadly leprosy, unaccompanied by pain, but eating to the bone. It is the white ant which has eaten away the frame of our spiritual house. It is the seed-bed of intellectualism, the handmaid of modernism. It is the fifth column boring from within, which has unseated and ousted the spirit of the Cross.[49]

Convictions like this were behind Maxwell's life-long suspicion of advanced education or higher learning and would have rendered him somewhat wary of the neo-evangelical emphasis on the importance of having well-educated spokesmen for Christianity who had been trained at the respected secular centers of academia.

Maxwell's opposition in the 1960s to PBI moving towards academic accreditation with the American Association of Bible College can be partly attributed to his affinity for a theology wherein man's intellect was viewed as a primary sphere in which "the self" or "the flesh" ruled supreme. In short, he considered intellectualism to be a prime symbol of the un-crucified life that sought to exalt self.

> The victorious believer will become aware of many forms of self which must yet be dealt with. We shall discover: In our service for Christ, self-confidence and self-esteem . . . in our relationships, self-assertiveness and self-respect . . . in our successes, self-admiration and self-congratulations . . . in life as a whole, self-love and selfishness. The flesh is an "I" specialist.
>
> These are but a few of the multiple forms of "the flesh" to be discovered and taken to the Cross . . . Although emancipated at the

---

[49] L.E. Maxwell, *Born Crucified*, 35.

life-center of our redeemed beings through the indwelling and infilling of the Spirit of life in Christ Jesus, we are still in a fight—albeit on the victory side. Vast areas of the flesh must yet be crucified. We must become Christ-like.[50]

Another facet of American fundamentalism that surfaces periodically in *Born Crucified* is Maxwell's strong belief in the necessity of the Christian being completely separated from the world. Although the second-order separation that became an essential attribute of American fundamentalism following the fundamentalist/neo-evangelical split in the 1940s never had the prominent profile at PBI that it did at a school like Bob Jones University, separation from this evil world and all of its subtle manifestations was always central to Maxwell's understanding of Christianity and to the PBI experience during his tenure.

> If ever I become so one with the world, so tolerant of its spirit and atmosphere that I reprove it no more, incur not its hatred, rouse not its enmity to Christ—if the world can find in me no cause to hate me and cast me from its company, then I have betrayed Christ and crucified Him afresh in the house of His friends. On intimate terms with this world that nailed Him to the tree? Perish the thought! In full identification with Christ the world can regard me as only fit for crucifixion. And as a disciple of Christ I should no more covet the favor of this crucified world than I would court and covet the smile of a cursed and crucified and expiring felon . . . Mark well, O popular Christian and worldly-wise preacher, venturing how far you must go with the world in order to win the world; never had the Church so much influence over the world as when she had nothing to do with the world.[51]

Maxwell's passion for "the crucified life" was undergirded by his affinity for the mysticism reflected in the work of several influential Roman Catholic writers including the renowned French mystic popularly known as Madame Guyon (1648-1717).[52] Although it is not within the purview of this book

---

50 Maxwell, *Born Crucified*, 87.
51 Ibid., 40-43.
52 Ian S. Rennie, "The Western Prairie Revival in Canada," 16: "He stressed holiness of the mystical Keswick type with his hero being—mirabile dictum—the extreme

to critique the theology set forth in *Born Crucified* in particular or by L.E. Maxwell in general, it bears repeating here to call the reader's attention to the work of Ian S. Rennie particularly in this regard.

Rennie's paper, *"The Doctrine of Man in the Bible Belt,"* is possibly the only document in print that notes Maxwell's curious affection for the writings of Guyon and raises several criticisms of the former's distinctive theological teachings regarding "the crucified life." The deficiencies that Rennie identifies in Maxwell's theology arise not only from Rennie's own expertise in theology and history but also from his acquaintance with a number of former PBI students whose subsequent rebellion, resentment and cynicism Rennie attributes at least in part to the views of God, man and the world advanced by Maxwell's mystical message of "the crucified life."[53]

2. *Crowded to Christ* and *Abandoned to Christ*

The Foreward to Maxwell's book, *Crowded to Christ*, is instructive for the purposes of this study on a couple of counts. For one thing, as with *Born*

French Roman Catholic Quietist, Madame Guyon." Rennie's surprise at Maxwell's sympathies for Guyon's perspectives ("mirabile dictum" is Latin for "strange to say" or "marvelous to relate") likely stems not only from Maxwell's consistent denunciation of Roman Catholicism in the *Pastor* and the *Overcomer*, but also from the fact that Guyon's views were condemned by the Roman Catholic hierarchy as bordering on pantheism and destructive of any recognizable form of Christianity. She was imprisoned for her views in 1695-1703.

[53] PBI Archives in Ted S. Rendall Library; L.E. Maxwell personal files contain a copy of Ian S. Rennie, "The Doctrine of Man in the Canadian Bible Belt."

After stating that L.E. Maxwell "is a man for whom I have the most profound respect" (5) and "I also agree with the major thesis of his book Born Crucified and with many of its sub-theses" (6), Rennie identifies what he considers to be several faults in the views advanced in *Born Crucified* (6-11): 1) An over-emphasis on 'crucifixion;' 2) The disparaging of the 'Self;' 3) The Doctrine of the World; 4) The broad definition of the 'World;' 5) A Two-Track Christianity; 6) The Concept of Spiritual Disciplines.

On the basis of my own theological education and personal experience, I concur with many of the deficiencies Rennie identifies in Maxwell's theology. Even more regrettably, I know numerous former PBI students and/or fellow "staff kids" who attribute their ongoing disdain for Christianity to the crushing guilt and sense of "never being good enough for God" that they encountered via Maxwell's views on "the crucified life" wherein there was always yet another undiscovered part of one's life that would invariably be ripe for crucifixion.

Crucified, the Forward was written by a fellow American and president of a prominent American Bible institute with whom Maxwell shared a close personal and professional relationship for decades.[54] The American orientation of Robert C. McQuilken, his minimization of the difference between the American and Canadian scenes in terms of their spiritual condition, his firm commitment to Biblical infallibility, and his fervent interest in missions are all evident when he states:

> All are aware that there is a moral breakdown in America today; there is an apostasy also among religious leaders who deny the infallible Word of God. Not all are awake to the deadly foes in camp of the orthodox who accept the Bible as God's infallible Word . . . One of the great missionary pioneers of the past generation, who day by day lived in the thick of the fight for souls in Africa[55]

Secondly, McQuilken affirms something of Maxwell's streak of independence with regard to any sense of complete alignment with the theology espoused by American fundamentalists.[56] In *Crowded to Christ* (and to a lesser extent also in *Abandoned to Christ*), Maxwell clearly indicates that his brand of fundamentalism did not hesitate to challenge certain tenets of premillennial dispensationalism that had come to be associated with American fundamentalism in the years prior to the fundamentalists

---

[54] Columbia, located in Columbia, South Carolina, USA, began formal operations in the fall of 1923, as Columbia Bible School. Although it changed its name to Columbia Bible College in 1929 when it began offering bachelor degrees (and graduate degrees in 1936), Maxwell and Robert C. McQuilken shared a kindred spirit based on their mutual respect for *The Sunday School Times*, the Keswick emphasis on "the victorious Christian life" and overseas missions. Evidence will be presented later in this book regarding Maxwell's relationship with McQuilken and Columbia.

[55] L.E. Maxwell, *Crowded to Christ*, (Grand Rapids, MI: Wm. B. Eerdmans Publishing Co., 1950), 9.

[56] Ibid., 9, 10: "Recently testimony has come from two leaders that the attitude of missionaries toward the observing of the Lord's Day has brought untold damage to the missionary work. Setting forth the true relation of the Christian to the law is one of the vital ministries of this book. It is a message that all of the great spiritual leaders of the church through the ages have agreed with. But our author has applied it in a magnificent way to the situation of our own day. More distinctly doctrinal and controversial aspects of law and grace are dealt with in five appendices which handle these problems in a warm and vital way."

and neo-evangelicals parting ways.[57] Like many American fundamentalist leaders, Maxwell had a strong personality that did not shrink from generating controversy when he considered such to be necessary in the articulation of correct theology. Whether it was the perceived heresies of Harry Emerson Fosdick, the United Church of Canada's aberrant perspectives, or the misguided teachings of the ultra-dispensationalists, Maxwell did not hesitate to be critical when, in his judgment, such was warranted.[58]

Any doubt that Maxwell definitely considered himself to be a fundamentalist is removed by noting his frequent references in this regard in *Crowded to Christ*. Among such are: "We are like Israel . . . We doubt not that God can do great and wonderful things. We are fundamental" (104), "much of our fundamentalism has unwittingly developed" (248), "Do we fundamentalists forget that . . ." (249), and "One can be as orthodox as

---

[57] With regard to Maxwell's resistance to certain tenets of the dispensational agenda, my experience while a student at PBI confirms the following judgment of Stackhouse in *Canadian Evangelicalism*, (241, note 36): "Prairie, like most Bible schools, taught dispensational eschatology. But it was not wholly dispensational. Maxwell, for instance, differed from dispensationalists in his holding of a Reformed understanding of the Old Testament Law as useful in the life of the Christian, while dispensationalists saw the Law to be utterly irrelevant to the dispensation of grace."

[58] L.E. Maxwell, *Crowded to Christ*, 138-139: ". . . His lack of conviction regarding Christ's last command arose from an ultra-dispensational handling of the Scriptures which furnishes Christians with an excuse from the obligations of obedience. It was the writer's rare privilege to have as one of his personal friends the late Dr. Robert H. Glover, one of the world's great missionary statesmen. In order to confirm the above conclusions regarding the detrimental effect of these extreme teachings of dispensationalism, we quote from his valuable book, *The Bible Basis of Missions* . . . Before leaving the consideration of how extreme dispensationalism militates against a wholehearted enthusiasm for missions . . ." See also, p. 156 and p. 249.

L.E. Maxwell, *Abandoned to Christ*, (Grand Rapids, MI: Wm. B. Eerdmans Publishing Co., 1955), 151: "At Jerusalem we were met by Dr. and Mrs. Lambdie, who are doing such a splendid work among the poor Arabs near Bethlehem. Thousands of these poverty-stricken souls, completely bereft of their homes, are being huddled together in great camps under the direction and meager supply of the UN. In this connection we learned a strange and almost unbelievable fact: No CARE parcel can go from the United States to a needy Arab of the Hashemite Kingdom of Jordan. Such is the hold of present Jewry on American mail channels to the Arabs. Some of these facts help those of us who are vitally interested in the prophetic future of the Jews to keep balanced in our thinking and sympathy."

Job . . . as fundamental as a Pharisee . . . but what is all this except a false glorifying in one's own fleshly elegance?" (262). Similar nomenclature is seen in *Abandoned to Christ* where he makes such statements as: "We fear that many of us, even many of us fundamental folk" (57), "Most of us fundamentalists say our prayers" (200), and "We are orthodox and fundamental like Jonah" (228).

These two volumes also show evidence of Maxwell's penchant to chastise fellow fundamentalists for refusing to die to self. In a section of *Crowded to Christ* where he spiritualizes the Old Testament story of the hanging of Haman as recorded in the book of Esther, he writes:

> Heaven's issues seem to hinge around His key men, men like Mordecai who by death to self build gallows on which to hang the Hamans . . . There are many middle-of-the-road ministers who may be excused for wishing that God would hang all the modernists, but there is first an Agag to be hanged in the fundamentalist. The sinful self-life in the fundamentalist is of all modernists the worst. Martin Luther said, "I am more afraid of my own heart than of the Pope and all his cardinals. I have within me that great Pope, Self." If the fundamentalist, whether within or without the modernistic machine, persists in saving self, in living for and bowing to self, on what is God to hang these modern Hamans? . . . We are convinced from Scripture that if fighting, militant, and daring fundamentalists would only sink into a selfless, carefree contempt for their own lives, forgetting their reputation and position, their cause and kingdom, and be willing to expose themselves to every battery the devil can muster against them we have little doubt that God could and perhaps would burn up His enemies round about and hang the Hamans of today as easily as He handled matters for Mordecai.[59]

Stackhouse, *Canadian Evangelicalism*, (241, note 36): ". . . according to Ted Rendall, Maxwell 'often quoted the original *Scofield Reference Bible's* comments on the giving of the law at Sinai to illustrate what he had concluded was an erroneous approach to the function of law.' This approach, says Rendall, made Moody Press, a dispensational publisher, reject Maxwell's [*Crowded to Christ*] while Wm. B. Eerdmans, of the Christian Reformed, published it." (Ted S. Rendall, 'L.E. Maxwell—His Literary Legacy,' *Prairie Overcomer* 57 [May 1984]: 27)."

[59] L.E. Maxwell, *Crowded to Christ*, 77.

Abandoned to Christ contains a challenge from Maxwell to "Let each one of us fundamentalists be searched by this penetrating insight into our own possible idolatries" (121) as well as a piece of poetry written by "one of our students" assailing fundamentalist Jonahs for relaxing at home while those in far-off Ninevah go to hell.[60]

It is apparent in both *Crowded to Christ* and *Abandoned to Christ* that Maxwell's theology and thinking represented the influences of numerous writers who contributed to a much broader definition of American fundamentalism than that associated with merely the militancy motif. For example, among the nineteenth century proto-fundamentalists whose writings Maxwell drew on in these volumes were A.J. Gordon, A.B. Simpson, A.T. Pierson and Dwight L. Moody.[61] He also made frequent use of articles in *The Sunday School Times* and the work of W.H. Griffith Thomas, a contributor to *The Fundamentals*.[62] Among the influential and prolific pastors and missionaries associated with the Keswick movement that Maxwell cited in *Crowded to Christ* were J. Hudson Taylor, Amy Carmichael, F.B. Meyer and the famous Canadian missionary to China, Jonathan Goforth.[63] *Abandoned to Christ* contains ideas borrowed from such fathers of American fundamentalism as C.I. Scofield (31) and Arno Gabelein (112).

In *Abandoned to Christ* Maxwell touches on a couple of themes that served as a kind of two sides of the same coin in American fundamentalism: worldliness in fundamentalist circles and the urgent need for revival among God's people. Herein we see his penchant for viewing God's law as a necessary instrument in awakening the unregenerate and even the complacent believer to sin, an emphasis that periodically earned him the charge of being a "legalist" in his understanding of how the Christian life was to be lived out:

---

[60] L.E. Maxwell, *Abandoned to Christ*, 231-232.

[61] References to Gordon in *Crowded to Christ* are found on 41, 87, 173, 183, 264; to Simpson on 50, 65, 113, 135, 144; to Pierson on 108; to Moody on 149.

[62] References to *The Sunday School Times* are found on 11, 34, 231 in *Crowded to Christ* and 15, 122, 134, 146 in *Abandoned to Christ*; to Thomas on 271 in *Crowded to Christ* and 71, 74-75 in *Abandoned to Christ*.

[63] References to Taylor in *Crowded to Christ* are found on 30, 57, 105, 143, 147, 173, 183 and in *Abandoned to Christ* on 30 and 106; to Carmichael on 39, 100, 181, 257, 258 in *Crowded to Christ* and 107, 172 in *Abandoned to Christ*; references to F.B. Meyer on 16, 117, 178, 235 in *Crowded to Christ*; to Goforth on 79, 94, in *Crowded to Christ* and 38, 43, 44, in *Abandoned to Christ*.

We need to get away from preaching merely academic or doctrinal truths. The best truths, doctrinally and coldly stated, will never break a heart. They fall like water off a duck's back . . . Let us have more heart preaching and heart dealing with sin. Let us get at the conscience and produce conviction for sin . . . Let us not be afraid to use the condemnations of God's law to produce a sense of sin . . . Let us as ministers being to denounce and uncover sin and worldliness. What about the worldly magazines and Sunday newspapers which flood millions of Christian homes? . . . Why should the Lord's Day be a day of entertainment and sightseeing and feasting and frolic and sports and fun? Let us deal a deathblow to fleshliness and worldliness, and see whether God will not produce some confession and forsaking of sin.[64]

In a chapter entitled "The Working of God in Africa" in *Abandoned to Christ*, Maxwell relates the accounts of trips he took to Japan and Africa to speak to missionaries concerning revival. His commitment to proclaiming this grand theme of American fundamentalism is obvious in statements such as: "There God visited us with great blessing in revival presence and power" (150), "Among them also God moved in blessed revival" (156), "Gradually God had His way, and confession followed confession while many missionaries in tears got right with God and their fellow-laborers" (159), and "We are especially thankful to the leaders of the S.I.M. for their appreciation and grateful co-operation in every way to see *revival*" (160).[65]

3. His other books

As is evident, Maxwell's commitment to the orientation and worldview associated with American fundamentalism was consistent throughout the first three and best-known of the books he authored. Most of the works to be considered now are from the second half of his tenure and were published by Prairie Bible Institute itself. They are indicative of Maxwell's affinity for the broader fundamentalist agenda that included such emphases as a fervent

---

[64] Maxwell, *Abandoned to Christ*, 41, 42.
[65] S.I.M. indicates Sudan Interior Mission, now known as Serving in Mission.

commitment to evangelism (missions) as the primary task of the church, personal holiness of life made possible through the continued infilling of the Holy Spirit, and an unswerving commitment to the absolute infallibility of the Bible.

Although Maxwell's booklet, *Capital Punishment*, is undated, the series of radio sermons it contains was likely broadcast during the early to mid-1970s since debate over capital punishment was vigorous at that point in Canadian history and eventually resulted in the abolition of capital punishment in the nation in 1976. Maxwell's remarks in this booklet also bear the marks of the controversy generated by the liberalization of laws affecting domestic and social policy in Canada that were associated with the early years of Pierre Elliot Trudeau's lengthy term as Canadian Prime Minister (mid-1968 thru early 1984).[66] The book is particularly useful for its insight into Maxwell's social views, most of which reflect the conservative perspectives of what by the end of the twentieth century would come to be known as the American "Religious Right."[67]

---

[66] Pierre E. Trudeau's (Liberal) government was briefly replaced by Joe Clarke's Progressive Conservatives in the last half of 1979.

[67] L.E. Maxwell, *Capital Punishment* (Three Hills, AB: Prairie Bible Institute, n.d.), 29: "Do we hear the voice of authority saying that the Canadian government has no rights in the bedrooms of Canadians? Does our government just wink at the sin of sodomy and seek to elevate these criminals to the place and plan of social respectability? Do our Western governments entirely pass over those who year after year live in adultery under what we call common law? Do we leniently conclude that rapists and kidnappers and skyjackers are just sick persons who need psychiatric treatment? These sex crimes we call by nice names. Adultery we call divorce or separation. Murder we call abortion. Sodomy is the "gay life."

Randall Balmer, *Encyclopedia of Evangelicalism*, 575: "Sometimes called the Christian Right or the New Christian Right, the Religious Right is a name applied to a loose coalition of personalities and organizations that arose in the late 1970s to articulate a politically conservative agenda. Although evangelicals have long been active in politics, many shied away from political engagement in the political arena in the middle decades of the twentieth century. The immediate catalyst for their return was the presidential campaign of Jimmy Carter, a Southern Baptist Sunday school teacher who openly declared that he was a "born-again Christian." While Carter lured many evangelicals out of their apolitical stupor (Southerners especially), many evangelicals turned against him when his administration's Justice Department sought to enforce anti-discrimination laws at Bob Jones University, a fundamentalist school in Greenville, South Carolina. This action represented an incursion into the evangelical sub-culture, which had been so carefully constructed in the decades following the Scopes Trial."

Arguing that capital punishment should be viewed as a divinely-constituted form of justice to be carried out by the state as opposed to the kind of random killing or murder prohibited in the Ten Commandments, the book reflects Maxwell's firm commitment to the fundamentalist's belief in the infallibility of Scripture, to the view that those ministers who argued otherwise were "liberal" or "modernist," and to insisting that the abolitionist view was based on an evolutionary understanding of man's character.[68] The volume also reveals how Maxwell often used such platforms to get in his customary dig at the intellectualism and godlessness propagated by such luminaries as Clarence Darrow, the famous criminal defense lawyer

---

By the end of the twentieth century, "the evangelical sub-culture" of which Balmer speaks, under the leadership of outspoken men like Jerry Falwell and Pat Robertson with their major television broadcasts in America, had identified abortion and homosexuality as the two primary social ills that fundamentalists-evangelicals needed to vehemently oppose.

[68] L.E. Maxwell, *Capital Punishment*, 3, 4: "Let it be said at once that the reason we have so many varied and diverse opinions, such an endless number of opposing views, so many arguments for and against capital punishment, so many pros and cons of debate—the reason, I say, for so much confusion is to be traced, not primarily to the perplexity of this moral and social problem, but because we lack a proper plumbline to determine the direction of our thinking. In this matter, as in every other moral issue, the "fear of the Lord" is indeed "the beginning of wisdom." Small wonder that God says, "The wise men are ashamed, they are dismayed and taken: lo, they have rejected the Word of the Lord; and what wisdom is in them?" (Jeremiah 8:9). That is, having rejected the Word of the Lord . . ."

5: "A certain noted rabbi in Toronto once said that the death penalty "is the most cold-blooded of murders." This liberal-minded rabbi . . ."

6: ". . . He went on to observe that the larger, older, and liberal-minded churches that have largely forsaken the Scriptures as their plumbline for faith and doctrine, are as a whole in favour of abolition. Those who believe the Bible to be God's Word simply accept what God says about the death penalty. Those who reject what God says in the Bible are against the death penalty."

6: "And I further notice that the liberals who reject capital punishment also reject the very heart of the Gospel . . ."

7: "Of course, the modernistic-minded minister does not believe in any kind of death penalty, much less the death penalty of Christ for sinners."

12: ". . . Some of this reasoning is based upon the false evolutionary theory of man. It is supposed that man has been ascending and coming up all the way to our civilized state of society, whereas the reverse is true."

associated with defending the teaching of evolution in Tennessee public schools at the infamous Scopes' "monkey trial" in 1925.[69]

Published in the early 1970s when the charismatic movement which emphasized the spectacular workings of the Holy Spirit such as speaking in tongues, healing and other miraculous manifestations was attracting considerable attention among North American evangelicals, Maxwell's *The Pentecostal Baptism* merits brief mention. For our purposes in this book, it is important to note that Maxwell's sources for the views he advanced on what was at the time a very controversial matter in fundamentalist-evangelical circles were figures such as Graham Scroggie, F.B. Meyer and Jonathan Goforth, men with strong connections to the Keswick movement. He also drew on the teaching of the noted revivalist, Rev. Armin Gesswein.[70] In characteristic Maxwell style which frequently reflected his affinity for Keswick theology, he warned against self-righteously dismissing the charismatic movement's emphasis on the gifts of the Holy Spirit as unbalanced and excessive while simultaneously defending a Christian experience that was icily barren of a passionate holiness.[71]

Maxwell prepared the booklet *Prairie Pillars* in anticipation of PBI's fiftieth anniversary in 1972. It is instructive to observe that part of his motivation for writing this volume was to reassure the school's supporting constituency that the school had remained faithful in its commitment to certain elements of the fundamentalism that it had embraced from its birth.

---

[69] Maxwell, 17: ". . . And modern psychologists and other men, men who are educated beyond their intelligence, believe that . . . Clarence Darrow, the great criminal lawyer, who cleared over 100 murderers without one being executed, thought the same way."

[70] L.E. Maxwell, *The Pentecostal Baptism: A Biblical Analysis and Appraisal*, (Three Hills, AB: Prairie Bible Institute, 1971): 4, 9, 15.

[71] Ibid., 1: "As ministers and missionaries we must face the humiliating fact that we are somewhat responsible, at least, in measure, for the drift of hungry hearts to those groups whose lives and teachings promise something more virile, more vital, more satisfying than the deadness and lukewarmness of today's evangelical Christianity. Sincere Christians become sick of shams and formalities and stagnations. Have many earnest believers asked us for the children's portion—the fullness of the Spirit is indeed the children's bread—only to be given a stone of cold and unsatisfying theology?"

Should the reader "go round about" our little "Zion" on a tour of inspection, "marking well" her bulwarks and towers and pillars, some questions like these might be in order:

Is Prairie still true to the great fundamentals of the Christian faith as set forth in her doctrinal statement?

Does she perseveringly adhere to those original standards upon which "wisdom hath builded her house?"

Is Prairie still distinctively a *Bible* school?

Is the Bible still at the heart of her curriculum?

Does Prairie remain true to her motto: "Training Disciplined Soldiers for Christ?"

Does she continue to emphasize the Spirit-filled life of Christian victory?

Is Prairie's focus still on the most needy and neglected areas of the world?

Does she maintain the principle of separation from the world and from alliance with modern religious liberalism?

In the face of our mounting Sodom-and-Gomorrah society can Prairie continue to uphold her unusual social regulations?

Does Prairie continue with her distinctive search-question method of Bible study?[72]

The answer to be found in *Prairie Pillars*, of course, was an unequivocal "yes!" In addition to featuring Maxwell's distinctive message of "dying to self" or "crucifying the flesh," the volume affirms historic fundamentalist ideals such as: the authority of Scripture, salvation through Christ alone, the centrality of the missionary endeavor as the primary work of the Church, and the necessity of a militaristic approach in carrying out the work of God.[73] *Prairie Pillars* again reveals Maxwell's fondness for citing authorities such as proto-fundamentalists D.L. Moody, Walter Wilson and A.T. Pierson, fundamentalists R.A. Torrey and Griffith Thomas along with the fundamentalist journal, *The King's Business*, as well as certain figures from the holiness-Keswick school including A.W. Tozer.

---

[72] L.E. Maxwell, *Prairie Pillars* (second ed.) (Three Hills, AB: Prairie Bible Institute, 1973); 8, 9.
[73] Ibid., 67-70, 73-78.

World Missions: Total War, first published the year I graduated from Prairie Bible Institute (1977), adequately summarizes both Maxwell's personality and his understanding of how the Christian life was to be lived out. The militant fundamentalism Maxwell affirmed seldom manifested itself in his later years with the kind of cantankerous and acerbic spirit that prompted the likes of T.T. Shields and Frank J. Norris to be on a seemingly perpetual hunt for evidence of advancing liberalism or heresy among the faithful. Nevertheless, it is apparent in this volume that Maxwell whole-heartedly embraced the militancy motif in his understanding of how the Great Commission was to be carried out.[74]

It was this conviction that created the strict discipline which prevailed at PBI throughout his tenure, a reality that prompted some critics to maintain that PBI was operated in a manner very similar to a military boot-camp.[75] Maxwell's usual response to such accusations was some kind of humorous rejoinder while maintaining that the record of Prairie graduates being sought out for leadership by Christian organizations spoke for itself.[76] Compared to the kind of rancorous in-fighting that Stackhouse rightly notes came

---

[74] Stackhouse, *Canadian Evangelicalism*, 21, claims T.T. Shields as the figure in Canadian church history who "marks out the fundamentalist limit of Canadian evangelicalism," a judgment that is generally well supported by the literature. See, for example:

John D.E. Dozois, "Dr. Thomas Todhunter Shields (1873-1955): in the stream of fundamentalism," (Bachelor of Divinity thesis, McMaster University, 1963).

David R Elliott, "Eight Canadian Fundamentalists," Chapter Seven: "T.T. Shields: The Baptist "Pope.""

Mark Parent, "The Christology of T.T. Shields: the irony of fundamentalism," (Ph.D. dissertation, McGill University, 1991).

Leslie K. Tarr, *Shields of Canada* (Grand Rapids, MI: Baker Book House, 1967).

Although Maxwell often came across to many as quite harsh in the rhetoric he employed in his preaching and teaching, he nonetheless had a reputation with others for being very approachable, kind and sensitive on the personal level. (For example, Spaulding in *Lion on the Prairies*, 74, includes an anecdote regarding Maxwell asking forgiveness of a large group as recalled by PBI graduate and former faculty member, the late Connie Kondos.) In addition to their differences in personality and temperament, it should also be noted that Maxwell and Shields moved in significantly different spheres throughout the course of their ministries.

[75] Stackhouse, *Canadian Evangelicalism*, 82, calls PBI's regulations "part of a missionary 'boot camp' experience" and appears to attempt a distinction between the concepts of "militant" and "military" or "militaristic."

[76] Ted S. Rendall Library, L.E. Maxwell, audio tape sermon entitled "The Inabilities of God," AC 231.4 MAX v. 2, n. d. In this sermon, Maxwell theatrically portrays a

to characterize many American fundamentalists in the 1920s and would eventually lead to the parting of the ways between fundamentalists and neo-evangelicals in the early 1940s, Maxwell's militaristic interpretation of the gospel was somewhat different. It focused rather on whatever stirring rhetoric was necessary to assault those far-flung regions of the world where animism, spiritism and heathendom prevailed as opposed to bickering over points of theology with his North American colleagues.

But let the record be clear, Maxwell loved to draw on the militaristic metaphors that appear in Scripture in order to set forth his understanding of precisely what was at stake in life. Not surprisingly, then, *World Missions: Total War* characteristically and repeatedly sets forth his convictions regarding missions as the heartbeat of the Biblical message and the importance of separation from the world:

> The Christian's calling is a summons, a call to arms. Paul's epistles bristle with battle terms. We are called not to a holiday, but to a campaign. Our tent is pitched not in a paradise, but on the field of battle . . . The only adequate figure of Christian service is that of the military muster . . . World missions under Christ's captaincy means war, total war, total mobilization for total conflict—"armed with complete steel." . . . We must confess that good soldiery is the lost chord of today's Christianity . . . [77]
>
> These sermons are sent forth with the hope that God's servants everywhere may come to revived missionary activity through a fresh insight into "Missions" as the main theme taught in the Scriptures.[78]
>
> "But there can be no reasonable doubt that that age in which the Church was so completely separated from the world was the age in which Christianity was the most victorious in the world." (Quoting "an old warrior-writer")[79]

---

conversation between two people: "What? You're going to go to Prairie, that Siberian prison camp?"

[77] L.E. Maxwell, *World Missions: Total War* (Three Hills, AB: Prairie Press, 1977); 13f.

[78] Maxwell, *World Missions—Total War*, 9.

[79] Ibid., 17-18.

Maxwell's sermons, lectures, interviews

The sampling of L.E. Maxwell's taped sermons, lectures and interviews consulted for the purposes of this book confirm and further illuminate what has already been noted regarding Maxwell's view of himself and Prairie Bible Institute as being a part of a broader fundamentalist fellowship. Among the familiar themes that regularly surfaced in his oratory were frequent references to "we fundamental folks," the Christian life as warfare, the desperate need for repentance and revival, and, of course, his trademark emphases on "crucifying the flesh" and missions.

As in his writings, his sermons and lectures were filled with citations from such authorities as Dwight L. Moody, J. Hudson Taylor, A.W. Tozer, Griffith Thomas and F.B. Meyer. In one of the sermons consulted for this study, he referred to "my dear friend, Howard of *The* Times," presumably a reference to Philip Howard Jr., editor of *The Sunday School* Times, the prominent fundamentalist journal that was published for more than a century.

Even in his later years, Maxwell's sermons were always given in an authoritative manner which both commanded and demanded his audience's attention.[80] His preaching was also frequently salted by his famous idiosyncrasies. For example, in establishing his belief in the depravity of mankind, he did not shrink from offering several verbal jabs at mainline denominations, psychology, "fool-osophy," and popular notions that he termed "nonsense" regarding the dignity of human nature. He preferred to view the latter as "man's inveterate anarchy."

On occasion he referred to people educated in what he considered the world's wisdom to be "ignoramuses" and generally seemed unconcerned whom he might offend with such rhetoric. He would summarize his

---

[80] Ted S. Rendall Library, L.E. Maxwell, audio tape sermon entitled: "The Laodicean Church," AC 228 MAXW: "There's some folks standing back there. Would you like to sit down? Or just "stand up, stand up" for Jesus? You can come on down here. Of course, that lady with the little one may want to be where she can get out. All right, let's get going here, go on and get settled . . . You two folks back there, you two folks right back there. Listen, listen, come over here and come right on down, here's two seats reserved for you . . . Lest if you want to stand—are you determined to stand? (nervous laughter from Maxwell). All right, I feel better when people are at least comfortable and can at least sit still and listen."

perception of worldly living with such descriptions as "going to this show, to that dance" or "loose-living fools."[81]

As well, there are clear indications of the conundrum that Maxwell represents when it comes to clearly delineating his relationship to fundamentalism. On the one hand, whereas Maxwell affirmed much of pre-millennial dispensationalism, he did not subscribe to the dispensationalist agenda in its entirety. For example, in a sermon entitled "The Laodicean Church," Maxwell calls the dispensational treatment of the letters to the seven churches found early in the book of Revelation as symbolic of seven drawn out periods at the end of the age "a gratuitous assumption." "Would the Laodiceans have understood that this epistle was written for somebody two thousand years later," he asks before sarcastically intoning, "only a twentieth-century fundamentalist would guess that!"[82]

On the other hand, in a 1970 radio interview on a Calgary radio station, Maxwell unashamedly identifies himself and PBI to the program's host by saying, "we would be reckoned old-fashioned fundamentalists." "Really!?" the host responds, somewhat perplexed. "Old fashioned fundamentalist? And why are you laughing?" "Because I enjoy it," Maxwell replies. "Oh yes, that's the reason!"[83]

What is both interesting and instructive in the radio interview is that although Maxwell's perspectives certainly reflect his fundamentalist orientation, his jovial personality is not at all what the host apparently associated with fundamentalism:

> Maxwell: (speaking of young people that some PBI students had worked with) "they were like a blind man in a dark room chasing a black cat that isn't there."

---

[81] Ted S. Rendall Library, L.E. Maxwell audio tape sermon entitled: "The Inabilities of God." AC231.4 MAX v. 2, n.d.

Ted S. Rendall Library, L.E. Maxwell audio tape sermon entitled: "The Three Rs of Redemption," 234.3 MAXW, n.d.

Ted S. Rendall Library, L.E. Maxwell audio tape sermon entitled: "Learning Obedience," 234.6 MAXW, n.d.

[82] L.E. Maxwell, audio tape sermon entitled "The Laodicean Church."

[83] Ted S. Rendall Library, "CHQR FORUM" radio interview with L.E. Maxwell; 207.71 MAXW, n.d. By virtue of the references Maxwell makes in the interview to PBI's history, it is evident this interview likely took place sometime during 1970.

Host:	"Isn't that rather arrogant, bigoted? Some would say it's very arrogant, very patronizing, a very bigoted way to talk toward others by saying that these young folks were going in circles and didn't know which end was up."
Maxwell:	"It could be that. It could be seen as Phariseeism, holier-than-thou, self-righteous . . ."
Host:	"But, Mr. Maxwell, I have to tell you sir, that I don't sense any superiority in your soul."[84]

Maxwell proceeds in the interview to affirm other of his fundamentalist affinities such as his complete abstinence from alcohol consumption, his disdain for the theory of evolution, his being a follower of D.L. Moody, and his regret regarding the contemporary church's failure in being "militant for God." In response to the host's summation of a year at PBI as "six months of fundamentalist study," Maxwell affirms "that's right."

Near the end of the program, the host confesses in good faith:

Mr. Maxwell, this is a disappointing program for me. You should be one of the most bigoted Bible-thumpers in all of western Canada, and you come in here and you're a reasonably healthy, happy individual who speaks his mind and doesn't condemn people at all. You've heard what I consider the bigoted Bible-thumper—if anybody should be this, it should certainly be the President of the Prairie Bible Institute. But you're not this at all—how do you explain that, sir?

✳   ✳   ✳

It is apparent that throughout his life L.E. Maxwell was both a fundamentalist in theology and considered himself a fundamentalist as evidenced by his consistently referring to himself and Prairie Bible Institute as such. Nonetheless, his personality as perceived by the host of the radio program just referred to (and, presumably, others) lends some credibility

---

[84] The host's surprise prompts one to wonder what his experience with other fundamentalists had been. Perhaps, to borrow from Stackhouse's portrayal of T.T. Shields, the host's notion of fundamentalists was that they were ever and always strident and cantankerous individuals, always looking to pick an ideological fight.

to the view inferred by Stackhouse. He claims that Maxwell was a likeable gentlemen who, generally speaking, did not share the cantankerous belligerence that defined certain leaders of twentieth-century American fundamentalism such as the prominent Canadian fundamentalist, T.T. Shields.[85]

---

[85] The subjective element of oral history needs to be acknowledged and emphasized here. As indicated earlier, several former "staff-kids" consulted during research for this book recalled Maxwell as quite cantankerous. For example, former PBI "staff-kid," graduate and eleven-year overseas missionary veteran, Wendell Krossa, retains many negative memories of Maxwell's character. In Chapter Two of the Spiritual Biography posted on his website (see Chapter One, footnote 40, of this book), Krossa states: "And according to LE, some Sunday mornings the chatter of people bothered God more than other Sundays. In one notable instance, during the opening of a morning service, LE sat on the platform of the Tabernacle watching people come in and take their seats. Many were engaging in friendly talk with others. It was just normal human interaction. LE impatiently waited till it was his turn to speak. He then strode quickly to the microphone and quite unexpectedly, shouted loudly in anger at the audience, "You came in here like a herd of stupid pigs. Don't you know that you are in the presence of God?" Everyone sat stunned and embarrassed, trying to think of others who had been talking more than they had. Maybe he was mad at someone else. It was a defensive response to try and deflect the shame. We did not realize that God was so pissed off with us just trying to be friendly to each other."

Such perspectives as Krossa's were and are frequently dismissed in the PBI constituency as the views of someone who has allowed "a root of bitterness to spring up." In other words, the real problem resides in the spiritual condition of the critic. Such a defense is standard fare among fundamentalists. In fact, many of Krossa's critical perspectives on PBI and fundamentalism reflect perspectives acquired via his missionary service in the Philippines and through undergraduate and graduate studies undertaken at Simon Fraser University and the University of British Columbia, both located in Vancouver, B.C., Canada.

CHAPTER NINE

Other prominent leaders at PBI

Hundreds of men and women served on the staff and faculty of Prairie Bible Institute during the Maxwell era. Most people conversant with this period of PBI's history would likely concur that the five individuals briefly introduced in this chapter merit specific identification. Their lengthy service at the school in combination with the prominence of the positions they held made a significant contribution to the fundamentalist orientation of PBI during the period under review.

J. Fergus Kirk

As previously documented, a Canadian farmer named J. Fergus Kirk (b. July 1, 1888) was the initial visionary of what eventually became Prairie Bible Institute. In addition to operating his own farm near Three Hills, he served as the school's President for its first forty years. He then held the title of President Emeritus until his death on September 15, 1981.[1] From 1929 to 1949, Kirk was also the pastor of a small congregation that met in the Ewing schoolhouse near Erskine, a community about an hour north of Three Hills.[2]

---

[1] Bernice A. Callaway, "PBI founder's history courageous and humble" *Three Hills Capital*; March 19, 1980, 23.

    Roy Davidson, "My Fellow Board Member," in *The Prairie Harvesters*, 29, No. 2, (April-August 1982); 2-3 reveals that the role of president was quite mundane in comparison to that associated with a Bible institute/college president today. Kirk regularly hauled coal and water for the school and tended an ample garden that provided vegetables for the student body.

[2] Yates and Ida Foxall, "Mr. Fergus Kirk—Pastor," in *The Prairie Harvesters*, 4-5: "Mr. Kirk faithfully and sacrificially served the group at Ewing until the late 1940s, sometimes spending two or three days in the area visiting and attending the weekly Bible study and prayer meetings. He continued even after the Presbyterian church was unable to give further financial assistance due to the depression . . . The little schoolhouse church . . . is now the Evangelical Free Church in the village of Erskine . . ."

A. His upbringing

Fergus Kirk was born into a Scottish home near Cornwall, Ontario, Canada, to Andrew and Maria Kirk, devout Presbyterians who raised their large family to value rigid self-discipline, material scarcity, the Scripture, Bible school training, missionary service and sacrificial support of Christian work.[3] One of the favorite books of Maria Kirk that influenced her understanding of Christianity as practiced in the Kirk home was *The Christian's Secret of a Happy Life* by Hannah Whitehall Smith, (published 1870).[4] Smith's thinking promoted the development of what became known as the "deeper Christian life" or "victorious Christian living" that came to be associated with the Keswick conferences in England and would have a prominent profile at PBI during the L.E. Maxwell era.[5]

Although several of Fergus Kirk's siblings attended Bible schools such as Nyack and went on to serve abroad as missionaries, he moved to western Canada as a young adult where establishing a successful farming career quickly became the governing priority in his life.[6] He succumbed to ill health while still a young man, however, and doctors advised that two years of complete rest would be necessary for him to make a full recovery.[7]

---

[3] Keller, 52-53, notes that "Mrs. Kirk never once iced a cake, feeling this to be an unwanted extravagance" (p. 50) and how following a "deep, Spirit-endowed quickening at a Christian conference held in their little Presbyterian church," Andrew cancelled all his insurance and diverted that money directly into God's work.

[4] Maxwell, *Crowded to Christ*, 98: "To my desk as I write, a similar word comes from Africa from Hector Kirk. Concerning the consecration, disappointment, and suffering of his mother (Grandma Kirk, as we knew her), he writes: "A book which came into her hand at that time, and which greatly influenced her life, was *The Christian's Secret of a Happy Life* . . .""

[5] Snyder, 17, 53.

[6] Charles Crawford, "Mr. Fergus Kirk—Christian Farmer," in *The Prairie Harvesters*, I: "As we worked together we talked of our plans for the future. Fergus told me his ambition was to have a good farm all paid for and a nice big house on it. With this as his goal, he worked hard!"

[7] The literature is unclear regarding the precise nature of Kirk's affliction. From what is said, however, it seems fair to conclude that he experienced some combination of a physical/emotional breakdown.

While chauffeuring a missionary around Alberta during his recuperation, Kirk heard the gentleman preach on 2 Samuel 24:24.[8] Leaving the meeting to sit in his vehicle, Kirk pondered the words "that which doth cost me nothing," wept at length and promised God that he was "prepared to sacrifice and sacrifice and sacrifice for my Savior."[9]

Upon recovery from his illness, Kirk began to sell off his land in keeping with the promise he had made to God. Using the "search questions" he had obtained from a sister who had attended Bible school at Nyack, Kirk initiated studying the Bible for himself. In time he acquired the use of a vacant schoolhouse where he offered Sunday school classes for interested residents of the community. He eventually became a respected lay preacher under the authority of the Presbyterian Church. It was during this period that "there grew upon him a great burden for the young people of the district." He thus wrote W.C. Stevens to ask if he might recommend someone who could teach them "the deeper walk with God."[10]

Factors such as Kirk's childhood home where Hannah Whitehall Smith's writing was influential, the family's connection with the Christian & Missionary Alliance school at Nyack and his affinity for language such as "the deeper walk with God," all point to Kirk's familiarity with some of the theology and educational philosophy that figured in the development of the movement that eventually fathered American fundamentalism. In this regard, readers are also reminded of the contents of Kirk's initial inquiry to W.C. Stevens concerning the need for a Bible teacher to come to Three Hills. Kirk had expressed alarm about the entrance of liberal teaching into churches, a concern that figured prominently among evangelicals in the years leading up to the eventual emergence of American fundamentalism.[11]

---

[8] 2 Samuel 24:24 in the King James Version reads: "And the king said unto Araunah, Nay; but I will surely buy it of thee at a price: neither will I offer burnt offerings unto the LORD my God of that which doth cost me nothing. So David bought the threshing floor and the oxen for fifty shekels of silver."

[9] Keller, 66.

Crawford, in *The Prairie Harvesters*, 2: "Fergus never looked back after he made this promise to God, and we who were close to him knew what it cost him. For one thing, he had bought a quantity of material for that new house he wanted. That house was never built."

[10] Keller, 67-69.

[11] Chapter One of this book, footnote 68.

B. His writings

Although Kirk was certainly not as prolific an author as L.E. Maxwell, two of the works he authored offer particular insight into the nature of the fundamentalism he embraced that in turn influenced the theological and cultural orientation of PBI.[12] *Jesus Christ the same yesterday, and today, and forever (Hebrews 13:8)* is an undated, self-published booklet containing a collection of essays by Kirk. "Social Credit and the Word of God" was written in April 1935 and reveals Kirk's assessment of the Social Credit political movement in Alberta as advocated by William Aberhart.[13]

Aberhart, a Calgary high school principal originally from Ontario, had also established himself as a Bible teacher, pastor, radio preacher, and founder of the Prophetic Bible Institute in that city during the 1920s. He was subsequently elected Premier of Alberta as head of the province's first Social Credit government in August 1935, a position he held until his death in 1943.

In the first publication noted above, Kirk reflects the type of Bible study promoted by the "search question" method of investigation. Numerous Bible verses are marshaled and cited one after another in the course of demonstrating his conviction that the Bible is the best interpreter of itself. Kirk interacts (by his own admission, somewhat legalistically (p. 6) with the matter of the relationship between the Old Testament's emphasis on law and the New Testament's focus on grace.[14] His conclusion is "that law and grace are not opposed, but work most harmoniously together."[15]

Although Kirk engages some of the tenets of dispensational theology throughout this work, he does so without any references to Darby, Scofield, Gabelein or other leading proponents of what had become a popular school of Biblical interpretation. This likely reflects the fact

---

[12] Doug Kirk, "Boyhood Memories Of My Dad," in *The Prairie Harvesters*, 7. Fergus Kirk apparently enjoyed writing as his son, Douglas, observed that even after the senior Kirk's retirement "... he did find considerable outlet for continued Christian service ... in the authoring of some pamphlets." The author encountered several of Kirk's pamphlets in the Ted S. Rendall Library Archives.

[13] J.F. Kirk, in David R. Elliott, (ed.) *Aberhart: Outpourings and Replies* (Edmonton, AB: Alberta Records Publication Board, 1991), 109-122.

[14] J.F. Kirk, *Jesus Christ the same yesterday, and today, and forever (Hebrews 13:8)* (Three Hills, AB: n.d.), 6.

[15] Ibid., 56.

that, during the Maxwell era, use of outside aids in Bible study at PBI was openly discouraged in the interests of "enabling each student to produce his own original findings from the Scriptures."[16] Nevertheless, it is apparent from this booklet that Kirk subscribed to many of the tenets of premillennial dispensationalism which, as has already been seen, is viewed by several authorities as a key component of American fundamentalism.

This independent approach to Bible study in tandem with the pietistic spirit with which it was employed at PBI often resulted in the utilization of a comparatively subjective approach in interpreting the Bible and in deriving corresponding applications. This is evident, for example, when Kirk writes: "Until recent years I personally have had difficulty in getting good sense from the parables; but recently I feel that the Lord has given me certain principles which can be applied to all of them."[17]

Such a statement connotes a significant presupposition that prevailed in the fundamentalism practiced at Prairie particularly in the first half of the period under review. The suggestion is that when God directly imparts to the Bible student the wherewithal to accurately interpret Scripture for himself, time spent studying ancient languages, cultures, history, patterns of communications in ancient genres of literature is comparatively unimportant, if not virtually unnecessary.

Although classes in Bible history, Biblical interpretation and the original languages in time came to be a part of the curriculum at Prairie during the Maxwell era, many were usually offered as electives or non-required courses and played a secondary role to the school's primary objective of directly immersing the student in the English text of the Bible. In such an environment where a subjective approach to the study of Scripture was given priority, it is not unreasonable to suggest that a conviction such as Kirk's that "the Lord has given me . . ." inevitably contributed to the abrasive dogmatism that came to be associated with some fundamentalists. In turn, such dogmatism was a potential contributor to the spirit of belligerence for which fundamentalism eventually acquired a reputation. After all, who dares to argue with insights gleaned from God himself?

---

[16] Chapter One of this book, footnote 9.
[17] J.F. Kirk, *Jesus Christ the same yesterday, and today, and forever;* 91.

Given PBI's insistence on students wrestling with the text for themselves, one of the puzzling aspects of life as a student at the school as encountered by many students concerned understanding why the instructors' subjective understanding of the Biblical text always prevailed when it came to the academic grading of assignments. Despite the encouragement we were given to search out the meaning of the text for ourselves, a low score on an assignment often left one with no other conclusion but that the Holy Spirit was invariably aligned with the particular instructor's perspectives rather than those purportedly revealed to the student. In other words, notwithstanding the emphasis at PBI that was placed on the Holy Spirit's teaching and leading students to find the truth for ourselves, apparently there was indeed some kind of an objective or preferred interpretation of the text that was used for the grading of assignments.

When combined with the beliefs that Christ's return was imminent and that millions around the world had yet to hear the Christian gospel without which they would suffer eternal conscious torment, the subjective nature of the fundamentalism which prevailed at Prairie was consistently undergirded by a sense of urgency. Kirk's booklet demonstrates that this urgency was enhanced by his perceptions of how current threats to the gospel such as atheistic communism were to be interpreted.[18]

"Social Credit and the Word of God" is an aggressive piece penned by Kirk which clearly demonstrates that something of the "battling," "militancy" and "contentiousness" that Stackhouse elects to reserve for Canadian fundamentalist pastor, T.T. Shields, could also be found in the perspectives of the Canadian co-founder of Prairie Bible Institute.[19] Social Credit as a political/social ideology, William Aberhart's theology, the Roman Catholic Church, some of

---

[18] J.F. Kirk, *Jesus Christ, the same yesterday, and today, and forever;* 107.

[19] Stackhouse, *Canadian Evangelicalism,* uses the terms "militant" (12, 21, 33), "contentiousness" (21) and "pugnacity" (33) to identify a unique form of (American) fundamentalism that characterized the personality and ministry of Toronto pastor, T.T. Shields, who regularly associated with prominent American fundamentalists of a militant inclination. Stackhouse also twice cites the title of a 1949 *Maclean's* magazine which referred to Shields as a "battling Baptist" (22, 34) to argue that Shields "marks out the fundamentalist limit of Canadian evangelicalism" (21, 23). That such descriptions of Shields are accurate is beyond dispute. My book contends, however, that the difference(s) in this regard between

the prominent Reformers as well as Protestantism in general are all indicted by Kirk in this tract.[20] Its primary purpose appears to be to fervently contend that the harsh economic depression of the 1930s

---

Kirk and Maxwell at PBI and T.T. Shields were not always as obvious or clear cut as Stackhouse implies.

Palmer, 263: "J. Fergus Kirk, president of PBI, warned that Aberhart was preaching materialism and communism."

[20] J.F. Kirk in Elliott, *Aberhart: Outpourings and Replies*:

116: "It is evident that Social Credit offers what it can never deliver, and it is a great pity that so many of God's dear people are so ready to seek shelter in such man-made security, which, in reality, bars Christ."

118: ". . . why is it that Social Credit appeals so readily, not only to most Christians, but also to every false sect, to the world in general, to atheists, Communists, and nearly every other class of people? Is it not because of the spirit of covetousness or the prospect of gain with little or no labor?"

119: "In other words Social Credit is simply the financial end of socialism . . . The method of action is somewhat different from radical socialism, but the objective is the same. All communists agree with the ideas of Social Credit, but many of them have little confidence in the method of action . . . I have interviewed several radical socialists on the matter and find them heartily in agreement with the movement . . . All the arguments of the Social Credit man brought forth regarding the poor can be had from the radical Communist by simply approaching him on the matter. The one great thing that made me question Social Credit was that I had heard most of their reasoning from radicals long before I heard of Social Credit. You don't get these arguments from any other class of people. Injustice, unfairness, inequality, etc., are the bases for practically all socialistic arguments."

113: "The founder of Social Credit in Alberta, until he took up Social Credit, was a strong dispensationalist teacher of the Word, but since, because it suits his business, has evidently dropped it altogether."

111: "Why did the early church lose out, and finally fail? Through fellowshipping with the world in love of position, praise, wealth, popularity, etc. Through these things the early Church, wide-awake, full of life and fire, became the worldly minded, worldly ambitious Roman Catholic Church."

111: "What is wrong with the Protestant Church today? Worldliness!"

112-113: "In studying the attitude which should be maintained by Gentile believers we should be careful about taking the lives of men, even of great reformers such as Luther, Wesley, Knox and others as a final rule. These men were not infallible, good as they were. Roman Catholics make this great mistake. Instead of going to the Word of God they study the lives of the church fathers. And so we find them exercising governmental authority where they have no right."

was attributable to the "judgment of God" on western civilization's "failure to walk with God."[21]

In addition to the stinging rhetoric he employs, Kirk's invective yields evidence of what various scholars have identified as defining influences that impacted the thinking and behavior of fundamentalists. These include: affinity for metaphysical dualism or Manichaeism; allegiance to dispensational millennialism; intentional separation from secular culture or "the world;" zealous commitment to Biblical authority, and preoccupation with alarmist prophecy and eschatology.[22] Aspects of some

---

[21] J.F. Kirk in Elliott, *Aberhart*, 109.

[22] J.F. Kirk, 117: "Isaiah 28:12-18 . . . This was spoken to Israel in regard to their looking to outside nations for support against their enemies instead of trusting only in the Lord. In supporting Social Credit, are we not doing the same thing? We are joining hands with the world against the evil day which we see right ahead, instead of looking to the Lord alone."

121: "We feel that the great blunder in this Social Credit movement is the failure to discriminate between things spiritual and things material. Accordingly, a political campaign is turned into a holy crusade and temporal matters are made to appear as spiritual. Unless Christians are alert to this confusion of things that differ they may easily be led to believe that unless they enlist in this holy (?) war they are not "doing God's service.""

Martin Riesbrodt, (trans. by Don Reneau) *Pious Passion: the Emergence of Modern Fundamentalism in the United States and Iran* (Los Angeles: Univ. of California Press, 1993), 61, 62: "The Manichaeism in fundamentalist thinking is, of course, already present in Christian thought in its distinctions between God and Satan, the forces of light and darkness, good and evil, and God's commandments and sin. These expressed dualisms rarely find application and largely disappear in pragmatic compromises in the everyday lives of most religious people, but they stand in the center of fundamentalist thought and are subject to continual actualization and dramatization. The effects of this dramatized Manichaeism are evident primarily in the representation of the enemy, in the self-perception of the movement, and in the categorical perception of society's crisis . . . The crisis in American society at the turn of the century was perceived not as a structural crisis caused by industrialization, urbanization, and mass immigration but as a moral crisis brought forth by unbelief."

Martin E. Marty and R. Scott Appleby, *The Glory and the Power: The Fundamentalist Challenge to the Modern World* (Boston: Beacon Press, 1992), 29: "Closely associated with the end-time thought of fundamentalisms is the embracing of a dualistic worldview which sharply divides the world into God's versus Satan's, Good versus Evil. The dualisms are extreme for a reason: they help fundamentalists see the enemy clearly and without flinching."

Nancy T. Ammerman, *Bible Believers in the Modern World* (New Brunswick, NJ: Rutgers Univ. Press, 1987), 82, notes that fundamentalists think in terms of polarities

of the idiosyncrasies of the fundamentalism that frequently surfaced at PBI are also evident: an elementary yet dogmatic understanding of civilization, history, economics and government; advocacy for a pietistic relationship to politics and government; the singular nature of the Church's mandate.[23]

---

[23] J.F. Kirk in Elliott, *Aberhart*, 109-110: "Our present civilization has been developed by Christianity and our present depression is caused by the breaking down of "that civilization" through failure to walk with God. It is remarkable that heathen countries such as China, India and Africa have been little affected by this great depression indicating that this depression is a judgment of God upon those nations which have once known Him and still profess Him, but whose hearts are far from Him. The above named heathen countries have, for many, many centuries, had no exalted position from which to fall for long ago they too forsook the God of heaven and ever since have been groveling in darkness and degradation—now they have no civilization to be affected. A few generations ago in the present so-called Christian countries, the Word of God was honored and obeyed and through righteousness these nations were "exalted"; in this generation the Word of God is dishonored and disobeyed, and "sin" which is becoming so prevalent is inevitably proving a "reproach." Without a doubt the present depression is the heavy hand of God upon these nations to bring them to repentance and to Himself, if possible. Otherwise, the warning, unheeded, can only be followed by utter ruin."

111: "Even so now, present depressing conditions are the outcome of the failure of the nations concerned to acknowledge God or to return to Him in their distresses."

115: "The believer is never to make temporal things a matter of concern . . . The Word throughout forbids stressing materialistic and temporal things . . . Social Credit will appeal to the man of the world and to the worldly minded Christian, because of its promise of plenty, ease and comfort with luxury and leisure."

113: "ARE WE TO HAVE NO PART IN GOVERNMENTAL AFFAIRS? By all means we are to have part. What saith the Word? Jeremiah 29:7 reads, "And seek the peace of the city whither I have caused you to be carried away captives, and pray unto the Lord for it; for in the pace thereof shall ye have peace,: and again in I Timothy 2:1,2, "I exhort therefore, that first of all, supplications, prayers and intercessions and giving of thanks, be made for all men; for Kings and for all that are in authority; that we may lead a quiet and peaceful life in all godliness and honesty." In James 5 we are told that "the effectual fervent prayer of a righteous man availeth much" (that some effectual, fervent prayer carries more weight than thousands of votes) . . . Yes, vote as God leads, in-as-much as popular vote is our present system, but don't count too much on the outcomes. Read Romans 13:1."

115: "The Social Credit advocate is not satisfied with what the Word allows ("Having food and raiment let us therewith be content" . . . but will be content with nothing less than the best the world can produce and plenty of it, without much to spare . . ."

C. His personality

When *Prairie Harvesters*, the alumni journal of Prairie Bible Institute, published a memorial issue following the death of J. Fergus Kirk in 1981, a number of recollections of the school's co-founder were included.[24] Among the memories that assist the attempt to construct an accurate profile of the man are tributes from a son and two grandsons.

One of his sons, Douglas, wrote, for example:

> I thank God for happy memories of my dad. In thinking of him, words come to my mind such as kind, gracious, helpful, generous, devout, and godly . . . Not only was my dad helpful but he was also kind and gracious. I cannot ever remember receiving a harsh word from him. I recall one particular incident in my boyhood that illustrates his graciousness. One day as I was leading a harnessed horse out of the barn, the traces caught on the latch of the door, pulling the door from its hinges. I felt devastated. Instead of scolding me

---

J.F. Kirk in Elliott, *Aberhart*, 114-115: "Paul in writing to the Christian Church (not to leaders particularly) says in 2 Corinthians 4:16: "While we look not at the things which are seen, but at things which are not seen, for the things which are seen are temporal, but the things which are not seen are eternal." The believer is never to make temporal things a matter of concern . . . Philippians 4:19 . . . Psalm 37:25 . . . Matthew 6:31 . . . The Word throughout forbids stressing materialistic and temporal things."

120: "It was the straight preaching of the Gospel in the power of the Spirit that finally changed the old Roman rule from pagan to Christian, introducing Christian freedom, therefore doing away with cruel slavery and many other evils. It was the straight preaching of the Gospel in Wesley's time that saved England from revolt and possible bloodshed. It was the straight Gospel message of days gone by which has given us our present high standard of morality and civilization. And it is the failure to still preach that same Gospel message that is causing that standard of morality and civilization to waver and break in our days . . . If we would save our land at this time, let us give ourselves to the proclamation of the Gospel of Christ, for IT only is the power of God unto salvation. It was Mr. Moody who said the old ship (this world) is doomed and is sinking fast. Don't waste time trying to save the ship, but get as many off as possible. Let us therefore give ourselves to the salvation of souls, rather than to patching up a world that is doomed to destruction."

24 *The Prairie Harvesters*, 1-12. Celebrating his 90th birthday in September 2012, Douglas Kirk served for most of his life as the resident electronics/recording/broadcasting expert at PBI. Bob Kirk is a business executive in Vancouver, Canada. Dr. Alan Kirk is Associate Professor of Religion at James Madison University in Harrisonburg, Virginia, USA.

for not having made sure that the door was opened wide enough, Daddy comforted me. This was typical of his graciousness with us boys.

Grandson Bob Kirk, son of Fergus's other son, Donald, and one of my chums in youth, identified another aspect of the senior Kirk's personality:

And what stubbornness! One dinner a dispute arose between Grandpa and Grandma about the spelling of a particularly simple word. When Aunt Catherine, Grandma's sister, tactfully suggested that a dictionary within easy reach on the sideboard might contain the answer, both nonagenarians, each afraid of being wrong perhaps, bluntly told her that it was their argument and to keep out of it![25]

Bob's younger brother, Alan, added:

I'll never forget the many summer and winter evenings spent sharing in Grandpa's, Grandma's and Ta's pre-bedtime cup of tea. After a cup or two, conversation ceased. Grandpa put on his reading glasses and reaching for *Daily Light*. With eyes almost closed so as not to miss a single word, Grandma and Ta listened in reverent silence to God's Word. All heads bowed as Grandpa prayed his lengthy evening prayer. I remember little of the content but their spirit of deep reverence for their Lord and Savior probably affected me more than I'll ever know. Yes, even the rebellious stirrings in possession of my heart when I was a teen-ager knew better than to express themselves in that "kitchen sanctuary." Other disconnected recollections of Grandpa flash by . . . old age never quenched his keen sense of humor which was always accompanied by twinkling eyes . . . How can I forget Grandpa's and Grandma's fiftieth wedding anniversary celebration in the dining room when Grandpa's "few words" stretched into a full-length sermon! Or how about the many times a passing glance into Grandpa's dim room revealed him sitting at his lamp-lit desk, glasses on, and Bible open.

These informative citations underscore the gracious and devout piety of J. Fergus Kirk, qualities that were openly promoted and expected in the course of

---

[25] *The Prairie Harvesters*, 9. Bob also noted his grandparents' lifelong commitment to material sacrifice: "To the day they were moved into a retirement home, they still had flour-sack sheets dating from the depression in their house."

daily life at PBI. At the same time, bearing in mind what was mentioned in the Introduction of this thesis with respect to the strength of Fergus Kirk's convictions, Bob again testified to the stubborn streak in his grandfather's character:

> But stubbornness over principles once occasioned a few hours in the local jail for Grandpa, who had enrolled my father, just turned fourteen, in Prairie's new and then unaccredited high school. The subtle influences of humanistic teaching in the English curriculum of the public school system had not escaped his discerning and largely self-educated mind, and if something had to give, it wasn't going to be he.

Along this line, as a youth I recall encountering the stubborn fervency of J. Fergus Kirk's adherence to the fundamentalist distinctive of separation from the world. When I was of junior-high school age, several of us who were a close-knit group of PBI "staff kids" at the time, persuaded our fathers to take us into Calgary for the annual Labor Day football game featuring the Calgary Stampeders of the Canadian Football League. This soon became an annual ritual and a highly-anticipated event among our group and often involved a caravan of several vehicles making the 1.5 hour trek to McMahon Stadium in Calgary for the game. Friends like Bob, Gordon, Alan, Stan and Gary Kirk (Fergus Kirk's grandsons) often participated in these outings.

Early in those years of attending the Labor Day games, my father informed my brothers and I that Fergus Kirk had paid him a visit. I do not recall precisely why it was our father that Kirk targeted in the offending group of fathers. Perhaps it was because he sat on the PBI board and some other prominent committees at the school alongside Kirk.

In any event, Victor Callaway advised us that Fergus Kirk was quite distressed that the fathers were taking us into an environment where alcohol was openly served, smoking was prominent and we would be subjected to possibly hearing the Lord's name taken in vain. I do not remember whether or not Kirk attempted to register a definitive prohibition against our going to the game in future years. What I do remember is the sense of annoyance many of us experienced as youngsters upon learning that someone in a position of authority over us was legalistically opposed to our participation in an event that held considerable enjoyment for us.

This incident is cited here to support the reality that the kind of fundamentalism that the co-founder of PBI was sympathetic to favored minimal exposure of the "redeemed" to worldly environments, entertainment or unbelievers in general. Such thinking was behind numerous stringent regulations at Prairie during the Maxwell era that prohibited our attendance at the theatre or the cinema, the presence of television on campus, and any meaningful interaction with the general population of the town of Three Hills.[26]

J. Fergus Kirk represented a dynamic that was true of many of the fundamentalist fathers. They were people of deep, personal piety. Nonetheless, in their efforts to take a stand for truth and holiness as they understood such, many did not hesitate to employ combative terminology or tactics in their public discourse and interactions. Insistence on a clear-cut, visible "separation from the world" was frequently a part of their understanding of what constituted authentic Christianity.

Dorothy Ruth Miller

As mentioned previously in this book, one researcher suggests that "Dorothy Ruth Miller was a stalwart of the newly established Prairie Bible Institute" and next to L.E. Maxwell "exercised the greatest influence in shaping the identity of the school."[27] A graduate of both New York (history major) and Columbia (English major) universities in New York City prior to launching a teaching career and then attending Bible school, Miller proceeded to teach in Bible schools of the Christian and Missionary Alliance in New York state and Seattle before arriving at PBI on June 29, 1928. She served as teacher, preacher, co-editor, residence administrator and counselor, and a board member at Three Hills until her death at age seventy-one in 1944.[28]

---

[26] PBI Archives in Ted S. Rendall Library: PBI Administrative Board minutes Box 31, May 15, 1963: "Parents of a local Prairie High student have requested that our high school young people, or local young people, be given the opportunity to play baseball with some of the town high school students. The present policy outlined in Motion 1014 of December 3, 1962 forbids this. Therefore permission was not granted."

[27] James Enns, *Hothouse Fundamentalism*, 2.

[28] L.E. Maxwell (with Ruth Dearing), *Women in Ministry: A Historical and Biblical Look at the Role of Women in Christian Leadership* (Wheaton, IL: Victor Books, 1987), 8. In the Foreword to this volume, Maxwell's long-time colleague, Ted S. Rendall states: "Miss Dorothy Ruth Miller . . . was a ten-talent Christian leader of stately Victorian appearance. At Mr. Maxwell's request she often preached to the congregation in Sunday services."

Miller had been one of Maxwell's instructors at Midland Bible Institute in Kansas City before she moved on to the Christian & Missionary Alliance school in Seattle. While teaching there Maxwell extended an invitation to her to come to PBI for the 1928-29 school term. (As an aside, it is likely that both Miller's role in Christian ministry as well as Maxwell's life-long openness to women serving in public teaching ministries reflected to some extent the influence of the perspectives of Christian & Missionary Alliance founder, A.B. Simpson, on that particular topic.)[29]

Enns' brief treatment of Miller's devout piety arises from portions of her diary that are preserved in the Prairie Bible Institute Library Archives. As with Maxwell, it is apparent that the holiness teaching of A.B. Simpson and of the Keswick movement played a very influential role in her thinking as to what the normative Christian experience should be. Accordingly, Enns states:

> the interpretive lens through which Miller records events is the importance of living a holy life. Holiness was measured by how well one gave evidence of living the crucified life of self-denial and total abandonment to divine leading into some form of Christian ministry and service. While students were expected to have had a specific conversion experience this did not signal the final victory in one's spiritual walk, rather it only marked the start of a new phase of spiritual warfare. This warfare usually took the form of a series of crises (or one major crisis) or tests of commitment, which usually involved a choice between following a more immediately desirable path of personal ambition, or the less desirable path of humility and self-sacrifice, usually culminating in some form of missionary service.[30]

This paragraph aptly communicates Miller's role in helping establish PBI's connection to the broader definition of fundamentalism that this

---

[29] PBI Archives in Ted S. Rendall Library: L.E. Maxwell personal file—"Women." The file contains an article by Miss D.R. Miller, "On Women Speaking," in *The Christian Reader's Digest*, May 1940, 10: ". . . later I was asked to become principal of an Alliance Bible school. This I declined, though Dr. Simpson urged it."

Janette Hassey, *No Time for Silence: Evangelical Women in Public Ministry Around the Turn of the Century* (Grand Rapids, MI: Zondervan Publishing House, 1986), 15-19.

[30] Enns, *Hothouse-Fundamentalism*, 7.

project calls for in evaluating Prairie Bible Institute during the Maxwell era. It also gives practical insight into the type of spiritual environment that prevailed at the school some twenty to thirty years after Miller's death when this author was a student there.

Fervent pleas to uncover new vistas of unsurrendered landscape in one's spiritual life were frequent in public meetings. Calls to publically rededicate some component of the "inner man" were often prolonged and frequently elicited intense weeping on the part of those in attendance at meetings of this nature.[31]

It was common for such appeals to take place within the context of an emotionally charged conference meeting or revival service wherein L.E. Maxwell would direct us to "do business with God." What this usually entailed was a professed willingness by those in the audience to abandon whatever vocational interests they might have in favor of committing themselves to missionary or pastoral services. These tasks were considered preferential pursuits for the truly committed at PBI.

During the annual Spring and Fall Conferences at Prairie, it was not uncommon for L.E. Maxwell to preach virtually another complete sermon after the main speaker had concluded in the course of passionately beseeching those in attendance to give God uninhibited control of some unsurrendered corner of their lives. Participants were consistently directed to "surrender all" including interests in the opposite sex, social standing, material wealth or vocational achievement in order to respond to a higher good, namely, the personal call of God to a life of "full-time Christian service."

Miller published *A Handbook of Ancient History in Bible Light* in 1937 "for the use of Bible schools and other institutions."[32] A number of the book's features reflect Miller's personal affinity for the more broadly defined fundamentalism being sought in this study of PBI.

Among these features are an Introduction written by Robert H. Glover, Director of the China Inland Mission, one of the great evangelistic faith-

---

[31] I remember how as a youngster I used to become extremely anxious in PBI conference meetings where proceedings of this nature occurred. It seemed to me that such prolonged pleas would invariably result in my mother crying. I recall wondering what could possibly be good about something that consistently achieved that result?

[32] Dorothy Ruth Miller, *A Handbook of Ancient History in Bible Light* (New York: Fleming H. Revell Company, 1937). The quotation is from Robert H. Glover's Introduction, 5.

missions with which PBI maintained a very close relationship.[33] In a tip
of the hat to one of the primary targets of American fundamentalism,
Glover states that the purpose of Miller's book is "to refute the outworn
but still advanced evolutionary hypothesis, and the false theories regarding
the remote antiquity of man," noting that "all of this will be welcomed by
Bible-believing people."[34]

Miller similarly claims in the Preface that previous works on ancient
history "all tend to undermine the Christian faith since all are based upon
the assumption that the evolutionary theory is true," a notion she concisely
refutes in the book's second chapter.[35] In identifying her aims in writing the
book, Miller includes an implicit affirmation of the inerrancy and authority
of Scripture.[36]

---

[33] Enns, 19-20 notes: "Miller noted with some pride that Dr. Glover had mentioned to
another missionary that CIM's best candidates came from PBI." Glover was a frequent
speaker at PBI's annual missionary conference.

Kevin Xiyi Yao, "The Fundamentalist Movement Among Protestant Missionaries
in China, 1920-1937," (ThD dissertation, Boston University School of Theology,
2000), 22-23: "The CIM is always claimed as the champion of the fundamentalist
cause. In many ways, this claim is correct since from the time of its founding the CIM
never wavered in its conservative evangelical doctrines and its doctrinal position had
much in common with fundamentalism . . . The CIM missionaries often accounted
for the majority of the fundamentalist forces [in China] . . . I acknowledge that an
important feature of the missionary fundamentalist movement in China was its
spirituality deeply rooted in the holiness movement and Keswick teachings. Spiritual
consecration and absolute surrender to Christ constituted powerful impetuses behind
the work of . . . the CIM."

[34] Miller, *Handbook of Ancient History*, 5-6.

[35] Miller, 7.

It is instructive to point out that whereas Stackhouse, *Canadian Evangelicalism*, 86,
takes pains to identify the lack of profile for anything opposing the theory of evolution
in *The Prairie Overcomer* during the years 1960-1964, he makes no reference whatsoever
to Dorothy Ruth Miller or her book's forthright challenge of evolution despite several
important facts: 1) Miller quite likely represented the best educated of all PBI faculty
during the Maxwell era; 2) she published the book during her tenure at PBI; 3) the
book was published by Fleming H. Revell Company, one of the most prominent
fundamentalist-evangelical publishers in the United States throughout the twentieth
century.

[36] Ibid., 12: "3. To show that history affords no evidence of the extreme antiquity of man
or of the slow emergence of primitive man from a state of barbarism; but that, on the
contrary, the findings of many of the greatest historians, archaeologists and biologists

As mentioned previously, Miller became co-editor of *The Prairie Pastor* shortly after coming to PBI. Since many of the general articles written by the editors are unattributed, it is occasionally difficult to determine whether a particular article represents the work of Maxwell or of Miss Miller, as she was known. Nevertheless, it is fair to suggest that, as co-editor of the *Pastor* during her years at Prairie, Miller would usually have been in agreement with publication of the fundamentalist themes that were attributed earlier in this chapter to Maxwell. In any event, her commitment to promoting PBI's fundamentalist orientation during her tenure at the school is indisputable.

Ruth C. Dearing

Following Dorothy R. Miller's tenure as a prominent player in the administration and faculty of PBI during approximately the school's first twenty years, another American woman emerged to maintain the feminine profile on the Institute's leadership team. Indeed, as one pages through copies of PBI's annual student yearbook, *The Prairian*, it is impossible not to notice the consistent presence of Ruth C. Dearing in photographs from the 1950s, 1960s and 1970s that depict the school's otherwise all male Board of Directors.

Miss Dearing, as she was always addressed, first met L.E. Maxwell when she was a college student in Seattle, Washington, in the early 1930s. Upon completion of a Bachelor of Religious Studies program at Seattle Pacific College, she enrolled in an intense one-year program of studies at PBI that enabled her to graduate in the spring of 1939. Following her PBI studies, she was appointed to work in the newly-opened Prairie High School where she eventually served as Principal for almost twenty years. In relating this information, James Enns writes:

> Maxwell also acknowledged her ability to lead by allowing her to fill roles in the school which were traditionally understood (and some would argue theologically ordained) to be the purvue (sic) of men. The first of these roles was teaching theology in the Bible College. In 1950 Maxwell asked

are in harmony with the teaching of the Scriptures as to the high degree of intelligence of primordial man; and that the savage state is one of degeneracy and degradation."

Dearing to teach an introductory Bible course to the first year students. Eventually this led to her becoming a full-time instructor in the Bible College after she resigned from the high school principalship in 1963. On different occasions male students would challenge her about her role as a Bible teacher, asking for a biblical justification. Dearing's measured response was that she had not placed herself in that position, but was put there by her administrative superior, Mr. Maxwell. Trusting that those over her were guided by God when asking her to take on these responsibilities gave her the freedom to teach without any sense that she was violating a Biblical commandment.[37]

During a lengthy career as an instructor in the Bible School division at PBI, Dearing regularly carried a full teaching load that included: Bible I, which consisted of an overview of The Pentateuch as well as the historical and poetical books of the Old Testament; Doctrine II, a survey of the theology of sin and salvation; New Testament Greek, which she learned herself for the first time quite late in her teaching career at the Bible school; various other courses as assigned by L.E. Maxwell.[38] She also spoke regularly in PBI's chapel sessions.

Regarding the roles of both Dorothy R. Miller and Ruth C. Dearing at PBI it should be noted that PBI was something of a trailblazer in the Bible institute movement in permitting women to play such a prominent role in leadership.[39] This is particularly noteworthy as it relates to the matter of a woman being allowed to teach Bible and theology courses or to fill any position that created the perception she was exercising authority over men.[40]

---

[37] James Enns, "Prairie Bible Institute" entry on the Alberta Online Encyclopedia website http://www.albertasource.ca/aspenland/fr/society/article_prairie_bible.html (accessed March 3, 2009).

[38] This is how these courses were identified at the time I attended Prairie Bible Institute in 1974-77.

[39] Clinton, *Focused Lives*, 401, footnote 19, suggests the key role played by women in L.E. Maxwell's own spiritual development in his early years had an influence on his theological affinity for promoting women in public ministries that many other Christian leaders of his era withheld from them.

[40] George M. Marsden, *Fundamentalism and American Culture* (1980), 249-250, note 40: "The fundamentalist movement generally allowed women only quite subordinate roles. When experiential emphasis predominated, the idea that Pentecost opened

Flory's research on the records of Wheaton College, Moody Bible Institute, Biola University and Bob Jones University up to 1991 as they relate to this theme is useful for comparative purposes. Early in his dissertation he identifies the very restrictive stance that most fundamentalists took on this matter.[41] His quantitative analysis then makes clear that, as compared to those leading Christian institutions in the United States, PBI was generally much further ahead of the times with respect to consistently allowing women to teach Bible and theology courses.

For instance, after noting that women taught as Bible professors prior to 1950 at Wheaton College in suburban Chicago, Flory reports that thereafter they were restricted to Christian Education courses before being completely eliminated from the religion faculty. He writes:

> What is particularly interesting about this is that women were teaching Bible classes, and that these women were teaching between 1928 and 1950, long before greater opportunities began to be available for women

---

a dispensation when women would prophesy (as the prophet Joel suggested) might be accepted . . . Apparently even in the Holiness traditions the role of women in the church declined during the fundamentalist era."

[41] Flory, 29: "An element of fundamentalist ideology that is found both in ideological statements and in social composition, concerns the legal and social position of women and their roles in these schools. Women's "place" has historically been a major preoccupation among various fundamentalist groups, and these schools are no exception. Fundamentalist leaders of the 1920s spoke against the provocative dress and lifestyles of some women and the adverse moral effect this had on men. They also debated the proper role of women in the church, the home and the work place. These themes have persisted over time and are a major symbolic issue for fundamentalists that intersect other issues such as the inerrancy of scripture, the family, morality, and the influence of the larger culture. That is, for fundamentalists, women and men each have separate and distinct roles which are ordained by God and neither is to intrude on the others' realm. Any changes in gender ideology and practice at these schools would be significant in terms of Riesbrodt's argument about the fundamental patriarchal nature of fundamentalism."

PBI Records Office files: *The Manual of the Prairie Bible Institute 1930-31*, 19, lists eighteen members of the Board of Directors including five women. *The Manual of the Prairie Bible Institute 1939-40*, lists thirteen faculty members (of which ten were women) along with the note "List of Teachers incomplete." Of the ten women, five taught subjects related to Bible and church life. *The Manual of Prairie Bible Institute 1931-32*, 18, identifies Miss Martha Pohnert as one of the speakers at PBI's 1931 Spring Convention.

in the workplace. Further, as the woman's movement of the 1960s and 1970s brought about greater opportunities, women were no longer included in the religion faculty.[42]

In summarizing his findings on the gender of instructors at Moody Bible Institute in Chicago, Flory states:

> The percentage of the faculty made up of women showed a general pattern of decline until 1975, and then a slight increase in 1980 after which it evened out ... In 1980 and 1985, one woman was teaching in the religion faculty in Christian Education and although the departmental breakdown was not available prior to 1980, it is not likely that any women taught anything other than Christian Education within the religion faculty. What is interesting is not that there weren't any women teaching something other than Christian Education in the religion faculty, but that after 1985, there were no women even teaching Christian Education. This area had long been associated with women in fundamentalist schools and churches, likely because it had mostly to do with children and young people, but this was apparently not a viable option for women at Moody.[43]

As for Biola University, now located east of downtown Los Angeles, Flory found:

> Within the religion faculty, there was an even lower percentage of women faculty members than in the rest of the faculty. In fact, no women were ever listed as teaching in the core Bible and theology curriculum, and the few women that were included in the religion faculty either taught in Christian Education or in missions concentrations. Although women were found teaching in these areas of the religion faculty, the same pattern was found at Biola as that found at each of the other schools in this study, that is, women initially taught in Christian education however, as this area became more professionalized, as indicated by more advanced degrees among the Christian education faculty, women were replaced by men.[44]

---

[42] Flory, 64-68.
[43] Flory, 132-136.
[44] Flory, 211-213.

Similarly, with respect to Bob Jones University in South Carolina, Flory learned:

> The faculty listings showed a particular emphasis on keeping the School of Religion, in particular the core theology and Bible courses, more purely fundamentalist. This was accomplished not only by having the vast majority of the faculty trained at BJU, but also by keeping it male dominated. This is a particularly important symbolic issue for fundamentalists because of their belief that women should not be allowed in positions of authority over men, particularly in the religious realm as ministers, or in this case as teachers of Bible and theology. In the view of BJU, these teachers are after all ministers, albeit in a formal educational, rather than a worship setting.[45]

To be clear, although the composition of the faculty at PBI throughout much of the Maxwell era was decidedly male, the distinguishing feature at PBI was that at least one woman taught Bible and theology courses at the school throughout most of Maxwell's tenure. Women were also regularly employed as instructors in the Bible school in such areas as Christian Education, music and language arts.

Appropriately then, toward the end of L.E. Maxwell's life, he asked Ruth Dearing to complete a manuscript for him that he was preparing for a book on the role of women in ministry.[46] The Maxwell/Dearing approach to the topic characteristically reflected a pragmatic concern:

> We make no claim to exhaustive research or high scholarship, nor do we make any pretence to great literary or exegetical value in connection with the subject at hand. Our prayer is that *Women in Ministry* may prove of practical value in the lives of godly women who long to be free from bondage and fruitful in the service of their Lord and Master.[47]

---

[45] Ibid., 302-305.

[46] In the Introduction to *Women in Ministry* (II), Dearing states concerning Maxwell and her role in completing the book: "He had already collected material on the subject when his health began to fail. Realizing he could no longer continue, in March of 1982 he asked if I would undertake the completion of the book. Suggesting that I would be the coauthor, he gave me liberty to add, omit, and change anything he had written. I agreed to attempt it, and he gave his endorsement. But in February of 1984 before the final chapters had been completed, he was called home."

[47] Maxwell (Dearing), 13.

Dearing's contribution to the project appears to have been primarily of an editorial nature. Nevertheless, it is useful to note that her participation can rightly be viewed as an implicit endorsement of the unreserved commitment to the authority of Scripture the volume reflects coupled with the interest of fundamentalists to avoid the perception of compromising with the world. The authors specifically distance their motivation in writing from anything to do with the agenda of the women's liberation movement that was so popular in the later years of the twentieth century.[48]

New students attending PBI were usually introduced to the school's widely known search-question method of study in the Bible I class which Dearing taught for many years. Part of the requirements for the course was the completion of a paper popularly known as "The Fall of Man."

It was commonly known among PBI students during the author's attendance at the school during 1974-77 that what our instructor was looking for in the papers was a virtual restatement of certain perspectives she had articulated in class. We were expected to have recorded these in our lecture notes. Submissions of a creative variety and those that did not clearly reflect the teacher's interpretations of the early chapters of Genesis invariably received low scores. Indeed, there was a standing joke that circulated in those days that the more citations one included in the paper from Miss Dearing's favorite and oft-quoted authority, Alfred Edersheim, the higher one's score would be.

The purpose of introducing this element of student life at Prairie is to briefly illuminate the nature of the fundamentalist education that was dispensed at the school. As previously noted, PBI earned a reputation for

---

[48] Maxwell (Dearing), 11, (Dearing writes): "For many years Mr. Maxwell had on his heart the urge to prepare a treatise on the ministry of women. His desire was that women might be set free from what he felt were unscriptural restrictions placed on them by many churches and Christian leaders: his only fear was that he might appear to endorse the "women's lib" movement which was then coming to the fore."

43, "We have not the least sympathy with the aims and goals of the ERA, which according to the literature of the radical feminists, are to "do away with family, love, marriage, heterosexuality, and religion." Certainly no Bible-taught believer can endorse or have sympathy with the ERA. This is idolatry's modern Moloch that sings and dances about such slogans as equality, human rights, social justice, and so forth."

148-149, Dearing concludes the book with a strong affirmation that true women's liberation is found in the Christian woman's freedom to exercise her gifts in Christian ministry.

its use of the inductive method of Bible study. This was proudly touted as a means whereby students could pursue the contents and the meaning of the Biblical text for themselves without being influenced by the views of various commentators and authors.

However, the ironic reality of the situation was that, as reflected by the previous anecdote regarding Miss Dearing's expectations related to the "The Fall of Man" paper, it was generally anticipated that the answers we uncovered in the text would be those that conformed to the predilections of our instructors or their favorite authorities. In other words, not only were we discouraged from using standard commentaries and reference books for Bible papers, minimal encouragement was given to students to present and defend anything of a creative or dissenting nature from the viewpoints dispensed in class lectures. The various interpretations of disputed portions of Scripture were therefore seldom encountered at PBI apart from learning the preferred view(s) of the instructors or their favorite sources.

This reality prompted some students on occasion to privately protest that what we were actually receiving at PBI was not education but more in keeping with indoctrination.[49] By virtue of the preferred pedagogical philosophy that prevailed, it was apparent that developing the ability to think critically and articulate one's perspectives accordingly was not high on the priority list the PBI administration held for its students. The underlying concern of our fundamentalist educators, some critics therefore asserted, was to control that which could potentially lead to the acceptance of or proliferation of liberal or otherwise heretical perspectives.

Paul T. Maxwell

Following a period of rebellion in his younger years against his father and the values of the institution that L.E. Maxwell had founded, Paul Maxwell

---

[49] A couple of books that address this aspect of fundamentalist education are: Christine Rosen, *My Fundamentalist Education: A Memoir of a Divine Girlhood* (New York: Public Affairs, 2005) and Shirley Nelson, *The Last Year of the War* (New York: Harper and Row, 1978), 17. The book is a novel that depicts life at a fictitious fundamentalist Bible school reminiscent of Moody Bible Institute: ""This has been called 'The Place of the Skull,'" she said cheerfully, "but that's unwarranted. The rules are much stiffer at other Christian schools. At Prairie Bible Institute in Alberta girls have to wear Ace bandages around their bazooms . . . Yes, I heard that!""

went on to graduate from PBI and to then engage in a lengthy period of missionary service in Colombia, South America. He returned to PBI in the early 1970s to become a Bible school instructor and then, to the surprise of many, was appointed in 1978 by the Institute's Board of Directors to succeed his father as PBI president. Among the courses the younger Maxwell taught in 1974-1977 when I attended Prairie were Bible III, Christian Counseling and a number of specialized classes on various topics related to missions.

Among the requirements for Bible III, which consisted in part of an overview of the Pauline epistles (with the exception of Romans), was a term paper popularly identified as "Law and Grace." A significant purpose of the paper was for students to identify in St. Paul's thought the role of the Old Testament law as a schoolmaster in pointing the people of God to the Christ of the New Testament as the authentic object of saving faith.

As noted regarding the "The Fall of Man" term paper that was a requirement of Bible I taught by Ruth C. Dearing, it was well known among Bible III students that papers that closely reflected the instructor's views as given in class were the most likely to receive a favorable score. Further, it was also common knowledge that the views set forth in class were a summation of those contained in L.E. Maxwell's book *Crowded to Christ* which the younger Maxwell frequently referenced. As was the case with the "The Fall of Man" paper, the understanding of what was expected for the "Law and Grace" paper again prompted certain students to quietly complain that they were being indoctrinated as opposed to being educated in the art of critical thinking or careful research.

A series of five radio messages preached by Paul Maxwell presumably on one of the various radio programs PBI sponsored over the years offers several useful insights into the thinking of the man who would succeed his father as president of Prairie Bible Institute.[50] Not surprisingly, certain

---

[50] Ted S. Rendall Library: audio tape sermons by Paul T. Maxwell entitled: "Signs of the Time," 236.61 MAXW, n.d. Although there is no date given when these messages occurred, given the frequent references Maxwell makes to current events, it is likely accurate to suggest they date to the early 1970s shortly after he had returned to PBI from Colombia, |south America where he had served as a missionary. This series may have been preached on "The Ambassador Hour," a radio program sponsored by PBI during the 1970s.

similarities to the themes identified in his father's preaching, teaching and writing are evident.

"Signs of the Time" begins with Maxwell sounding a strong note of warning regarding the increasing decadence of modern society. He likens the spirit of the age to the days of Noah and Belshazzar when people were complacent and unconcerned about their sinful ways. He compares Western nations to an incident recorded in *Reader's Digest* regarding a town in Quebec that partially slid into a giant crater despite the fact that huge cracks appeared in the streets days in advance of the catastrophe. Suggesting that society was possibly headed for World War III, Maxwell's opening message sets an alarmist tone similar to that which can be ascertained in the writings and sermons of some of the proto-fundamentalists of the late nineteenth and early twentieth centuries. They similarly pointed to specific flaws in the social habits of the day to suggest that time was short and judgment certain.[51]

In the second message, Maxwell refers to conditions in the day of Lot before going on to catalogue a number of specific ills he sees in North American life. Like certain fundamentalists of the 1920s and 1930s, he identifies alcohol as the top U.S. "drug problem." He also decries materialism, idleness as seen in the push for a four-day work week, and the multi-million dollar salaries being paid sports stars. He summarizes that "God will not allow this to go on indefinitely" and, inferring the need for revival, concludes that "the only answer is to cry to God for an awakening to eternal realities."

The third message of the series specifies a number of current examples of society's godlessness. Maxwell speaks of "a holy admixture" in the world of advertising and cites a TV advertisement for flea powder that stated "in the beginning, not God, but dog." Invoking a prophetical tone, Maxwell declares, "such a twist in the use of Scripture and the name of God is downright blasphemy." Another TV ad is referenced that portrayed Eve suggestively tempting Adam to try "Cranapples." Reflecting fundamentalism's firm commitment to the infallibility of Scripture, Maxwell warns:

---

[51] Marsden, *Fundamentalism and American Culture* (1980), 156: "Methodist church choirs, for instance, allowed young women to display "brazen bared knees." "Who is responsible for this change of custom from the bended knee . . . ?" queried *The King's Business*.

Such advertising is more than a cute adaptation by a clever advertising agency . . . in the flea powder ad, the eternal God is reduced to the level of a dog . . . the second advertisement, the very reason for man's condemnation and death is treated as a joke . . . Such devilish playing with God's Word is to flirt both with one's immediate judgment and to confirm one's ultimate damnation. As Christians we should raise such a voice that these Satanically-inspired perversions would have to be removed from the nation's TV screens.[52]

He continues the third message with a verdict that "Belshazzar was sick, but we are sicker" and substantiates his claim with references to:

- an article in a recent TIME magazine that spoke of "shops offering Jesus Christ jockey shorts for men and Jesus Christ bikinis for ladies . . . it went on to tell of a Jesus watch (Mickey Mouse style) for children"
- a newspaper article about an art dealer in Toronto who was selling "life-like replicas of all parts of the human anatomy displayed as if for sale in a delicatessen type setting . . . as if this was not revolting enough, the artist made an elaborate setting of The Lord's Supper with a human torso and organs heaped on gravy-filled plates."

He noted that hundreds had flocked to see the exhibit just mentioned that was scheduled for a cross-Canada tour later that year. Maxwell then registered his belief that the judgment of God was imminent by exhorting his listeners to "use the few remaining hours that we have to snatch a few from the burning wrath of God."

Maxwell turned his attention in the fourth message of the series to a topic that by the late 1950s had replaced Hollywood as a favorite whipping boy for

---

[52] Maxwell's concerns here curiously presage the kind of outrage that fundamentalist Muslims began to articulate and demonstrate toward the Western world in the latter years of the twentieth century. In 1989 Islamic leaders declared a "fatwa" or death sentence on author Salman Rushdie for purported blasphemy against Allah in his book *The Satanic Verses*. See Bruce Bawer, *Surrender: Appeasing Islam; Sacrificing Freedom*, and the chapter entitled "Docile Provocateurs," 214f, for documentation of the growing controversy in the United States and Europe regarding the West's commitment to freedom of speech and Islam's intolerance of blasphemy.

fundamentalists: rock and roll music.[53] The rock opera *Jesus Christ Superstar* was in circulation at the time of Maxwell's messages and was being widely indicted by fundamentalists as particularly offensive to Bible-believing Christians.

Referring to an October 25, 1971, cover story in TIME magazine regarding the musical, Maxwell scorns the production by responding to the suggestion that the rock opera was "show 'biz with a twist" with an emphatic "twisted is right!" He then uses *Jesus Christ Superstar* as a point of departure to address the rising popularity of "gospel rock" or Christian rock music.

Maxwell maintained that "the very name sets forth an unholy mixture, gospel is the message of Christ's glorious salvation" whereas rock was "originally the message of heathendom in dark Africa, but today the message of sensual America." He then proceeded to argue that "just like Belshazzar's use of holy vessels for unholy ends, gospel rock takes the unholy vessel of rock music and combines it with a holy theme somehow daring to hope that it will accomplish sanctified ends."

Addressing "enthusiastic but misinformed Christian young people," Maxwell asks, "What are you worshipping with this type of music? Belshazzar also worshipped, but not the God of heaven!" He closes the message with an appeal to the holiness motif in the assertion:

> Your confession of compatibility between these two—the gospel and rock music is a confession of your lack of complete compatibility with God. This is not a question of a generation gap, it's a question of a holiness gap.

The concluding message in the series addresses the rise of involvement in the occult among North Americans which Maxwell takes as an indication the last days spoken of in 1 Timothy 4:1-2 and Revelation 16:13-14 have arrived. Noting the increase in astrology columns in American daily newspapers, he quotes a Victor Ernest as an authority who contended that "extended gospel meetings or revival sessions are essential to counter the decline in spiritual vitality in our churches."

Theologically speaking, it appears fair to conclude that Paul Maxwell was loyal to the historic tenets of fundamentalism such as the infallibility of Scripture, separation from the world, the essential pursuit of holiness of life, and revival. And,

---

[53] This mid-century component of fundamentalism is discussed at greater length in Chapter Eleven of this book.

similar to the fundamentalists of days gone by, he did not shrink from sounding a prophetic warning concerning the social ills of the day such as rock music, maintaining that "gospel rock" was merely a sign of the contemporary Church's failure to maintain a circumspect separation from the world.

From a practical perspective, his years of foreign missionary service reflected his affinity for that key distinctive of fundamentalism as more broadly defined. His missionary experience also helped equip him for leadership at one of the most famous missionary-sending academic institutions in the world.

Ted S. Rendall

In the winter of 1976 when I was a second-year student at PBI, a classmate in what was then called Bible II boldly raised his hand and inquired if it was permissible to write the required term paper on the book of Daniel from a post-millennial perspective. The instructor, Ted S. Rendall, was clearly not amused and curtly reminded the inquirer that when the latter had applied to attend Prairie he had signed a statement indicating he was in agreement with the school's doctrinal statement. Such, of course, clearly spelled out that PBI adhered to a pre-millennial stance on matters related to eschatology.

This incident is particularly memorable for a couple of reasons. For one thing, Rendall's response was uncharacteristically sharp for a typically gracious man held in high regard across Canada for his voracious reading and studied ability to interact with numerous theological perspectives.[54] A native of Scotland who had attended the Bible Training Institute in Glasgow and the London Bible College prior to coming to PBI in the early 1950s, Rendall quickly earned the respect of L.E. Maxwell and had a significant influence in broadening both pedagogical and theological horizons at Three Hills.[55] As mentioned before in this book, while I was a student at PBI

---

[54] During my junior and senior years of high school, I attended a small church a few miles east of Three Hills where T.S. Rendall was the pastor. Consequently, I was aware of Rendall's breadth of knowledge prior to sitting under his instruction while a student at PBI.

[55] Ted S. Rendall, personal interview, August 14, 2006: "I'd been exposed to the British approach to exegesis having studied at London Bible College and the Bible Training Institute in Glasgow before I came to Prairie. So I was accustomed to using all the resources of the library and felt that insisting on the inductive method alone was like trying to fly with one wing. I plucked up enough courage to suggest to Mr. Maxwell

during the mid-1970s, it was widely assumed that T.S. Rendall would succeed L.E. Maxwell as president of PBI.

Viewed from another angle, Rendall's brusque answer to the student with the post-millennial inclination that day perhaps reflected something of the difficult role the Scottish gentleman had to fill at Prairie from essentially the outset of his time at the school. When Rendall arrived at Prairie in the early 1950s, winds of change were blowing in North America's conservative Christian community. Neo-evangelicalism was aggressively seeking to establish itself following its break with fundamentalism. Billy Graham was rapidly gaining recognition around the globe for the evangelistic crusades he was holding in large sports stadiums.[56]

The American evangelist's rise to prominence in the 1950s would eventually widen the rift between the American fundamentalist and neo-evangelical communities to the point where the fundamentalists were inclined to determine theological orthodoxy simply on the basis of where an individual or organization stood with relationship to being supportive of or opposed to the ministry of Billy Graham.[57] Accordingly, schools like Prairie were now being subjected to heated queries by pastors and parents of prospective students concerning their institution's stance with respect to Billy Graham.[58]

Academic accreditation of Bible institutes and colleges was another issue that arose comparatively early in Rendall's tenure at PBI.[59] Suggestions

---

that it would be very helpful if the student could learn how to use the tools of the library as spades rather than crutches. He listened carefully to me and said "yes" so I came up with the idea of offering a number of exegesis courses in the curriculum where students were taught to use all those tools. That way they had the inductive approach which led them directly into Scripture and the exegesis course that taught them how to use the tools of the library."

[56] Joel A. Carpenter, "Fundamentalist Institutions and the Rise of Evangelical Protestantism, 1929-1942," in *Church History*, Vol. 49, No. 1 (March 1980), 62-64, offers a succinct overview of developments in the early 1950s in American fundamentalism-evangelicalism.

[57] Dalhouse, 83-84: "One observer noted that shortly after New York, "at the grass roots level the question soon became simply 'are you for or against Graham?'"

[58] As will be documented in Chapter Thirteen of this book, L.E. Maxwell's personal files in the PBI Archives in Ted S. Rendall Library contain numerous letters written in the 1950s and 1960s from pastors, parents and supporters pointedly inquiring where Prairie stood with regard to supporting Billy Graham.

[59] This topic as it related to PBI during the L.E. Maxwell era is addressed further in Chapter Thirteen.

that the PBI administration reconsider the school's stringent social regulations also surfaced during those years.[60] By the time the 1970s arrived, emotionally-charged debates over the North American church's changing standards in music and entertainment standards posed major challenges for the leadership of some Christian colleges.

In hindsight, therefore, it is not difficult to speculate that Ted Rendall, widely perceived as the heir-apparent to L.E. Maxwell at PBI, would have experienced significant pressures in preparing to lead a renowned institution into changing times.[61] It is therefore possible that the question posed to Rendall that day in Bible II regarding post-millennialism merely served to remind him of the numerous issues rife with controversy and potential conflict that awaited L.E. Maxwell's successor.[62]

Notwithstanding the modest changes Rendall implemented at PBI following the period of time under review in this project, it is important to point out that he consistently reflected his adherence to the broader definition of fundamentalism that this book affirms. His extensive teaching, preaching and writing ministries regularly affirmed the authority (or "inerrancy" of Scripture, which became the operative term in the mid-1970s) of Scripture, the primary

---

[60] PBI Archives in Ted S. Rendall Library: L.E. Maxwell personal file—"Social Regulations." A December 3, 1962, four-page letter from Karl Janzen, Dean of Men, written to the PBI Board on behalf of all the deans, contains: "To sum up all these questions, we are wondering if, in the light of recent changes in the administrative set-up of our Institute, recent changes in the academic standards of our Institute, the board feels that the time has come for modification in our social standards as well.

[61] T.S. Rendall, *In God's School*, (Three Hills, AB: Prairie Press, 1971); 9: Dr. Alan Redpath, at one time the pastor of Moody Church, Chicago, writing in the book's *Foreword* stated: "The author is personally known to me, and he has stepped in to a great responsibility following in the steps of the Rev. L.E. Maxwell as Principal of Prairie Bible Institute. All who have any knowledge of what it means to step into the shoes of this spiritual giant and seek to maintain the ministry of past years and to make it relevant to a contemporary scene will recognize something of the immense personal pressures involved."

[62] Ted S. Rendall, personal interview, August 14, 2006: "Paul Maxwell wanted to maintain Prairie's policy of not permitting television on campus. I, however, felt it was hypocritical to have so many staff members going into community homes to watch Hockey Night in Canada. I don't think you can condone that kind of inconsistency. As well, when I became president, I appointed three ad-hoc committees to re-evaluate our policies on sports, music and social regulations." Indeed, while growing up at Prairie, my father and my siblings frequently visited "Uncle" Charlie Crawford in Three Hills on Saturday nights to catch the weekly Hockey Night in Canada television broadcast.

importance of evangelism in general and foreign missions in particular, holiness of life, revival, and the imminent, pre-millennial second coming of Christ.

A. His writings

Since several of T.S. Rendall's books are compilations of articles he published in the *Prairie Overcomer* while serving as the journal's Associate Editor and then Editor, his writings will be considered here in a collective category. Upon joining PBI staff in 1956, Rendall regularly wrote a "Young Overcomer" feature in *Prairie Overcomer*, an initiative that eventually led to the launch of *Young Pilot* in the late 1950s, a monthly magazine designed for children that Rendall edited and was published by PBI.

Rendall's regular articles for young people in the *Overcomer* consistently featured an emphasis on standard fundamentalist themes such as the necessity of salvation, the primary importance of foreign missions, the need for holiness of life, and the authority of Scripture.[63] With respect to L.E. Maxwell's writings in the *Prairie Pastor* and the *Prairie Overcomer*, it should be noted that even after Rendall joined the *Overcomer*'s editorial staff, the section entitled "The World of Today in the Light of the Word" continued to profile such favorite fundamentalist whipping-posts as the theology of the Roman Catholic Church, women's dress, Hollywood and the tobacco industry.[64]

Consider, as an example, just one edition of "The World of Today in the Light of the Word" compiled some five or six years after Rendall became Associate Editor of the *Overcomer*. It yields abundant evidence of the overtones of the kind of fundamentalism that prevailed at Prairie during the Maxwell era:

> In these days when "all roads lead to Rome," may the Protestant Church awaken to the real issues of the hour and keep herself absolutely separate from the conniving of Rome. (Fresh, or Foul?)
>
> No man, therefore, be he the Archbishop of Canterbury or any other dignitary of the Church, can classify the book of Jonah as fiction when

---

[63] *The Prairie Overcomer*, 31, No. 2; (February 1958), 73; 31, No. 3; (March 1958), 113; 31. No. 5; (May 1958), 192; 31, No. 6; (June 1958), 233; 31, No. 8; (August 1958), 313; 31, No. 9; (September 1958), 353; 31, No. 10; (October 1958), 393; 31, No. 11; (November 1958), 433; 31, No. 12; (December 1958), 473.

[64] See footnote 65 in this chapter.

the Son of God has accepted it as fact. We bow our knees to the authority of Jesus. (Fact, or Fable?)

As well try to wash up a mud floor as to clean up the movie business. In a tirade against the attendance at hopeless and "dirty" movies John Crosby (*Saturday Evening Post*, Nov. 10) cries out: "Enough! Enough! For God's sake, let's quit it—not leave these matters to some censor." After attempting to pick and choose to find a good movie, he concludes it to be hopeless: "how do you know in advance?" He finally concludes what we have long known: "Perversion is coming in strong" as putrefied as described in Romans chapter one.

How some Christians can contend that converted actors can continue in the show business is beyond us. If redemption is real it spells deliverance "from this present evil world." (Gal.I:14). It is a grand escape from "the corruption that is in the world through lust" (II Peter I:4). ("Dirty" Movies)

Is it sufficient, then, to say each dedicated Christian will instinctively sense what is right and wrong in deportment and in dress? Or do Christian women need to be told that short, tight, form-fitting dresses are a disgrace to grace and to their profession of godliness?

Worldly, lustful, and loose-living saints come up with the common excuse: "It is all in your mind; it all depends upon how you look upon these things." This reasoning may in some instances have a measure of truth and plausibility. But the common fault of such inferences—that it is only "as a man thinketh"—lies in the fatal presumption that human nature is not too depraved after all. (Worldliness)

These poor slaves of smoking can be shown all the terrible results of lung cancer, but such is the grip of the habit that they cannot free themselves. There are some who give it up, but the majority carry right on—their eyes open. Information is not enough to set a man free. He needs a power above himself, the power of God, to liberate him from the tyranny of sin. (Film Scare)

Within the Christian Church are those who attempt to live in both spheres. "I looked for the Church," says Horatius Bonar, "and I found it in the world; I looked for the world, and found it in the Church. (Home Aquaticus)[65]

---

[65] *The Prairie Overcomer*, 35, No. 12; (December 1962), 445-450.

Rendall's primary strength as a writer was demonstrated in his widely-recognized ability as a capable expositor of Scripture. Accordingly, this was a primary role he eventually undertook with the *Prairie Overcomer* and led to the publication of several books consisting of articles originally prepared for publication there. Among his favorite topics was revival as evidenced in the volume *Fire in the Church* which reflected Rendall's affinity for that particular proto-fundamentalist concern.[66] It was a theme that surfaced frequently in his writings.[67]

Rendall's love for exposition was predicated on his firm commitment to the inerrancy of Scripture, a topic that surfaced for lively debate within North American neo-evangelical circles in the latter half of the 1970s. On this matter, Rendall was unequivocal: both he and Prairie Bible Institute adhered to a high view of Scripture that was similar if not identical to the stance articulated by the fundamentalists in the early part of the twentieth century. Rendall often cautioned, however, that a commitment to the authority of Scripture had to be balanced with a commitment to the application of Scripture.[68]

A strong dedication to evangelism, particularly as it related to the missionary endeavor, was of course essential for any man considered to succeed L.E. Maxwell. Accordingly, Rendall was clear as to where he stood in this regard.[69] He also acknowledged his awareness that the aftermath of the fundamentalist-

---

[66] Ted S. Rendall, *Fire in the Church* (Chicago, Moody Press, 1974). The book was reprinted by Toronto: G.R. Welch Co., 1982.

[67] T.S. Rendall, *Jeremiah: Prophet of Crisis* (Three Hills, AB: Prairie Press, 1979): 175-184.
T.S. Rendall, *Nehemiah: Laws of Leadership* (Three Hills, AB: Prairie Press, 1980): 197f.

[68] Rendall, *Nehemiah*, 9-10: "Currently, in "the battle for the Bible," attention is being focussed (sic) on Paul's first proposition—"all Scripture is given by inspiration of God." But we must not overlook Paul's second proposition, which is of equal value—"all Scripture . . . is profitable." Thus, while on the one hand, we defend the authority of the Bible, on the other hand, we must involve ourselves in the application of the Bible. To defend the inerrancy of the Scriptures without allowing the Holy Spirit to correct our errors, both of theory and practice, would be to miss a major purpose of God in giving us the Bible.

[69] Ibid., 27: "Nehemiah's example might well be followed by those seeking to give leadership in the Church today. In the area of missions, for example, many Christians have a very nebulous idea of the real need of the world; their ideas about the evangelization of other countries are vague and indefinite. It is the duty of Christian leaders to bring the real need of the nations into focus so that Christians may understand the demands that are being placed upon missions today."

modernist debate lingered in some circles and directly addressed such.[70] As well, on occasion Rendall spoke pointedly to the matter of believers being separated from the world and sometimes appeared to raise concerns about the kind of cooperative evangelism practiced by Billy Graham.[71]

B. His preaching and teaching

Ted Rendall's preaching and teaching style was one that paid close attention to the context and details of any portion of Scripture being considered. He regularly made it his duty to be aware of the various interpretations of difficult passages and was always concerned to identify the practical implications of the text.

Not surprisingly, his interpretation and application of Scripture faithfully emphasized PBI's commitment to "training disciplined soldiers for Christ" and the cultivation of a pietistic devotion to Christ in the lives of listeners. As a consequence, his public discourse frequently touched on practical themes that emphasized holiness of life, support of home and foreign missions, greater commitment to God and the affirmation of a high view of Scripture that was demonstrated by faithfully living in accordance with the directives of the Bible.

For example, in a Father's Day message entitled "The Father Who Sat on the Fence" based on II Kings 4, Rendall asked fathers in attendance a series of probing questions including:

---

[70] 81-82: "We think of evangelical denominations which have lost their testimony and lost their heritage through their compromise with error and evil, and now liberal men who deny all the fundamentals of the faith have taken over the inheritance of God's people. We think, too, of evangelical schools that have been taken over by liberal professors, and now those facilities which were brought into being through the stewardship of God's people are being used to promote the cause of liberalism and unbelief.

[71] 250: "The Word of God is crystal clear on the matter of separation from the enemies of God's people

251: ". . . But inviting a poisonous snake into our living room does not make him a friend. This is one of the serious consequences of modern day co-operative evangelism. During the duration of the evangelistic crusade, men who are known to be liberal in their theology are invited to associate with men holding to the fundamental doctrines of God's Word. The people on "the outside" are led to believe that all those cooperating in the campaign share the same views, and that the liberal pastors endorse the preaching of the evangelist; whereas in actual truth there has been no change in the view of the majority of the liberal participants. Tobiah does not have a change of heart because he has a room in the Temple; nor does a liberal preacher have a change of heart because he participated in a fundamental evangelistic campaign."

Do you encourage your wife in her desire to have family devotions or does she always have to remind you to accept that responsibility?

Do you encourage your wife in her desire to have missionaries into your home for a meal?

Do you encourage your wife in her desire to give to God's work?

Do you personally have a burden for the salvation of your children, do you pray for their salvation?

Are you conscious of the spiritual warfare that involves your family and children and do you know how to win in the spiritual conflict?

Do you cultivate your relationship with God on a daily basis?

Do you seek to minister to others?[72]

A sermon entitled "Men of Fire—Messages of Flame" from Zephaniah 3:14-17 showcased Rendall's fondness for the theme of revival. "Restored fellowship is what revival is all about," he declared, "reconciliation, restitution, the renewed enjoyment of God." At the conclusion of the message, Rendall stated "you must walk the road of repentance to experience revival."[73]

Indeed, revival was far more than something merely talked about at PBI. In the winter of 1972 when I was a student at Prairie High School, a series of revival meetings came to PBI under the leadership of two American evangelists known as the Sutera Twins. They had been holding meetings in various churches across Western Canada where people responded with spontaneous confessions of sin and a desire to "get right with God."

With the full support of L.E. Maxwell and T.S. Rendall, classes at PBI were suspended for several days in favor of lengthy meetings wherein the Sutera brothers sang and preached. This was usually followed by some form of call for confession or commitment that resulted in lengthy lines of students coming to the microphone to confess sin and express renewed determination to pursue their walk with God with greater vigilance and fervor. Small groups of students would cluster about campus in spontaneously organized assemblies to pray and repent. These informal groupings and the

---

[72] Ted S. Rendall Library audio tape sermon by Ted S. Rendall entitled: "The Father Who Sat on the Fence" 2 Kings 4, delivered June 15, 1997, to Prairie Tabernacle Congregation; PBI Library: Cassette #AC 248.8421 REND

[73] Ted S. Rendall Library audio tape sermon by Ted S. Rendall entitled: "Men of Fire—Messages of Flame #8: Restored fellowship" Zephaniah 3:14-17, delivered January 28, 1996, to Prairie Tabernacle Congregation; PBI Library: Cassette #269.5 REND V8.

public meetings often involved weeping and other demonstrations of strong emotion on the part of those coming to terms with their sin.

In short, such events were often spoken of at Prairie as "but a taste" or "just a sample" of spiritual awakenings that had swept parts of the United Kingdom and North America (Great Awakenings) in previous centuries. Because of Ted Rendall's Scottish background, he was instrumental in bringing to PBI a number of speakers who were knowledgeable and experienced with regard to spiritual awakenings in that part of the world. Comparisons with the working of God at Keswick conferences in England and the bygone era of camp-fire revivals in the United States contributed to placing the desired impact of such sessions at PBI within the context of those influences that contributed to the rise of American fundamentalism.

Ted S. Rendall was held in high regard by the PBI community throughout his tenure at the school.[74] This reality was due not only to his own carefully-honed expertise as an exegete and communicator, but was also a natural response from the constituency to the fact that he was recruited, groomed and mandated by L.E. Maxwell to be the latter's successor. Even after Maxwell passed away, it continued to be generally accepted that Rendall had always functioned with Maxwell's seal of approval and blessing.

*　*　*

Each of the individuals profiled in the last two chapters made unique contributions to the fundamentalist identity of Prairie Bible Institute as it existed during the L.E. Maxwell era. As has been seen, the school collectively made a somewhat unique contribution to the constitution of American fundamentalism by virtue of the prominent roles given to women in teaching theology at PBI. In this way, PBI thus helped establish the reality that twentieth-century fundamentalism was definitely not a monolithic entity, entirely bereft of diversity.

---

[74] Following his retirement from PBI, Rendall relocated to Memphis, Tennessee, where he is Institute Lecturer & Curator of the T.S. Rendall Collection at The Stephen Olford Center, Union University. I am very grateful to Dr. Rendall for his participation and assistance in research conducted for this book.

CHAPTER TEN

Evaluating Stackhouse's view
of fundamentalism

Having identified something of the kind of fundamentalism that prevailed at PBI during the Maxwell era, this chapter now offers a brief critique of Stackhouse's focus on militancy as _the_ defining characteristic of American fundamentalism. The conclusion reached is that while such an approach to fundamentalism has certain attractions, it is ultimately inadequate in identifying a complex movement wherein several dynamics coalesced.

This chapter will prepare readers for the final four chapters of the book. It is shown there that, in addition to militancy, certain common theological and cultural themes characterized the fundamentalism found in both American fundamentalism in general and in the fundamentalism that typified PBI in particular during the Maxwell era.

In the Introduction to _Canadian Evangelicalism in the Twentieth Century_, Stackhouse offers his understanding of fundamentalism noting that it "derives from the American scene." He observes that "originally it was a positive term" coined by American magazine editor Curtis Lee Jones in 1920 to describe:

> those who maintained the essential 'fundamentals of the faith' against modern attacks from liberal or modernist theology (following the publication between 1910 and 1915 of the booklet series known as _The Fundamentals_.) In this positive sense the term was used in America, and in Canada and Britain as well, at least into the 1950s. The controversies of the 1920s, however, brought out its chief characteristic of militancy, of a crusading spirit against what it saw to be modern threats to the faith. Following the debacle of the Scopes 'monkey trial' over evolution in 1925, fundamentalism became stereotyped as Southern, rural, and anti-intellectual. In fact, fundamentalism was more typically led by Northern, urban, educated men who industriously set about building a network of

institutions that would substitute for the colleges, seminaries, missionary societies, and so on that they had lost to their enemies[1]

It is instructive to note in the citation above that Stackhouse acknowledges fundamentalism began as a positive concept and links the positive element of fundamentalism to the theology set forth in *The Fundamentals* that were published prior to fundamentalism adopting a militant orientation. Presumably, this is the very same theology that forms the theological essence of what he later describes as a "sectish" form of Canadian evangelicalism since he offers nothing that would lead one to conclude otherwise. It was after fundamentalism had established its initial positive theological orientation then that it acquired what Stackhouse identifies as "its chief characteristic of militancy" or "a crusading spirit." It is useful to observe that the militancy of which he speaks introduced a psychological component into fundamentalism's identity.

I.   Allowing a part to represent the whole

A problem emerges when, on the basis of what transpired in the mid-1920s by way of the introduction of "a crusading spirit" to the defense or articulation of fundamentalism's positive theology, Stackhouse permits militancy to essentially become synonymous for American fundamentalism. In other words, a part of fundamentalism's identity is essentially permitted to represent the whole.

Granted, this militancy unquestionably became a highly visible attribute and one that created a lasting legacy for fundamentalism. Nonetheless, it needs to be maintained that militancy was but a part of a larger organism that came to be identified as fundamentalism. Considered from another perspective, Stackhouse's approach enables the psychological component of fundamentalism to dominate the theological and certain cultural components of fundamentalism. He offers no proof, however, that all who adhered to fundamentalist theology necessarily also embraced fundamentalism's acerbic bent. According to this schema, the mere absence

---

[1]   Stackhouse, *Canadian Evangelicalism in the Twentieth Century*, 10-11.

of militancy apparently qualifies fundamentalism to be labeled something else—"sectish" Canadian evangelicalism, in this case.[2]

However, it begs to be asked, did the original positive theology and emerging cultural orientation become any less important characteristics of fundamentalism than they were before the militant psyche bared its fangs. The answer to that question must be "no" if one is to give due respect to the theological and cultural uniqueness of fundamentalism. Accordingly, Marsden appears to have no problem in seeing fundamentalism as a movement that was always something more than merely what its militant component represented.[3]

Perhaps a better way of understanding the dynamic then, as even Stackhouse seems to infer in the citation above, is to acknowledge that American fundamentalism went through a notorious phase of militancy yet outlasted such to sustain as an identifiable religious subculture with

---

[2] Stackhouse, 51: "[Prairie Bible Institute] stood as the central institution and representative of a "sectish" sort of evangelicalism common especially outside urban areas but present in cities across Canada as well."

75: "Prairie Bible Institute, by contrast, represented the 'sectish' form of Canadian evangelicalism. . ."

31: ". . . this bastion of 'sectish' evangelicalism."

[3] Even Marsden does not completely lose sight of fundamentalism's theological moorings or its theological overlap with other expressions of evangelicalism. To at least some extent, the distinctive theological emphases of fundamentalism both preceded and outlasted its militant phase. (Parts of the following citation from Marsden are *underlined for my emphasis* to indicate this.)

Marsden, *Fundamentalism and American Culture* (1980), 4: "[Fundamentalism] was militantly anti-modernist Protestant evangelicalism. *Fundamentalists were evangelical Christians, close to the traditions of the dominant American revivalist establishment of the nineteenth century*, who in the twentieth century militantly opposed both modernism in theology and the cultural changes that modernism endorsed. Militant opposition to modernism was what most clearly set off fundamentalism from a number of *closely related traditions*, such as evangelicalism, revivalism, pietism, the holiness movements, millenarianism, Reformed confessionalism, Baptist traditionalism, and other denominational orthodoxies. Fundamentalism was a "movement" in the sense of a tendency or development in Christian thought that gradually took on its own identity *as a patchwork coalition of representatives of other movements*. Although it developed a distinct life, identity, and eventually a subculture of its own, *it never existed wholly independently of the older movements from which it grew*. Fundamentalism *was a loose, diverse, and changing federation of co-belligerents* united by their fierce opposition to modernist attempts to bring Christianity into line with modern thought." (*emphasis* added)

distinctive theological and cultural emphases drawn from the larger evangelical brotherhood. Such an approach might better justify Stackhouse's contention that, with a few notable exceptions such as T.T. Shields, the psychological or temperamental component of American fundamentalism was generally not as pronounced among Canadian fundamentalists.

The cogent point, as the following chapters will document, is that militancy was not the sum of fundamentalism and presenting it as such creates not a few problems. Fundamentalism originated and, at least to some extent, sustained as a theological framework that in time translated into a veritable Christian sub-culture.[4] To view fundamentalism only in terms of its militancy to the virtual neglect of its theological and cultural infrastructure risks courting a misunderstanding of what was actually a much more broadly nuanced movement than that represented by the attribute of militancy alone.

Drawing on "definitive" works by Marsden as well as Marty and Appleby's massive *The Fundamentalism Project*, Stackhouse nevertheless identifies the comparatively negative attribute of militancy as the primary characteristic of fundamentalism as he proposes to use the term.[5] While there is doubtless some legitimacy in this approach, in the interests of both accuracy and clarity this book seeks a broader definition of fundamentalism. Any comprehensive understanding of fundamentalism should reflect and include the positive elements of the movement's pre and post-militancy days that Stackhouse himself affirms to have existed "at least into the 1950s."

A natural starting point for understanding the positive element of fundamentalism as Stackhouse himself speaks of it is to pick up on the movement's indebtedness to both the contributors to and the contents of *The Fundamentals*, an important work that Stackhouse specifically identifies.

---

[4] Joel A. Carpenter, "Fundamentalist Institutions and the Rise of Evangelical Protestantism, 1929-1942," in *Church History* Vol. 49, No. 1, March 1980; 64: "Fundamentalism was a popular movement, not merely a mentality; it had leaders, institutions and a particular identity. Fundamentalists recognized each other as party members as it were, and distinguished themselves from the other evangelicals listed above."

[5] Stackhouse, 208-209, footnote 25: ". . . On the more generic contemporary usage of 'fundamentalism,' see Marty and Appleby 'The Fundamentalism Project vii-x. The definitive account of the origins of fundamentalism in America is found in George M. Marsden, *Fundamentalism and American Culture*; see also his *Understanding Fundamentalism and Evangelicalism*."

The role of *The Fundamentals* in establishing a definition of fundamentalism that is broader than merely a pre-occupation with its militancy motif is a pursuit even Marsden considers legitimate.[6] Indeed, to refrain from emphasizing this broader orientation of fundamentalism risks perpetuating the misleading notion that fundamentalism originated solely due to developments in the 1920s and that it was primarily a psychological dynamic void of any theological context.

II. Militancy is not the sum of fundamentalism

My argument maintains that an accurate definition of fundamentalism must reflect the movement's indebtedness to its positive origins as spelled out in *The Fundamentals*, the theological affirmations of more congenial people than the likes of such cantankerous figures as T.T. Shields and J. Frank Norris who never came to prominence until the 1920s. Failure to do so, I suggest, risks focusing on the negative polarity of fundamentalism to the detriment of adequate consideration of those positive realities of the movement that even Stackhouse acknowledges did exist.

To omit these positive components of fundamentalism from a basic understanding of the movement renders Stackhouse's argument as quoted above somewhat difficult to sustain. For instance, it is somewhat perplexing to state that the positive sense of fundamentalism lasted "at least into the 1950s" while simultaneously maintaining that the controversies of the 1920s brought out the movement's "chief characteristic of militancy, of a crusading spirit against what it saw to be modern threats to the faith."

If the positive aspects of fundamentalism survived its negative attribute of militancy, in what sense does militancy then qualify as fundamentalism's "chief characteristic?" To restrict the meaning of fundamentalism in this way clouds the reality that, as even Stackhouse acknowledges, fundamentalism

---

[6] Marsden, *Fundamentalism and American Culture* (1980), 119: "*The Fundamentals*, however, had a long-term effect of greater importance than its immediate impact or the lack thereof. It became a symbolic point of reference for identifying a "fundamentalist" movement. When in 1920 the term "fundamentalist" was coined, it called to mind the broad united front of the kind of opposition to modernism that characterized these widely known, if little studied, volumes. In retrospect, the volumes retain some usefulness in tracing the outlines of the emerging movement. They represent the movement at a moderate and transitional stage before it was reshaped and pushed to extremes by the intense heat of controversy."

lasted into the middle decades of the twentieth century. Or, as Carpenter infers, at a minimum one would have to acknowledge that mid-twentieth century fundamentalism was a significantly different fundamentalism than the variety Stackhouse speaks of wherein militancy was the "chief characteristic."

By the 1930s, Carpenter says: "If fundamentalism was viewed as the organized offensive against liberalism in the denominations and evolution in the schools, then it was a spent force."[7] It thus appears that the positive qualities of fundamentalism outlived its militancy motif. This therefore begs the question: in what sense then can the militancy motif be considered fundamentalism's "chief characteristic" as Stackhouse claims? Fundamentalism, it would appear, was a larger entity of which a militant psyche was but a transient, albeit conspicuous, component.

Carpenter points in the direction of adopting such a more-encompassing definition of fundamentalism. He offers the following more broadly nuanced understanding of the movement:

> Simply put, fundamentalism in the 1930s and 1940s was not to be found primarily within the broken ranks of the antimodernist crusades, nor was it limited to the small and alienated groups of separatists or the "super-church" empires of some of its chieftains. Fundamentalism was a popular movement . . . So if we are to see how fundamentalism was doing in the 1930s, we must explore its major network of operations, the grid of institutions bequeathed to it by the revivalistic and pre-millennial pastors, evangelists, missions leaders, and the Bible teachers who had laid the foundations of the movement at the turn of the century.[8]

Was fundamentalism truly more clearly defined by a particular psychological make-up than it was by particular theological or cultural orientations? At times, Stackhouse himself appears prepared to allow for both the negative (militancy) and the positive (pietistic emphasis, missions, Keswick, etc.) components of fundamentalism.[9] On other occasions, however,

---

7 Carpenter, *Revive Us Again*, 13.
8 Ibid., 16.
9 Stackhouse, 71–75: In his depiction of a day in the life of a typical PBI student, Stackhouse notes the conservative dress, segregation of the genders, pietistic emphasis,

he is reluctant to label L.E. Maxwell a fundamentalist because Maxwell lacked a temperamental belligerence equal to that of T.T. Shields.

The fact of the matter remains however that, as has been shown, although the two may have had disparate temperaments, the differences in their theology were comparatively inconsequential. Perhaps then, they are better defined as merely different types of fundamentalists. In any event, one cannot help but question if Stackhouse's "sectish" form of Canadian evangelicalism is truly any different than that type of American fundamentalism which Carpenter demonstrates to have outlasted bombastic controversialists like Shields, Norris, and Riley?

Stackhouse's own words reflect the relatively short-lived period that characterized the kind of militant fundamentalism he champions. He refers on page 11 of *Canadian Evangelicalism in the Twentieth Century* to the rapid rise of the moderate fundamentalists (or neo-evangelicals) and such organizations as the National Association of Evangelicals, Wheaton College and Fuller Theological Seminary. It is necessary to underscore that, as Carpenter points out, these developments were well underway by the mid-1940s precisely because by then these positive voices within fundamentalism were already fed-up with the never-ending strife and division generated by the negative voices that had dominated American fundamentalism throughout the 1920s and 1930s.[10]

Further, Stackhouse's assertion that fundamentalism, "especially after 1960," became characterized by "separatism and, in particular, by the distinctive practice of 'second-degree separation,'" merits some qualification.[11] By the 1960s, to cite Stackhouse himself, those who eventually became known as neo-evangelicals had been denouncing American fundamentalism's "insularity . . . its fear of modern learning, and its abandonment of social

---

missions focus, deeper-life teachings, etc. that were all a part of mid-twentieth century American fundamentalism.
[10] Carpenter, 187-195. See especially 192: "Indeed, one of the important discoveries these [conservative] graduate students made was that their liberal mentors were admirable people . . . For conservative graduate students reared on stories about believers being ridiculed and browbeaten in university classrooms, this was something of a revelation. Some suspected that they were being treated more kindly in the liberals' home institutions than the liberals would be in theirs. Personal graciousness and a willingness to engage in a civil debate, the graduate students were learning, should be the marks of the conservative no less than the liberal."
[11] Stackhouse, 11.

responsibility" for almost twenty years already.[12] Similarly, by the 1960s, the debate over first and second-order separation had been underway for at least several years, having come to a head in the mid-1950s when Billy Graham's New York evangelistic crusade openly adopted an ecumenical orientation.

III. Seeking a more encompassing definition of fundamentalism

These weaknesses in Stackhouse's argument reflect language that is not as precise as it might be. They are cited to underscore the reason this book calls for a more encompassing definition of fundamentalism than Stackhouse's work represents.[13] Conspicuous as it was, the militancy motif that arose within American fundamentalism in the 1920s does not conclusively define a movement that began to congeal in the later years of the nineteenth century and lives on still today in the rhetoric of the American Religious Right.

In recommending a definition of fundamentalism that is suitable for the Canadian setting, Stackhouse writes:

> In arriving at a Canadian definition then, to distinguish 'fundamentalist Protestantism' from the larger category of 'evangelicalism' that includes it as a constituent, we can provisionally appropriate the leading characteristics of American fundamentalism: militant opposition to modernity—especially modern ideas (liberal theology, biblical criticism, and evolution chief among them)—and separation from all who are not wholly pure in their convictions and associations. This study will demonstrate that there was a Canadian fundamentalism *of this sort* in the twentieth century) (exemplified by T.T. Shields and discussed in part I, chapter I), but that it was not in fact central to Canadian evangelicalism.[14]

---

[12] Stackhouse, 11.

[13] Ron Sawatzky, "Book Review: Canadian Evangelicalism in the Twentieth Century: An Introduction to Its Character," *Church History*, Vol. 63, No. 3, 486, picks up on the element of imprecision in Stackhouse's work when he states: "The discussion of the elements which are used to define evangelicals is particularly interesting although the various nuances that are introduced seem less precise than one would expect. The reader may wonder if the definition is designed to fit the institutions under study or if it is a delineation of a discrete religious movement which has clear, distinguishing boundaries from any other." Carpenter, 33-88.

[14] Stackhouse, 11-12.

In adopting such a limited definition of fundamentalism, Stackhouse risks arbitrarily jettisoning the positive sense of fundamentalism that he himself acknowledges was in existence prior to the arrival of the militancy motif and lasted "at least into the 1950s." Such a definition, especially absent a mutually agreed upon definition of "militancy," promotes a subjectivism that could spawn endless debate.

Debate might ensue, for example, regarding degrees of militancy or whether or not said militancy requires only aggressive rhetoric or also requires sufficient physical aggression to necessitate the summoning of law officers.[15] The problem is both underscored and exacerbated when Stackhouse periodically uses the term "fundamentalist" to refer to parties such as PBI that elsewhere in his work he disqualifies as fundamentalists on the basis of the militancy motif alone.[16]

Whereas from the outset of his work Stackhouse spotlights the psychological element that typified American fundamentalism—and it was indeed a prominent one—this book maintains that certain theological and cultural convictions must also be factored in to adequately understand those who became known as American fundamentalists. To truly grasp the spirit of American fundamentalism requires that we inquire as to what it was these people were militant about and why.

In so doing, it becomes apparent that specific theological and cultural beliefs were already at work well before the cantankerous and belligerent psyches of the prominent American fundamentalists came to prominence in the 1920s. Establishing a broader definition of fundamentalism than that which merely focuses on the militancy factor thus helps account for those who considered themselves fundamentalists yet were not prepared to fight about it to the extent demonstrated by others of their brethren.

---

[15] For example, were Carl McIntire and John R. Rice any less militant because their actions over the years did not include brushes with the law such as that incurred by Frank J. Norris who shot and killed a man or by T.T. Shields in the Des Moines University debacle where law officers were summoned? See Marsden, *Fundamentalism and American Culture* (1980), 190.

[16] After going to some length in stating that he classifies PBI as a "sectish" form of Canadian evangelicalism, for example, Stackhouse periodically overtly refers to PBI as "fundamentalists." See p. 86 where he states: "As did other fundamentalists, Prairie's leaders . . ." and acknowledges "Prairie's avowed identity as a militant opponent of modernism."

To summarize, as opposed to Stackhouse's definition of fundamentalism that primarily stresses the militancy motif or the psychological element in the behavior of those who defended and advanced evangelical doctrine, this author calls for an understanding of fundamentalism that is more positive and more theologically and culturally nuanced. It proposes an understanding of fundamentalism that views it as an offspring of turn of the twentieth century proto-fundamentalism which propagated particular theological emphases in the context of exclusive communities of believers that firmly rejected the values and influences of popular culture. Certain leaders of such communities, but definitely not all, were for a time particularly acerbic in defending their theological views.

At a minimum, such a definition should account for several key fundamentalist theological emphases and at least one fundamentalist cultural distinctive.[17] The next three chapters thus take a look at where Prairie Bible Institute during the Maxwell era stood with regard to several major planks in American fundamentalism's theological platform and with regard to fundamentalism's defining stance toward culture. As well, two transient issues that proved, to varying degrees, to be particularly divisive within fundamentalist ranks are discussed owing to their significant contribution to the fundamentalist identity of PBI that this book seeks to establish.

---

[17] D. Bruce Hindmarsh, "The Winnipeg Fundamentalist Network, 1910-1940: The Roots of Transdenominational Evangelicalism in Manitoba and Saskatchewan," *Didaskalia*, Fall 1998, 2, contends that ". . . the Winnipeg fundamentalist network was closely linked with Protestant fundamentalists in the United States and elsewhere, and while there are points of discontinuity, the overwhelming continuity of the Winnipeg fundamentalism must not be obscured. Moreover, a convincing case has been made for the fact that within American fundamentalism itself there was a moderate, centrist tradition which was defined less by militancy, by defensive positions and controversies, than by its focus upon evangelization, world missions, and personal holiness." Hindmarsh refers to Michael S. Hamilton's PhD thesis in this regard which was earlier identified in this book (Introduction: footnote 10). During the period under review in this project, L.E. Maxwell and PBI gave evidence of both the militant (negative) component of American fundamentalism that Stackhouse reserves for T.T. Shields in Canada and the more moderate (positive) aspects of American fundamentalism that both Hindmarsh and Hamilton acknowledge.

CHAPTER ELEVEN

PBI and the theological milieu of fundamentalism

The next four chapters focus on elements of PBI's ethos during the Maxwell era that warrants a closer association of the school with American fundamentalism than is reflected in Stackhouse's views. This chapter reviews several theological distinctives of fundamentalism that require inclusion in a broader understanding of the movement. It also documents how each of these theological emphases had a prominent profile at PBI.

In establishing a broader understanding of fundamentalism than Stackhouse employs, it is important to note well the link between American fundamentalism and a particular theological emphasis that came to the fore in American society around the middle of the nineteenth century. Although the work of Ernest R. Sandeen is not without its critics, *The Roots of Fundamentalism* makes an invaluable contribution to documenting that fundamentalism did not just arrive on the scene in the 1920s from out of nowhere. That component of theology known as eschatology played a prominent role in bringing about the kind of theological and psychological orientation for which fundamentalism would eventually become famous.

The importance of Sandeen's claim that it was "millenarianism which gave life and shape to the Fundamentalist movement" cannot be overlooked in attempting to establish the broader understanding of fundamentalism for which this book contends.[1] Sandeen aptly points out the seminal influence of "Darbyite dispensationalism" as "one of the most significant elements in the history of Fundamentalism."[2] Of particular import, Sandeen claims, was John N. Darby's teaching about the second coming of Christ, "known at that time and since as the secret rapture and one of the most distinctive teachings of dispensationalism."[3] Among other things, Darby, an English gentleman from a Plymouth Brethren background, believed that this "secret

---

[1]   Sandeen, *The Roots of Fundamentalism*, xix.
[2]   Ibid., 60-61.
[3]   62.

rapture" of the church "could occur at any moment." This prompted some to refer to this element of his teaching as "the doctrine of the any-moment coming."[4] Sandeen thus notes: "This expectation of the imminent advent, with no obstacle in the way of Christ's return, proved to be one of the greatest attractions of dispensational theology."[5]

As noted earlier in this volume concerning the definition of fundamentalism, scholars such as Carpenter, Ammerman and Marsden all identify the close relationship between Darby's dispensational theology and emerging fundamentalism. Marsden, for example, calls dispensational pre-millennialism "one of the distinctive emphases that came to characterize fundamentalism."[6]

The "any-moment" return of Christ was a key component of the dispensational theology Darby brought with him from England when he visited both Canada and the United States seven times between 1862 and 1877. Sandeen reports that an annual summer conference for Brethren was begun in Guelph, Ontario, as a result of Darby's visits and that Darby himself crossed the Atlantic in 1870 specifically to attend the Guelph meetings that attracted some four hundred people from Canada and different parts of the United States.[7]

It was during these visits to some of the large cities of eastern North America that Darby encountered proto-fundamentalist leaders such as Dwight L. Moody and A.J. Gordon. Although it is not entirely clear how successful Darby was in initially convincing them of the entirety of his entire dispensationalist agenda, there is little doubt that certain elements of Darby's theology had an enormous impact on them. Such a conclusion is supported, for example, by the strong convictions and fervent actions of the proto-fundamentalists that Sawatzky speaks of in connection with the various late nineteenth-century Bible and prophecy conferences such as that held at Niagara-on-the-Lake, Ontario, Canada from 1883-1897.[8] It is certainly possible that the Guelph conferences inspired by Darby may have

---

[4]   Sandeen, 63.

[5]   Ibid., 64.

[6]   Marsden, *Fundamentalism and American Culture* (1980), 6.

[7]   Sandeen, 71.

[8]   Sawatzky, "Looking for that Blessed Hope," 19-20.

      Sandeen, 134: "Virtually everyone of any significance in the history of the American millenarian movement during this period attended the Niagara conference."

helped launch the Bible and prophecy conferences that became a staple of late nineteenth-century proto-fundamentalism.

The kind of considerable influence that certain aspects of Darby's dispensationalism had on North American proto-fundamentalists is evidenced by a couple of citations from Sandeen. First, regarding Darby's influence on participants in the Niagara Conferences, he writes:

> Although not every Niagara participant can automatically be assumed to have accepted these views, most of the speakers and leaders of the conference do seem to have accepted the Darbyite view of the second coming for a time at least. One of the members of the executive committee, Robert Cameron, a Brantford, Ontario, Baptist pastor, stated that the 1884 conference witnessed a special emphasis upon the doctrine of the any-moment coming: "At the 1884 Conference it came to be the "fashion" of every speaker to "ring the changes" on the possibility of Christ coming any moment—before the morning dawned, before the meeting closed, and even before the speaker had completed his address."[9]

Regarding dispensationalism's eventual influence on the unordained Dwight L. Moody, whom Sandeen claims "was the most influential "clergyman" in America" during the last two decades of the nineteenth century, Sandeen states:

> While still known only locally for his Sunday school work in Chicago, Moody met and fell out with J.N.Darby . . . the writings of C.H. Mackintosh, Darby's popularizer, were apparently even more significant. Moody wrote about them: "Some time since I had my attention called to C.H.M's Notes, and was so much pleased and at the same time profited by the way they opened up Scripture truths, that I secured at once all the writings of the same author, and if they could not be replaced, would rather part with my entire library, excepting my Bible, than with these writings. They have been to me a very key to the Scriptures." Moody was too independent and eclectic to tie himself completely to Plymouth Brethren theology, but there can be no question that it had significant influence upon him. As early as 1877 Moody had become a millenarian

---

[9] Sandeen, 139-140.

and was teaching, in his own rough style, that Christians ought to be ready to welcome Christ's second advent at any moment.[10]

Sandeen's work is rife with references to dispensationalism's influence on other proto-fundamentalists such as A.J. Gordon, A.T. Pierson, James M. Gray and A.C. Dixon as well as Keswick speakers such as F.B. Meyer, Andrew Murray and G. Campbell Morgan.[11] It is useful to point out that the writings of each of these men were consistently popular and influential at Prairie Bible Institute during the period under review.

There is at least some validity in suggesting that the dispensationalists' teaching concerning the "any moment" or imminent return of Jesus Christ was the theological spark that ignited what in time became the fundamentalist fire. The rise of German rationalism in the 1870s with its implications for the evangelical understanding of Biblical authority as well as the publication in 1859 of Darwin's *On the Origin of Species* were interpreted by some as indisputable evidence of the kind of rampant unbelief pre-millenarians believed pointed to the imminence of Christ's return. The prospect of Christ's soon return gave a sense of urgency to several realities that came to characterize proto-fundamentalist culture in the last quarter of the nineteenth century and that of their fundamentalist protégés well into the twentieth century.

There is justification, then, in positing some variety of a cause and effect relationship between an urgent theology and a militant psychology. The militant psychology that emerged among some in the fundamentalism of the 1920s might be directly linked with the urgent theology embraced by the proto-fundamentalists of the late nineteenth century and its attendant implications for evangelical culture.

Accordingly, I propose that certain theological and cultural distinctives that both nurtured the advent of militant fundamentalism and outlasted fundamentalism's militant phase need to be accounted for by way of a broader definition of fundamentalism than that allowed for in Stackhouse's summary. It was precisely because certain people felt so strongly about specific points of theology and their attendant cultural implications that certain militant behaviors were demonstrated and defended. These were

---

[10] Sandeen, 173.
[11] Ibid., 179-181.

the beliefs and the practices of Americans who identified themselves as fundamentalists.

It is probable that any attempt to identify a complete list of the core theological distinctives of American fundamentalism will not win the approval of all authorities on the topic. Accordingly, the following list is not intended as an exhaustive condensation of fundamentalist theology. Rather, what is offered here is simply an enumeration of the primary points of the fundamentalist theological regimen that governed and was reflected in day-to-day life on the campus of Prairie Bible Institute during the period under review.

That being said, readers should bear in mind the statement referred to earlier in this book as contained in an early Prospectus of the Bible school established at Three Hills: "The school stands for every whit of the "Fundamentals," presumably a reference to the early twentieth-century essays financed by the Stewart brothers and edited by A.C. Dixon."[12] PBI initially and overtly linked itself with the document that scholars such as Stackhouse, Marsden and others specifically associate with the rise of American fundamentalism.

It is also accurate to suggest, however, that the school could have very well made the very same affirmation regarding adherence to *The Fundamentals* in 1980, the year L.E. Maxwell formally retired from teaching at PBI. In other words, it is legitimate to state that *The Fundamentals* accurately reflected the basic theological orientation of Prairie Bible Institute throughout the L.E. Maxwell era. Any disagreements with that declaration would have required but minor modification or clarification.

Several specific theological emphases contained in *The Fundamentals* governed life at PBI throughout the Maxwell era thereby placing the school within the broader definition of American fundamentalism for which this book contends. The core theological beliefs linking PBI with American fundamentalism included:[13]

---

[12] See Chapter Three of this book, footnote 29.
[13] Feinberg, *The Fundamentals* (vol.I): see Articles I-20; *The Fundamentals* (vol. 2): see Articles 61-62.

I. Unyielding allegiance to Biblical authority

David O. Beale makes a useful observation regarding the fundamentalism that ruled the day at Prairie Bible Institute during the L.E. Maxwell era when he states:

> Fundamentalism is not a philosophy of Christianity, nor is it essentially an interpretation of the Scriptures. It is not even a mere literal exposition of the Bible. The essence of Fundamentalism goes much deeper than that—it is the *unqualified acceptance of and obedience to the Scriptures.*[14] (*emphasis in original*)

Implicit in Beale's observation is a nuance that is helpful in grasping the difference between neo-evangelicalism and fundamentalism as far as their respective approaches to Scripture is concerned. Whereas neo-evangelicals are usually open to dialogue regarding their claims concerning the Bible's divine origins and authority, such is consistently a matter of unqualified dogmatism for fundamentalists.

That is, for fundamentalists, the absolute authority and accuracy of the Christian Scriptures is non-negotiable.[15] The Bible is a document of divine origin that serves as the cornerstone of everything else one believes regarding spiritual matters. Fundamentalism assumes Biblical authority and has little regard for the need to defend that stance.

For this reason, many Bible institutes such as PBI did not see the need to offer courses in apologetics or basic philosophy. Nor was time spent investigating and refuting prominent aspects of higher criticism such as the Graf-Wellhausen school of thought regarding the Bible's composition.

---

[14] David O. Beale, *In Pursuit of Purity: American Fundamentalism Since 1850* (Greenville, SC: Unusual Publications, 1986), 3.

[15] For some fundamentalists, although this was not the case at PBI, the Scripture that is in view at this point is the original King James Version or The Authorized Version of the Holy Bible. The New American Standard Bible was the recommended version for study during my attendance at PBI, 1974-1977. This reality rendered Prairie more "liberal" in the minds of some of my wife's relatives who were heavily involved at Berean Bible College in Calgary where the KJV reigned supreme. Berean was the mid-twentieth century successor of The Prophetic Bible Institute where eventual Alberta premiers William Aberhart and E.C. Manning once held prominent roles in the 1920s and early 1930s.

It was generally assumed that the best defense of the Bible's supernatural nature was simply to unleash its power just as one would demonstrate the power of a lion by letting the creature out of its cage. The best argument for the Bible's authority, it was believed and advanced, was to consider the changes in the lives of people who had turned from unbelief to an acceptance of its teachings regarding mankind's need for deliverance from sin. The Bible was clear that on the basis of Christ's atoning death and subsequent resurrection, repentant sinners could partake in a personal relationship with God.

Among the numerous gospel songs this writer sang time and time again while a youngster in the elementary school on the campus of Prairie Bible Institute during the 1960s was *The Bible Stands*.[16] Its words are as follows:

The Bible stands like a rock undaunted
'Mid the raging storms of time;
Its pages burn with the truth eternal,
And they glow with a light sublime.

(Refrain)The Bible stands though the hills may tumble,
It will firmly stand when the earth shall crumble;
I will plant my feet on its firm foundation,
For the Bible stands.

The Bible stands like a mountain towering
Far above the works of men;Its truth by none ever was refuted,
And destroy it they never can. (repeat Refrain)

The Bible stands and it will forever,
When the world has passed away;
By inspiration it has been given,
All its precepts I will obey. (repeat Refrain)

---

[16] The curriculum of Prairie's elementary, junior high and senior high schools always included Bible. Regular and special chapel services were also a staple of school life at every level of a PBI education.

The Bible stands every test we give it,
For its Author is divine;
By grace alone I expect to live it,
And to prove and to make it mine. (repeat Refrain)[17]

By fervently singing this song we affirmed our unalterable belief in the authority of the Bible as it was interpreted for us by those who were or had been associated with American and Canadian proto-fundamentalists and, in turn, with American fundamentalism.[18] Among the prominent names connected with proto-fundamentalism and familiar to us even as children at PBI were Dwight L. Moody, A.J. Gordon, A.T. Pierson, C.I. Scofield, R.A. Torrey, to name a few. To cite Carpenter, these were names that were part of:

> a movement which later was transformed into fundamentalism [and] began in the last quarter of the nineteenth century as an interdenominational revivalist *network* . . . The characteristic beliefs and concerns of this movement came to be the hallmarks of fundamentalism[19]

The small home our family occupied on the campus of Prairie Bible Institute during my early childhood required my father to keep part of his ample library in the bedroom I shared with two brothers. As both a 1952 graduate of PBI and a staff member in the Institute's Book Room for several years, he had accumulated scores of volumes by authors bearing names such as James Orr, W.H. Griffith Thomas, James M. Gray, A.T. Pierson, Arno Gabelein, Benjamin B. Warfield, R.A. Torrey, W.J. Erdman,

---

[17] Words and Music by Haldor Lillenas, 1917. Public Domain. http://library. timelesstruths.org/music/The_Bible_Stands/ (accessed January 3, 2013). It should be noted that this portion of the book had already been completed before I came across a reference to the same song in Opp, *Culture of the Soul*, 63: "The militancy of the fundamentalist-modernist controversy also placed a new emphasis on the bible (sic) . . . Typical of this imagery is Haldor Lillenas' "The Bible Stands.""

[18] Both David Beale and George W. Dollar wrote as professors at Bob Jones University and speak of fundamentalism as a movement that began with resistance to German rationalism and its attack on the authority of Scripture and continued up to the post World War II split with neo-evangelicals. In other words, they don't make a distinction between proto-fundamentalists and fundamentalists.

[19] Carpenter, *Revive Us Again*, 6.

Bishop H.C.G. Moule, Charles G. Trumbull, Bishop J.C. Ryle, A.C. Dixon, and G. Campbell Morgan. Each of these men had made at least one contribution to *The Fundamentals*, an unofficial theological statement of American fundamentalists.[20]

Many of the books in my father's library addressed and defended the topic of Biblical authority, inspiration or inerrancy as it was proclaimed at PBI. As another indication of PBI's connection with American fundamentalism's commitment to defending and promoting Biblical authority, it should be noted that by the time I reached junior high school I was regularly perusing my father's subscription to *The Sunday School Times*, the religious newspaper published for over one hundred years that had become the authoritative periodical of record for American fundamentalism.[21] The journal frequently featured articles regarding the imperative nature of a high view of Biblical authority. My father conversed regularly with L.E. Maxwell concerning which books and publications the latter used and recommended. Maxwell invariably commended publications that had come to his attention via *The Sunday School Times*.

PBI, in other words, was committed to a strong view regarding Biblical authority partly because that was the perspective advanced by the theological authorities that J. Fergus Kirk and L.E. Maxwell were exposed to in their formative years at home (Kirk) and at Bible school (Maxwell). The validity of the views of Moody, Gordon, Simpson and others on Biblical authority were dogmatically assumed as were those of Warfield and Machen.

To sing a song like *The Bible Stands* was to affirm our "unqualified acceptance" (Beale) in a literal interpretation of the historical sections of the Bible including:

---

[20] The reason I recall these names is that I now possess most of my father's library.

[21] As mentioned earlier, L.E. Maxwell was a contributor to *The Sunday School Times* and a close friend with Philip Howard, Jr., who once served as the now defunct journal's editor. Howard recommended his daughter attend PBI for one year prior to missionary service after she had graduated from Wheaton College. Prairie advertised regularly in *The Sunday School Times* (e.g. January 29, 1944, 78 and February 5, 1944, 93) as did Canada's Keswick (June 1, 1940, 452). Carpenter, 26, states: "Getting on the *Times*' endorsement list was a great boon to these organizations; conversely, being removed from it, with editorial explanation appended, was similar to being excommunicated from the movement." The January 21, 1933, issue of the *Sunday School Times* indicated that along with PBI, the other Canadian schools on the *Times*' endorsement list at the time were Moose Jaw Bible Institute, Toronto Bible College, Vancouver Bible Training School and Winnipeg Bible Institute.

the creation of the earth in seven twenty-four hour periods; the complete rejection of Darwin's notion of evolution including the suggestion that man evolved from primates; the preservation of Noah and his family aboard the Ark as God's provision to escape judgment via a destructive flood that destroyed all other living beings; the rolling back of the waters of the Red Sea to enable the children of Israel to elude the pursuing Pharoah; Daniel and his friends' survival despite being thrown into a fiery furnace, Jonah's being swallowed whole by a great fish prior to recanting of his stubbornness and being regurgitated thereby granting him a second chance to preach at Nineveh; etc. It was also an articulation of our belief in cardinal Christian doctrines such as: mankind's total depravity, the virgin birth and deity of Jesus Christ: the vicarious atonement for sin offered by Jesus on Calvary's cross: the literal, bodily resurrection and return to life of Jesus following his crucifixion; the personality and deity of the Holy Spirit; salvation by faith alone in Christ alone by virtue of the grace of God alone; and the eternal dwelling of all mankind who have ever lived in either a literal heaven or a literal hell.

The following comments by Carpenter regarding fundamentalism's affinity for an inerrant Scripture aptly summarize the Prairie Bible Institute of the L.E. Maxwell era with respect to the matter of Biblical authority.[22] They also help us grasp that this perspective was one of those positive points of fundamentalist theology articulated in *The Fundamentals* which pre-dated the militant component of fundamentalism.

> Fundamentalists' commitment to being New Testament Christians was based on their belief that the Bible communicated God's sure, clear, and unchanging will. They were self-styled "Bible-believing Christians," by which they meant that they upheld the Bible as the verbally inspired, inerrant word of God, as trustworthy in its references to matters of nature and history as in its teaching of religious and moral precepts. This was one of several keystone beliefs upon which fundamentalism rested as both an ideology and a way of life ... New Testament Christianity was still available to modern people, fundamentalists insisted, because the Bible spoke timeless truth.[23]

---

[22] L.E. Maxwell, "Jonah and His Gourd," in *The Prairie Overcomer*, 20, No. 9, (September 1947); 237: "As Bible-loving fundamentalists we claim that "there is none other name under heaven given among men, whereby we (yea, and all others) must be saved."
[23] Carpenter, 69-70.

II. The imminent return of Christ

It has already been noted that L.E. Maxwell did not endorse the entire theological framework of pre-millennial dispensationalism.[24] Nonetheless, Prairie Bible Institute did unreservedly embrace dispensational eschatology and its emphasis on the pre-millennial return of Christ. This included the acceptance of Darby's teaching regarding Christ's "any-moment" return.

From the earliest days as students in PBI's Sunday School and daily Kindergarten, we were taught that Jesus might return at any moment hence the importance of being found ready should such occur. By being found ready our teachers emphasized that this meant not being found engaged in sins such as lying to our parents, smoking cigarettes or being unkind to our friends at the precise moment of Christ's return which would occur "in the twinkling of an eye." In later years when we were older, the definition of "being found ready" was expanded to mean not being caught in such sins as fornication or in attendance at the movie theatre at the time Christ "descended from the heavens with a shout."

While a Prairie High School student in grade 11 in the spring of 1973, I participated as an actor in a drama featuring the story of a young man who became caught up in the attractions of this world including a fascination with motorcycles, party life and the opposite gender. Sadly, he was left behind when Jesus returned and the final act of the drama portrayed him sitting with his head in his hands as a mournful lament underscored the importance of being found ready for Jesus to return at any moment.

Part of the point of identifying memories such as these is to underscore a possible difference between fundamentalists and neo-evangelicals with respect to their view of Christ's return. In keeping with fundamentalism's focus on separation from the world and a corresponding emphasis on holiness of life, as opposed to the neo-evangelical perception of Christ's return as "the blessed hope," there is a sense in which fundamentalists view Christ's return more in keeping with what might be termed "the blessed threat."

---

[24] Feinberg, *The Fundamentals* (vol. 2): see Articles 63-64. As opposed to dispensationalism's view of the Old Testament Law, for example, Maxwell adopted the Reformed understanding of the Law as relevant for modern Christian's in performing the role of "schoolmaster" to point mankind to Christ.

For instance, the drama just referred to was intentionally designed to warn people regarding the risks of not being ready to meet Christ at a moment's notice or of being caught engaged in sin at his return. Exposure to popular fundamentalist films such as *Thief in the Night* that were occasionally shown at PBI also helped accomplish this objective. The film warned of the possibility of being "left behind" when Jesus returned for the saints and of being subjected to the terror of being branded with the number 666 or forced to serve anti-Christ.

Suffice it to note that by the time one had completed Kindergarten through Bible school at PBI, he was well schooled in how to use the possibility of Christ's any-moment return as a fear-inspiring motivation factor. The school's preaching and teaching frequently warned listeners to be sure their relationship with God was in an appropriate condition lest they unexpectedly meet him face to face.

As demonstrated by the prophecy conferences of the late nineteenth century, a firm belief in the any-moment nature of Christ's return as advanced by Darby and pre-millennial dispensationalism served as a powerful motivating factor in reminding believers concerning the urgency of both personal holiness and world evangelization. Public services and classes at PBI during the Maxwell era consistently emphasized both of these themes. Believers needed to be living in a state of holiness in preparation for Christ's imminent return. Unbelievers needed to be evangelized as quickly as possible in light of the prospect of Christ's imminent return and their impending judgment.

III. Holiness and revival

Another quotation from Carpenter appropriately introduces the affinity American fundamentalists had for individual holiness and ongoing personal revival:[25]

> Fundamentalism taught that living a separated life implied two-distinct actions: pulling away from the world and its values, and drawing closer to Jesus Christ to become his disciple. It is common to think about fundamentalism in reference to the first part of this formula—as a

---

[25] Feinberg, *The Fundamentals* (vol. 2): Articles 40, 48, 51, 52, 59.

separatistic, militantly reactionary, and radically Biblicist persuasion. But fundamentalism has had a softer, more experiential side as well, and one cannot have a fully dimensional understanding of the "separated life" without considering it. Fundamentalist piety was dominated by two spiritual experiences: conversion, or the New Birth, as it was often called; and an event subsequent to conversion commonly called entering into the "higher Christian life." These two experiences did much to shape the fundamentalist movement's structure, ethos, and sense of mission.[26]

L.E. Maxwell's writing on "the crucified life" is the primary public indicator of Prairie Bible Institute's close association during his tenure with the teaching that came to be known as "the higher Christian life" and popularized by the Keswick movement.[27] Although "the higher Christian life" was also known by various labels like "the deeper life," "the victorious life" or other terms such as Maxwell's "the crucified life," what such designations held in common was the belief that the secret to an effective and rewarding Christian life was an on-going, post-conversion experience in which the believer consciously and daily yielded their life to God on a moment-by-moment basis.[28]

---

[26] Carpenter, 76.

[27] See in particular *Born Crucified*. Maxwell frequently affirmed that missionary leaders had advised him that the reason PBI students were in such demand in their organizations was because they had been schooled in "the crucified life." One of the "Five Smooth Stones" that Maxwell often spoke of with regard to PBI's essential distinctives was "The Keswick testimony concerning the deeper Christian life." *Principles and Practices of Prairie Bible Institute* (located in Box 80 of the PBI Library Archives) states (I-7,8): "The Editor of the Sunday School Times, after stating that leaders of various missions "speak well of their missionaries who are graduates of Prairie," asked the question: "What is the secret of its spiritual vitality and answered it as an editorial comment upon Born Crucified: Undoubtedly one reason why the lives of so many students are transformed is because of the emphasis upon the necessity for every believer to be identified with Christ in His death and resurrection." (underline in original)

[28] Elmer Towns, *Understanding the Deeper Life: A Guide to Christian Experience* (E-book available at http://www.elmertowns.com/books/online/Understanding_the_Deeper_Life%5BET%5D.pdf (accessed September 19, 2009) is a very affirming treatment of "the deeper life." He refers to Maxwell's teaching on the "crucified life" on pp. 55 (footnote 3), 57.

Douglas W. Frank, *Less Than Conquerors: How Evangelicals Entered the Twentieth Century* (Grand Rapids, MI: Wm. B. Eerdmans Publishing Co., 1986), 103-166, offers a critical assessment of Keswick and "the higher Christian life" teaching.

Steven Barabas writes that it was the publication of W.E. Boardman's *The Higher Christian Life* in 1859 that first popularized "higher life" teachings in a substantial way in both America and England. He also relates that it was the efforts of Mr. and Mrs. Robert Pearsall Smith of Philadelphia "in whom the Keswick movement had its genesis."

> Mrs. Pearsall Smith says that she knew herself to be a child of God, but was unable to act like one, and this made her wonder whether she had not missed something which would have given her victory . . . In her discouragement she began to be afraid that she would lose every bit of religion she possessed. She and her husband, she says, had "learned thoroughly the blessed truth of justification by faith, and rejoiced in it with great joy. But here we had stopped. The equally blessed twin truth of sanctification by faith had not yet been revealed to us.[29]

This new revelation came to Ms. Pearsall Smith about 1867 through a young Baptist theological student who lived in their home as a tutor and a Methodist dress-maker who resided in their village. Barabas states:

> From the tutor she learned that the way of victory was by faith; and from the dressmaker, that there was an experience called the "second blessing" which brought one into a place of victory. She says that she now learned a secret of the Christian life which she had never learned before—the secret of committing her daily life as well as her future destiny to Christ; and she found that when she did that, He gave her deliverance from the power of sin, as well as from its guilt.[30]

Smith's husband initially thought she was delving into heresy but he eventually joined her in disseminating these views via speaking and writing.[31] Ordered to England by a doctor for health reasons in 1872, the Smiths discovered their teachings had preceded them there. The following

---

[29] Steven Barabas, *So Great Salvation: The History and Message of the Keswick Convention* (Eugene, OR: Wipf & Stock Publishers, 2005), 16-17.

[30] Ibid., 18.

[31] Mary Agnes Rittenhouse Maddox, "Jesus Saves Me Now: Sanctification in the Writings of Hannah Whitall Smith," (PhD dissertation, The Southern Seminary, 2003) provides a fascinating and comprehensive overview of Smith's life.

year, Mr. Smith and W.E. Boardman were asked to speak on the topic of the higher Christian life to evangelical ministers and others in London. Twenty-four hundred preachers heard the message.

Regular conventions related to "the higher Christian life" began to be held in England. Eventually, conference grounds at Keswick in the country's northwest became the regular host location for these sessions. Dwight L. Moody encountered the "higher life" emphasis while on a preaching mission to England in 1875 and gave it his endorsement and prayer support.[32]

As for how the Keswick influence eventually reached Prairie Bible Institute, readers are reminded that one of the books that had a prominent profile in the boyhood home of J. Fergus Kirk was Hannah Whitall Smith's (Mrs. Robert Pearsall Smith) *The Christian's Secret of a Happy Life*.[33] With respect to how the Keswick movement influenced L.E. Maxwell and PBI, Carpenter is again helpful here:

By the time of the fundamentalist-modernist controversies, Keswick holiness teaching was thoroughly integrated into the fundamentalist network of Bible schools, summer conferences, and faith missions. Although these beliefs had been accepted and widely disseminated by D.L. Moody's associates in the late nineteenth century, the movement's foremost twentieth-century promoter was Charles G. Turnbull. He was converted to the doctrine in 1910, and in 1913 helped to found the "America's Keswick" conference center in southern New Jersey. Trumbull also . . . promoted the larger movement and its views in the *Sunday School Times*. Other leading speakers on the Higher Life circuit were Trumbull's protégé, Robert C. McQuilken, who was the president of the Columbia Bible College, and Rowland V. Bingham, the director of the Sudan Interior Mission, editor of the *Evangelical Christian*, and founder of "Canadian Keswick" in northern Ontario. By the 1930s Keswick holiness teaching had become the most prominent model of the "separated life's" spiritual dimension, and it pervaded the popular biographies of the

---

[32] Barabas, 23-24.
[33] Dollar, *A History of Fundamentalism in America*, 21: "Later, Keswick made more of an impact on American evangelicals and influenced some schools to follow its basic concerns and answers, notably Columbia Bible College in Columbia, South Carolina and Prairie Bible Institute in Three Hills, Alberta, to which many American students have gone for training."

time, such as *Borden of Yale* (1926), *Hudson Taylor's Spiritual Secret* (1932), *The Triumph of John and Betty Stam* (1935) by the prolific Mary Guinness ("Mrs. Hudson") Taylor of the China Inland Mission, and the several memoirs of Amy Carmichael, the British missionary to India's temple children. Keswick's pervasiveness in fundamentalist circles is by now fairly well known, but its impact has been largely taken for granted. It is important to stress how important this "surrendered life" ideal was to the fundamentalist ethos.[34] (emphasis added)

L.E. Maxwell, of course, had a life-long appreciation for Dwight L. Moody, Moody Bible Institute and Moody Press by virtue of early influences via a pastor and the evangelist Walter L. Wilson. I earlier identified Maxwell's affinity for *The Sunday School Times* and his close friendship with Robert C. McQuilken of Columbia Bible College who wrote the Foreword to Maxwell's book *Crowded to Christ*. Maxwell's writings and sermons are filled with anecdotes and quotations from the works of J. Hudson Taylor and his wife, Mrs. Howard Taylor. Amy Carmichael's writings also had a major impact on Maxwell's thinking as is evident in his written work.

From a personal perspective, it may be useful to point out that all of the books referred to by Carpenter above were included in the library in the home of my youth. In particular, my mother read and re-read *Borden of Yale* and *The Triumph of John and Betty Stam* and, on the personal recommendation of L.E. Maxwell, she was greatly attracted to the writings of Mr. and Mrs. Howard Taylor and Amy Carmichael. She frequently read portions of these works to us at the dinner table or before we went to bed at night. Their presence in our home was testimony to their availability and popularity at the Prairie Book Room, Prairie Bible Institute's campus bookstore. Similarly, their popularity and presence in the Prairie Book Room was indicative of the fact that the message of Keswick was a vital part of Prairie Bible Institute's culture during the L.E. Maxwell era.[35]

---

[34] Carpenter, 81-82.

[35] Cheul Hee Lee, "Sanctification by Faith: Walter Marshall's Doctrine of Sanctification in Comparison With the Keswick View of Sanctification," (PhD dissertation, Westminster Theological Seminary, 2005). See particularly Chapter V for Lee's concise summation of the Keswick views of God's Standard of Holiness, the Nature of Human Inability for Holiness, God's Provision in Christ for Holiness, and the Manner of Practicing Holiness.

Numerous conferences were held at or sponsored by Prairie throughout the early decades of the school.[36] During my years of living on campus, two major conferences occurred annually. The Spring Missionary Conference was timed to serve as the conclusion of the school year in April and culminated with Bible School graduation. Another conference was held in October of the school year and for a time was regularly called the Fall Keswick Conference.[37] These days following fall harvest were intentionally designed for teaching on "the deeper life" and revival.[38]

It was not uncommon, however, for both of these conferences to feature speakers from the Keswick circuit or from organizations similarly sympathetic to the Keswick message. Among the numerous Keswick-oriented speakers that visited PBI during the L.E. Maxwell era were Rowan C. Pearce (Fall 1947), Harold Wildish (Spring 1958 and frequently thereafter), Philip Newell (Fall 1958), S. Franklin Logsdon, (Spring 1962), Stanley Collins (Fall 1962), Roy Hession and Alan Redpath (several times each).[39]

---

[36] For example, the April-May 1947 issue of *The Prairie Overcomer* advertises the Overcomer Bible Conference to be held June 1-8 that year at Burrard Inlet Bible Camp in suburban Vancouver with L.E. Maxwell as one of the main speakers. The same issue advertises a Summer Bible Conference and High School Graduation at PBI for June 15-18, 1947.

[37] An announcement in *The Prairie Overcomer* 30, No. 5, (May 1958); 200, read: The Northwest Keswick Conference which has been held in previous years in the month of August will not be held at this time this year. Instead it will be held in October. Further announcements will be made as to dates, speakers, etc. There will be no Prairie Children's Camp."

[38] Larry J. McKinney, "The Growth of the Bible College Movement in Canada," *Didaskalia*, 10, No. 1; (Fall 1998), 32: "The Bible college movement in Canada grew out of a strong revivalist tradition which had a significant impact on religious life in the late nineteenth and early twentieth centuries, particularly in the western provinces."

[39] PBI Archives in Ted S. Rendall Library: L.E. Maxwell personal files—"Keswick." The file contains a letter dated November 19, 1954, to Maxwell from Redpath who was then the pastor of Moody Church, Chicago, and also the Chairman of Mid-America Keswick. The letter invites Maxwell to speak at Mid-America Keswick to be held October 15-22, 1955. In responding positively to the invitation, Maxwell wrote: "You will be interested to know that for the past month or two we have been considering the possibility of instituting a Keswick conference for northwest North America. We are two thousand miles from Chicago and are quite conveniently situated both as to facilities and geography to care for a large convention crowd."

Similarly, PBI publications regularly included articles from the pens of men and women who had been active in Keswick circles.[40]

As noted earlier, Ted S. Rendall had a personal interest in the topic of revival. His book *Fire in the Church* explored the subject which was also regularly addressed in the pages of the *Prairie Overcomer* during Rendall's involvement with that publication. Speakers from the United Kingdom such as Duncan Campbell and Mary Morrison visited PBI during this writer's residency to testify concerning the Welsh revivals. Periods of what was often called "divine visitation" were both sought and welcomed at PBI. Classes would then be suspended in favor of prolonged sessions of prayer, confession and "waiting on God."

IV. The primacy of missions

The Prairie Bible Institute of the L.E. Maxwell era was unashamedly first and foremost a missionary training center.[41] It is decidedly not an overstatement to suggest that Maxwell's primary passion in life was training men and women to carry the Christian gospel to people living in spiritual darkness in lands afar. As Maxwell once stated:

> "Don't go to P.B.I. or they will make you a missionary"—is the warning given to many young people before applying to us for admission. So we are accused of being *too missionary*? Would GOD we could plead 'guilty'

---

[40] L.E. Maxwell, "The Holy Spirit in Missions," in *The Prairie Overcomer*, 20, No. 2; (February 1947), 41-47 is part of an address delivered by L.E. Maxwell at the Missionary Conference of the Student Foreign Missions Fellowship (held in Toronto, December 27-31, 1946). He draws at length on the experience and testimony of Canadian missionary to China, Jonathan Goforth, who was strongly influenced by Keswick teaching. The same issue (49-50) quotes from "an Excerpt from a Recent Letter by Miss Amy Carmichael of Dahnavur Fellowship, India, to one of our Senior Students." Carmichael was similarly strongly influenced by Keswick.

[41] Feinberg, *The Fundamentals* (vol. 2): Articles 30-47, 49-50, 55.
See James Enns, "Every Christian a Missionary." Also L.E. Maxwell, "Every Christian a Missionary" in *The Prairie Pastor*, 2, No. 2; (January 1929), 7: "We maintain that if the West is to be evangelized as it should be, the standard of discipleship will have to be raised. Our motto must be—"Every Christian a Missionary." This is but the normal condition of spiritual life and growth. Anything less means certain decay and death.

to such a blessed accusation. But we must confess that we are utterly unworthy to bear such a holy reproach.[42]

So too the following quotation from Maxwell indicates that one topic he was unashamed to become belligerent over was the matter of missions being the primary business of contemporary Christians:

Christianity is missionary. And the spiritual depth of any institution may be measured by the percentage of its graduates who obey Christ's last command. Any church or school will produce missionaries as soon as the Cross has dealt a death blow to fleshly self-centeredness and where the Spirit of God holds sovereign sway. But some Christian leader objects: "Our aim is not to make missionaries. We have other objectives." And you are a Christian? Shame on you! But my contention is still deeper and more serious. If the Cross were allowed to make its own legitimate inroads into your aims and objectives, you would find yourself automatically corrected and aflame with obedience.[43]

From its inception, PBI intentionally aligned itself with independent faith missions in keeping with its identity as an inter-denominational institution. Although some of the school's students went to a foreign mission field under the auspices of a denominational mission, the majority of Prairie's students opted for affiliation with faith mission agencies such as China Inland Mission (now known as Overseas Missionary Fellowship), Sudan Interior Mission (now SIM International), The Evangelical Alliance Mission, Japan Evangelical Mission, The West Indies Mission and Regions Beyond Missionary Union (the latter two eventually merged as WorldTeam).[44] Faith

---

[42] L.E. Maxwell, "Too Missionary?" in *The Prairie Pastor*, II, Nos. 1-2; (January-February 1938), 9.

[43] L.E. Maxwell, "Conflict and the Campus" in *The Prairie Overcomer*, 21, No. 2; (February 1948), 44-45.

[44] Alvyn Austin, *Saving China: Canadian missionaries in the Middle Kingdom* (Toronto: Univ. of Toronto Press, 1986), 1-17. The chapter "Journeying Mercies" contains important information that ties the China Inland Mission (CIM) with the late nineteenth century proto-fundamentalist movement in the U.S. and Canada. An example of the kindred spirit that united J. Hudson Taylor, the founder of CIM, and L.E. Maxwell is evident in Taylor's words to a Niagara-on-the-Lake conference (6): "The gospel must be preached to these people in a very short time," he pleaded, "for they are passing

missions were given a high profile at PBI from the earliest days when records indicate Robert H. Glover, Director of the China Inland Mission, was a frequent conference speaker at the school.[45]

Carpenter calls attention to the strategic link in fundamentalism between the Keswick emphasis on the deeper life of holiness and self-surrender with a carefully-crafted focus on missionary service when he notes:

> "the life of faith" taught at Keswick was at the very heart of the fundamentalists' missionary impulse . . . the very act of fully surrendering one's will and all claims to one's life seemed to fundamentalists to point

---

away. Every day, every day, oh how they sweep over . . . There is a great Niagara of souls passing into the dark in China. Every day, every week, every month, they are passing away. A million a month in China are dying without God!"

Irving Alfred Whitt, "Developing a Pentecostal Missiology in the Canadian Context (1867-1944): The Pentecostal Assemblies of Canada;" (D.Miss. dissertation, Fuller Theological Seminary, 1994), 81-86, offers a concise overview of how proto-fundamentalists such as A.T. Pierson, A.J. Gordon, A.B. Simpson and R.A. Torrey were very influential in the establishment of modern faith missions.

Dana Lee Robert, "Arthur Tappan Pierson and Forward Movements of Late-Nineteenth Century Evangelicalism;" (PhD dissertation, Yale University, 1984). Robert perceptively argues that Pierson and A.J. Gordon should be considered fathers of the modern faith-missions movement.

Brian Alexander McKenzie, "Fundamentalism, Christian unity and pre-millennialism in the thought of Roland V. Bingham, 1872-1942," (PhD dissertation, University of St. Michael's College, 1986). McKenzie's work represents an insightful look at the life and theology of Canadian-born Sudan Interior Mission founder, Roland V. Bingham.

Carpenter, 29: "The China Inland Mission (CIM), a non-denominational agency of British origin that became a favorite of North American fundamentalists, experience remarkable growth during the 1930s. In 1929, just after the anti-foreign and anti-Christian campaigns subsided in China, D.E. Hoste, CIM's director, issued a call for two hundred new recruits in two years. He got them, and ninety-two were North Americans who came largely from fundamentalist Bible institutes. But that was just the beginning. Even though China was suffering from internal strife and from Japanese aggression, CIM sent out 629 new missionaries between 1930 and 1936, raising its total force to almost 1,400." It is fair to say that a sizeable percentage of the North Americans would have come from PBI (see Chapter I of this book, footnote 41).

[45] Carpenter, "Fundamentalist Institutions and the Rise of Evangelical Protestantism, 1929-1942," 72: "Fundamentalists supported independent, "faith" missions which were not denominationally connected and did not solicit funds directly."

to the missions field . . . Responding to the call of missions . . . seemed to many to be the sign and seal of their full surrender.[46]

At PBI, regular courses on evangelism and missions in tandem with daily chapel sessions that frequently featured visiting missionary speakers served to stimulate students to consider the urgent need for willing workers to carry the gospel around the world. Students were also urged to regularly participate in a prayer group for a particular region of the world that interested them. We were also encouraged to publicly testify concerning any developing sense of call we were experiencing, be it to a particular country or to a particular people group. Weekly Friday night missionary meetings, frequent opportunities to personally interact with visiting missionaries, periodic "biography nights" along with the annual Spring Missionary Conferences were other means in the regular PBI routine whereby one might expect to discern the voice of God calling him or her to a far-off destination.

As indicated in the preliminary pages of this book, throughout the years that I was growing up at PBI, a large motto was prominently displayed at the front of the Prairie Tabernacle, a cavernous auditorium which served as the primary meeting facility for the entire PBI community. Its words reflected the intensity of the passion for foreign missions that prevailed at the school throughout the Maxwell era:

> *Is there a soul who died, who died because of me*
> *Forever shut away, from heaven and from Thee?*
> *Because I tightly clutched my little earthly store,*
> *Nor sent Thy messenger to some distant shore?*

Included in the scores of popular missionary songs that frequently reverberated among the rafters of the Prairie Tabernacle on PBI's campus while I was a student there was one that included these lines:

> *Untold millions are still untold, untold millions are outside the fold*
> *Who will tell them of Jesus' love, and of heavenly mansions awaiting above*
> *Jesus died, on Calvary, to cleanse each one from sin,*

---

[46] Carpenter, *Revive Us Again*, 82.

Now He calls to you and me, to go and bring them in
for many . . . (repeat)[47]

In an environment that was frequently charged with emotion, public meetings at PBI often concluded with a call for a visible indication of one's personal willingness to go "anywhere at any time at any cost" in response to the call of God to serve in a particular region of the world.[48] Given these realities, Carpenter's summation is very precise with regard to the PBI experience during the Maxwell era:

> The sincerity of one's commitment to Christ often was reduced, then, to acquiescence to at least the possibility of accepting a missionary call. Did you trust fully in God? Were you fully surrendered to his will? Was the life which you were now living in fact being lived through the indwelling Christ? If so, then you would be willing to go anywhere, do anything.[49]

Fully supportive of such probing concepts as these, L.E. Maxwell made no apology for daily challenging the students of Prairie Bible Institute to consider service on the foreign mission field as the highest calling possible.[50] The following comments on Luke 24:46-47 are an example of how unashamedly he consistently stated his case in this regard:

---

[47] Words & Music attributed to Franklin F. Ellis; http://gospelmusic.org.uk/s-u/untold_millions.htm (accessed June 16, 2009).

[48] Carpenter, *Revive Us* Again, 77: "Since conversion happened only once, fundamentalists developed ways for born-again Christians to "come forward" more often. By broadening their altar call into an invitation for believers to receive further assurance of their salvation, to dedicate or rededicate their lives to God, to surrender themselves to God's service, or to testify to a "definite call" to a particular field of service, fundamentalists found a way to meet their thirst for holy moments. "Going forward" became a fundamentalist sacrament."

[49] Carpenter, 82.

[50] It may be helpful to point out with regard to oral history that, on this point, my memory concurs with the judgment of Wendell Krossa's when he writes of his PBI experience: "On the ladder of spiritual status, becoming a missionary was the highest rung of attainment or service. It was the real 'work of God', more than any other kind of work." www.wendellkrossa.com Spiritual Autobiography, (accessed September 19, 2009).

Thousands of pages have been penned by our theologians to fortify and further the great fundamentals of Christ's redemptive work. Other thousands have been written to promote particular Christian doctrines, to prove the plenary inspiration of the Scripture, to preserve precious Church ordinances—things which are good in themselves, all very good as far as they go.

But we must read on. The Lord of the harvest did not stop with the "thus-is-is-written" of His "dying and rising." He went on to point out the ultimate purpose of His glorious redemption: "And that repentance and remission of sins should be preached in His Name among all nations" (v. 47).

Even as Christ was involved in the terrible necessity—"thus it is written, and thus it behoved (sic) Christ "to suffer and to rise again (v. 46), not less is coupled the inseparable and terrible necessity charged upon us: "And that repentance and remission of sins should be preached in His Name among all nations" (v. 47). These twin necessities God has joined together. Let not man put them asunder."

However, as we search theological works, we can find volumes on verse 46 regarding the atoning work of Christ, but seldom can we discover so much as a paragraph on verse 47, which declares the ultimate purpose of Christ's redemptive work, viz. that the glad tidings should be "preached in His Name among all nations." Manifestly the Great Commission (of verse 47) is the one great omission of most theologians. Yet here is the one great universal command to the Church to preach the Gospel to every creature; and he who is wise above that command is wise at his own risk and peril. The present missionary blight which has befallen us is the direct result of our downright disobedience to the ultimate purpose of our grand redemption.[51]

An unwavering belief in the authority of Scripture, the imminent return of Christ, the urgency of individual holiness in the pursuit of "the deeper life" and ongoing revival, and the primacy of missions represent four key components of fundamentalist theology articulated in the movement's original theological treatise, *The Fundamentals*.

---

[51] L.E. Maxwell, *World Missions: Total War*, 8.

These themes continue to play an important role in certain fundamentalist circles today. As demonstrated in the PBI context, these emphases continued long past the movement's militant era in the 1920s-1930s although fundamentalist spokesmen such as L.E. Maxwell continued to militantly articulate their importance. Such a reality lends support to this book's call for a broader understanding of American fundamentalism than that which is evident in Stackhouse's volume.

CHAPTER TWELVE

PBI and the cultural milieu
of fundamentalism

The theological themes just reviewed are important in attempting to capture something of the positive component of American fundamentalism that was an integral part of the movement. Yet Nancy T. Ammerman properly reminds us that such dynamics as conservative orthodoxy, evangelism, inerrancy, and pre-millennial eschatology do not ultimately define fundamentalism in a satisfactory manner. There are, she notes, many theological conservatives who in fact likewise subscribe to these theological perspectives yet do not consider themselves fundamentalists.

In order to identify the true trademark of fundamentalism, Ammerman suggests, one must look to the cultural and/or social realm(s) and grasp something of the way fundamentalists related to one another, to those who did not share their views and to the world in general.[1]

By 1925 fundamentalists realized they were now "outsiders" to the mainstream of American religious life. Accordingly, they advanced that the denominations were "hopelessly apostate, no better (and perhaps worse) than the secular world" and internal controversy eventually developed regarding how to relate to these apostates.[2] "The choice facing the movement," asserts

---

[1] Nancy T. Ammerman, "North American Protestant Fundamentalism," in Martin E. Marty and R. Scott Appleby, *Fundamentalisms Observed*, vol. I, 7-8. "The ultimate characteristic that has distinguished fundamentalists from other evangelicals has been their insistence that there *can be* tests of faith. Fundamentalists insist on uniformity of belief within the ranks and separation from others whose beliefs and lives are suspect. The fundamentalist, then, is very likely to belong to a church with strict rules for its own membership and for its cooperative relations with others. It is likely to be an "independent" church, since so many of the denominations are seen as affected with apostasy and compromise."

[2] Ibid., 28. "Now they saw the entire culture dominated by non-Christian influences. They became convinced that all of society had come under the sway of ideas that excluded God, ideas they saw as forming a pattern and an ideology that they eventually termed "secular humanism.""

Ammerman, "was between cultural relevance and cultural separation."[3] Many, if not most fundamentalists, chose cultural separation.[4]

Clark Pinnock picks up on Ammerman's observation regarding fundamentalism's proclivity for separatism but suggests a distinction be made between "strict fundamentalism" and "open fundamentalism." Nevertheless, concerning the former he identifies that which most people today think of when they hear the term "fundamentalist:"

> These are people who want to be different from the world and to separate from those Christians who compromise their witness. They want to be a distinct people, which means adopting a different way of living in the world. It means refusing to cooperate with those who do not observe the same strict standards of belief and behavior. Compromise and accommodation are what they want most to avoid. Strict fundamentalism is a world in opposition, a sacred world which offers meaning and direction in contrast to the deteriorating world outside.[5]

This separation from liberals, apostates and compromisers eventually came to be known as "first-order" or "primary" separation.

Humphreys and Wise call attention to another form of separatism that developed within this initial separatism when they speak of "second-order separation." Whereas "first-order" or "primary" separation consists of separating one's self, congregation or institution from theological liberals generally considered unregenerate, "second-order" or "secondary" separation requires that one also separate from fellow fundamentalists who will not completely separate from theological liberals. The lengths to which some fundamentalists have been prepared to resort to on the matter of separatism are evident in an anecdote they relate|:

---

3   Ammerman, 36.

4   Dalhouse, 117f, makes a number of important comments regarding "educational and cultural separatism" that accurately depict the identical thinking at PBI in this regard during the Maxwell era. "Their separatist, premillennial doctrine compelled them to announce the inevitable demise of their culture and society, yet they retained the desire to build a "city upon a hill.""

5   Clark Pinnock, "Defining American Fundamentalism: A Response," 44, in Norman J. Cohen (ed.), *The Fundamentalist Phenomenon.*

In Fundamentalism there is a tradition of second-degree separatism. This is separatism from people who are Fundamentalists themselves but who are willing to relate to and work with people who are not Fundamentalists. In some Fundamentalist circles there is contempt for conservative Christians who are irenic. Bob Jones III has described such people as *pseudo-Fundamentalists*. George W. Dollar, a historian of Fundamentalism who is a Fundamentalist, has described how in 1978 Fundamentalist Wendell Mullen condemned John R. Rice because Rice had supported Jerry Falwell, who had sinned by standing next to Warren Wiersbe, who had approvingly quoted Helmut Thielicke, who was not an inerrantist.[6]

Joel Carpenter's work is unparalleled when it comes to a comprehensive discussion of "the separatist impulse" that, by the 1930s, throbbed within the collective breast of many fundamentalists. Many of the ideas he articulates in Chapters 2, 3 and 4 of *Revive Us Again* accurately capture both the spirit and the nature of the separatism that prevailed at Prairie Bible Institute during the L.E. Maxwell era.[7]

Because of PBI's geographical location on the vast, remote prairie of western Canada, both "first-order separation" and "second-order separation" were not as immediately relevant to its regular routine as compared to those fundamentalist congregations and institutions located in the large, urban centers of North America.[8] Indeed, the scores of students who

---

[6] Humphreys and Wise, 60.

[7] Carpenter, 33-88.

[8] Anderson, 92-93: "After high school, I enrolled in the Prairie Bible Institute . . . Like the surrounding prairies, the campus was austere, and the smallest details of our personal lives were regulated by rules or bells. It was a bit like a Protestant monastery. Everything was designed to turn one's attention from the distractions of common life to the more serious business of learning the Bible. This we undertook with boot-camp zeal."

Although it is not uncommon to hear PBI's rural location linked to notions of a religious commune or a monastic type establishment, no evidence was uncovered in the research undertaken for this book to suggest that the remote location of Three Hills was intentionally chosen as the location for the Bible school in order to remove students from the temptations and evils of the "big, bad world." Three Hills simply happened to be where the Kirk family had settled and where a vacant farmhouse that was suitable for Bible classes was available. Although the school's remote location certainly had some advantages in helping students remained undistracted by the world, I believe it would be inaccurate to suggest the location was part of any strategic design

made the trek to Three Hills, Alberta, from highly-populated regions needed no convincing they were coming to a "separated" community. The simple fact of the matter was that PBI's rural setting largely ruled out the possibility of having to rub shoulders with liberal Christians and compromising modernists on a regular basis.[9] In this regard, the world as experienced at PBI was significantly different than what many of the school's fundamentalist brethren in more populated areas regularly faced.[10]

Nevertheless, L.E. Maxwell's personal files contained well-marked articles on separation by authorities like Graham Machen and Charles E. Fuller and give ample indication that "separation" was a topic of considerable importance to PBI's president. In addition to hand-written notes possibly for use in an address to the PBI staff or student body, one finds a paper on "separation" that Maxwell wrote "as a member of a committee to consider the subject of separation." In short, the paper reveals that whereas Prairie unequivocally adhered to "primary" or "first-order" separation, the school preferred a gentler and more congenial approach to the matter of "secondary" or "second-order" separation" from those it considered brothers and sisters in Christ.[11]

---

to remove students from the mainstream of society or to intentionally be separated from the larger world.

[9] To be sure, as this book documents in Chapter Fourteen, there were periodic clashes between the fundamentalist orientation of L.E. Maxwell at PBI and mainstream denominations in the area. But by and large, PBI operated without many of the pressures faced by fellow-fundamentalists in urban areas.

[10] As Shirley Nelson depicts in *The Last Year of the War*, students at fundamentalist institutions in urban settings rode public transit and worked off-campus which brought them into regular contact with outsiders. Given Prairie's remote location, its rules and the virtual self-sufficiency of the Institute community, about the only contact students had with the outside world was in the periodic shopping they did in the town of Three Hills and in contacts made while conducting chaperoned street evangelism, jail visitation or other "outreach" activities in larger centers not far from Three Hills such as Drumheller, Red Deer or Calgary.

[11] PBI Archives in Ted S. Rendall Library: L.E. Maxwell personal file—"Separation." An undated paper titled "Separation in the Scriptures" authored by Maxwell states: "However, we are compelled to call for a final word of caution. Separationism has almost become a sect, a veritable obsession with some. It leads them to indulge in sniping at their fellows. They cannot live and let live. They find it difficult to abide by Augustine's word of wisdom: "In essentials, unity; in doubtful questions, liberty; in all things, charity."

As Carpenter points out, the most obvious sign of the priority that fundamentalists placed on separation from the world and from worldly Christianity was "their commitment to a "separated life.""[12] External indications that one did not subscribe to popular culture's values, fashions or past-times was a primary means by which living "a separated life" was communicated by these Christians. Certain external signs of separation from the world were the most visible and audible expression of this school of thought's commitment to the "separated life." Indeed, the following description from Carpenter of what it meant to be visibly "separated" from the world is as accurate with regard to the Prairie Bible Institute of the L.E. Maxwell era as it was concerning any of the fundamentalist Bible institutes in urban North America at the time:

> The separated life for fundamentalists meant a variety of things, but most visible, of course, was their desire, in the midst of the Jazz Age, to uphold the behavioral standards of nineteenth-century evangelicalism. In addition to abiding by principles of strict sexual chastity and modesty in dress, fundamentalists were to abstain from alcoholic drink, profane or coarse language, social dancing (and dance music), and the theater— including the movies. Using tobacco, playing cards, gambling and working on Sunday (or even playing too strenuously) were also forbidden. Extremes in fashion and heavy use of cosmetics were considered worldly; the ideal was to look clean-cut and "wholesome."[13]

As discussed in Chapter Eight of this book, L.E. Maxwell's writing, teaching and preaching did not shrink from pointedly articulating the believer's need to live a life of separation from the world.[14] The "world"

T.S. Rendall personal interview, August 14, 2006. Dr. Rendall confirmed that "PBI believed in separation from liberalism and would not consciously have a liberal on campus representing anything or speak from the pulpit. So, "yes" on Prairie's adherence to first-order separation, but "no" with regard to second-order separation." In support of the latter point, Rendall stated that Stephen Olford was a regular speaker at PBI and had preached L.E. Maxwell's funeral sermon. "Olford was a long-time friend of Billy Graham and, in fact, led Graham into an experience of the fullness of the Holy Spirit as well as prepared messages for Graham at Harringay."
[12] Carpenter, 57.
[13] Carpenter, 58.
[14] Chapter Eight of this book, footnote 51.

as spoken of in Scripture, he believed, refers to "the whole orbit and life of the natural man." And, he asserted:

> Since the world slew Christ, and hates God, its whole ambition and passion and swagger, its popularity and pleasure—yea, its ten thousand enchantments all contradict the Cross and exclude "the love of the Father.[15]

Staff and students at PBI therefore had minimal contact or association with the unbelieving population of Three Hills. Apart from shopping at some of the local stores, we seldom interacted with the residents of the town.[16]

Maxwell was adamant that such association would eventually lead to worldliness and pointedly identified:

> a few subtle forms of worldliness which lure us to the rocks, and wreck our Christian testimony. Note:
>
> Our dread of the faces and frowns of worldly men. On the other hand, what a pleasant morsel is the world's favor and flattery!
>
> The unwarranted time we can spend over some trifling hobby instead of "redeeming the time." We call it relaxation, but there may be much worldliness in it.
>
> The ease with which we can sit in slippered feet noting the world's news when we might be giving the "good news" to lost men . . . The prevalent lust for late night lunching and vainglorious witticisms—cheating ourselves of the time needed for God's fellowship in the Word and prayer next morning . . .
>
> The great place we give to likes, dislikes, and personal choices.
>
> How much we are regulated by public opinion, perhaps religious opinion, rather than scriptural principle.
>
> How easily we are content to allow this or that thing, be it ever so innocent or lovely, to becloud the world to come.

---

15 L.E. Maxwell, *Born Crucified*, 34-35.

16 It didn't take long for PBI "staff kids" such as me who would have liked to play sports with fellow residents of Three Hills to identify one of the enduring paradoxes of fundamentalism. On the one hand, fundamentalism taught that it was the Christian's primary mandate in life to evangelize unbelievers. Simultaneously, we were told to have nothing to do with unbelievers lest we be infected by their worldliness. It is obvious one is hard pressed to simultaneously or effectively practice both directives.

How little we count it a privilege to suffer shame for His name.

What expectations we have of great contentment and satisfaction from certain earthly comforts. How fond we are of nice things and luxuries, and how unwilling to forego them for the sake of sending the gospel to the heathen.

How we abhor being counted eccentric! How unquestioningly obedient we are to fashion's decrees, not because the styles are reasonable or right or decent. We are so worldly-minded we would rather be indecent than different . . .

The whole root of our ruin is found in worldliness.[17]

The purpose for using this extended quotation from Maxwell's first book is to establish the depth of his animosity for worldliness and the specific nature of some of the behaviors and attitudes he believed believers needed to separate themselves from. His passion with regard to how easily believers are influenced by the world was no less pointed in the last book he penned:

Too many young people from Christian homes are being trained, not to be disciplined soldiers for Christ, but to fulfill professional positions, to secure good jobs, to qualify as teachers, to be competent businessmen—in other words, trained with ability to make a good living in this world and to enjoy a measure of ease and comfort. To put the question squarely: For which world are our children being trained?[18]

To underscore a theme noted previously in these pages, the perspective that ruled the day at PBI throughout the Maxwell era was unequivocal in its emphasis that serving on the foreign mission field was the noblest pursuit any Christian could undertake. Toward that end, anything that looked like the world, sounded like the world or could possibly be confused with the world was best rejected and avoided. This aspiration to be separate from the world was reflected over the years by PBI's policies with regard to the following components of popular culture. These regulations placed the school firmly

---

[17] Maxwell, 36-37.
[18] Maxwell, *World Missions: Total War*, 29.

in the mainstream of twentieth century American fundamentalism following the upheaval of the 1920s.[19]

I. Dress and appearance

The fundamentalist alarm regarding inappropriate changes in the fashion industry surfaced early in the pages of PBI's primary publication, *The Prairie Pastor*. Such indicated just how conversant with and influenced by American fundamentalism L.E. Maxwell was in his early years. For example, he cites an incident from the life of American president Calvin Coolidge regarding women's immodest dress before asking: "Christian woman, what excuse have you for wearing clothes which excite the baser passions of men?"[20]

Similarly, he introduced an article reprinted from the American-based *The Sunday School Times* just a few weeks later in this way:

> While we do not wish to make the subject of women's dress a hobby, we recognize it as of no slight importance. The Lord's redeemed people constitute "a royal priesthood." . . . Does not a Christian woman affront God, when she, an intercessor, "a priest" appears before Him in the livery of the world? Can she thus appear and not "bear iniquity?[21]

The reprinted article reflects fundamentalism's keen belief that one's dress was a primary sign of either separation from the world or of accommodation to the world:

---

[19] Flory documents similar policies on these issues that existed at Wheaton (94, 99f, 106f), Moody (181-189), Biola (259, 264), Bob Jones University (325, 343, 344).

Martin Riesebrodt, *Pious Passion*, 54: "The central sign of crisis for fundamentalists was the change in sexual morality. Their publications and pamphlets were filled with complaints about prostitution and venereal disease, about dance halls and indecent dress on women, about music and dance, about the cinema and theater . . . equally condemned were the changes in personal habits and leisure-time pursuits. Most important here, of course, was alcohol consumption . . ."

[20] L.E. Maxwell, "The Modern Goddess, FASHION!" in *The Prairie Pastor*, I, No. 5, (May 1928); I.

[21] L.E. Maxwell, "Women's Dress," in *The Prairie Pastor*, I, No. 9, (September 1928); I.

Christian women must choose between Christ and the world. If they choose to please the world they cannot please Christ, and if they choose to pleas Christ they cannot please the world.

If women and girls despise and cast from them the glory that God has placed on their head as a mark of special favor to them, how can they expect that God will trust the eternal glories to them?

Men are guilty of other forms of worldliness equally serious. All of us, both men and women, have great need of repentance.

Difficult as it may be for those living in the twenty-first century to comprehend, concern regarding this matter was sufficient for Maxwell to publish a lengthy article in 1940 entitled "Christ or Fashion." Drawing on the words of Charles G. Finney to the effect that every Christian makes an impression by virtue of their conduct, looks, dress and demeanor, the writer of the article declared:

In these days when the sins of a Sodom-soaked world are mounting to High Heaven it is time that women cease cutting off their skirts and bowing to the goddess Fashion. We are to "present our bodies a living sacrifice, holy, acceptable unto God." But Christian women, along with all the rest of the worldlings, are presenting their bodies a living sacrifice, unholy, to the goddess Fashion, and to the gaze of men. And any Christian woman who persists in wearing short skirts loves to show herself off.

To help drive home their point, the writer relates the experience of "one of our young men" engaged in gospel literature distribution work in a large city. They happened to be working that day in a district "in which there were houses of ill fame." Handing a tract to a young woman coming out of one of these houses, he was startled to learn that she was actually one of the Christian young women on his team. In defending himself, the young man exclaimed that he could not tell by her appearance "but what she was one of the whores." [22]

By the mid-1900s PBI's student handbooks regularly contained lengthy sections outlining what the school considered to be the appropriate length

[22] "Christ or Fashion," in *The Prairie Pastor*, 13, No. 11, (November 1940); 7ff. The writer's identity is not clear in the original publication.

of women's skirts and blouse sleeves.[23] Women were not permitted to wear jewelry such as earrings or make extensive use of cosmetics. The specific nature of men's haircuts was carefully worded so that nothing reminiscent of the "hippie" era, an anti-establishment movement popular in North America in the late 1960s and early 1970s, was evident among male students.[24] "Button flies" on men's trousers were prohibited during the brief time such were in style during the 1970s. It was not uncommon for the student deans at PBI to monitor for skirt and hair lengths as well as "button flies" as students lined up for meals in the dining room. Offending students were directed to immediately change clothes or get a haircut.[25]

---

[23] PBI Records Office files: *Manual of the Prairie Bible Institute 1930-31*, 21: "We do not approve of short skirts, low necks, short sleeves, sheer or gaudy material in waists or dresses, flesh-colored or otherwise attractive stockings, or the use of cosmetics of any kind; believing that Christians should dress Scripturally, not conforming to the fashions of this world, but obeying the Word, "as obedient children, not fashioning yourselves according to the former lusts in your ignorance." Young women with bobbed hair are expected to let their hair grow when they come to the Institute. We strongly recommend that no young woman wear her skirts shorter than eight or nine inches from the floor. We see no reason why Christian women should bow to the modern Goddess, Fashion. We agree with one writer that . . . ""During this last year the limit of vulgarity in female dress has been reached.""

[24] Male "hippies" often wore beards and shoulder-length or longer hair as a sign of their anti-establishment philosophy.

[25] L.E. Maxwell personal file—"Prairie Social Regulations." In what appears to be an undated letter to PBI staff, Maxwell laments the recognition that most PBI women graduates did not maintain the school's strict dress regulations following graduation from the school. "I am of the conviction that this can be almost entirely accounted for on the basis of a remaining worldly-mindedness. The spirit of the world is so strong that these young folks little know its grip upon them." He goes on to comment: "I am 100% for what is regarded as the extreme long dress. I would rather see them "sacky" than short . . . I am coming to believe that God's testimony through P.B.I. is somewhat more blasphemed and rendered unsuccessful and ineffective through a too close adherence to the eleven inches. I believe, however, that on account of the hardness of heart so evident everywhere, and even in our very midst, that it will be necessary to make the concession. I mean by concession, this: that we shall have to have the fraction such that it will hit about the calf of the leg, whether it varies between ten and thirteen inches. It seems to me that our testimony with regard to self and sin and human depravity and our emphasis upon the Cross as the way of life are somewhat discountenanced through the fact that our graduates go out and do not observe that which we have taught them for three or four years."

Interestingly enough, although Stackhouse demonstrates his awareness of the strict rules that prevailed at Prairie with regard to women's dress standards and men's hairstyles, he minimizes the connection of such standards at PBI with either American fundamentalism or the American influence at the school.[26] In fact, it might be charged that he conveniently fails to mention that the *Prairie Pastor* article he cites in his work is the very *Sunday School Times* reprint identified in footnote 21 of this chapter.

It is such realities as these that prompt one to question if what Stackhouse labels as Canadian "sectish" evangelicalism is truly as different a creature from American fundamentalism as he asserts. In any event, it should be duly noted that many of the identical behaviors that Carpenter and others report came to define American fundamentalists with regard to external matters of dress and appearance also apparently defined those whom Stackhouse identifies as Canadian "sectish" evangelicals.

II. "Worldly" habits

Similar to regulations at large American fundamentalist educational institutions like Biola, Moody, and Columbia, so too PBI students during the Maxwell era were not permitted to participate in habits that the school's leadership associated with "worldliness." This included such activities as consumption of alcohol, smoking or chewing tobacco, dancing, attending movie theatres, or the reading of pornographic or risqué literature. Although PBI students were strongly encouraged to maintain these standards even while they were away from the school during winter and summer breaks, the author can attest from personal observation and experience that not all students cooperated in this regard.

Again, L.E. Maxwell's personal files contain numerous clippings and articles testifying to the evil nature of pursuits such as those just listed above. Clippings from *The Dawn* refer to dancing as "a whirl of promiscuous caress" while attendance at the cinema is summarized with "the immoral aspect gets a grip on you, and once it has got you, it is impossible to get away. It is like smoking or drinking. It is a habit. The pictures affect the mind. They are a drug."[27]

---

[26] Stackhouse, 83.
[27] L.E. Maxwell personal file—"Pleasures."

Many of the clippings in Maxwell's "Pleasures" file come from either the *Prairie Pastor* or the *Prairie Overcomer*, PBI's own magazines, and contain statements such as:

> We have been insisting that the Holiness people should boycott the miserable movie picture show business. Crimes among young people and children are fearfully increasing.
>
> We read that a New York chief of police spoke out in these plain terms against the dance: "Three fourths of the fallen girls of New York were ruined by dancing."
>
> There are a few questions which help us to settle the matter of amusements . . . Would I be ashamed to be caught doing this or that when Jesus comes?
>
> From a moral standpoint [Christians] should be against the dance. From the Christian viewpoint they should shun and hate it as from the very pit of hell.

A letter dated November 2, 1953, to Maxwell from a Mr. and Mrs. Ben Findley of Lewiston, Idaho, reads: "We thought this article printed in our daily paper recently might be of some interest to you." The attachment from American Press/New York entitled "Church Opposition to Dancing, Cards on Wane, Survey Shows" begins:

> Old-time religious disapproval of ballroom dancing and card playing isn't what is (sic) used to be in many churches today. The opposition generally has modified, denominational leaders say . . . said Dr. Ralph Stoody, information director of the Methodist Church, "there is much more positive preaching nowadays, and less of the negative type.

In his written and oral communication, L.E. Maxwell consistently cited the decline in standards as documented in such articles as this as evidence that the time was fast approaching for Christ's return.

While I was a student at PBI in 1976, the school was confronted with a significant obstacle to its policy regarding attendance at the cinema. A Christian movie entitled *The Hiding Place* featuring the popular, true story of Corrie ten Boom and her Dutch family was released to cinemas around the world. Several members of ten Boom's family including herself, her father and her sister were imprisoned by the Nazis in concentration camps in punishment for giving shelter to Jews.

After considerable discussion by the Institute's Board of Directors, it was decided that a one-time exception would be made so that with proper supervision PBI students could see the movie at a Calgary or Red Deer cinema. In time, as the release of additional Christian films to community cinemas became a popular practice, it became evident this policy would have to be reconsidered.[28]

III. Radio and television

As far as I can discern, although radios were always permitted in the homes of PBI staff members, they were not allowed in the residential dormitories at Prairie except in the offices of the Dean of Men and Dean of Women.[29] Therefore, unless they purchased a newspaper or news magazine or sought out such in the Bible school library, residential students at PBI were largely dependent on reports from deans, teachers, staff members or their children, or letters and phone calls from back home for information concerning major developments in world news.[30]

---

[28] PBI Archives in Ted S. Rendall Library: PBI Administrative Team minutes, January 25, 1980: "We have been informed that the film "Joni" is to be released in Calgary very shortly. It will be shown in the Brentwood Mall Theatre. We agreed that if the same general arrangements that pertained to the showing of "The Hiding Place" exist in respect to "Joni," then we would adopt the same policy as we had for "The Hiding Place." In essence this recognizes that the film is being shown under the auspices of World Wide Pictures not the theatre, and that the theatre is only being rented for the purpose of projecting the film."

Following L.E. Maxwell's retirement, a number of rules at PBI with regard to behavior and dress were altered. PBI Archives in Ted S. Rendall Library: PBI Administrative Team Minutes, February 17, 1982: "As a general practice staff members will not attend theatres. However, when a Christian film is being shown, attendance at that film will be a matter of a staff member's personal conscience." PBI Administrative Team Minutes, June 10, 1982, report revisions to a number of issues including permission for women to wear pants in the residences, the tasteful use by women of cosmetics and ear-rings, and women's blouse sleeves shortened from completely covering the elbow to being half-way between the shoulder and elbow.

[29] Phonographs and tape recorders were also not permitted in students' dorm rooms until the mid-1970s.

[30] For most of the time period under review in this project, of course, "the news" did not have the kind of prominent profile it does in the daily life of the twenty-first century

The arrival of television in mid-century North American society met with a different response, however. Television was not permitted on the campus of Prairie Bible Institute or in the homes of staff members who lived off campus until several years following L.E. Maxwell's death.[31] Evidence from his personal files suggest Maxwell maintained an affinity for perspectives which argued that much of television programming openly and ominously undermined Christian values. Ted Rendall confirmed that with the numerous reports that circulated regarding violence and obscenity on TV, "L.E. just swept it aside.[32]

when media are now a part of Big Business. I vividly recall a number of American students coming to our home to listen to radio news reports of American president John F. Kennedy's assassination in November 1963. When I was in the seventh and eighth grades, I delivered the major daily, *The Calgary Herald*, to the PBI Library and to subscribers in the PBI dormitories. Mike Bartlett, a native of Texas, diligently subscribed only to the Monday edition of the newspaper so that he could follow the scores for American college football games played the previous weekend.

31 PBI Archives in Ted S. Rendall Library, Box 80: "Principles and Practice of Prairie Bible Institute" (n.d.). XI-3 reads: "While we recognize that the occasional program on television is worthwhile, and while we appreciate the fact that God has blessed this medium to the saving of souls; nevertheless, we do not permit our staff members on or off campus to have television sets. It is our conviction that Prairie's staff members see too many profitable areas of time investment in the timeless potentialities latent in the students God sends us, to demand a tabulated list of reasons for this regulation."
The energetic debate over permitting television on PBI campus is evident in the Board of Directors' minutes throughout 1986. Television on campus was eventually approved in 1987. By way of comparison, when I was a student at Trinity Divinity School in suburban Chicago in the early 1980s, students at Moody Bible Institute advised me that televisions were permitted in the lounge areas of Moody dorms. Such were, nonetheless, strictly monitored by dormitory supervisors.

32 L.E. Maxwell personal file—"Television." The contents of this file are entirely negative on the moral implications of television: "Important! Some Things You Should Know Before You Turn on Any Television," published by the Fundamental Evangelistic Association of Los Angeles; "Alistair Cooke - What TV is Doing to America," an interview in *U.S. News & World Report*, April 15, 1974, wherein Cooke claims that next to parents, television most affects the development of a child, far ahead of school and church influences; "Fifteen Reasons Why Television is Wrong," by Huey Gillipsie, Evangelist, published by Pilgrim Tract Society, Randleman, NC, subtitled "Hell's Pipeline Into the Home;" a newspaper clipping in which The Archbishop of Canterbury views television's influence with alarm; "Should a Christian Have Television In His Home?" in which Evangelist Joseph W. Arnett states: "I am firmly convinced that a Bible-believing Christian should not have a television set in his home for these reasons . . ." "Television: What is Wrong with It for the Christian?" stating,

Symbolic of the viewpoints that seemed to best resonate with Maxwell regarding TV is that of *Newsweek* columnist, Colman McCarthy, who opined that "TV is a wasteland, with irrigation offered only by the rare trickle of a quality program."[33] In another clipping located in Maxwell's files, A.W. Tozer of the Christian and Missionary Alliance warned:

> Be serious-minded. You can well afford to see fewer comedy shows on TV. Unless you break away from the funny boys, every spiritual impression will continue to be lost to your heart, and that right in your own living room. The people of the world used to go to the movies to escape serious thinking about God and religion. You would not join them there, but you now enjoy spiritual communion with them in your own home. The devil's ideals, moral standards and mental attitudes are being accepted by you without your knowing it.[34]

The prohibition of television on PBI campus was not without its problems. Rumors abounded frequently during my youth that certain families harbored television sets in the attics of their homes although such was never actually verified as far as can be determined. A zealous campus milkman once reported a neighbor who had erected a FM antenna on his roof, the former suspecting it was actually a TV antenna. Many PBI staff members conveniently visited off-campus homes on Saturday night when *Hockey Night in Canada* was broadcast on CBC-TV.[35] PBI broadcast a Christmas

---

"Television is a rival of schools and churches, the feeder of lust, a perverter of morals, a tool of greed, a school of crime, a betrayal of innocence . . ." etc.
  Ted S. Rendall, personal interview, August 14, 2006.
[33] L.E. Maxwell personal file—"Television." Colman McCarthy, "Ousting the Stranger From the House," *Newsweek*, (March 25, 1974), 17.
[34] L.E. Maxwell personal file—"Television." See article by A.W. Tozer, "How to Have a Personal Revival."
[35] T.S. Rendall, personal interview, August 14, 2006; Rendall stated he felt it was hypocritical that so many staff members went to community homes to watch *Hockey Night in Canada* on Saturday nights which was one of the reasons he pushed for allowing television on campus following the L.E. Maxwell era. "You can't condone that kind of inconsistency," Rendall remarked. Indeed, as noted previously, the Callaway boys and their father could frequently be found at "Uncle" Charlie Crawford's home on winter Saturday evenings!

television program over a regional television channel for several years which earned the school some criticism for a purported double standard.

Ultimately however, it was a pragmatic reality that played a decisive role in television being allowed on PBI campus. The invention of video cassette recorders which required a monitor (i.e. television set) had, of course, significant implications for an educational institutional such as PBI. This eventually resulted in television becoming a staple in the homes of many staff members.[36]

IV. Films and drama

Like many fundamentalist organizations that were committed to being visibly separated from the world, PBI periodically wrestled with how to make a proper distinction between the message of popular culture and the medium employed by popular culture to dispense its message. Given what was mentioned earlier in this chapter regarding how PBI handled the matter of its students viewing the movie *The Hiding Place*, it should be noted that the introduction of "Christian" motion pictures or films in the early 1950s was cause for controversy among some who were affiliated with PBI. Certain members of PBI's leadership team believed that drama or acting of any kind intruded a "make-believe" or "fairy tale" element into the presentation of sacred matters.

A brief but critical essay entitled "Films" penned by L.E. Maxwell for the October 1954 issue of the *Prairie Overcomer* earned the following responses from PBI's supporting constituency:

> You are to be commended for as fine an analysis and balanced understanding of the gospel movie problem as I have ever heard. My soul has been deeply grieved because many of the films produced and

---

[36] My youngest brother, Phil, joined PBI staff in the early 1980s and acquired a "monitor" shortly thereafter. He insisted he had obtained it with the proviso that it was only to be used for viewing appropriate video products. When visiting Three Hills from time to time, however, as his older brother, I was more than happy to demonstrate that, owing to the wonders of modern science, the "monitor" could also be "converted" for other appropriate purposes such as tuning in *Hockey Night in Canada* or, memorably, the January 1985 Super Bowl game between the Miami Dolphins and the San Francisco 49ers.

widely distributed today have counter-acted some of our best efforts to keep the world out of the churches and lives of our people. Some of us have felt deep convictions regarding make-up, jewelry, the slavish fashion of the day, etc., and had succeeded to some degree in keeping our young people free from these damaging things, until prominent actors in gospel films were shown wearing these things, and it did more damage in one evening that (sic) faithful preachers have been able to build up in years of labor. (Lawrence R. Cartwright, Yakima Free Methodist Church, Yakima, Washington)

God bless you for your courage and you spoke the truth with authority. Your message carried a weightiness that exceeded opinion; I believe you spoke for God. Oh, will not Fundamentalism open her eyes these days to her worldly approach to sacred things! (Rev. George Smith, Plattsmouth, Nebraska)

Last week there were three arrivals in Provost which were related to one another, namely, the *Overcomer*, a copy of A.W. Tozer's seven reasons why he is opposed to religious films, and a kindly old gentleman, _____ _____ of Billy Graham Evangelistic Films. Mr. _____'s head office had been advised more than a month ago that there was not an opening in Provost for the showing of the film. The office acknowledged receipt of our letter but failed to notify Mr. _____. The fact that the film wasn't wanted here, and the news that anyone had written anything about films in other than an enthusiastic vein, seemed to trouble Mr. _____ (I showed him both the *Overcomer* and A.W. Tozer's material.) The good Brother appeared to be doing some deep thinking—he frankly admitted that he was "disturbed." (W.H. Elliott, Provost Gospel Mission, Provost, Alberta)[37]

Previous mention was made in this chapter regarding a dramatic play I was part of while a student at Prairie High School in 1973. The drama created something of a stir among PBI's administration since, generally speaking, any form of live drama or acting was not encouraged at PBI. Such

---

[37] L.E. Maxwell personal file—"Films." W.H. Elliott later became a Bible school instructor at PBI for a lengthy period that included my childhood and training at PBI. His children remain my friends today.

was considered by some outspoken staff members as the domain of the sinful world from which the school was to be clearly separate.[38]

During my time at PBI, however, missionary films and Moody Bible Institute's film series entitled *Sermons From Science* were standard fare in public meetings. As well, the Christmas holiday season featured daily screenings in the Prairie High School auditorium of scientific, historical and biographical offerings from The National Film Board of Canada.

V. Music

A photograph from the 1930s located in the PBI Records Office during the course of researching this book is labeled "The Ladies" String Band" and shows a sizeable group of female PBI music students.[39] Several of the young ladies are holding guitars.

The photo is particularly significant for one who grew up at PBI during the 1960s and 1970s in an era when a guitar was seldom seen or heard on campus. This reality existed because of that particular instrument's association with rock-and-roll music that had come to prominence in North America in the mid-1950s.

---

[38] My father was a member of the PBI Board of Directors at the time. My mother wrote the script for the drama and I played the role of the lead character. As readers might appreciate, several "interesting" conversations ensued over the Callaway family's dinner table while this matter was discussed among PBI's leadership.

The Berg Chorale, a Christian choir from Calgary led by one-time PBI "staff kid" and music faculty member, the late Ferdinand "Ferd" Berg, occasionally incorporated drama into their musical presentations. I recall one occasion in my high school years when the Chorale performed at PBI and included a dramatic segment in its presentation. Again, some of the PBI leadership was upset and my father shared the details over an evening meal. I remember him saying something to the effect that: "They say this time Ferdie's gone too far!"

L.E. Maxwell often took the brunt of the criticism for such matters as prejudice against drama that existed among some at Prairie. The fact of the matter was, as documented in personal conversation between my father and I, others often pressured Maxwell into a more conservative stance on some issues than he was personally comfortable with.

In 1995 a drama team from PBI performed in the Calgary church where I was the pastor at the time, indicative of the kind of changes that came to PBI in the post-L.E. Maxwell era.

[39] PBI Records Office file: *Manual of the Prairie Bible Institute 1931-32.*

Like most fundamentalist organizations, PBI associated rock-and-roll with a worldview that advocated the kind of sensuality and rebellion that flourished in the drug and sex-fueled "hippie" sub-culture that engulfed the North American continent in the 1960s. Thus, both the driving beat of rock-and-roll, as well as many of the musical instruments responsible for the distinctive rock-and-roll sound, were, for all practical purposes, banned from campus. The few guitars that occasionally were in evidence were virtually always played in a subdued, classical manner and seldom used in the public services associated with regular school life.[40]

This reality needs to be interpreted against the background of PBI's declared affinity for the style of Christian music affiliated with nineteenth-century American evangelicalism and proto-fundamentalism as well as twentieth-century fundamentalism.[41] The hymns and gospel songs of Dwight L. Moody's song-leader, Ira Sankey, and those written by holiness-era songwriters like Fanny J. Crosby, Frances R. Havergal, Philip P. Bliss

---

[40] PBI Records Office file: *PBI Bible School Handbook 1973-74*, L-8, 9: ". . . Certain types of music in popular use are regarded as musically inferior, inconsistent with a sacred message, and potentially detrimental to spiritual health. We include blues, jazz, and rock of all types in this category, and we therefore do not sanction their use in any phase of our music program. For the same reason we do not approve certain styles of performance, such as cowboy style and "show biz" style . . . We recognize the guitar as a legitimate musical instrument, useful in a wide variety of situations; however, we do not wish to feature the guitar in our worship services. Guitars will not be used, therefore, in our Sunday services, in Bible School and High School Chapel services, or in meetings at Spring and Fall Conferences." Those who attended Prairie High School c. 1970-73 will recall that this policy was not strictly enforced as Mr. Fred de Vos, Dean of Boys, frequently used the guitar in high school chapels and other services.

Mark Taylor Dalhouse, *An Island in the Lake of Fire*, 143. PBI's views on music closely resembled those at Bob Jones University: "Rock music is banned because, again as Jones III explains, "the very beat of it is sensual. It makes animals out of the hearers, to appeal to their passions." Rock is not the only music banned at BJU. According to the handbook, "jazz, folk-rock, country and western, and 'so-called religious music that is performed in folk-style, country-western style, Southern gospel style or nightclub style'" is also prohibited."

[41] Opp, 56-66, offers some perceptive insights regarding how the genre of the "gospel song," so popular in fundamentalist circles, was not appreciated by the mainline Christian churches or even by all fundamentalists who preferred "a higher standard of hymnody."

and others were staples of the PBI environment.[42] The music of more contemporary writers of gospel songs such as Merrill Dunlop and John W Peterson was also occasionally used.[43] The hymnbooks that served for congregational singing at PBI as well as the songs that were performed in public worship services, chapels and by PBI music groups travelling away from the school generally reflected the holiness-fundamentalist heritage the school was proud to be associated with.

For a number of years, PBI presented an annual "Music Night" at public auditoriums in Calgary and Edmonton that featured various music groups from the school. Virtually all of the music used on these occasions was at least several decades old and reflected the school's preference for themes uplifting both the holiness-revivalist message and a strong missionary emphasis.[44]

In describing fundamentalism's appeal to various immigrant groups, Marsden states:

> In twentieth-century America many Scottish and English Protestants could sing one of the most popular fundamentalist songs together with newer Americans:

> > *I am a stranger here, within a foreign land*
> > *My home is far away, upon a golden strand*
> > *Ambassador to be, of realms beyond the sea*
> > *I'm here on business for my King"*[45]

This gospel song served as the "theme song" for PBI's Ambassador Choir for a period of time during this writer's youth in the 1960s. The songs of American fundamentalists were our songs too! This is not too surprising since most of the music used at PBI during the Maxwell era came

---

[42] George M. Marsden, *Fundamentalism and American Culture* (1980), 36; 75-77;
   One of my vivid memories from my youth is of lengthy conference meetings where I passed the time paging through the hymnbook counting the number of songs published in the 1800s versus the number of songs published in the 1900s.

[43] Carpenter, 128. Merrill Dunlop played the organ at several PBI conferences during my youth. Because my mother also played the organ and had several of Dunlop's recordings, Dunlop was often a dinner guest in our home when visiting PBI.

[44] Exceptions were made for recent songs written by PBI personnel.

[45] Marsden., 205.

from hymnbooks and music books published by the standard American fundamentalist publishers.[46]

---

[46] My good friend and former fellow "staff kid," Mark Imbach, kindly loaned me a letter he came across in his mother's possessions following her death in Three Hills (July 2006) at 96 years of age. The letter from L.E. Maxwell to Mrs. Faith Imbach (director of PBI's Radio Choir) is dated February 2, 1961 and portions of it read as follows:

"I greatly appreciate the fact that our Radio Choir numbers have beauty and simplicity and, what I might call, finesse, yet I have long felt the need of more than delicacy and perspicuity of performance. While you know that I have no capacity or right to judge you and Miss Dearing in the matter of your public musical presentations, I must confess, and I am far from being alone in this conviction, *that we need more virility and masculinity and attack in our radio numbers*. There is too great a disparity between the finesse of our performance and the gospel message to which we give top priority here at Prairie. I think we need not be afraid of losing our gospel simplicity and our delicacy of platform performance. *We need virility, and we need to charge and challenge red-blooded young people to good soldiery.* It seems to me that *we may seem to lack that which the Moody Choral* (sic) *seems to have. We can make up by having sharpness and attack and good martial numbers.* At least have more of these numbers sprinkled in the midst of our present platform performances.

"For the first time in our conversation I mentioned this matter to Mr. Snyder today. He agrees that this is a complaint commonly voiced to him. I did not know that he even had this in mind . . . I therefore suggested to him the *possibility of having a man lead at least some of these numbers on the forthcoming tour.* I do not wish in any way to hurt you, nor am I voting you out or setting you aside. *I would like to see numbers that have more virility and with more sharpness and attack.*" (*emphasis* added)

This letter reflects several points relevant to matters touched on in this book, such as:

1) Maxwell's affinity for the militancy motif in declaring the Christian gospel.
2) An American institution, Moody, was Maxwell's template for how Prairie should be operated.
3) Despite his openness to women in ministry, Maxwell still believed there were certain qualities of leadership that men were most suited for and should/must be called upon to provide.

A February 14, 1963, letter from Mrs. Imbach to Mr. Robert Snyder, Chairman of the PBI Music Department, reads in part: "Because there are now two men in the voice department who, as far as we know feel God's call to stay in our music department, and, because I have been unqualified to do for the department what could and should be done, and because the department needs a man's decisiveness, vision and full time to promote the work, I feel I should withdraw from the place as head of the Voice Department of Prairie Bible Institute . . . I can say with a heart full of gratitude to the Lord and my fellow workers for patience, mercy and tender dealings . . ."

In addition to PBI's almost exclusive use of the religious music spawned in the proto-fundamentalist/fundamentalist era, the school also had a distinct predilection for classical music.[47] Indeed, anyone taking a stroll past PBI's Music Building late on an average school-day would invariably encounter a cacophony of sound created by vocalists, pianists and orchestra instrumentalists all busily practicing pieces of music from the turn-of-the-century and older eras. Any music that was to be publicly performed on or off campus by PBI students was vetted by a member of the music faculty for theological and artistic integrity in keeping with PBI's strict standards.[48]

My high school and Bible school education at Prairie Bible Institute coincided with the advent in North America of a style of music that went by a number of names including "gospel rock," "Christian rock" and/or "Jesus music." Inspired by the work of Christian musicians like Ralph Carmichael and Otis Skillings who were committed to speaking to and for modern youth by putting Christian lyrics to up-tempo music, "gospel rock" received a significant boost from the "Jesus People" in the late 1960s and early 1970s.[49]

---

[47] Negro spirituals and classical religious music such as pieces from "The Messiah" were another popular source of the music used at PBI during the Maxwell era.

[48] Like many who grew up at PBI, I was enrolled in music lessons early in life. After five or six years of piano lessons I advised my parents I was weary of playing hymns and select classical pieces such as "The Spinning Wheel." Having discovered an LP recording by The Blackwood Brothers in my parents' extensive record collection, I was convinced the only interest I had in piano was if I could learn to play Southern gospel music made famous by the likes of The Blackwood Brothers. When I shared this desire with Ms. Eleanor Lyn, my piano teacher at the time and a member of the Bible school music faculty, I was curtly advised that such music was mere "show-biz" and "ungodly." My budding piano career came to an abrupt halt shortly thereafter.

[49] I was a seventh grade student when Becky Graham, a classmate whose family was from West Virginia, U.S.A., showed up one day with a copy of Carmichael's album, I Looked for Love. Suggesting that her mother would "kill" her if she was found with the record, Becky (now Rebecca Graham Philpott of suburban San Deigo, CA) gave it to the Callaway boys for "safe keeping." Upon listening to the disc numerous times, in our completely objective judgment, this was something far superior to even The Blackwood Brothers. Thus, we played the record frequently and loudly—usually when our parents were away at Saturday morning PBI "staff" meetings. We were "heroes" in the collective estimation of the staff-kids who lived on 9th Avenue North, Prairie Heights.

The "Jesus People" were "hippies" who had "dropped out" of mainstream North American society to join that sub-culture before becoming disenchanted with the movement's "anti-establishment" ethos and turning to faith in Christ. Chuck Smith was one pastor at a church in southern California who invited "hippies" who were disappointed and disheartened by their quest for meaning in an alternative world to attend Bible studies at his church. Through the ministry of Calvary Chapel in Costa Mesa, California, many young people trusted Christ and began to put their faith to song using the only type of music they knew, rock-and-roll.[50]

The arrival of "gospel rock" on the scene presented a prime opportunity for PBI to demonstrate its commitment to the principle of cultural separation from the world. By the early 1970s the school's student handbooks and publicity catalogues contained lengthy statements regarding the Institute's music policy. These documents were clear that listening to or performing "gospel rock" was strictly forbidden at PBI. Chapel services were occasionally devoted to presentations that outlined the subtle evils of a form of music that was now making its way into the life of a Church that was spiritually asleep.[51] In the judgment of PBI's administration, "gospel rock" was but

---

[50] Lori Jensen, "(Re)Discovering Fundamentalism in the Cultural Margins: Calvary Chapel Congregations as Sites of Cultural Resistance and Religious Transformation," (PhD dissertation, Univ. of Southern California, 2000), 38-99, offers a concise overview of the history of the Calvary Chapel phenomenon. Chuck Girard, now one of my dear friends, was converted through the ministry of Calvary Chapel and became one of the fathers of what came to be known as "Jesus music" or "contemporary Christian music."

[51] L.E. Maxwell personal file—"Music." Among only two documents contained in this file was the text of a March 13, 1968, chapel address given by PBI faculty member Alban Douglas. Douglas likened the inevitable effects of rock-and-roll to the drunken orgy that resulted in the children of Israel constructing the golden calf as recorded in Exodus 32.

One of the primary authorities to influence the views presented by PBI regarding music was American evangelist Bob Larson, a self-proclaimed ex-rock star, who wrote extensively on the evils of rock-and-roll. See, for example, his books: *Rock and Roll: The Devil's Diversion* (Denver, CO: Bob Larsen Ministries, 1970); *Hindus, Hippies and Rock & Roll* (Carol Stream, IL: Creation House, 1972); *Rock and the Church* (Carol Stream, IL: Creation House, 1971); *The Day Music Died* (Denver, CO: Bob Larsen Ministries, 1978); *Rock: Practical Help for Those Who Listen to the Words and Don't Like What They Hear* (Wheaton, IL: Tyndale House Publishers, 1980); *Your Kids and Rock* (Wheaton, IL:

another lamentable indication that North American evangelicalism was beset by a lukewarm spirituality similar to what the church at Laodicea was indicted for by Christ in Revelation 3.[52]

It is significant for the purposes of this book to point out that throughout the L.E. Maxwell era at PBI, a significant number of Americans consistently held strategic positions in the school's music department. Beginning in the early years with L.E. Maxwell's own aunt, Katherine Anderson, the music program at PBI regularly featured American instructors such as Kathleen Dearing, Robert Snyder, Edward Rosevere, Faith Imbach, Lyle Birch, Deanna Lockwood, Jean Boswell, Dan Kennedy, Ray Olson, Lowell Hart and Paul Rausch, to name some of the more prominent individuals who served during the author's years at PBI.[53]

Some of these people brought a few of the more extreme elements found within American fundamentalism along with them. Lowell Hart, for example, who oversaw music in the high school when the author was a student at Prairie High, was in effect a neo-fundamentalist as it related to his animosity toward rock 'n roll music.[54] Not only did Hart frequently

---

Tyndale House Publishers, 1988). Bob Larsen is still on "the circuit" in late 2012, now functioning as an exorcist.

[52] Carpenter, 49-50, makes a useful observation that helps explain PBI's opposition to "gospel rock" when he writes: "Several historians have pointed out that the separatist position drew much support from fundamentalists' widespread pessimism about the future of the church. The dispensationalist doctrinal view, which dominated the movement, predicted the ruin of the church. As we have seen, this belief was one of the key alienating factors in the movement and it carried an explicit mandate for true believers to separate themselves from the coming Great Apostasy."

[53] This is not to suggest that all members of the music department staff at PBI were always Americans or that there was a strategic plan to hire Americans. This data simply reflects the reality that, as in many of the school's departments during the L.E. Maxwell era, the staff consisted of a significant number of Americans. See Appendix I of this book. Ferd Berg, Art Wiebe, Ernie James, Gordon Head and Evelyn Charter were among the many Canadians who served in the PBI music department during the Maxwell era. In the personal interview with Ted Rendall that I conducted on August 14, 2006, Rendall remarked: "I'm sorry we lost that trio of James, Wiebe and Berg. They would have been a great contribution to staff for maybe twenty years or so of ministry."

[54] Jack Van Impe, *Heart Disease In Christ's Body: Fundamentalism . . . Is It Sidetracked?* (Royal Oak, MI: Jack Van Impe Ministries, 1984), 25. Van Impe uses the term "neo-fundamentalist" ". . . to designate an unscriptural movement within true fundamentalism that would rather fight than switch. Neo-fundamentalists seemingly ignore what the Scriptures say about love and unity among Christians and present a lopsided view of what

address the topic of music in high school classes and chapels, he eventually ran into conflict with PBI's administration over the proposed manuscript for a book he was writing entitled *Satan's Music Exposed*.[55]

Paul Rausch, on the other hand, occasionally incurred the disfavor of some Canadians at PBI owing to his fondness for using music associated with American civil religion such as "The Battle Hymn of the Republic" in public performances by those representing a Canadian institution.[56] Like Hart, he too was obstinate in his insistence that contemporary Christian music such as that popularized by Bill and Gloria Gaither and widely received in North American evangelical churches at the time, was superficial

---

constitutes orthodoxy. They preach and teach a misinterpreted message on separation, and then view themselves as the only ones who understand such truth."

[55] PBI Archives in Ted S. Rendall Library: Administrative Team minutes of December 17 & 18, 1980, and January 6 & 7, 1981, reveal lengthy discussions with Hart regarding PBI's hesitation over being identified with the book for numerous reasons. In other words, some of Hart's views were too extreme even for certain of PBI's administrators. For example, the following is from the December 17 minutes: "3. A question was raised concerning the difference between worldly music that is wrong because of its close association with the world and the apparent endorsation of the classical music which could also be closely associated with the world. Mr. Hart in passing stated that classical music does not appeal to the flesh. This was challenged. Mr. Hart pointed out that worldly music such as rock music has a fleshly appeal whereas the classical music has intellectual appeal."

Regrettably, in my view, the kind of arrogance demonstrated by Hart and others was permitted to rule the day at PBI throughout the 1970s as evidenced by these words from the Prairie Music Standards published in the *PBI Bible School Handbook 1973-74*, L-8: "Certain types of music in popular use are regarded as musically inferior . . . we include blues, jazz and rock of all types in this category, and we therefore do not sanction their use in any phase of our music program." It was dogmatic opinions such as this that used to annoy those who felt that perhaps history itself might ultimately have something to say about the intellectual appeal of rock or folk acts such as The Beatles, Bob Dylan, The Eagles or Canadian musicians like Joni Mitchell, Leonard Cohen, The Guess Who (Burton Cummings, Randy Bachman), Neil Young, and Anne Murray, to name but a few of some of the aging artists who are still writing and performing in the twenty-first century.

[56] This insight was gleaned from lengthy conversations with my father who, along with other PBI staff members such as John Thompson, Don Powell and Clarence Strom, were particularly proud and loyal Canadians.

"show-biz" and would not stand the test of time as had the old hymns of the faith.[57]

*　*　*

Being visibly and audibly separated from the transient fashions and pursuits of the unbelieving masses was a matter of urgent importance to American fundamentalists in the twentieth century. As has been documented in this chapter, this particular association with fundamentalism was also very prominent in both standard and creative ways at Prairie Bible Institute during the L.E. Maxwell era.

---

57 Both Hart and Rausch would often assert that "Christian rock" music was all show and would not sustain or that the Christian commitment of the performers was either suspect or tenuous or that their personal lives did not and eventually would not withstand careful scrutiny. The lengthy ministries and marriages of fathers of contemporary Christian music such as Dallas Holm (our second son's namesake) and Chuck Girard, testify to the foolishness of such generalities. Such judgmental attitudes have rightly earned fundamentalism a negative reputation among many Christians and non-Christians alike.

CHAPTER THIRTEEN

Two key issues in PBI's fundamentalist identity

This chapter examines two additional spheres of life at PBI during the Maxwell era that support our contention that the Prairie Bible Institute of the L.E. Maxwell era was indeed more closely aligned with American fundamentalism than what Stackhouse suggests. The purpose for including these chapters in the study is to offer insight into both the somewhat unique nature of Prairie's brand of fundamentalism as well as to detail the struggle the school had in fully embracing the neo-evangelical agenda.

The academic accreditation issue

Another dimension of life at PBI under Maxwell's tenure that reflected the school's firm commitment to separation from the world relates to the matter of academic accreditation. Readers are again reminded that one of the motivating dynamics in the original founding of PBI was J. Fergus Kirk's concern that liberal or modernist teaching was entering many churches.[1] The blame for this development was frequently laid at the gates of established universities and colleges, many of which had been founded my Christian denominations but were now viewed by fundamentalists to be functioning as greenhouses of theological modernism.

As was the case with numerous North American evangelicals in the late nineteenth and early twentieth centuries, the solution to this problem concerning suitable education was deemed to be the establishment of indigenous educational institutions that would produce theologically orthodox graduates to staff evangelical churches and missionary agencies.[2] Out of this sensitivity arose scores of small Bible institutes across North America. Several grew to be sizeable entities such as Biola, Columbia Bible College, Moody Bible Institute, and Prairie Bible Institute.

---

[1] See Chapter One of this book, footnote 9.
[2] See Chapter Two of this book where this theme is reviewed.

From the early days at PBI, L.E. Maxwell was emphatic and unequivocal that both the content of the school's curriculum and the manner in which study was carried out at PBI would be unique. Students would receive maximum and direct exposure to the whole of the Biblical text. Using the method of inductive Bible study in combination with prayerfully seeking the illumination of the Holy Spirit, earnest students would plumb the meaning of the text without the use of commentaries or other aids.[3]

Given the rapid growth of the student body at PBI in the early years, Maxwell was properly confident that this approach was both what churches were looking for and what God was choosing to bless.[4] Similarly, he was consistently caustic and skeptical toward what he perceived to be the nefarious influence of secular universities on young people.[5]

As time passed in the twentieth century, however, there was a movement among some of the established Bible institutes and newer Bible colleges to seek some form of academic accreditation in order to facilitate the matter of transfer credit to or from and recognition by other schools.[6] Ringenberg relates that in the late 1940s, after years of discussions and exploration, the

---

[3] See Chapter One of this book, footnote 8.

[4] See Chapter Eight of this book, footnote 23.

[5] See Chapter Eight of this book, footnotes 19, 25.

  PBI Archives in Ted S. Rendall Library: L.E. Maxwell personal file—"Education." Random notes in Maxwell's handwriting communicate the depth of Maxwell's conviction in this regard: "William R. Harper of Chicago University once said: "The probability is that the young people who attend our universities will come out infidels." And no less than Clarence Darrow, the great infidel lawyer of Chicago, admitted that even Leopold and Loeb's cold blooded killing was "sanctioned by the philosophy taught in American universities today (Gilbert)."

[6] PBI Archives in Ted S. Rendall Library: L.E. Maxwell personal file—"Accreditation." The file contains a request dated December 5, 1951, from Lois L. Weyhe of The William Jennings Bryan University in Dayton, TN, stating: "Would you please send us a copy of your latest catalogue. We have a few students who have transferred from Prairie Bible Institute and we would like to know the educational standing of the school." Maxwell's response reads: "I might say that young folks who are graduated from our high school department are accepted without examination at Seattle Pacific College and accepted upon examination by Wheaton and Bob Jones. Columbia Bible College has been considering the granting to our students a special concession for the reason that they have found their general biblical knowledge of a sufficient caliber to warrant their doing so. They have taken no actual steps in this direction, but Dr. McQuilkin wrote me such an encouragement at one time. The thought at the time was that they might consider granting our graduates one year graduation from Columbia."

Accrediting Association of Bible Institutes and Bible Colleges (AABIBC) was formed in the United States. It was guided by the leadership of Howard Ferrin, president of Barrington College in Providence, Rhode Island, president Safara Witmer of Fort Wayne Bible College in Indiana, and dean Samuel Rutherford of Biola. In the late 1950s the AABIBC shortened its name to the Accrediting Association of Bible Colleges (AABC) and hired Witmer as its first full-time executive secretary.[7]

Although such developments helped address a number of concerns between like-minded institutions, Ringenberg writes:

> Not all of the Bible schools accepted the accreditation movement as desirable, however. For example, L.E. Maxwell, whose Prairie Bible Institute in Alberta, Canada, was widely respected among Bible college officials in the United States, frankly stated:
>
> "We are not personally concerned about becoming uniform with others, or in becoming accredited. God has given us a special method of Bible study second to none, and we are content to do what God wants us to do without having to adjust to that which others feel led to do . . . We are convinced that many of the present trends will ultimately take these very Bible institutes into modernism"[8]

This perspective was consistent with that which Maxwell had been advancing for years:

> Why should we seek to be standardized and recognized? We have one aim and one purpose. We do not want our young people to take up with worldly occupation and preoccupations. We do not care to have them pursue worldly professions. "If we give them degrees, they will go into nursing, school teaching, commerce and various professions. We want them to stick to missions." Are there not already scores of schools, yes Christian schools (at least by profession) which claim to prepare young people for all these worthy walks of life? But we want no detracting influence. God help us keep single-eyed and pursuing this one thing.[9]

---

[7]   Ringenberg, 169-170.
[8]   Ringenberg, 170.
[9]   L.E. Maxwell, "Mold and Motive," in *The Prairie Pastor and Overcomer*, 18, No. I; (January 1945), 11-12.

It is instructive to note that even decades after PBI was established and had met with considerable success, Maxwell's mistrust of modernism lingered as did, presumably, his determination to fight it. Clearly, this was a deeply embedded concern for him and indicative of the fear that some have identified as a primary characteristic of devout fundamentalism.[10] Note also the element of skepticism regarding other "Christian" schools that surfaces in the last citation above. Some would suggest this has overtones of the kind of skepticism and subtle pride that some fundamentalists traditionally exhibited. They believed they alone were the loyal remnant of God's people in a final age of desperate unbelief and thus had the inside track with God.[11]

It should be noted that Maxwell's thinking with regard to the potential dangers of accreditation was not without some cause. For one thing, as documents from his personal files attest, PBI had a strong constituency of

[10] Armstrong, *The Battle for God*, 135: "By the end of the nineteenth century . . . People felt obscurely afraid . . . some would project their fears onto imaginary enemies and dream of universal conspiracy." 143: "The chief bone of contention at the end of the nineteenth century was not evolution but Higher Criticism . . . for the traditionalists, "Higher Criticism" was a scare term. It seemed to symbolize everything that was wrong with the modern industrialized society that was sweeping the old certainties away." 171: "But during the Great War, an element of terror entered conservative Protestantism and it became fundamentalist." 178: "Fundamentalist faith was rooted in deep fear and anxiety that could not be assuaged by a purely rational argument."

Humphreys and Wise, 58: "Fundamentalism was born from the fear that aspects of the modern world were threatening the faith of the Christian community, and many Fundamentalists continue to live their lives in an elevated state of fear."

Hood, Hill and Williamson, 11-46, discuss the importance of a sacred text to fundamentalism as a meaning system and the subsequent anxiety that is created when the absolute truth and values they believe are communicated by the sacred text are attacked.

PBI Archives in Ted S. Rendall Library; Box 65 contains an interesting survey of PBI graduates from 1931-32 through 1954-55 regarding their motives for placing their faith in Christ. On a declining scale from a high of 76.8% in 1931-32 to a low of 45.6% in 1954-55, students stated their primary motivation was fear.

[11] Humphreys and Wise, 58: "For many Fundamentalists though, suspicion is a continuing state of mind."

Frank, 224: "American evangelicals, from the beginning of their history, have lived within a national ethos whose unquestioned and proudly advertised assumptions receive no support whatever in the biblical text." See also Chapter VI, "Put No Confidence in the Flesh" for a probing and insightful treatment of the matter of pride among fundamentalists.

supporters across North America that validated Maxwell's intentions to maintain the school as an unaccredited Bible institute. Wrote J.A. Burleigh of Seattle, Washington on 10 December 1964:

> I have sent $1000.00 to Stearns Missionary Fund in Philadelphia for Prairie's general operations. The more I learn of "modern" Christian (?) Colleges, the more convinced I am of Prairie's place in our Lord's earthly affairs.

In an address to PBI's fortieth anniversary banquet in 1962, Stan Jesperson, then a member of the school's Advisory Council, stated:

> Let us not apologize to the sophisticated of the educational world for our designation as a 'Bible Institute.' It is a badge of honor. To take the infallible and inerrant Word of God as the centre of our curriculum is neither narrow nor naïve. We firmly believe the Scriptures and hold no mental reservation whatsoever. It is just good judgment to centre on the best rather than the second best. I commend the Prairie Bible Institute for demanding that no peripheral studies and interests supplant the first hand study of the Scriptures. The trend today is to regard the Bible School as a half-way house to a regular college. Let us be sure of this—the Bible School is an institution in its own right and under God has its own distinctive contribution to make. [12]

Witmer visited numerous Bible institutes in western Canada during the winter of 1960 including a visit to PBI on February 19-20. The only Canadian schools that were accredited members of the AABC at the time were London Bible Institute in London, Ontario, and Mennonite Brethren Bible College in Winnipeg. With the exception of Bob Jones University, the larger American schools with which PBI was often associated were all accredited members of the AABC as well: Biola, Columbia, and Moody.[13] Representatives of Canada's Bible colleges began to meet annually in 1959 at

---

[12] L.E. Maxwell personal file—"Accreditation." The D.M. Stearns Missionary Fund in Philadelphia was regularly advertised in PBI's promotional literature as the avenue via which American residents could support the school and realize some element of benefit on their U.S. income tax returns.

[13] Ibid., AABC News Letter, Vol. IV, No. 1; (February 1960).

what was called the Canadian Conference of Christian Educators. Delegates to that conference in May of 1968 established The Association of Canadian Bible Colleges.[14]

Following Witmer's visit to PBI he submitted a follow-up analysis in which he acknowledged his recognition of the school's somewhat unique situation regarding accreditation. He wrote: "First, your institution is of such magnitude with so many facets that one would need to spend considerable time to know enough facts to make a valid appraisal."[15] Nonetheless, he proceeded to outline twelve recommendations for PBI including the suggestion "that consideration be given to strengthening PBI's standards in other academic areas—faculty, library." Perhaps the most important comments he made were these:

One of the central problems at PBI has to do with faculty and staff personnel. The academic program cannot be appreciably strengthened until more qualified teachers are secured . . . The question has arisen in my mind as to why PBI has not grown more of its personnel from its own superior graduates who go on to advanced studies. (emphasis in original)

PBI did not proceed with seeking accreditation with the AABC at this time. Among what was likely a variety of reasons for this decision are two that warrant specific mention.

On one hand, as suggested above, many of the credible supporters of PBI that Maxwell apparently chose to listen to did not encourage the school to pursue accreditation. These included missions leaders that Maxwell held in high regard. In an April 24, 1961, letter to PBI's Advisory Council Members, he wrote:

May I make mention of one further matter. It concerns the swing of the present day toward accreditation. We are frank to say that the more we look into this matter, the more shy we are becoming of going with the wind in this direction. Actually the more we think of this the less we think of it. And a recent conversation with Mr. Mathews of the CIM, whose messages we so much appreciated lately, is illuminating in this

---

[14] Pamphlet entitled "Association of Canadian Bible Colleges."
[15] Letter to A.H. Muddle, Institute Secretary.

connection. A certain professor in a Bible School (now a Bible college) lamented to Mr. Mathews the small number of registrations in his missionary course. He was wondering to Mr. Mathews regarding the cause of the same. Mr. Mathews replied: "You get what you aim for: if you aim at college training and accreditation, that is what you will get." He was telling this man that having shifted their emphasis from a Bible and missionary training school they had gone collegiate in focus and the students had come to them in line with the collegiate objective rather than the missionary objective. We feel, therefore, that we must remain true to our objective.[16]

A letter from Elden Whipple, Candidate Secretary for an unnamed mission, who had just concluded a trip "among Bible Schools and Colleges in the Northeastern part of the USA and Canada," similarly read:

Lack of interest in missions was most discernible in the few schools that have changed from a Bible-centred curriculum to an academic program leading to the granting of academic degrees. It seemed to us that the temper and purpose of the student body in these schools had altered . . . The danger in perhaps too many of our Christian schools is the sacrificing of the spiritual to the intellectual and academic.[17]

Secondly in this regard, an exchange of letters with staff at Columbia Bible College is illuminating for a couple of reasons. First, they represent a reality that is obvious in perusing L.E. Maxwell's correspondence files. When it came to important decisions regarding the direction PBI should take, his frame of reference was found at American institutions like Moody and Columbia as opposed to Canadian institutions like Briercrest Bible Institute, a comparative stone's throw away in geographical terms.[18] Further,

---

[16] L.E. Maxwell personal file—"Accreditation,"
[17] L.E. Maxwell personal file—"Accreditation."
[18] L.E. Maxwell personal file—"Revised Standard Version." Another example of Maxwell's clear affinity to seek the counsel of his American brethren with regard to controversial decisions is an exchange with Wilbur M. Smith at Fuller Theological Seminary in Pasadena, California, that is dated in January of 1953 and found in this file. In the context of the debate that was brewing over methods of translation used in the Revised Standard Version, Maxwell asked Smith regarding his understanding of the "virtual worshiping of the King James version as the only inspired version in the

as the following correspondence demonstrates, Columbia's experience with the AABC likely confirmed some of Maxwell's original hesitations with regard to the matter of accreditation. G. Allen Fleece, Columbia's president wrote Maxwell on March 7, 1960:

> The matter of accreditation and the pertinent questions which were raised in your recent letter do present some considerations which are not too easily answered. I can say, to begin with, that we have experienced no problems whatever thus far as a result of our membership in the Accrediting Association. Generally speaking, I have found that the leaders of the Association have been much more understanding of our local situation than the printed criteria of the Association would seem to suggest. I had the opportunity of seeing things from the inside when it was my privilege to serve for two years on the executive committee of the Association . . .
>
> In view of what I have just said I would also say that I fear that there are pressures from within the Association that could easily change the general attitude of the Association from what has been the prevailing attitude and spirit until now. We have thought here at Columbia that the day might come when there would be such a change in the Association in the direction of unreasonable academic demands that we ourselves would no longer be able to remain a member. Thus far this has not been the case. Personally, I would never favor accreditation on any other basis than the one which we now enjoy. I would surrender it at once rather than start in the direction which we would both fear.
>
> I am in full accord with your attitude toward degrees . . .

On October 22, 1965, Fleece wrote again:

> Several years ago you wrote me asking some question about the Accrediting Association of Bible College (sic). You will be interested to know that we have found it necessary to withdraw from the Association due to the increasing demands of the Association for worldly academic standards.

---

world." Smith's two-page, single-spaced response begins: "With the terrific pressure of work I seem to be under just now, normally I would be answering a question like this in about one paragraph, <u>but coming from you, I cannot dismiss it so briefly.</u>" (<u>emphasis</u> added)

This was done by unanimous vote of our Trustees and with the complete harmony of the faculty.

This note was followed on July 5, 1966, by a letter signed only "Ray (or Roy?) & Helen, Mark, Suzanne & Karen," from an address in Columbia, SC, where Columbia Bible College (CBC) is located. It read in part:

> You probably have heard that CBC withdrew from the Accrediting Assoc. of Bible Colleges last September. Confidentially, the Accrediting Assoc. had evaluated our program the preceding year, and was probably going to kick us out anyway. The CBC Board felt that the AABC has shifted during the years to a wrong emphasis on intellectualism. Actually they charged CBC with being anti-intellectual and Dr. Fleece told them that we are not anti-intellectual but we are anti-intellectualism.[19]

The Columbia experience with the AABC likely confirmed for Maxwell the accuracy of his concerns about having to cede some element of control over PBI via the accreditation process. Note also that Fleece makes mention that the reason Columbia withdrew from the AABC was "due to the increasing demands of the Association for worldly academic standards." This explanation would certainly have resonated with Maxwell's consistent desire to be loyal to fundamentalism's over-arching commitment to be separated from the world.[20]

It is important to point out that the entire process of the limited negotiations that went on between PBI and the AABC in the early 1960s was quite likely overshadowed by the fact that Maxwell had faced a taxing challenge during the mid-1950s from some of PBI's own faculty with regard to the issue of accreditation. David Enarson, a PBI alumnus and a Bible school faculty member at PBI from 1952-1957, offers this succinct notation in his memoirs regarding his PBI experience:

---

[19] L.E. Maxwell personal file, "Accreditation."

[20] Although the research for this project found no indication that Maxwell ever consulted with the leaders at Bob Jones University on anything, it should be noted that with respect to the matter of accreditation, the administrations of both schools indicated their reluctance to be controlled by any "outside" agency. See Dalhouse, 42; 137-140. Several comments to this effect are found in Maxwell's personal files located in the PBI Archives in the Ted S. Rendall Library.

As a student at Prairie, Dave had been unhappy that the credits he earned there would not transfer to Canadian universities; now as a faculty member and administrator at P.B.I. he had that same concern for the student. He was to push hard for the accreditation of Prairie's elementary and high school, and would also work (in vain) towards P.B.I.'s initiating a degree program—an innovative and divisive idea which would be a factor in his eventually leaving P.B.I.[21]

After leaving PBI, Enarson would become one of the founders of Trinity Western University in suburban Vancouver, British Columbia. Today, Trinity Western is a fully accredited Christian university, one of only a handful of such institutions that exist in Canada.[22]

It is evident that a couple of factors were crucial for L.E. Maxwell with regard to his thinking about academic accreditation. Clearly, he was adamantly opposed to any changes he believed would serve to bifurcate PBI's primary calling and obvious success as a missionary-producing school. His passion in that regard was as fervent in 1962 as it was in 1922. As well, believing that, by and large, academia promotes an environment wherein the intellect roams uncontrolled thus leading to a form of what he ultimately considered worldliness, Maxwell was determined to resist pressure on his watch for Prairie to become accredited. Accordingly, his mistrust of academia prevailed virtually to the end of his tenure at PBI.

The Billy Graham debate

The rise to prominence in the mid-twentieth century of American evangelist Billy Graham proved to be somewhat of a watershed event in the history of American fundamentalism. Beginning with the eight-week 1949 Los Angeles evangelistic crusade that quickly brought Graham to fame among North Americans, devout fundamentalists became quietly skeptical of a methodology that featured the professed conversions of famous individuals

---

[21] David E. Enarson, *Thine Hand Upon Me: He Tells It Like It Was* (self-published, c. 1996), Chapter 28.

[22] See Spaulding, 44, "An Institutional Threat," for additional information regarding this rift at PBI and the emotional toll it apparently exacted of Maxwell.

from the entertainment, sports and criminal worlds.[23] A prolonged series of meetings in the United Kingdom in the early 1950s introduced the young American evangelist to Europe and the wider world.

It was the appearance of modernists and Roman Catholics on the platform at Graham's New York crusade in 1957, however, that fuelled the smoldering coals of controversy into a roaring conflagration within fundamentalist circles. Dalhouse succinctly summarizes the ultimate significance of the fracture when he writes:

> One observer noted that shortly after New York, "at the grass roots level the question soon became simply, 'are you for or against Graham?' Individuals like the Bob Joneses, evangelist John R. Rice, and denominations such as the GARBC quickly aligned against Graham, while J. Elwin Wright, Carl F. Henry and the NAE supported him. Twenty years earlier, they had all been allies united against modernism. Graham's ministry also hastened the redefinition of the once synonymous "fundamentalist" and "evangelical." Graham himself disavowed the fundamentalist label.[24]

Which side of this fissure did Prairie Bible Institute identify with? The available evidence suggests that PBI eventually elected to try and walk a middle ground on the Billy Graham controversy. This reality partly explains why it is ultimately somewhat difficult to decisively label the school with either the "fundamentalist" or "neo-evangelical" designation. For that reason, and others, the facts regarding PBI's view of Billy Graham merit documentation here.

Shortly after Billy Graham came to international attention as a result of the 1949 Los Angeles evangelistic crusade, L.E. Maxwell contacted the evangelist to inquire concerning Graham's availability to come and speak at PBI.[25] Jerry Beaven, Graham's Executive Secretary at the time, responded

---

[23] Carpenter, *Revive Us Again*, 225-231.
    Dalhouse, 76: "Five years before Graham held his 1957 New York crusade with the help of "modernists," when he was still very much a part of the fundamentalist community, the Joneses were already criticizing their former student."
[24] Dalhouse, 83-84.
[25] L.E. Maxwell personal files—"Billy Graham." There are three files labeled "Billy Graham" in Maxwell's personal files in the Rendall Library Archives. Except where noted for purposes of clarification or elaboration, all letters and documents referred to in this section are from these files. As early as November 22, 1951, Maxwell contacted

TIM W. CALLAWAY

"we will certainly keep Canada in mind as we look forward to the plans for 1953." Maxwell advised in his response that such a visit would be timely since PBI had plans to erect a new "tabernacle" of a size that would qualify the facility as one of the largest auditoriums in Canada used for religious purposes. The men agreed to stay in contact with a goal in mind to having Graham come to PBI at some point in the future.

A form letter dated December 29, 1953, from Billy Graham to the editor of the *Prairie Overcomer* reminds the recipient that "our London evangelistic campaign begins March first at Harringay Arena in London." Graham asks that the March, April and May issues of the school's publication carry "full reports—and, if possible, editorials" and adds his expectation that "the secular press here in America will be giving full coverage."

A March 7, 1954, telegram to "Dr. L.E. Maxwell" reads in part: "Please urge continued prayer by your students for London crusade. More than 1500 decisions for christ (sic) first week greatest spirit of revival we have ever known." A note at the bottom of the telegram in Maxwell's handwriting states: "Folks: that is an everyday prayer request for the next weeks. Who knows, maybe these mtgs will turn into revival such as was seen under the Wesleys."

On March 11, 1954, Maxwell enthusiastically wrote Graham in London to this effect:

We have taken this to the student body and prayer is being offered continually. We are also having the telegram put in on the first page of our School publication, the *Prairie Overcomer*. We are also carrying the content of the telegram to radio land in this area. Thanking God for your testimony and may God bless you "real good" . . .

Graham responded on March 26 by writing:

Dear Dr. Maxwell:

We are in the middle of our fourth week here in London . . . total attendance has been 338,600 . . . 7, 458 recorded decisions for Christ and 75% of those have been first time decisions for salvation. 60% of the

the Billy Graham Evangelistic Association extending an invitation for Graham to come to PBI under several proposed scenarios.

decisions have been on the part of people who had no previous Church connection . . . We are deeply grateful for the prayers of the Faculty and staff. We feel their prayers! . . .

And from Scotland on February 17, 1955, Graham wrote:

Dear Mr. Maxwell:

The repercussions and implications of this crusade will be the most far-reaching we have ever had. Therefore I am asking you if you will ask the faculty, staff and students of Prairie Bible Institute to pray as they have never prayed. We believe that effectual, fervent praying on the part of God's people can be used to bring about a great spiritual revival in Scotland. (emphasis in original)

As far as can be determined, although Billy Graham never ever did visit PBI to speak, it is significant to note that one of his more famous converts from the 1949 Los Angeles crusade apparently did so. Jim Vaus, who had garnered some measure of infamy as a wiretapper for a notorious West Coast gangster, Mickey Cohen, shared his testimony at PBI on April 13, 1954. His message was subsequently edited for publication in the June 1955 issue of the *Prairie Overcomer*.

That Maxwell and PBI were initially recognized as openly supportive of Graham is evident by the fact that on March 16, 1956, a Dr. H.M. Dudley, representing an initiative called The Washington Pilgrimage, wrote "Dr. Maxwell" advising him that Dr. Billy Graham would receive the Clergy Churchman of the Year 1956 award on April 28 in Washington, D.C. Dudley noted that a book of letters from Graham's "friends and admirers" would be presented to him and stated: "You are cordially invited to write a brief message of congratulations and good wishes for this occasion."

No indication was found as to whether or not Maxwell compiled anything in response to this invitation. There is, however, abundant evidence in Maxwell's files that by the mid-1950s the president of PBI was hearing no small amount of criticism from the school's constituency regarding his public support of Billy Graham. The majority of the letters on file came from American readers of the *Prairie Overcomer* or other supporters of Maxwell and the school who lived in the United States.

As early as late 1952, in fact, a Mrs. W.O. Andrews of Webster Groves, Missouri, wrote Maxwell to inquire regarding Billy Graham's support of the newly published Revised Standard Version (RSV) of the Bible as well as Graham's endorsement of a prominent Catholic bishop, Fulton Sheen. Maxwell responded: "I am rather of the opinion that Mr. Graham will yet have to back down in his endorsement of this new Bible" and proceeded to state that the *Prairie Overcomer* did not endorse the RSV nor did the Prairie Book Room sell it. He went on to say that PBI agreed with *The Sunday School Times'* "carefully worded, yet genuine, reproof of Mr. Graham for having endorsed Bishop Sheen in any way." Maxwell then makes a statement that he would reiterate numerous times in years to come to those who were critical of Graham and his ministry:

> Personally, I hesitate to sit in judgment on the man that God is using far more to the winning of souls than He is using those who judge him. I think the habit which has grown up all over this country of knifing fellow-members of the body of Christ has become a spreading fretting leprosy. Contentious for the faith is not the same as "contending for the faith."

In an April 4, 1955, letter from Maxwell to James P. Welliver of Virginia, Minnesota, Maxwell affirmed: "I, too, had wondered about [Graham's] connection with modernists in these large campaigns." In a characteristic Maxwell-ism, he responded to the matter of new converts being sent to modernist churches for follow-up by expressing concern about "putting live chickens under a dead hen." Nonetheless, he again sought the middle ground by writing:

> I am not sure about my own ability to just tell every man where God would have him to serve. I think sometimes of the prophets of old who, in the midst of an apostate nation, stood with their backs to the wall and protested against sin everywhere and anywhere.

As noted previously, it was the 1957 New York City crusade at Madison Square Garden that threw wide the floodgates of criticism toward Billy Graham and his association with modernists. Long before the New York meetings began, however, George Edstrom from the Billy Graham office in Minneapolis telegraphed the *Prairie Overcomer* on September 22, 1956, asking for the magazine's help in clarifying a misrepresentation by media regarding Billy Graham's statements concerning the purpose of his coming to New York City. Obviously, the Billy Graham people felt they had reason to believe Maxwell and PBI would speak in their defense.

But storm clouds were indeed gathering. PBI alumnus George Bethune of Brooklyn, New York, wrote Maxwell in April 1957 as follows:

> The campaign is quite a controversial issue here among the Fundamentalists, and has caused a split in the camp. Many feel that they can give full support to the campaign regardless of the overwhelming majority representation by Modernists on the Committees, etc. Others feel that they cannot give this support because the alliance with our Modernistic enemies is one which has no scriptural support. In many of the churches here there are the "for" and "against" elements, which puts many a pastor "on the spot." . . . I remember when back in Three Hills, I couldn't understand why fundamentalists could be so opposed to the New York campaign and I prematurely judged that such people were jealous of Billy Graham's success as a servant whom the Lord was pleased to use in an outstanding way, but since coming to New York and seeing the situation as it is I now have the deepest sympathy with those (or most of those) whom I had already prejudged. I now realize that with many of the fundamentalists here who feel that they cannot take part in the campaign as it is being planned at present, it is not so much a matter of being jealous in respect to the success of the Billy Graham team's success but being jealous of the name and work of Christ. Although many of us feel that we cannot identify ourselves with the modern prophets of Baal . . .

Maxwell assured Bethune in his response that "a number of us have for some months, or perhaps years, been somewhat alarmed over Billy Graham's latitudinarianism" and registered concern that Graham's "concessions to the modernists" may eventually become "plain compromise."

Missionaries Edith and Stephen Knights wrote Maxwell on June 5, 1957, from "on board J.V.O" concerning the New York crusade with an alternative perspective:

We were sorry we did not get the opportunity to hear Billy Graham, but from all reports the Lord is doing a wonderful work. I have checked up with reliable sources and could not find any confirmation that the counseling was in the hands of the modernists. In fact, this was flatly denied by many good friends whose judgement (sic) I appreciate very much. It appears that this criticism came first from John Rice and is unfounded. But those who have attended the meetings have told us of the Spirit coming down in remarkable power. You will know that the campaign has been extended until July 31st. The numbers that have professed conversion have been very large and there is no doubt that God is laying bare His arm. Some missionaries on board who have attended the meetings have spoken of "the amazing visitation of the Spirit" and of more than 200 prayer meetings spending all night in prayer for the Crusade.

These last two communications indicate something of the difficult position Maxwell faced in knowing how to best handle the growing controversy: he was receiving conflicting perspectives from his own constituency. Nevertheless, it was a problem that was not going to merely disappear.

Articles that Maxwell penned in the August 1957 and November 1957 issues of the *Prairie Overcomer* were perceived as supportive of the New York crusade and met with strong criticism from some of the magazine's readers. Howard B. Carey, Jr., who identified himself as a director of the Christian Business Men's Committee in Oceanside, California, advised Maxwell that his suggestion that it was "the stronghold of prayer for Billy Graham" that was "the one strong front the devil would like to overthrow" was inaccurate. "There is a bigger front Satan would like to destroy; namely, the barrier between the true believers and the unbelievers, between the church and the world," Carey declared.

Maxwell was pointed in his response to Carey making it clear that he had little sympathy for those representing the critical extreme of American fundamentalists on the issue:

Personally, I am glad that we have kept as free as we have from the present controversy over Billy. I have tried to get at the facts and am doing my bet to view impartially this whole matter. Personally I want to beware of the jealousy which has taken hold of certain of our other evangelists relative to Billy Graham. When Bob Jones refuses to graduate anybody who prays for or stands up for Billy Graham—so I am told on good authority—then I think it is too bad. When a leading ACC man wires Billy somewhat to this effect: "We are praying for you that you will either quit preaching or die, "I think that is going pretty far, far too far.

I had Billy Scholfield here and he says you couldn't find a modnerist (sic) anywhere in the organizational functions of the New York campaign, and Billy Scholfield was there for quite some time.

Some of my near and dear friends in the east were very severe in their criticism of Billy Graham . . . In spite of some weaknesses which I see, and which I shall not take the time to mention, I am rather forced to admit that the hand of God is on Billy Graham. This does not mean that I agree with everything he is doing; it simply means that God is using most any of us not because of us but rather in spite of us . . . Many, many souls are being converted through [Graham's] ministry, ten times more than are being converted through the critics of Billy Graham. While there are some things I terribly dislike, I feel that spiritual judgment demands that I keep from straining at the gnats while swallowing the camel. You may be sure that if the time ever comes that I feel God would have me bludgeon the whole matter, I shall very gladly and frankly do so. (emphasis in original)

Ernestine Matthews of Washington, D.C., wanted documentation for Maxwell's claim in the November 1957 *Overcomer* that eleven Catholic priests had come to faith in Christ at the New York campaign. Maxwell advised her that he had heard the report from a Dr. Savage, a speaker at Canadian Keswick that summer. In a letter to Maxwell, Savage stated his information had come from Bob Pierce who had spoken at MARANATHA. Although both inquired, neither Maxwell nor Matthews were able to get confirmation of the story from the Billy Graham Evangelistic Association.

Pastor R.E. Stanley Hunt of Vancouver, Washington, wrote Maxwell on February 22, 1958, expressing reservations about Maxwell's apparent endorsement of Billy Graham. He claimed he had learned that over $16,000.00 of the New York crusade's finances had gone into the treasury of the Council of Churches. Maxwell responded emphasizing his concern that Graham's "very graciousness and generosity with others has rendered him open to weakness in the direction of compromise."

In a letter to Sylvia Ellen Miller of St. Albans, West Virginia, on March 20, 1958, Maxwell again sought a middle ground. "I think that Billy Graham's generosity, which is his strong point and which has been so commendable in the face of a cold, calculating and callous fundamentalism, is turning out to be his greatest weakness." He informed Miller that PBI had recently declined to show the Billy Graham film "Miracle in Manhattan" because "we did not see that we would be much advantaged in having it."

Likewise, Maxwell told William R. Grant in St. Lucia, British West Indies, of his belief that "Billy's strong point is his graciousness." Maxwell went on to warn that "this could prove to be his grave and great weakness" before adding:

> As of now, however, I am of a feeling that I should not come out in any public denunciation of the man. I would rather be careful what I say either in the way or endorsation or condemnation—lest I prove to be an accuser of the brethren. It is easy to be a wholesale critic. It is difficult to find the path of God in the midst of a time of confusion.

"I grant that there are weaknesses and flaws in Billy Graham's inclusiveness," Maxwell stated to Mr. and Mrs. C.W. Powell of Central Point, Oregon. He went on to point out that although Billy Graham had promised to hold meetings in Chicago under the evangelical banner only, certain "dogmatic fundamental men" had stated they would hold a simultaneous evangelistic program "in order to reveal their manifest disagreement with the other entirely evangelical group." Maxwell's frustration is evident as he asks, "Where do we go from here?"

Although Maxwell backed off in his public endorsements of Billy Graham after the late 1957 articles in the *Prairie Overcomer* mentioned above, an event in 1959 is perhaps indicative of the price he believed PBI was paying and would continue to absorb as a result of the ongoing controversy over Billy Graham's public profile. The ministry of a Rev. Larry Love had been recommended to Maxwell by a trusted colleague and Maxwell subsequently inquired of Love as to his availability to speak at PBI's Spring Missionary Conference scheduled for April 17-24, 1960.

When Love responded to Maxwell on November 9, 1959, he informed the PBI president that he was no longer serving as pastor of the church Maxwell had sent the invitation to but had recently taken a position as Missions Representative and Overseas Director for the Billy Graham Evangelistic Association. Nonetheless, Love wrote: "you may be sure that I count it a real privilege to have the opportunity of ministering the Word of God at P.B.I . . ."

Maxwell's enthusiastic response on November 13 directed that Love "should count on some eight to ten messages during the week, making them focus on the deeper Christian life coupled with a missionary emphasis." For some indiscernible reason(s), however, these plans were soon derailed.

Maxwell wrote to Love on December 3 that upon receiving Love's affirmation of his availability to come to Three Hills, the former had been "caught in the cross-fire of things." Maxwell then makes a somewhat curious comment to Love when he states that "ever since your first letter came, <u>with the letterhead</u>, questions have faced us" (<u>emphasis</u> added). The problem, Maxwell said, was Love's affiliation with the Billy Graham Evangelistic Association because of "Billy Graham's inclusivist policies and program." Instructively, Maxwell wrote:

> I want to assure you personally I can have nothing to do with the spirit of fight and protest such as comes out in the "Sword of the Lord" and other such publications. I heartily recognize that the hand of God is on Billy Graham. To me it seems very wicked to shred a man anointed of God as Billy Graham must be. On the other hand, there are many true Christian ministers who sense and feel the weaknesses of the inclusivist policy, so much so that while not wanting to touch the Lord's anointed feel that they cannot on the other hand endorse certain trends of inclusivism.
>
> I am therefore caught in the cross-fire of things. Some of my close associates feel that if you knew of the delicate and touchy situation in our Northwest world you would not wonder at our inability just to snap our fingers in the face of those who can, and may, do us unending injury. Temperamentally, I am given to snapping the finger at the thoughts of other men, but a number of my fellow-workers feel we will have to forego your coming at this time. I am compelled to agree . . . Brother, it pains me thus to write you. I only do so to save us all from a possible worse regret later. Please do not I feel I am against you or Billy or your God-honoured efforts.

This is a remarkable statement by Maxwell from a number of perspectives. Obviously, he either already was or believed he very easily could become enmeshed in a significant controversy over a Billy Graham associate coming to PBI as a conference speaker. Beyond this lone reality, however, numerous important questions emerge.

How did the letterhead on Love's letter contribute to Maxwell's predicament? What was the "delicate and touchy situation" he made reference to? Was this pressure primarily an internal matter at PBI or primarily originating from beyond the campus? Who and what is intended by Maxwell's reference to "our Northwest world?" What did the word "inability" convey? And who would have been capable of doing the school "unending injury?"

Ted S. Rendall told me he had no immediate recollection of this event when interviewed for this book. He did remark, however, that it was not uncommon during the years he worked with Maxwell for PBI to have a number of American staff members, including Bible school faculty, who harbored strong views against Billy Graham for the evangelist's perceived associations with modernists. Rendall indicated it was possible some of these may have approached Maxwell privately and threatened some kind of public showdown if Rev. Love was permitted to speak at Prairie.

Perhaps some clue to Maxwell's decision with regard to Love is found in considering the increasing number of letters that came to Prairie well into the 1960s that conveyed very strong opinions regarding the school's perceived stance on the Billy Graham issue. Despite Maxwell's belief that "Billy Graham is blessedly anointed and blessedly used of God," a number of letters suggested, both explicitly and implicitly, that continued support for Graham could cost PBI in perhaps more ways than one.

For instance, a May 15, 1960, letter from E.J. Brandt of Renton, Washington, advised Maxwell that the letter-writer's step-daughter was thinking of applying to PBI. However, a close friend of hers had informed them that "the Billy Graham films are used there and that Prairie Bible School, or rather the institute, contributes toward Billy Graham's work." Accordingly, wrote Brandt:

> If it is true, then my step-daughter _____ _____ will not receive any financial help whatsoever from me. I will not have any part in the awful apostasy of which Billy Graham is the "king pin." (emphasis in original)

When Maxwell spoke positively in the January 1967 *Prairie Overcomer* of the Billy Graham sponsored Congress on Evangelism that was held in Berlin in 1966, Mrs. J.A. Watson of Ordway, Colorado, wrote the editor on March 6, 1967, saying that her pastor had read Maxwell's words "to cast suppission (sic) upon you and the school." She concluded by stating:

> We have a son who wishes to come to school at Prairie Bible Institute and I suppose that is partly behind [the pastor's] remarks as his sons are attending B.J.U. in South Carolina . . . What I really want is your personal testimony on where you stand, not only for me but for many others who now have a doubt planted in their minds.

Dr. Jack W. Murray, President of Bible Evangelism, Inc., wrote Maxwell on February 17, 1967. "As far as I am concerned," he stated, "the Berlin Congress on Evangelism was the "mush of concession to the ecumenical movement"" and urged Maxwell to reconsider his opinion.[26]

A November 12, 1965, letter to Victor L. Callaway, my father and then Extension Director at PBI (thereby in charge of scheduling the school's music teams for promotional ministry in churches), offers another angle on the Billy Graham matter. Pastor Frank R. Hamblen of Lima, Ohio, stated that before his church would confirm the visit of a musical team from Prairie, the church board had asked him to write to ask regarding "the position of P.B.I. concerning Ecumenical Evangelism." In a day when some outstanding evangelists had begun using unbelievers and enemies of the Gospel in their sponsoring bodies, Hamblen informed PBI that "Calvary Bible Church is taking a firm stand against this method of evangelism."

Following a PBI Board of Administrators discussion on this particular letter, Maxwell responded to Hamblen on January 6, 1966, saying:

> Although the Board of Administrators of the Prairie Bible Institute cannot endorse some of the alliances and affiliations entered into by the Billy Graham Evangelistic Association, we must recognize that God has greatly used their ministry of the Graham team to the salvation of many souls.

---

[26] L.E. Maxwell personal file—"Berlin Congress."

The Board of Administrators' minutes from that occasion shed additional light on the nature of the board's discussion and read:

A.H. Muddle moved and H. Elliott seconded that Mr. Maxwell respond to Rev. Hamblen of Lima, OH, pointing out that certain good students here at PBI would be grieved and unable to understand if we take a strong position against the God-owned instruments of their salvation.[27]

Hamblen responded to Maxwell with almost four pages of single-spaced text, contending that as for those students who purportedly came to faith in Christ under Graham's ministry, he had similar folk in his church. "If they are grieved," he argued, "let it be at the Word of God. It is hardly my responsibility to withhold truth because someone might be hurt by it."

Such correspondence as this indicates that despite Maxwell's attempts to walk and his preference for pursuing a middle ground on the Billy Graham controversy, he grasped that such a stance would come with a steep price attached. To thus have openly supported Graham by permitting a member of his staff to speak at a PBI conference may have become untenable given that the price tag may well have included possible strife among PBI's own faculty/staff, the loss of prospective students and/or financial support, inaccessibility to some churches for PBI and a loss of respect for Maxwell personally and PBI collectively among other fundamentalist organizations.

In essence, it is apparent that both Maxwell and PBI eventually and perhaps somewhat reluctantly conceded to the anti-modernists in the Billy Graham dispute. Although this may be perceived as significantly different from actually siding with the anti-Graham forces, it was also demonstrably something less than a full-throated endorsement of the American evangelist and the neo-evangelical agenda he represented.

On what was to emerge as the defining issue of mid-twentieth century fundamentalism, Maxwell's initial enthusiasm for Graham eventually dwindled into a mediocre endorsement fraught with reservations and caveats. Such a conclusion is reached on the basis of several indicators.

Firstly, in one of the last personal letters found in Maxwell's file on the topic, he writes the following to Mrs. Clyde W. Painton of Poplar

---

[27] L.E. Maxwell personal file—"Accreditation," and PBI Board of Administration minutes, January 5, 1966.

Bluff, Missouri, who had stated her concern that "some of our preachers are wanting to use the Billy Graham films to win the young people to Christ." Maxwell responded in a manner in keeping with his long-standing adherence to fundamentalism's preference for a clear line of demarcation between the church and the world.

> I think, however, many of [Graham's] methods will lead the next generation to compromise with the show business. I fear that some of his methods even in his inclusivist policies will lead to a breakdown between fundamentalism and modernism and between the church and the world. It is difficult to draw the line between the church and the world after his presentations. These are some of the regrettable features from which the church may yet reap a bad harvest. In fact, we are already in days of confusion and compromise and worldliness, such as you knew nothing of in your younger days.

Secondly, in an undated paper that Maxwell prepared on "Separation in the Scriptures—as it is related to present-day religious problems" (of which the Billy Graham controversy may well have been one the writer had in mind) he summarized his thinking by applying it to Billy Graham in this way:

> And it seems evident to us that it is just at the same point of his graciousness and generosity that Billy Graham, so much like the great and godly Jehoshaphat and so used of God, is likewise sowing the seeds of compromise that will reap a frightful harvest in the course of time. The God-ordained gulf calling for Scriptural protest and separation is disappearing. The liberals are capitalizing on his compromise. Their organizational life is being re-invigorated and perpetuated by his inclusivism. Evangelical Christians are losing their ability to say No. Their unprotesting presence can not only be tolerated abut be converted into a contribution to keep alive those very hierarchies that are an abomination to God and a stumbling block to men.

Note that whereas Maxwell had previously spoken of Graham's "concessions" to modernists, in this document he conclusively states that "the liberals are capitalizing on his compromise."

Lastly, when Billy Graham came to Alberta for evangelistic crusades in August of 1980 at Edmonton and in August of 1981 at Calgary, PBI's response to these initiatives in Maxwell's last year in the classroom was, at best, tepid. Minutes of the school's Administrative Team regarding the Billy Graham Crusade in Edmonton on August 10-17 read:

> It was agreed that we will not take an official Institute position, but will leave the matter to individuals to determine whether they will attend or participate. It was noted with regret that in a recent article of Mr. Graham's in *The Saturday Evening Post*, he has spent the entire article eulogizing the pope.[28]

* * *

In summation, the evidence is clear that L.E. Maxwell consistently opposed any form of academic accreditation during his primary years in leadership at PBI. As well, the enthusiasm he initially demonstrated in the early 1950s in terms of a willingness to be associated with Billy Graham's ministry waned considerably over the next thirty years.

Research suggests that despite some of his personal regrets regarding Graham's willingness to associate with modernists in his crusades, Maxwell nevertheless attempted to focus on what he considered to be the more important reality: souls were being converted to Christ as a result of Graham's ministry. As the end of the 1950s neared, however, Maxwell concluded that bringing a Graham representative to PBI as a conference speaker would cause some sort of irreparable damage to the school. As reluctant as he may have been to do so, with regard to what came to be the most controversial issue in fundamentalist circles in the mid-twentieth century, Maxwell permitted the fundamentalist forces to prevail. There is thus a sense in which, at least as it relates to this most definitive of issues among mid-twentieth century fundamentalists, the "fighting fundamentalist" of Prairie's early years became, to borrow from the title of a recent book, "the reluctant fundamentalist."[29]

---

[28] PBI Archives in Ted S. Rendall Library: PBI Administrative Team minutes, January 30, 1980.

[29] Mohsin Hamid, *The Reluctant Fundamentalist* (New York: Harcourt, Inc., 2007) is a fascinating novel depicting the personal tensions encountered by a Princeton University educated young man from Pakistan who was working in the financial world in New

CHAPTER FOURTEEN

The militancy factor
in PBI's fundamentalism

Even if we were to uncritically accept Stackhouse's view that militancy was the primary distinguishing characteristic of American fundamentalism in the twentieth century, there is ample evidence that, contrary to what Stackhouse argues, such militancy did, in fact, thrive at PBI during the L.E. Maxwell era. This reality was largely due to the personality and theological perspectives of Maxwell himself. As previously noted, although there is some legitimacy in suggesting that Maxwell's vehement rhetoric mellowed with age, the title of the last book he compiled toward the end of his active teaching career, *World Missions: Total War*, is an apt reminder of the pugilistic mindset that typified the former member of the U.S. Army throughout his life.

Stackhouse, we have seen, states that the theological controversies of the 1920s brought out fundamentalism's "chief characteristic of militancy." This he succinctly defines as "a crusading spirit against what it saw to be modern threats to the faith." To this he adds:

> In arriving at a Canadian definition, then . . . we can provisionally appropriate the leading characteristics of American fundamentalism: militant opposition to modernity—especially modern ideas (liberal theology, biblical criticism, and evolution chief among them)—and separation from all who are not wholly pure in their convictions and associations. This study will demonstrate that there was a Canadian fundamentalism *of this sort* in the twentieth century (exemplified by T.T.

York City at the time of the terrorist attacks on that city on September 11, 2001. Surprisingly and reluctantly, he found his sympathies returning to his Muslim roots despite the fact that he was now earning a very comfortable living as a member of an affluent Western society. He eventually left his job in New York to return to his original home in Lahore, Pakistan.

Shields and discussed in part I, chapter I), but that it was not in fact central to Canadian evangelicalism.[1] (*emphasis* in original)

An important matter that requires brief attention here is objectively establishing how the terms "militant" or "militancy" are to be understood in concluding whether or not the terms can or cannot be accurately used with respect to L.E. Maxwell. In this regard, the 2009 edition of *The Random House Dictionary* assigns the following virtually identical meanings to both "militant" and "militancy." When used as an adjective, the term means: "1) vigorously active and aggressive, esp. in support of a cause: *militant reformers*; and 2) engaged in warfare, fighting." When employed as a noun, the term means: "3) a militant person, or 4) a person engaged in warfare or combat." The synonyms listed are: "belligerent, combative, contentious."[2]

Based on Stackhouse's lone chapter on T.T. Shields, whom he cites as the primary Canadian example of what a militant fundamentalist looked like or sounded like, it is apparent that Stackhouse's portrayal of Shields does indeed reflect the definition of "militancy" as supplied by *The Random House Dictionary*. In Stackhouse's judgment, Shields was consistently belligerent, combative and contentious in his attempts to defend orthodox theology.[3]

As for our purposes, this chapter will demonstrate that, in his own way het similar to T.T. Shields, L.E. Maxwell was likewise a militant fundamentalist. He not only proudly embraced militancy, but was more

---

[1]   Stackhouse, *Canadian Evangelicalism in the Twentieth Century*, 11.

[2]   *The Random House Dictionary* (New York: Random House, 2009).

[3]   It bears repeating that ascribing such terms as "belligerent" and "contentious" to any individual has its problems. For example, Leslie K. Tarr's sympathetic treatment of the life of T.T. Shields in *Shields of Canada* (Grand Rapids, MI; Baker Book House, 1967) suggests he would presumably have interpreted such terms more positively with regard to Shields than does Stackhouse. Further, see David T. Priestley, ed., *Memory and Hope: Strands of Canadian Baptist History* (Waterloo, ON: Wilfred Laurier University Press, 1996) where Mark Parent, "The Irony of Fundamentalism: T.T. Shields and the Person of Christ," 183-196, argues that the type of fundamentalism practiced by Shields was owing to his theological conviction regarding inerrancy of Scripture, not his psychological make-up. That being said, in the same collection of essays, David R. Elliott writes in, "Three Faces of Baptist Fundamentalism in Canada: Aberhart, Maxwell, and Shields," 177: "The most militant fundamentalist in North America during the first half of the century was T.T. Shields of Toronto." Note in particular Elliott's judgment that Shields was the most militant fundamentalist, not just in Canada, but in North America!

than capable of periodically demonstrating belligerence, combativeness and contentiousness in his attacks on modernism.

It should be pointed out for the sake of those who may wish to split hairs, semantically speaking, that *The Random House Dictionary* defines "militarism" as a noun with three facets of meaning: "I) a strong military spirit or policy, 2) the principle or policy of maintaining a large military establishment, 3) the tendency to regard military efficiency as the supreme ideal of the state and to subordinate all other interests to those of the military."[4] Reference has been previously made to the slogan that ruled at PBI throughout the Maxwell era—Training Disciplined Soldiers for Christ. The spartan conditions of student and dormitory life at the school have been noted along with the strict regulations that governed such matters as dress and gender relations. Each of these factors contributed to the militaristic ambience that prevailed at PBI during the period of time under evaluation here.[5] The salient point to be made is to affirm that both "militancy" and "militarism" were active factors in the kind of fundamentalism exemplified at PBI from 1922 until virtually the end of L.E. Maxwell's career as the primary administrator and instructor at Prairie.

By way of a final introductory comment to this chapter, a somewhat lengthy citation from Stackhouse is offered. Readers are encouraged to bear in mind Stackhouse's assertion concerning Prairie's stance on such topics as the United Church of Canada and evolution when reading the contrary evidence that is advanced in this chapter. As will become evident, L.E. Maxwell did in fact excel in employing militant rhetoric on some of the very themes Stackhouse claims he was silent on. Curiously, in the brief portions of this citation we have chosen to underline, Stackhouse appears to essentially contradict himself with respect to the perspective he maintains throughout his book with regard to Prairie's identity as an institution that was significantly different from that associated with American fundamentalism. He wrote:

> L.E. Maxwell and other leaders at Prairie Bible Institute were alert to changes not only in Canadian society but also across the world. In the Institute magazine, Maxwell and his associate editors regularly

---

4   *The Random House Dictionary.*
5   Many of the news stories written on PBI during its first thirty or forty years referred to conditions at the school as "spartan."

commented on 'The World in the Light of the Word.' In this column the editors concentrated on the forces of evil they saw to be most dangerous to the health of the church and the spread of the gospel. The three most frequently mentioned foes were modernism (and its supposed offspring, the ecumenical movement), communism and Roman Catholicism. As did other fundamentalists, Prairie's leaders often linked the three. All opposed the gospel, all were militant, and all posed some threat to the church in some part of the world. Communism and Roman Catholicism especially were dangerous because of their commitments to world domination, and the Prairie editors were quick to spot attempts by either to extend its influence in Canada or the United States. Modernism was an internal problem, a cancer in the church—although Prairie's leaders seem to have had little first-hand contact with it: most of their references are to newspaper articles and their most frequent target was the distant fundamentalists' favourite foil, liberal preacher Harry Emerson Fosdick of New York City.

Indeed, as the years rolled on and Prairie continued to expand, there is little evidence of actual engagement with these foes, whether in debate, public protest, or political action. The enemies, even modernism, seem at one remove at least from Prairie and its constituency: dangers against which Prairie was bulwark, but still distant dangers for most readers of its warnings. This apparent absence of contact is extraordinary when one considers the large presence of the United Church on the prairies, the church most evangelicals viewed with disaffection if not outright hostility, and Prairie's avowed identity as a militant opponent of modernism. Unexpectedly rare, also, are references to evolution. Prairie clearly eschewed anything close to evolutionary science, but this was not at all the animating issue it was in American fundamentalism. Indeed, in at least one five-year period, 1960-4, the *Prairie Overcomer* did not mention evolution at all. Prairie Bible Institute, then, seems a centre of a community only indirectly involved with these forces of evil, content to set out its alternative rather than contend with them directly. This lack of engagement makes sense, therefore, only if Prairie is not seen as essentially a 'fighting fundamentalist' school, but rather as an evangelical institution preoccupied with preparing missionaries.[6] (emphasis added)

---

[6]   Stackhouse, 85-86.

What follows is an examination of several specific areas wherein something of the militant nature of L.E. Maxwell's orientation is apparent. In at least two of these spheres, the United Church and the topic of evolution, it will be obvious that Maxwell was far more combative and belligerent than Stackhouse allows. Accordingly, let the record show what those of us who sat under his teaching knew well: L.E. Maxwell did not hesitate to militantly contend for what he believed to be historic theological truth. Were he alive today, he would no doubt consider it an honor to be labeled as one who militantly contended for the faith.

Militantly defending the Christian faith

A casual review of the contents of a file labeled "Militancy" in L.E. Maxwell's personal files yields ample evidence of how interested the former United States Army soldier was with respect to any proposed changes affecting the rigid discipline that governed life in the U.S. military. As well, there is an abundance of material in the file reflecting Maxwell's keen sensitivity to engaging the militaristic themes in Scripture with regard to living the Christian life.[7]

Among the file's documents is a hardback booklet entitled *Salvation Soldiery* authored "By The General of the Salvation Army." It is particularly noteworthy that the chapter called "A Good Soldier of Jesus Christ" contains a significant amount of underlining and numerous marginal notes in Maxwell's handwriting.[8] Maxwell seems particularly taken with two of the author's descriptions of a good soldier for he underlined both "A Good Soldier Makes War His Business" and "A Good Soldier of Jesus Christ is Always a Fighting Man."

In the margin next to the former theme Maxwell wrote: "Shoot to kill—don't be forever aiming, aiming to do this and that but never shooting—shoot to kill." Among the sentences he underlined under the latter designation are: ". . . is not fighting the very essence of and meaning, and bone and marrow of a good soldiery? And you cannot have it without.

---

[7] PBI Archives in Ted S. Rendall Library: L.E. Maxwell personal file—"Militancy."
[8] The Founder of the Salvation Army, *Salvation Soldiery* (London: The Salvationist Publishing & Supplies, Ltd., n.d.). 39-46.

And is not fighting, the spirit of war, the liking for it, and the habit of it, the very essence of all true Christian Soldiery likewise . . . ?"

Maxwell expected his fellow staff members at PBI to likewise embrace the significance of the militaristic motif. As he wrote in *Principles and Practices of Prairie Bible Institute*, the official policy manual for staff at PBI: "A soldierly attitude is fundamental in our close inter-relationships, especially toward our intimate campus friends."[9] From other documents found in the "Militancy" file, it is apparent that Maxwell periodically addressed regular staff meetings along these lines. Hand-written notes labeled "Militant Men and Women" and dated "Staff: February 11/67" contain statements such as: "Who is on the Lord's side? There is no neutrality in this war nor is there any discharge, for the multitudes and masses are in entrenched rebellion against King El Shaddai;" "I get concerned when I hear that we talk warfare but fear it. I don't resent the charge. One day when I resented it I learned that I must be guilty or I'd not feel that way;" "I feel we need to examine ourselves—whether ye be in the faith that fights!" and "We are orthodox, learned, theological, proper and precise, but where is the fight?"

Another loose document written by Maxwell's hand and located in the file states: "Peaceful co-existence: 'O God, save me from any doctrinal anodyne that breeds: That fatal inertia on the eve of battle.'" In a third set of notes called "The Lost Chord of Christianity," dated October 8, 1961, and sounding like it was also the text for an address to a meeting of PBI's staff, Maxwell says:

> As hundreds of young people are coming to us for training, and since our motto is "Training disciplined Soldiers for Christ" then we must face the fact that complete capitulation to the Captain of our salvation spells conscription for total war on every front. Christian friend, did you ever notice how Paul's epistles fairly bristle with battle terms? He speaks of fighting the good fight and warring the good warfare. But good soldiery is largely the lost chord in our Christianity. We have gone soft. We have sheathed the sword. We draw no blood. Many of our churches have become lovely Kinsman's clubs. As Christians we want no war, no conflict, no fighting—no fighting, mind you, no fighting. I would sound the trumpet alarm against the deadly foe of aggressive Christian warfare.

---

[9]   Principle and Practices of Prairie Bible Institute, (n.d.), 1-2.

Maxwell's American identity and his affinity for militarism are both evident via the markings on a loose newspaper clipping also located in the "Militancy" file. Speaking of a new hymnbook proposed for use by both the Anglican and United Churches of Canada, Maxwell isolated the following words by Canadian reporter Sidney Macbeth:

Apparently the book will not contain "Onward Christian soldiers, marching as to war . . ." This should surprise no one . . . perhaps it is a mite too militaristic in this United States draft-dodger and armed forces deserter-infested country. That the "war" of the hymn is against the causes of the dodged and deserted wars is beside the point; sin, evil, war, soldier, Devil and fight are taboo words in today's tangle-footed large "established" churches.[10]

Maxwell's high regard for the military metaphor and his capacity to conduct himself accordingly with respect to living the Christian faith was not lost on those he met even on a casual basis. For example, a reporter for the Medicine Hat Daily News wrote:

The Brooks Gospel Mission hall was filled to capacity last night as eager listeners thronged to hear Rev. L.E. Maxwell, principal of the Prairie Bible Institute at Three Hills. For the militant, steel-haired Kansas-born leader of the largest Bible college in Canada, it may have appeared a small crowd compared with his regular audience of over 1,200 students[11]

J.B. Tweter, in a 1949 feature for *Christian Life* magazine, described Maxwell as follows:

Despite his mere 170 pound weight, Maxwell has the constitution of an ox and the rugged physique of a pugilist. The tremendous drive which these give him is easily his outstanding visible characteristic. His preaching is like his personality—razor-sharp, pungent, uncompromising[12]

---

[10] L. E. Maxwell personal file—"Militancy;" Sidney Macbeth, "Gates of Hell Can Never . . . ," unknown newspaper, September 5, 1970.

[11] "L.E. Maxwell personal file—"Militancy;" Prairie B.I. Started on Shoestring Now Flourishes with 1,200 Enrolment," Medicine Hat Daily News, November 13, 1948.

[12] Ibid., J.B. Tweter, "Prophet of the Plains," Christian Life, 18, May 1949.

Maxwell's fascination with the Christian life as warfare consistently flowed in both his spoken and written communication. Consider, for example, this "personal word from the Principal of Prairie Bible Institute" located in the "Militancy" file which states:

> Dear Fellow Soldiers: And soldiers we are if we are saved—enlisted for life in the King's own command. John Bunyan was right when he called ours a "Holy War." All the true and faithful have "climbed the steep ascent of heaven through peril, toil, and pain." Paul's epistles bristle with battle terms. At peace with a world that is at war with God? Never! Not till sin's fierce war has ceased. But today's war rages on and on, ruthless, unrelenting, unrepenting.[13]

So too, an article by Maxwell entitled "A Militant Faith" advised readers of the *Prairie Pastor* that "warfare with the world" should be the norm and not the exception for true believers.[14]

The annual "Music Nights" that PBI's Music Department coordinated for several years for presentation at large auditoriums in Edmonton and Calgary were replete with numerous songs advancing both the missionary theme and the notion of the Christian life as warfare.[15] Prairie's 1972 Jubilee Service that was presented in the same cities as well as at Three Hills featured missionary songs such as "How Long Must They Wait?" "Coming, Coming, Yes They Are," "Ten Thousand Times Ten Thousand." As well, pieces with a distinct military theme such as "Onward, Christian Soldiers," "As a Volunteer," and "I'm on the Battlefield," were included. Maxwell's message for the event was entitled "Disciplined Soldiers."

An important question is appropriate at this point. Given L.E. Maxwell's firm commitment to a militant expression of the Christian life, what did such look like or sound like in his day to day ministry at Three Hills and beyond? What follows might be described as an attempt to hear L.E. Maxwell at work.

---

13 The document is dated March 1947.

14 L.E. Maxwell, "A Militant Faith," in *The Prairie Pastor*, 4, No. 12; (December 1931), I.

15 See Chapter Twelve in this book, footnote 46, regarding Maxwell's letter to Mrs. Faith Imbach.

His militancy versus modernism in general

Chapter Eight cited several examples from Maxwell's writing wherein he boldly warned of and challenged the dangers of both modernist theology and those who advanced the same such as Harry Emerson Fosdick, the famous modernist pastor in New York City. As was evident in those citations, Maxwell's rhetoric at times could be razor-like.

Part of the purpose of this chapter is to go beyond the general brickbats that Maxwell periodically hurled from afar at modernists and their messages. We will note several specific instances where he aggressively went on the offensive in challenging Canadian figures who publicly advanced perspectives contrary to his understanding of the basic tenets of the historic Christian faith.

On January 27, 1961, L.E. Maxwell penned what he labeled "An Open Letter" to Dr. Frank Jones, a professor at McMaster University in Hamilton, Ontario, Canada. Jones had been featured on a radio program over the Canadian Broadcasting Corporation on January 23.[16] Somewhat ironically, it was his suspicion of theological modernism at McMaster that helped earn Toronto pastor T.T. Shields the reputation of a militant fundamentalist as presented by Stackhouse and others. As well, given what we have previously noted regarding there being some indication that Maxwell's rhetoric mellowed as he aged, it should be pointed out that in 1961 when this letter was written he would have been 65 years of age.

Maxwell begins the letter on a cordial enough note, explaining "I write as Principal of the Prairie Bible Institute, a school with over 1,200 students already on the foreign fields, and as editor of the *Prairie Overcomer*, a paper with some 60,000 subscribers." He acknowledges that he knows what it is to receive letters from "mere ranters trying to set me right" and states that he trusts Jones "can appreciate that I am not merely railing or ranting." He concludes the first paragraph with "while I do write without rancour (sic) I write as resolutely as you spoke on the radio."

In the second paragraph of the typewritten letter of almost four pages, Maxwell however becomes noticeably combative. Due to the frequency of the rhetorical barbs he offers Jones, the letter is quoted here at some length:

---

[16] L.E. Maxwell personal file—"Philosophy."

Let me say at once that I most thoroughly abominate your false infidelic philosophy. I must deny your arrogant and presumptive a priori—that Christ and true Christianity (two inseparables), are like heathen religions, merely "man-made". How can you presume, for instance, that the martyrs for Christ died for a daydream, died for a faith that was a cipher, an empty abstraction, a mere faith in their faith. Of course you first declined to this false philosophy by stripping God of His Personality. After that Christian faith can be but fiction, a mental hallucination—"man-made". Don't you think you would be more honest by ceasing to pay lip-service to the benefits, so-called, of religions? Why not at least be consistent by lining up with your company, the infidel communists?

How can you, by the wildest imagination, account for the conversion of Saul of Tarsus? Don't come up with that unbelievable excuse that the man suffered an epileptic fit on the Damascan road. Am I to believe that this man under a mental fit of some kind become so transformed thereby that he wrote what scholars of all these ages have declared to be "the profoundest book in existence" (Coleridge)? Of course I refer to the epistle to the Romans. That book carefully studied might do you a world of good.

I suspect you may still agree with that maxim of Christ: "By their fruits ye shall know them." And I find it not difficult to behold the kind of fruit which your sociological reasonings produce. The present delinquencies among the young cry aloud their accusations from the house-tops. "The curse uncaused does not come." On the other hand we here at Prairie Bible Institute have witnessed hundreds of heart-and-life transformations, all through what you so conclusively call a "man-made" faith, a mere make-believe . . . When I face your glaring conclusions about the "man-made" Christian religion, and then turn to the facts of gospel transformations, I am compelled to ask, "Do men gather grapes of thorns, or figs of thistles?" Plain honesty compels me to conclude, Dr. Jones, that your "thorn" and "thistle" philosophies, have not, and cannot, produce this kind of good fruit. Is it any wonder under such false tutelage frustrated young folks become like the blind man in the dark room chasing the black cat that is not there. Yet you keep avowing that such religions, any and all, have their benefits—if only the illusioned believe sufficiently in the black cat to keep up the chase. Small wonder that Paul said of such philosophers: "Professing themselves to be wise, they became fools." (Rom. 1:22).

Presumably you have Baptist forbears, or Baptist connections, since you are in (what was once) an honourable Baptist University You are well aware that McMaster was founded by Bible-believing men who would turn over in their graves if they had heard your bold unbelief over the C.B.C. on January 23. You cannot brush off the fact that you owe your present position and compensation to the Blood—bought faith you patronizingly deny. What can truth lovers conclude as to such ethics? Presumably they are quite in keeping with your sociological meanderings. "By their fruits we know them.

As a matter of ethics I must ask: May Christ's sentence upon your unbelief be applicable when He said: "Light is come into the world; and men love darkness rather than light because their deeds are evil?" So said the keenest and the kindest Judge you and I will ever face, and face Him we must. If we are refusing Him our faith—His resurrection is one of the best attested facts of history—we had better make doubly sure that the Judge's condemnation has no least application to us. Make doubly sure there is no secret passion that bribes and suborns the intellect. (Be assured that "the lusts of the mind" are more fallen and treacherous than those of the drunkard or the dopester). Make doubly sure there is no inner desire that dreads Christ's entrance. I say in all sincerity, make sure there are no dark deeds, whether manifest or merely mental, that shelter themselves from His accusing light. And as you honestly and fearlessly conduct such an unshrinking search you may soon discover that the solution to spiritual darkness lies not via the test tube of a sociological analysis, but in the natural, the hidden, the age-long refusal of man to submit to Christ.

You and I may be about the same age. There was a day in 1923 when I had an interview with a professor of McMaster University. I had contemplated attending that school. But as I listened to your "University of the Air" lecture I could not help but wonder whatever a Christian young man or woman would do after he had undergone your bold unbelief and brainwashing. Let me pass on the picture left me, and not left me alone, by your lecture. I could only see a man of abounding self-confidence away yonder in his self-constructed minaret, calling for, and himself paying, unquestioning obeisance to an undoubted ability, apart from any least experience with the Lord Christ, to assay any and all religions, all the while condescendingly permitting the Son of God a place in his religious polyglot. I wonder if you realize the eminence from which you purveyed such a conclusive assay. God's word has you photographed as one who goes in circles: "Ever learning and never able to come to the knowledge of the truth." And from Paul this appropriate word: "But the natural man receiveth not the things of the Spirit of God: for they are foolishness unto him: neither can he know them, because they are spiritually discerned," (I Cor. 2:14).

Why not come down to the foot of the Crucified where the rest of us have had to learn and unlearn—unlearn all but Christ? If you are an honest doubter and not a mere trifler with truth, then I believe you will follow the clue of Christ laid down in John 7:17, where He puts into the hand of every honest skeptic a key that will unlock the truth as to His deity . . .

That clue given by Christ in John 7:17 will lead to certainty. At the same time it is at once a perfect test of any man as to whether he is a sincere skeptic or a trifler. Don't follow the clue if you do not want to obey the light. There is light enough in God's revelation to guide any man who wants to know, in order that he may do, God's will. There is left darkness aplenty to confound those who are willfully blind. God's word thus takes the wise in their own craftiness, and by a stethoscopic test, not of the head acumen but of heart willingness, lets each man determine his own destiny . . .

Trusting to hear from you and that we may together meet Him who loved us and gave Himself to the Cross for our redemption, I am,

Yours cordially in Christ,
PRAIRIE BIBLE INSTITUTE

L.E. Maxwell, Principal [17]

I found no indication as to whether or not Dr. Jones ever responded to Maxwell's letter. Nonetheless, a few comments are in order with respect

---

[17] Every attempt was made to reproduce the letter as originally written including certain spelling and punctuation errors such as the absence of question marks where they would have been appropriate.

to elements of Maxwell's letter that prompt me to submit it as an example of his capacity for the kind of militancy Stackhouse maintains was the exclusive domain of the strident T.T. Shields in Canada during the twentieth century.

Despite Maxwell's initial assertion that he writes "without rancour" (sic), one cannot help but wonder how any gentleman would respond to a communication from an unknown source informing him that "I most thoroughly abominate your false infidelic philosophy." In this context as in perhaps any similar context, it seems obvious that the words "abominate," "false" and "infidelic" serve as combative and contentious terminology hardly conducive to constructive dialogue. It is not difficult to conceive that any self-respecting individual so addressed would immediately feel under attack and inclined to assume a defensive frame of mind. Given the nature of Maxwell's opening salvo, one cannot help but wonder why Jones would seriously consider the former's invitation in the conclusion of the letter for further interaction from Jones.

Further, Maxwell makes several bold insinuations regarding the character of Jones' integrity suggesting that the professor is arrogant, presumptive, not completely honest, inconsistent and unethical. At one point Maxwell claims communists would be right at home in Jones' ideological camp. Elsewhere, he infers that if Jones was truly ethical he would recognize that both his employment and compensation are illegitimate since they are owing to "the Blood-bought faith you patronizingly deny."

Maxwell's well-documented disdain for advanced education comes through in his references to Jones' "sociological reasonings" and "sociological meanderings" and the reference to "the blind man in the dark room chasing the black cat that is not there." He castigates the professor's "thorn" and "thistle" philosophies, accuses him of "false tutelage" and implies that he qualifies as one the Apostle Paul had in mind when he wrote "professing themselves to be wise, they became fools." In essence, Maxwell at one point essentially demeans man's intellect by informing Jones that "'the lusts of the mind' _are more fallen and treacherous_ than those of the drunkard or the dopester." (emphasis added)

It is useful to bear in mind here what has been previously stated regarding a term such as "militant" and associated words such as "combative" or "belligerent" being somewhat necessarily subjective in nature depending on variables like the experience of the person applying the designation or the context in which the term is used. Nonetheless, it is my judgment that Maxwell's letter to Dr. Jones contains rhetoric that unquestionably affirms the qualifications of the long-time president of Prairie Bible Institute to belong to that sector of North American twentieth-century fundamentalists who displayed a decided propensity for militancy.

Such was articulated by said fundamentalists by militantly advocating what they considered "the truth" and militantly attacking what they considered falsehood. Nor did they hesitate, as the above letter to Jones indicates, to come perilously close to employing *ad hominem* attacks in such diatribes. This was often done at the expense of compassion thereby lending credibility to George Marsden's claim that "a fundamentalist is an evangelical who is angry about something."[18]

His militancy versus The United Church of Canada

Contrary to Stackhouse's claim that L.E. Maxwell had minimal engagement with the United Church of Canada, the research conducted for this book discovered the very opposite to be true. Abundant evidence exists that Maxwell did in fact interact with local United Church parishoners and clergy concerning the modernistic teachings of the denomination. Included here are selected letters from Maxwell's personal files as well as reference to several articles in the *Prairie Pastor* wherein he publicly reproaches specific United Church clergymen.

An undated, hand-written letter on PBI letterhead from Maxwell begins with the salutation "Dear Swalwell-ites." Presumably the recipients are residents of Swalwell, Alberta, a small hamlet just a few miles south of Three Hills. The letter's contents make it clear that Maxwell did not mince his words in offering advice as to whether or not these people should prolong their affiliation with the local United Church and its minister. Of particular note here is his use of some of the standard texts of Scripture employed by American fundamentalists regarding the necessity of separation from modernists.

I hear you have the intention of going to the United Church minister tomorrow—to threaten him that you will leave the church unless he

---

[18] See Chapter Three of this book, footnote 65.

preaches the gospel. The plan is not very good, I fear, for the following reasons:

1. If a man does not preach the gospel of his own volition how can he do so by compulsion.
2. If such a preacher does preach the gospel in a measure as a result of your threatening, you are obliged to stay to keep your end of the bargain.
3. You heard the quotations, infidelic and atheistic, which I read you last evening, and which I could multiply. <u>Where is your heart</u> if you can still have any hankering for antichrist?

"Come out and be ye separate" is God's word to you people—and I have no hesitation to say so. Cease to compromise and God will bless you. "Let us therefore go forth unto Him without the camp (outside the camp of false religion) bearing His reproach." Heb. 13:13.

Yours for God's greater glory,
L.E. Maxwell[19]
(emphasis in original)

Although irenic in tone, a March 27, 1958, letter from Maxwell to a Rev. J. Wood of Three Hills further reveals Maxwell's general skepticism with regard to the theology of the United Church of Canada. It is apparent that his point of reference in critiquing the statement would have been standard fundamentalist works such as *The Fundamentals*.

I have before me the Statement of Faith put out by the United Church of Canada. I would say, in the first place, that there is nothing especially wrong in the Statement of Faith. I think, however, it is not what is said, but what is left unsaid that matters. I note that the Virgin Birth is omitted. I note also that there seems to be a studied omission of chapter and verse for any particular doctrine. While there is mention of the Resurrection there is nothing about the Bodily Resurrection. Even

---

[19] L.E. Maxwell personal files—"United Church."

Fosdick believes in the "risen Lord," but denies the bodily resurrection. In the matter of the Scriptures I would say that position is Barthian rather than scriptural. And, finally, there seems to be nothing too definite as to the eternal destiny of the lost.

I note concerning this Statement of Faith that it is with the "general approval" of the Church as it sat in General Council. Personally, I would expect that most any modernist could subscribe to this Statement of Faith—with certain reservations in his own mind.

I recall that very shortly after church union was effected in 1925 that the United Church paper stated that the doctrinal statement of faith was, if anything, too conservative. I think you will agree with me that had it been a downright statement of modernism's position it would not have been acceptable to the rank and file of the good old Methodists and Presbyterians. We are both acquainted with the fact that a modernist can utter all these statements with his tongue in cheek.

While we must be careful not to be too technical as to precise verbiage we must also beware of en who do not "hold fast the form of sound words" (II Tim. 1:13).[20]

Maxwell was not the only faculty member at PBI to view the United Church of Canada as modernistic. In fact, as the following PBI inter-office memo dated April 9, 1948, relates, both Maxwell and J.M Murray, who had a lengthy career as both instructor and traveling representative for PBI, harbored suspicions that the United Church and Communism had much in common. "Dear Brother Maxwell," wrote Murray:

In connection with something you said at the Baccalaureate service, I feel constrained to send you this bit of information. You said, as I recall, something to the effect that you felt that the United Church and Communism were bosom companions in spirit. I can readily confirm that.

In the fall of 1926 I attended what was called the "Alberta School of Religion," being a series of lectures put on by the United Church of Canada the fall of each year. The main speaker at that particular time

---

[20] L.E. Maxwell personal files—"United Church"

was James Woodsworth, who was to found in a few months' time the political party known as the C.C.F.

Mr. Woodsworth had abandoned the Methodist Church ministry in the year 1918 or thereabouts. That was right after the Bolshevist Revolution, which occurred in 1917. In the early 20's Mr. Woodsworth went to Russia. I remember his telling us all this.

When he returned, naturally he was full of Communistic principles; and undoubtedly having the thought of a new political party in mind, he was invited to be the main speaker at this United School of Religion. And it seemed without exception almost that this entire assembly swallowed him and his doctrines hook, line, and sinker. I can almost hear now one minister's wife saying something to this effect: "This man is wise; he knows what he is talking about." To her it seemed as if Woodsworth was a new kind of savior.

I might add, too, that I can remember even now after over 21 years that his attitude was as sneeringly derisive of the basic principles of Christianity as a renegade "minister's" could be.

One more thought comes to me. When I was leaving the Peace River district (and the Methodist Church, thank God) in the fall of 1924, I heard a young candidate newly arrived in the country distinctly say, "Well, I am determined to know nothing here save Jesus Christ, and Him crucified." His words even now ring in my ears. About twelve years later I met that same man right here in Three Hills. He had finished his college course and lost his faith. Old Mr. White had heard him a short time before preach a funeral sermon in this district, and Dr. White was absolutely shocked at the things he said. I could tell when I met him that his text was no longer the one just quoted.

I have said many times in past years that Communism, the C.C.F., and the United Church were essentially three-in-one.[21]

A couple of points in Murray's note merit comment. Firstly, he states that Maxwell's original comments were made "at the Baccalaureate service." PBI's Baccalaureate service was a regular part of the school's annual Spring Conference that concluded with graduation. Accordingly, given the realities associated with Spring Conferences at PBI, it is safe to conclude that

---

[21] L.E. Maxwell personal files—"United Church"

Maxwell's comments would have been heard by several thousands of visitors, some of whom would have presumably repeated Maxwell's allegations back in their home districts.

Secondly, as is frequently evident in both the *Prairie Pastor* and the *Prairie Overcomer*, Maxwell did periodically evidence something of American fundamentalism's mid-twentieth century preoccupation with Communism or "the Red Scare."[22] For example, early in the *Pastor's* tenure, Maxwell did not hesitate to suggest that even Harry Emerson Fosdick was stoking the fires of Bolshevism. In a sermon reprinted from "the regular Sunday afternoon service of the Prairie Bible Institute on January 11, 1931," Maxwell said:

> But that such damnable heresy is the ally of Russia, we quote a portion of an open letter from an orthodox missionary from China, addressed to Dr. Harry Emerson Fosdick, the recognized leader of the Modernists of America:
>
> *"While on furlough in 1922, I was invited to the home of one of the leading Christians in New York City, and was shown a catalogue published by the "Reds" in which a number of your well-known books were listed, along with books by Socialist and Communist authors, all being recommended as suitable for use by the "Reds" for propaganda among Church people and various other classes of people. I wondered if you were aware of the fact that your books were thus listed, although I was not surprised that the Bolshevik leaders realized that no books were better suited for undermining the faith of Christian people than your popular volumes."*
>
> The "Reds" recognize these Modernistic doctrines as identical with those which "turned Russia upside down" and are everywhere busy following up their deadly work in our land. Who can be surprised if they make many followers from among the cold and lifeless churches of today?[23]

Indeed, the Communist threat was something that was frequently profiled at PBI throughout the Maxwell era via such means as conference speakers whose ministry consisted of smuggling Bibles behind what was then referred to as "The Iron Curtain." As mentioned before in this book, I vividly recalls the fear that swept over me as a seventh-grade student when

---

[22] Louis Gasper, *The Fundamentalist Movement*, 46-71, contains an excellent overview of the attention paid the Communist factor by the American fundamentalist movement.

[23] L.E. Maxwell, *The Prairie Pastor*, 4, No. 3; (March 1931), 3. (*italics* in original)

various leaders at PBI repeatedly warned that Pierre Elliott Trudeau, elected Prime Minister of Canada in June 1968, was either a "Fabian socialist" or an outright communist.

As acknowledged in an earlier chapter, the *Prairie Pastor* was the popular forum that both Maxwell and co-editor Dorothy Ruth Miller often utilized to vent their criticism of modernist churches and preachers in general and the United Church of Canada and its ministers in particular. Excerpts from some of their more general bromides include:

The principal of a school in an Alberta town was recently talking to us at a Convention. During the conversation he said, "You know that a few years ago I got under awful conviction for sin. It was pressing in upon me until I could scarcely endure it longer, so I called upon a pastor of the town where I was. (And that pastor is still preaching not one hundred miles from the editor's desk). I told him just how I felt. My eyes were almost filled with tears, I was under such conviction. That pastor just laughed at me and said that everyone goes through something like that once in a while—and that I must not take it so seriously. Then he brought out a bottle of whiskey and gave me a good drink—passing around the bottle to all the boys." Later this young man was led to one who showed him the plan of salvation and he was wonderfully delivered from sin.

Another young school teacher and business man, just converted two years ago, and who with his wife came to Bible School one year ago, recently approached his old modernistic pastor and said, "Pastor, you know I was a member of your church for a year, and I was living deep in sin—Why did you not tell me about how to be saved. You never told me about a Saviour." The pastor, a noted Modernist, replied in anger, "What right have you to come down here and ask me that?" But, thank God, that young man fell into better hands, found the Lord Jesus Christ, and during this past summer has witnessed the salvation of about two hundred souls. Hallelujah forever! But, oh! oh! oh! How about the hundreds of young lives blasted by the booze of Modernism. This modern adultery in religion is slaying its thousands . . . [24] (L.E.M.)

---

[24] L.E. Maxwell, "False Guides of Youth," *The Prairie Pastor*, 5, No. 10; (October 1932), 3.

In a large church in one of our cities the pastor openly denies the fundamentals of the Christian faith, and is of the world worldly. Is there a decline in the membership or in the size of the congregation? Quite the contrary. The church is crowded Sunday after Sunday with people who hang eagerly upon his words . . . The separation of the orthodox from the unorthodox, of the spiritually living from the spiritually dead, by the withdrawal of those who trust in the blood of Christ, from churches that do not present the atoning work of the Lord Jesus Christ, the eternal Son of God come in the flesh, as the only ground of salvation will increase. Not only so but more and more will rejecters of the atoning blood whether from nominally christian (sic) or from nominally heathen sources seek fellowship in the organizations thus abandoned by the children of God . . . What is the course to be taken by God's children in relation to religious organizations that no longer hold to and proclaim the Word of God? What does God say? "Come out of her, my people, that be not partakers of her sins, and that ye received not of her plagues . . . for she saith in her heart, I sit a queen and am no widow, and shall see no sorrow. Therefore shall her plagues come upon her in one day, death, and mourning and famine; and she shall be utterly burned with fire: for strong is the Lord who judgeth her."[25] (D.R.M.)

In a more particular vein, Maxwell's assault on the theological condition of the United Church of Canada is evident in a *Prairie Pastor* piece referred to earlier in this project but deserving of a second mention. In a succinct comment fraught with theological, sociological and cultural implications, Maxwell responded to the assertion of a Dr. Ernest Thomas, United Church leader and regular contributor to the denomination's publication *New Outlook*. Thomas suggested that "Every element of 'possessive morality' in the relations of men to women is being rejected. Every vestige of the idea of a man's property or monopoly in his wife must be set aside." Maxwell fired back: "We say, 'Rotten.' Sunken doctrine leads to sunken living."[26]

Maxwell then proceeded to recommend and advise readers how to obtain a booklet entitled "The Looting of a Legacy" by "a preacher of the United Church who has rendered a valuable service to all the members of

---

[25] Dorothy Ruth Miller, "A Temple or a Cage?" *The Prairie Pastor*, 8, No. 1; (January-February 1935), 3-4.

[26] L.E. Maxwell, "Rotten!" *The Prairie Pastor*, 4, No. 10; (October 1931), 1.

that constituency who wish to know the truth about the official teachings of their denomination." Maxwell claimed the book showed how the current teachings of the United Church "are contradictory to all the historic creeds of Christendom" and asserts that the author, J.N. Sturk, a United Church lay-preacher from Winnipeg:

> shows by authentic and verbatim quotations and comparisons how that the teachings of the United Church leaders, while worded differently, are quite in harmony with those of Pres. Chas. H. Smith of the American Association for the Advancement of Atheism.

Assuming the role of prophet, Maxwell then goes on to predict:

> It scarcely need be remarked that Modernist preachers who have rejected the plenary inspiration of Scripture and other essentials will openly and privately persecute Mr. Sturk and do as much as possible to prevent this book from getting into the hands of the membership of the United Church. While we do not know Mr. Sturk, nor can we say that we would have adopted just his methods of combating such error, we must confess that here is a preacher who has dared to speak the truth and consequently expose himself to all the calumny and ostracism that will be heaped upon him. Mr. Sturk will be branded as a "dogmatist, quarrelling over things that do not matter. Had he lived in a barbarous age and country he would be branded and persecuted at the stake and thumbscrew, but in this cultivated age he will be the victim of an envenomed speech from religious politicians. And we make bold to say that the rank and file of church members know nothing of the manifold ramifications of corrupt politics and party wire-pulling indulged in by ministerial associations, councils and assemblies. It is pathetically tragic but terribly true.[27]

Maxwell continues by offering a lengthy treatise on the importance of resisting the "peace at any price" approach to doctrinal disputes in which, as was noted with respect to his handling of the Billy Graham issue in later years, he states his preference to walk a sort of middle-ground in the fundamentalist debates. Admitting "we confess that we have little time or

---

[27] L.E. Maxwell, "Rotten!" I-2.

patience with those who spend their energies criticizing modernists and modernist ministers," he nonetheless affirms "we believe, however, that God calls some men to expose the pernicious doctrines of these blind leaders." Perhaps he had the likes of T.T. Shields in mind with such a statement.

Maxwell then sums up the kind of advice he would give to those still attending modernist congregations such as many in the United Church of Canada in this manner:

> After some years of study we insist upon it that no Christian or group of Christian should continue to listen to ministers who do not unquestionably and fearlessly exalt the Virgin Birth of Christ, His Deity, Bodily Resurrection, and His precious Blood as the only remedy for doomed sinners. "Let them alone" "From such turn away"—"From such withdraw . . ."

A good portion of the April 1932 edition of the *Prairie Pastor* was taken up with excoriating the views of the United Church of Canada. The issue leads off with the testimony of a modernist preacher, Rev. Munro, who had a dramatic death-bed conversion experience. There then follows a section entitled "Further Exposure of United Church Teachings" in which Maxwell castigates the denomination's publication, *New Outlook*, with comments such as "We do not suppose the *New Outlook* will give much attention to the above testimony for it contradicts their statements about *"conversion"* being an *"old fashioned revivalistic and catastrophic kind of thing* (Vol. 6, No. 34, P. 103);" "Mr. Munro had a revival of soul such as Moody and all other godly evangelists have witnessed; but the *New Outlook* has no use for Moody's revivals or Moody's Bible. It says: *". . . we are not able to use the Bible in our Christian work as it was used in the enquiry rooms of the Moody revival,"* (Vol. 2, No. 7, P. 5); "But behold the blatancy of the *New Outlook*! In Vol. 5, No. 9, P. 233, the Bible process of getting rid of sin is referred to as *"the old-fashioned and troublesome way of repentance.*"[28]

---

[28] David B. Marshall, *Secularizing the Faith: Canadian Protestant Clergy and the Crisis of Belief, 1850-1940* (Toronto: Univ. of Toronto Press, 1992), 192: "The 'most-advanced Methodist views' published in the *New Outlook* were singled out for attack. The dreaded descent to complete denial of the resurrection, then agnosticism and a conviction that there was no deity, and finally atheism seemed to be an unavoidable one, according to some critics."

After devoting a full page to the heresies outlined in the *New Outlook*, Maxwell then summarized:

> The facts are so evident regarding the awful swing from God's Word in the United Church of Canada that no true Christian can continue to support it as an Institution. What could the infidels 'more say' to destroy God's Word, that the United Church has not already said?[29]

In no uncertain terms he presents his conviction that the United Church of Canada was among the zenith of those who sought to destroy God's Word.

Beginning in the December 1934 edition of the *Prairie Pastor*, Maxwell set his editorial sights on a local United Church pastor with the words: "The Calgary papers have been printing the religious vapourings of one Norwick Kelloway, the new pastor at Knox United Church. It seems that Mr. Kelloway is even more blatant than his predecessor Dr. Dickson" whom Maxwell had earlier chastised in the pages of the *Pastor*.[30] Concerning Kelloway, Maxwell remarked very pointedly:

> It is interesting to note that Mr. Kelloway's deeds and doctrines go together. Just subsequent to denouncing the Bible as "myths, superstitions, fallacies, deceits, etc., Mr. Kelloway went to the theater to see the rather indecent show, "World O' Girls." We do not blame Mr. Kelloway for going to such a show. Such conduct is in perfect keeping with his infidelic utterances. And in spite of all that Mr. Kelloway saw at the show he could have seen nothing there any more indecent than his doctrines. It is very evident that this poor preacher has not "escaped the corruption that is in the world through lust."

---

[29] L.E. Maxwell, "Further Exposure of United Church Teachings," *The Prairie Pastor*, 5, No. 4; (April 1932), 7.

[30] L.E. Maxwell, *The Prairie Pastor*, 5, No. 12; (December 1931), 2. "'Is Rev. Dr. Dickson preaching for the Bible or against it? He picked out a passage . . . picked it to pieces and ridiculed it." This inquiry in Open Letters of the *Calgary Herald* was answered by a young skeptic, a student of science (so called). He commended Dr. Dickson for *"thus saving the Bible for the younger generation by overthrowing its fundamental doctrines. Listen to this fifth report of the "American Association for the Advancement of Atheism," on how Modernism Aids Atheism . . ."'*

A few paragraphs later in the same article, PBI's leader continued his verbal battering of Kelloway's perspectives:

We want to say that Mr. Kelloway's dangerously smooth way of treating sex matters—even to the point of comparing them to excessive eating, drinking and other common places of life—is a far more subtle and insidious form of sin than the theatrical exhibition. The show business does not claim to be anything but sinful, but Mr. Kelloway as a religious leader would go a step farther down the scale and teach us how to call evil good. Mr. Kelloway's sense of sin, if he has any at all, is less than that of the average worldling. His view of sin is refined (?) and polite (?) and polished (?), without a horn or hoof—while that of the average man is just unhypocritically wicked—but to the discerning Christian Mr. Kelloway's doctrines and views of sin smell the more strongly of brimstone and the pit . . . Mr. Kelloway's philosophies are the product of our positively putrid professors and philosophers, who pose as educators of our youth."

We do not write concerning the personal and private life of Mr. Kelloway. Concerning this we have nothing to say. But from his own utterance as reported in the *Herald* we regard his doctrines as more dangerous and destructive than a "World O' Girls." From a Christian standpoint his conception of sin is infidelic and heathenish. Imagine for a moment a preacher telling youth—the lust loving youth of today—to treat all matters of sex just as they would the daily exercises of eating and drinking. How far will the false philosophies and psychologies of modern education carry their victims?

Moreover, Maxwell did not hesitate to speculate as to whether the board of Knox United Church would rebuke the pastor before concluding that Knox was too spiritually dead for such to happen. He deemed Kelloway to be even more depraved that the noted atheist Robert Ingersoll:

We wonder whether Mr. Kelloway will be rebuked by his church board for his lining up with atheistic professors against the supernatural of God's Word. It is not likely there is sufficient spiritual life in his church to call forth a lively protest, let alone put him out of the church for his infidelity. A few years ago his utterances regarding sex would have shocked such men as Ingersoll and other atheists, but today even the people have become so accustomed to the language of Satan that his assertions do not seem so bad after all . . .

We venture to say that in spite of his stout assertions against God's word that Mr. Kelloway's church will be quite filled. The late Dr. Dickson had these people about ready to receive the next degree in the distructive (sic) criticism of the Bible. And apparently Mr. Kelloway is the man to give that destructive teaching. Only by degrees can the people be brought to swallow these Satanic assertions against God.[31]

Maxwell again takes Rev. Kelloway to task at some length in the January-February 1935 issue of the *Prairie Pastor* for preaching "folly." Someone had mailed Maxwell a sermon by Kelloway entitled "Finding a Religion to Live By." Included in Maxwell's lengthy comments on the sermon are the following:

In this sermon Mr. Kelloway ridicules the old faith and claims with great gusto to be coming to the rescue of youth, giving them *"a religion to live by."* This religion (?) he calls, not the 'religion *about* Jesus,' but the 'religion *of* Jesus.' . . . we need no Saviour according to Mr. Kelloway. The virgin birth, the Blood-shedding of Christ, the bodily resurrection and other great essential doctrines *about* Jesus, Mr. Kelloway can brush aside with all the haughtiness of a Voltaire, an Ingersoll or a Tom Paine . . .

Now as to the religion *of* Jesus. We are first told that it is of no vital matter to be a Christian *who* Jesus was, or *what* we believe about Him. We are then bidden to practice His ethics, just live the religion *of* Jesus. Jesus is just a Model: we need Him not as a Saviour. What a two-faced business is this? We are told that it matters not to a Christian whether Jesus was the Son of God, the Redeemer, the Lord of Glory—it matters not whether He was virgin born or His mother of a questionable character—it matters not whether He was a sinner or His Blood provides a covering for sin—it matters not whether He was He arose triumphant over sin and death and hell—all of these foundations of the Christian faith may be brushed aside at a stroke. Then we are told to mimic His

---

[31] L.E. Maxwell, "Deeds and Doctrine," *The Prairie Pastor*, 7, No. 12; (December 1934), 4, 7-8.

religion. What a hopeless task to place before sinful, depraved and unborn again young people. Resolutions to live as Jesus lived! What folly! . . . Any man who can so haughtily brush aside all the sacred facts *about* Jesus should not have the face to pretend to imitate Jesus."

. . . Mr. Kelloway would deride those who call Jesus Lord, virtually accusing them in every mention he makes of such persons that they have only a theoretical lip profession. According to his own printed sermons he hates the thought of the next world. He abhors the thought of personal salvation. He despises the way which Jesus said was 'narrow.' May this poor preacher awaken before he deceives multitudes leaving them nothing to live for and nothing to die by.[32]

In late 1936 Maxwell focused his criticism on another United Church pastor in Calgary and used the occasion to offer a sweeping censure of modernist congregations such as those that populated the United Church of Canada. He wrote:

In the *Calgary Herald* of October 10 appeared a letter from Rev. Dr. R. Paton of the Scarboro United Church, in which he tears the Bible to pieces in the very same fashion that Tom Paine or Bob Ingersoll used to do it—but with this difference, they did it *outside the church.* Today pious people in the pews pay preachers to do the infidel's dirty work. Is it not amazing how people will pay a false shepherd to tear the Bible into shreds?—and the very Bible they profess to believe.

We know of people, Christian people we believe, who stay with, defend and support the old church where their folks attended from olden days. No matter how far the preacher departs from the old moorings in parading his modern views, they would not "come out and be separate" as the Word commands. The Lord Jesus may be slighted, ignored, and denied yet these friends are sentimentally married to the dear old building, the windows, the pews, the associations, their dead relatives, etc. If their dead relatives should ever be as ignored, slighted and belittled as the Lord of glory is year after year in their pulpits they would never darken the door of the place again. But they can much easier see their

---

[32] L.E. Maxwell, "A Religion to Die By," *The Prairie Pastor*, 8, No. 1; (January-February 1935), 4, 7. (*italics* in original)

Lord maltreated than their dead relatives, so little do they care for the crucified Saviour. They can support a system that will crucify Him afresh and put Him to an open shame. One wonders: "Are such people born again?"[33]

The advice Maxwell dispensed to one United Church member who advised him that "my husband and I have been dismissed from the United Church here for teaching the Bible" offers evidence that Maxwell did not deter from publicly advising the orthodox to leave the denomination:

"To the above we replied in a way that may open the eyes of many of our readers to the apostasy of the United Church. Our reply was, for the most part, as follows:

"My dear Mrs. S_____:

I deeply thank God for your letter. For years I have maintained that real Christians could not conscientiously continue to stand in fellowship with the anti-Christ teachings of the United Church of Canada. I have seen this work out time and again in just the way it has proved true in your case. The official hierarchy of the United Church do not want the Bible taught as the inspired Word of God. It is to me a source of thanksgiving that you should have been so sufficiently awake and faithful to your testimony that you have been put out of the United Church.

We are told in Luke 6:22, 23: 'Blessed are ye, when men shall hate you, and when they shall separate you from their company, and shall reproach you, and cast out your name as evil, for the Son of man's sake. Rejoice in that day and leap for joy: for, behold, your reward is great in heaven: for in the like manner did their fathers unto the prophets.'

And I am sure that you are now experiencing the blessedness promised by the Lord Jesus in these verses (Luke 6:22, 23). I might say, on the other hand, that the reason some Christians are still able to stay in fellowship with such connections is because they do not get sufficiently close to the Lord to incur the hatred which would cast them out . . ." [34]

---

[33] L.E. Maxwell "Modernism, or The Devil's Dirty Water," *The Prairie Pastor*, 9, Nos. 11-12; (November-December 1936), 3, 4. (*italics in original*)

[34] L.E. Maxwell, "Modernism," *The Prairie Pastor*, 13, Nos. 4-5; (April-May 1940), 3.

Predictably, Maxwell's frequent rhetorical attacks on the United Church earned him little favor with the hierarchy of that organization. As a result, leaders of the United Church were not inclined to look with favor on "Three Hills" as critics of PBI often called the Institute. The following, for example, is a letter written in 1944 by a Superintendent of Missions for the United Church of Canada to a new minister in United Church Circles, a Rev. S. Medhurst of Viewfield, Saskatchewan.[35]

It has come to my attention that you have arranged for special services May 17th to 31st, and that you have invited in to assist you in this work a minister from another religious group which I am credibly informed has for reasons best known to its own leaders been very critical of the United Church. I was very much surprised to hear of this. I feel you have not given this matter the consideration it should have been given. We are all anxious to win all possible for the service of Christ's Kingdom and to give them the instruction and inspiration which they require. There is no Church more willing than the United Church to cooperate with those who are willing to work with it on the basis of mutual confidence, but such cooperation is not likely to be a success when the other involved make it a practice to try to impress upon their people that the regular Churches are sadly amiss in their doctrine and this I have learned has been the practice of the Three Hills leaders.

You are a minister ordained by another Church whom tentatively we have employed in the service of our United Church. Would it not have been a wise and right course before arranging with a minister of still another religious body to come with you into your United Church charge to have consulted with the Presbytery or myself? I realize how you may not have been informed concerning relations in the past between our United Church and the Three Hills Bible Institute and I have no doubt your intentions are of the best but more is involved than you are likely to have understood.

Your services begin today. I hope that it may turn out that Professor Miles preaches a positive message and refrains from criticism of the Church to one of whose charges he is at present preaching. For whatever

---

[35] L.E. Maxwell personal file—"United Church."

may be done in the way of winning souls for the way of Christ and for the service of His Church we shall be glad.

As regards the future however, while you are supplying for the United Church it will be well to remember that there we (sic) have courses of procedure to be followed and ways of doing things which have proved their worth in the past. I shall hope to see you at Conference and shall be glad to discuss the matter further.

Rev. R.J. McDonald
Supt of Missions
United Church of Canada

The pastor of Westminster United Church wrote Maxwell on December 14, 1950, to complain about an assertion the latter had made in a recent issue of the *Prairie Overcomer* concerning the United Church of Canada:[36]

My December issue of the Prairie Overcome (sic) arrived this week. In it I found an article entitled "Union", page 260, which was most ambiguous and did not come up to the usual good standard of the "Overcomer". Furthermore, in its vagueness its references were subtle and dangerous.

Am I right in concluding from the article that, as a member of the United Church of Canada referred to in the second sentence of that article, I and my Church are therefore classified by the Institute as a co-worker with the Communist and Catholic forces, being "organized enemies out for blood"?

In all fairness to your many readers who, being resident outside of Canada, will know of the United Church of Canada by name only, I believe you are obliged to clarify fully in a future issue of the "Overcomer" the reference made to the United Church.

I should like personally to hear from you in this matter, also.

Yours very truly,
Wm. A. Harvey
A Subscriber

---

[36] L.E. Maxwell personal file—"United Church"

Maxwell's response, albeit pleasant, was emphatic:

Your letter of December 14th is at hand. I was not aware that my article in the *Overcomer* was vague in its references. I have read it again and feel that it is quite plain.

I have not thought that the United Church is a co-worker with the Catholics. My impression is that they are not. Of course, you know that a good many of your ministers are Communist inclined. Otherwise they would not have had Mr. Endicott, who is very friendly with Moscow and has been there as Moscow's guest, in their churches I am sure you know that it would be contrary to fact to say that many of the United Church ministers are not friendly with Moscow's doctrines. However, I am glad to admit (I think I am right) that the United Church had to dismiss Mr. Endicott for his pronouncedly Communistic views.

The rigt (sic) between the orthodox faith and modernism is so great that, as the "Christian Century" has plainly said, "The God of the Fundamentalist is one God and the God of the Modernist is another." In view of this fact one can understand how that modernism is out to league up against, and bring legislation against minority orthodox groups. Whether the United Church of Canada has done this I cannot say.

If you are prepared to state that the United Church of Canada is not modernist controlled and if your official organ is willing to make a bold statement on behalf of the orthodox faith and against modernism, then I think it would be quite in order for me to make a very sincere apology and state, which I would gladly do, that the United Church is fundamental and orthodox and in no sense modernistic. I happen to know, however, that one of your own orthodox ministers down east feels that there may be as many as a half dozen true-to-the-orthodox-faith ministers in Ontario.

I hardly see how I could come out in your paper and state that the United Church of Canada is modernistic. Do you think I could? If I were to judge by the number of old-fashioned conversions, or lack thereof, in the United Churches across the country what have I to conclude? I will leave the matter to your own judgment.

Assuring you that I bear no ill will toward any personal member of the United Church, and believing you will rejoice to know that we have in our midst persons out of 100 different denominations—born again with a know-so salvation based upon the eternal Word of God—and with kind personal regards to you as a reader of the *Overcomer*, I am,

Sincerely, yours in Christ,
PRAIRIE BIBLE INSTITUTE

L.E. Maxwell, Principal

Lastly, an exchange of personal letters that Maxwell had in late 1965 with a resident of Norwich, Ontario, a Mrs. Evelyn Bishop, helps establish that Maxwell's battle with the theology and orientation of the United Church of Canada was carried out at both the public and private levels.[37] Maxwell's November 5 response to Bishop's letter of September 2 appears to be a response to an indication of surprise from her that he considered the United Church to be modernistic:

I cannot imagine that you are entirely unaware of the doctrinal trends in the United Church of Canada. There are so many United Church people who have recently become so consciously aware of this trend that they are not only alarmed, but are doing just what you say you would do, namely, "not be a member of that organization." One of the finest pastors of Saskatoon wrote a red-hot letter of resignation a few months ago. I know of a fine druggest (sic) here in western Canada who also with his family left the church some months ago. I know of another area where a group of people asked for an evangelical organization to come in and open up a church. This group was a solid group leaving the modernistic United Church . . .

I have lately received an article by the Rev. Ben Smillie, writing in the United Church journal in which he berates Billy Graham for using the phrase "the Bible says," and then this man Smillie, who is a United Church Chaplain in the University of Saskatchewan in Saskatoon goes on to say: "Nothing is said about the Bible being composed partly of legend and myth and allegory, and so Christians continue to hear the word of God ignorantly. They go on believing in clay-made man, a floating zoo, an amphibious-footed Jesus, a son of God who demonstrated his divinity

---

[37] L.E. Maxwell personal file—"United Church"

as a home brew artist by turning water into wine and topped it with an ascension that looks like a Cape Kennedy blast-off."

I must say that the above statement has been regarded as so blasphemous, almost outdoing Tom Paine, or Voltaire, or Bob Ingersoll, that I have been reluctant to even reprint the same as an exposure of departure from Bible truth and doctrine. If the official editors of the United Church Observer are not in favour of such frightful and blasphemous statements and charicatures (sic) of Christ Jesus our Lord, why on earth do they print such mockeries of Christ?

Bishop's November 11 response to Maxwell's first letter clearly disappointed him as is evident by several comments he makes in his November 16 reply to her:

May I quote from your letter? You say that you have "yet to find anything that the United Church teaches that I cannot accept." If indeed you are ready to accept whatever the Liberals teach, well, that is that.

You mention that some minister said that "many scholars did not believe Jonah was swallowed by a whale." This sounds like the question: "Have any of the Scribes and Pharisees believed on Him?" Remember it was the scholarly religious world that crucified Christ.

Again you say: "Our minister's explanation of the book of Jonah suited me fine, and I was glad I did not have to believe the story of Jonah and the whale." If you had said your heart was "grieved" instead of being "glad" that you did not have to believe the story of Jonah and the whale then there would be more hope for your being recovered to a Bible believing position. Remember that honest double always causes grief of heart, never gladness of heart . . .

You may be sure that I shall not further bother you about these matters, for your word "glad" and your word "prefer" indicate, as you say, that "no amount of criticism from another group will change our views." I had thought from your first letter that you were perhaps an honest doubter. But pardon me if I say very frankly that I am reminded of the man who says, "Don't bother me with the facts; my mind is already made up." I trust that you will at least recognize that in denying the book of Jonah and other miracles of the Old and New Testaments, you will have to deal with Jesus Christ who put His stamp of approval upon all of these miracles and Himself said, "the Scripture cannot be broken."

As a "P.S." to his letter, Maxwell scrawled: "If modern critics of the Word of God are not "false prophets" in sheep's clothing then there are no false prophets? Are there none? LEM"

It is evident from the material presented above that L.E. Maxwell's public and private sparring with the theology as well as the clergy and laity of the United Church of Canada played a much more prominent role in his overall career than what Stackhouse acknowledges. Accordingly, as indicated in the Introduction to this book, scholars such as Michael S. Hamilton believe there is indeed sufficient evidence to consider Maxwell a "militant fundamentalist."

While the evidence suggests Maxwell was often careful to be pleasant and diplomatic in his personal correspondence, when it came to editorializing in the *Pastor* or the *Overcomer* about the teachings of the United Church and some of its ministers, he did not hesitate whatsoever to employ combative terms such as "Satanic," smelling of "brimstone and the pit," "rotten" and "infidelic." Nor did he shy from alleging that United Church pastors like Kelloway and Dickson were "false shepherds" and those who remained under their teaching were likely not truly born again.

True, unlike a personality such as T.T. Shields, there is no record that L.E. Maxwell ever disrupted any denominational conferences or engineered protests at public gatherings. In all likelihood, such would have indeed been beyond what he would have been comfortable in doing. On the other hand, it is important to bear in mind that, unlike Shields, Maxwell spent the balance of his career outside denominational and urban settings where there would have been significantly fewer opportunities for such demonstrative actions.

His militancy versus Evolution

Perhaps the most militant action anyone associated with Prairie Bible Institute ever exhibited was the occasion in the late 1930s when J. Fergus Kirk, president of PBI at the time, was jailed for keeping his sons from attendance at the Three Hills public school. Part of the motivation for Kirk's rebellion was his opposition to having his sons instructed in accordance with humanistic thought including the assumptions associated with an evolutionary approach to science.[38]

It was likely no coincidence that at precisely the same time Kirk was waging his battle with the authorities in the provincial Education department, Maxwell was writing prolifically about the topic of evolution in the *Prairie Pastor.*[39] Apparently, as is evident from Maxwell's editorials, Kirk's protest had aroused significant interest related to evolution. Interestingly enough, as the following citation displays, Maxwell again acknowledges that his first love is not hammering away at error. Stackhouse might fairly respond that such an admission suggests the PBI president was, generally speaking, less cantankerous than the likes of T.T. Shields.

> We have been receiving requests from various sources for quotations from Alberta school text-books which are evolutionary in their teaching. We are accordingly printing a few this month. We could quote many more such passages but we like to keep for the most part to that which is a real contribution to the spiritual life of our readers. While people must be warned concerning these destructive teachings, we grow weary of writing or preaching on subjects that merely prevent the acceptance of error.[40]

The publication Maxwell refers to in the above quote was a simple, two-page document that read (in part) as follows:

> We have been receiving requests from various sources for quotations from Alberta school text-books which are evolutionary in their teaching. We are accordingly printing a few.
>
> "World History is a story of mankind. It is a long story covering hundreds of thousands of years." A Brief World History, page 4-N. DeWitt

---

[38] See Chapter Four of this book under *Legacy* by Bernice Callaway. See also Chapter Nine of this book under J.F. Kirk's personality.

[39] "Evolutionary Teaching Prepares for Anti-Christ," in *The Prairie Pastor*, 10, No. 9-10; (September-October 1937), 5.
"Agassiz's Exposure of Darwinism," in *The Prairie Pastor*, 10, No. 9-10; (September-October 1937), 3f.

[40] L.E. Maxwell, "Evolution in Our Text-Books," in *The Prairie Pastor*, 12, No. 7; (July 1939), 2.

"The art of the stone-mason also had its origin in Egypt. This, too, was developed step by step. Its beginnings are found far back in the Stone Ages, 10,000 years before Christ or earlier." DEWITT, Page 74.

"In Europe the Stone Age began at least 100,000 years ago." A Short History of Early Peoples, Page I—West.

"But through all their tens of thousands of years the Chipped Stone men were hunters merely. They never learned to farm." West, Page 2.

These foregoing statements absolutely set aside the Scripture chronology which places Creation some 4000 years before Christ.

"In the neighborhood of a million years ago primitive man first wandered through the forests and over the plains of Europe . . . He ate seeds, leaves, roots and berries. He may even have stored some against the needs of winter." Powers, Meuner and Bruner, Man's Control of His Environment, page 5.

"This (the cerebrum) in man is far more highly developed than in other animals, and in this respect indicates the growth of man toward intelligence." Powers, Menuer and Bruner, page 573.

Notice that none of these excerpts so much as hint that man possesses an immortal spirit. He is spoken of as a mere animal. Nothing beyond the physical is recognized.[41] (emphasis in original)

In the *Prairie Pastor* version of this document, Maxwell elaborated more fully than he did in the original statement. For example, with regard to the first quotation he stated:

These assertions absolutely set aside the Scripture chronology. The evolutionist must teach that man has been on the earth for an extremely long time since it is certain that two thousand years before Christ man was as intelligent as he is now and some forms of art were as highly developed as they have ever been. But the evolutionist likes to deceive himself and others by giving man a history of hundreds of thousands or millions of years and by supposing that in that extremely long time he has developed from a man only a trifle above the ape.[42]

---

[41] L.E. Maxwell personal file—"Evolution."
[42] L.E. Maxwell, "Evolution in Our Text-Books," in *The Prairie Pastor*, 12, No. 7; (July 1939), 3.

In the March 1939 issue and then again in the April-May 1939 issue of *Prairie Pastor*, Maxwell penned a two-part lengthy article entitled "Trends In Modern Education." He lamented therein:

> There was a day in our land when the old log schoolhouse stood for all that was wholesome and holy. It was supposed to set the best moral standards for the community and to be a powerful factor for good—an elevating influence with very ethical, if not Christian, ideals. When such was the general condition in the educational realm how beneficial was compulsory education! But now the tables have been turned. How dangerous and damning are the pernicious influences of the average school! And yet children are compelled to sit there and take a lot of rubbish from men and women whose lives are often loose and whose principles in many cases are wax.[43]

As evidence that the dispute PBI was having with the education authorities in Alberta was quite well known in Alberta, Maxwell cites a letter-writer to the *Calgary Herald* who opined:

> 'If the *Herald* believes in the right of people to their own religious convictions, it should not object to certain steps taken by the Prairie Bible Institute. There would seem to be no good reason why children should be forced to study the theory of evolution or any other theory that directly or indirectly undermines the Christian faith, nor any kind of literature that in the estimation of the parents has a band influence of the mind of either child or adult. The church may teach what it likes, but no one is compelled to attend any particular church or any church at all. But school attendance is compulsory, and for that very reason should be freed from a lot of rubbish that has nothing to do with education in the best sense of the word.
>
> There is a rapidly increasing tendency to spread propaganda under the guise of education, and to treat unsound, unproven theories as actual facts. However, in these matters everyone has a right to his own opinion, but no right to force it on others.'

---

[43] L.E. Maxwell, "Trends in Modern Education," in *The Prairie Pastor*, 12, No. 3; (March 1939), 3-10.

Proceeding into a lengthy exposition of Roman 1:18f, Maxwell eventually indicts evolutionary theory and those who advance it in this manner:

> In order to get away from this immediate personal responsibility to the infinite God of glory, evolution would fain bid us behold a long, slow, difficult process which led through far lower forms of thought, the fetish, the nature power, the tribal god, the national god, and then finally to Abraham there was conceived in the mind of man the idea of one God supreme. But such a false conception is found contrary to the facts, contrary to history and, of course, contradicted by Scripture. . . .
>
> Note what these philosophers (rightly called fool-osophers) have done. "They changed the truth of God into a lie" verse 25. God's glorious Person has been *"changed into the lie"* of evolution. These "modern" shallow-pan days are taking us back to the pit, the old pits of paganism, just as fast as possible. Evolution relegates God (if there be any such thing as God left) to the utmost confines of time and space. He is no larger than the amoeba. He is no longer personal or powerful. He is tied by the hands of nature. He will never judge men for sin. So now every man can do that which 'is right in his own eyes.'
>
> Evolution and sin are bed-fellows. They both change the truth of God into a lie. And evolution is known by its fruits. This doctrine is basic to most of the increasing falsehood in our social, moral and educational life. It has paralyzed many a preacher, and is literally "poisoning human life and civilization with the lethal gases of communism and free love" (Gilbert). This statement we shall expect to prove by citing instances from experience before we conclude this series. The catalogue of sin concluding Romans 1 is returning swiftly to society on this continent through our educational literature.

Maxwell concluded the first part of his treatise against evolution by suggesting the theory was part of a conscious conspiracy by godless and unethical educators:

> Professor Haeckel, the greatest German evolutionist, was so bent upon demonstrating the theory of evolution as a fact that he doctored up his diagrams, fraudulently foisting them on the public. Six to eight per cent

of them "are really forgeries . . . to fill in and reconstruct the missing links." Then he goes on to say, "I should feel utterly condemned and annihilated by the admission were it not that hundreds of the best observers and most reputable biologists lie under the same charge." He further admits that "the great majority of . . . diagrams (pretentiously proving organic evolution) are more or less doctored." At the close of his life he said in 1919: "Most modern investigators of science have come to the conclusion that the doctrine of evolution, and particularly Darwinism, is an error, and cannot be maintained.

Perhaps there is no better succinct summation of Maxwell's combative attitude toward the topic of evolution than to draw attention to editorial notes he inserted before a couple of articles on the topic that he chose to reprint in the *Prairie Pastor*. Prior to the piece "Agassiz's Exposure of Darwinism" published in the September-October 1937 issue, Maxwell inserted this statement:

> The following article is a portion of an editorial published in *The Sunday School Times* for August 7. We take pleasure in reprinting it. Scientists well known that the evolutionary hypothesis is an exploded theory. Is it not about time that Christian parents refuse to have their children taught as a fact a theory which is clung to only because those who advocate it are determined not to acknowledge a God who by the word of His mouth created the universe and every living creature? Are men who refuse to have God in their knowledge to fill the minds and hearts of your children with their own arrogant unbelief?

A similar notation accompanied a reprinted article by Robert L. Cooke entitled "What is Wrong with American Education?"[44] (Readers will note again that the title and nature of the article is an apt reminder that Maxwell seldom made any distinction between Canadian or American society when it came to passing comment on the broader culture's deteriorating standards.) Wrote Maxwell in a militant tone:

---

[44] L.E. Maxwell, editorial insertion prior to Robert L. Cooke, "What is Wrong with American Education?" in *The Prairie Pastor*, 14, No. 7; (July 1941), 3.

Pagan philosophy and Satanic worldly wisdom are doing infinitely more to undermine the faith and morals of our young people than we realize. When we opened our Christian High School, refusing to include soul-ruining text-books there was an amazing outcry against us. Newspapers and radio hook-ups all "agreed together" that such a move was "a dangerous precedent." We had touched Satan's chief seat. We had cast down the Baal of worldly wisdom. Such a challenge and exposure brought fire from the enemy's many mouthpieces. Such a reaction revealed how deep the grip of this poisonous plague. (This article is condensed from *The Sunday School Times*.—Ed.)

Lastly for my purposes here, in a *Prairie Pastor* article entitled "Is It True? Is Man Coming Up- or Going Down?" Maxwell again displays his fondness for tackling the topic of evolution.[45] This is apparent by comments such as:

Is man coming up or going down? This vital question is one that I will gladly discuss with every reader of what is here written. Almost everywhere now throughout the world of learning, and, even by many in the Christian Church itself, the theory of man's evolution from the lowest possible form of life is really assumed to be beyond all dispute. Science, it is claimed, traces man right back through the animals, from one form to another, until an original life germ is presumed . . .

But this is all rank, rationalistic speculation! For the materialistic bishop can only say "probably," while Darwin, elaborating his theory, could never go any farther than "We may well suppose," which phrase occurs over eight hundred times in his two principal works. Other authorities contend that evolution is, and never can be anything else but theory. Regarding it, Professor Everett, of Harvard University, says: "Evolution, or this story of transformation and activity is a dream." As a paleontologist, the late Professor Agassiz wrote: "I am compelled to say that the theory is a scientific mistake, untrue in its facts, unscientific in its methods and mischievous in its tendency." Sir Wm. Dawson also wrote of it that "The records of the rocks are decidedly against evolutionists." Dr. Etheridge, Fossiologist of the British Museum, says: "Nine-tenths of the talk of evolutionists is sheer nonsense, not founded

---

[45] *The Prairie Pastor*, I, No. 9; (September 1928), 4-8.

on observations and wholly unsupported by the facts. This museum is full of proofs of the utter falsity of their views. Professor Fleischman, of Erlangen, as definitely affirms that "The Darwinian theory has in the realms of Nature not a single fact to confirm it. It is not the result of scientific research, but purely the product of the imagination." Many other scientists could here be quoted showing that there is not really the faintest shadow of evidence to support the astonishing theory that man has come up from the lower animals. It is all a stupendous guess . . .

The facts then with regard to PBI's public stance against evolution are that the co-founder of Prairie Bible Institute, J. Fergus Kirk, once withdrew his children from attendance at the Three Hills public school. He subsequently went to jail for his actions that were due in part to his firm opposition to the teaching of evolution in text-books used at the school. His concerns about the teaching of evolution in time contributed to the founding of Prairie High School.

The other co-founder of PBI, L.E. Maxwell, supported the former's actions by circulating evidence of what the leadership at PBI considered to be offensive material in the text-books under protest. The latter also publicly derided the integrity of the evolutionary theory on numerous occasions, charging that educators knowingly propagated false data to advance the notion, an insinuation of no small significance in academic circles. He boldly went on the public record in calling evolution a "deception," "rubbish," "poison," "an exploded theory" and "a stupendous guess."

Did the actions and rhetoric of J. Fergus Kirk and L.E. Maxwell in this regard qualify as militant fundamentalism? I have already consistently suggested that Maxwell's barbed rhetoric certainly had similarities with the kind of contentious rhetoric that flourished in such circles. With regard to Kirk's actions of promoting truancy, it is revealing to point out that by running afoul of the law, he thereby placed himself in the company of J. Frank Norris and T.T Shields, whom Stackhouse identifies as authentic representatives of militant American/Canadian fundamentalism.[46]

---

[46] George M. Marsden, *Fundamentalism and American Culture* (1980), 190-191, refers briefly to Norris's shooting a man to death which a jury eventually ruled as self-defense and to the debacle involving Shields at Des Moines University where police were eventually called to quell a riot.

CONCLUSION

The primary objective of this book has been to refine how Prairie Bible Institute during the L.E. Maxwell era should be understood by students of North American church history. As a significant component of its quest, the work represents both a belated response to and an eager interaction with the valuable foundational efforts of Canadian scholar, Dr. John Stackhouse, Jr., in this regard. His efforts are set forth in a 1993 book entitled *Canadian Evangelicalism in the Twentieth Century: An Introduction to Its Character*, a revision of his doctoral dissertation at the University of Chicago.

Drawing on my own insider perspective of PBI as well as on research undertaken since Stackhouse conducted his investigation more than twenty years ago, I have herein challenged both Stackhouse's narrow definition of fundamentalism and his accompanying claim that PBI under Maxwell was an "indigenous Canadian product." The focus of my work included the articulation of an informed skepticism regarding Stackhouse's notion that the kind of "sectish evangelicalism" he claims typified PBI in the twentieth century was truly of any substantial difference to the broader definition of American fundamentalism proposed here. I suggest the net effect has been to credibly argue that the following conclusion reached by Stackhouse, at least as it relates to Prairie Bible Institute, is, if not demonstrably false, regrettably misleading:

> "The institutions portrayed here as central in the life of Canadian evangelicalism in the twentieth century were, without exception, indigenous Canadian products. However much they benefited in typical Canadian style from British or American initiative (for instance . . . the American model of Moody Bible Institute for PBI . . .) or from leaders from either place (for example, L.E. Maxwell at PBI . . .), the institutions were founded and funded and staffed predominantly by Canadians.[1]

Following an Introduction that discussed the strengths and weakness of the "insider" perspective employed in the thesis and noted various important

---

[1]   Stackhouse, 196.

parameters that served to delimit my work, Chapter One outlined a brief history of PBI's founding in 1922 leading to its achievement by mid-century of an international reputation as one of the top two or three largest Bible institutes in the world. The book's first chapter also established a working hypothesis.

Chapters Two and Three identified a number of key terms used throughout the book and indicated how these terms would be employed. The following two chapters then exhaustively identified particularly influential popular and academic written works that address some element of PBI's history. These chapters did not include writings by any of the key leaders at PBI during the L.E. Maxwell era. Such works were, however, identified in later chapters where attention was paid to the individual authors in the course of discussing their respective contributions to PBI's fundamentalist identity.

Chapter Six surveyed a selection of books that outline general and specific elements of the history of Canada, "The West," and/or the province of Alberta. Chapter Seven then presented the views of a dozen scholars regarding some aspect of Canada's religious history. The purpose of these two chapters was to establish a broader background than just the religious sector against which to consider the scope of American influence in Canada as well as to verify the inescapable and powerful sway of American religious life on the ecclesiastical orientation of its northern neighbor. Such an overview was very important in helping me arrive at the judgment that Stackhouse's inaccurate portrayal of PBI in *Canadian Evangelicalism in the Twentieth Century* is due in part to an inadequate consideration of the ubiquitous American influence in Canadian history in general.

Chapter Eight was devoted to a discussion of L.E. Maxwell himself and his American roots. It was shown that Maxwell's conversion took place within fundamentalist circles and that his formal theological training was obtained at the feet of those whose theological sympathies resided with the proto-fundamentalist personalities and themes of the late nineteenth and early twentieth centuries. It was further revealed that through his writings and preaching in his primary years at PBI, Maxwell faithfully echoed American fundamentalist emphases with respect to theology and the social issues of the day.

That Maxwell did not hesitate at all in the early years at PBI to proudly associate himself and PBI with the American fundamentalist cause by referring to himself and the school as "fundamentalist" was made apparent. The articles he penned for the *Prairie Pastor* and the *Prairie Overcomer* repeatedly denounced the social ills identified by fundamentalism such as diminishing standards in women's dress, alcohol, dance, Hollywood, evolution and Communism. Maxwell's unique and popular teaching on "the crucified life" facilitated his association with two of fundamentalism's popular themes: separation from the world and the primacy of world missions. His fraternities with American fundamentalists like Philip Howard, Jr. of *The Sunday School Times* and Robertson McQuilken of Columbia Bible College as well as PBI's affinity with Keswick helped make Maxwell popular in the more moderate American fundamentalist circles. Indeed, as was shown, the evidence of Maxwell's fraternal relationships with his American colleagues vastly outweighed any similar relationships with his colleagues at Canadian Bible institutes.

Something of Maxwell's militaristic orientation and firm predilection to being in control at all times was evident in the various quotations derived from his writings, particularly his book, *World Missions: Total War*, and in comments taken from his sermons. Maxwell himself openly joked about how outsiders viewed life at that "boot camp" in Three Hills. It was noted that several newspaper reporters picked up on his militant nature when he visited churches away from Three Hills.

Chapter Nine offered a brief overview of five other figures that occupied strategic roles in the leadership of PBI during the L.E. Maxwell era and contributed to its fundamentalist orientation. The resilient piety of J. Fergus Kirk maintained a firm commitment to the separation of believers from the world, a matter over which he took William Aberhart to task when the latter left the Christian ministry to enter Alberta politics. That fundamentalism was not and is not a monolithic entity was apparent in the sections on Dorothy Ruth Miller and Ruth C. Dearing where it was shown that, with respect to the role of women in theological training, Maxwell and PBI were certainly well ahead of their day. It was observed that Paul Maxwell and Ted Rendall, who served successive terms as PBI presidents following the senior Maxwell's tenure, both made their own unique contributions to ensuring that PBI retained its affiliation with certain traits of American fundamentalism.

The last five chapters of the book represent the core of my challenge to the conclusions that Stackhouse posits regarding PBI. In Chapter Ten, I argued that Stackhouse is misguided in arguing that militancy or its psychological component was the key characteristic of American fundamentalism and therefore essentially ends up committing the error of allowing a part to represent the whole. In any event, a closer look revealed that Maxwell was certainly militant enough both in his personal nature and in the manner he operated PBI to merit at least some association with the militant nature of certain American fundamentalists. Nevertheless, the book calls for a more nuanced definition of American fundamentalism than a focus on militancy alone offers, one that gives greater attention to the theological components of the movement after the initial decade of rancor.

In Chapter Eleven I maintained that at least four theological themes characterized the mainstream of American fundamentalism in the majority of the twentieth century and that each of these was consistently woven into the environment that prevailed at PBI. These motifs were: an unyielding allegiance to Biblical authority, a pervasive emphasis on the imminent return of Christ, a relentless focus on holiness and revival, and an overarching commitment to the primacy of missions. Joel Carpenter's work, *Revive Us Again*, was referred to at several points to show how these themes were dominant in that fundamentalist branch of American Christianity that eventually resulted in the establishment of neo-evangelicalism. I pointed out that the very same authors, speakers, books, hymns and gospel songs that typified mainstream American fundamentalism in the middle decades of the twentieth century were welcomed and utilized at Prairie Bible Institute during the L.E. Maxwell era.

I employed Chapter Twelve to underscore that many of the cultural distinctives of American fundamentalism as well found a home at Prairie Bible Institute during the Maxwell era. A significant amount of administrative energy was placed on ensuring that students at PBI not only were literally kept separate from the world but were also required to look and sound like they were separate from the world. In addition to PBI's overarching and rigid social regulations that prevailed for almost the entirety of the Maxwell era, the spheres of campus life where separation was particularly visible and audible pertained to students' dress and appearance, zero tolerance for worldly habits, the non-use of various media or communication devices, and the school's policy regarding music. The American influence in PBI's Music Department was particularly underlined.

Chapter Thirteen documented two elements of PBI's unique culture that were directly tied to the school's fundamentalist alignment: the school's reluctance to engage academic accreditation and it's vacillation on endorsing the ministry of Billy Graham. Both of these realities also served to establish that PBI during the Maxwell era never did fully embrace the neo-evangelical agenda. A residual fear that accreditation would lead to PBI's being unable to control its own destiny and possibly cause the school to drift into liberalism was at least part of the reason for the firm resistance to academia that prevailed during Maxwell's tenure at Prairie. His personal suspicion of the perils of higher education was closely linked to fundamentalism's obsession with separation from the world.

On what was perhaps the defining issue that fundamentalists faced in the twentieth century, Maxwell elected to backtrack on his initial endorsement of and enthusiasm for the ministry of the Billy Graham Evangelistic Association. Although the evidence for this "waffling" is inconclusive in terms of leading to a dogmatic explanation as to why he did what he did, what is apparent is that Maxwell opted to defer to the very vocal "anti-Billy Graham" lobby so abundantly evident in the correspondence located in Maxwell's personal files in the PBI Archives. No other conclusion can be drawn except to say that on this definitive issue that divided American fundamentalism in the mid-twentieth century, Maxwell allowed the perception to emerge and prevail that on the Billy Graham question, PBI would side with the anti-Graham fundamentalists.

Chapter Fourteen concludes the book by citing abundant material from Maxwell's writings particularly in the early years at Three Hills that directly refute Stackhouse's reluctance to place either Maxwell or PBI in the camp of militant fundamentalism. Indeed, sufficient citations are included with respect to Maxwell's battle against the United Church of Canada and the theory of evolution to demonstrate that Stackhouse is simply wrong in his assertion that these issues had minimal profile at PBI. In fact, Maxwell's running battles with the United Church of Canada and particularly some of its Calgary-based pastors and churches is impossible to miss in even a casual perusal of the early issues of the *Prairie Pastor.* When it came to the use of militant rhetoric, L.E. Maxwell could slug it out with the best of them!

In summation, with respect to challenging Stackhouse's narrow definition of fundamentalism, this book demonstrates that twentieth century American fundamentalism was more broadly nuanced than what the militancy motif alone permits. Fundamentalism's theological and cultural legacy indeed survived its initial militant orientation. It was also shown that on the basis of Stackhouse's own words, fundamentalism both preceded and outlasted its militant phase when a broader definition of the movement is considered.

The review of its various theological and cultural attributes helped establish that American fundamentalism had a much broader identity than strictly the militancy motif that Stackhouse identifies. Certain theological distinctives and many cultural attributes of American fundamentalism could be distinguished in the movement both before and after its militancy period during the 1920s-1930s.

In the course of documenting the very strong American presence and influence at Prairie Bible Institute, this book has identified several specific areas in which the school during the L.E. Maxwell era demonstrated solidarity with the importance that American fundamentalists placed on visible separation from the world. On some of these matters, PBI demonstrated thinking similar to that which prevailed at places like Moody Bible Institute, Biola College, or Columbia Bible College. On other occasions, the school's philosophy was more closely aligned with the kind of fundamentalism that ruled the day at Bob Jones University.

For Stackhouse to assign the designations "trans-denominational evangelicals" and "sectish evangelicals" to PBI may be accurate and legitimate to some extent. Clearly, there was significant overlap between the evangelical and fundamentalist identities particularly in the first half of the twentieth century. However, it must be noted that, in the course of so doing he ends up applying the term "evangelicals" to people who advocated virtually the identical theology and exemplified virtually the same behavioral and cultural distinctives as did self-described American fundamentalists. This might be considered pure coincidence were it not for the fact that, as this book suggests, a thorough quantifiable analysis of the staff, faculty and student body at Prairie Bible Institute during the period under review would, in all likelihood, demonstrate that the school consistently had a decidedly large American component among its personnel.[2] Additional research of

---

[2] Stackhouse, 84: "Most of [PBI's] students came from the Canadian and American west (from 1949-50 until 75-6, in fact, more students came from the United States than from Canada . . .)

a quantifiable nature would be beneficial in establishing this assumption, however.

The distinction that Stackhouse infers between Canadian "sectish" evangelicals and American fundamentalists is therefore useful only if one accepts the very restricted definition of "fundamentalism" for which Stackhouse argues. As has been documented in this book, not only do several scholars not share such a limited definition of fundamentalism, there is substantial evidence to indicate that Stackhouse attempts a distinction that even he is hard pressed to sustain.

Comments in Stackhouse's work such as "Prairie Bible Institute maintained its separatist stance," or "as did other fundamentalists, Prairie's leaders often" and "Prairie Bible Institute's distinctiveness" indicate that the distinction between American fundamentalism and the Canadian "sectish" evangelical label that Stackhouse assigns PBI is simply not as clear-cut as he would like us to believe.[3] It bears repeating that just sentences after stating that the *Prairie Overcomer* during the Maxwell era "was decidedly not preoccupied with any of these matters as a typical fundamentalist magazine would be," Stackhouse writes: "The usual fundamentalist targets of alcohol, dancing, television, and rock-and-roll do come in for frequent attack in these pages."[4] In this regard, I must respectfully, yet pointedly, ask: so which will it be?

Even from his outsider perspective and given his narrow definition of fundamentalism, Stackhouse himself found it relatively easy to verify that PBI often strayed very close to if not directly into fundamentalist territory. Indeed, the school identified itself as "fundamentalist!"

Given the insights into life at Prairie Bible Institute that I—a former insider—have presented, it should be readily apparent to readers that PBI shared ideological and behavioral patterns with schools that met the broader definition of American fundamentalism such as Columbia, Biola,

---

See Appendix I of this book. While the first twenty-five years saw PBI's student body consist primarily of Canadians, that changed noticeably by mid-century. In any event, it is fair to say that PBI's staff and administration during the Maxwell era consistently reflected a considerable number of Americans. Based on the data in Appendix I of this book, by "a considerable number," I suggest readers can legitimately think in terms of approximately 50% of the PBI community being Americans at any one time during the L.E. Maxwell era.

3   Stackhouse, 14, 86, 145.
4   Ibid., 86.

and Moody. Accordingly, I retain a firm confidence in the validity of my governing hypothesis in this book: it is indeed accurate to refer to Prairie Bible Institute under L.E. Maxwell's leadership from 1922 to 1980 as a fundamentalist organization.

APPENDIX I

Although a quantifiable analysis of Prairie Bible Institute's staff and student body during the period under review in this book did not form a major part of the research reflected herein, the following information is included as a suggestion of where such an analysis might lead an investigator who was to pursue quantifying the American factor at PBI during the L.E. Maxwell era. The specific purpose of including the selected statistics below is to counter Stackhouse's assertion on page 196 of *Canadian Evangelicalism in the Twentieth Century*:

> "The institutions portrayed here as central in the life of Canadian evangelicalism in the twentieth century were, without exception, indigenous Canadian products. However much they benefited in typical Canadian style from British or American initiative . . . the institutions were founded and funded and staffed predominantly by Canadians."

The author of this book spent 1960-1977 growing up on a part of Prairie Bible Institute's campus popularly known as Prairie Heights, a collection of some twenty-six homes on the campus's east side. The staff families who were my neighbors on "the Heights" during my youth are identified below along with their place of residence or citizenship prior to coming to PBI. Prairie Heights would have represented a typical PBI staff community in this regard.

Table I.I

Residents of "Prairie Heights" (c. 1962-1976) and their nationality:

J. Huckaby	USA	U. Janz	Canada
L. Rudderow	USA	W. Jack	Canada
R. Boutwell	USA	R. Wilson	Canada
A. Peterson	USA	J. Vert	Canada
C. Graham	USA	D. Berg	Canada
F. Thompson	USA	R. Butler	Canada
R. Ladewig	USA	C. Wright	Canada
F. deVos	USA	V. Callaway	Canada
R. Jordahl	USA		
J. Silver	USA	G. Head	Canada
A. Lovejoy	USA	W. Major	Canada
M. Wright	USA	H. Muddle	Canada
R. Pulliam	USA	N. Charter	Canada
J. MacLennan	USA	A. Wiebe	Canada
A. Freeman	USA	W. Elliott	Canada
D. Masterson	USA	D. Kirk	Canada
R. Snyder	USA	T. Ewing	Canada
R. Reed	USA	S. Hanson	Canada
F. Hoehnle—	USA	G. MacPherson Canada	Canada
F. Pike	USA	S. Estabrooks	Canada
		G. Lewis	Canada
J. Pace	USA	S. Hanson	Canada
R. Cline	USA	N. Wilkins	Canada
J. Sylvania	USA	C. Creasser	Canada
G. Ross	USA	A. Bienert	Canada
L. Workentine	USA	L. Lindbergh	Canada
L. Couse	USA		
E. Bowling	USA		
V. Keller	USA		
L. Hart	USA		
D. Adkins	USA	D. Zweifel	Switzerland
D. Long	USA		

R. Porr	one parent from USA, the other from Canada
S. Erickson	one parent from USA, the other from Canada

Table I.2

My elementary school teachers (1961-1970) and their nationality:

1961	Kindergarten	Mrs. Ross	USA
		Mrs. Mumford	USA
1962	Grade One	Mrs. Steele	Canada
1963	Grade Two	Mrs. McLennan	USA
1964	Grade Three	Mrs. Dolsen	USA
		Mrs. Rosevere	USA
1965	Grade Four	Miss Hurl	Canada
1966	Grade Five	Mr. Blake	USA
1967	Grade Six	Mr. Janz	Canada
1968	Grade Seven	Mr. Silver	USA
1969	Grade Eight	Mr. Pike	USA
	Miss Gale	Canada	

Table I.3

My high school teachers (1970-1974) and their nationality:

W. Akers	USA
K. Amstutz	Canada
R. Armbruster	Canada
C. Baines	USA
H. Bradley	Canada
G. Bryant	USA
K. Capps	USA
J. Carroll	USA
L. Couse	USA
F. deVos	USA
E. Ely	USA
E. Firth	Canada
L. Freswick	USA
R. Gamache	USA
L. Hart	USA
J. McClenahan	USA
P. Norbo	USA

K. Penner	Canada
A. Peterson	USA
W. Pike	USA
W. Shewell	USA
W. Tilzey	USA
H. Tromsness	USA
M. Wright	USA
J. Yule	USA

Table I.4

My Bible School teachers (1974-1977) and their nationality:

B. Bates	Australia
J. Boswell	USA
R. Boytim	USA
A. Burgess	USA
A. Chamberlain	Canada
E. Charter	Canada
R. Cline	USA
G. Crouch	Australia
A. Douglas	Canada
K. Dearing	USA
R. Dearing	USA
S. Erickson	USA
H. Elliott	Canada
N. Garwood	USA
S. Hanson	Canada
K. Haynes	USA
G. Head	Canada
M. Hoath	USA
G. Imbach	USA
W. Irving	Canada
R. Jordahl	USA
D. Kennedy	USA
J. Kayser	USA/Canada (dual citizen)
C. Kinvig	Canada
P. Kinvig	Canada

C. Kondos	USA
R. Malesky	USA
A. Martin	USA
D. Masterson	USA
L. Maxwell	USA
P. Maxwell	Canada
P. Meier	Canada
E. Mumford	USA
R. Murray	Canada
R. Olson	USA
A. Olver	Canada
G. Poehnell	Canada
D. Powell	Canada
R. Rakestraw	USA
L. Rausch	USA
P. Rausch	USA
N. Reed	USA
T. Rendall	Scotland
L. Robinson	South Africa
J. Strakbein	USA
L. Teale	USA
G.Trevalyan	Canada
N. Wilkins	Canada
B. Witherspoon	USA

Table 1.5

PBI Administration during my years at PBI (1960-1977)

1960 Administrative Board of Directors

President	L.E. Maxwell	USA
Co-Founder	J.F. Kirk	Canada
Secretary	A.H. Muddle	Canada
Personnel	D.E. Crites	USA
Business	G.R. Imbach	USA
Registrar	R. Dearing	USA
Member at L	M. Olson	Canada

Phys Plant	S. Hanson	Canada
Member at L	J.M. Murray	Canada

1966 Administrative Board of Directors

President	L.E. Maxwell	USA
Co-Founder	J.F. Kirk	Canada
Vice-Pres	T.S. Rendall	Scotland
Registrar	R.C. Dearing	USA
Exec Dir	A.H. Muddle	Canada
Bus Mgr	G.R. Imbach	USA
Personnel	D.E. Crites	USA
Secretary	D. Powell	Canada

1966 Board of Governors

J. Murray	Canada
C. Strom	Canada
D. Masterson	USA
H. Dolsen	USA
M. Olson	Canada
K. Westfall	USA
J. Powles	Canada
H. Elliot	Canada
R. Snyder	USA
G. Imbach	USA
D. Crites	USA
S. Hanson	Canada
R. Bicknell	USA
D. Powell	Canada
L. Maxwell	USA
R. Dearing	USA
JF Kirk	Canada
A. Muddle	Canada
T. Rendall	Scotland
R. Kirk	Canada
R. Gamache	USA
A. Freeman	USA

1970 Administrative Board of Directors

L.E. Maxwell	USA
D.E. Crites	USA
A.H. Muddle	Canada
W.H. Elliot	Canada
T.S. Rendall	Scotland
H. Dolsen	USA
R.C Dearing	USA
A.C. Strom	Canada
G.R. Imbach	USA
J.F. Kirk	Canada

Table 1.6

PBI's North American graduates during L.E. Maxwell tenure at PBI (1922-1980)

Year	Canadians	Americans
1927	7	
1929	14	5
1930	7	2
1931	5	-
1932	12	2
1934	19	3
1935	48	1
1936	61	8
1937	48	8
1938	41	13
1939	52	15
1940	34	15
1941	45	17
1942	53	17
1943	48	14
1944	52	18
1945	49	19
1946	31	16
1947	68	24
1948	60	17
1949	63	36

Year	Canadians	Americans
1950	92	58
1951	71	83
1952	62	54
1953	53	77
1954	50	63
1955	36	44
1956	32	54
1957	52	61
1958	41	52
1959	46	49
1960	40	48
1961	37	52
1962	53	72
1963	44	70
1964	44	57
1965	37	51
1966	30	51
1967	37	53
1968	46	90
1969	35	80
1970	34	61
1971	55	60
1972	54	57
1973	50	50
1974	61	46
1975	48	68
1976	40	61
1977	69	46
1978	62	46
1979	76	63
1980	67	38

APPENDIX II

(additional works on PBI)

I.   A variety of early booklets

Several small booklets summarizing the history of PBI and the school's distinctives were published by the Institute during its first fifty years. These include *First Things First* by Hector Kirk, one of J. Fergus Kirk's brothers. The undated tract-like booklet gives a brief account of how the godly Kirk family eventually arrived in Three Hills. *Hoping for Nothing*, dated 1955, is a similarly sized booklet containing an article of that title by Philip E. Howard, Jr., editor of *The Sunday School Times*, a dominant periodical that circulated among North American fundamentalists for a century. *Hoping for Nothing* also includes a "Further Sketch of History" by L.E. Maxwell that concludes with an invitation to young people to consider attending PBI. Another booklet entitled *The Miracle of Prairie Bible Institute* dated 1959 is an update by Maxwell of the *First Things First* tract and reprints Howard's *Hoping for Nothing* and Maxwell's "Further Sketch of History" pieces. These three pieces were eventually published in numerous editions under the title With God on the Prairies which was the standard publicity statement the school circulated until the publication of *Expendable!*

2.   *Nothing in my hand*—by Mrs. Mabel Kirk McElheran (Printed in Canada with Forward dated December, 1960)

This autobiography by J. Fergus Kirk's oldest sister was originally published a couple of years before her death in 1963 and is now available online at: http://iam.homewithgod.com/byhisgracealone/nothinginmy/indexlhtml (accessed April 9, 2009). PBI officially started with classes held in an abandoned farmhouse on the McElheran family's property. The primary value of the book to this study is the insight it gives into the very devout

Christian piety that Mabel learned growing up in the Andrew and Maria Kirk home which she then practiced throughout her life. The pietism the Kirk family contributed to the embryonic PBI stressed frequent spiritual crises often involving deep guilt. It also emphasized the importance of surrendering legitimate pursuits in society (i.e. classical music) as worldly distractions in order to go to the foreign mission field. PBI considered such sacrifices to be the supreme display of Christian devotion.

3. *Raise up the Foundations!*—by Juanita C. Snyder (Three Hills, AB: Prairie Bible Institute, 1966) 69 pp.

This short book, penned by the wife of a PBI music faculty member at the time, tells the story of J. Fergus Kirk's parents, Andrew and Maria (Marshall) Kirk from their youth to the time of their death. Several points with some minor relevance to the present project include: their meeting at a Methodist church in Ontario; Maria's deep appreciation for Hannah Whitehall Smith's classic *The Christian's Secret of a Happy Life*; the Kirk's sacrificial support of foreign missions; Andrew Kirk's encounter with the Holy Spirit and subsequent Christian service; the attendance of Edward, Hattie and Elsie, siblings of J. Fergus Kirk, at the Missionary Training Institute at Nyack, New York; Andrew's acceptance in 1908 as a full-time missionary with the Presbyterian Board which eventually brought them to Three Hills.

4. *She Has Done What She Could*—by John Cunningham (Three Hills, AB: Prairie Bible Institute, 1976) 55 pp.

This brief work outlines the biography of Mrs. Catherine Cunningham, Dean of Bible School Women at Prairie Bible Institute, 1955-1962, for whom Cunningham Memorial Residence on the school's campus is named. The book is a sympathetic view of a saintly woman as seen through the eyes of her eldest son who, along with his three brothers, all graduated from PBI and entered full-time Christian service. In addition to highlighting the story of a Canadian family that was profoundly influenced by and contributed to the work of PBI, the slim volume's Introduction is written by Betty (Howard) Elliot, a PBI alumni and one of the American heroes of the twentieth century missionary movement that was spurred on by schools such as PBI. The work helps underscore the prominent role capable women were given at PBI throughout the L.E. Maxwell era.

5. *The Spirit of Prairie*—by Bernice and Victor Callaway (Three Hills: Prairie Bible Institute, 1997) 78 pp.

This piece of pictorial memorabilia was prepared for Prairie's 75th anniversary and Homecoming in 1997 by my own parents. The book's text gives a brief, historical summation of the school's 75 years and includes brief tributes from a sampling of its alumni.

6. **Culture of the Soul: Fundamentalism and Evangelism in Canada, 1921-1940—by James W. Opp, MA thesis at the University of Calgary, Calgary, Alberta, Canada; 1994, 150 pp.**

This brief thesis examines several different aspects of Canadian fundamentalism in the early twentieth century. Although the work touches only occasionally on PBI, its primary value for the purposes of this study is the clarity that Opp demonstrates in portraying L.E. Maxwell and Prairie Bible Institute as promoters of the fundamentalist cause. As well, Opp's work contributes to my skepticism regarding the legitimacy of making the kind of clear-cut distinctions between Canadian and American forms of fundamentalism that Stackhouse attempts.

7. **A Comparative Study of the Doctrine of the Christian Life As Set Forth by Dr. Robert C. McQuilken and Reverend Leslie E. Maxwell—by Jeanne Schaufelberg, MA thesis at Columbia International University, Columbia, SC; 1984, 93 pp.**

This thesis was not examined for the purposes of this study. It is mentioned here in the interests of compiling as complete a record as possible concerning the academic work done on PBI.

8. **Learning Strategies of Bible College freshmen: A case study of Prairie Bible College—by Lynn H. Wallace, EdD dissertation at Montana State University; 1994, 145 pp.**

The impact of selected demographic characteristics and use of ten learning strategies upon first semester GPA is examined among 122 freshmen at Prairie Bible College (PBC) in Three Hills, Alberta. As above, this work was not examined for the purposes of this book but is nevertheless listed in the interests of compiling as complete a record as possible regarding the academic work that has been done on PBI.

BIBLIOGRAPHY

I. Primary Sources

A. Books

Kirk, Hector. *Balanced Security.* Maple, ON: The Beacon Press, *n.d.*

————. *First Things First.* Three Hills: Prairie Press, *n.d.*

————. *With God on the Prairies.* Three Hills: Prairie Press, *n.d.*

Kirk, J. Fergus. *Jesus Christ: the same yesterday, and today, and forever.* Three Hills: J.F. Kirk, *n.d.*

Kirk, J. Fergus. "Social Credit and the Word of God," In *Aberhart: Outpourings and Replies,* edited by David R. Elliott, 109-122. Edmonton: Historical Society of Alberta, 1991.

Maxwell, L.E. *Abandoned to Christ.* Grand Rapids: William B. Eerdmans Publishing Co., 1955.

————. *Born Crucified.* Chicago: Moody Press, 1945.

————. *Capital Punishment.* Three Hills: Prairie Bible Institute, *n.d.*

————. *Crowded to Christ.* Grand Rapids: William B. Eerdmans Publishing Co., 1950.

————. *Prairie Pillars.* Three Hills: Prairie Bible Institute, *n.d.*

————. *Quips & Quotes.* Three Hills: Action International Ministries, 1992.

————. *The Pentecostal Baptism: a Biblical analysis and appraisal.* Three Hills: Prairie Bible Institute, 1971.

————. *World Missions: Total War.* Three Hills: Prairie Press, 1977.

———— with Ruth C. Dearing. *Women in Ministry: A Historical and Biblical Look at the Role of Women in Christian Leadership.* Wheaton, IL: Victor Books, 1987.

Miller, Dorothy Ruth. *A Handbook of Ancient History in Bible Light.* New York: Fleming H. Revell Co., 1937.

Principles and Practice of Prairie Bible Institute. Three Hills: Prairie Bible Institute, *n.d.*

Rendall, T.S. *In God's School.* Three Hills, Prairie Press, 1971.

————. *Jeremiah: Prophet of Crisis.* Three Hills, Prairie Press, 1979.

_____. *Nehemiah: Laws of Leadership.* Three Hills: Prairie Press, 1980.

The Miracle of Prairie Bible Institute. Three Hills: Prairie Press, *n.d.*

B. Archival materials

Maxwell, L.E. Personal files located in the PBI Library Archives.

Prairie Bible Institute Administrative Team files located in the PBI Library Archives.

Prairie Bible Institute Board of Directors files located in the PBI Library Archives

Prairie Bible Institute Catalogs and Student Handbooks files located in the PBI Records Office.

Prairie Bible Institute Education Committee files located in the PBI Library Archives.

Prairie Bible Institute Operating Executive Committee files located in the PBI Library Archives.

C. Journals:

The Prairie Harvester. (Selected issues)

The Prairie Overcomer. 1946-1988.

The Prairie Pastor. 1928-1943

The Prairie Pastor and Overcomer. 1943-1945

D. Websites:

McElheran, Mabel Kirk. "Nothing In My Hand." http://iam.homewithgod.com/byhisgracealone/nothinginmy/index.html (accessed March 16, 2009).

II. Secondary sources

A. Anthropological perspectives

Langness, LL. *The Life History in Anthropological Science.* New York: Holt, Rinehart and Winston. 1965.

B. Articles in books

Acheson, T.W. "Evangelicals and Public Life in Southern New Brunswick, 1830-1880." In *Religion and Public Life: Historical and Comparative Perspectives*, edited by Marguerite Van Die, 50-68. Toronto: University of Toronto Press, 2001.

Ahlstrom, Sydney E. "From Puritanism to Evangelicalism: A Critical Perspective." In *The Evangelicals: What They Believe, Who They Are, How They Are Changing*, edited by David F. Wells and John D. Woodbridge, 289-309. Grand Rapids: Baker Book House, 1977.

Allen, Richard. "The Social Gospel as the Religion of Agrarian Revolt." In *The Prairie West: Historical Readings*, edited by R. Douglas Francis and Howard Palmer, 439-449. Edmonton, AB: Pica Pica Press/University of Alberta Press, 1985.

Almond, Gabriel A., Emmanuel Sivan and Scott R. Appleby. "Fundamentalism: Genus and Species." In *Fundamentalisms Comprehended*, edited by Martin E. Marty and Scott R. Appleby, 399-424. Chicago: University of Chicago Press, 1995.

Ammerman, Nancy T. "North American Protestant Fundamentalism." In *Fundamentalisms Observed*, edited by Martin E. Marty and R. Scott Appleby, 1-65. Chicago: University of Chicago Press, 1991.

Askew, Thomas A. "The Shaping of Evangelical Higher Education Since World War II." In *Making Higher Education Christian*, edited by Joel A. Carpenter and Kenneth W. Shipps, 137-152. Grand Rapids: William B. Eerdmans Publishing Co., 1987.

Austin, Alvyn J. "The Transplanted Mission: The China Inland Mission and Canadian Evangelicalism." In *Aspects of the Canadian Evangelical Experience*, edited by G.A. Rawlyk, 351-368. Montreal & Kingston: McGill-Queen's University Press, 1997.

Barr, John J. "The Impact of Oil on Alberta: Retrospect and Prospect." In A.W. Rasporich (ed.), *The Making of the Modern West: Western Canada Since 1945* Calgary: University of Calgary Press, 1984), 98-99

Brereton, Virginia Lieson. "Bible Schools and Evangelical Higher Education." In *Making Higher Education Christian*, edited by Joel A. Carpenter and Kenneth W. Shipps, 110-136. Grand Rapids: William B. Eerdmans Publishing Co., 1987.

Burkinshaw, Robert K. "Evangelical Bible Colleges in Twentieth-Century Canada." In *Aspects of the Canadian Evangelical Experience*, edited by G.A. Rawlyk, 369-384. Montreal & Kingston: McGill-Queen's University Press, 1997.

Carpenter, Joel A. "The Fundamentalist Leaven and the Rise of An Evangelical United Front." In *The Evangelical Tradition in America*, edited by Leonard I. Sweet, 257-88. Macon, GA: Mercer University Press, 1997.

Carter, Paul A. "The Fundamentalist Defense of the Faith." In *Change and Continuity in Twentieth Century America: the 1920s*, edited by John Braeman, Robert H. Bremner, and David Brody, 183-197. Columbus, OH: Columbus State University, 1968.

Cook, Sharon Anne. "Evangelical Moral Reform: Women and the War Against Tobacco, 1874-1900." In *Religion and Public Life in Canada: Historical and Comparative Perspectives*, edited by Marguerite Van Die, 177-195. Toronto: University of Toronto Press, 2001.

Dayton, Donald W. "The Limits of Evangelicalism: The Pentecostal Tradition." In *The Variety of American Evangelicalism*, edited by Donald W. Dayton and Robert K. Johnston, 36-56. Downers Grove, IL: Inter-Varsity Press, 1991

Elliott, David R. "Three Faces of Baptist Fundamentalism in Canada: Aberhart, Maxwell, and Shields." In *Memory and Hope: Strands of Canadian Baptist History*, edited by David T. Priestly, 171-182. (Waterloo, ON: Wilfred Laurier University Press, 1996).

Gerstner, John H. "The Reformed Perspective." In *The Evangelicals: What They Believe, Who They Are, Where They Are Changing*, edited by David F. Wells and John D. Woodbridge, 21-37. Grand Rapids: Baker Book House, 1977.

Hindmarsh, D. Bruce. "The Winnipeg Fundamentalist Network, 1910-1940: The Roots of Transdenominational Evangelicalism in Manitoba and Saskatchewan." In *Aspects of the Canadian Evangelical Experience*, edited by G.A. Rawlyk, 303-319. Montreal & Kingston: McGill-Queen's University Press, 1997.

Hall, D.J. "Clifford Sifton: Immigration and Settlement Policy 1896-1905." In *The Prairie West: Historical Readings*, edited by R. Douglas Francis and Howard Palmer, 281-308. Edmonton, AB: Pica Pica Press/University of Alberta Press, 1985.

Hiller, Harry H. "Alberta and the Bible Belt Stereotype." In *Religion in Canadian Society*, edited by Stewart Crysdale and Les Wheatcroft, 372-383. Toronto: Macmillan of Canada, 1976.

Hunter, James Davison. "Fundamentalism in Its Global Contours." In *The Fundamentalist Phenomenon: a view from within; a response from without*, edited by Norman J. Cohen, 56-72. Grand Rapids: William B. Eerdmans Publishing Co., 1990.

Kantzer, Kenneth S. "The Future of the Church and Evangelicalism." In *Evangelicals Face the Future*, edited by Donald E. Hoke, 125-135. South Pasadena, CA: William Carey Library, 1978.

――――――. "Unity and Diversity in Evangelical Faith." In *The Evangelicals: What They Believe, Who They Are, Where They Are Changing*, edited by David F. Wells and John D. Woodbridge, 58-87. Grand Rapids: Baker Book House, 1977.

Marsden, George M. "Defining American Fundamentalism." In *The Fundamentalist Phenomenon: a view from within; a response from without*, edited by Norman J. Cohen, 22-37. Grand Rapids: William B. Eerdmans Publishing Co., 1990.

――――――. "Evangelical and Fundamental Christianity." In *The Encyclopedia of Religion* (Vol. 5), edited by Mircea Eliade, 190-197. New York: Macmillan Publishing Co., 1987.

――――――. "Fundamentalism." In *Encyclopedia of the American Religious Experience: Studies of Traditions and Movements* (Vol. II), edited by Charles H. Lippy and Peter W. Williams, 947-962. New York: Charles Scribner's Sons, 1988.

――――――. "Fundamentalism and American Evangelicalism." In *The Variety of American Evangelicalism*, edited by Donald W. Dayton and Robert K. Johnston, 22-35. Downers Grove, IL: Inter-Varsity Press. 1991.

――――――. "The Evangelical Denomination." In *Evangelicalism and Modern America*, edited by George M. Marsden, vii-xix. Grand Rapids: William B. Eerdmans Publishing Co., 1984.

Marty, Martin E. "Tensions Within Contemporary Evangelicalism: A Critical Appraisal." In *The Evangelicals: What They Believe, Who They Are, How They Are Changing*, edited by David F. Wells and John D. Woodbridge, 190-208. Grand Rapids: Baker Book House, 1977.

Mitchinson, Wendy. "Women's Christian Temperance Union." In *An Introduction to Canadian History*, edited by A.I. Silver, 614. Toronto: Canadian Scholars' Press, Inc., 1991.

Noll, Mark A. "Canadian Evangelicalism: A View from the United States." In *Aspects of the Canadian Evangelical Experience*, edited by G.A. Rawlyk, 3-20. Montreal & Kingston: McGill-Queen's University Press, 1997.

_____. "Princeton Theology, Old." In *Evangelical Dictionary of Theology*, edited by Walter A. Elwell, 877-878. Grand Rapids, Baker Book House, 1984.

_____. "The Revolution, the Enlightenment, and Christian Higher Education in the Early Republic. In *Making Higher Education Christian*, edited by Joel A. Carpenter and Kenneth W. Shipps, 56-76. Grand Rapids: William B. Eerdmans Publishing Co., 1987.

_____. "The University Arrives in America, 1870-1930." In *Making Higher Education Christian*, edited by Joel A. Carpenter and Kenneth W. Shipps, 98-109. Grand Rapids: William B. Eerdmans Publishing Co., 1987.

Ostow, Mortimer. "The Fundamentalist Phenomenon: A Psychological Perspective." In *The Fundamentalist Phenomenon: a view from within; a response from without*, edited by Norman J. Cohen, 99-125. Grand Rapids: William B. Eerdmans Publishing Co., 1990.

Palmer, Howard. "Strangers and Stereotypes: The Rise of Nativism—1880-1920." In *The Prairie West: Historical Readings*, edited by R. Douglas Francis and Howard Palmer, 309-333. Edmonton, AB: Pica Pica Press/University of Alberta Press, 1985.

Parent, Mark. "The Irony of Fundamentalism: T.T. Shields and the Person of Christ." In *Memory and Hope: Strands of Canadian Baptist History*, edited by David T. Priestley, 183-196. Waterloo, ON: Wilfred Laurier University Press, 1996.

Pierard, Richard V. "Evangelicalism." In *Evangelical Dictionary of Theology*, edited by Walter A. Elwell, 379-382. Grand Rapids: Baker Book House, 1984.

Pinnock, Clark H. "Defining American Fundamentalism: A Response." In *The Fundamentalist Phenomenon: a view from within, a response from without*, edited by Norman J. Cohen, 38-55. Grand Rapids: William B. Eerdmans Publishing Co., 1990.

Ringenberg, William C. "The Old-Time College, 1800-1865." In *Making Higher Education Christian*, edited by Joel A. Carpenter and Kenneth W. Shipps, 77-93. Grand Rapids: William B. Eerdmans Publishing Co., 1987.

Stackhouse, John G., Jr. "Who Whom?: Evangelicalism and Canadian Society." In *Aspects of the Canadian Evangelical Experience*, edited by G.A. Rawlyk, 55-70. Montreal & Kingston: McGill-Queen's University Press, 1997.

Stump, Roger W. "Fundamentalism." In *St. James Encyclopedia of Pop Culture*, edited by Sara Pendergast & Tom Pendergast, 181-183. Detroit: St. James Press, 2000.

Sweet, Leonard I. "Nineteenth-Century Evangelicalism." In *Encyclopedia of the American Religious Experience: Studies of Traditions and Movements* (Vol. II), edited by Charles H. Lippy and Peter W. Williams, 875-899. New York: Charles Scribner's Sons, 1988.

——————. "The Evangelical Tradition in America." In *The Evangelical Tradition in America*, edited by Leonard I. Sweet, 1-86. Macon, GA: Mercer University Press, 1984.

Synan, Vinson. "Theological Boundaries: The Arminian Tradition." In *The Evangelicals: What They Believe, Who They Are, Where They are Changing*, edited by David F. Wells and John D. Woodbridge, 38-57. Grand Rapids: Baker Book House, 1977.

Thomas, Lewis H. "A History of Agriculture on the Prairies to 1914." In *The Prairie West: Historical Readings*, edited by R. Douglas Francis and Howard Palmer, 221-236. Edmonton, AB: Pica Pica Press/University of Alberta Press, 1985.

Weber, Timothy P. "Premillenialism and the Branches of Evangelicalism." In *The Variety of American Evangelicalism*, edited by Donald W. Dayton and Robert K. Johnston, 5-21. Downers Grove, IL: Inter-Varsity Press, 1991.

Wright, Robert A. "The Canadian Protestant Tradition 1914-1945." In *The Canadian Protestant Experience*, edited by George A. Rawlyk, 141-160. Burlington, ON: Welch Publishing Company, 1990.

Young, Walter D. "The C.C.F.: The Radical Background." In *The Prairie West: Historical Readings*, edited by R. Douglas Francis and Howard Palmer, 538-558. Edmonton, AB: Pica Pica Press/University of Alberta Press, 1985.

C. Articles in journals

Armstrong, Karen, Susannah Heschel, Jim Wallis & Feisal Abdul Rauf. "Fundamentalism and the Modern World." *Sojourners*, March-April 2002; 20-26.

Bibby, Reginald W. "Religion and Modernity: The Canadian Case." *Journal for the Scientific Study of Religion* 18 (March 1979): 1-17.

Boyer, Peter J. "The Big Tent: Billy Graham, Franklin Graham, and the transformation of American evangelicalism." *The New Yorker,* Vol. 81, No. 24; August 22, 2005: 42f . . .

Carpenter, Joel A. "Fundamentalist Institutions and the Rise of Evangelical Protestantism, 1929-1942." *Church History* 49, No. 1 (March 1980): 62-75.

Chandler, Graham. "Loosening our Bible Belt: The Changing Faith of Alberta." *Alberta Views,* November/December 2001: 30-36.

Coreno, Thaddeus. "Fundamentalism as a class culture." *Sociology of Religion* (Fall 2002), 1-24.

Farley, Edward. "Fundamentalism: A Theory." *Crosscurrents* (Fall 2005): 378-402.

Fuller, W. Harold. "The Legacy of Leslie E. Maxwell. *International Bulletin of Missionary Research* 28 (July 2004), 126-130

Grenz, Stanley J. "Book Review: *Canadian Evangelicalism in the Twentieth Century.*" *Christian Century,* Vol. 111, No. 9, March 16, 1994: 288-289.

Guenther, Bruce L. "Slithering Down the Plank of Intellectualism? The Canadian Conference of Christian Educators and the Impulse Towards Accreditation Among Canadian Bible Schools During the 1960s." *Historical Studies in Education* 16, No. 2 (2004): 197-228.

Hiller, Harry H. "Continentalism and the Third Force in Religion." *Canadian Journal of Sociology* 3 (Spring 1978): 183-207.

Jacobsen, Douglas. "Book Review: *The American Evangelical Story.*" *Church History* 75, No. 2: 464-465.

LeVine, Mark. "What is Fundamentalism, and How Do We Get Rid Of It?" *Journal of Ecumenical Studies* 42: No. 1 (Winter 2007): 15-28. .

McKinney, Larry J. "Protestant Fundamentalism and Its Relationship to the Bible College Movement in North America." *North American Religion* 5 (1996/7): 90-113.

_____. "The Growth of the Bible College Movement in Canada." *Didaskalia* 10:1, (Fall 1998): 31-48.

McLoughlin, William. "Is There a Third Force in Christendom?" *Daedalus* 46 (Winter 1967): 43-68.

Numrich, Paul David. "Fundamentalisms and American Pluralism." *Journal of Ecumenical Studies* 42, No. 1 (Winter 2007): 9-14.

Rawlyk, George A. "Religion in Canada: A Historical Overview." *The Annals of the American Academy AAPSS* 538 (March 1995): 131-142.

Ryan, M.B. "Provinces of Western Canada Call for the Restoration Message." *Christian Standard*, LXIII, No. 8, (February 25, 1928).

Sawatzky, Ron. "Book Review: Canadian Evangelicalism in the Twentieth Century." *Church History*, Vol. 63, No. 3, 485-487.

Smith, Timothy L. "The Evangelical Kaleidoscope and the Call to Unity." *Christian Scholar's Review* 15, No. 2 (1986): 125-140.

Stewart, Kenneth J. "Did Evangelicalism Predate the Eighteenth Century? An Examination of David Bebbington's Thesis." *Evangelical Quarterly* 77, No. 2; April 2005: 135-153.

Sweet, Leonard I. "Wise as Serpents, Innocents as Doves: The New Evangelical Historiography." *Journal of the American Academy of Religion* 56 (Fall 1988): 397-416.

Woodbridge, John D. "The Fundamentalist Label" (an interview). *Trinity Magazine*, (Spring 2009): 7f.

D. Books

I. History of Alberta/The West

Barr, John J. *The Dynasty: The Rise and Fall of Social Credit in Alberta.* Toronto: McClelland and Stewart Ltd., 1974.

Brennan, Brian. *Building a Province: 60 Alberta Lives.* Calgary: Fifth House Publishers, 2000.

Byfield, Ted (ed.). *Alberta in the 20th Century* (vol. 2). Edmonton, AB: United Western Communications Ltd., 1992.

Conway, J.E. *The West: The History of a Region in Confederation.* Toronto: James Lorimer & Company, Publishers, 1983.

Ford, Catherine. *Against the Grain: An Irreverent View of Alberta.* Toronto: McClelland & Stewart Ltd., 2005.

Francis, R. Douglas and Howard Palmer (Eds). *The Prairie West: Historical Readings.* Edmonton: Pica Pica Press, 1985.

Friesen, Gerald. *The Canadian Prairies: A History.* Toronto: University of Toronto Press, 2002. (repr.)

Hamilton, Jacques. *Our Alberta Heritage Series: People.* Calgary: Calgary Power Ltd., 1971.

_____. *Our Alberta Heritage Series: Places.* Calgary: Calgary Power Ltd., 1971.

_____. *Our Alberta Heritage Series: Progress.* Calgary: Calgary Power Ltd., 1971.

Hanson, Eric. *Local Government in Alberta.* Toronto: McClelland & Stewart Ltd. 1956.

Kennedy, Fred. *Alberta Was My Beat.* Calgary: The Albertan, 1975.

MacEwan, Grant. *Eye Opener Bob: The Story of Bob Edwards.* Edmonton: Institute of Applied Art, 1958.

_____. *Fifty Mighty Men.* Saskatoon, SK: Western Producer Prairie Books, 1975.

Macpherson, C.B. *Democracy in Alberta: Social Credit and the Party System* (Second Ed.). Toronto: University of Toronto Press, 1962.

Palmer, Howard (with Tamara Palmer). *Alberta: A New History.* Edmonton, AB: Hurtig Publishers Ltd., 1990.

Van Herk, Aritha. *Mavericks: An Incorrigible History of Alberta.* Toronto: Penguin Canada, 2002. (repr.)

2. History of Canada

Brown, Craig (ed). *The Illustrated History of Canada:* Toronto: Lester Publishing, 1991.

Careless, J.M.S. *Canada: A Story of Challenge.* Toronto: Macmillan of Canada, 1970.

Francis, R. Douglas and Donald B. Smith. *Reading Canadian History.* Scarborough, ON: Nelson Thomson Learning, 2002.

Francis, R. Douglas and Donald B. Smith. *Readings in Canadian History: Post-Confederation* (Second Ed.). Toronto: Holt, Rinehart and Winston of Canada, 1986.

Francis, R. Douglas, Richard Jones and Donald B. Smith. *Destinies: Canadian History Since Confederation* (4th ed.). Scarborough, ON: Nelson Thomson Learning, 2000.

Grant, W.L. *Ontario High School History of Canada.* (Revised & Enlarged Ed.) Toronto: The Ryerson Press, 1926.

Gray, James H. *The Roar of the Twenties.* Toronto: Macmillan of Canada, 1975.

Masters, D.C. *The Coming of Age.* Montreal: Canadian Broadcasting Corporation, 1967.

McClung, Nellie. *Clearing in the West: An Autobiography.* Toronto: Thomas Allen & Son Limited, 1976.

Morton, Desmond. *A Short History of Canada*. Edmonton: Hurtig Publishers Ltd.,1983.

Rawlyk, G. A. *Revolution Rejected 1775-1776*. Scarborough, ON: Prentice-Hall of Canada, Ltd., 1968.

Silver, A.I. *An Introduction to Canadian History*. Toronto: Canadian Scholars' Press, Inc., 1991.

Wrong, George M., Chester Martin and Walter N. Sage. *The Story of Canada*. Toronto: The Ryerson Press, 1935. (repr.)

3. History of Canadian religion

Berton, Pierre. *The Comfortable Pew*. Toronto: McClelland & Stewart Ltd., 1965.

Burkinshaw, Robert K. *Pilgrims In Lotus Land: Conservative Protestantism in British Columbia 1917-1981*. Montreal & Kingston: McGill-Queen's University Press, 1995.

Clark, S.D. *Church and Sect in Canada*. Toronto: University of Toronto Press, 1948.

Crouse, Eric R. *Revival in the City: The Impact of American Evangelists in Canada 1884-1914*. Montreal & Kingston: McGill-Queen's University Press, 2005.

Crysdale, Stewart and Les Wheatcroft (Eds). *Religion in Canadian Society*. Toronto: Macmillan of Canada, 1976.

Enarson, David E. *Thine Hand Upon Me: He Tells it Like it Was*. n.p., n.d.

Gauvreau, Michael. *The Evangelical Century: College and Creed in English Canada from the Great Revival to the Great Depression*. Montreal and Kingston: McGill-Queen's University Press, 1991.

Graham, Ron. *God's Dominion: A Skeptic's Quest*. Toronto: McClelland & Stewart Inc., 1990.

Grant, John Webster (ed). *The Churches and the Canadian Experience: A Faith and Order Study of The Christian Tradition*. Toronto: The Ryerson Press, 1966. (repr.)

Grant, _____. *The Church in the Canadian Era* (Updated and Expanded). Burlington, ON: Welch Publishing Co., 1988.

Hanson, Calvin B. *The Trinity Story*. Minneapolis: Free Church Press, 1983.

Mann, William E. *Sect, Cult and Church in Alberta*. Toronto: University of Toronto Press, 1972. (repr.)

Marshall, David B. *Secularizing the Faith: Canadian Protestant Clergy and the Crisis of Belief, 1850-1940.* Toronto: University of Toronto Press, 1992.

Murphy, Terrence and Roberto Perin. *Concise History of Christianity in Canada.* Toronto: Oxford University Press, 1996.

Priestley, David T. (Ed.). *Memory and Hope: Strands of Canadian Baptist History.* Waterloo, ON: Wilfred Laurier University, 1996.

Rawlyk, George A. (Ed). *Aspects of the Canadian Evangelical Experience.* Montreal & Kingston: McGill-Queen's University Press, 1997.

_____. *Champions of the Truth: Fundamentalism, Modernism, and the Maritime Baptists.* Montreal & Kingston: McGill-Queen's University Press, 1990.

_____. *Is Jesus Your Personal Saviour? In Search of Canadian Evangelicalism in the 1990s.* Montreal & Kingston: McGill-Queen's University Press, 1996.

_____. *Ravished by the Spirit: Religious Revivals, Baptist, and Henry Alline.* Montreal & Kingston: McGill-Queen's University Press, 1984.

_____. *The Canada Fire: Radical Evangelicalism in British North America 1775-1812.* Montreal & Kingston: McGill-Queen's University Press, 1994.

_____. (Ed). *The Canadian Protestant Experience.* Burlington, ON: Welch Publishing Co., 1990.

_____. *Wrapped Up in God: A Study of Several Canadian Revivals and Revivalists.* Burlington, ON: Welch Publishing Co., 1988.

Rawlyk, George and Kevin Quinn. *The Redeemed of the Lord Say So: A History of Queen's Theological College 1912-1972.* Kingston: ON: Queen's Theological College, 1980.

Renfree, Harry A. *Heritage and Horizon: The Baptist Story in Canada.* Mississauga, ON: Canadian Baptist Federation, 1988.

Reynolds, Lindsay. *Rebirth: the redevelopment of the Christian and Missionary Alliance in Canada.* Willowdale, ON: C&MA in Canada, 1992.

Tarr, Leslie K. *Shields of Canada: T.T. Shields 1873-1955.* Grand Rapids: Baker Book House, 1967.

Taylor, Bill. *From Infancy to Adolescence: The Evangelical Free Church of Canada, 1984-2005.* Belleville, ON: Guardian Books, 2007.

Van Die, Marguerite (Ed). *Religion and Public Life in Canada: Historical and Comparative Perspectives.* Toronto: University of Toronto Press, 2001.

Walsh, H.H. *The Christian Church in Canada.* Toronto: The Ryerson Press, 1956.

Westfall, William. *Two Worlds: The Protestant Culture of Nineteenth Century Ontario.* Montreal & Kingston: McGill-Queen's University Press, 1989.

Wilson, Douglas J. *The Church Grows in Canada.* Toronto: Canadian Council of Churches, 1966.

4. History of Christian Education in Canada

Hiebert, Al, with Char Bates and Paul Magnus. *Character with Competence Education: The Bible College Movement in Canada.* Steinbach, MB: Association of Canadian Bible Colleges, 2005.

Rawlyk, G.A. (Ed). *Canadian Baptists and Christian Higher Education.* Montreal & Kingston: McGill-Queen's University Press, 1988.

5. History of Christian Education in the United States

American Association of Bible Colleges: *S.A. Witmer . . . Beloved Educator.* Wheaton, IL: American Association of Bible Colleges, 1970.

Brereton, Virginia Lieson. *Training God's Army: The American Bible School, 1880-1940.* Bloomington, IN: Indiana University Press, 1990.

Bechtel, Paul M. *Wheaton College: A Heritage Remembered 1860-1984.* Wheaton, IL: Harold Shaw Publishers, 1984.

Carpenter, Joel A. and Kenneth W. Shipps (Eds). *Making Higher Education Christian: The History and Mission of Evangelical Colleges in America.* Grand Rapids: William B. Eerdmans Publishing Co., 1987. (Christian College Consortium)

Dalhouse, Mark Taylor. *An Island in the Lake of Fire: Bob Jones University, Fundamentalism & The Separatist Movement.* Athens, GA: The University of Georgia Press, 1996.

Getz, Gene A. *MBI: The Story of Moody Bible Institute.* Chicago: Moody Press, 1986. (Revised and updated by James M. Vincent)

Marsden, George M. *The Outrageous Idea of Christian Scholarship.* New York: Oxford University Press, 1997.

―――――――――. *The Soul of the American University: From Protestant Establishment to Established Nonbelief.* New York: Oxford University Press, 1994.

McKinney, Larry J. and Joniva M. Mondragon. *Equipping for Service: An Historical Account of the Bible College Movement in North America.* Accrediting Association of Bible Colleges, 1997.

Ringenberg, William C. *The Christian College: A History of Protestant Higher Education in America.* William B. Eerdman's Publishing Co., 1984 (Christian College Consortium)

Witmer, S.A. *The Bible College Story: Education With Dimension.* Manhasset, NY: Channel Press, Inc., 1962.

6. History of Christianity

Bainton, Roland H. *Christianity.* Boston: Houghton Mifflin Company, 1987. (repr.) for The American Heritage Library)

Dowley, Tim (Ed). *Introduction to The History of Christianity.* Minneapolis: Fortress Press, 2002. (repr.)

Gaustad, Edwin S. and Mark A. Noll (Eds). *A Documentary History of Religion in America Since 1877* (Third ed.). Grand Rapids: William B. Eerdmans Publishing Co., 2003.

Latourette, Kenneth Scott, *A History of Christianity* (Vol. II): *Reformation to the Present* (Rev. Ed.). New York: Harper and Row, 1975.

Noll, Mark A. *A History of Christianity in the United States and Canada.* Grand Rapids: William B. Eerdmans Publishing Co., 1992.

7. History of Evangelicalism

Balmer, Randall. *Mine Eyes Have Seen the Glory: A Journey Into the Evangelical Subculture in America* (Third Edition). New York: Oxford University Press, 2000.

Bebbington, D.W. *Evangelicalism in Modern Britain: A history from the 1730s to the 1980s.* London: Routledge, 2002. (repr.)

Bloesch, Donald G. *The Future of Evangelical Christianity: A Call for Unity Amid Diversity.* Garden City, NY: Doubleday and Co., 1983.

Dayton, Donald W. *Discovering an Evangelical Heritage.* New York: Harper & Row, Publishers, 1976.

Dayton, Donald W. and Robert K. Johnston. *The Variety of American Evangelicalism.* Downers Grove, IL: Inter-Varsity Press, 1991.

Elwell, Walter A. (Ed). *Evangelical Dictionary of Theology.* Grand Rapids: Baker Book House, 1984.

Frank, Douglas W. *Less Than Conquerors: How Evangelicals Entered the Twentieth Century.* Grand Rapids: William B. Eerdmans Publishing Co., 1986.

Fuller, Daniel P. *Give the Winds a Mighty Voice: The Story of Charles E. Fuller.* Waco, TX: Word Books, 1972.

Gabelein, Frank E. *Christianity Today: Voices of evangelical Christianity in penetrating analyses of current issues of life, thought and faith.* New York: Pyramid Books, 1968.

Haykin, Michael A.G. and Kenneth J. Stewart, (eds). *The Emergence of Evangelicalism: Exploring Historical Continuities.* Nashville, TN: B&H Academics, 2008.

Hoke, Donald E. (Ed). *Evangelicals Face the Future.* South Pasadena, CA: William Carey Library, 1978.

Hunter, James Davison. *Evangelicalism: The Coming Generation.* Chicago: The University of Chicago Press, 1987.

Lovelace, Richard F. *Dynamics of Spiritual Life: An Evangelical Theology of Renewal.* Downer's Grove, IL: Inter-Varsity Press, 1979.

Noll, Mark A., David W. Bebbington and George W. Rawlyk (Eds). *Evangelicalism: Comparative Studies of Popular Protestantism in North America, The British Isles, and Beyond.* New York: Oxford University Press, 1994.

Noll, Mark A. *The Rise of Evangelicalism: The Age of Edwards, Whitefield, and the Wesleys.* Downers Grove, IL: Inter-Varsity Press, 2004.

_____. *The Scandal of the Evangelical Mind.* Grand Rapids: William B. Eerdmans Publishing Co., 1994.

Rawlyk, George A. and Mark A. Noll: *Amazing Grace: Evangelicalism in Australia, Britain, Canada, and the United States.* Grand Rapids: Baker Book House, 1993.

Smith, Christian. *American Evangelicalism: Embattled and Thriving.* Chicago: The University of Chicago Press, 1998.

Stone, Jon R. *On the Boundaries of American Evangelicalism: The Post-War Evangelical Coalition.* New York: St. Martin's Press, 1999.

Sweeney, Douglas A. *The American Evangelical Story: A History of the Movement.* Grand Rapids: Baker Academic Books, 2005.

Webber, Robert E. *Evangelicals on the Canterbury Trail: Why Evangelicals Are Attracted to the Liturgical Church.* Waco, TX: Word Books, 1985.

Webber, Robert E and Donald Bloesch, (Eds). *The Orthodox Evangelicals: Who They Are and What They Are Saying.* Nashville, TN: Thomas Nelson Inc., 1978.

Weber, Timothy P. *Living in the Shadow of the Second Coming: American Premillennialism 1875-1982.* Grand Rapids: Zondervan Publishing House, 1983.

Wells, David F. and John D. Woodbridge (Eds). *The Evangelicals: What they Believe, Who They Are, Where They Are Changing.* Grand Rapids: Baker Book House, 1977.

8. History of Fundamentalism in the United States

Beale, David O. *In Pursuit of Purity: American Fundamentalism Since 1850.* Greenville, SC: Unusual Publications, 1986.
Cole, Stewart G. *The History of Fundamentalism.* New York: Richard R. Smith, Inc., 1931.
Dollar, George W. *A History of Fundamentalism in America.* Greenville, SC: Bob Jones University Press, 1973.
Furniss, Norman F. *The Fundamentalist Controversy, 1918-1931.* Hamden, CT: Archon Books, 1963.
Humphreys, Fisher and Philip Wise. *Fundamentalism.* Macon, Ga: Smyth & Helwys Publishing Inc., 2004.
Kaplan, Esther. *With God on Their Side: How Christian Fundamentalists Trampled Science, Policy, and Democracy in George W. Bush's White House.* New York: The New Press, 2004.
Marsden, George M. *Fundamentalism and American Culture.* New York: Oxford University Press, 1980.
_____. *Fundamentalism and American Culture* (New Edition). New York: Oxford University Press, 2006.
Sandeen, Ernest R. *The Roots of Fundamentalism: British and American Millenarianism 1800-1930.* Chicago: University of Chicago Press, 1970.
_____. *The Roots of Fundamentalism: British and American Millenarianism 1800-1930.* Grand Rapids: Baker Book House, 1978. (repr.)
Stonehouse, Ned B. *J. Gresham Machen: A Biographical Memoir.* Grand Rapids: Wm. B. Eerdmans Publishing Co., 1954.

9. History of Fundamentalism beyond the United States

Ali, Ayaan Hirsi. *Infidel.* New York: Free Press, 2007.
Armstrong, Karen. *The Battle for God.* New York: Ballantine Books, 2000.
Brouwer, Steve, Paul Gifford and Susan D. Rose. *Exporting the American Gospel: Global Christian Fundamentalism.* New York: Routledge, 1996.

Marty, Martin E. and R. Scott Appleby (Eds). *Accounting for Fundamentalisms: The Dynamic Character of Movements*. Chicago: University of Chicago Press, 1994.

—————. *Fundamentalisms and Society*. Chicago: University of Chicago Press, 1993.

—————. *Fundamentalism and the State*. Chicago: University of Chicago Press, 1993.

—————. *Fundamentalisms Comprehended*. Chicago: University of Chicago Press, 1995.

—————. *Fundamentalisms Observed*. Chicago: University of Chicago Press, 1991.

10. History of Missions

Austin, Alvyn. *Saving China: Canadian Missionaries in the Middle Kingdom*. Toronto: University of Toronto Press, 1986.

Conley, Joseph F. *Drumbeats That Changed the World: A History of the Regions Beyond Missionary Union and The West Indies Mission 1873-1999*. Pasadena, CA: William Carey Library, 2000.

Elliot, Elizabeth. *Shadow of the Almighty: The Life and Testimony of Jim Elliot*. New York: Harper and Brothers, Publishers, 1958.

Fuller, W. Harold. *Run While the Sun is Hot*. Sudan Interior Mission, n.d.

Michell, David. *A Boy's War*. Overseas Missionary Fellowship, 1988.

Richardson, Don. *Eternity in Their Hearts* (Revised). Ventura, CA: Regal Books, 1981.

—————. *Lords of the Earth*. Glendale, CA: Gospel Light/Regal Publications, 1977.

—————. *Peace Child*. Glendale, CA: Gospel Light/Regal Publications, 1974.

Stickley, Caroline. *Broken Snare*. London: OMF Books, 1975.

11. History of Prairie Bible Institute

Callaway, Bernice A. *Legacy*. Three Hills: MacCall Clan Publishing, 1987.

Callaway, Bernice and Victor. *The Spirit of Prairie.* Three Hills: Prairie Bible Institute, 1997.

Cunningham, John. *She Has Done What She Could.* Three Hills: Prairie Press, 1976.

Davidson, Roy L. *God's Plan on the Prairies.* Three Hills: Roy L. Davidson, 1986.

Epp, Margaret. *Into All the Word: the missionary outreach of Prairie Bible Institute.* Three Hills: Prairie Press, 1973.

Fieldhouse, Marvin L. *The Prairie Bible Institute . . . whither bound?* Nagano Ken, Japan: Bibla-Books/Oriental Bible Study Fellowship, *n.d.*

_____. *The Prairie Bible Institute . . . whither bound?* (Second Edition). Nagano Ken, Japan: Bibla-Books/Oriental Bible Study Fellowship, *n.d.*

Fuller, W. Harold. *Maxwell's Passion and Power.* Memphis: The Master Design, 2002.

Howard, Jr., Philip E. *Hoping For Nothing.* Three Hills: Prairie Press, *n.d.*

Keller, W. Phillip. *Expendable! With God on the Prairies: the Ministry of Prairie Bible Institute, Three Hills, Alberta, Canada.* Three Hills: Prairie Press, 1966.

Snyder, Juanita C. *Raise Up the Foundations!* Three Hills: Prairie Bible Institute, 1966

12. History of Religion in the United States

Bloom, Harold. *The American Religion: The Emergence of the Post-Christian Nation.* New York: Simon and Schuster, 1992.

Finke, Roger and Rodney Starke. *The Churching of America 1776-1990: Winners and Losers in Our Religious Economy.* New Brunswick, NJ: Rutgers University Press, 1992.

Hordern, William E. *A Layman's Guide to Protestant Theology* (rev. ed). New York: Macmillan Publishing Company, 1968.

Hudson, Winthrop S. *American Protestantism.* Chicago: The University of Chicago Press, 1961.

Marty, Martin E. *Modern American Religion* (Volume 1): *The Irony Of It All 1893-1919.* Chicago: The University of Chicago Press, 1986.

_____. *Modern American Religion* (Volume 2): *The Noise of Conflict 1919-1941.* Chicago: The University of Chicago Press, 1991.

_____. *Modern American Religion* (Volume 3): *Under God, Indivisible 1941-1960.* Chicago: University of Chicago Press, 1996.

Williams, Peter W. *Popular Religion in America: Symbolic Change and the Modernization Process in Historical Perspective.* Englewood Cliffs, NJ: Prentice-Hall, Inc., 1980.

13. Other books

Agar, Michael H. *Speaking of Ethnography* (Qualitative Research Methods Series 2). Beverly Hills, CA: Sage Publications, Inc., 1986.

Agar, Michael H. *The Professional Stranger: An Informal Introduction to Ethnography.* New York: Academic Press/Harcourt Brace Jovanovich, Publishers, 1980.

Axline, Andrew, James E. Hyndman, Peyton V. Lyon & Maureen A. Molot (Eds). *Continental Community? Independence & Integration in North America.* Toronto: McClelland and Stewart Ltd., 1974.

Balmer, Randall. *Thy Kingdom Come: How the Religious Right Distorts the Faith and Threatens America, An Evangelical's Lament.* New York: Perseus/Basic Books, 2006.

——————. *Encyclopedia of Evangelicalism* (Revised and Expanded Edition). Waco, TX: Baylor University Press, 2004.

——————. *Growing Pains.* Grand Rapids: Brazos Press, 2001.

Barabas, Steven. *So Great Salvation: The History and Message of the Keswick Convention.* Eugene, OR: Wipf & Stock, 2005. (repr.)

Barr, James. *Fundamentalism.* London: SCM Press, 1981. (repr.)

Bawer, Bruce. *Stealing Jesus: How Fundamentalism Betrays Christianity.* New York: Crown Publishers, Inc., 1997.

Berger, Carl. *The Writing of Canadian History: Aspects of English-Canadian Historical Writing Since 1900.* Toronto: University of Toronto Press, 1986.

Bloesch, Donald G. *The Future of Evangelical Christianity: A Call for Unity AmidDiversity.* Garden City, NY: Doubleday & Co., Inc., 1983.

Blumhofer, Edith L. *Aimee Semple McPherson: Everybody's Sister.* Grand Rapids: William B. Eerdmans Publishing Co., 1993.

Bradley, James E. and Richard A. Muller. *Church History: An Introduction to Research, Reference Works, and Methods.* Grand Rapids: William B. Eerdmans Publishing Co., 1995.

Braeman, John, Robert H. Bremner and Everett Walters (Eds). *Change and Continuity in Twentieth-Century America.* New York: Harper and Row, 1966.

Brant, Albert E. *In the Wake of Martyrs: A Modern Saga in Ancient Ethiopia.* Abbottsford, B.C.: Omega, *n.d.*

Bruce, Steve. *The Rise and Fall of the New Christian Right: Conservative Protestant Politics in America 1978-1988.* Oxford: Clarendon Press, 1990.

Cantor, Norman F. and Richard I. Schneider. *How to Study History.* Arlington Heights, IL: Harlan Davidson, Inc., 1967.

Carpenter, Joel A. *Revive Us Again: The Reawakening of American Fundamentalism.* New York: Oxford University Press, 1997.

Clinton, J. Robert. *Focused Lives: Inspirational Life-Changing Lessons From Eight Effective Christian Leaders Who Finished Well.* Altadena, CA: Barnabas Publishers, 1995. (E-book edition)

Cohen, Norman J. (Ed). *The Fundamentalist Phenomenon: A view from within; a response from without.* Grand Rapids: William B. Eerdmans Publishing Co., 1990.

Cooper, Barry. *Sins of Omission: Shaping the News at CBC TV.* Toronto: University of Toronto Press, 1994.

Currie, David B. *Born Fundamentalist, Born Again Catholic.* San Francisco: Ignatius Press, 1996.

Dayton, Donald W. *Discovering An Evangelical Heritage.* New York: Harper and Row, 1976.

DeBerg, Betty A. *Ungodly Women: Gender and the First Wave of American Fundamentalism.* Minneapolis: Fortress Press, 1990.

Emberley, Peter C. *Divine Hunger: Canadians on Spiritual Walkabout.* Toronto: HarperCollins Publishers, 2002.

Ellingsen, Mark. *The Evangelical Movement: Growth, Impact, Controversy, Dialog.* Minneapolis: Augsburg Publishing House, 1988.

Feinberg, Charles L. (Ed). *The Fundamentals for Today.* (2 vols.) Grand Rapids: Kregel Publications, 1958.

Grenz, Stanley J. *Renewing the Center: Evangelical Theology in a Post-Theological Era* (Second Ed.) Grand Rapids: Baker Publishing Group, 2006.

Guyon, Madame. *Experiencing the Depths of Jesus Christ.* Gardiner, ME: Christian Books, 1975. (repr.)

Haiven, Judith. *Faith, Hope, No Charity: An Inside Look at the Born Again Movement in Canada and the United States.* Vancouver: New Star Books, 1984.

Hamid, Mohsin. *The Reluctant Fundamentalist.* New York: Harcourt, Inc., 2007.

Harris, Harriet A. *Fundamentalism and Evangelicals.* Oxford: Clarendon Press, 1998.

Hart, D.G. *Deconstructing Evangelicalism: Conservative Protestantism in the Age of Billy Graham.* Grand Rapids: Baker Publishing Group, 2004.

Hassey, Janette. *No Time for Silence: Evangelical Women in Public Ministry Around the Turn of the Century.* Grand Rapids: Zondervan Publishing Co., 1986.

Hawley, John Stratton (Ed). *Fundamentalism & Gender.* New York: Oxford University Press, 1994.

Hedges, Chris. *American Fascists: The Christian Right and the War on America.* New York: Free Press, 2006.

Henry, Carl. F.H. *The Uneasy Conscience of Modern Fundamentalism.* Grand Rapids: William B. Eerdmans Publishing Co., 2003. (repr.)

Hexham, Irving. *A Concise Dictionary of Religion.* Downer's Grover, IL: Inter-Varsity Press, 1993.

Hofstadter, Richard. *Anti-Intellectualism in American Life.* New York: Vintage Books, 1963.

Hood, Ralph W., Jr., Peter C. Hill and W. Paul Williamson. *The Psychology of Religious Fundamentalism.* New York: The Guilford Press, 2005.

Hoornaert, Eduardo. *The Memory of the Christian People.* Maryknoll, NY: Orbis Books, 1988.

Howard, Thomas. *Evangelical is Not Enough: Worship of God in Liturgy and Sacrament.* San Francisco: Ignatius Press, 1984.

Hunter, James Davison. *American Evangelicalism: Conservative Religion and the Quandary of Modernity.* New Brunswick, NJ: Rutgers University Press, 1983.

Hutchison, William R. *The Modernist Impulse in American Protestantism.* Cambridge, MA: Harvard University Press, 1976.

Keating, Karl. *Catholicism and Fundamentalism: The Attack on "Romanism" by "Bible Christians."* San Francisco: Ignatius Press, 1988.

Klein, Patricia, Evelyn Bence, Jane Campbell, Laura Pearson and David Wimbish. *Growing Up Born Again: a whimsical look at the blessings and tribulations of growing up born again.* Old Tappan, NJ: Fleming H. Revell Co., 1987.

Lawrence, Bruce. *Defenders of God: The Fundamentalist Revolt Against the Modern Age.* San Francisco: Harper & Row, 1989.

Lipset, Seymour Martin. *Continental Divide: The Values and Institutions of United States and Canada.* New York: Routledge, 1990.

Marsden, George (Ed). *Evangelicalism and Modern America.* Grand Rapids: William B. Eerdmans Publishing Co., 1984.

_____. *Reforming Fundamentalism: Fuller Seminary and the New Evangelicalism.* Grand Rapids: William B. Eerdmans Publishing Co., 1987.

_____. *Understanding Fundamentalism and Evangelicalism.* Grand Rapids: William B. Eerdmans Publishing Co., 1991.

Marty, Martin E. and R. Scott Appleby. *The Glory and the Power: the Fundamentalist Challenge to the Modern World.* Boston: Beacon Press, 1992.

Marwick, Arthur. *The Nature of History.* London: Macmillan and Company Ltd., 1970.

McCutcheon, Russell T. (Ed). *The Insider/Outsider Problem in the Study of Religion: A Reader.* London: Cassell, 1999.

Mouw, Richard J. *The Smell of Sawdust: What Evangelicals Can Learn From their Fundamentalist Heritage.* Grand Rapids: Zondervan Publishing Co., 2000.

Murphy, Nancey. *Beyond Liberalism & Fundamentalism.* Harrisburg: Trinity Press International, 1996.

Nelson, Shirley. *The Last Year of the War.* New York: Harper and Row, 1978.

Noll, Mark A. *Between Faith & Criticism: Evangelicals, Scholarship and the Bible in America.* San Francisco: Harper and Row, 1986.

_____. *What Happened to Christian Canada?* Vancouver: Regent College Publishing, 2007.

Packer, J.I. *'Fundamentalism' and the Word of God.* London: Inter-Varsity Fellowship, 1963. (repr.)

Penning, James M. and Corwin E. Smidt. *Evangelicalism: The NEXT Generation.* Grand Rapids: Baker Book House, 2002.

Quebedeaux, Richard. *The Young Evangelicals: The Story of the Emergence of a New Generation of Evangelicals.* New York: Harper and Row, 1974.

Ramm, Bernard. *The Evangelical Heritage: A Study in Historical Theology.* Grand Rapids: Baker Book House, 1981. (repr.)

Reimer, Sam. *Evangelicals and the Continental Divide: The Conservative Protestant Subculture in Canada and the United States.* Montreal & Kingston: McGill-Queen's University Press, 2003.

Riesebrodt, Martin. *Pious Passion: The Emergence of Modern Fundamentalism in the United States and Iran.* (trans. By Don Reneau) Berkeley: University of California Press, 1993.

Rosen, Christine. *My Fundamentalist Education: A Memoir of a Divine Girlhood.* New York: Public Affairs/Perseus Books Group, 2005.

Russell, C. Allyn. *Voices of American Fundamentalism.* Philadelphia: The Westminster Press, 1976.

Ruthven, Malise. *Fundamentalism: The Search for Meaning.* London: Oxford University Press, 2004.

Sauve, Roger. *Borderlines: What Canadians and Americans Should—But Don't—Know About Each Other . . . a Witty, Punchy and Personal Look.* Toronto: McGraw-Hill Ryerson, 1994.

Schaeffer, Frank. *Crazy for God: How I Grew Up as One of the Elect, Helped Found the Religious Right, and Lived to Take All (Or Almost All) of it Back.* New York: Carroll & Graf Publishers, 2007.

Sheler, Jeffery L. *Believers: A Journey Into Evangelical America.* New York: Viking, 2006.

Smith, Hannah Whitall. *The Christian's Secret of a Happy Life.* New York: The Fleming H. Revell Company, 1952.

Stackhouse, John G. Jr., *Canadian Evangelicalism in the Twentieth Century: An Introduction to Its Character.* Toronto: University of Toronto Press, 1993.

Stevens, W.C. *The Book of Daniel.* Harrisburg, PA: Christian Publications, Inc., *n.d.*

Sweet, Leonard I. (Ed). *The Evangelical Tradition in America.* Macon, GA: Mercer University Press, 1997. (repr.)

Thomas, David (Ed). *Canada and the United States: Differences That Count.* Peterborough, ON: Broadview Press, 1993.

Ulstein, Stefan. *Growing Up Fundamentalist: Journeys in Legalism & Grace.* Downer's Grove: Inter-Varsity Press, 1995.

Upham, Thomas C. *The Life of Madame Guyon.* London: Allenson & Co., Ltd., 1961. (repr.)

Van Impe, *Heart Disease in Christ's Body: Fundamentalism . . . Is It Sidetracked?* Royal Oak: Jack Van Impe Ministries, 1984.

Webber, Robert and Donald Bloesch (Eds). *The Orthodox Evangelicals: Who they are and what they are saying.* Nashville: Thomas Nelson, Inc., 1978.

Wells, David F. *God in the Wasteland: The Reality of Truth in a World of Fading Dreams.* Grand Rapids: William B. Eerdmans Publishing Co., 1994.

_____. *No Place for Truth: Or Whatever Happened to Evangelical Theology?* William B. Eerdmans Publishing Co., 1993.

Wilson, Walter Lewis. *A Sure Remedy Prescribed by the Doctor.* Chicago: Moody Press, 1938.

_____. *The Romance of a Doctor's Visits.* Chicago: Moody Press, 1935.

Woodbridge, John D., Mark A. Noll and Nathan O. Hatch. *The Gospel in America: Themes in the Story of America's Evangelicals.* Grand Rapids: Zondervan Publishing House, 1979.

Young, Perry Deane. *God's Bullies: Power Politics and Religious Tyranny.* New York: Holt, Rinehart & Winston, 1982.

14. Social history perspectives

Thompson, Paul. *The Voice of the Past: Oral History.* Oxford: Oxford University Press, 1978.

15. Sociological perspectives

Adams, Michael. *Fire and Ice: The United States, Canada and the Myth of Converging Values.* Toronto: Penguin Canada, 2003.

_____. *Sex in the Snow.* Toronto: Viking/The Penguin Group, 1997.

Ammerman, Nancy T. *Bible Believers in the Modern World.* New Brunswick, NJ: Rutgers University Press, 1987.

Berger, Peter L. *The Sacred Canopy: Elements of a Sociological Theory of Religion.* New York: Doubleday/Anchor Books, 1969. (repr.)

Bibby, Reginald W. *Fragmented Gods: The Poverty and Potential of Religion in Canada.* Toronto: Irwin Publishing, 1987.

_____. *Unknown Gods: The Ongoing Story of Religion in Canada.* Toronto: Stoddart Publishing, 1993.

_____. *Restless Gods: The Renaissance of Religion in Canada.* Toronto: Stoddart Publishing, 2002.

_____. *The Boomer Factor: What Canada's Most Famous Generation is Leaving Behind.* Toronto: Bastian Books, 2006.

Boyer, Patrick. *The Peoples' Mandate, Referendums and a More Democratic Canada.* Toronto: Dundurn Press, 1992.

Braeman, John, Robert H. Bremner, and David Brody. *Change and Continuity in Twentieth Century America: the 1920s.* Columbus, OH: Ohio State University Press, 1968.

Troeltsch, Ernest. *The Social Teaching of the Christian Churches* (2 vols.). New York: Harper and Brothers, 1960. (Trans. by Olive Wyon)

Wach, Joachim. *Sociology of Religion.* Chicago: The University of Chicago Press, 1962.

Weber, Max. *Essays in Sociology.* London: Routledge and Keegan Paul Ltd., 1974.

Wuthnow, Robert. *Christianity in the 21ˢᵗ Century: Reflections on the Challenges Ahead.* New York: Oxford University Press, 1993.

E.   Dissertations—Theses

Enns. James. *Every Christian a Missionary: Fundamentalist education at Prairie Bible Institute 1925-1947.* M.A. thesis, University of Calgary, 2001.

Epp, Kenneth A. "The Impact of the Theological Views of William Jennings Bryan on His Educational Ideas." PhD diss., Loyola University of Chicago, 1995.

Elliott, David R. "Studies of Eight Canadian Fundamentalists." PhD diss., University of British Columbia, 1989.

Flory, Richard W. "Development and Transformation Within Protestant Fundamentalism: Bible Institutes and Colleges in the U.S. 1925-1991." PhD diss., University of Chicago, 2003.

Gauvreau, Michael. "History and Faith: A Study of Methodist and Presbyterian Thought in Canada 1820-1940." PhD diss., University of Toronto, 1985.

Goertz, Donald A. "The Development of a Bible Belt." M.C.S. thesis, Regent College, Vancouver, B.C., Canada, 1980.

Gregory, Chad Alan. "Revivalism, Fundamentalism and Masculinity in the United States, 1880-1930." PhD diss., University of Kentucky, 1999.

Guenther, Bruce L. "Training for Service: The Bible School Movement in Western Canada, 1909-1960." PhD diss., McGill University, Montreal, Canada, 2001.

Hamilton, Michael S., "The Fundamentalist Harvard: Wheaton College and the Continuing Vitality of American Evangelicalism, 1919-1965." PhD diss., University of Notre Dame, 1994.

House, Sean David. "Pentecostal Contributions to Contemporary Christological Thought: A Synthesis With Ecumenical Views." ThM thesis, University of South Africa, 2006.

Jensen, Lori. "(Re)Discovering Fundamentalism in the Cultural Margins: Calvary Chapel Congregations as Sites of Cultural Resistance and Religious Transformation." PhD diss., University of Southern California, 2000.

Lee, Chul Hee. "Sanctification by Faith: Walter Marshall's Doctrine of Sanctification in Comparison With the Keswick View of Sanctification." PhD diss., Westminster Theological Seminary, 2005.

Lewis, Camille Kaminski. "Whatsoever Things are Lovely: Bob Jones University and the Romantic Rhetoric of Separation." PhD diss., Indiana University, 2001.

McKenzie, Bryan Alexander. "Fundamentalism, Christian unity and pre-millennialism in the Thought of Roland V. Bingham, 1872-1942." PhD diss., University of St. Michael's College, 1986.

McKinney, Larry J. "An Historical Analysis of the Bible College Movement During Its Formative Years: 1882-1920." EdD diss., Temple University, Philadelphia, 1985.

Moore, Howard Edgar. "The Emergence of Moderate Fundamentalism: John R. Rice and *The Sword of the Lord*." PhD diss., George Washington University, Washington, D.C., 1990.

Opp, James W. "Culture of the Soul: Fundamentalism and Evangelicalism in Canada 1921-1940." MA thesis, University of Calgary, 1994.

Robert, Dana Lee. "Arthur Tappan Pierson and Forward Movements of Late-Nineteenth Century Evangelicalism." PhD diss., Yale University, 1984.

Sawatzky, Ronald George. "Looking for that Blessed Hope: The Roots of Fundamentalism in Canada, 1878-1914." PhD diss., University of Toronto, 1985.

Trollinger, William Vance., Jr. "One Response to Modernity: Northwestern Bible School and the Fundamentalist Empire of William Bell Riley." PhD diss., University of Wisconsin-Madison, 1984.

Whitt, Irving Alfred. "Developing a Pentecostal Missiology in the Canadian Context (1867-1944): The Pentecostal Assemblies of Canada." DMiss diss., Fuller Theological Seminary, 1994.

Yao, Kevin Xiyi. "The Fundamentalist Movement Among Protestant Missionaries in China 1920-1937." ThD diss., Boston University, School of Theology, 2000.

F.   Movies

Jesus Camp. A&E IndieFilms and Magnolia Pictures, c. 2006 A&E Television Network.

G. Unpublished papers

Enns. James. *"Hothouse Fundamentalism on the Prairies: The early years of Prairie Bible Institute through the private eyes of Dorothy Ruth Miller."* (PBI Library Archives, *n.d.*)

Rennie, Ian. "The Doctrine of Man in the Bible Belt." The transcription of a talk delivered at a conference on the Bible College movement, <u>circa</u> 1977 in Calgary.

──────────. "Theological Education in Canada: Past and Present." Paper presented at a conference at Ontario Bible College in 1974.

──────────. "The Western Prairie Revival in Canada: During the Depression and World War II."

Spaulding, Stephen M. *"Lion on the Prairies: An interpretive analysis of the life and leadership of Leslie Earl Maxwell."* Paper prepared at Fuller Theological Seminary, 1991

H. Websites

Bill Gothard—Institute in Basic Life Principles
http://www.billgothard.com/bill/about/lifechapters/3/

Canadian Chautauquas/Dominion Chautauquas
http://www.thecanadianencyclopedia.com

Elmer Towns—(e-book) Understanding The Deeper Life
http://www.elmertowns.com/books/online/Understanding_the_Deeper_Life%5BET%5D.pdf

Prairie Bible Institute
http://www.albertasource.ca/aspenland/fr/society/article_prairie_bible.html

The Famous Five
http://www.abheritage.ca/famous5

The Institute for the Study of American Evangelicals
http://www.wheaton.edu/isae/defining_evangelicalism.html

The Southern Baptist Convention in Canada
http://www.ccsb.ca/national-ministries/the-history-of-the-ccsb

The United Farmers' Wives of Albert
http://www.thecanadianencyclopedia.com

Wendell Krossa—Former PBI "staff-kid" and graduate's Spiritual
Autobiography www.wendellkrossa.co

ACKNOWLEDGEMENTS

I am deeply indebted and ever grateful to my wife, Joyce, and our children Travis, Dallas, and Karis, for their patience, love, and support extended so faithfully and selflessly over the years I talked about, researched, and wrote this manuscript. Every husband/father should be so blessed!

I acknowledge the eager assistance and encouragement of my parents (both of whom passed away during my research—hopefully not as a result of my research! Dad and Mom both wrote about PBI long before I did). Appreciation is also due my siblings Dave, Dan, Ruth and Phil for their interest and help—you're stuck with me; please commence dealing with it!

I am very thankful to the following professionals for their roles in inspiring, enabling, and guiding my efforts, particularly my doctoral supervisors Dr. Paul Gundani (University of South Africa) and Dr. Irving Hexham (University of Calgary). Others who merit my heartfelt applause are (the late) Rev. Graeme Crouch (PBI), Dr. Al Hiebert (Providence University College), Dr. David Larsen (Trinity Divinity School), Dr. Robert Rakestraw (PBI), Dr. Ted S. Rendall (PBI), Rev. Harold Peters (my ordination mentor), Dr. David Taras (Mt. Royal University, Calgary), and Dr. William Willimon (Duke Divinity School), as well as my physicians—Dr. Curtis Bell, Dr. John Toews and Dr. Doug Watson, all of Calgary, Alberta.

Three fine people at the Ted S. Rendall Library on the campus of Prairie Bible Institute were most helpful and patient throughout my frequent forays into the PBI archives and merit acknowledgement for their professional assistance: Veronica Lewis, Deanna Lockwood, and Bill Nyman.

Similarly, I am indebted to former colleagues who contributed to my undertaking this work in more ways than they can know: Shawn Anderson, Linda Andreasen, Bob Bahr, Shane Bassen, Mark Bezanson, Brian Burkhart, Denise Daniel, Myrna DeFehr, Fraser Edwards, Tony Hanson, Gary Hellard, Cathy Irwin, Gord Klassen, Heather McKeeman, John Miller, Marlene Nordstrom, Doug Pippus, Don Somerville, and Tammy Virr.

My thanks also to former fellow-PBI "staff kids" Bryan Butler, Dr. Paul Chamberlain, Larry and Pixie Charter, Mark Imbach, Dr. Glenn Kowalsky, Wendell Krossa, Brenda (Boytim) Morrison, John Pace, Robert Pace, and

Paul Workentine, for helpful memories, insights, clarifications and humor regarding days long ago. Friends such as Dr. Ron Galloway, Rev. Mike Jones, Tim and Rita MacKay, Don McAreavy, Candace McLean, Bob and June Neufeld, Hal and Joan Rainforth, Bas and Marieke Zohlandt, and the "Friday Afternoon Crew," also provided unique forms of encouragement.

Lastly, the outstanding and motivating music of gifted friends Steve Archer, Chuck Girard and Dallas Holm sustained me throughout this project—as it has throughout most of my life. Thank you, gentlemen!

I, of course, assume full responsibility for any errors found herein.

Tim W. Callaway
Calgary, Alberta, Canada
Easter Sunday 2013

ABOUT THE AUTHOR

Timothy Wray. Callaway (b. 1956) grew up as a "staff kid" at Prairie Bible Institute in Three Hills, Alberta, Canada, from 1960-1977. In addition to completing each of the four levels of education that existed at PBI during that era (kindergarten, elementary, high school, Bible college), he is a graduate of Providence University College (B. Rel. Ed) in Otterburne, Manitoba, Canada; the University of Waterloo (B.A.) in Waterloo, Ontario, Canada; Trinity Evangelical Divinity School (MDiv and ThM) in Deerfield, Illinois, U.S.A., and the University of South Africa (ThD) in Pretoria, South Africa. He and his wife Joyce are parents to three adult children and reside in Calgary, Alberta, Canada, where Tim is active in a variety of roles including pastor, professor, writer, and social justice advocate.

CPSIA information can be obtained at www.ICGtesting.com
Printed in the USA
BVOW031942180613

323665BV00001B/4/P